RESEARCH IN ECONOMIC ANTHROPOLOG

Supplement 7 • 1993

ECONOMIC ASPECTS OF W
IN THE PREHISPANIC NEW

RESEARCH IN ECONOMIC ANTHROPOLOGY

ECONOMIC ASPECTS OF WATER MANAGEMENT IN THE PREHISPANIC NEW WORLD

Editors: VERNON L. SCARBOROUGH
             University of Cincinnati

             BARRY L. ISAAC
             University of Cincinnati

SUPPLEMENT 7 • 1993

 JAI PRESS INC.

Greenwich, Connecticut   *London, England*

CONTENTS

PART III.   WEST MEXICO AND THE U.S. SOUTHWEST

PART IV.   THE CENTRAL ANDES

PART V.   DISCUSSION

LIST OF CONTRIBUTORS

Jorge Angulo V.

Instituto Nacional de
    Antropología e Historia
Mexico, D.F.

Clark L. Erickson

Department of Anthropology
University of Pennsylvania,
Philadelphia

Charles D. Frederick

Department of Geography
University of Texas-Austin

Peter D. Harrison

Maxwell Museum of Anthropology
University of New Mexico-
Albuquerque

Jerry B. Howard

Mesa Southwest Museum
Mesa, Arizona

Barry L. Isaac

Department of Anthropology
University of Cincinnati

Deborah L. Nichols

Department of Anthropology
Dartmouth College
Hanover, New Hampshire

C.R. Ortloff

FMC Corporation
Santa Clara, California

Vernon L. Scarborough

Department of Anthropology
University of Cincinnati

Phil C. Weigand

Museum of Northern Arizona
Flagstaff, Arizona

SERIES EDITOR'S PREFACE

The *Research in Economic Anthropology* series consists of two types of books: (1) Research Annuals and (2) Supplements. Research Annuals (1978 to the present) contain a mixture of ethnology and archaeology, and each covers several topics and areas. Supplements are devoted entirely to archaeology and (occasionally) ethnohistory, and each volume is thematic, restricted to a particular topic or region.

Supplement 1 (1980), issued while George Dalton was series editor (1978-1983), was John Murra's *The Economic Organization of the Inka State* (1980). It is the only single-author Supplement. Excluding the present volume, the Supplements issued during my editorship (1983 to present) are:

#2. *Economic Aspects of Prehispanic Highland Mexico* (1986).

#3. *Prehistoric Economies of the Pacific Northwest Coast* (1988).

#4. *Prehistoric Maya Economies of Belize* (1989), co-edited with Patricia A. McAnany.

#5. *Early Paleoindian Economies of Eastern North America* (1990), co-edited with Kenneth B. Tankersley.

#6. *Long-Term Subsistence Change in Prehistoric North America* (1992), co-edited with Dale R. Croes and Rebecca A. Hawkins.

Plans for the present volume were laid in 1988, as Scarborough was joining the Department of Anthropology at the University of Cincinnati. At that point, we knew only that we would put together a volume reflecting our common interests in Mesoamerica, complex societies, and long-term evolutionary change—as well as economic anthropology. By 1991, when we at last had time to plan this volume in earnest, Scarborough's research had become more and more centered upon water management. Thus, that topical focus seemed the natural one.

A volume of essays gains coherence through its topical, temporal, or geographical focus. The choice of one of these three foci as primary leaves the other two to be defined, and at least one of them must be brought under fairly tight control. Having decided upon the topical focus, we wrestled with geographical coverage—whether to restrict the volume to the New World or to try for worldwide coverage. Once we opted for the former, we had to decide whether to focus exclusively on Mesoamerica or to extend coverage northward and/or southward. We soon agreed that hooping in the Greater Southwest and the Andes would make a more interesting volume.

Those decisions made, we decided to strive for a mixture of Mexican and U.S. authors. Accordingly, we invited essays from six Mexican anthropologists (archaeologists or ethnohistorians) whose recent work on water management we had read. Luck was not with us in this matter. In three cases, we received no response, despite duplicate mailings from Cincinnati and Mexico City; perhaps we were victims of the two countries' postal (dis)services. Two others of the six were overwhelmed with administrative responsibilities. Imagine our dismay, then, upon learning in Spring 1992 that a computer virus had destroyed Jorge Angulo's draft manuscript! Fortunately, he was able to reconstruct it in time for its inclusion.

As with all the volumes in the *Research in Economic Anthropology* series, this one's general concern is livelihood in the sense of "getting a living." More elegantly, we are interested in the economy—the processes of *production* (extraction, transformation, elaboration, storage), *consumption* (use—whether instrumental or final), *distribution* (circulation; transfers from one social node to another), and *exchange* (two-way, hand-to-hand movements) of materials and services that sustain or reproduce humans both as individuals and as members of sociocultural units. (For elaboration, see Supplement 5, pp. 331-334, 342-346.)

Barry L. Isaac
Series Editor

ACKNOWLEDGMENTS

We are much in debt to this volume's contributors, who were unusually quick and cooperative in writing and revising their chapters. We also thank Matthew Becher, undergraduate major in the Department of Anthropology, University of Cincinnati, for producing or enhancing many of the volume's illustrations; and James Litfin, Graduate Assistant in Anthropology, for help in computer matters. Scarborough thanks the Competitive Taft Faculty Fellowship fund and the McMicken College of the University of Cincinnati for research leave in Autumn Quarter 1992. Isaac thanks the McMicken College for academic leave in Winter 1993. In both cases, the leave of absence has been crucial in the preparation and completion of this volume.

INTRODUCTION

Vernon L. Scarborough

Water management is the interruption and redirection of the natural movement or collection of water by society. With or without living consultants or extant texts, dams, reservoirs, canals, and wells reveal alterations to a landscape that permit an evaluation of a group's land-use practices. The scale and complexity of these features provide archaeologists, ethnographers, and geographers a powerful database for examining economic behavior.

The first individual to develop and articulate a theory of water management was Karl Wittfogel (1957, 1972). Together with Julian Steward (1949) and the first Pan American Union Conference (1955), Wittfogel championed a deterministic role for the influence that water management played in early states, arguing that state controlled bureaucracies evolved as a consequence of expanding irrigation systems. Wittfogel proposed that, in arid and semiarid

Research in Economic Anthropology, Suppl. 7, pages 1-14.
Copyright © 1993 by JAI Press Inc.
All rights of reproduction in any form reserved.
ISBN: 1-55938-646-0

zones occupied by populations economically more complex than simple subsistence farmers and not based on private property, despotic state predictably developed. The Hydraulic Hypothesis stimulated a series of debates about its primacy for stratified society (Hunt & Hunt 1976, Leach 1959, Millon 1962, Mitchell 1973, Service 1975). An emphasis on political transformations and the sometimes strident tone of Wittfogel's work made for a comparably strong reaction to the importance of his contribution.

Although the Hydraulic Hypothesis cannot be regarded as the primary explanation for the origins or development of complex society, viewed in the historic context of the discipline, the theory did permit anthropologically-oriented archaeology the opportunity to test the merits of the Hypothesis (Harris 1968: 685). Steward's interest in integrating archaeology more closely with developments in cultural anthropology provided an early forum for material-based explanations of the processes exciting state origins. The nomothetic structure of the Hydraulic Hypothesis allowed both cultural anthropologists and archaeologists to evaluate the argument explicitly and thereby pose other stimuli assailable from the archaeological record—trade, warfare, resource symbiosis, demographic pressure. Perhaps the most damning of arguments against the Hydraulic Hypothesis was presented by Robert McCormick Adams (1966, 1981), who argued from extensive field survey data that truly complex irrigation schemes followed the establishment of urbanism in ancient Sumeria. Nevertheless, Adams' explanations for the rise of civilization featured the role of irrigation as a key variable in the multicausality of state origins.

The Pan-American Union monograph, *Irrigation Civilization: A Comparative Study* (1955), edited by Steward, was followed by *Irrigation's Impact on Society* (Downing & Gibson 1974) nearly two decades later. In that time, water management was defined as a significant anthropological interest, but its primacy for explaining state origins was no longer a critical issue. Adams was the only participant to be published in both collections, and his influence steered the direction of water studies in the latter volume. Following Robert and Eva Hunt's classic article, "Canal Irrigation and Local Social Organization" (1976), most scholars argued that small-scale irrigation systems were responsible for immediate "man-land" relationships in many complex societies. The focus of anthropological analysis was on ecological relationships rather than political transformations. Although the theoretical implications of water management had changed, the two volumes established irrigation as an important consideration for anthropology.

Nearly 20 years after the last major edited volume examining water management, the present book is offered. In keeping with the 1974 precedent, this volume takes a different approach to the management of water than the previous volumes. Water management is defined more broadly than irrigation and includes reservoirs, lake-margins, and wetland reclamation efforts.

Furthermore, the focus of the present volume is on New World systems, water management adaptations quite different from classic Old World irrigation models. Finally, the rationale for examining water management is placed in an explicitly economic context.

IRRIGATION VS. STILL-WATER SYSTEMS

Ecologically, water management has been examined mainly as a process of allocation, with canal systems distributing water over a landscape. Much has been written about canal systems and the techniques used to relocate water and the labor force necessary to construct and maintain an adequate water supply. Although sizable natural watersheds—and the rivers and streams issuing from them—provide permanent and predictable quantities of water,[1] shortages can occur, induced principally by human agents (Scarborough 1991). Nevertheless, seasonal as well as annual fluctuations are generally understood by a group and water allotments are scheduled accordingly. Attention in these water systems is directed to allocation decisions. Based on an irrigation model, management practices involve (1) the size of the area to be watered, (2) the amount and timing of the release, and (3) the established rules and traditional formulas affecting distribution (Scarborough 1991).

Although two of the eight papers in this volume focus on irrigation systems, the remainder emphasize still-water adaptations. While distributional systems have been studied extensively, still-water sources that are almost completely constructed by humans—reservoirs—have received little research attention. In still-water systems, allocation decisions remain important, but other factors weigh more heavily. Where water collection is a deliberate action requiring construction and maintenance, a different set of organizational principles is implied than is the case with irrigation systems. In some areas of the world dependent on reservoir sources, entire watersheds were created to accommodate the water demands of a thriving community. The Classic period Maya Lowlands are a specific case (Harrison, this volume; Scarborough, this volume). The adaptations made by the ancient Sinhalese are another (Gunawardana 1971, Leach 1961). Note that the elevated seepage rates of the karstic terrain associated with the Maya Lowlands made site pavements absolutely necessary, while the Sinhalese of northern Sri Lanka adapted to the paucity of water by damming small rivers behind huge collection tanks.

Unlike canal distributary systems that assume the overall availability of water from a faraway and sizable watershed, reservoir/catchment-basin systems demand immediate and persistent attention to a watershed. The physical positioning of goods and people over the landscape in this adaptation is expectedly different from that associated with a canalized system.

Another variety of still-water management is the modification of lake margins and internally drained, seasonally inundated wetlands. These systems assume the availability of source initially, but with sizable reclamation projects investing in raised or drained fields; access to acceptable water levels and water purity depend on landscape engineering. How water is stored in the still-water channels between fields is critical. Too much water and the fields are flooded, too little water and plant desiccation results. Further, accelerated sedimentation rates or uncontrolled mineralization are as much a concern to still-water managers as to irrigation managers.

Storage is a driving force in organizing still-water systems. The seasonal availability of water, coupled with its sometimes erratic appearance even during the rainy season, makes the physical preparation and maintenance of the rainfall runoff catchment area critical for establishing sufficient quantities of water in storage.

NEW WORLD VS. OLD WORLD

Four principal landscaping techniques comprise most water manipulations among early states. Wells, reservoirs, dams, and canals represent major earth-moving investments demanding significant labor, exact timing, and precision in both construction and maintenance. Some societies emphasize reservoir management, while others focus on canal distributary systems. The physical investments dichotomize between collection and diversion, source as opposed to allocation. Although considerable variability exists, this division is further defined by environments with arid settings associated with navigable rivers and those identified with humid settings without navigable rivers—a division apparent between Old World and New World settings, respectively, and the earliest experiments in civilization. This separation is a useful one for the earliest states, but collapses with the spread of stratified society globally. Not surprisingly, the incidence of reservoir construction does appear to correlate with the absence of perennial drainages, while canal systems are associated with more predictable riverine flow.

In the New World, primary states did not evolve in proximity to the hemisphere's great rivers as states did in the Old World. As Wittfogel's work implies, the reasons for this may include the less arid settings in which the Mississippi and the Amazon flow, or the levels and kinds of technology that developed in the New World. In any case, it was the exception in the New World that large urban settlements developed over broad, flat tracts of land, as they did in the Old World on the great flood plains of the Tigris-Euphrates, Indus, Huang-ho and, to a somewhat lesser extent, on the Lower Nile. The great cities of the Valley of Mexico indicate that the adaptation was made to flat land, but here an ancient lacustrine environment—not the abundance of a permanent river—accommodated urbanism. Even the great urban center of Chan Chan on the north coast of Peru was dependent on a canalization scheme very different from those of the Old World (Moseley 1983; Ortloff, this volume). Here, a relatively small, incised river, knifing through a tectonically-active environment, forced frequent canal abandonment and a heavy investment in "sunken gardens" (excavated, water-table fields).

ECONOMIC ASPECTS OF WATER MANAGEMENT

The fundamental difference in water availability between the New and the Old Worlds, and the economic challenges posed by this condition, distinguish this volume from other studies of water management. As noted above, water systems in either hemisphere have been viewed primarily as a set of ecological relationships between humans and the natural world. Clearly, this approach has merit, providing valuable information about the spatial positioning of resources and their extraction and distribution by humans. Because water management has focused on irrigation schemes and the allocation of water to individuals and communities, the literature has emphasized the distributional character of water management systems. Water management has been seen as the relocation of water within and between small-scale irrigation systems, and economic discussions have focused on the method and rationale of water exchange. If water is a scarce resource, it can even be considered a commodity when a market-economy approach is taken.

Halperin (1988, 1989) has recently reintroduced Polanyi's (1957) concept of the "economy as instituted process." She suggests that a formal model for the economy should include more than "locational movement," or the physical changes induced by humans in the material stuff of livelihood and/or the relocation of goods or people from one area to another. Her analysis indicates that ecological studies have emphasized locational movements but have devoted less attention to the principles underlying human organization and factors relating to the transfer of rights, or "appropriational movements." Halperin (1989: 18) writes:

> Appropriational movements...consist of: (1) organizational changes, or (2) transfers of rights.... Transfers of rights change people's access to and control over goods and resources. The ability to control goods and resources used in the production of surpluses to maintain large populations and the ability to acquire goods for simple and direct consumption by producers are both examples of appropriational movements.

Such movements as an aspect of economic behavior related to water management provide meaning to the organizational differences between those seldom assessed systems that emphasize source as opposed to irrigation, or allocation, systems.

The organization of labor associated with the construction and maintenance of a watershed source differs from that of a purely distributary system. Where the watershed of a community is its residential locus, a community-wide investment in watershed maintenance is required from a wide variety of spatially separated areas—unlike the maintenance organization associated with a ditch master's obligations to fixed points along narrowly defined canal lengths. The water draining a human-modified catchment area and the associated reservoirs built to receive that water are not accessible or divisible until the source is canalized. Source systems emphasize community-wide activity, while allocation systems are more readily exploited by the special interests of an individual or a group.

How might the physical disposition of people and things over a landscape influence the organization of labor and resources? The task demands of maintenance on a reservoir system are legion. Although certain times of the year are more demanding in monitoring flows and generating water stores, focused maintenance of the catchment emphasizes seepage-proof surfaces and waste debris removal even during the dry season. Heavy rainfall is a period of community coordination to make sure that runoff is directed to reservoirs and that the scouring action of moving water is minimized. In the somewhat exaggerated case of the southern Lowland Maya, the entire site was the catchment surface, with each household having a direct and immediate link to the quality and quantity of water.

Both locational and appropriational movements were fundamentally different in the reservoir/catchment area systems than in canal distributary systems. It is posited that people did not relocate great distances to plant, maintain, or harvest their agricultural plots in the still-water model. Although reservoirs reached sizable proportions, they were finite in capacity. The farther a household plot was from a reservoir source, the greater the likelihood that neighboring households would exhaust the water supply. The adaptation was one to the immediate margins of the reservoir; the larger the capacity of the reservoirs in a system, the larger the population in proximity.

Canal distributary organization encouraged field plots at any distance from the source, given the abundance of a perennial riverine setting. When postioned on a plain, ancient cities were frequently horizonally gridded or radially planned with a set of field systems following the riverine course as far as transportation networks would accommodate. Communities compacted themselves at periodic intervals within the riverine system and still maintained their field plots some distance away. Because of the potential distances between communities and field plots, the agriculturalist operated in a more independent manner than did the agriculturalist using a reservoir system. As Wittfogel championed, a bureaucracy was necessary in a canal distributary system to control land and water allotments and to prevent abuses.

These two adaptations (reservoir/catchment and canal/distributary) existed in the earliest states. It is presumed that the immediate economic organization within a community dependent on catchment runoff reservoirs demanded a community integration different and more focused than that defined by outfield canalized plots. Given the volume of literature examining canal systems, perhaps a closer view of reservoir-dependent water systems is appropriate.

As suggested elsewhere (Scarborough & Gallopin 1991), reservoir-dependency centralized the water resource and may have influenced the political organization of the prehispanic Maya. Nevertheless, the Maya did not nucleate into large urban aggregates like those of some early states based on canal distributary systems. The appropriational movements associated with water systems that emphasize watershed construction and maintenance may entail (1) a less routinized scheduling of labor based on the less precise knowledge of when and how much rain actually will fall on a human-made watershed, and (2) a tendency to settle the landscape in a dispersed manner to maintain and deploy a labor force over a spatially-wide water catchment area; the settlement is partially determined by the natural contours of the watershed. Although factors other than water clearly influenced the locational and appropriational movements of Maya economy, watershed maintenance was a significant organizing principle—less apparent in many riverine-based, canal-dependent states.

The concepts of locational and appropriational movements provide a useful approach for assessing the economic organization of ancient water systems. The locational movements concept illuminates the physical dichotomy between water systems that emphasize source, or watershed dependency, and those emphasizing distribution, or canal-oriented systems. The appropriational movements concept allows a window into how watershed systems might organize their labor force; dispersed settlement, in part, was designed to accommodate the uncertainty of fluctuating and seasonal rainfall.

ABOUT THE ESSAYS

The essays in this volume present critical research on prehispanic water management systems in the New World. As indicated above, most of the essays examine human adaptations to static bodies of water—reservoirs, lake margins, or swamp settings—as well as settlement associated with nearby run-off catchment areas or water sources. The two essays that focus on canal/distributary systems come from the northern- and southern-most reaches of our coverage. Such grand canal systems were less widely occurring in the New World than was the case in many Old World states. Nevertheless, the Peruvian case demonstrates the complexity of an irrigation system associated with one of the world's greatest primary states.

The eight essays in the volume were selected for both geographic coverage and topical interests (Figure 1). Although Mesoamerica receives significant attention, we have attempted to emphasize those areas where formative state development in the New World was initiated. Coverage is not complete, given the limitations of a single volume, and many would deny the label of formative state to the Hohokam (though this should be rereasoned carefully in light of Howard's paper).

The volume has been organized into four parts of two essays each: (1) The Southern Maya Lowlands, (2) The Central Mexican Highlands, (3) West Mexico and the U.S. Southwest, and (4) The Central Andes. The first part examines the swampy Maya Lowlands and the still-water systems that most typify the New World. The next section shows that Highland Mexico shares many of the adaptations outlined in the Maya realm but also draws upon small-scale flow irrigation systems. Jorge Angulo's broad-based survey (Chapter 4) of the literature provides a clear transition into Phil Weigand's pioneering

Figure 1.   Geographic Coverage of the Essay in This Volume

contribution examining West Mexico. Weigand acknowledges the inspiration of Angel Palerm and Pedro Armillas, vanguards of subsistence and economic studies in Highland Mexico, who each predicted the abundance of swamp agriculture in ancient West Mexico. Jerry Howard's essay in Part 3 represents the northern limits of our coverage; it changes the focus to irrigation systems and presents a remarkable new synthesis for water management from the arid Hohokam region. Introducing Part 4, on the Central Andes, is the only other essay devoted entirely to irrigation. This essay, by C. R. Ortloff, presents recent interpretations of canalization along the North Coast of Peru. The other essay in Part 4, by Clark Erickson, is a stimulating account of the high altitude, ancient Bolivian raised field systems. Barry Isaac concludes the volume with an assessment of earlier concepts, such as Marx's "Asiatic Mode of Production," which continue to influence our thinking about water management.

Closer inspection of the essays reveals several shared aspects worthy of emphasis. My essay (Chapter 1) examines the issue of accretionary development of cultural landscapes and the significance of reservoir-adapted water systems. It introduces the idea that the Maya, and perhaps many other semitropical civilizations, evolved in their environmental backdrop by way of a slow, additive modification of the landscape. This slow development permitted the initial flexibility necessary to accommodate the vagaries of climate, vegetation, and soils by the earliest colonizers, but it eventually culminated in a human-made environment capable of supporting extremely high population densities and a very complicated economic and political organization. The essay contrasts with Jerry Howard's (Chapter 6) on the canal systems of the Hohokam and further illustrates the dichotomy between irrigation and still-water systems.

Peter Harrison's essay (Chapter 2) defines the varied water management techniques employed by the ancient Maya. It suggests the accretional construction of terraces and the incremental reclamation of raised and drained field swamp localities. Of particular interest is his acknowledgement that recent rainfall data collected from three areas within and near Tikal indicate the erratic nature of the precipitation from year to year and station to station. Nevertheless, over an extended period of years the actual monthly differences appear to even out. This observation may have a significant bearing on our assessments of the organization and flexibility associated with still-water reservoir systems. Polity divisions, as suggested by various epigraphers through emblem glyph assignments and related textual decipherment, argue for a range of territorial sizes in the Maya area. Considerable debate revolves around the size of these polities and, by extension, the significance of regional state organization (Culbert 1991) vs. smaller, more volatile segmentary states (Demarest 1992). Perhaps a closer examination of the variability apparent in precipitation within and between polity divisions will suggest the limits to which a governed territory expanded. Given that rainfall was seasonal and the sole source of water for many of these polities, it follows that "statelets" as small as suggested by Mathews (1991) would have been difficult to maintain from year to year because of their inability to subsume enough land (catchment area) to assure at least some significant rainfall in major portions of a polity's holdings. The absence of rainfall in one area of a polity would be compensated by its availability somewhere else within the territory. This would be much less likely if the polity were quite small and autonomously governed.

The essay by Deborah Nichols and Charles Fredrick (Chapter 3) argues that environmental risk management stimulated intensive agriculture in the Basin of Mexico. They suggest that the greater productivity of fertile alluvium, degraded from swidden practices on the adjacent piedmont slopes, promoted land ownership and the elevation of a controlling elite. (Chapter 1 describes a similar trend at a comparable time during the Middle and Late Preclassic, with populations gravitating toward swamp settings associated with the cutting of swidden plots in uplands and resulting in soil replenishment in low-lying areas of the Maya Lowlands.) In addition to the identification of Terminal Formative canals in the Basin, Nichols and Fredrick present early dates for chinampa fields. They remain uncomfortable with the absolute dates, however, and prefer to associate the fields with a pre-Aztec context. Interestingly, they note the presence of a dike between two small lakes in the far north of the Basin's lake system, suggesting lake level control at a pre-Aztec moment. Even the huge urban adaptations of the Central Valley are supported by swamp margin watershed controls.

Jorge Angulo (Chapter 4) provides a summary statement from his many years of examining water management systems and their implications. His access to sources less well-known to many of us and his familiarity with the ethnohistoric record make this contribution highly valuable. His introduction emphasizes the biases we have inherited from Old World expectations of how early complex societies should behave and then proceeds to provide definitional rigor to the many types of water and land management tools and features used in ancient Mesoamerica. Angulo stresses the antiquity of water management technology, suggesting that most of the means of production were in place by the Middle Formative. His concluding statements concerning *tequio*, or obligatory labor, as a driving force in water and land management indicate the importance of a coordinated work force for stimulating early state development. The role of both Armillas and Palerm in directing the study of landscape archaeology is clearly implied.

Phil Weigand (Chapter 5) provides the first empirical data for the extensiveness and complexity of West Mexican agricultural systems. Acknowledging the predictions of Palerm and Armillas with respect to the widespread presence of wetland agriculture, Weigand documents over 30 km^2 of raised and drained fields. The dimensions of these features are more akin to those identified in the Maya area, but they fall into the range documented by Nichols and Fredrick for the pre-Aztec exposures mentioned above.

Jerry Howard's contribution (Chapter 6) is a detailed examination of the canal systems associated with present-day Arizona and the extremely well-developed canalization efforts of the 8th-century Hohokam. His essay confirms one of William Doolittle's (1990) recent points from his useful compendium of irrigation practices in ancient Mexico, namely, that the extent of canal length used by the Hohokam overshadowed the irrigation works of most of ancient Mexico. Howard shows that most of the canals identified in the Hohokam area were built and operated contemporaneously, further indicating the irrigation investment made by this group. His work has wide-ranging implications in two arenas. First, his data indicate that irrigation schemes of scale require an "explosive," or rapid investment in labor and resources, not a slow, incremental development. Adherence to the incremental viewpoint has historically kept Southwest prehistorians away from questions that address complex chiefdom levels of social organization and allowed little mention of water management bureaucracy and nascent state development. Secondly, at a worldwide level, Howard's work shows that irrigation systems are likely to be implemented as grand schemes, planned and organized by an authority or power above the immediate community. This is indeed the position advocated by Wittfogel but dismissed by many others following the careful work of Robert Adams and others in the Near East (Adams 1965, 1981; Adams & Nissen 1972). If the kinds of dating techniques Howard advances could be used in dating the canal systems of the southern Mesopotamia area, we might want to reassess Wittfogel's perspective. The inter-community cooperation emerging from the rapid construction of these interconnected distributary systems appears to stimulate centralization and formative state development rather than the reverse.

Charles Ortloff's essay (Chapter 7) employs the same engineering rigor that Howard uses for Hohokam canal systems, but brings it to bear upon a highly dynamic natural environment. The orogenic processes at work near the Peruvian coast forced the continual modification of canal systems. But this was not accretional or incremental change: major canal networks were planned and constructed rapidly to take advantage of the immediate topography before moments of uplift and subsequent degradation. The ill-fated Intervalley Canal represents one of the great canalization efforts in the New World, but even its singularity of purpose was broken by the forces of nature. Ortloff argues that the centralizing bureaucracy associated with canalization at this scale, coupled with the mountain-building disruptions of the Andes, resulted in the advanced technologies developed in ancient Peru. Here, the rapidly evolving irrigation technology forced developing states into the realm of predictive engineering and science. Though some may disagree, stargazing—eclipse predictions, positioning of Venus, etc.—or the cultivation of ritual knowledge were not the major catalysts for science in Peru.

The final field essay, by Clark Erickson (Chapter 8), forces us to assess the role of ancient state control and *tequio* labor (à la Angulo) on extensively modified landscapes. His point is more than a cautionary tale; it is one that emphasizes a bottom-up vs. a top-down view of the management of water and land. Through the incorporation of new archaeological survey and excavation data as well as the replication of raised field agriculture methods, Erickson argues that an accretionary model is responsible for the engineered landscape associated with Tiwanaku. He sees little connection between state centralizing forces and raised field production systems, and even less of a relationship between either of the former and population growth. Angulo as well as Nichols and Fredrick indicate the lack of a necessary demographic trigger for explaining intensive landscaping techniques (but see Isaac 1992).

A term coined by Valerio Valeri (1991) and adapted by Erickson is "centering," as opposed to centralization, when discussing community organization of the water and land management system. Centering suggests the cooperative forces developing from traditions rooted in greater antiquity than that of the state itself. Elsewhere (Scarborough 1991) I have referred to these forces as traditional formulas having developed from a series of short-term trials within a given environment and social context. The long-term adaptation by a community can be very resilient and flexible if the formulas develop in a dynamic social and physical environment.

Although Erickson's essay is an important balance to the volume, he may be understating the significance that early states—even reservoir-dependent and/or lake-margin adapted types—had over their landscapes. Do raised field systems accommodating sizable prehispanic populations represent less cooperation? As stated above, scheduling differences exist between irrigation and reservoir-dependent systems, but we must wonder if the state and its client support population are any less dependent on one another. The marvelous restoration program that Erickson has initiated, which has forced us to grapple with a bottom-up orientation, is probably still too small in scale to allow us to generalize to the entirety of the ancient landscape. How would many more thousands of residents have affected lake levels or water catchment areas? And what about the stimuli for cross-country causeways in an autonomous agricultural setting? Nevertheless, it is because of Erickson's challenging perspective that his essay concludes the geographic coverage of the volume, forcing us to assess our expectations and biases.

NOTE

1. It is important to note that catastrophic floods have influenced canal-dependent riverine states from the outset. Nevertheless, the frequency of inundation events may be greater than a century, effectively interrupting collective generational memory and the development of well-defined technical or social adaptations to curb devastation.

REFERENCES

Adams, Robert McCormick (1965) *Land Behind Baghdad.* Chicago: University of Chicago Press.
———— (1966) *The Evolution of Urban Society.* Chicago: Aldine Publishing.
———— (1981) *Heartland of Cities.* Chicago: University of Chicago Press.
Adams, Robert McCormick, and Hans J. Nissen (1972) *The Uruk Countryside.* Chicago: University of Chicago Press.
Culbert, T. Patrick (1991) "Polities in the Northern Peten, Guatemala." Pp. 128-146 in his (ed.) *Classic Maya Political History.* Cambridge, ENG: Cambridge University Press.
Demarest, Arthur A. (1992) "Ideology in Ancient Maya Cultural Evolution." Pp. 135-158 in Arthur A. Demarest & Geoffery W. Conrad (eds.) *Ideology and Pre-Columbian Civilizations.* Santa Fe, NM: School of American Research Press.
Doolittle, William E. (1990) *Canal Irrigation in Prehistoric Mexico.* Austin: University of Texas Press.
Downing, Theodore E., and McGuire Gibson, eds. (1974) *Irrigation's Impact on Society.* Tucson: Anthropological Papers of the University of Arizona, No. 25.
Gunawardana, R. A. L. H. (1971) "Irrigation and Hydraulic Society in Early Medieval Ceylon." *Past and Present* 53:3-27.
Halperin, Rhoda H. (1988) *Economies Across Cultures.* London: Macmillan Press.
———— (1989) "Ecological Versus Economic Anthropology: Changing 'Place' vs. Changing 'Hands'." Pp. 15-41 in Barry L. Isaac (ed.) *Research in Economic Anthropology, Volume 11.* Greenwich, CT: JAI Press.
Harris, Marvin (1968) *The Rise of Anthropological Theory.* New York: Thomas Y. Crowell Co.
Hunt, Robert C., and Eva Hunt (1976) "Canal Irrigation and Local Social Organization." *Current Anthropology* 17:389-411.
Isaac, Barry L. (1992) "Discussion." Pp. 441-452 in Dale R. Croes, Rebecca A. Hawkins & Barry L. Isaac (eds.) *Long-term Subsistence Change in Prehistoric North America, Suppl. 6, Research in Economic Anthropology.* Greenwich, CT: JAI Press.
Leach, Edmund R. (1959) "Hydraulic Society in Ceylon." *Past and Present* 15:2-26.
———— (1961) *Pul Eliya: A Village in Ceylon.* Cambridge, ENG: Cambridge University Press.
Mathews, Peter (1991) "Classic Maya Emblem Glyphs." Pp. 19-29 in T. Patrick Culbert (ed.) *Classic Maya Political History.* Cambridge, ENG: Cambridge University Press.
Millon, Rene (1962) "Variation in Social Responses to the Practice of Irrigation Agriculture." Pp. 56-88 in Richard B. Woodbury (ed.) *Civilization in Arid Lands.* Salt Lake City: University of Utah Anthropological Papers, No. 62.
Mitchell, William P. (1973) "The Hydraulic Hypothesis: A Reappraisal." *Current Anthropology* 14:532-534.
Moseley, Michael E. (1983) "The Good Old Days Were Better: Agrarian Collapse and Tectonics." *American Anthropologist* 85:773-799.
Polanyi, Karl (1957) "The Economy as Instituted Process." Pp. 243-269 in Karl Polanyi, Conrad M. Arensberg & Harry W. Pearson (eds.) *Trade and Market in the Early Empires.* New York: Free Press.
Scarborough, Vernon L. (1991) "Water Management Adaptations in Non-Industrial Complex Societies: An Archaeological Perspective." Pp. 101-154 in Michael B. Schiffer (ed.) *Archaeological Method and Theory, Volume 3.* Tucson: University of Arizona Press.
Scarborough, Vernon L., and Gary Gallopin (1991) "A Water Storage Adaptation in the Maya Lowlands." *Science* 251:658-662.
Service, Elman R. (1975) *Origins of the State and Civilization: The Process of Cultural Evolution.* New York: W. W. Norton.
Steward, Julian H. (1949) "Cultural Causality and Law: A Trial Formulation of the Development of Early Civilization." *American Anthropologist* 51:1-27.

―――――― (1955) *Irrigation Civilizations: A Comparative Study*. Washington, DC: Pan American Union.

Valeri, Valerio (1991) "Afterward." Pp. 134-144 in J. Stephen Lansing (ed.) *Priests and Programmes*. Princeton, NJ: Princeton University Press.

Wittfogel, Karl A. (1957) *Oriental Despotism: A Comparative Study of Total Power*. New Haven: Yale University Press.

―――――― (1972) "The Hydraulic Approach to Pre-Spanish Mesoamerica." Pp. 59-80 in Frederick Johnson (ed.) *Chronology and Irrigation: The Prehistory of the Tehuacan Valley, Volume 4*. Austin: University of Texas Press.

PART I

THE SOUTHERN MAYA LOWLANDS

WATER MANAGEMENT IN THE SOUTHERN MAYA LOWLANDS:
AN ACCRETIVE MODEL FOR THE ENGINEERED LANDSCAPE

Vernon L. Scarborough

INTRODUCTION

The study of water management practices and scale allows one approach to the causal factors resulting in state formation (Scarborough 1991a, Wittfogel 1957). Nevertheless, water management in wet semitropical and tropical settings has not received the same consideration that it has in arid and semiarid environments (Doolittle 1990, Downing & M. Gibson 1974, Steward 1955, Wittfogel 1957). One such wet semitropical setting is the Maya Lowlands of upper Central America, the focus of this essay.

The ancient Maya of the southern Yucatan Peninsula represent one of the few semitropical civilizations that developed independently from other neighboring states. Furthermore, unlike the riverine-dependent primary states

Research in Economic Anthropology, Suppl. 7, pages 17-69.

17

of arid zones that developed sustained canal or distributional water systems, Maya polities maintained an extremely flexible water manipulation system that helped shape their landscape and the scale and complexity of their society (Scarborough 1992a-b, Scarborough et al. 1992, n.d.).

Water technology and landscape alterations in the Maya Lowlands are best characterized by a model of accretionary growth. State formation occurred as early as 600 B.C. in the southern Lowlands, associated with human-modified watersheds and reservoir systems. By A.D. 600, the Maya of Tikal had centralized a rainfall catchment area and the associated reservoirs, permitting hydraulic control across an urban core. The slow, accretive development of sophisticated water systems in the Maya area reflects the adaptability and longevity of this semitropical culture.

WATER MANAGEMENT DEFINED

Water management is the interruption and redirection of the natural movement or collection of water by society. The technology associated with water's manipulation is strongly constrained by the local environment. Although exceptions are found, a dichotomy exists between early complex societies developing along the great semiarid and arid waterways of the world—the Nile (Butzer 1976), Tigris-Euphrates (R. M. Adams 1980), Indus (Allchin & Allchin 1982, Scarborough 1988), and Huangho (Chang 1986, Hsu 1980)—and the semitropical civilizations which have appeared in Java (see Bronson 1978), Cambodia (Briggs 1951, Higham 1989, Van Liere 1980), Sri Lanka (Gunawardana 1971, 1981; Leach 1959), and the Maya Lowlands (Flannery 1982, Harrison & Turner 1978). The former depended on canalization and/or floodplain sediment renewal to support the populations necessary to sustain their urban aggregates. The latter drew most of their water from tanks or reservoirs. In the New World, the great semiarid states of Peru and highland Mexico were associated with rugged topography and less consequential drainages when compared to their semiarid state equivalents in the Old World. Nevertheless, water management technique was heavily dependent on terraces, diversion dams, aqueducts, and canal networks within valley-limited drainages which were knit together by expanding empires.

In the case of the Maya Lowlands, the semitropical setting significantly influenced the settlement pattern and land-use adaptations of the Maya. When contrasted with the high population densities and rigid grid plan of cities as large as Teotihuacan in the temperate highlands of Mexico (Millon 1973, Sanders et al. 1979) or upland Chan Chan, Peru (Moseley & Day 1982), the Maya appear to be a series of loosely-organized, independent units—household to household, village to village. Nevertheless, the Maya represent one of the most long-lived of early civilizations, with the earliest sophisticated evidence

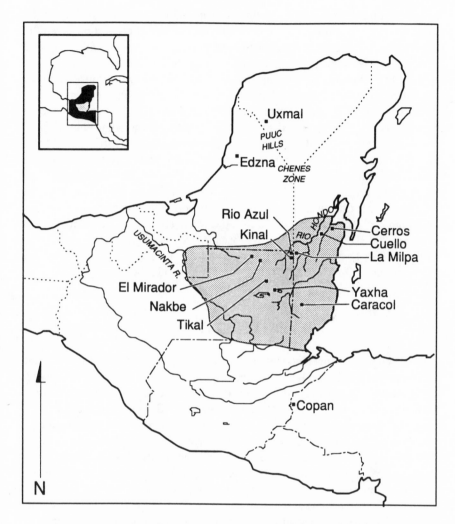

Figure 1.   Map of Maya Lowlands, with Boundaries for the
Southern Lowlands (after Folan et al. 1983, Harrison, this volume)

for monumental architecture by 600 B.C. (Hansen 1991). Until A.D. 900 and
its economic and political collapse (Culbert 1973, 1988), Maya civilization
continued with limited interruption and without wholesale replacement of
culture (Culbert 1991a), a period of longevity seldom sustained by other early
experiments in statecraft (Yoffee & Cowgill 1988).

My thesis is that the longevity of the Maya can be attributable to their
successful, uninterrupted, accretive landscape engineering, an adaptation in

part conditioned by a seasonally-limited water supply and the fragility of the wet-dry tropical forest. Unlike ancient civilizations that occupied rapidly transformable landscapes associated with permanent, year-round rivers and streams, where intensive canalization and/or flood recession management (Park 1992) allowed the rise and fall of many great civilization, the Maya contoured their landscape in an additive manner, expanding over centuries on the earlier techniques and initially modified land surfaces. The lowland Maya densely occupied a comparatively non-riverine area larger than that of most other early states and had a dispersed population identified by strikingly similar material culture from the Usumacinta in Chiapas, Mexico, to the Rio Hondo in Belize (Figure 1).

Siltation, erosion, and salinization rapidly accelerate over a semiarid landscape with the diversion of water from permanent streams into canals. Although evidence does show that lowland Maya civilization's abrupt collapse in A.D. 900-1000 occurred partly because of environmental degradation (Culbert 1988, Deevey et al. 1979, Harrison 1977, Rice et al. 1985),[1] it survived for more than 1,500 years as a well-defined culture, identifiably very differently from that of neighboring states (Scarborough 1991b).

HISTORY

Although Karl Wittfogel is credited with the presentation of water management as a deterministic causal factor for the origin of states, Karl Marx anticipated the Hydraulic Hypothesis. Marx argued that Asiatic societies were ahistorical in the sense that small, self-sufficient villages altered their environments only marginally and without the physical changes that intensive farm labor induced (see Avineri 1969:40). Here, a town or village could be destroyed and what emerged on its leveled foundation was a village of identical complexity and scale, prone to the same routines and events of its predecessor. Marx's yardstick for history, of course, was Europe and ancient society in Greece and Rome (see Kohl 1983). To Marx, no significant historical change was possible without humans changing the environment. Further, the development of truly complex and interdependent economic units resulting in cities as he defined them was less possible in the Asian example because of the self-sustaining economy of the village and the absence of a concept for private property (Engels 1972, McGuire 1992:24).

Foreshadowing Wittfogel, Marx evaluated the concentration of state power in Asiatic societies based on the control of irrigation systems. Kin-based village insularity, coupled with an increasing population, resulted in loosely organized, segmental groups evolving around a common water system. Under the inspiration of religion, a despot arose to receive tribute and connect the various economic and political units of society (Giddens 1971:26).

As a student of Max Weber, Wittfogel emphasized the bureaucratic organization apparent in state formation. Agreeing with Marx's notions of an Asiatic Mode of Production, Wittfogel argued that the early Chinese state tied to an irrigation scheme promoted despotic control by expanding the division of labor to all levels of society. The bureaucracy did not require private property or individual notions of ownership; rather, it was based on what Giddens would call "possession," or the privilege of use (Giddens 1971:26).

Oriental Despotism: A Comparative Study of Total Power was published in 1957 and was immediately heralded as a landmark in political economy. In it, Wittfogel argued that Hydraulic Society was synonymous with Oriental Despotism. If a society were (1) more economically complex than that of simple subsistence agriculture, (2) outside the influence of successful rainfall agriculture, and (3) not based on a property-ownership industrial model, then Hydraulic Society could develop. Either water was relocated at great effort by mass labor allotment, or not at all.

This model for the origin of the state was promoted for each of the primary loci of early state development in the Old World and later generalized to the Western Hemisphere (Wittfogel 1972). Although Wittfogel's thesis has been severely criticized for its determinism (R. M. Adams 1966, Leach 1959, Mitchell 1973, Scarborough 1991c), it does demonstrate a well-defined role for irrigation, landscape modification, and "prehistoric" history (à la Marx) in semiarid seats of early state formation.

But what about wet semitropical and tropical environments? Although Wittfogel argued that portions of China and much of India invested considerable energy in landscape modification, those societies organized in geographic zones capable of successful rainfall agriculture were less likely to evolve complex state-level political economies. Wittfogel did show the magnitude of landscape alteration in semiarid Asia and argued for the importance of a non-European model for state development. However, in both Marx's and Wittfogel's interpretations, semitropical civilizations are dismissed as derivative of other, well-established states with identifiable histories (Wolf 1982). In their view, semitropical states are transient, without history, and without intense landscaping modifications—the latter defined as water management investments, principally canalization.

Lansing (1991) has recently reassessed Balinese history in light of the influence of Marx's paradigm. Bali is a semitropical setting shown to have been severely landscaped over a sustained period. Lansing's thesis is that, contrary to Marx and perhaps Wittfogel, the Balinese irrigation system represents a long-term cooperative undertaking, functioning at times independently of the island's political divisions or states. Nevertheless, there exists a clear investment in long-term and sustained land-use modification and, therefore, history.

Lansing's perspective for Bali also characterizes the lowland Maya case. Although massive labor projects directed by despotic rulers did play a role

in state formation in semiarid settings, other adaptations leading to state
complexity are possible. The argument that states arise based on the amount
of corvée labor made available to a select elite is simply one model, one that
may describe the intense and explosive appearance of Sumer, Old Kingdom
Egypt, Harappa (but see Miller 1985), Shang China, Moche Peru, and
Teotihuacan—basically the first indigenous states of the temperate world. In
each example, there exists a heavy and concentrated investment in landscape
alteration, much of it associated with water management technology. These
primary states rose precipitously and were vital enough to spawn the institution
of state complexity and a series of subsequent secondary states. Nevertheless,
the initial brilliance of the primary state was the intensive resource investment
in place (Gilman 1981), an investment previously unrealized at anything
approximating that scale. Few of these early temperate states lasted more than
800 years, or half the longevity of the lowland Maya,[2] and though many of
the former had a spatial radius seemingly as wide as that of the Maya, these
other civilizations were restricted to the dendritic distances of principal
waterways—unlike the dispersed land use and occupation of the non-riverine
Maya.

Lansing's *accretive model* suggests that, in areas of the world where
successful rainfall agriculture is possible but principal waterways are lacking,
other adaptations leading to state complexity are likely. The adaptation to the
environment in the semitropical setting of the Maya Lowlands was toward the
use of reservoirs and the long-term modification of local watersheds. Here,
the "mysterious" Maya, a people supposedly without history, are now
understood to have had the most complete record of their own past of any
of the prehispanic states (Schele & Freidel 1990). It was an accretionary history,
strongly dependent on the ancestry of kings and deities and the political
alliances they established through time. The great earth-moving enterprises of
Han China (Hsu 1980) or Moche-Chimu Peru (Moseley 1983; Ortloff, this
volume), associated with canalization, were not attempted in the Maya area—
not because of limited resources or small population aggregates, but because
of the near absence of permanent rivers, streams, or springs. Theirs was a
generational accretion, a modification of the environment in increments over
a 1,500-year period, extending across a vast, pocked, pitted, and folded
limestone plain.

THE MYSTERIOUS MAYA

Although we know much more about the scale and organization of the ancient
Maya than we did a generation ago, the perception continues that the Maya
states were not simply different from semiarid states, but less complicated
(Sanders & Webster 1978, 1988). In part, this view is predicated on the dispersed

settlement pattern of the Maya and the implication that populations were less controllable or rapidly mobilized to support state institutions. This interpretation, coupled with a belief that the Maya were less engaged in intensive agricultural production, has lead some researchers to implicitly dismiss the Maya as a series of complex state developments (Sanders 1979). Such an orientation is influenced by a notion that the Maya did not have the socioeconomic wherewithal to significantly alter their environment and, in Marx's terms, were unable to define "history." Because of the undeniable investment in architecture, art, and early writing and calendrical systems— material underpinnings associated with the inference of state complexity elsewhere—the Maya are thus rendered enigmatic. An alternative view of the Maya, championed here, sees their culture as less mysterious and as complicated as other primary states based on sizable population aggregates and intensive agricultural practices.

Environmental Setting

The purview of this essay is the southern Maya Lowlands extending over 68,000 km^2 and occupying Belize, central and northern Guatemala, and adjacent areas of Mexico and Honduras (Figure 1). This was the principal seat for Preclassic and Classic Period Maya civilization (600 B.C.-A.D. 900), which will be shown to be a case example of state complexity and "history" in a semitropical setting. Although subsequent developments in Maya statecraft continued in the northern Maya Lowlands following the collapse and abandonment of the south, primary, less interrupted state developments occurred principally in the south.

Rainfall is seasonal in the southern Lowlands, defined by a tropical wet-dry forest with an annual average precipitation of 1350-2000mm and interrupted by a four-month period of drought from January through April. The thin soils are fertile on the hills and better-drained flatlands (mollisols), but thick, viscous clays (vertisols) obstruct utilization of the low-lying *bajos* (seasonal, internally drained swampland) today. Approximately 30 percent of the area is covered by *bajo*, though in the most densely occupied zone, from Tikal to Rio Azul, during the Classic Period over 40 percent of the landscape was *bajo* (Culbert et al. 1989). During the dry season, water is at a premium because of the paucity of springs and permanent rivers and streams.

External drainages do exist, though they chiefly drain only the eastern and western margins of the greater Maya Lowlands. The western Usumacinta drainage carries the most water, but its incised channels and/or poorly-defined floodplain preclude well-developed canalization. The eastern Rio Azul/Rio Hondo system allows slow-moving, backwash, floodplain channelizing, but because of the absorption/dispersion characteristics of the porous limestone watershed, which permits a slow-release discharge during both the dry and wet seasons, little annual water level fluctuation results (Siemens 1978). Generally, this condition prevents a yearly floodplain sediment renewal, precluding the deployment of complicated water diversion techniques. This is not to say that the meandering course of the Rio Hondo or its tributaries will not yield evidence of intensive forms of agriculture based on water manipulation. To the contrary, the annually stable water levels have been argued to have allowed drained or raised field agriculture to flourish in northern Belize (Harrison & Turner 1983; Scarborough 1991d; Siemens 1978, 1982; cf. Pohl 1990, Pope & Dahlin 1989). Nevertheless, classic forms of riverine canalization or predictable flood sediment deposition have not occurred in the lowland Maya area.

Nor is the incidence of artesian springs or hand-excavated wells suggestive of a predictable water source available year around. Springs have been noted at some Lowland Maya communities, but generally the limestone strata defining the northeastern Peten core zone of the southern Maya Lowlands are not condusive to permanment spring activity (N. Dunning, pers. comm.). Topographically and geologically elevated from the remainder of the Yucatan Peninsula, the northeastern Peten is defined by the largest cities in the Maya area.

Where springs have been detected, however, wells have been frequently identified (see, e.g., Scarborough et al. 1992). Wells also appear in proximity to tanks or *aguadas* (natural, clay and silt-laden sinks), indicative of an elevated or perched water table and the attempt to obtain a filtered, less surface-exposed drinking source (Scarborough et al. n.d.). In the northern Maya Lowlands, greater emphasis was placed on *cenotes*, or open, vertical walled, karstic sinks defined by well water (Matheny 1978, 1982). These natural features were frequently modified to form walk-in wells. Few of these modified *cenotes* are identifiable in the south, however, except perhaps in the low-lying Petexbatun area, where they are still relatively rare (N. Dunning, pers. comm.). Generally speaking, *cenotes* are most abundant within and to the north and east of the Chenes region, though the Puuc Hills do not accommodate *cenotes* development (see Figure 1).

It is apparent that, during the dry season, water availability in the Maya area was at a premium. What adaptations were available to the Maya in coping with this critical liability? Given the economic and political complexity to which the Maya were to aspire, treating the water deficit issue was of principal importance. This essay will show that water management was a gradual, additive process, one initiated even earlier than monumental building projects.

Climatic Change

Given the seasonal rainfall budget, weather patterns through time have had a severe impact on ancient Maya land use and water management adaptations.

Unfortunately, the number and kind of variables influencing climatic reconstruction are difficult to control. Nevertheless, two pioneer attempts have been made to model climate change in the Maya area. Folan et al. (1983) present evidence for four periods of climatic oscillation extending over the Preclassic and Classic Periods, drawing on the initial work of Gunn and Adams (1981). From 1400 B.C. to 500 B.C., the weather was wetter and perhaps cooler than at present. A drier, warmer cycle prevailed during the Formative period, which introduced statecraft to the Maya from 500 B.C. to A.D. 600. The Late Classic cultural zenith in the southern Maya Lowlands, A.D. 600-900, was identified with heavier rainfall and cooler temperatures, while the period associated with the cultural collapse of the south, A.D. 900-1200, revealed drier, warmer conditions. Folan et al. (1983:Figure 8) also provide complementary data on sea level fluctuations, indicating that the sea level rose over 2.5m from the Late Preclassic (300 B.C.) until the end of the Early Classic (A.D. 550), but subsequently dropped to present-day levels by the Terminal Classic Period (A.D. 950)(cf. Dahlin 1983).

In a recent study, Messenger (1990) argues that the southern Maya Lowlands are especially difficult to model climatically because of the apparent discrepancy between mean annual precipitation and January mean precipitation for the region. Nevertheless, he indicates that, from A.D. 200 to 900 (Classic Period), this core area received 0-10 percent less annual precipitation than normal (defined as mean annual precipitation during the 1960s), while receiving 75-100 percent more rainfall during especially cool years for January. During the Early and Middle Preclassic periods (1400-500 B.C.), the climate appears unstable, ending with cooler, wetter conditions. From 500 B.C to A.D. 200 (inclusive of the Late Preclassic), the annual average was warmer and drier. During the Terminal Classic (800-1000 A.D.), the climate was again warmer and drier, though unstable.

The two interpretations of rainfall for the southern Maya Lowlands (Folan et al. 1983, Messenger 1990) do not align chronologically, but they do tend to agree with one another. The major conflict between them occurs over the Classic Period. Messenger views climatic conditions then as drier overall, but with a winter-time precipitation increase; Folan et al. imply an Early Classic desiccation, followed by a Late Classic wet phase. Nevertheless, both of these positions are reconcilable with the water management data presented below.

Dispersed Settlement

The Lowland Maya occupied the landscape in a dispersed manner (Ashmore 1981, Culbert & Rice 1990, Scarborough & Robertson 1986). Early attempts to explain this adaptation presumed limited productivity of the land and the restrictions of slash-and-burn agricultural technology (Sanders 1963, Willey 1956). Although a new "swidden hypothesis" allowing for intensively maintained and cropped swiddens is receiving considerable attention (Ford 1986:77; Netting 1977; Sanders 1977, 1979), it does not fully address the large populations across the entirety of the Maya Lowlands (Baker 1992; Culbert & Rice 1990; Harrison, this volume). Populations appear to have been in excess of the arable uplands necessary to feed them using even intensive slash-and-burn techniques.

There is little disagreement about the dispersed population characteristic of Maya cities. The largest of the well-mapped cities demonstrate densities of little more than $900/km^2$ (Culbert et al. 1990), markedly less than those associated with Classic Period Highland Mexico, Middle Horizon Peru, Shang China, Sumer, Harappa, or even the towns attributable to Old Kingdom Egypt (Fletcher 1986). Nevertheless, the "sustaining population" outside the urban core in the Maya area did not abruptly decrease, as it did in the other examples of semiarid state formation tethered to permanent water courses. Population densities during the Classic Period were $180/km^2$ (inclusive of vast tracts of *bajo*), among the highest for any preindustrial state in the world when density is evaluated across the greater cultural landscape (Rice & Culbert 1990:26).

Although the earliest Maya may have tethered their settlements to the courses of stream channels, initially colonizing the southern Maya Lowlands by moving up the slow-moving and seasonally less predictable streams flanking the interior of the Peninsula (Puleston & Puleston 1971), subsequent populations were less inclined to accept this settlement adaptation. Because of the heavy rainfall during eight months of the year, people could venture away from riverine settings and occupy the margins of natural *aguadas* (sinks) and *bajos* (swamplands). If the water-retaining character of a natural depression were enhanced by human alteration, then long-term residency at that location was possible. Further, the construction of formal reservoirs and diversion features by the Late Preclassic Period (300 B.C.-A.D. 150) opened the landscape in ways not possible in more arid state experiments. Dense population aggregates comparable to those defined at Teotihuacan in Highland Mexico or Chan Chan, Peru, were less likely. Nevertheless, reservoirs at the household and village level permitted ready access to collected water, with the size of the village dependent on the capacity of the tank. Today, this model of "one tank, one village" is the organizing principle across the densely occupied landscape of semitropical South India and Sri Lanka, an environment similar in many respects to the southern Maya Lowlands (Chambers 1980, Leach 1961, Scarborough 1991a).

LAND AND WATER

In most discussions of agricultural potential, water is mentioned as a critical resource, but attention is focused upon the kind and amount of land in production as well as the crop and associated technology used to develop the land. Seldom is water considered beyond the technology to relocate it. For early states in semiarid settings, where rivers provide the canalized source for irrigation, water availability is assumed. Seasonal fluctuations are apparent but predictable, and greater scholarly attention is directed toward the preparation and yield of the land. The ultimate source of the water is seldom in question, located in a faraway and immense watershed. The ethnographic literature does recognize conflict resolution associated with limited access to canalized sources (Hunt & Hunt 1976, Scarborough 1991a), but ultimate source is less commonly examined, in part because the community or site lies some distance from it.

Water must be considered an independent variable in any land-use study. If it can be assumed or predicted along a stream course or canal system, other variables can take on greater significance. In the Maya Lowlands, ultimate source could not be assumed, though through time, greater predictability for the resource developed as the reservoir technology evolved. Nevertheless, this dependence on capturing rainfall from diminutive and immediate catchment areas, or "micro-watersheds," which in turn directed runoff into depressions or tanks, presents water as the unequivocal independent variable for the Maya Lowlands.

In a recent article, Drennan (1988) has suggested that intensification of land use was most pronounced in settings like the Maya Lowlands, because the dispersed population base lived in immediate proximity to their plots. This adaptation was unlike those practiced in the highlands of Mexico, where compaction and nucleation were the more common settlement pattern. Drennan suggests that compaction is a normal condition for settlements and that a dispersed population is an anomaly. However, the settlement pattern in the Maya area is not a biased-random distribution of households on the landscape. Rather, it represents a set of decisions to best secure a predictable water source at the micro-watershed level, initially for potable water supplies and subsequently for agricultural ends. Land and soil fertility in this context are most dependent on water and its source.

Emphasis on source and the construction and maintenance of micro-watersheds in the southern Maya Lowlands evolved through time. From the Late Preclassic Period (300 B.C.-A.D. 150) until the Late Classic Period (A.D. 600-900), significant changes in the overall watershed-dependent adaptation occurred, induced by increased population densities and possible fluctuations in climate. Although water management adaptations were altered, the slow, accretionary development of the engineered landscape continued.

PRECLASSIC PERIOD (1000 B.C.-A.D. 150)

The earliest evidence for water manipulation in the Maya Lowlands is reported from Albion Island, Belize (Bloom et al. 1985; Pohl 1990) and most recently from Cobweb Swamp, Belize (Jacob 1991). Shallow ditches draining the margins of the swamps are interpreted as an elevated water table cropping technique dating as early as 1000 B.C. As documented today in southern Belize (Wilk 1985), riverbank (dry-season, floodwater recessional) farming would entail the type of ditching identified during the Preclassic. In swamp-like settings modified by drainage ditches and less encumbered by vegetation requiring considerable energy to clear, incipient agriculture demanded less labor than that practiced in adjacent upland regions.

Although speculative, it is possible that the acceleration of sediment fill, the so-called Maya Clays, found in core samples taken from the above two swamps and the Central Peten Lake Region (Rice et al. 1985) may reflect upland clearance during and following the Late Preclassic Period, when swamp-margin soils were becoming exhausted by repeated use. Such upland clearance may have had two ends: (1) to increase agricultural yields by swidden cropping of the uplands and, (2) to accelerate erosional rates as a method of replenishing depleted soils in the lowlying depressions and *bajos* (swamplands) adjacent to the uplands.

From the beginning, water management in the Maya Lowlands was a different construct than was found in the temperate riverine zones. If seasonal runoff and associated alluvium were directed crudely to lowlying crop lands and into the gravity-fed swamp depressions, their diversion represents an adaptation to water catchment maintenance, an early introduction to the later complicated systems based solely on a human-made watershed (see below).

Cuello

Throughout much of the Yucatan Peninsula, early quarrying of the elevated limestone bedrock produced basins, tanks, and cisterns. With greater antiquity than the other known examples, Cuello, Belize, is arguably associated with the earliest cistern (Hammond 1991). Two limestone rock carved cavities are identified within the domestic locus of the carefully exposed Platform 34. The function of these constricted oriface, subterranean chambers (*chultuns*) may have been food or beverage storage, as suggested for Tikal at a slightly later time (Coe 1990, Dahlin & Litzinger 1986, Puleston 1971), but in at least one case the construction and shape of the feature suggest a water holding function at Cuello (Miksicek et al. 1991). By 300 B.C., the deliberate quarrying of cisterns and/or wells into the limestone carapace underlying most of the Yucatan was established.

Early in the first millennium B.C., the Maya were already landscaping their environs, even prior to monumental architecture. The two main components defining water management in the Lowlands were established: (1) channelizing or ditching, and (2) basin construction (i.e, *chultuns*). Perhaps catchment clearance had also begun.

Nakbe

The initial appearance of public buildings has been reported at Altar de Sacrificios (Willey 1977), Tikal (Laporte & Fialko 1990), and Nakbe (Hansen 1991) by 600-400 B.C. The most impressive energy investment in architecture at this time comes from Nakbe, where an undecorated 20m-high pyramid was constructed as well as several smaller structures. Hansen (1991) indicates that such grand public architecture may have been precipitated by a need for a water-collecting facility at the Middle Preclassic community. Without explicitly stating so, he suggests that the quarried depressions created to produce the pyramidal concentrations of stone and clay would have functioned as one or more tanks, and that the pavements designed to define courtyards and plazas would have provided ready catchment surfaces for directing runoff into such tanks, with a minimum of erosion, sedimentation, or seepage. Today, there are no water sources at the site, and Hansen's team must travel 5.6 km by muleback to obtain water for camp.

El Mirador

It is likely that the largest site in the Maya area is El Mirador, Peten, Guatemala (Dahlin 1984; Graham 1967; Matheny 1980, 1986), lying only 13 km from water-deficient Nakbe and set on the immediate margins of a sizable *bajo* (Figure 2). Recent excavation programs indicate an explosive Late Preclassic construction episode followed by a less well-defined Early Classic occupation. An immense investment was made in the volume of monumental architecture at the site. Where the fill for these structures was obtained is not apparent from the presently available maps. Nevertheless, water shortfalls are again pronounced, perhaps indicating that the visible architectural volume at the site is to a degree an inverted image of the easily hidden and severely degraded depression volume.[3] Two of the largest acropolis complexes at El Mirador have an architectural volume of well over 1,000,000 m^3, a figure comparable to the construction fill composing the Pyramid of the Sun at Teotihuacan. Although resourceful landscaping probably took advantage of any natural promontories to further elevate the grand pyramidal structures at the site, major quarrying operations were clearly conducted. The large *bajo* (swampland) upon which El Mirador rests has four lengthy causeways traversing it, each radiating from the site's core. Removal of quarried fill used to construct these causeways modified the existing depression (Dahlin 1983).

Generally, causeways are viewed as traffic corridors with no function other than the relocation of people and things. This interpretation assumes that *bajos* are primarily wasted environmental space, which was, when unavoidable, crossed as expeditiously as possible. In the case of El Mirador, initial testing suggests that the causeways were elevated only slightly above the swamp

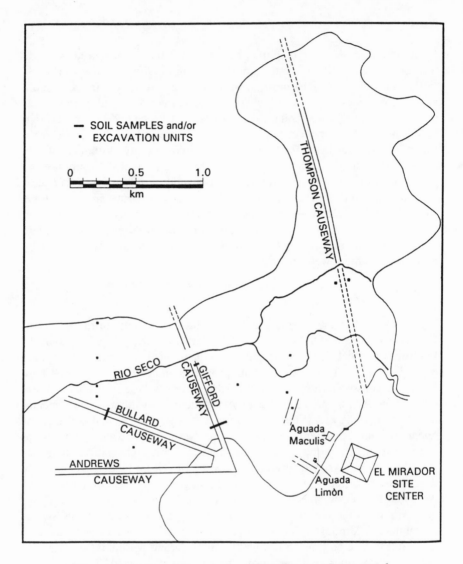

Figure 2.   Map of Causeways at El Mirador (Courtesy of
New World Archaeological Foundation and B. Dahlin)

margins (Dahlin et al. 1980). Given the quantity of clay and limestone used
in the construction of the structures at the site, and the absence of huge quarry
scars (at least within the massive West Group), *bajo*s are postulated as the
source for much of the fill used in constructing El Mirador. The causeways,
then, are accessways into the *bajo*s, and they may represent the original, slightly

elevated ground of the *bajo* surface. The causeway strips were scraped around to produce their elevated, linear appearance, as demonstrated during the Late Preclassic Period at Cerros (see below).

Of special interest are the breaks in the four major causeways, reported on the immediate flanks of El Mirador, that otherwise would connect to high ground opposite the trajectory of each causeway (Dahlin 1984, Graham 1967). Although erosion of a causeway's margins is predictable over a nearly 2,000-year period of disuse, the fact that a 300-600m gap exists in each of the causeways except the shortest one may be more than coincidental. This same clear termination of a causeway prior to traversing a final portion of a *bajo* depression is apparent at Terminal Classic Kinal, dating over half a millenium later (see *Kinal*, below).

The likelihood exists that *bajo*s were managed at a very early date. In addition to the causeways, several housemounds were mapped in the *bajo* below El Mirador, and the excavation of four of them predictably revealed a Terminal Preclassic date (Dahlin 1983). The argument that vast tracts of the Lowland Maya area represent former shallow lakes cannot be dismissed (Cooke 1931, Harrison 1977, Palerm & Wolf 1957), though the seasonally inundated *bajo*s have not yet been shown to have functioned in this manner. Nevertheless, a desired gradient during the rainy season may have been achieved by scraping the shallow bed of the *bajo* floor. Not only would structural fill be made readily available for pyramids and courtyard groups, but portions of the *bajo* would be used to promote agricultural ends. The lateral stripping of construction fill has been well documented at Cerros for a comparable period (Scarborough 1983, 1991d). The absence of a connecting link at the termination of the causeways suggests a necessary passage for water around the causeway system. Presumably, a perishable wood structure would have bridged the channel at the terminus of the causeway, allowing its traditionally accepted function.[4] It is important to note, however, that no fields or related agricultural features are yet distinguishable in the Mirador *bajo* system (Dahlin 1983).

In addition to the causeways identified at El Mirador, several roads have been noted by Ian Graham (1967), one extending 12 km from the site and defined by the *bajo*s it has breached (Figure 3). Although their function as traffic corridors remains unchallenged, the position of these causeways across sometimes wide segments of shallow *bajo* but in proximity to already high ground suggests additional use. The energy and time necessary to construct some causeways may reflect attempts to impound runoff or divert it to locations better suited for human use. Causeways functioned as dams or dikes in later periods.[5]

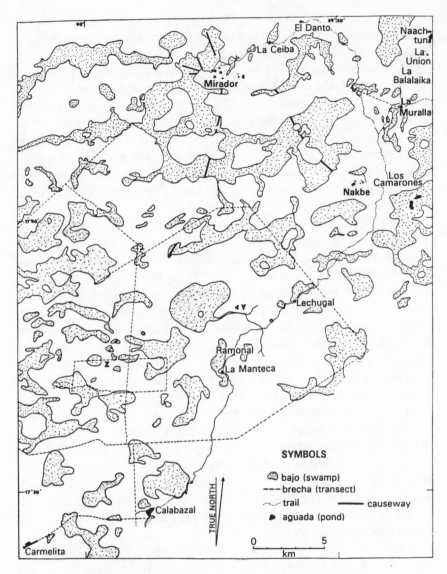

Figure 3.   Map of Causeways in the Vicinity of El Mirador
(Courtesy of Middle American Research Institute and I. Graham)

Edzna

A second Late Preclassic site associated with massive landscape modification
is Edzna, Campeche (Matheny 1976, Matheny et al. 1983). Edzna occupies

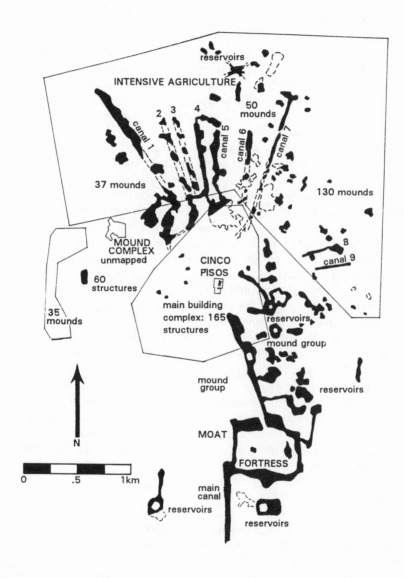

Figure 4. Map of Edzna (Courtesy of University
of New Mexico Press and R.T. Matheny)

a shallow valley in northwestern Yucatan Peninsula (Figure 4). Although technically in the northern Maya Lowlands, Edzna receives 1000mm of rainfall during the rainy season and resembles other Late Preclassic water management adaptations further south.

Matheny (1976) argues that over 20 km of canal length at Edzna, coupled with numerous reservoirs, compose a huge hydraulic system comparable in scale of the earth moving expenditures to the construction of both the Pyramid of the Sun and the Pyramid of the Moon at Teotihuacan. Such massive construction projects required the quarrying of volumes of earth and stone similar to those necessary for the erection of the immense acropolises and pyramid complexes at El Mirador.

The main canal at Edzna is 12 km long, and about 1.5m deep and 50m wide for at least half its length. At its north end, the canal connects a large moat system which, in turn, joins a radiating series of spoke-like channels. The latter canals converged on the civic center and were associated with several residential reservoirs. The entire storage capacity of the canal basins was 2,000,000 m^3.

Although the water retaining purpose of the hydraulic system is clear, given the extended dry season in northern Yucatan, the precise function of the water adaptation remains unclear. Because the greater site area has not been contour mapped, the directional flow within this human-modified watershed is not well understood. Nevertheless, Matheny (1976) indicates that the movement of water was from the splayed canal system toward the center of the site, which was elevated on a rock outcrop. I suggest that, during the rainy season, water would not inundate this area of the site, while in the dry season water would be concentrated in immediate proximity to the center. In the northwest sector of the site, Matheny (1976:642) indicates that the reservoirs are higher than the connecting canals, arguing that water was released from these reservoirs to the southern ends of the canals which, in turn, carried water by way of small feeder channels to other reservoirs near civic structures. If Matheny is right, Edzna represents in reverse the centralizing influence and controlled movement of water away from the site core, as demonstrated in the Late Classic Period (600-900 B.C.) (see below).

Cerros

The Late Preclassic community of Cerros, Belize, reveals a water management system which supports the interpretations provided by Matheny (1976) at the much larger site of Edzna and which lends further backing to the previously suggested functions of hydraulic manipulations at El Mirador (Figure 5). Considerable energy was invested in the engineering of a low-lying landscape, as was the case with the other two sites, a Late Preclassic adaptation.

As in Edzna, the community core of Cerros rests at the lowest margin of the terrain on a bight or peninsula that projects into Chetumal Bay. An

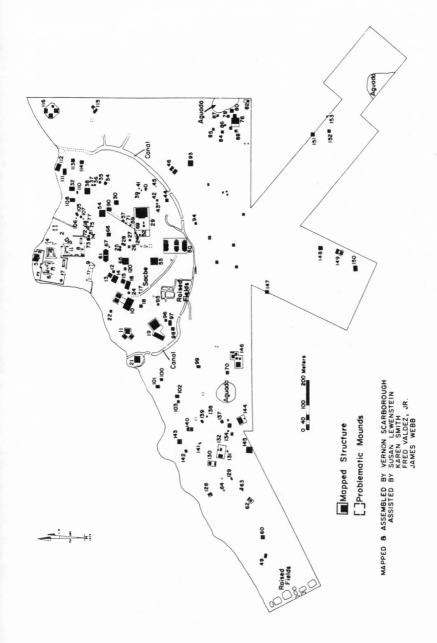

MAPPED & ASSEMBLED BY VERNON SCARBOROUGH
ASSISTED BY SUSAN LEWENSTEIN
KAREN SMITH
FRED VALDEZ, JR.
JAMES WEBB

■ Mapped Structure

[ ] Problematic Mounds

Figure 5. Map of Cerros

35

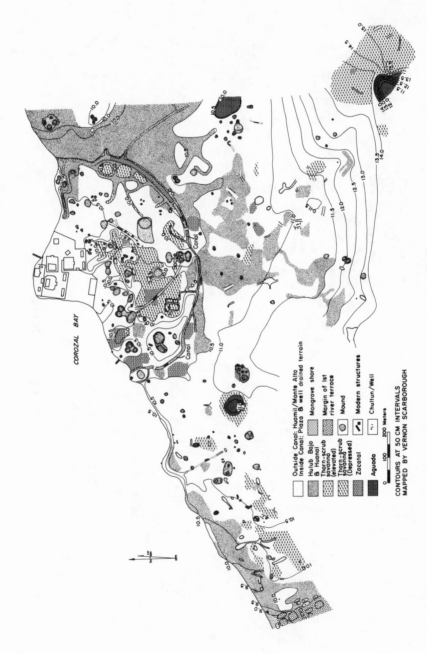

Figure 6. Map of Cerros Environs

environmental reconstruction of the setting was carried out (Scarborough 1983, 1991d; see Figure 6), showing that the water table/sea level has risen at least 1m since the site was occupied and the engineered landscape filled with aggrading sediment. Representative of approximately 200,000 m³, or one-tenth the quarried fill suggested by the storage capacity of the basin canals and reservoirs at Edzna, the Cerros survey and excavation program demonstrates the systematic horizontal stripping of the underlying limestone in producing a human-made watershed. Within the contour mapped area of 1.5 km, vertical critical relief only undulated by 4m excepting structure height, which climbed to a maximum of 22m. The core area of the site enclosed by the main canal extended over 37 ha and contained 99 percent of the structural fill volume identified at the site (Scarborough 1991d:183), yet registered only a 2m relief differential across its surface, excluding elevated structure height. Quarry fill was obtained principally from within the core area, and removed systematically to produce the catchment surface and depression volume defining the water management system.

The main canal at Cerros was 1.2 km long, approximately 6m wide and 2m deep, and graded less than 1m from west to east (Figure 7). Because of the system of reservoirs, feeder canals, sills, and dikes, runoff during the rainy season was directed into tanks and basins throughout the settlement. Although

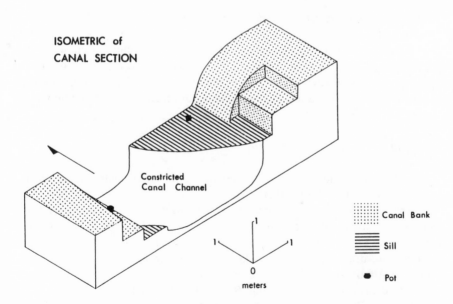

Figure 7. Isometric Cross-section of the Main Canal at Cerros

the main canal could hold 14,400 m^3, it would take fewer than 5 cm of runoff across the core site area to fill and overflow the canal immediately. Wright et al. (1959:17) state, "Falls of rain are often of an intense kind; 5 inches [12.8 cm] in 24 hours is experienced not infrequently." Given the impermeable clays underlying quarried depressions as well as the exposed indurated limestone caprock, relatively little seepage loss was possible. Cowgill and Hutchinson (1963:20) indicate that only 20 percent of the runoff into Bajo de Santa Fe was absorbed by the soil. At Cerros, the chest-high water levels negotiated at the 9.5m contour interval near the center of the core area in July of 1976 strongly indicate the community-wide hydraulic system necessary to prevent soil damage as well as household disruption. The contours at the site indicate that high ground connected all civic and residential space, yet provided ready access to water.

A portion of the site that received considerable attention was a low relief zone featuring a limited number of raised fields separated by a causeway (*sacbe*) from two reservoirs and a concentration of housemounds (Figure 8). The causeway was constructed principally by quarrying the margins of the feature to produce the adjacent low-lying areas. Although the road functioned to connect the residential area to the northwest with the ballcourt group to the southeast, it also acted as a dike. Functioning as a dam, it divided the private and (presumably) potable water source of the reservoirs from the more public and agricultural water source of the raised fields and main canal.

Water stores were retained and distributed across the Cerros settlement as a consequence of the severity of the four-month annual drought. Because water was readily available to any spatial sector of the community, it could not be easily controlled by a limited few elites. Although corporate labor and town planning are well attested by this hydraulic system (Scarborough 1991d), evidence does not suggest that water was a centralizing force in sociopolitical control at Cerros.

Summary

By the Late Preclassic Period (300 B.C.-A.D. 150), water management adaptations within the southern Maya Lowlands are viewed as deliberate systems. Several experiments by the ancient Maya at the community level suggest a modification of low-lying settings. The Late Preclassic Period emphasized the alteration of swamp margin habitats, and much of our best evidence for drained and raised field agriculture has been recovered from this time. At Albion Island, Pulltrouser Swamp, and Cerros, early canalization is associated with swamp-like settings (Scarborough 1991d:187).

The Late Preclassic Period was a time not only of swelling population densities and staggering investments in public architecture (Scarborough

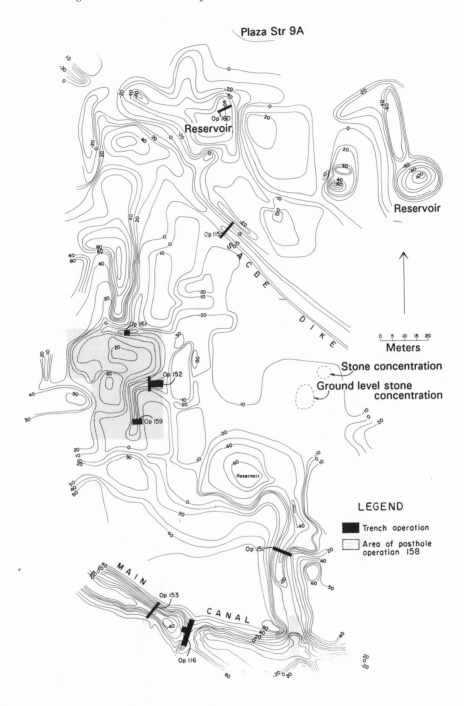

Figure 8. Raised Field Area and Associated Causeway (*Sacbe*) at Cerros

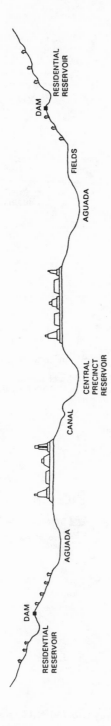

CONCAVE MICRO-WATERSHED

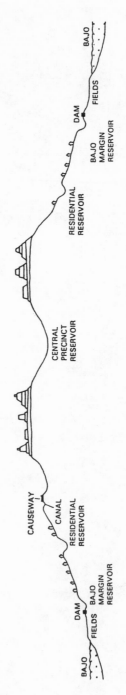

CONVEX MICRO-WATERSHED

Figure 9. Concave (Late Preclassic) and Convex (Late Classic) Micro-Watersheds

40

1991d:175-196), but also of a decrease in rainfall, as indicated by both the Folan et al. (1983) and the Messenger (1990) climatic reconstructions. Many of the larger Late Preclassic sites were positioned near swamp margins, perhaps a consequence of the shrinking availability of the source and the need to modify these depressions to cope best with the water deficit.

The latter three Late Preclassic communities examined above provide our best information concerning water management adapations during this time. In part precipitated by a climatic drying trend and an increasing population density, considerable time and energy were invested in swamp-margin manipulation. These sites can be characterized as dependent on "concave" micro-watersheds, or the movement of water from little altered, upland settings into well-managed, low-lying zones (see Figure 9). Given an established tradition of swamp-margin utilization during the Early and Middle Preclassic, the subsequent effects of an extended drought may have forced populations to concentrate land and water resources. Regardless, true control of the water resource by a formidable elite is not demonstrable.

EARLY CLASSIC PERIOD TRANSITION (A.D. 150-600)

The Classic Period in the Maya Lowlands introduced a greater emphasis on upland landscaping than was the case in the Late Preclassic. Although more extensive use of the uplands may be revealed for the Late Preclassic Period in the future, the presently identifiable terracing in the Lowlands appears to date to the Classic Period (Eaton 1975, Healy et al. 1984, Matheny & Gurr 1983, Turner 1974). Furthermore, regional survey transects by Ford (1986) and Rice and Rice (1980) indicate a clear settlement gravitation toward compacted upland centers during the Early Classic, manifesting less dispersal of housemounds between centers. Generally, large Classic Period sites are located on elevated terrain, but in proximity to a *bajo* (swampland) or related depression (R. E. W. Adams 1980).

The reasons for this settlement shift are not altogether clear. Nevertheless, it does suggest that the immediate *bajo* margins were not the attractive locations that they had once been. Two factors may have seriously affected the dislocation: (1) a water table rise and (2) an accelerated sedimentation rate, in amounts exceeding those manageable during the Late Preclassic— precipitating Classic Period upland terracing.

Although climatic reconstructions for the transition from Late Preclassic to Early Classic are difficult, some researchers have argued that the period of desiccation beginning in the late Middle Preclassic continued through the Early Classic (Dahlin 1983, Folan et al. 1983), with a complementary rise in sea level (Bloom et al. 1985; Scarborough 1983, 1991d). If such were the case, the impoundment of water in the relatively shallow basin canals and reservoirs

Figure 10.   Flagstone Walkway across In-filled Main Canal at Cerros

(Edzna and Cerros) as well as in the modified *bajo* flats (El Mirador) would be jeopardized eventually by the elevated evaporation rate across the broad surfaces involved. At Cerros, directly on the sea, even a minor sea level rise would introduce brackish water contamination into the freshwater catchment.

Although truly elevated sedimentation rates are attributable to Late Classic upland deforestation (Deevey et al. 1979, Rice et al. 1985), siltation problems are evident by the end of the Late Preclassic. At Cerros, the main canal was infilled with fine silts and clays to a depth of 2m, at which point an Early Classic flagstone walkway was placed across it in at least one of the excavated sections (Scarborough 1983, 1991d) (Figures 7 and 10). The near abandonment of Cerros and other Late Preclassic communities in northern Belize and elsewhere appears to be a consequence of these environmental adjustments, though complementary sociopolitical developments also affected change (Scarborough 1991d:190-196).

The accelerated population growth identified with the Late Preclassic Period forced the intensification of the agricultural base. Because of the early attraction to the elevated water table associated with *bajo* margins, settlement concentrated in these zones. Clearly, other factors—such as defensibility, trade and exchange networks, access to the most favorable soil, etc.—influence the precise location of a site. Nevertheless, the ready availability of water was a primary factor in *bajo*-margin occupation. Population growth, however, did push communities to expand away from swamp margins into the flanking uplands. The subsequent sedimentation increase is likely a product of these latter populations' exploitation of the more fragile uplands. Initially, this land-use exploitation may have been encouraged, not simply for the dispersal of people away from overpopulated *bajo* margins, but for the increased water catchment area exposed as a consequence of cutting down the jungle vegetation. Reduced evapotranspiration and greater runoff from the uplands would have increased water supplies in the natural and artificial depressions throughout the Lowlands.

During the Early Classic, the environmental situation may have severely deteriorated. Though drought-like conditions prevailed, the exposed upland margins of the Lowlands would have allowed increased sediment loads into the modified *bajos* and related depressions. This may have resulted in more maintenance labor than *bajo*-margin dwellers could expend. Although a minority opinion, some now suggest that the initial attraction that Preclassic peoples had to the swamps was never again fully realized, given the investment necessary to reclaim them (Pohl et al. 1990; Pope & Dahlin 1989).

Terracing would have been a transitional development set in place by the displacement of Late Preclassic populations. Terraces may have been built in the beginning as an attempt to slow the erosion of soils into the *bajos*. Although erosion control remained an important aspect of upland terracing, cropping on the leveled surfaces became the desired end. Turner states that "tens of thousands of relic terraces crisscross the hillsides of southern Campeche and Quintana Roo, encompassing an area exceeding 10,000 square kilometers" (Turner 1974:119, cited in Matheny & Gurr 1983).

Coupled with the movement into the uplands and the terracing of slopes was the increased need for water sources. Although the *bajo* margins were never abandoned, due to the ponding of water from even unmanaged upland sources, greater emphasis through time was placed on the collection of the water source higher up the slope. Messenger (1990) does argue for slightly drier conditions than today in the southern Maya Lowlands by A.D. 200, but he suggests that January rainfall may have been higher than normal. Reservoirs and efficiently paved catchment areas would have been designed and built to stave off overall Early Classic drought-like conditions but maximized to collect as much water as possible during the wet season. We have few examples of well-dated Early Classic reservoir complexes, though Rio Azul suggests such an adaptation and Harrison (this volume) indicates an Early Classic date for the inception of the Palace Reservoir at Tikal. Even though positioned in immediate proximity to the only significant river in northeastern Peten, the occupants of Rio Azul constructed one of the largest reservoirs of the time within the central precinct (Adams 1990). Other sites near former water sources also suggest reservoir construction—such as Yaxha, overlooking Lake Yaxha (D. Rice, pers. comm. 1991). Clearly, the Early Classic Period forced even seemingly water abundant communities to accommodate water shortages.

LATE CLASSIC PERIOD (A.D. 600-900)

For the Classic Period in the southern Maya Lowlands, significant increases in population densities and monumental construction programs are widely reported. Nevertheless, the commonly accepted regional political instability (Willey 1974) indicated between Early and Late Classic times (ca. A.D. 550) does correlate to a climatic shift from dry to wet, according to the Folan et al. (1983) model. The political turbulence during this transition is attributable to many factors (Culbert 1991b), but an increased sophistication in water management technique gained during the Early Classic at some sites and not others may have preadapted these same communities to greater resource centralization and economic expansion given an increase in precipitation.

Tikal

By the Late Classic Period, Tikal manifests one of the most sophisticated water control systems in the New World (Scarborough & Gallopin 1991). A heavy investment in upland water containment during the drought-like conditions postulated for the Early Classic Period allowed the refinements of

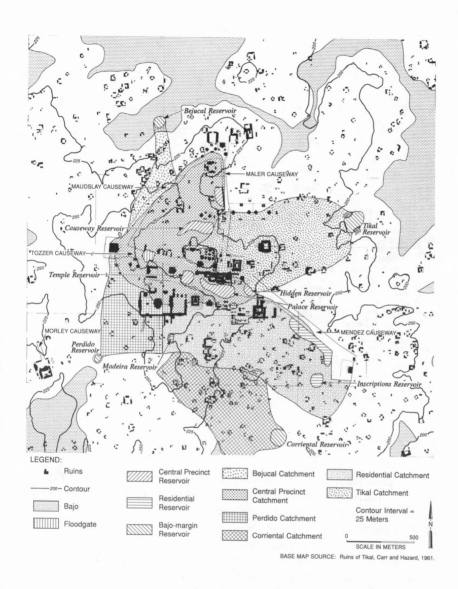

Figure 11. Map of Tikal Catchments

the Late Classic. The water system at Tikal was defined by six major reservoir catchment areas, or drainage divides, directing runoff from the summit of the site core (Figure 11). Unlike the low-lying "concave" catchment systems of the Late Preclassic Period, Tikal's system carefully controlled the movement of

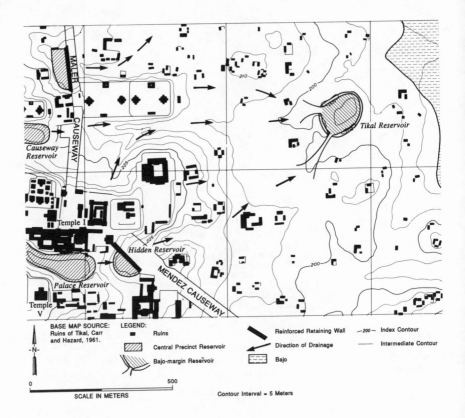

Figure 12.   Close-up Map of Causeways and Reservoirs at Tikal

runoff across the surface of a "convex" catchment and thereby held sway over an entire micro-watershed (see Figure 9). This "convex" catchment system permitted vastly greater control over the resource than did the earlier systems in the Lowlands. The most elevated "central precinct catchment" at Tikal covered an area of 62 ha and—because of limited seepage loss owing to the impervious plaza pavements and plastered monumental architecture—alone could collect over 900,000 m^3 of water (based on 1500 mm of rainfall annually). The runoff from this and adjacent catchment areas easily filled the associated reservoirs during the eight-month wet season (Gallopin 1990). Eventually, each catchment area terminated in the *bajo*-margin reservoirs or natural *aguadas*, ultimately leading into the flanking *bajo*s (Figure 12).

Three reservoir types have been defined at Tikal, based on reservoir location and amount of water contained: (1) central precinct reservoirs, (2) residential reservoirs, and (3) *bajo*-margin reservoirs. The six central precinct reservoirs contained 100,000-250,000 m^3 of water and were formed behind well-defined causeways, which connected portions of the city's core but dammed water within the major catchment area. Residential reservoirs were positioned immediately below the central precinct within the most densely settled area of the community. Near the foot of the hillock upon which the core area of Tikal rests were the *bajo*-margin reservoirs, four in number and located away from the dense population aggregates found further upslope. Of the same scalar order as the central precinct reservoirs, the *bajo*-margin reservoirs were designed to capture water released from the more elevated tanks after it had been used and contaminated by upslope residents. *Bajo*-margin reservoirs are presumed to have been holding basins for agricultural fields maintained at the margins of the *bajo* during the dry season.

The Tikal system represents the most complicated example of water management in the Maya Lowlands. Although one the largest Classic Period cities, Tikal is not unique in the southern Maya Lowlands in having neither rivers nor springs in proximity. Most Classic Maya cities of Tikal's complexity, if not its size, are located on natural promontories away from permanent water sources. Because of the size, location, and density of reservoirs within the spatial core of the city, the water management system indicates resource centralization. The Tikal data suggest that greater urban compaction was possible during the Late Classic, in part because water storage facilities were centralized.

Tikal does not represent the only Late Classic community to have been examined for water control systems. Caracol (Chase & Chase 1987, Healy et al. 1984), Copan (Turner & Johnson 1979), and Uxmal (Barrera 1987) in the northern Maya Lowlands all reveal component parts of the water system defined at Tikal. These techniques illustrate the pervasiveness of the shared hydraulic knowledge in the Maya Lowlands during the Late Classic.

La Milpa

In an effort to identify the variation, scale, and complexity of Lowland Maya water management systems, a multi-year program of regional survey and excavation has been initiated in northeastern Peten and western Belize (Scarborough 1991e). In cooperation with Richard E. W. Adams, Fred Valdez, Norman Hammond, Gair Tourtellot, and the Guatemalan and Belizean authorities, the "Ancient Maya Water Management Project" has examined two large Late Classic Period cities, La Milpa and Kinal, and several less complicated rural adaptations in proximity.

Like Tikal, the city of La Milpa in northwestern Belize (Guderjan 1991) has revealed a complicated water system at a site with no permanent water source for four months of the year (Scarborough et al. 1992) (Figure 13). The central precinct of the site dominates the summit of a hillock with three reservoirs positioned at the heads of three gently sloping arroyos, naturally draining the

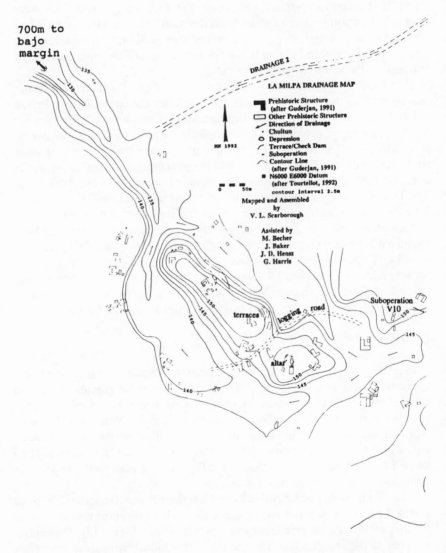

Figure 13. Preliminary Drainage Map of La Milpa

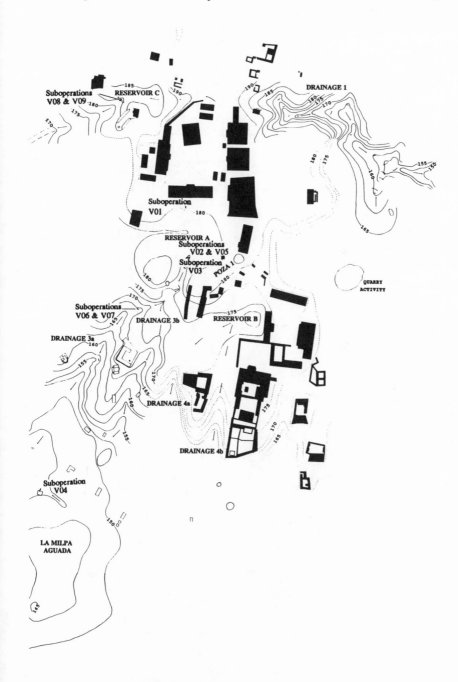

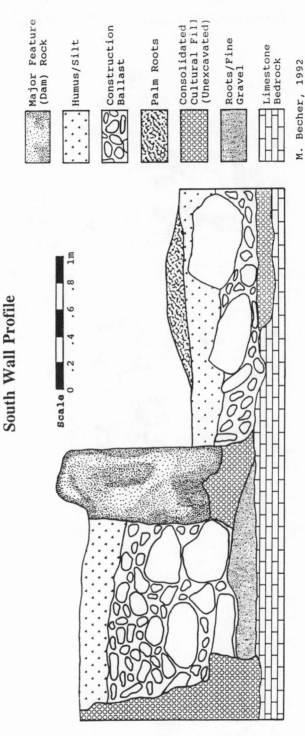

South Wall Profile

Scale 0 .2 .4 .6 .8 1m

Major Feature (Dam) Rock

Humus/Silt

Construction Ballast

Palm Roots

Consolidated Cultural Fill (Unexcavated)

Roots/Fine Gravel

Limestone Bedrock

M. Becher, 1992

Figure 14. Excavation Profile of the Tabular Limestone Dam at La Milpa

site. Survey conducted by Gair Tourtellot (pers. comm.) indicates that most of the runoff from the main plaza associated with the grand architecture at the site was directed into the northwestern arroyo. A dam approximately 17.5m long was mapped and test-excavated 200m down the channel from the plaza edge (Figure 14). The dam was U-shaped in longitudinal section, contouring to the eroded channel bed, but is likely to have been considerably built up when operational. Given the similar gradient on either side of the dam and the breached character of the feature, it does not hold ponded water today. Excavations demonstrate that large, tabular limestone slabs measuring 1.5m × 1.5m × 0.4m were placed on end, one next to the other, spanning the channel and effectively abating the movement of water. The stones were anchored in a wet marl and rubble fill 1m deep. It is likely that the dam was much higher when originally used, given the care taken to secure the foundation stones and the height of the flanking stone outcrops that constrict this location of the arroyo channel.

The second reservoir dam was an earthen feature that has severely eroded (Figure 15). The reservoir is positioned to the south of the main plaza and received runoff from the southern third of the summit catchment. Excavations suggest that a series of sluices may have deliberately cut through the embankment in an attempt to better control the passage of water. Given the volume of water contained, a single large sluice moulded into an earthen weir would easily rupture. Although constructed of stone, the three pylons identified at Tikal and associated with the "Floodgate" may have had a similar function (Scarborough & Gallopin 1991).

The third reservoir to the southeast was relatively large and appears to have provided potable water to a complex of elite courtyard groups at its margins and further downslope. Each of these reservoirs drained into channels carrying water to the south and southwest.

The above channels were flanked by ridges occupied by courtyard groups and housemounds. An occasional check dam controlled the velocity of the water as it issued from the reservoir, probably to prevent unnecessary erosion during the rainy season. After leaving the reservoirs and the inclined channel drainage, water fanned out over a series of flats believed to be fields, an adaptation not unlike that of the *akchin* reported in the dry North American Southwest (Castetter & Bell 1942). A system of shallow earthen canals is indicated by one of the excavation units. Further, at least one *chultun* was discovered within the drainage margins of the field zone, suggesting its use as a cistern (Figure 16). *Chultuns* as cisterns have been demonstrated in the much drier northern Lowlands, where dish-shaped household catchments direct water into cavernous subterranean pits (McAnany 1990). In the south, *chultuns* are generally assumed to have been used for food storage, but the location of the bell-shaped *chultun* within the drainage system and the presence of a disproportionate number of broken water jars argue for a water storage adaptation in proximity to the fields.

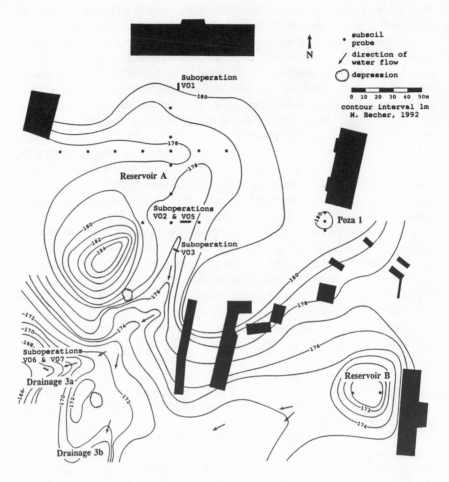

Figure 15.   Map of Reservoirs A and B at La Milpa

An *aguada* modified to improve water retention was mapped and cored for pollen and soil samples within 600m of the central precinct and south of the field area. It appears to be recharged during the rainy season by runoff from the south and southeast channelized arroyos. Water from all three reservoirs and arroyos converged on a densely settled zone immediately below the principal field locus. The consolidated channel at this location was deeply incised (as much as 2m) and eventually terminated in a small *bajo*, 2 km from the central precinct.

This western *bajo*, one of two in immediate proximity to the site, may have been used as another field location. The terminus of the main channel,

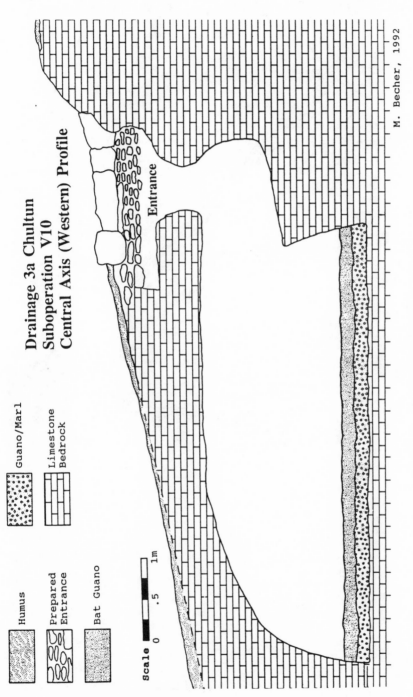

Drainage 3a Chultun
Suboperation V10
Central Axis (Western) Profile

Entrance

M. Becher, 1992

Humus

Prepared
Entrance

Bat Guano

Guano/Marl

Limestone
Bedrock

Scale   0   .5   1m

Figure 16. Profile of *chultun* at La Milpa

53

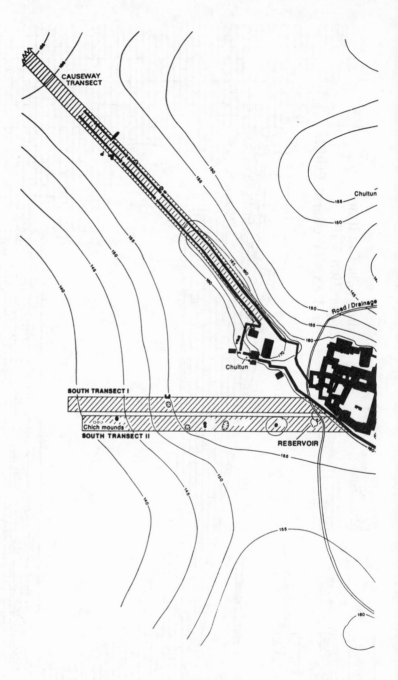

Figure 17. Map of Kinal

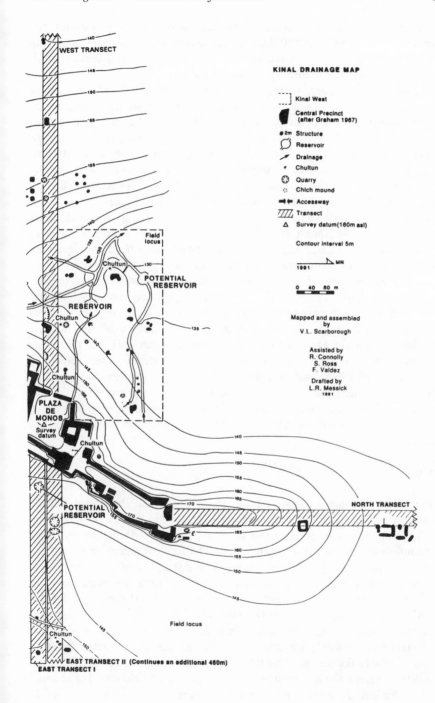

KINAL DRAINAGE MAP

Kinal West

Central Precinct
(after Graham 1967)

● 2m Structure

⬭ Reservoir

✐ Drainage

• Chultun

⊕ Quarry

○ Chich mound

➡ ⬅ Accessway

▨ Transect

△ Survey datum(160m asl)

Contour interval 5m

1991 ➘ MN

0 40 80 m

Mapped and assembled
by
V.L. Scarborough

Assisted by
R. Connolly
S. Ross
F. Valdez

Drafted by
L.R. Messick
1991

representing the combined force of all three arroyo catchment zones, was dammed by a 1m high earth and stone plug before issuing into the *bajo*. Time did not permit excavation of the feature but, if aboriginal, this feature would strongly suggest water manipulation within the *bajo*.

Although the data suggest the presence of a sophisticated water management system, the La Milpa system does differ from the Tikal model in one critical respect. Water appears to travel through an elevated field area before entering a second and more densely occupied zone, thus allowing potential agricultural pollutants to contaminate a residential drinking supply. The possibility does exist, however, that the large *aguada* immediately to the south functioned as a filtering system for the second residential zone. From this residential zone, the system drained into potential *bajo*-margin fields (see Figure 13).

The central precinct at La Milpa was defined by one other major drainage issuing to the east/southeast. It differed from the other three drainages by virtue of its precipitous, incised incline and the absence of a head-end reservoir. Although few check-dam terraces were identified along the other arroyos (only one clearly enough defined to warrant excavation), several well-defined terraces were mapped here. These check-dam terraces represent erosional control features that may have been seasonally planted, but which were not involved in reservoir release. A *bajo* does exist at the terminus of this arroyo, approximately 3 km northeast from the central precinct area, but the severe gradient within the immediate area of the site core indicates a less integrated residential spatial relationship when compared to the southern and western drainages previously described. Control and access to water along this channel were too difficult, though an investment in terrace erosion control was made. The latter is hypothesized to have reduced the sedimentation rate into the *bajo* margins.

Kinal

During the Terminal Classic Period, the site of Kinal, Peten, only 25 km southwest of La Milpa, was most intensively occupied (Adams 1989, Graham 1967). The site rests on a ridge dividing two immense *bajo*s to the northeast and southwest (Figure 17). Although the site had a clear defensive advantage, accented by a massive parapet wall circumscribing the summit central precinct, the paved courtyards and monumental architecture again preserved and directed runoff into a well-conceived reservoir system (Scarborough et al. n.d.).

Unlike the central precinct reservoir adaptation, in which water was collected from the summit catchment and held in sizable tanks for release downslope, the Kinal system was only dependent on the summit catchment for the diversion of runoff. The tanks at Kinal were located downslope from the central precinct, within the residential core but in proximity to presumed field loci. The channel gradient feeding the Kinal reservoirs was steep, in excess of that identified at

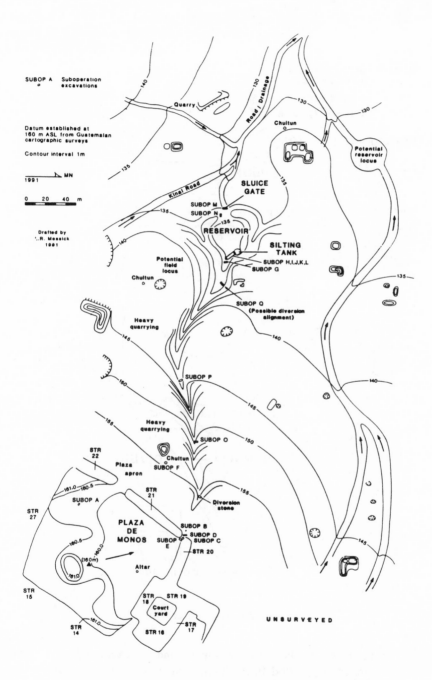

Figure 18. Map of Kinal West

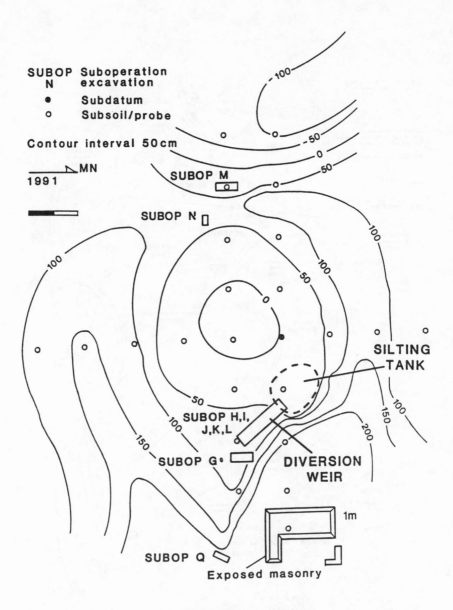

Figure 19.   Kinal Reservoir

Tikal or La Milpa. In the carefully mapped and test-excavated Kinal West zone, the precipitous, well-defined channel extended for nearly 300m before debouching into a reservoir 25m (vertical) below (Figure 18). As identified at

La Milpa, a method to slow the movement of water into the reservoir was necessary, including check-dams, a one-piece diversion stone, and a pooling area, each designed to retard erosion.

The Kinal West Reservoir received focused attention with the exposure of a dam or weir, approximately 8m in length, which directed channel water from the central precinct into a diminutive silting tank before it entered the main body of the reservoir (Figure 19). In addition to preventing large particulate matter from entering the potable water supply, the reservoir was designed to systematically release water during the dry season. A V-shaped outlet was identified, positioned at a depth in the reservoir embankment indicating that the entire volume of the reservoir could be drained (Figure 20).

The Kinal reservoir system represents a less centralized form of water management when compared to the Tikal and La Milpa systems. The site received its greatest architectural and residential investment at the end of the Classic Period, when militarism and fractious polity intrigue were probably charting the subsequent collapse of the Lowland Maya. Nevertheless, Kinal provides hydraulic details about the technology incorporated at all three sites. Reflecting the reservoir dependency of the Lowland Maya, the care taken to control erosion and sedimentation was pronounced and well-defined at Kinal.

The Classic Period sites highlighted here demonstrate the "convex" modified watershed adaptation (see Figure 9). These watersheds allowed the collection and control of the water source in a manner unlike any before. Centralized water control permitted greater sociopolitical control, given sole-source resource control. The technology and landscape engineering leading to the convex system was initiated by the Middle Preclassic Period. By the Late Preclassic Period most of the principles had been established in the "concave" watershed setting. With the changes associated with the end of the Late Preclassic, the water adaptation migrated upslope. By the Late Classic Period, however, true control over the most precious of resources—water—was possible at the larger sites. This development of control and complexity was accretional, unlike the more explosive developments associated with irrigation schemes.

CONCLUSIONS

The development of Maya civilization in the southern Maya Lowlands was a consequence of several factors. One underestimated influence was the availability and enhancement of water access. Although the stimulus for monumental building was complex, with important sociopolitical and religious inspiration, the creation of human-made watersheds from the same contoured and sculpted surfaces suggests an additional, economic end. Like the pyramids of the Old Kingdom Egypt, the ziggurats of Sumer, the citadels of the

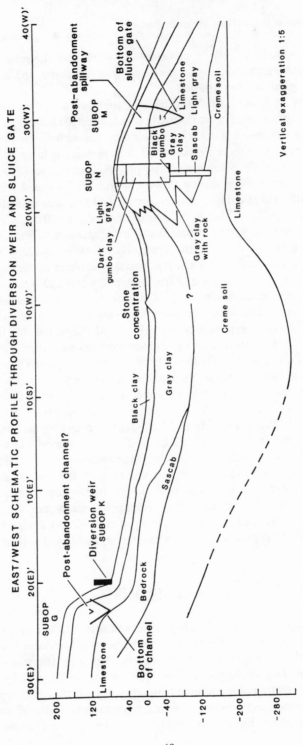

Figure 20. Schematic Cross-section of Kinal Reservoir

Harappans, and the pyramids of the Sun and Moon at Teotihuacan, monumental architecture was built by the Maya to eulogize rulers, deities, and a cultural identity. Nevertheless, the Maya had another, more immediate agenda in their landscape engineering. By systematically quarrying at some locations and elevating at others, they replaced the natural terrain with a carefully contoured cultural relief.

The lack of midden debris noted in epicentral Tikal (Harrison, this volume) indicates the importance of such water catchment surfaces. Clearly, the inadvertant addition of household waste to the main water supply was discouraged. The dispersed household and public building pattern in Maya centers reflects in part an attempt to maximize the quality of the water source. The cooperation associated with this kind of water control was not the same as that found in distributary/canal systems.

The process of Maya watershed management was an accretional one. The Late Preclassic "concave" landscapes evolved into Classic Period "convex" watersheds of urban proportions. These developments may have been partially triggered by climatic change, but increases in population, coupled with adjustments in resource availability, conflictual political relationships, alliance formation, and exchange access clearly impacted settlement growth and development. Nevertheless, the seasonal water deficit represented a constant pressure upon an expanding state. Runoff modifications made to the environment were initiated as early as 1000 B.C. At sites such as Tikal, a continuous record of occupation spans nearly 1,500 years, demonstrating the successful transformation of the environment in accommodating the growing population. On the other hand, Cerros and El Mirador did not fare as well; they reveal a necessary stage in the development of water manipulation in the Lowlands, but one unable to adjust to the changing human-made environment. The knowledge gained from these failed examples was reapplied by the Maya to slightly new circumstances, leading to greater adaptability and cultural longevity.

In contrast, Howard (this volume) demonstrates the explosive growth of canal systems among the Hohokam. They show that accretionary growth in an extensive network of canals, fields, and communities is a difficult proposition, given topographic relief and the physical properties of water. Unlike the slow, additive growth of canal length posed by Woodbury's initial model (1961), the rapid deployment of canal schemes along the Gila and Salt rivers is evidence of "history" as defined by Marx and, therefore, greater complexity.

Although the contribution in this volume by Howard does demonstrate the rapid landscape modifications associated with early canal systems, it implies that Woodbury's accretive explanation for less advanced sociopolitical organization was correct. My essay shows that Woodbury was doubly wrong; not only are canal systems explosive in their appearance in early complex society, but slowly developing water systems can introduce very complicated economic and political systems.

ACKNOWLEDGMENTS

I thank the students who have shown dedication and patience in the recent acquisition of field and archival data. Gary Gallopin, Robert Connolly, Steven Ross, Matthew Becher, Jeffrey Baker, Dr. Garry Harris, and J. D. Hensz have assisted me closely with the initiation of the "Ancient Maya Water Management Project." Richard E. W. Adams, Fred Valdez, Jr., Norman Hammond, Nicholas Dunning, and Gair Tourtellot have been strong supporters of this research, lending logistical aid in the field. I have benefited from conversations and correspondence with the above scholars as well as T. Patrick Culbert, Barry Isaac, Andy Hoffling, and Rhoda Halperin. My wife, Pat Mora, has helped me to clarify my argumentation. Grants from the National Geographic Society and the University of Cincinnati have made the recent field work at Kinal and La Milpa possible. Further support for this manuscript was made possible by a Charles Phelps Taft Memorial Fund Competitive Faculty Fellowship.

NOTES

1.   The extent of economic and political disruption to the lowland Maya during the 9th century has been recently questioned (Sabloff & Andrews V 1986). Nevertheless, few researchers contest the catastrophic changes recorded within the southern Lowlands, the core of formative and classic state development.

2.   It is difficult to firmly fix the uninterrupted temporal range of early states. The following time spans represent the periods during which early states formed and matured, based on a constellation of shared material remains and their implications for state complexity (cf. Childe 1950, Flannery 1972): (1) Sumer—3500-2350 B.C. (Crawford 1991, Redmond 1978), (2) Old Kingdom Egypt—3200-2180 B.C. (Aldred 1965, Redmond 1978), (3) Harappa—2500-1750 B.C. (Allchin & Allchin 1982), (4) Shang China—1765-1123 B.C. (Chang 1986), (5) Moche Peru—A.D. 100-800 (Lumbreras 1974; cf. Conklin & Moseley 1988), and (6) Teotihuacan—100 B.C.-A.D. 700 (Millon 1988, Sanders et al. 1979). Unlike the remainder of these primary states, the Egyptian state continued in a politically unified form until the beginning of the Christian era (Yoffee 1991:292)—although the instability associated with the end of the Old Kingdom and the beginning of the Middle Kingdom cannot be minimized. In each of the above cases, significant disorder and internal reorganization occurred at the end of the initial florescence of the primary state. The intrusion of foreign goods and material symbols suggests military conquest in most cases. The Maya do evidence militarism and periodic internal upheaval, but not on the scale demonstrated by these other states, until the Classic Maya collapse.

3.   Dahlin (1983; Dahlin et al. 1980) does note the presence of two Late Preclassic upland reservoirs and two *bajo*-margin *aguadas* in immediate proximity to the site.

4.   Dahlin et al. (1980) suggest that the Gifford Causeway at El Mirador functioned to dam water behind its length. They also conjecture that the area behind the uppermost Thompson Causeway was a lake.

5. The manipulation of ancient lake levels by causeway construction, functioning in part as dikes, is well reported among the Aztecs. It probably has an earlier inception in Highland Mexico than that associated with the Aztec capital of Tenochtitlan; see Doolittle (1990), Scarborough (1991a), and Nichols & Frederick (this volume) for a review of this material.

REFERENCES

Adams, Richard E. W. (1980) "Swamps, Canals, and the Locations of Ancient Maya Cities." *Antiquity* 54:206-214.

————, ed. (1989) *Rio Azul Reports, Number 4: The 1986 Season.* San Antonio: University of Texas-San Antonio.

———— (1990) "Archaeological Research at the Lowland Maya City of Rio Azul." *Latin American Antiquity* 1:23-41.

Adams, Robert McC. (1966) *The Evolution of Urban Society: Early Mesopotamia and Prehistoric Mexico.* Chicago: Aldine.

———— (1980) *Heartland of Cities.* Chicago: University of Chicago Press.

Aldred, Cyril (1965) *Egypt to the End of the Old Kingdom.* London: Thames & Hudson.

Allchin, Bridget, and Raymond Allchin (1982) *The Rise of Civilization in India and Pakistan.* Cambridge, ENG: Cambridge University Press.

Ashmore, Wendy, ed. (1981) *Lowland Maya Settlement Archaeology.* Albuquerque: University of New Mexico Press.

Aviner, Shlomo (1969) *Karl Marx on Colonialism and Modernization.* Garden City, NY: Anchor Books.

Baker, Jeffrey L. (1992) *Ecology, Population and Subsistence in Late Classic Maya Lowlands.* M.A. Thesis, University of Arizona, Department of Anthropology.

Barrera Rubio, Alfredo (1987) "Obras hidráulicas en la región Puuc, Yucatán, México" ("Hydraulic Works in the Puuc Region, Yucatan, Mexico"). *Boletín de la Escuela de Ciencias Antropológicas de la Universidad de Yucatán* 15:3-19.

Bloom, Paul R., Mary Pohl, and Julie Stein (1985) "Analysis of Sedimentation and Agriculture along the Rio Hondo, Northern Belize." Pp. 21-34 in M. Pohl (ed.) *Prehistoric Lowland Maya Environment and Subsistence Economy.* Cambridge, MA: Harvard University, Papers of the Peabody Museum of Archaeology and Ethnology, Vol. 77.

Briggs L. P. (1951) *The Ancient Khmer Empire.* Philadelphia: Transactions of the American Philosophical Society, Vol. 4, Pt. 1.

Bronson, Bennet (1978) "Angkor, Anuradhapura, Prambanan, Tikal: Maya Subsistence in an Asian Perspective." Pp. 255-300 in P. D. Harrison & B. L. Turner II (eds.) *Pre-Hispanic Maya Agriculture.* Albuquerque: University of New Mexico Press.

Butzer, K. W. (1976) *Early Hydraulic Civilization in Egypt: A Study in Cultural Ecology.* Chicago: University of Chicago Press.

Castetter, Edward F., and Willis H. Bell (1942) *Pima and Papago Indian Agriculture.* Albuquerque: University of New Mexico Press.

Chambers, Robert (1980) "Basic Concepts in the Organization of Irrigation." Pp. 28-50 in E. W. Coward, Jr. (ed.) *Irrigation and Agricultural Development in Asia.* Ithaca, NY: Cornell University Press.

Chang, K. C. (1986) *The Archaeology of Ancient China.* New Haven, CT: Yale University Press.

Chase, Arlen F., and Diane Z. Chase. (1987) *Investigations at the Classic Maya City of Caracol, Belize: 1985-1987.* San Francisco, CA: Pre-Columbian Art Research Institute, Monograph 3.

Childe, V. Gordon (1950) "The Urban Revolution." *Town Planning Review* 21:3-17.

Coe, William R. (1990) *Excavations in the North Acropolis, North Terraces, and Great Plaza of Tikal.* Philadelphia: University Museum, University of Pennsylvania, Tikal Report 14, Vol 3.

Conklin, William J., and Michael E. Moseley (1988) "The Patterns of Art and Power in the Early Intermediate Period." Pp. 145-163 in R. W. Keatinge (ed.) *Peruvian Prehistory.* Cambridge, ENG: Cambridge University Press.

Cooke, C. W. (1931) "Why the Mayan Cities of the Peten District, Guatemala, Were Abandoned." *Journal of the Washington Academy of Sciences* 21(13):283-287.

Cowgill, Ursula M., and G. Evelyn Hutchinson (1963) *El Bajo de Santa Fe.* Philadelphia: Transactions of the American Philosophical Society, New Series 53, Pt. 7.

Crawford, Harriet (1991) *Sumer and the Sumerians.* Cambridge, ENG: Cambridge University Press.

Culbert, T. Patrick, ed. (1973) *The Classic Maya Collapse.* Albuquerque: University of New Mexico Press.

———— (1988) "The Collapse of Classic Maya Civilization." Pp. 69-101 in N. Yoffee & G. L. Cowgill (eds.) *The Collapse of Ancient States and Civilizations.* Tucson: University of Arizona Press.

———— (1991a) "Maya Political History and Elite Interaction: A Summary View." Pp. 311-346 in his (ed.) *Classic Maya Political History.* Cambridge, ENG: Cambridge University Press.

————, ed. (1991b) *Classic Maya Political History.* Cambridge, ENG: Cambridge University Press.

Culbert, T. Patrick, Laura J. Kosakowsky, Robert E. Fry, and William A. Haviland (1990) "The Population of Tikal, Guatemala." Pp. 103-122 in T. P. Culbert & D. S. Rice (eds.) *Precolumbian Population History in the Maya Lowlands.* Albuquerque: University of New Mexico Press.

Culbert, T. Patrick, Laura J. Levi, and Luis Cruz (1989) "The Rio Azul Agronomy Program: 1986 Season." Pp. 189-214 in R. E. W. Adams (ed.) *Rio Azul Report, No.4: The 1986 Season.* San Antonio: University of Texas at San Antonio.

Culbert, T. Patrick and Don S. Rice, eds. (1990) *Precolumbian Population History in the Maya Lowlands.* Albuquerque: University of New Mexico Press.

Dahlin, Bruce H. (1983) "Climate and Prehistory on the Yucatan Peninsula." *Climatic Change* 5:245-263.

———— (1984) "A Colossus in Guatemala: The Preclassic Maya City of El Mirador." *Archaeology* 37(5):18-25.

Dahlin, Bruce H., J. E. Foss, and Mary E. Chambers (1980) "Project Acalche: Reconstructing the Natural and Cultural History of a Seasonal Swamp at El Mirador, Guatemala." Pp. 43-57 in R.T. Matheny (ed.) *El Mirador, Peten, Guatemala: An Interim Report.* Provo, UT: Papers of the New World Archaeological Foundation, No. 45.

Dahlin, Bruce H., and William J. Litzinger (1986) "Old Bottles, New Wine: The Function of *Chultuns* in the Maya Lowlands." *American Antiquity* 51:721-36.

Deevey, E. S., Don S. Rice, Prudence M. Rice, H. H Vaughan, Mark Brenner, and M. S. Flannery (1979) "Maya Urbanism: Impact on a Tropical Karst Environment." *Science* 206:298-306.

Doolittle, William E. (1990) *Canal Irrigation in Prehistoric Mexico.* Austin: University of Texas Press.

Downing, Theodore, and McGuire Gibson, eds. (1974) *Irrigation's Impact on Society.* Tucson: Anthropological Papers of the University of Arizona, No. 25.

Drennan, Robert D. (1988) "Household Location and Compact Versus Dispersed Settlement in Prehispanic Mesoamerica." Pp. 273-293 in R. R. Wilk & W. Ashmore (eds.) *Household and Community in the Mesoamerican Past.* Albuquerque: University of New Mexico Press.

Eaton, Jack D. (1975) *Ancient Agricultural Farmsteads in the Rio Bec Region of Yucatan.* Berkeley: Contributions of the University of California Archaeological Research Faculty, No. 27.

Engels, Friedrick (1972) *The Origins of Family, Private Property and the State.* (Introduction and Notes by Eleanor B. Leacock.) New York: International Publishers.

Flannery, Kent V. (1972) "The Cultural Evolution of Civilizations." *Annual Review of Ecology and Systematics* 3:399-426.

————, ed. (1982) *Maya Subsistence: Studies in Memory of Dennis E. Puleston.* New York: Academic Press.

Fletcher, Roland (1986) "Settlement Archaeology: World-Wide Comparisons." *World Archaeology* 18:59-83.

Folan, William J., Joel Gunn, Jack D. Eaton, Robert W. Patch (1983) "Paleoclimatological Patterning in Southern Mesoamerica." *Journal of Field Archaeology* 10:453-468.

Ford, Anabel (1986) *Population Growth and Social Complexity: An Examination of Settlement and Environment in the Central Maya Lowlands.* Tempe: University of Arizona, Anthropological Research Paper No. 35.

Gallopin, Gary G. (1990) *Water Storage Technology at Tikal, Guatemala.* M.A. Thesis, Department of Anthropology, University of Cincinnati.

Giddens, Anthony (1971) *Capitalism and Modern Social Theory.* Cambridge, ENG: Cambridge University Press.

Gilman, Antonio (1981) "The Development of Social Stratification in Bronze Age Europe." *Current Anthropology* 22:1-23.

Graham, Ian (1967) *Archaeological Exploration in El Peten, Guatemala.* New Orleans: Tulane University, Middle American Research Institute, Publication 33.

Guderjan, Thomas H. (1991) *Maya Settlement in Northwestern Belize: The 1988 and 1990 Seasons of the Rio Bravo Archaeological Project.* Culver City, CA: Labyrinthos.

Gunawardana, R. A. L. H. (1971) "Irrigation and Hydraulic Society in Early Medieval Ceylon." *Past and Present* 53:3-27.

———— (1981) "Social Function and Political Power: A Case Study of State Formation in Irrigation Society." Pp. 133-154 in H. J. M. Claessen & P. Skalnik (eds.) *The Study of the State.* The Hague: Mouton.

Gunn, Joel, and Richard E. W. Adams (1981) "Climate Change, Culture, and Civilization in North America." *World Archaeology* 13:87-100.

Hammond, Norman, ed. (1991) *Cuello: An Early Maya Community in Belize.* Cambridge, ENG: Cambridge University Press.

Hansen, Richard D. (1991) "The Road to Nakbe." *Natural History*, May, pp. 8-14.

Harrison, Peter D. (1977) "The Rise of the *Bajo*s and the Fall of the Maya." Pp. 470-509 in N. Hammond (ed.) *Social Process in Maya Prehistory: Studies in Honour of Sir Eric Thompson.* New York: Academic Press.

Harrison, Peter D., and B. L. Turner II, eds. (1978) *Prehispanic Maya Agriculture.* Albuquerque: University of New Mexico Press.

————, eds. (1983) *Pulltrouser Swamp: Ancient Maya Habitat, Agriculture, and Settlement in Northern Belize.* Austin: University of Texas Press.

Healy, Paul F., John D. H. Lambert, J. T. Arnason, and Richard J. Hebda (1984) "Caracol, Belize: Evidence of Ancient Maya Agricultural Terraces." *Journal of Field Archaeology* 10:397-410.

Higham, Charles (1989) *The Archaeology of Mainland Southeast Asia.* Cambridge, ENG: Cambridge University Press.

Hunt, Robert C., and Eva Hunt (1976) "Canal Irrigation and Local Social Organization." *Current Anthropology* 17:389-411.

Hsu, C. (1980) *Han Agriculture: The Formation of Early Chinese Agrarian Economy [206 B.C.-A.D. 220].* Seattle: University of Washington Press.

Jacob, John S. (1991) *The Agroecological Evolution of Cobweb Swamp, Belize.* Washington, DC: Report submitted to National Geographic Society, Grant No. 4274-90.

Kohl, Philip L. (1983) "Archaeology and Prehistory." Pp. 25-28 in T. Bottomore, L. Harris, V.
    G. Kiernan & R. Miliband (eds.) *Dictionary of Marxist Thought*. Cambridge, MA: Harvard
    University Press.
Lansing, J. Stephen (1991) *Priests and Programmers: Technologies of Power in the Engineered
    Landscape of Bali*. Princeton, NJ: Princeton University Press.
Laporte, Juan Pedro, and Vilma Fialko C. (1990) "New Perspective on Old Problems: Dynastic
    References for the Early Classic at Tikal." Pp. 33-66 in F. S. Clancy & P. D. Harrison
    (eds.) *Vision and Revision in Maya Studies*. Albuquerque: University of New Mexico Press.
Leach, Edmund R. (1959) "Hydraulic Society in Ceylon." *Past and Present* 15:2-26.
_____ (1961) *Pul Eliya: A Village in Ceylon*. Cambridge, ENG: Cambridge University Press.
Lumbreras, Luis G. (1974) *The Peoples and Cultures of Ancient Peru*. Washington, DC:
    Smithsonian Institution Press.
Matheny, Ray T. (1976) "Maya Lowland Hydraulic Systems."*Science* 193:639-646.
_____ (1978) "Northern Maya Lowland Water-Control Systems." Pp. 185-210 in P. D.
    Harrison & B. L. Turner II (eds.) *Pre-Hispanic Maya Agriculture*. Albuquerque: University
    of New Mexico Press.
_____, ed. (1980) *El Mirador, Peten, Guatemala: An Interim Report*. Provo, UT: Papers of
    the New World Archaeological Foundation, No. 45.
_____ (1982) "Ancient Lowland and Highland Maya Water and Soil Conservation Strategies."
    Pp. 157-180 in K. V. Flannery (ed.) *Maya Subsistance: Studies in Memory of Dennis E.
    Puleston*. New York: Academic Press.
_____ (1986) "Investigations at El Mirador, Peten, Guatemala." *National Geographic Research*
    2:332-353.
Matheny, Ray T., and Deanne L. Gurr (1983) "Variation in Prehistoric Agricultural Systems of
    the New World." *Annual Reviews in Anthropology* 12:79-103.
Matheny, Ray T., Deanne L. Gurr, Donald W. Forsyth, and F. Richard Hauck (1983)
    Investigations at Edzna, Campeche, Mexico, Vol. 1 Part 1: The Hydraulic System. Provo,
    UT: Paper of the New World Archaeological Foundation, No. 46.
McAnany, Patricia A. (1990) "Water Storage in the Puuc Region of the Northern Maya Lowlands:
    A Key to Population Estimates and Architectural Variability. Pp. 263-284 in T. P. Culbert
    and D. S. Rice (eds.) *Precolumbian Population History in the Maya Lowlands*.
    Albuquerque: University of New Mexico Press.
McGuire, Randall (1992) *A Marxist Archaeology*. New York: Academic Press.
Messenger, Jr., Lewis C. (1990) "Ancient Winds of Change: Climatic Settings and Prehistoric
    Social Complexity in Mesoamerica." *Ancient Mesoamerica* 1:21-40.
Miksicek, Charles H., Elizabeth S. Wing, and Sylvia J. Scudder (1991) "The Ecology and Economy
    of Cuello." Pp. 70-97 in N. Hammond (ed.) *Cuello: An Early Maya Community in Belize*.
    Cambridge, ENG: Cambridge University Press.
Miller, Daniel (1985) "Ideology and the Harappan Civilization." *Journal of Anthropological
    Archaeology* 4:34-71.
Millon, René (1973) "The Teotihuacan Map," in his (ed.) *Urbanization at Teotihuacan, Mexico,
    Vol. 1 Pt.1*. Austin: University of Texas Press.
_____ (1988) "The Last Years of Teotihuacan Dominance." Pp. 102-164 in N. Yoffee & G.
    L. Cowgill (eds.) *The Collapse of Ancient States and Civilizations*. Tucson: University of
    Arizona Press.
Mitchell, William P. (1973) "The Hydraulic Hypothesis: A Reappraisal." *Current Anthropology*
    14:532-34.
Moseley, Michael E. (1983) "The Good Old Days Were Better: Agrarian Collapse and Tectonics."
    American Anthropologist 85:773-799.
Moseley, Michael E., and Kent C. Day, eds. (1982) *Chan Chan: Andean Desert City*. Albuquerque:
    University of New Mexico Press.

Netting, Robert M. (1977) "Maya Subsistence: Mythologies, Analogies and Possibilies." Pp. 299-333 in R. E. W. Adams (ed.) *The Origins of Maya Civilization*. Albuquerque: University of New Mexico Press.

Palerm, Angel, and Eric R. Wolf (1957) "Ecological Potential and Cultural Development in Mesoamerica." *Pan American Union, Social Science Monographs* 3:1-38.

Park, Thomas K. (1992) "Early Trends toward Class Stratification: Chaos, Common Property, and Flood Recession Agriculture." *American Anthropologist* 94:90-117.

Pohl, Mary D., ed. (1990) *Ancient Maya Wetland Agriculture: Excavations on Albion Island, Northern Belize*. Boulder, CO: Westview Press.

Pohl, Mary D., Paul R. Bloom, and Kevin O. Pope (1990) "Interpretation of Wetland Farming in Northern Belize: Excavations at San Antonio Rio Hondo." Pp. 187-254 in M. D. Pohl (ed.) *Ancient Maya Wetland Agriculture*. Boulder, CO: Westview Press.

Pope, Kevin D., and Bruce H. Dahlin (1989) "Ancient Maya Wetland Agriculture: New Insights from Ecological and Remote Sensing Research." *Journal of Field Archaeology* 16:87-106.

Puleston, Dennis E. (1971) "An Experimental Approach to the Function of Classic Maya Chultuns." *American Antiquity* 36:322-35.

Puleston, Dennis E., and Olga S. Puleston (1971) "An Ecological Approach to the Origins of Maya Civilization." *Archaeology* 24:330-337.

Redman, Charles L. (1978) *The Rise of Civilization*. San Francisco: W.H. Freeman.

Rice, Don S., and T. Patrick Culbert (1990) "Historical Contexts for Population Reconstruction in the Maya Lowlands." Pp. 1-36 in T. P. Culbert & D. S. Rice (eds.) *Precolumbian Population History in the Maya Lowlands*. Albuquerque: University of New Mexico Press.

Rice, Don S., and Prudence M. Rice (1980) "Northeastern Peten Revisited." *American Antiquity* 45:432-454.

Rice, Don S., Prudence M. Rice, and Edward S. Deevey (1985) "Paradise Lost: Classic Maya Impact on a Lacustrine Environment." Pp. 91-106 in M. Pohl (ed.) *Prehistoric Lowland Maya Environment and Subsistenc Economy* . Cambridge, MA: Harvard University Press, Papers of the Peabody Museum of Archaeology and Ethnology, Vol. 77.

Sabloff, Jeremy A., and E. Wyllys Andrews V, eds. (1986) *Late Lowland Maya Civilization*. Albuquerque: University of New Mexico Press.

Sanders, William T. (1963) "Cultural Ecology of the Maya Lowlands, Part 2." *Estudios de Cultura Maya*3:203-241.

———— (1977) "Environmental Heterogeneity and Evolution of Lowland Maya Civilization." Pp. 287-298 in R. E. W. Adams (ed.) *Origins of Maya Civilization*. Albuquerque: University of New Mexico Press.

———— (1979) "The Jolly Green Giant in Tenth-Century Yucatan, or Fact and Fantasy in Classic Maya Agriculture." *Reviews in Anthropology* 6:493-506.

Sanders, William T., Jeffrey R. Parsons, and Robert S. Santley (1979) *The Basin of Mexico: Ecological Processes in the Evolution of a Civilization*. New York: Academic Press.

Sanders, William T., and David L. Webster (1978) "Unilinealism, Multilinealism, and the Evolution of Complex Society." Pp. 249-302 in C. L. Redman et al. (eds.) *Social Archaeology: Beyond Subsistence and Dating*. New York: Academic Press.

———— (1988) "The Mesoamerican Urban Tradition." *American Anthropologist* 90:521-546.

Scarborough, Vernon L. (1983) "A Preclassic Maya Water System." *American Antiquity* 48:720-744.

———— (1988) "Pakistani Water: 4500 Years of Manipulation." *Focus* 38(1):12-17.

———— (1991a) "Water Management Adaptations in Nonindustrial Complex Societies: An Archaeological Perspective." Pp. 101-154 in M. B. Schiffer (ed.) *Method and Theory in Archaeology*. Tucson: University of Arizona Press.

———— (1991b) "Courting in the Maya Lowlands: A Study in Prehispanic Ballgame Architecture." Pp. 129-144 in V. L. Scarborough & D. R. Wilcox (eds.) *The MesoamericanBallgame*. Tucson: University of Arizona Press.

_____ (1991c) Review: *Canal Irrigation in Prehistoric Mexico: The Sequence of Technological Change*, by William E. Doolittle (1990). *Journal of Field Archaeology*18:518-520.

_____ (1991d) *Archaeology at Cerros, Belize, Central America, Volume III: The Settlement System in a Late Preclassic Maya Community.* Dallas, TX: Southern Methodist University Press.

_____ (1991e) "Water Management Among the Ancient Maya." Washington, DC: National Geographic Society Grant Proposal No. 4595-91.

_____ (1992a) "The Flow of Power." *The Sciences* 32:38-43.

_____ (1992b) "La Distribution de l'Eau dans l'Empire Maya." ("The Distribution of Water in the Maya Empire.") *La Recherche* 23:924-926.

Scarborough, Vernon L., and Gary G. Gallopin (1991) "A Water Storage Adaptation in the Maya Lowlands." *Science*251:658-662.

Scarborough, Vernon L., and Robin A. Robertson (1986) "Civic and Residential Settlement at a Late Preclassic Maya Center." *Journal of Field Archaeology* 13:155-175.

Scarborough, Vernon L., Matthew Becher, Jeffrey L. Baker, J. D. Hensz, and Garry Harris (1992) *Water Management Studies atLa Milpa, Belize.* Washington, DC: Report submitted to National Geographic Society, Grant No. 4595-91.

Scarborough Vernon L., Robert P. Connolly, and Steven P. Ross (n.d.) "Water Management Studies of Kinal and Adjacent Areas," in R. E. W. Adams (ed.) *Ixcanrio Regional Archaeological Survey Report.* San Antonio: University of Texas at San Antonio.

Schele, Linda, and David A. Freidel (1990) *A Forest of Kings: Royal Histories of the Ancient Maya.* New York: William Morrow.

Siemens, Alfred H. (1978) "Karst and the Pre-Hispanic Maya in the Southern Lowlands." Pp. 117-144 in P. D. Harrison & B. L. Turner II (eds.) *Pre-Hispanic Maya Agriculture.* Albuquerque: University of New Mexico Press.

_____ (1982) "Prehistoric Agricultural Use of the Wetlands of Northern Belize." Pp. 205-222 in K. V. Flannery (ed.) *Maya Subsistence: Studies in Memory of Dennis E. Puleston.* New York: Academic Press.

Steward, Julian, ed. (1955) *Irrigation Civilizations: A Comparative Study.* Washington, DC: Pan-American Union.

Turner, B.L., II (1974) "Prehistoric Intensive Agriculture in the Maya Lowlands." *Science* 185:118-124.

Turner, B.L. II, and W.C. Johnson (1979) "A Maya Dam in the Copan Valley, Honduras." *American Antiquity* 44:299-305.

Van Liere, W.J. (1980) "Traditional Water Management in the Lower Mekong Basin." *World Archaeology* 11:265-80.

Wilk, Richard R. (1985) "Dry Season Agriculture Among the Kekchi Maya and Its Implications for Prehistory." Pp. 47-57 in M. Pohl (ed.) *Prehistoric Lowland Maya Environment and Subsistence Economy.* Cambridge, MA: Harvard University, Papers of the Peabody Museum of Archaeology and Ethnology, Vol. 77.

Willey, Gordon R. (1956) "Problems Concerning Prehistoric Settlement Patterns in the Maya Lowlands." Pp. 107-114 in his (ed.) *Prehistoric Settlement Patterns in The NewWorld.* New York: Viking Fund Publication in Anthropology,No. 23.

_____ (1974) "The Classic Maya Hiatus: A Rehearsal for the Collapse?" Pp. 417-430 in N. Hammond (ed.) *Mesoamerican Archaeology: New Approaches.* Austin: University Texas Press.

_____ (1977) "The Rise of Classic Maya Civilization: A Pasión Perspective." Pp. 133-158 in R. E. W. Adams (ed.) *The Origins of Maya Civilization.* Albuquerque:University of New Mexico Press.

Wittfogel, Karl A. (1957) *Oriental Despotism: A Comparative Study of Total Power.* New Haven, CT: Yale University Press.

———— (1972) "The Hydraulic Approach to Pre-Spanish Mesoamerica." Pp. 59-80 in F. Johnson (ed.) *Chronology and Irrigation: The Prehistory of the Tehuacan Valley*, Vol. 4. Austin: University of Texas Press.

Wolf, Eric (1982) *Europe and the People without History*. Berkeley: University of California Press.

Woodbury, Richard (1961) "A Reappraisal of Hohokam Irrigation." *American Anthropologist* 63:550-560.

Wright, A. C. S., D. H. Romney, R. H. Arbuckle, and V. E. Vial (1959) *Land in British Honduras: Report of the British Honduras Land Use Survey Team*. London: Her Majesty's Stationery Office.

Yoffee, Norman (1991) "Maya Elite Interaction: Through a Glass, Sideways." Pp. 285-310 in T. P. Culbert (ed.) *Classic Maya Political History*. Cambridge, ENG: Cambridge University Press.

Yoffee, Norman, and George L. Cowgill, eds. (1988) *The Collapse of Ancient States and Civilizations*. Tucson: University of Arizona Press.

ASPECTS OF WATER MANAGEMENT IN THE SOUTHERN MAYA LOWLANDS

Peter D. Harrison

INTRODUCTION

Among the ancient Maya of the southern Lowlands, water management may be divided into two major and an number of minor functions. The first of these is the collection and storage of water for daily use, primarily for consumption but for other household uses as well (Scarborough 1991a). The methods by which this most simple function was achieved themselves illustrate the basic feature of variety that characterizes the Maya adaptation to their environment. The second function of water management is far more complex. This is the control of water for purposes of facilitating food production. While both functions relate directly to survival, they differ in their reflection of population sizes. A sedentary population of any size requires the storage of water for daily use, while water control and management for purposes of agricultural intensity have a more direct relationship to the pressures of population (Sanders et al. 1979:384). Water management for agricultural purposes is the more complex

Research in Economic Anthropology, Suppl. 7, pages 71-119.
ISBN: 1-55938-646-0

topic, relating as it does to differing soil conditions as well as to the distribution of natural bodies of water.

In this essay, I examine and discuss the varieties of both of the aforementioned functions of water management and examine their distribution within the Maya Lowlands according to present knowledge. Much of the material remains controversial as well as speculative. The greatest hinderance to such a discusssion is the relative lack of direct archaeological investigation in the face of the enormous diversity of adaption across the Lowlands. A specific solution for any particular problem of water control at one locality will not necessarily apply directly at a few kilometers' distance. This diversity is in part due to the largely uncredited heterogeneity of landscape in the Lowlands, but it also reflects the ingenious and seemingly limitless solutions to local problems that the Maya were able to conjure.

In the face of this variety of both landscape and ability to cope with it, reliable "rules" of how the Maya managed problems of water control cannot be stated simply. At best, we can hope to categorize the types of landscape that were subject to water management problems and then classify within these a number of known ways that management was achieved. It is useful at the same time to note the presence of as yet poorly understood situations, ones in which the problem of water management was approached but for which we have only the broadest outline of the solutions.

THE PHYSICAL ZONE AND ITS CHARACTERISTICS

The cultural boundary between the Northern and Southern Maya Lowlands was established with reference to the recognizeable cultural zones that formed each (Culbert 1973:5).[1] The resulting irregular line which crosses the Yucatan Peninsula is based partly upon the assumed locations of known cultural dividers (especially architectural style) and partly on certain geographical features recognized in the 1960s. The Alluvial Plain of the Uscumacintla/ Grijalva river basins is separated from the rest of the State of Campeche (see Figure 1). Then an arc spreads north from the Petén/Campeche boundary, based upon the known distributions of architectural styles (the Central, or Petén style in the south, and the Río Bec/Chenes, or Central Yucatecan styles in the north). The eastern remainder of the boundary follows the Hondo River, which is also the modern boundary between Quintana Roo in Mexico and Belize. The arc to the north of the Petén extends for an approximate distance not greater than 40 km north of the Guatemalan/Mexican border.

If the geophysical features are consulted, as well, we find that this area is characterized as the Hilly Karsted Zone (West 1964:71) and is also noted for the occurence of wetlands, otherwise known as *bajos*, *akalche*, and *polje* (Rice 1993:17). This karsted zone extends from a line near the 17th parallel, at about

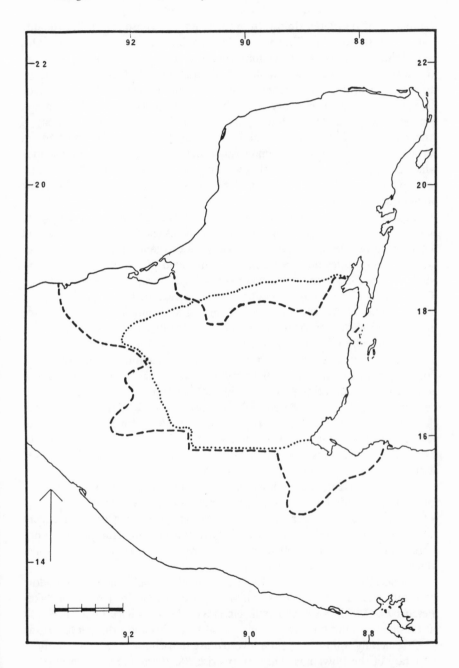

Figure 1.　Boundaries for the Southern Lowlands (Heavy dashed line is after Culbert [1973]. Dotted line is zone discussed in this essay.)

the middle of the Petén (ibid.), to an inverted arc whose zenith lies roughly 160 km north of the Guatemalan/Mexico border. In other words, this geographic zone crosses the recognized cultural boundary, extending some 120 km further north than the established cultural zone (Culbert 1973:5). Thus, the recognized cultural and geophysical features of the ancient Maya landscape do not coincide with reference to the boundaries between the Northern and Southern Lowlands (see Figures 1 and 2). For the purposes of this essay, a compromise has been sought, establishing an artificial boundary some 60 km further north than Culbert's boundary, in order to include a group of wetlands which geographically belong with a wetland region to the south. This feature was neither recorded nor recognized for its significance when the Culbert boundaries were first established.

The southern boundary of the Maya Lowlands is no simpler in definition. A series of low mountain ranges (*sierras*), such as the Sierra de Chama and the Sierra de las Minas, interrupt the concept of Lowlands but occur well north of certain major sites that are traditionally included within the core of ancient Maya culture. Specifically, the major sites of Quiriguá and Copán lie outside of the physical Lowlands in a subzone that is regarded and published as a recognizeable cultural entity under the rubric of the Southeast Maya Zone (see Boone & Willey 1988). Although remote and frontier in many respects, this zone is culturally related to the Lowlands proper and is linked to the rest of the Lowlands by river systems from the Gulf of Honduras. This Southeast Zone has been excluded from the present survey because of the distinctness of its cultural characteristics and physical separation from the southern Lowlands as well as its intense publication elsewhere (Baudez 1983, Willey et al. 1978, Webster 1985). For lack of data, the Southwest Zone is also excluded. The configuration resulting from these alterations in the traditional shape of the southern Lowlands is shown in Figure 1, which defines the area under discussion.

Despite the caveats noted above, there are significant correlates within the southern Lowlands between geography and cultural development, especially with regard to settlement around natural bodies of water. Conversely, there are enough non-correlations to avoid determinism—for example, the non-correlation of the N-S cultural boundary and the boundary of the wetland zone, which are independant of each other.

Geologically, the southern Lowlands are divided roughly across the middle by a fault line that marks the southern edges of a series of permanent lakes (Petén-Itzá, Quexil, Sacnab, Yaxhá, etc.) (West 1964:71, Rice 1993:15). South of this dividing fault line are a series of east-west folds and ridges of limestone which generally follow the gentle inverted arc that characterizes the southern boundary of the Lowlands. These ridges rise 100-300m above sea level (Rice 1993) and extend northwest toward the central string of lakes. To the north of the lake/fault line is the hilly, karsted zone with wetlands, described above.[2]

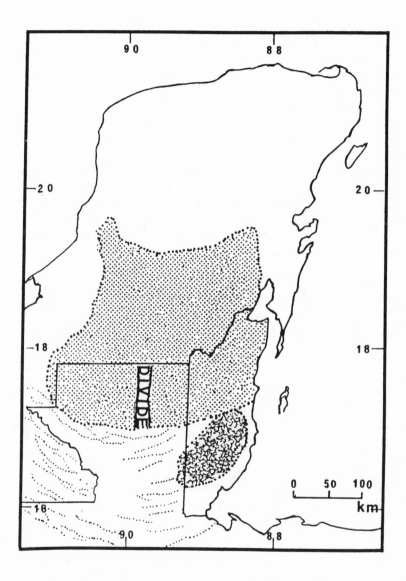

Figure 2. The Physiographic Zones within the Southern
Lowlands (The stippled area marks the karsted, hilly wetlands
and extends across the North-South border. Folded ridges lie
to the south with the Maya Mountains on the lower right.)

A drainage divide extends from near the east end of Lake Petén-Itzá and angles northwards and slightly east, roughly following the line from Tikal to Calakmul. Thus, the northern wetland, karstic zone is itself divided into eastern and western drainages but with a number of major sites sitting along the divide: Tikal, Uaxactún, and Calakmul slightly northeast of the trajectory. Major drainages with their headwaters near the divide are the Hondo to the east and the San Pedro Mártir to the west, providing access to either side of the greater Yucatan Peninsula from the divide (see Figure 3).

Comparison of the known population distribution with the three drainage zones shows that correlations with water are riparian in southern Zone 1 and wetland-edge in Zones 2 and 3. There are, of course, exceptions to this sweeping characterization, such as El Perú in Zone 2 and Lamanai and Nakum in Zone 3. This northeastern drainage is the most densely populated according to present demographic knowledge. Further, Adams (1981) has already noted that the northeastern sector of the Petén contains the densest number of sites within this modern political unit. The concept can be extended to include northern Belize and southern Quintana Roo. The relative lack of population in the

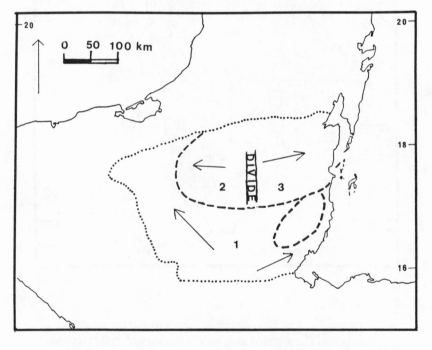

Figure 3.   Drainage Zones within the Area of Discussion
(Arrows indicate riverine and drainage directions.)

northwestern zone may be in part attributable to the relative lack of exploitable agricultural ground or lack of archaeological exploration.

Throughout the southern Lowlands, the preferred locations for settlement can be summarized as follows: (1) uplands, on the littorals of what today are seasonal wetlands; (2) riveredge, presumably to exploit the fast moving routes of long-distance communication; and (3) the littorals of permanent bodies of deep water (lakes), which the settlement patterns indicate were the least preferred location. The citeable examples of large sites in this third position are few: Tayasal, Topoxche, Ixlu, Yaxhá, to name a sample.

Within the context of this varied geography, a significant factor for both water supply and the potential uses of permanent and seasonal bodies of water is variation in the water level. This variation is considerable and the predictability only moderate (Rice 1993:21-22), a factor with some serious economic implications. Even lake levels can fluctuate widely for geomorphologic reasons as yet unexplained. For example, since the massive (7.8 Richter scale) earthquake in Guatemala in 1976, the water level of Lake Petén-Itzá has risen steadily. Whole communities, much private property, and touristic facilities once on the lake shore are now inundated. Until the water level within the lake basin reaches the elevation at which artifically cut drainage tunnels can be effective, no human manipulation can stop the rise. Loss of agricultural and pastoral lands as well as negative impact on tourism have reached serious levels, a circumstance defying water management today.

Little is known of how the prehistoric Maya coped with such disaster situations or, for that matter, even with the annual fluctations of river and lake levels. It is an area requiring study. The Maya have, however, demonstrated a broad range of ingenuity in solving the problems and exploiting the opportunites offered by water resources, variously for purposes of survival, state development, and political control.

DIRECT CONSUMPTION

Citing White et al. (1972:252), Scarborough (1991a:102) has pointed out that humans require 2-3 liters of water per day in a sedentary economic environment. Minimum requirements, however, seldom reflect the waste occurring in an advanced society, if availability allows (ibid.).

In his review of comparative Old and New World technologies, Scarborough (1991a) highlighted a number of properties of water which aid and inhibit economic manipulation, of which the following is a summary. Control systems are divided between systems of collection and allocation. Gravity flow is the friend of collection but can be an obstacle to allocation in situations of complex surface relief. In some complex Old World societies, systems for lifting water have been devised, but evidence for such systems has not been recovered in the New World, even though they can be postulated on the basis of simple hand watering for local garden situations.

Plumbing and Incidental Sources

A vaulted aqueduct has been noted at Palenque (Weaver 1981:315), together with a three-seater latrine in the Palace, which has been presumed to empty into the controlled flowing water system that passes this structure. The question of how waste was safely disposed without pollution of the water supply is unresolved. Similarly, a one-seater example of indoor plumbing has been cited for the site of Becan (Potter 1977:44), an unusual example of a shaft located in a alcove on an upper story of an elite palace structure. Just where the shaft exited or how waste was collected or otherwise disposed of is not known in this case, either.

While sweat houses depend upon a very limited use of water, their principal purpose is ritually oriented rather than serving any economic purpose. Their presence in the society does not represent conspicuous consumption of a commodity for purposes of impressing the populace (Satterthwaite 1952).

The use of wells was apparently not successful in the southern Lowlands. The level of the water table was too unpredictable or too deep for practical use at these latitudes. Wells occur in the Chenes (meaning "wells") architectural district of Campeche and Quintana Roo (Nelson 1973:33, Harrison n.d.a). Wells are more generally associated with the Northern Lowlands. However, within the slightly expanded northern frontier used in this essay (see Figure 1), it is useful to mention a distribution of wells found in southern Quintana Roo.[3] Wells of ancient construction were found there at the sites of Chacchoben, Margarita Maza de Juárez and Chichmuul; for site locations, see Figure 10.1 in Harrison (1981). Information retrieved from one of these southern Quintana Roo wells is of particular interest here because it was possible to measure the present depth and determine some features of its construction. The opening was 93 cm in diameter (see Figure 4). Mortared stones surrounded the shaft in a circular fashion to a depth of 5.4m, at which point the remainder of the shaft was simply cut through the limestone bedrock (see Figure 5). Constricting rings occurred at depths of 12.5m and 17.7m below the ground level and may represent excavation units during construction. The present bottom is at 22.65m below ground level and undoubtedly consists of a good bit of fallen debris. The bottom is dry. Villagers presently occupying the site reopened another well, which they claimed had the same depth. Two meters of new excavation into the bedrock were necessary before a water table was found once again. Ceramics recovered in direct association with the mouth of this well and with other wells in the survey area were of Late Postclassic strap-handled water storage vessels. This suggests that, as late as the 12th century, such wells were still functioning as a water source. Since the 12th

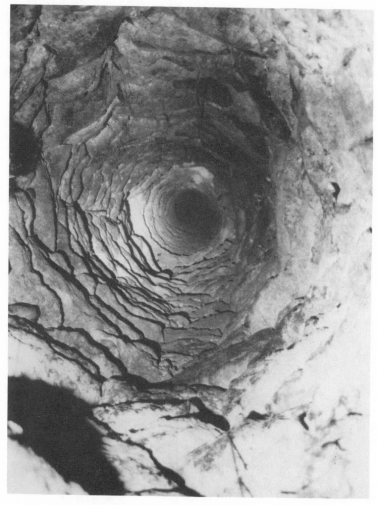

Figure 4. Masonry Construction at the Top of an Ancient Well at Margarita Maza de Juárez in Southern Quintana Roo, Mexico

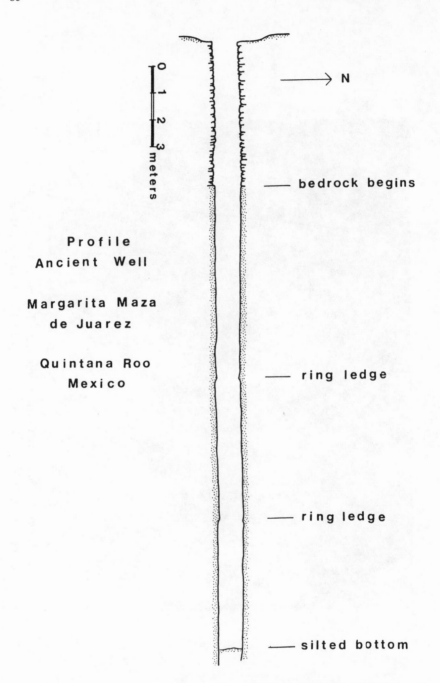

Figure 5. Profile/Section of the Well in Figure 4

century, the well shown in Figures 4 and 5 became disfunctional due to change in the level of water, which, if our informants were reliable, consisted of a drop of 2m. The location is south-central Quintana Roo in the midst of the karsted hilly region of wetlands. Information is not presently available about how localised such a change in water table might be, but within the karsted topography it could be a local example.

Chultuns

Chambers excavated into the bedrock, called *chultuns,* occur in both the southern and northern Lowlands but seem to have served a different purpose in the two locales. While it has been firmly established that they served as water catchment and storage chambers in the north (McAnany 1990), no such function has been established in the south. Other functions have been convincingly argued, while that of water storage has been largely discredited by the demonstrably porous quality of the limestone base into which they are cut (Puleston 1968). The alternative functions include food storage (Puleston 1965, 1968, 1971) and human burial (Chase & Chase 1987).

Reservoirs

The types of reservoir constructed by the Maya have been analysed and described by Scarborough and Gallopin (1991:659) with reference to the features found at Tikal, Guatemala: *central precinct, residential, bajo margin, pozos*, and *aguadas.* This range covers factors of size, location, and function in a series of water catchment strategies. Their analysis demonstrates that the techniques of collecting water utilize monumental architecture, causeways, reservoirs, and other types of holding basins. The size of the collection area varies according to the rate of delivery. For example, monumental, vertical stone structures act as inverted funnels, spreading rainfall to be collected on the paved "catchment" surfaces of plazas and patios (see Figure 6). These surfaces, in turn, are sloped to collect the runoff and divert it to one of several collection basins, or reservoirs. The model is Tikal, and an example of a specific mechanism of catchment is provided below. An important assumption should be noted here, namely, that the engineering aspects which made the water management possible at Tikal were handled at the elite level, while the labor which made it happen was provided from below this level. It has been suggested that control of water for consumption and its conspicuous use may have served the purpose of consolidating power for the ancient Maya (ibid.:661). An example of catchment control by architectural devices from the Central Acropolis at Tikal is described latter in this essay.[4]

Figure 6. Multi-storied Structures in the Central Acropolis, Tikal, Which Serve as Rain Catchment for the Palace Reservoir

Rainfall and Catchment

In the Petén, as well as elsewhere in the Lowlands, rainfall quantities vary dramatically in both time and space. The zone falls within the rainfall contours of 2000-3000mm annually. Lundell (1937:7) noted that an average above 1250mm qualifies the zone as rain forest. His cited records for the Petén over 11 years (1924-34) showed an average of 1762mm. Rainfall records were maintained at two locales at Tikal by the University of Pennsylvania Project: one at the Project camp, adjacent to the Tikal Reservoir; the other in the Great Plaza, reflecting the rainfall within the catchment area that served the Palace Reservoir, the Hidden Reservoir, and the Causeway Reservoir. The only other comparative record for the same time period (1956-69) was that maintained by FYDEP (Fomento y Desarrollo Económico del Petén) at the airport in Santa Elena, at the west extremity of Lake Petén-Itzá. The two stations at Tikal were located at a distance of a little more than 1 km apart, while the FYDEP station was some 60 km distance from Tikal. While these records are not at this time available to me, my recollection of them is that the results showed certain consistent differences over the period of collected data. These differences showed a relatively stable relationship among the three stations, despite wide variation from year to year. The camp station by the Tikal Reservoir received the least rainfall; the Plaza station was noticeably and consistently higher, and the Santa Elena station received dramatically higher rainfall than either station at Tikal. The range at each station had its variation over time. For example, on a certain day in November 1965, more than 75mm fell in several hours, while none fell for the entire month of November 1968. The latter year was one of remarkable drought, illustrating the unpredictability of rainfall in modern times at least.

In the Plaza zone, located on one of the highest ridges that form the site center and with a higher rainfall, the monumental architecture and the connecting plastered floors served as a gigantic water collector with runoff drainages in several different directions. Runoff is rapid even today in a heavy rainfall, and when the plastered floors were fresh and well maintained the degree of loss by absorbtion and evaporation would have been minimal. A secondary function of water collection for the architecture and courtyard floor slopes in particular, is clear in the field record in the Central Acropolis. The relatively small size and proximity of the Palace Reservoir to the densest core of monumental architecture implies that this feature was intended for collection of water to be consumed there rather than distributed for agricultural purposes.

Given the force and speed of runoff, it would be undesireable for the Maya to have allowed middens containing food or human waste to accumulate in places where the runoff could deliver such potentially toxic waste directly into the water supply. It would not take many years of experience to learn that such waste should not be permitted within a water catchment zone, which indeed would be the whole of the Central Acropolis. With the exception of one enclosed court, the runoff from all five other courtyards had access to the Palace Reservoir on the south side of the Acropolis. It has been suggested elsewhere (Harrison 1970:252, Sanders & Price 1968:146) that human waste from ceremonial precincts was likely collected for economic use as fertilizer at some distance from the sources of water catchment for consumption. The absence of stratified middens all around the core of the Plaza zone at Tikal was demonstrated during the Pennsylvania excavations. The conventional explanation for the absence of such middens is that they had been removed annually as part of the ritual calendar cycle and that the refuse so removed was utilized as construction fill. This interpretative explanation may or may not have been true, but if such middens accumulated at all within the ceremonial catchment precincts, they would have had to be removed regularly by May, before the seasonal rains normally begin, and not allowed to accumulate again until December, when the rains normally end. However, the unpredictability of the onset of rains could make the practice of middening in the catchment zone very risky.

The Palace Reservoir at Tikal

Ceramic refuse stratified in the lower levels of the Palace Reservoir showed the presence of Early Classic sherds at the bottom and even mixed among the basal "liner" stones that formed the foundation of the reservoir. These stones had been sealed with impermeable black montmorillonitic clays, without doubt imported from the nearby Bajo de Santa Fe at the east edge of the site. Thus, the porous limestone bedrock was covered with a lining of stone and clay, ensuring that the catchment basin would be effective. The Early Classic ceramics provide a *terminus post quem* for the construction. It is likely that the present reservoir began as a quarry located in a shallow arroyo that separated the ridge of the Great Plaza from the next nearest ridge to the south, where Temple V is now located. The quarry must have served as the source of building blocks for the Central Acropolis during the Late Preclassic and early stages of the Early Classic ceramic periods (250 B.C.-A.D. 350). Sometime during the Early Classic ceramic phase (A.D. 350-650), the former quarry was converted into a reservoir in a feat of engineering that required coordination with the construction of the eastern dam *cum* causeway at the eastern end of the present reservoir. This latter served as a multi-purpose construction, providing a level crossing over the former arroyo from the zone called the East Plaza to the south bank of the arroyo. It also served to dam the east end of the former arroyo and create a basin for a reservoir.

By approximately A.D. 450, the Central Acropolis was developing into a complex of multi-level courtyards and becoming a viable catchment for rainfall. The dating of construction is subject to the usual caveats that are demanded by a *terminus post quem*. The vagaries of casual deposition of debris ceramics

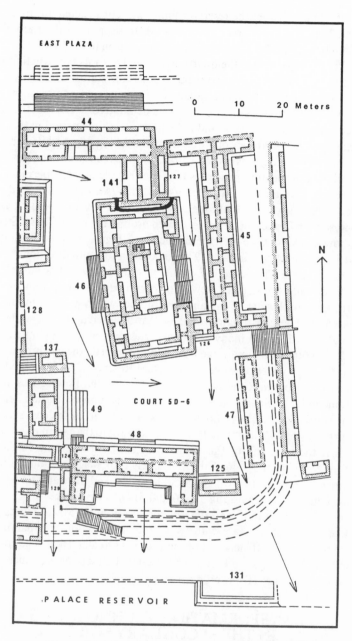

Figure 7. Location of Drain (in black) around
Structure 5D-141 and Rain Flow Pattern through Court
6 from the Central Acropolis to the Palace Reservoir

do not inform us whether the reservoir lining was constructed during the Late Preclassic Period or the Early Classic Period. In support of the Early Classic date, it can be argued that there is so little construction in the Central Acropolis of Late Preclassic date that the quarry associated with its construction would not yet have warranted the conversion to reservoir status. The Early Classic date is consistent with both the quantity of accelerated construction in the adjacent Central Acropolis and the increased demand for water that the implied increased population density would indicate for this time period in this locale.

Maintenance of the efficacy of the catchment quality of the architecture within the confines of the courtyards of the Central Acropolis can be attested by a specific example that occurred during the growth of the architectural complex in the Late Classic period. The slopes of the flooring of Court 6 (see Figure 7) were designed to direct rainfall southwards through the courtyard toward the now existing Palace Reservoir. These runoff waters flowed around the Early Classic Structure 5D-46, now known to have been the clanhouse of Jaguar Paw the Great (Schele & Freidel 1990:464-465, Harrison 1970), in a north to south direction.

During the Late Classic period, someone—probably a descendant of the Jaguar Paw clan—constructed new patios with surrounding rooms on both the north and south sides of the ancestral home, which at this time was 350-400 years old. The construction of these patios interrupted the water flow, which had been designed many years earlier as part of the catchment for the Palace Reservoir. To maintain the flow and not impede the catchment quality of Court 6 as a provider of water to the Palace Reservoir, a low vaulted tunnel was constructed beneath the north patio, allowing the flow of runoff water to continue in its original path (see Figure 8). This tunnel, or drain, let runoff from the south side of 5D-44 flow in its usual pattern, to the east side of the ancestral home (5D-46) and into the small courtyard to the east of this structure. Eventually, the west end of this tunnel was sealed, preventing further flow toward the east side of 5D-46. This event likely took place in conjunction with the construction of 5D-126, which would have blocked the water flow through the small court space separating 5D-46 and 5D-45 (see Figure 7).

The details of operation and date of the drain under 5D-46 represent but a single example of the care with which water collection was handled and modified to maintain efficiency in the confines of Greater Tikal. The collection zone and catchment system that served the Tikal Reservoir are much greater in size and complexity (Bronson n.d.).[5]

TRANSFORMATION TECHNOLOGIES IN THE SECONDARY SOILS

Rice (1993:42) compared population estimates against land productivity for certain cultivars, using the Lake Yaxhá-Sacnab basins as his model. The

Figure 8. Entrance to the Drain Constructed under the North Patio of 5D-46 to Allow Water to Bypass 5D-141

resulting ratios demonstrated that a severe strain existed in the 8th century, when population was at its peak. The test was for non-intensive forms of agriculture and took into account all categories of land form in the study area. The resulting shortage of arable land within this set of assumptions was great, even in a study region that Rice has demonstrated was relatively sparse in population in ancient times.

The gap between high population levels and the potential for low levels of non-intensive food production was most likely filled through water management techniques of agricultural intensification. The gaps in research data on questions about these techniques of agricultural intensification are enormous. Most data available derive from the environs of large sites, loci of dense population. While data from the less dense zones do exist, they are in the minority (Ford 1985, 1986; Fedick 1989; Rice 1976, 1978, 1988; Harrison n.d.a, 1981; Turner & Harrison 1981, 1983). However, the situation is not quite as bad as it might at first appear. A misdirected perspective on the nature of soils has been a major culprit in the history of Maya studies of ancient economics. A serious difficulty lies in the fact that few, if any, archaeologists are skilled in the chemical analysis of soils, although a rudimentary concept of the importance of this factor has been part of archaeological training since the early 1950s. In order to fill a gap which basically lies outside the humanistic framework, archaeologists have sought field participation of "soil scientists" whose background, in turn, lacked the framework of dealing with man as an integer in the scientific equation. This difference in the academic frameworks of collaborating colleagues introduces the possiblity of differences of focus and interpretation of field data. In the short term, the effort to enlist the aid of "hard science" as an quick route to solving complex problems about ancient societies has brought about some disagreement concerning the relevance of cultural content within disturbed soils. These problems will be apparent in the discussion of wetland manipulation, but first this essay will deal with the upland solutions that were employed by the ancient Maya.

Terracing

The record of agricultural terraces in the southern Lowlands has been noted since 1927 (Ower 1927). In the intervening 65 years, knowledge of the distribution, prevalence, and variety of terracing has improved only marginally. Early observations were made by Thompson (1931) for the South Cayo District in Belize, basically on the Vaca Plateau, between the regions of Xunantunich and Mountain Cow, a linear distance of nearly 40 km (ibid.:30). Lundell (1940:9-11) noted terracing in the Petén, as did Turner (1974) near Lake Macanche, south of Tikal. The area best known for terracing to date is the Río Bec region, where the combination of karst hills and wetlands has produced some of the best evidence of agricultural intensification and water management.

Terraces in this region were first reported by Ruppert and Denison (1943:13) in the vicinity of both Calakmul and Oxpemul. The latter site lies 48 km west of Rio Bec, while Calakmul is 26 km south of Oxpemul (ibid.:50). Sharer (in Morley & Brainard 1983:193) has described the area of terraced hills in this region as encompassing 150,000 ha. This could still be an underestimation of their extent in this region. It is known that the terraced hillslopes begin in the east, in the locale of the modern town of Nicolás Bravo on the Chetumal-Escarcega highway (Turner 1974). The distance from Nicolás Bravo to Oxpemul in the west, if this site is taken to represent the western limits of the terraced hills, is about 96 km. Whether this distance contains unbroken terracing of the hills is not known, but terraces have been observed in dense clusters from Nicolás Bravo to Becan (Turner 1974; Harrison n.d.c), a distance of some 60 km. What is not known is the north-south extent of terracing along this belt. The greater region known loosely as the "Río Bec terrace region" encompasses roughly 5,000 sq. km and includes 14 known large ceremonial centers. The region is adjacent to a complex of wetlands, also known for the presence of agricultural land transformations (see below).

Other important zones of reported terraces include the environs of the site of Caracol on the north flank of the Maya Mountains (Healy et al. 1983; Chase & Chase 1987, n.d.) and the Petexbatun region in the western Petén (Dunning & Beach, n.d.). The use of terracing and construction of non-agricultural walls is reported to be extensive but to date only partially explored. On the basis of what has already been recorded, it appears that slope terracing was a significant factor in the Late Classic economy of the Petexbatun escarpment zone. Finally, survey in the upper reaches of the Belize River Valley (Fedick 1989) has reported occurrences of agricultural terracing and check dams on the valley flanks.

The term "terrace" is used rather broadly to describe a variety of forms and, even, functions. The linear sloping dry-field terrace was described by Spencer and Hale (1961), and the term was adopted by Turner (1974, 1979) and Healy et al. (1983) for occurrences of this type in the Río Bec, Vaca Plateau, and Caracol regions (see Figure 9). The second type, found in Zone 3 drainage (see Figure 3), is the weir terrace, also referred to as "check dams" (Ruppert & Denison 1943:14, 50) and *terraplenes agrícolas* (Blom 1946:5). The weir terrace is an embankment constructed across small drainage channels to create level planting surfaces (Turner 1979:107) (see Figure 10). While both forms of terrace retard soil erosion by runoff, the weir terrace also spreads the natural water flow to a more even and broader surface.

In the Petexbatun study, three types of terraces were distinguished. Of these, the *footslope terrace* is a new one in the lexicology of this form of land transformation (Dunning et al. n.d.) (see Figure 11). Found especially in association with the site of Tamarindito, such terraces occurred at the base of hillslopes ranging from 30 to 60 degrees. This ingenious form of terrace is

Figure 9. Embankment Terrace Wall in Southern Quintana Roo, in the Rio Bec Terrace Region

Figure 10. Weir Terraces South of Lake Macanche (courtesy of B.L. Turner II)

Figure 11. Footslope Terrace near Laguneta Tamarindito in a
Recently Burned Milpa (Terrace is positioned to catch sediments
eroded off adjacent slope.) (Courtesy Dr. N. P. Dunning)

not presently known outside of the Petexbatun area, where it seems to be an
adaptation to the escarpment situation. Now that this terrace form and its
topographically specific location have been identified, more examples may be
expected to be found, commensurate with re-examination of the landscape. The
footslope terrace catches soil and water runoff from the slope of the escarpment,
exploiting a dramatic geologic situation. It is an excellent example of the Maya
propensity to exploit every variation in their topography, no matter how extreme.

Hillslope terraces are found in two types along the Petexbatun escarpment:
box terracing and contoured embankments. The former are descending
rectangular or ridged benches, as found near Tamarindito. The description of
contouring embankments in the Petexbatun case seems to agree with the basic
description of a linear sloping dry terrrace, as found elsewhere in Belize and
in the northern karsted hilly region (see Figure 3). In other words, the "box"
and "embankment" terraces defined by Dunning et al. (n.d.) seem to be
subtypes of the more familiar hill-slope terrace found elsewhere, probably with
local adaptations. These distinctions are quite valid, reflecting once again the
Maya cultural characteristic of adaptation to local features. The investigator
makes the distinctions, and sometimes it is difficult to find common functions

in the realm of water control that separate the different forms that terraces assume for different topographies. Dunning and Beach (n.d.) note that both the "box" and "embankment" types of terrace in their classification serve the same purpose of preventing erosion of the rendoll soils, providing relatively level cultivation surfaces, and thickening the A-horizon (ibid.).

Detailed descriptions of the varieties of construction used for terrace walls will not be included here. These have been adequately described elsewhere by Turner (1974, 1979), Healy et al. (1983), and others. Suffice it to say that a variety of constructional techniques were used, varying from the subtle, and in some cases barely detectable (Rice 1993), to the extravagant (Turner 1979). Rice's observation that the presence of terraces in certain topographic environments can easily be overlooked because of the subtle, approaching ephemeral, nature of the constructs is important. This was particularly true of the gently sloped grasslands of the savannahs (Zones 1 and 2 in Figure 3).

The energetics that enter into the construction of this form of land/water control vary considerably, and the problem of effort versus yield has been approached by Turner (1983). For broad-based, linear terraces, the wall is constructed of two parts, a dry-laid front wall and a rubble buffer, or fill, of small, "uniformly-sized" stones to the rear and under the front wall. Typically, a broad-based wall is about 1m high and 1m wide. Turner (1983) found that the average length of terrace walls from six mapped sites was 424m. Calculating labor costs on the basis of hauling earth and excavating and hauling stone, the range of cost was 105-848 days/ha for terrace construction. The average translated into 250 worker days/ha without including the costs of stone haulage. This heavy output in labor means that the need had to be great enough and the output in food production sufficient to offset the costs (Turner 1983).

Dunning and Beach (n.d.) suggest that, despite their complexity, terraces protected less than 25 percent of the sloping terrain from erosion and that even the best constructed terraces served to reduce soil loss by a factor of not more than 50 percent. These labor intensive efforts served only as a check on the natural degradation of the sloped lands. They further suggest that systems of less permanent record may have been in use alongside the stone terraces. Land transformations such as earthen berms, which have no present (or as yet observed) record, may have been as or even more common than the more permanent stone terrace (Rice 1993:38). This concept is analogous to the "invisible house mound," structures now recognized as having both economic and population implications but which leave no visible trace on the unexcavated surface (Pyburn 1990:191). The importance of such "temporary" constraints on water flow should be seriously considered for their impact on ancient economics and become a subject of concern in field strategies, even though the physical evidence may be difficult to retrieve.

Dunning and Beach (n.d.) suggest that the apparent absence of techniques of slope conservation in the central Petén (a large portion of Zone 3) may be due to a distortion in data recovery. If constructs of very low relief had been built in ancient times, such constructs in present condition could very well be ephemeral and very difficult to detect. Rice (1993:38) made the same point independently. It is interesting that Zone 3 (see Figure 3), which has the highest postulated regional population density, is also the region with the least recorded occurrence of terraces. This zone is also the location of the highest concentration of monumental architecture, and it is curious that these construction techniques were not applied to slope conservation, unless for some reason such conservation was not necessary. As already noted, artificial constructs related to water collection and conservation were utilised in Zone 3. Finally, the zone is not devoid of sloped terrain that would have benefited by the use of terraces. Perhaps historic accident of investigation has led to the overlooking of slope conservation features, or perhaps Dunning's explanation accounts for the apparent absence.

Wetland Manipulation

In archaeology, evidence is seldom, if ever, unequivocal. Rather, many lines of evidence point toward a particular interpretation. The researcher must balance absence of evidence, the data that would have been useful but were not retrieved, against the concrete evidence retrieved. The interpretation that follows is a "best fit" for the balance. This is particularly true for the interpretation of the evidence for wetland manipulation, touching upon the role of human intervention in the creation of raised fields. A controversy presently exists, and some background for it is presented here.

Drained and raised fields are found in many cultures, both ancient and modern. As a device of agricultural intensification, the construction of such fields is probably the most significant form of water manipulation next to complex systems of water dispersal. In this regard, Scarborough and Gallopin (1991:658) have noted the distinction between water allocation and collection, and the fact that examples of allocation in the Maya Lowlands are rare but not nonexistent. The evidence for irrigation in the Highlands of Mesoamerica has been strong (Sanders et al. 1979:280-281), while the evidence for post-12th-century use of raised field technology (called *chinampas*) in highland Mexico is conclusive (Blanton 1972a-b, Parsons 1976). The *chinampas*, or raised fields, of the Ixtapalapa district of Mexico, D.F., continue to produce food today. Field systems originally constructed by the Aztec hierarchy served as a significant part of the economic base for the city of Tenochtitlan. Their shape and technology have altered through time, but they continue to serve as a significant source of food supply for modern Mexico City. Other areas in the New World that supported societies which successfully embraced this system include the altiplanos of Bolivia, Ecuador, and Peru (Denevan 1970, 1982:195; Kolata 1986, 1991; Binford 1991, Binford et al. n.d., Erickson 1988, Erickson & Candler 1989). These examples of New World non-Maya societies that constructed water-dependent agricultural platforms also demonstrate an association of this system with state development and organization (Aztec, Inca, Tiahuanaco). In other words, adding the ancient Maya to the list of those New World civilizations which utilised wetland manipulation as a tool for food production does not radically alter the accepted view of New World prehistory. Yet, a persistent resistance to admitting that the Maya did in fact utilise wetland manipulation to any significant degree continues even today. Perhaps this resistance is due to the complex nature of the archaeological evidence, as mentioned above.[6]

There is another way to explain this resistance to a change in view of ancient Maya food strategies, which has been couched in terms of intellectual clinging to entrenched models (Sabloff et al. 1987, McAnany 1989). For nearly a century, the Maya were believed to have developed their society on the basis of a simple swidden economy. The discovery of new evidence (albeit imperfect) has failed to convince some researchers that Maya economies were complex and included wetland manipulation.

It is not appropriate here to reiterate the history of the research and interpretation of raised fields over the last 20 years in the southern Lowlands. This has been recently accomplished most eloquently by Rice (1993). However, some discussion of the background of the controversy and one example that characterizes it—lack of communication on the use of terms—is useful. The example discussed here is the difference in usage of the terms "ditches" and "canals."

The resistance began with an excavation on Albion Island in northern Belize initiated by archaeologist Puleston—a program which has currently grown into a soil study of the northern half of Belize. Puleston (1978) made the non-controversial observation that all platforms used as raised fields may not have been artifically constructed. At the same time, Puleston suggested that such platforms and their attendant canals may have originated as natural *gilgai*. This

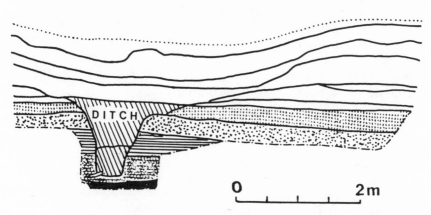

Figure 12. Profile of a "Ditch" Excavation at Albion Island (after Bloom et al. 1983:Fig. 2)

suggestion has been rejected by archaeologists largely on the basis of associated
cultural evidence that belies the existence of *gilgia*, but it has been kept alive
by soil scientists and archaeologists Dahlin and Pohl (Antoine et al. 1982,
Bloom et al. 1983, Pope & Dahlin 1989, Pohl 1990).

The excavations on Albion Island revealed that lands that would be
agriculturally fertile had been cut by ditching (see Figure 12) (Bloom et al.
1983:418). A "ditch" is a narrow, V-shaped linear excavation usually connecting
to a permanent body of water, in this case the Río Hondo. In this form, it
can serve the purpose of either admitting or draining the water to or from the
adjacent agricultural plain, according to the slope of the ditch bottom.[7] There
are certain physical characteristics of this form of water manipulation. The
energetics are low, as little earth volume is removed compared to other such
systems requiring excavation (canals). The narrowness and V-shape prohibit
the practice of "mucking" (Denevan 1982:186). Periodic re-excavation is
required if maintenance and sustainability are associated with this simplest
form of water control. The rate and degree of side slumpage is expected to
be high. In other words, "ditches" are of limited economic value, especially
with regard to their potential for longevity.

The evidence from the Albion Island prototype ditch does not indicate its
specific hydraulic function—allocation or drainage—although drainage has been
assumed (Bloom et al. 1983:417). Further assumed is that drainage was required
during the Maya occupation due to rises in sea level that led to inundations of
the lower Río Hondo basin, depositing sediments and flooding the agricultural
lands. Since the landscape in this scenario is assumed to be already inundated,
just how ditching would remove the water is not explained. Sedimentary clays
are indeed a feature of the stratigraphy in northern Belize, and a difference of
interpretation exists between those that are deposited naturally and those that
were manipulated by humans. To the east of Albion Island, adjacent to the New
River, excavations in the fields of Pulltrouser Swamp demonstrate that deposition
of the clays contained in the field "fill" could not have occurred in the manner
described by Bloom et al. (1983) through natural flooding. It has been claimed
that the same stratigraphy found at Albion Island pertains to the landscape
surrounding Pulltrouser Swamp (Pohl & Bloom n.d.).

The Evidence from Pulltrouser Swamp

The excavated features that have convinced most archaeologists that raised
field/canal systems are anthropogenic, as opposed to being produced by forces
of nature, are discussed below. Pulltrouser Swamp serves as the basic model,
but corroborative findings at other locations are cited.

(*a*) *Form* The fields at Pulltrouser are found in a variety of shapes and
sizes (see Figure 13). "Channelized fields" have been described as having

Figure 13. Raised Fields at the North End of Pulltrouser Swamp (courtesy of B. L. Turner II)

growing surfaces that are partially artificial (anthropogenic) and partially natural, while the side canals are wholly artificial (Turner & Harrison 1981, Turner 1983, Harrison n.d.b). The basic finger shape is known to vary only in length. This shape represents the least amount of labor for production, involving the excavation of the canals and the addition of a varying amount of new soil to extend the "finger" into the swamp basin.

"Islands," or basic raised fields conforming to the typology recognized on a world distribution (Denevan 1970, 1982; Devenvan et al. n.d.), are interpreted as having been wholly constructed in shallow water, while the surrounding canals are excavated to a depth greater than the original swamp bottom (Denevan & Turner 1974, Turner 1983).[8] These fields (see Figure 14) are found in a large variety of shapes. Naturally, there has been considerable degradation and slumping in the near millenium during which these fields have seen disuse. Nevertheless, shapes can be characterized from their present state as oval, square, L-shaped (often integrated with a square field in the crook of the L), and Y-shaped. There are also differences in height, or absolute elevation above the water level. In one instance, low, simply shaped fields (oval or square, without appendage formations) at site RF 9 on the western littoral of Pulltrouser South are presently elevated less than 1m above the water line. Across the open and permanent water of this arm of the basin lies site RF 7, a Y-shaped raised field rising 1.92m above the water line (see Figure 15) (Harrison n.d.b).[9] The complex shape of RF 7, which was formed by cutting channels through the swamp border and by artificially raising the arms of the "Y", in addition to its elevation well above the opposite site RF 9, establish that a natural origin by sedimentation resulting from inundation is physically impossible. Sediments cannot be deposited during flood conditions at highly differential elevations (a difference of nearly 1m) across a shared body of water. Nor could rapid runoff account for the complex and steep configuration of RF 7. In addition, these formal differences (shape and elevation above water) have implications for economic microniches deliberately created around the borders of the swamp in order to establish different moisture requirements for differing cultigens, for example maize or root crops versus cotton or cacao.

Functionally, the canal/field system found at Pulltrouser Swamp and elsewhere in northern Belize (Cobweb Swamp, Nohmul, Cerros) is very different from the ditching system described by Bloom et al. (1983) on Albion Island. Canals are flat or concave-bottomed and at least 1m in width. "Mucking" is part of the process of maintaining a canal/field system, which is designed for sustainability. Annually or less often, men walk the canal, collecting the nutrient rich muck from the canal floor and placing it on the surface of the adjacent fields (Denevan et al. n.d., Denevan 1982). As noted above, this is not possible for a narrow ditch system. Various hydraulic and non-hydraulic functions have been described for raised fields, relating to the variable needs of soil moisture (Denevan & Turner 1974:26-29). These varied functions can be reflected in the

Figure 14. An "Island," or Raised Field, Surrounded by Canals in Pulltrouser Swamp

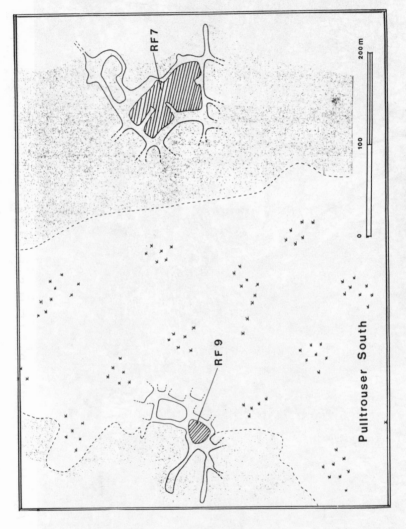

Figure 15. A Portion of the Map of Pulltrouser South, Showing Locations of RF 9 and RF 7 Across Open Water

100

various shapes, such as found in the Pulltrouser assemblage of fields. Today, this swamp system is connected hydrologically to the New River, and the water levels in the swamp basin fluctuate in accordance with the river level, as well as with the annual rainfall flowing from the surrounding terrain. In this sense, the Pulltrouser basin does not function in the same way as a land-locked *bajo* (*akalche*, or swamp) lacking a presently active riverine connection.

Whether the Maya of Pulltrouser devised a sluice dam to maintain constant water levels is not known. The economic advantage and relative ease with which such a device could be constructed suggest its likelihood, but material evidence is lacking. Today, the water levels within the swamp rise and fall, leaving some canals dry (see Figure 16) while deeper and wider ones remain inundated (see Figure 17). The unpredictability of the rainfall and, thus, the river level results in uncertainty of moisture retention in the canals without any sluice control. If these conditions prevailed in ancient times, they would have been a liability to the efficiency of the system.

(*b*) *Stratigraphy and Content*   The topography around the swamp basin has an organic, surficial "A-horizon" representing the activity from late Maya times (8th-12th century A.D.) until the present. On the surface of the fields, this *solum* contains a substantial incidence of artifacts, including both ceramics and lithics (Fry 1983:202-203, Shafer 1983:243). The condition of fluctuating water levels is not amenable to good ceramic preservation, so a majority of recovered ceramics were not clearly identifiable by period. Yet, enough were identifiable to indicate a preponderance of Late Classic (Santana Tepeu) period ceramics on the surface and sides of the fields.

The mottled fill that comprises the part of the field interpreted as man-made has the following characteristics: (a) mottling from gray to black clay, often in curvilinear formations (see Figure 18); (b) inclusions of angular limestone, not native to sedimentary deposits (Turner, pers. comm., 1983); (c) both ceramic and lithic artifacts, the latter of a type (biface ovates) associated with the working of agricultural fields (Shafer 1983:242-243); (d) phytolithic and pollen remains of water lilies (discussed below); and (e) maize and gossypian (cotton) pollen, both near surface and at depth in several fields (Wiseman 1983, n.d.), as well as three examples of corn stalk macrofossils (Miksicek n.d.). Palynological and macrofossil evidence for many other non-cultigens was recovered, but direct evidence of cultigens remains sparse (but not absent) to date.[10]

The macrofossil and pollen returns from the field constructs have produced some provocative results, despite the sparsity of cultigens. One of these is the differences in malacologic and floral assemblages shown between raised and channelized fields. Miksicek (n.d.) says the following:

Figure 16. A Drying Canal as Water Seasonally
Recedes Near the South End of Pulltrouser West

Figure 17.   Water Lilies in Broad Branch of Open Water, Pulltrouser Swamp

Figure 18. Excavations into a Raised Field at Site 1, 1979, Showing the Mottling of the Clay Fill, Pulltrouser Swamp

Despite the lack of cultigen evidence, the ground pattern flotation samples do suggest some interesting patterns ecologically. One group of samples is characterized by high proportions of lake snails (*Pyrgoebocus* and *Cochlioena*), little disturbance charcoal, no *Cladium* seeds, and the presence of calcite casts of palm roots. These types of sample were collected from raised or island-type fields (3-50A, 3-51A, 4-71A, 4-72A,7-1B, 3-80A and 3S-81A). These fields appear to have been artificial platforms constructed predominantly from lake muck. The second group of samples is dominated by disturbance snails (*Hawaiia, Lamellaxis,* Unknown A) mixed with a few shallow water species (*Biomehalacia, Gundlacchia,* and *Stenoehysa*). These samples also produced *Cladium* seeds or stems, and disturbance charcoal (*Hamelia* and *Solanum*). Flotation samples with this upland disturbance-shallow water assemblage were generally collected from finger or channelized fields.

Disappearance of the lake snail was noted in the raised fields but not in the channelized fields—a fact which, in combination with the appearance of the *Cladium* seeds, strongly indicates a change in the hydraulic regime between the two types, i.e., a change from lake regime to swamp regime (ibid.). These facts not only provide clues to a possible chronology of field types but provide critical evidence of their artificial construction.

Yet another line of evidence derives from the clay fill of the fields. Wiseman's (1983:115) discussion of the role of the water lily, for which pollen and phytolith remains were recovered from several field sources, has bearing upon the anthropogenic source of the fields. He (Wiseman 1983:115) writes:

> Another economic implication concerns the water-lily evidence in the upper samples, which probably are from maintenance additions, as opposed to initial construction. This plant, while not a primary economic taxon, may have been an important second-level component of the raised field system. First it provides a suitable microenvironment for numerous invertebrates, recycles organic detritus, and produces dissolved oxygen. These factors provide an ideal habitat for fish, an important protein source for the Maya. This association between fish and *Nymphaea* is often represented in Maya art (Puleston 1977:458). Second, the rapidly growing water lily provides an on-site, abundant source of mulch.

The implied association of fish and *Nymphaea* is confirmed at Pulltrouser even today. The same conditions must occur as in ancient times in the broader and deeper canals, which do not have the overhead swamp cover that would inhibit water lily growth. In one such canal, the remains of a recent historic fish weir partially block the intersection of the canal with the open water of Pulltrouser South. Harvesting fish in these ancient canals has continued into recent times, underscoring the economic value of this subsidiary function of water control (see Figure 19).

(*c*) *Settlement*   The population trajectories for settlement history in the environs of the swamp littorals clearly indicate an interest in the swamp by the Late Preclassic (Harrison 1983, 1990, n.d.b). Populations around the borders of the basin showed a dramatic expansion in the Late Classic, with an apparently substantial survival into the Terminal Classic.

Figure 19. Remains of a Recent Historic Fish
Weir in an Ancient Canal, K'axob, Pulltrouser Swamp

Of the 11 communities settled around the littorals, five display some urban characteristics in the sense of functional diversification, but only two were truly nucleated (Harrison 1989). The same two communities, K'axob and Kokeal, have the shared longest time depth of occupation from the Middle Preclassic period through Terminal Classic. The majority of settlements—six communities—are rural in quality, with a population expansion (in the Late Classic) that demonstrates a rural focus for the study zone. The distributions of these small communties and of the raised fields have no direct correlation. Other factors, such as location on elevated sandy ridges, seem to have influenced the choice of location, although no settlement is more than 400m from the swamp littorals.

The evidence that does exist, both directly from the fields and in the associated communities, indicates that some development of swamp agriculture took place during the Late Preclassic, probably as initial experimentation. The florescence of swamp agriculture is dated to the Late Classic by direct association of artifacts as well as the population trajectories for the settlement as a whole. Extended use continues into the Terminal Classic. Much of this dating is by association in the best archaeological tradition and, thus, is inferential, but it is supported by the ceramic evidence from the fields themselves.

Other Sites

In discussion of similar features in Cobweb Swamp, adjacent to the site of Colha and south of the Pulltrouser system, Jacob and Hallmark (n.d.) have used the terms "ditched" and "canal" interchangeably, without recognizing any formal or functional differences. Recent investigators working in northen Belize (Jacob n.d., Pohl & Pope n.d., Bloom & Pohl n.d.) have interpreted the soil stratigraphy of a series of alleged fields and canals at Cobweb Swamp with emphasis on the chemistry rather than the cultural context and reached the conclusion that the mottled fill soils found therein are natural in deposition. In doing so, they agree with the arguments (basically their own) originally presented in Bloom et al.(1983) concerning the interpretation of the evidence from Albion Island. The setting at Cobweb Swamp is quite similar to that of Pulltrouser, in that water drainage in the basin is associated with Lopez Creek and, thus, has an external outlet. Pohl and associates have concluded (Pohl & Bloom n.d., Jacob n.d., Pohl & Pope n.d.) that Preclassic ditching in an early A-horizon (paleosol) was buried at a much later date by sediments derived from upland erosion (as opposed to rising sea level). Artifacts in part of this "sedimentary" deposit are dismissed as secondary in origin. This condition of early "ditching" buried by clay sediments is extended to regional interpretation including most of northern Belize (Pohl & Pope n.d.). This point of view has some longevity in the literature, as noted earlier, and has been espoused principally by pedologists (Antoine et al. 1982, Bloom et al. 1983,

Pope & Dahlin 1989). As a regional explanation, this interpretation is clearly at odds with the facts, as known, from Pulltrouser Swamp. A summary of the argument and its rebuttals have been stated most eloquently by Rice (1993).

Research on the extent of raised fields in wetlands was pioneered by Siemens (Siemens & Puleston 1972) and produced the greatest amount of evidence for northern Belize (Siemens 1978, 1982). Siemen's (1982:215) map illustrating distribution of raised fields in northern Belize demonstrated the extent of wetland patterning and its distribution in riverine as well as *bajo* (swamp) wetlands. Investigations at the site of Cerros by Scarborough (1983, 1991a-b) illustrated the complexity of hydraulic systems that the urban Maya were capable of achieving as well as their adaptation into urban and suburban settings.

At the northern extreme of the southern Lowlands (see Figure 1) lies the wetland complex known as Bajo Morocoy/Acatuch, immediately adjacent to the eastern limits of the Río Bec terrace region discussed above. This complex has figured in the literature as an example of one of the areally largest expanses of raised fields known in the Lowlands (Harrison 1977, 1978; Gleissman et al. 1983). In an attempt to correlate the presence/absence of canals (and, thus, of raised fields) with varied hydrologies, Pope and Dahlin (1989) erroneously classified the Morocoy/Acatuch complex as perennially wet. Adams et al. (1990) countered with the observation that the complex is in fact seasonal. A photograph of a roadway in the middle of Bajo Morocoy taken during the dry season had been published in 1977 (Harrison:482).

The aerially viewed pattern in Bajo Morocoy represented the second set of data, following Siemens and Puleston (1972, and Siemens 1982) to draw attention to the raised field phonomenon in the southern Lowlands (Turner 1974, Harrison & Turner 1978, Turner & Harrison 1983). In fact, the complex of wetlands in this zone is greater than the named *bajo*s would indicate (see Figure 20). Here, the combined sets or groups of visible fields amount to 246 sq. km of field/canal combinations.[11] One such group is pictured in Figure 21, with an "island" of high ground visible to the lower right and a north-oriented roadway originating on the Chetumal highway on the left. A group of fields and canals lies between. Examination of the detailed aerial photographs of this zone suggests that the fields are not continuous throughout the various *bajo* basins.

In Figure 20, several drainage systems are also shown, the largest of which has its headwaters in the uplands near the major cermonial center of Tzibanche, shown here as a large black blob near the center of the map. In the high ground, where the site is located, this body of water is a flowing permanent river called X'Kan Río. This river meanders eastwards through a part of Bajo Morocoy, where no field patterns are visible. Passing eastward through an interface of semi-*bajo* and upland, it becomes a narrow, rushing creek and then meanders again through slender arms of the wetland complex. By the time it reaches Bajo Acatuch (the right hand *bajo* and field complex in Figure 20), it has become

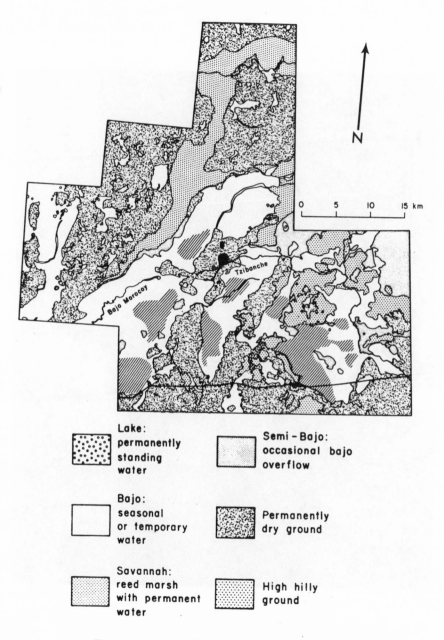

Figure 20. Land Form Map of Bajo Complex
Morocoy/Acatuch. (Hatched areas are patterned vegetation
interpreted as raised fields. Sites are noted in black.)

Figure 21.   A Field/Canal Group North of Nicolás
Bravo in Bajo Morocoy, Southern Quintana Roo

the Río Ucum, which crosses the Chetumal highway at the town of Ucum and empties as a tributary into the Río Hondo. This drainage cannot today be traced above ground for its full length. In the fashion of hilled karstic drainages, it occasionally disappears underground for some distance to reappear again in its eastward and southerly course. Segments of other water courses are visible in the photographs of Bajo Morocoy, and they likely represent portions of a dendritic pattern of drainage for the Morocoy basin as a whole. However, too many segments are missing on both the 1:50,000 and 1:20,000 composite areal photographs to confirm a single dendritic drainage.

Ground proof of the efficacy of the aerial pattern of raised fields has been accomplished by Gleissman et al. (1983), who testify to the similarity of the profiles of the field/canal constructs to those excavated at Pulltrouser Swamp. A difference in hydraulic regimes between the Morocoy/Acatuch system and the Pulltrouser system is hereby acknowledged. Today, the former is unquestionably seasonal while the latter is perennial in part.[12]

An important comparison can be made between the Morocoy/Acatuch complex in southern Quintana Roo and the Bajo de Santa Fe adjacent to Tikal in the central Petén. The Morocoy complex lies at about 100m asl[13] while Bajo de Santa Fe lies at roughly 225m asl.[14]

Drainage in the Bajo de Santa Fe begins with headwaters slightly to the south and east of the Tikal upland ridges. It then curves northwards to a point south of the site of El Encanto and swings southwards to become the Río Folmul outside of the Bajo de Santa Fe (Map Hoja NE 16-9E, Guatemala Forestal), passing directly by the site of Nakum, then swinging northwards to the lagoon and *bajo* complex at the south edge of the site of Yaloch. At this point a narrow drainage divide must be crossed to join a series of drainages flowing west to east. After crossing the modern border of Belize, named drainages flowing west to east include Pescado Creek, Crique Negro, Yalbac Creek, and Labouring Creek. The latter flows directly into the northern arm of the Belize River at latitude 19° 31″. The similarity of this drainage pattern to that in Bajo Morocoy, from an upland *bajo* to a major river system, is striking. Several researchers have observed vegetal patterns in the Bajo de Santa Fe (Dahlin 1979:308, Harrison 1978:247-53, Siemens 1978:139), but minimal attempts to locate them on the ground have failed (Dahlin 1979:307). The need for further investigation has been noted a number of times (Adams et al. 1990).

The same situation is true for other karsted wetland systems north of the lakes fault divide (see Figure 2). Tantalizing patterns are noted in *bajo* Mirador (Stuart 1975:785), and the great causeways crossing the *bajo* to the south of the major site appear to interrupt the direction of flow of the internal *bajo* drainage. Investigations here, too, have failed to discover any association of the features in question with water control and agriculture (Pope & Dahlin 1989:98).

CONCLUSIONS

The karstic nature of the landscape in the southern Lowlands and the natural drainages produced by it have influenced the development of Maya civilization in a number of ways. Drainage patterns account for part of the population distribution, with riparian settings preferred in the folded hills of the southern zone. In the northern, karsted wetlands, it is drainage patterns through the wetlands which have influenced the choice of settlement. However, in this northern zone, control of the water flow was possible. Manipulation of the wetland basins as well as riverine levee swamps (Siemens 1978, 1982) made the northeastern sector of the southern Lowlands most attractive. Here are found the densest known concentrations of population.

On the sloped uplands, water control in the form of terracing designed for purposes of food production (rather than residential use) occurs in the folded hills of the south and in the extreme north of the karsted wetlands, a region where terraces appear to be most prevalent (the so-called Río Bec region). The relative absence of terraces in the central portion of the Petén, which is also part of the karsted wetlands, is noted as curious, and a number of explanations have been considered.

Architecturally constructed controls for the collection of water for household use are elaborate. The rapidly increasing data base for such constructs probably reflects a new awareness on the part of researchers. The use of wells as a water resource is restricted geographically to the northern portions of the karsted wetlands. The water source, whether water table or subterranean aquifer, for a number of known wells has changed, rendering the wells unusable. The causes of such change since the Late Postclassic are not known.

This survey of the complexities evident in ancient water management gives rise to provocative inferences for societal organization and state developement. The suggestion of elite control over the collection and consumption of water and large-scale organization of "managed" food production in the wetlands are indications, if not of an organized central state, then of a shared knowledge of organization on a regional basis at least.

The role of trade has not been addressed in this essay, but the water routes that provide access from the hinterlands to either side of the Yucatan Peninsula were undoubtedly a major economic factor. "Control" of these routes would undoubtedly have had economic, social, and military ramifications.

The least known region within this study zone is the Northeast drainage of the wetlands, where the Río San Pedro Mártir provides access from the west side of the divide to the Uscumacintla. Here lie the important sites of El Perú and El Mirador, where an impressive florescence occurred in the Late Preclassic (Matheny et al. 1980, Hansen 1990).

As a prognosis for future work, study of the area's environmental heterogeneity is the most immediate need, requiring equal focus on the upland ridges and the wetlands. Solutions devised by the ancient Maya for all problems of water management have proven to have been as diverse as is the topography of the southern Lowlands. We must better understand this diversity to gain knowledge of both the mechanisms of water management and their effect on ancient Maya societal development.

NOTES

1. This map was republished virtually unchanged in Rice and Culbert (1990:29) as Map 1.1.

2. Within this zone a great deal of variability exists in the hydrological and vegetal regimes of the wetlands. The most common condition today is one of seasonal water with accompanying xerophytic regimes, but a number of these so-called wetlands are in fact shallow lakes whose borders shrink and swell with the seasons. These are particularly common in southern Quintana Roo (Harrison 1978).

3. Site survey and investigations were conducted in Quintana Roo in the old Uaymil Province of Postclassic times, under the auspices of the Royal Ontario Museum (Toronto) between 1971 and 1974. Partial reporting has been published (Harrison 1972, 1979, 1981; Fry 1972, 1987). The complete report will be published by the Royal Ontario Museum (Harrison n.d.a).

4. Detailed description, together with corroborative sections, plans, and photographs concerning water management in the Central Acropolis will be published in Tikal Report 15 (Harrison), The University Museum, University of Pennsylvania.

5. Publication of Bronson's work on water distribution and dispersal will likely be included in Tikal Report 23, University Museum, University of Pennsylvania.

6. Apart from arguments about the reality of wetland manipulation by the Maya, there are also arguments concerning the association of wetland manipulation with state development. Raised fields in New Guinea have been cited frequently as an instance where sizable congregations of agricultural platforms were managed on a family cooperative basis without the benefit of state organization (Denevan 1982, Denevan & Turner 1974). It must be noted, however, that the relative levels of material culture and socioeconomic development of New Guinea do not correspond to those of the ancient Maya, who had achieved state development, in the view of this author. The example from New Guinea demonstrates that sizable (not large) zones of raised fields *can* be managed without state development.

7. Denevan (1982:188) addresses only the function of drainage with respect to ditches, while Scarborough and Gallopin (1991:658) raise the distinction between allocation and dispersal as water management techniques, although not in specific reference to ditches.

8. A variant interpretation would allow a natural origin for part or all of the growing surface, which is surrounded by wholly artificial canals. In such an interpretation, a segment of the swamp littoral would have been wholly separated from the parent "mainland" by the excavation of canals. Renewal and addition to the growing surface would occur by mucking.

9. This field at site RF 7 represents a third classified form of growing platform at Pulltrouser Swamp. It combines features of channelized and raised fields in that the growing surface is partly natural and partly artificial (Harrison n.d.b).

10. Soil cores taken directly through raised fields and in one canal in 1981 penetrated to a depth of 2m without reaching the underlying native sascab of the swamp basin. These cores did pass through multiple soil laminae, resembling varves, that *underlay* the mottled clay fill of the field in each situation, or were truncated by the canal bottom. Presentation of the analysis of these cores is pending (Wiseman pers. comm., 1992).

11. This group of fields was incorrectly reported in 1977 by Harrison (1977:478) in a series of escalating miscalculations. The entire group of visible grid patterns was reported as comprising

23 percent of 10,700 sq. km, which should have read 1,070 sq. km. Further, it was stated that the lower block alone (Bajo Morocoy) contained minimally 1461 sq. km. The error has been noted by both Denevan and Turner.

12. The west arm of the Pulltrouser system is seasonally wet, while the East and South arms are perennially wet.

13. Map sheet Chetumal 16Q-V y Rio Azul 16Q-VII, Estados Unidos Mexicanos, published by Comisión Intersecretarial Coordinadora del Levantamiento de la Carta Geográfica de la República Mexicana, 1958.

14. Mapa Forestal de la República de Guatemala, Hoja NE 16-9F, Tikal, United Nations Development Program, 1966.

REFERENCES

Adams, R. E. W. (1981) "Settlement Patterns of the Central Yucatan and Southern Campeche Regions." Pp. 211-257 in Wendy Ashmore (ed.) *Lowland Maya Settlement Patterns*. Albuquerque: University of New Mexico Press, School of American Research.

Adams, R. E. W., T. P. Culbert, W. E. Brown, Jr., P. D. Harrison, and L. J. Levi (1990) "Rebuttal to Pope and Dahlin." *Journal of Field Archaeology* 17:241-244.

Antoine, P. P., R. K. Scarie, and P. R. Bloom (1982) "The Origin of Raised Fields near San Antonio, Belize: An Alternative Hypothesis." Pp. 227-236 in K. V. Flannery (ed.) *Maya Subsistence, Studies in Memory of Dennis E. Puleston*. New York: Academic Press.

Baudez, C. F. ed. (1983) *Introducción a la arqueología de Copán, 3 vols. (Introduction to the Archaeology of Copan, 3 vols.)*. Tegulcigalpa, Honduras: Secretaría de Estado en el Despacho de Cultura y Turismo.

Binford, M. W. (1991) "Testing Sustainable Landscapes: Lessons from Ancient Agroecosystems Practices in the Bolivian Altiplano." *Landscape Ecology and Environmental Planning*. Logan: Utah State University Press.

Binford, M. W., A. L. Kolata, and M. Brenner (n.d.) "Rehabilitating Ancient Raised Fields in the Bolivian Altiplano: Paleoecological and Archaeological Evidence for Sustainable Agriculture." Paper presented before the International Society of Ecological Economics Conference, Washington, DC, May 21-23, 1990.

Blanton, R. E. (1972a) *Prehispanic Settlement Patterns of the Ixtapalapa Peninsula Region, Mexico*. University Park: The Pennsylvania State University, Department of Anthropology, Occasional Papers in Anthropology, 6.

_____ (1972b) "Prehispanic Adaptation in the Ixtapalapa Region, Mexico." *Science* 175:1317-1326.

Blom, F. (1946) "Apuntes sobre los ingenieros mayas" ("Notes on Maya Engineers"). *Irrigación en México* 27:5-16.

Bloom, R. B., and M. Pohl (n.d.) "Soils and Ancient Maya Agriculture in the Lowlands of Northern Belize." Paper presented before the Society for American Archaeology, Pittsburgh, PA, 1992.

Bloom, R. B., M. Pohl, C. Buttleman, F. Wiseman, A. Covich, C. Miksicek, J. Ball, and J. Stein (1983) "Prehistoric Maya Wetland Agriculture and the Alluvial Soils Near San Antonio, Rio Hondo, Belize." *Nature* 301 (5899):417-419.

Boone, E. H., and G. R. Willey, eds. (1988) *The Southeast Classic Maya Zone*. Washington, DC: Dumbarton Oaks.

Bronson, B. (n.d.) "Field Notes for the 1966 Season." Notes taken for the Tikal Project, The University Museum, University of Pennsylvania. (Forthcoming in *Tikal Report No. 23*.)

Chase, D. Z., and A. F. Chase (1987) *Investigations at the Classic Maya City of Caracol, Belize: 1985-1987*. San Francisco, CA: Pre-Columbian Art Research Institute, Monograph 3.

——— (n.d.) *Investigations at Caracol, Belize: 1988-1991* (2 vols.). San Francisco: Pre-Columbian Art Research Institute.

Culbert, T. P. (1973) "Introduction: A Prologue to Classic Maya Culture and the Problem of Its Collapse." Pp. 3-19 in T. P. Culbert (ed.) *The Classic Maya Collapse*. Albuquerque: University of New Mexico Press, School of American Research.

Dahlin, Bruce H. (1979) "Preliminary Investigations of Agronomic Potentials in 'Bajos' Adjacent to Tikal, Peten, Guatemala." Pp. 305-312 in *Actes du XLIIe Congrès International des Americanistes, Vol. VIII* (Paris).

Denevan, W. M. (1970) "Aboriginal Drained Field Cultivation in the Americas." *Science* 169:647-654.

——— (1982) "Hydraulic Agriculture in the American Tropics: Forms, Measures, and Recent Research." Pp. 181-203 in K. V. Flannery (ed.) *Maya Subsistence: Studies in Memory of Dennis E. Puleston*. New York: Academic Press.

Denevan, W. M., and B. L. Turner II (1974) "Forms, Functions and Associations of Riased Fields in the Old World Tropics." *The Journal of Tropical Geography* 39:24-33.

Denevan, W. M., W. M. Kent, and R. Whitten (n.d.) "Mounding, Mucking and Mangling: Recent Research on the Raised Fields in the Guayas Basin, Ecuador." Paper presented before the Conference on Prehistoric Intensive Agriculture in the Tropics, Canberra, Australia, 1981.

Dunning, N. P., and T. Beach (n.d.) "Soil Erosion, Slope Management, and Ancient Terracing in the Maya Lowlands." Paper presented before the Society for American Archaeology, Pittsburgh, PA, April 1992.

Dunning, N. P., T. Beach, and D. Rue (n.d.) "Ecology and Ancient Settlement in the Petexbatun Region: Preliminary Findings of the 1991 Season." Report to the Petexbatun Regional Archaeological Project, Vanderbilt University.

Erickson, C. L. (1988) *An Archaeological Invesitgation of Raised-Field Agriculture in the Lake Titicaca Basin of Peru*. Ph.D. dissertation, University of Illinois, Champaign-Urbana.

Erickson, C. L., and K. L. Candler (1989) "Raised Fields and Sustainable Agriculture in the Lake Titicaca Basin." Pp. 230-248 in J. Browder (ed.) *Fragile Lands of Latin America: Strategies for Sustainable Development*. Boulder, CO: Westview Press.

Fedick, S. L. (1989) "The Economics of Agricultural Land Use and Settlement in the Upper Belize Valley." Pp. 215-255 in P. A. McAnany & B. L. Isaac (eds.) *Prehistoric Maya Economies of Belize, Supplement 4, Research in Economic Anthropology*. Greenwich, CT: JAI Press Inc.

Ford, A. (1985) "Maya Settlement Pattern Chronology in the Belize River Area and the Implications for the Development of the Central Maya Lowlands." *Belcast Journal of Belizean Affairs* 4(2):13-31.

——— (1986) *Population Growth and Social Complexity: An Examination of Settlement and Environment in the Central Maya Lowlands*. Tempe: Arizona State University, Anthropological Research Paper No. 35.

Fry, R. E. (1972) "The Archaeology of Southern Quintana Roo: Ceramics." Pp. 487-493 in *Atti del XL Congresso Internazionale degli Americanisti* (Rome).

——— (1983) "The Ceramics of the Pulltrouser Area: Settlements and Fields." Pp. 194-211 in B. L. Turner II & P. D. Harrison (eds.), *infra*.

——— (1987) "The Ceramic Sequence of South-Central Quintana Roo, Mexico." Pp. 111-122 in P. M. Rice & R. J. Sharer (eds.) *Maya Ceramics: Papers from the 1985 Maya Ceramic Conference*. Oxford: British Archaeology Reports, International Series, 345(i).

Gleissman, S. R., B. L. Turner II, R. May, and M. F. Amador (1983) "Ancient Raised Field Agriculture in the Maya Lowlands of Southeastern Mexico." Pp. 91-110 in J. P. Darch (ed.) *Drained Field Agriculture in Central and South America*. Oxford: British Archaeological Reports, International Series, 189.

Hansen, R. D. (1990) *Excavations in the Tigre Complex, El Mirador, Petén, Guatemala.* Provo, UT: New World Archaeological Foundation, Paper No. 62 (El Mirador Series, Part 3).

Harrison, P. D. (1970) *The Central Acropolis, Tikal, Guatemala: A Preliminary Study of the Functions and Its Structural Components during the Late Classic Period.* Ph.D. Dissertation, University of Pennsylvania.

_____ (1972) "Precolumbian Settlement Distribution and External Relationships in Southern Quintana Roo, Part 1: Architecture." Pp. 479-486 in *Atti del XL Congresso Internazionale degli Americanisti* (Rome).

_____ (1977) "The Rise of the Bajos and the Fall of the Maya." Pp. 469-508 in N. Hammond (ed.) *Social Process in Maya Prehistory.* London: Academic Press.

_____ (1978) "Bajos Revisited: Visual Evidence for One System of Agriculture." Pp. 247-253 in P. D. Harrison & B. L. Turner II (eds.), *infra.*

_____ (1979) "The Lobil Postclassic Phase in the Southern Interior of the Yucatan Peninsula." Pp. 189-207 in N. Hammond & G. Willey (eds.) *Maya Archaeology and Ethnohistory.* Austin: University of Texas Press.

_____ (1981) "Some Aspects of Preconquest Settlement in Southern Quintana Roo, Mexico." Pp. 259-286 in W. Ashmore (ed.) *Lowland Maya Settlement Patterns.* Albuquerque: University of New Mexico Press, School of American Research.

_____ (1983) "The Pulltrouser Settlement Survey and Mapping of Kokeal." Pp. 140-157 in B. L. Turner II & P. D. Harrison (eds.), *infra.*

_____ (1989) "Functional Influences of Settlement Pattern in the Communities of Pulltrouser Swamp, Northern Belize." Pp. 460-465 in S. MacEachern, D.J.W. Archer & R. D. Garvin (eds.) *Households and Communities.* Calgary: Proceedings of the 21st Annual Chacmool Conference, The Archaeological Association of the University of Calgary.

_____ (1990) "The Revolution in Ancient Maya Subsistence." Pp. 99-113 in F. S. Clancy & P. D. Harrison (eds.) *Vision and Revision in Maya Studies.* Albuquerque: University of New Mexico Press.

_____ (n.d.a) Uaymil Project Field Notes, 1974 Season. Studies in South-Central Quintana Roo, Mexico. Forthcoming publication by Royal Ontario Museum, Toronto.

_____ (n.d.b) "Asentamiento en la zona arqueológica en el norte de Belice" ("Settlement in the Archaeological Zone of Northern Belize"). Paper presented before the Conference on Ancient Maya Agriculture and Biological Resources Management, University of California, Riverside, August 1991.

_____ (n.d.c) "Archaeology in Southwestern Quintana Roo: Interim Report of the Uaymil Survey Project." Paper presented before the XLI Congreso Internacional de Americanistas, Mexico City, 1974.

Harrison, P. D., and B. L. Turner II, eds. (1978) *Prehispanic Maya Agriculture.* Albuquerque: University of New Mexico Press.

_____ (1983) "Pulltrouser Swamp and Maya Raised Fields: A Summation." Pp. 246-270 in B. L. Turner II & P. D. Harrison (eds.), *infra.*

Healy, P. F., J. D. H. Lambert, J. T. Arnason, and R. J. Hebda (1983) "Caracol, Belize: Evidence of Ancient Maya Agricultural Terraces." *Journal of Field Archaeology* 10:397-410.

Jacob, J. S. (n.d.) "The Maya Clay: Late Classic Sedimentation in the Wetlands of Northern Belize." Paper presented before the Society for American Archaeology, Pittsburgh, PA, April 1992.

Jacob, J. S., and C. T. Hallmark (n.d.) "Maya Ditched Fields in Cobweb Swamp, Belize: A Pedological Assessment." Ms, Department of Soil and Crop Sciences, Texas A & M University, 1990.

Kolata, A. L. (1986) "The Agricultural Foundations of the Tiwanaku State: A View From the Heartland." *American Antiquity* 51:748-762.

————— (1991) "The Technology and Organization of Agricultural Production in the Tiwanaku State." *Latin American Antiquity* 2:99-125.

Lundell, C. L. (1937) *The Vegetation of the Peten.* Washington, DC: Carnegie Institution of Washington, Publ. No. 478.

————— (1940) "The 1936 Michigan-Carnegie Botanical Expedition to British Honduras." Pp. 1-58 in *Botany of Maya Area.* Washington, DC: Carnegie Institution of Washington, Publ. No.522, Misc. Paper No. 14.

McAnany, P. A. (1989) "Economic Foundations of Prehistoric Maya Society: Paradigms and Concepts." Pp. 347-372 in P. A. McAnany & B. L. Isaac (eds.) *Prehistoric Maya Economies of Belize, Supplement 4, Research in Economic Anthropology.* Greenwich , CT: JAI Press.

————— (1990) "Water Storage in the Puuc Region of the Northern Maya Lowlands: A Key to Population Estimates and Architectural Variability." Pp. 263-284 in T. P. Culbert & D. S. Rice (eds.) *Precolumbian Population History in the Maya Lowlands.* Albuquerque: University of New Mexico Press.

Matheny, R. T., R. D. Hansen, and D. L. Gurr (1980) "Preliminary Field Report, El Mirador, 1979 Season." Pp. 1-23 in R. T. Matheny (ed.) *El Mirador, Peten Guatemala, An Interim Report.* Provo, UT: New World Archaeological Foundation, Paper No. 45.

Miksicek, C. (n.d.) "Paleoecology and Subsistence at Pulltrouser Swamp: The View From the Float Tank." Unpublished MS, 30 pp.

Morley, S. G., and G. W. Brainard (1983) *The Ancient Maya* (4th ed., rev. by R. J. Sharer). Stanford, CA: Stanford University Press.

Nelson, F. W., Jr. (1973) *Archaeological Investigations at Dzibilnocac, Campeche, Mexico.* Provo, UT: New World Archaeological Foundation, Paper No. 39.

Ower, L. H. (1927) "Features of British Honduras." *Geographical Journal* 70:373-386.

Parsons, J. R. (1976) "The Role of Chinampa Agriculture in the Food Supply of Aztec Tenochtitlan." Pp. 233-257 in C. E. Cleland (ed.) *Cultural Change and Continuity.* New York: Academic Press.

Pohl, M. D., and P. R. Bloom (n.d.) "Soils and Ancient Maya Agriculture in the Lowlands of Northern Belize." Paper presented before the Society for American Archaeology, Pittsburgh, PA, April 1992.

Pohl, M. D., and K. O. Pope (n.d.) "Prehistoric Farming in Wetlands of Northern Belize." Paper presented before the Conference on Ancient Maya Agriculture and Biological Resource Management, University of California, Riverside, August 1991.

Pope, K. O., and B. H. Dahlin (1989) "Ancient Maya Wetland Agriculture: New Insights from Ecological and Remote Sensing Research." *Journal of Field Archaeology* 16:87-106.

Potter, D. F. (1977) *Maya Architecture of the Central Yucatecan Peninsula, Mexico.* New Orleans, LA: Tulanbe University, Middle American Research Institute, Publ. 44.

Puleston, D. E. (1965) "The Chultuns of Tikal." *Expedition* 7(3):24-29.

————— (1968) *Brosimium Alicastrum as a Subsistence Alternative for Classic Maya of the Central Southern Lowlands.* M.A. Thesis, University of Pennsylvania.

————— (1971) "An Experimental Approach to the Function of Classic Maya Chultuns." *American Antiquity* 36:322-335.

————— (1977) "The Art and Archaeology of Hydraulic Agriculture in the Maya Lowlands." Pp. 449-467 in N. Hammond (ed.) *Social Process in Maya Prehistory.* London: Academic Press.

Pyburn, K. Anne (1990) "Settlement Patterns at Nohmul: Preliminary Results of Four Excavation Seasons." Pp. 183-197 in T. P. Culbert & Don S. Rice (eds.) *Precolumbian Population History in the Maya Lowlands.* Albuquerque: University of New Mexico Press.

Rice, D.S. (1976) *The Historical Ecology of Lakes Yaxha and Sacnab, El Peten, Guatemala.* Ph.D. dissertation, Pennsylvania State University.

————— (1978) "Population Growth and Subsistence Alternatives in a Tropical Lacustrine Environment." Pp. 35-61 in P. D. Harrison & B. L. Turner II (eds.), *supra.*

_____ (1988) "Classic to Postclassic Maya Household Transitions in the Central Peten, Guatemala." Pp. 227-247 in R. R. Wilk & W. Ashmore (eds.) *Household and Community in the Mesoamerican Past.* Albuquerque: University of New Mexico Press.

_____ (1993) "Eighth-Century Physical Geography, Environment, and Natural Resources in the Maya Lowlands." Pp. 11-63 in J. A. Sabloff & J.S. Henderson (eds.) *Lowland Maya Civilization in the Eighth Century A.D.*. Washington, DC: Dumbarton Oaks.

Rice, D. S., and T. P. Culbert (1990) "Historical Contexts for Population Reconstuction in the Maya Lowlands." Pp. 1-36 in T. P. Culbert & D.S. Rice (eds.) *Precolumbian Population History in the Maya Lowlands.* Albuquerque: University of New Mexico Press.

Ruppert, K., and J. H. Denison, Jr. (1943) *Archaeological Reconnaissance in Campeche, Quintana Roo, and Peten.* Washington, DC: Carnegie Institute of Washington, Publ. 543.

Sabloff, J. A., L. R. Binford and P. A. McAnany (1987) "Understanding the Archaeological Record." *Antiquity* 61:203-209.

Sanders, W. T., and B. Price (1968) *Mesoamerica, The Evolution of a Civilization.* New York: Random House.

Sanders, W. T., J. R. Parsons, and R. S. Santley (1979) *The Basin of Mexico: Ecological Processes in the Evolution of a Civilization.* New York: Academic Press.

Satterthwaite, L. S., Jr. (1952) *Piedras Negras Archaeology: Architecture, Part V, Sweathouses.* Philadelphia: University of Pennsylvania, The University Museum.

Scarborough, V. L. (1983) "Raised Field Detection at Cerros, Northern Belize." Pp. 123-136 in J. P. Darch (ed.) *Drained Field Agriculture in Central and South America.* Oxford, ENG: British Archaeological Reports, International, Series 189.

_____ (1991a) "Water Management Adaptation in Non-Industrial Complex Societies: An Archaeological Perspective." Pp. 101-154 in M. B. Schiffer (ed.) *Archaeological Method and Theory, Vol. 3.* Tucson: University of Arizona Press.

_____ (1991b) *Archaeology at Cerros, Belize, Central America Volume III, The Settlement System in a Late Preclassic Maya Community.* Dallas, TX: Southern Methodist University Press.

Scarborough, V. L., and G. G. Gallopin (1991) "A Water Storage Adaptation in the Maya Lowlands." *Science* 251:658-662.

Schele, L., and D. Freidel (1990) *A Forest of Kings, The Untold Story of the Ancient Maya.* New York: William Morrow & Co.

Seimens, A. H., (1978) "Karst and the Prehispanic Maya in the Southern Lowlands." Pp. 117-43 in P. D. Harrison & B. L. Turner II (eds.), *supra.*

_____ (1982) "Prehispanic Cultural Use of the Wetlands of Northern Belize." Pp. 205-25 in K. V. Flannery (ed.) *Maya Subsistence: Studies in Memory of Dennis E. Puleston.* New York: Academic Press.

Seimens, A. H., and D. E. Puleston (1972) "Ridged Fields and Associated Features in Southern Campeche: New Perspectives on the Lowland Maya." *American Antiquity* 37:228-239.

Shafer, H. J. (1983) "The Lithic Artifacts of the Pulltrouser Area: Settlements and Fields." Pp. 212-245 in B. L. Turner II & P. D. Harrison (eds.), *infra.*

Spencer, J. E., and G. A. Hale (1961) "The Origin, Nature and Distribution of Agricultural Terracing." *Pacific Viewpoint* 2:1-40.

Stuart, G. E. (1975) "The Maya Riddle of the Glyphs." *National Geographic Magazine* 148(6):768-791.

Thompson, J. E. S. (1931) *Archaeological Investigations in the Southern Cayo District, British Honduras.* Chicago: Field Museum of Natural History, Publ. 301, Anthropological Series, Vol. XVII(3).

Turner, B. L. II (1974) "Prehistoric Intensive Agriculture in the Mayan Lowlands." *Science* 185:118-124.

———— (1979) "Prehispanic Terracing in the Central Maya Lowlands: Problems of Agricultural ✓ Intensification." Pp. 103-115 in N. Hammond & G. R. Willey (eds.) *Maya Archaeology and Ethnohistory*. Austin: University of Texas Press.

———— (1983) *Once Beneath the Forest. Prehistoric Terracing in the Rio Bec Region of the Maya Lowlands*. Boulder, CO: Westview Press, Dellplain Latin American Studies, No. 132.

Turner, B. L. II, and P. D. Harrison (1981) "Prehistoric Raised-Field Agriculture in the Maya Lowlands." *Science* 213:399-405.

———— eds. (1983) *Pulltrouser Swamp. Ancient Maya Habitat, Agriculture, and Settlement in Northern Belize*. Austin: University of Texas Press.

Weaver, M. P. (1981) *The Aztecs, Maya and Their Predecessors* (2nd ed). New York: Academic Press.

Webster, D. L. (1985) "Recent Settlement Survey in the Copan Valley, Copan, Honduras." *Journal of New World Archaeology* 94:39-63.

West, R. C. (1964) "Surface Configuration and Associated Geology of Middle America." Pp. 33- ✓ 83 in R. C. West (ed.) *Natural Environment and Early Cultures, Handbook of Middle American Indians, Volume 1* (R. Wauchope, gen. ed.). Austin: University of Texas Press.

White, G. E., D. F. Bradley, and A. U. White (1972) *Drawers of Water: Domestic Water Use in East Africa*. Chicago: University of Chicago Press.

Willey, G. R., R. M. Levanthal, and W. L. Fash (1978) "Maya Settlement in the Copán Valley." *Archaeology* 31(4):32-43.

Wiseman, F. M. (1983) "Analysis of Pollen from the Fields at Pulltrouser Swamp." Pp. 105-119 ✓ in B. L. Turner II & P. D. Harrison (eds.) *supra*.

———— (n.d.) "Palynology and Vegetation Analysis, Pulltrouser Swamp, Belize." Unpublished MS written at MIT, Cambridge, MA, 1983.

PART II

THE CENTRAL MEXICAN HIGHLANDS

IRRIGATION CANALS AND CHINAMPAS:

RECENT RESEARCH IN THE NORTHERN BASIN OF MEXICO

Deborah L. Nichols and Charles D. Frederick

Settlement pattern surveys of the Basin of Mexico had as one of their objectives tracing the development of agriculture, with particular attention to hydraulic systems. After completion of the surveys, Sanders et al. (1979:222-280) wrote a comprehensive review of the region's agricultural history; however, for the pre-Late Aztec periods (before ca. A.D. 1350; see Table 1) much of their reconstruction derived from indirect data on site locations. Over the last 15 years, a series of excavations in the northern Basin have recovered archaeological remains of prehispanic hydraulic agricultural systems, including Formative period irrigation canals in the Guadalupe Range, irrigation networks at Teotihuacan and to the north dating to the Classic and Postclassic periods, and Postclassic *chinampas* (raised fields) at Xaltocan in Lake Xaltocan (Figure 1). In this essay we will revisit the agricultural history of the northern

Research in Economic Anthropology, Suppl. 7, pages 123-150.

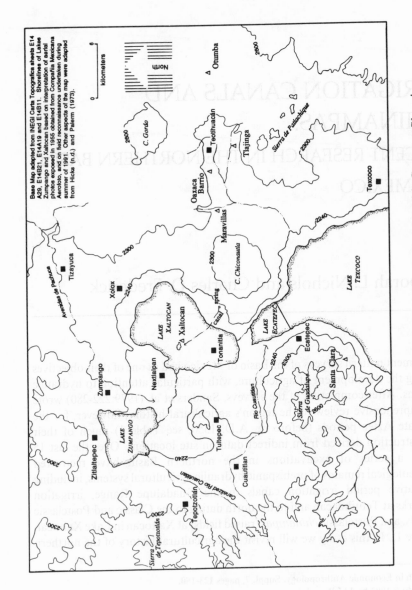

Figure 1. The Northern Basin of Mexico during the 16th Century, Showing Major Towns (Localities mentioned in text are indicated by triangles.)

Base Map adapted from INEGI Carta Topografica sheets E14 A29, E14B21, E14A19 and E14B11. Shorelines of Lakes Zumpango and Xaltocan based on interpretation of aerial photos exposed in 1955 obtained from Compañía Mexicana Aerofoto, and on field reconnaissance undertaken during summer of 1991. Other aspects of the map were adapted from Hicks (n.d.) and Palerm (1973).

Table 1.   Archaeological Period and Phase Names Used in the Text

Period	Phase	Dates	Local Phase	Dates
Postclassic		A.D. 750-1519		
	Late Aztec	A.D 1350-1519	Aztec III-IV	A.D. 1350-1519
	Early Aztec	A.D.1150-1350	Aztec I-II	A.D.1150-1350
	Late Toltec	A.D. 1000-1150	Mazapan	A.D. 1000-1150
	Early Toltec	A.D. 750-1000	Coyotlatelco	A.D. 750-1000
Classic		A.D. 200-750		
	Late Classic	A.D. 500-750	Metepec	A.D. 650-750
			Xolalpan	A.D. 400-650
	Early Classic	A.D. 200-500	Tlamimilolpa	A.D. 200-400
Formative		1400 B.C.-A.D.200		
	Terminal	150 B.C.-A.D. 200	Miccoatli	A.D. 150-200
			Tzacualli	0-A.D.150
			Patlachique	150 B.C.-0
	Late	650-150 B.C.	Cuanalan	650-150 B.C
	Middle	1050-650 B.C.	Chiconautla	900-650 B.C.
			Altica	1050-900 B.C.
	Early	1400-1050 B.C.		

Basin to synthesize these new findings and complement Jeffrey Parsons' (1991) recent discussion of hydraulic agriculture in the southern Basin. We will conclude with thoughts about future directions for research in this area.

THE FORMATIVE PERIOD (1400 B.C.-A.D. 200)

The first documented occupation of the northern Basin by people who grew maize and other cultigens took place during the Early Formative phase (1400-1150 B.C.), when a few small, scattered settlements occur in the Cuauhtitlan Valley, the Guadalupe Range, and the upper Papalotla Basin in the Texcoco region. Given the low population density, Sanders (1981:164) suggests that agriculture served as an adjunct to wild food collection in the northern Basin until the succeeding Middle Formative phase (1050-650 B.C.), when we find the earliest evidence for the use of hydraulic agriculture, at the Santa Clara site (Nichols 1982).

Located on the alluvial plain of a subvalley of the eastern Guadalupe Range and now covered by the modern town of Santa Clara Coatitlan, the Santa Clara site consists of a stratified series of floodwater irrigation canals originally exposed in the profiles of two large barrow pits dug to obtain fill for highway construction. Excavations identified a total of 25 artificial canals. All are simple earthen ditches, U-shaped in cross-section, and averaging 1m wide at the top,

50-60 cm wide at the bottom, and approximately 50-60 cm deep. The features represent two types of canals, primary (or distribution; see Doolittle 1990:14-15) and secondary. Primary canals, which had to be periodically reexcavated as they filled with sediments, took fast-moving surface runoff water from a *barranca* (a gully with a seasonal stream) into the secondary canals, which irrigated individual fields. The technology of this early irrigation system was simple and, as Doolittle (1990:24) notes, the coarse sediments that comprise the canal fill indicate that no attempt was made to regulate the water flow with reservoirs. Analysis of digitized data from infrared aerial photographs of the area identified a grid of linear features, similar in size and configuration to the excavated secondary canals, 30m north of the excavated area (Nichols 1988:18).

Based on the water-deposited pottery in the fill of the canals and the stratigraphic sequence, the most recent canals have been dated to the late Middle Formative phase (900-650 B.C.). The system might have been constructed in the preceding early Middle Formative phase (1050-900 B.C.), when permanent villages occur in the area for the first time; the presence of Terminal Formative, Tzacualli (0-A.D. 150) pottery in a stratum above the canals indicates that the excavated canals were abandoned by that time, or perhaps by the Late Formative phase. While the features seem to be restricted to the Middle Formative phase, the excavations explored only a tiny fraction of the alluvial plain in this area; thus, later irrigation features may also be present.

In addition to documenting an early date for this irrigation system, the excavations also revealed that a striking amount of deposition had taken place on the alluvial plain. Nearly 7m of soil were deposited on the alluvial plain in the Santa Clara area during the Middle Formative phase, compared with less than 1m of deposition since that time. This deposition would have had several important implications for agriculture. Soil suspended in fast-moving floodwaters would normally have flowed through the *barranca* and been deposited on the lakeshore plain and in the lake; however, when the water was diverted for irrigation, the sediments were deposited on fields. The regular addition of this material would have maintained soil fertility and, thus, permitted more frequent plantings without a drop in yields. On the other hand, a shallow soil cover on the slopes probably could not have retained enough moisture for cultivation without some kind of terracing system (Donkin 1979:26). In fact, cultivation of these slopes without erosion controls might have precipitated erosion.

Sanders et al. (1979) proposed that the early agricultural utilization of the Basin involved a highland variant of swiddening called *tlacolol*. In support of this interpretation, they pointed to the pattern of site locations in the lower and middle piedmont, where rainfall is higher and the chance of frost lower than on the alluvial plains. Based on carrying capacity estimates, they argued that populations in the most densely settled areas of the northern Basin, the Texcoco piedmont and Guadalupe Range, would have exceeded the productive limits of *tlacolol* during the Late Formative phase, necessitating a shift to more intensive systems. The Santa Clara system, however, seems to have been started before the limits of *tlacolol* were reached (Nichols 1987a:597). If the piedmont erosion around Santa Clara was caused in part by *tlacolol* cultivation, then the long-term effect of this system might have prompted the early development of irrigation on the deep-soil alluvial plain.

Nichols (1987a, 1989) has also argued that unpredictable annual variations in rainfall posed sufficient risks (cf. Cancian 1980:162-163) for rainfed farming to cause the shift to small-scale irrigation systems at relatively low levels of population density. Feinman and Nicholas (1989), however, feel that the greater drought resistance of Formative maize varieties would have reduced risks for rainfed farming and obviated the need for irrigation. The archaeo-botanical evidence indicates that the trend during the Formative period was toward *greater* use of less drought-resistant but higher-yielding maize varieties, a change that only makes sense with irrigation.

In addition to environmental conditions and agroeconomic factors such as technology, yields, and labor input, the sociopolitical milieu must also be considered to understand the development of hydraulic agriculture. Hereditary ranking was already present in the southern Basin when farming populations colonized the northern regions (Tolstoy 1989) and, by the Middle and Late Formative phases, ranked status differentiation is evident in the northern Basin at El Arbollio and Ticoman in the Guadalupe Range (Tolstoy 1989:109) and at Loma Torremote in the Cuauhtitlan Valley (Sanders et al. 1979:331).

The small size of early irrigation systems like the one at Santa Clara, which could have irrigated at most several hundred hectares, would not have necessitated a hierarchical management system (Hunt 1988), although it would have reinforced intra-community cooperative arrangements. As Netting (1990) has recently shown, no simple correlation exists between agricultural intensification, in general, and stratification. The development of irrigation in the northern Basin, however, provided new opportunities for economic manipulation by emerging elites through the creation of limited zones of high productivity (Sanders & Webster 1978), and the situation in the Basin is similar in important respects to that described by Earle (1987:295) for prehistoric Hawaii:

> Following initial colonization, population grew and spread through the islands, initially emphasizing marine resources but gradually shifting towards cultivation of the uplands. The farming of the uplands gradually resulted in the degradation of this fragile resource and the alluviation of the valley floors. Influenced by these human-induced environmental changes, chiefs promoted a rapid shift to irrigated agriculture on the new alluvial soils as a means to maximize their competitive position. The irrigated soils were but a small fraction of the agricultural soils on the island, and their development made ownership feasible.

Unpredictable crop losses from annual variations in rainfall and frost and, possibly, diminishing yields from erosion in the piedmont posed potential problems for all households, but they presented an additional difficulty for emerging elites. Elites, including big men and chiefs, require surpluses, not only to support their households but also for activities such as the feasting and exchanges of prestige items that figure so prominently in the competitive status systems of middle-range societies. Erratic surpluses undermine the ability of such elites to attract and hold followers. The development of stratification, thus, acted as an additional stimulus to intensification (Nell 1979). Irrigated land, in turn, provided more secure surpluses but, because it was more limited than rainfed land, competition for control of it could have reinforced the position of elites (Netting 1990:57). We are not arguing that irrigation alone caused stratification during the Formative period, but that the two processes were mutually reinforcing.

While early agriculturalists no doubt understood the basic principles of gravity-fed irrigation, some uncertainty always accompanies the implementation of a new land-use system, and during the Middle Formative phase this was probably offset by a diversified exploitive strategy that included rainfed cultivation, farming of *humedad* (high watertable) lands near rivers and springs in the northern Basin, and use of lacustrine resources along the lakeshore. The start of the Late Formative phase marks a shift in zonal settlement patterns in the Cuauhtitlan Valley onto the alluvial plain; however, the amount of naturally irrigated (*humedad*) land was too small (600-700 ha) by that time (Santley 1977:428) to support the regional center's population of nearly 3,000 people at San José Cuauhtitlan. Thus, it seems likely that small-scale permanent irrigation was in use in the Cuauhtitlan Valley. Sanders (1976:117-119), citing pollen and other data, argues that, in the Teotihuacan Valley, permanent irrigation and *chinampa* cultivation began at this time. These data suggest that irrigation became widely practiced during the Late Formative phase in the northern Basin (Doolittle 1990:44). Increasing reliance on small-scale irrigation at this time in the southern Basin is suggested by the expansion of settlement in the piedmont (Parsons 1991:23-25). Recent excavations confirm that irrigation was practiced at the ancient city of Teotihuacan by the succeeding phase.

THE CLASSIC PERIOD (A.D. 200-750)

In 1987 and 1989, Michael Spence excavated a large residential structure in Tlailotlacan, the Oaxaca Barrio, near the western periphery of the city of Teotihuacan, and uncovered the remains of an earlier floodwater irrigation system (Nichols et al. 1991). The features consist of nine artificial earthen-ditch channels excavated into soil or bedrock and filled with water-deposited sand, gravel, and cobbles in varying proportions. The excavations were confined to the area of the residential structure (260m^2); nonetheless, two superimposed floodwater canal networks are represented by the excavated features. The early network consists of secondary, or branch, canals (Doolittle 1990:11-13), while the late network includes both secondary and tertiary canals that channeled water onto fields. The canals average 20-40 cm wide and 20-40 cm deep. Rising ground elevation from sediments deposited by the canals apparently caused the early network of canals to be abandoned, as about 30 cm of alluvial soil separates the two sets of canals.

The canals presumably drew water from the Barranca de Cerro Colorado, which lies northwest of the Oaxaca Barrio (Figure 1) and was artificially canalized (as were other major streams) to accommodate the grid plan of Teotihuacan. The irrigation canals, however, follow the natural contours. Because of the limited scope of the excavations, we do not know if diversionary structures were employed or when the Barranca was routed to its present course. Further investigations are also required to determine the size of the Tlailotlacan system.

The residential structure built by Zapotec immigrants (Spence 1990) during the Tlamimilolpa phase (ca. A.D. 200-300) securely dates the abandonment of the irrigation system. Ceramic and stratigraphic data indicate that the system was begun during the Terminal Formative (Tzacualli) phase and that the latest canals ceased to function sometime during the Miccoatli phase (A.D. 150-200). It is not yet known how much time elapsed between the abandonment of the canals and the construction of the Zapotec compound. This system represents the first definitive evidence of irrigation at Teotihuacan; however, around the periphery of the early Classic city other, less securely dated hydraulic features indicate a pattern of intensive agricultural landuse that included most of the major floodwater sources.

The Tlailotlacan irrigation system lies at the edge of a Tzacualli settlement cluster on the western periphery of Teotihuacan (Cowgill 1974:386); during the Terminal Formative phase, when most of the Basin's population aggregated at Teotihuacan, settlement was concentrated in the northwestern section of the city. Farther to the west, Sanders (1965, 1976:117-119) found floodwater irrigation canals that extend along a group of Classic period sites near Maquixco Alto, representing the first documented inter-village irrigation network, which Sanders thinks may date to the Terminal Formative phase. To the east of Teotihuacan, Charlton (n.d. a-c) discovered a series of stratified floodwater irrigation canals on the alluvial plain on the north edge of the Aztec town of Otumba. His excavations in 1977-1978 suggested that the earliest canals were constructed during the Late or Terminal Formative phase; a light late Terminal Formative (Tzacualli phase) occupation also occurs at Otumba. Charlton's findings raise the possibility that irrigation was developed much earlier in this part of the Teotihuacan Valley than previously thought and that it was probably prompted by the growth of Teotihuacan. In 1989, Charlton (1990:202) reexcavated the area of the earliest canal at Otumba and found water-laid sand and gravel deposits containing water-rolled Late and Terminal Formative phase pottery; however, he thinks these deposits are associated with a natural drainage and are not the same as those found in his 1977 excavations.

On the eastern edge of the city of Teotihuacan, Rattray (Nichols et al. 1991:128) found features similar to the Tlailotlacan canals underneath structures that date to the Tlamimilolpa phase in the Merchants Barrio. Construction of irrigation canals might also have begun during Terminal Formative times in the Tlajinga (southern) section of the city. The Tlajinga features, located on the alluvial plain, were investigated as part of a project to assess the effectiveness of infrared aerial photography for discovering buried prehispanic irrigation canals and *chinampas* (Nichols 1987b, 1988; Sanders et al. 1982). Excavations near the Barranca de San Mateo, just below the piedmont-plain juncture, uncovered a complex series of features that included stratified artificial floodwater irrigation canals filled with sand, gravel, and cobbles. The canals range from 30 cm below the present ground surface to 2.0m where the canal beds lie in the natural *tepetate* (compacted volcanic ash) bedrock. They are 0.6-1.1m wide and 0.5-0.6m deep and include both primary and branch canals. The excavations also uncovered the original bed of the Barranca de San Mateo, which originally flowed in a southeast-northwest direction across the Tlajinga plain. Like other streams that ran through Teotihuacan, this *barranca* was canalized, and its present course runs in a north-south direction that accommodates the city's grid.

Because of the limited area exposed by the excavations, we cannot precisely sort out the relationship of the features to one another, and mixing of deposits further complicates their dating. Rising ground elevation caused by deposition from the canals and alluviation from the nearby slopes necessitated the excavation of new canals. The most recent canals (discussed below) clearly date to the early Postclassic period; the relative proportions of water-rolled pottery suggest some canals were used during the Classic period. The presence of water-rolled Tzacualli pottery raises the possibility that the earliest canals were constructed during the Terminal Formative phase (see Table 1).

Nichols now suspects that, like the Tlailotlacan system, the earliest canals on the Tlajinga plain were constructed in Terminal Formative times, possibly prior to rerouting of the Barranca de San Mateo; the Teotihuacan Mapping Project recorded a scattered Tzacualli occupation in the area (Millon et al. 1973). Angulo (1987:401) has argued that some of these early irrigation systems were incorporated into the city's drainage system, and perhaps this was the case on the Tlajinga plain. With the expansion of the city during the Classic period, the area that could have been irrigated on the alluvial plain from the Barranca de San Mateo would have included about 20 ha, just enough land to support the occupants of a single Teotihuacan apartment compound.

As Spence and Nichols (Nichols et al. 1991:126-128) have pointed out, irrigated land on the periphery of the city would have been highly valuable because of its proximity to the urban population. The fact that some of this land was taken out of production, which is clearly demonstrated in the case of the Tlailotlacan system, and how it was taken out of production have important implications. Spence and Nichols suggested that, at the start of the Tzacualli phase, local kin groups who resided in scattered household clusters controlled the Tlailotlacan irrigation system and probably other floodwater systems, as well. During the early Classic period, some of these systems were abandoned, as in the case of Tlailotlacan, and some were reduced in size, as in the case of Tlajinga. At Tlailotlacan, not only did the pattern of land use change from agricultural to residential, but the landusers also changed, from local inhabitants to foreigners from Oaxaca, and this change might have occurred within a very short span of time, possibly no more than one year. A similar change may have taken place in the Merchants Barrio that Maya immigrants occupied (Rattray 1987:26).

Since it seems unlikely that local cultivators would have readily relinquished control over valuable irrigated land, the Teotihuacan state had probably by this point become directly involved in the allocation of land and other resources (Nichols et al. 1991:127-128). The massive movement of most of the Basin's population into Teotihuacan during the Tzacualli phase (Sanders et al. 1979:107) would have necessitated some kind of coordinated land allocation system, since the majority of the city's residents were engaged in agriculture (Millon 1976:228). The reorganization of streams in and around the city (Drewitt 1967:80-88, Millon et al. 1973, Monzón 1982), which would have also affected floodwater and permanent irrigation systems, represents a deliberate, large-scale undertaking that bespeaks centralized planning and administration. It appears that, by the start of the Classic period, if not before, some control over irrigation resources in Teotihuacan's immediate hinterland had shifted from local kin groups to the state. Scarborough (1991:131-132) suggests that such state control of irrigation systems in the Basin was temporary and limited to large-scale projects with high costs that may or may not have benefited local farmers. Parsons (1991:36), on the other hand, sees this as a deliberate political strategy of "firm and immediate control over both the agricultural land and the agricultural labor that most directly affected its [Teotihuacan's] subsistence base."

At this time, we still lack direct archaeological data on permanent irrigation and *chinampa* cultivation at Teotihuacan during the Classic period. The area immediately south of the archaeological zone of Teotihuacan was converted to *chinampas* at the time of the Spanish conquest. Sanders (1976:117-118) thinks the *chinampa* cultivation began during the Late or Terminal Formative phase based on the changes in plant pollen in this area and the depiction of what appears to be a *chinampa* plot on a mural in the Classic period apartment compound of Tepantitla (Miller 1973:98, Figures 166/167). The infrared photos, however, failed to reveal traces of buried *chinampas* (Sanders et al. n.d.; Nichols 1988). The photos showed that the area between the Ciudadela and Barranca de San Lorenzo, where no mounds are visible on the surface, contains Teotihuacan apartment compounds, which could have been built over earlier *chinampas* (Sanders et al. n.d.:9). Similarly, no buried irrigation canals were identified from infrared photographs of the alluvial plain, which was irrigated from the springs at Teotihuacan in the 15th century. The failure to find such remains is perhaps due to heavy deposition on the plain and the conditions under which the photographs were taken (Nichols 1988).

Infrared photographs were also taken of the deep soil plain east of the town of Cuauhtitlan along the original course of the Río de Cuauhtitlan between Tultitlan and Ecatepec, where Teotihuacan-period sites concentrate on the plain and on the piedmont overlooking the plain. Resettlement of this area, along with other selected parts of the Basin during the Miccoatli and Tlamimilolpa phases, has been interpreted as a Teotihuacan-directed colonization program to exploit resources for the urban population (Sanders et al. 1979:116, Parsons 1991:36). The Río de Cuauhtitlan is one of the major permanent irrigation sources in the Basin. Infrared photos showed linear features resembling buried irrigation canals, and ground reconnaissance by Sanders found that the features were not superficial (Sanders et al. n.d.:10). While these features are intriguing, they need further study to establish their significance. The Teotihuacan site of Chingu, near Tula, also seems to have been associated with a permanent irrigation system, as Mastache (1976:57-68) found that one edge of the site borders precisely an irrigation canal that runs near several other Early Classic sites.

Recent research has shown that the growth of Teotihuacan stimulated significant changes in agricultural land-use throughout the Basin and adjoining areas (Parsons 1991). Investigations over the last 15 years have documented an intensive use of floodwater irrigation in Teotihuacan's immediate hinterland, which strongly suggests an equally intensive development of the larger and more secure permanent irrigation sources in the northern Basin. Teotihuacan's expansion and its hyper-nucleated settlement pattern prompted greater intensification and expansion of irrigation systems and possibly more direct state control than during periods when the population was more dispersed.

THE POSTCLASSIC PERIOD (A.D. 750-1519)

Hydraulic agriculture reached its maximum extent in the northern Basin during the Late Aztec period (A.D. 1350-1519), for which there is both documentary and archaeological data, and which has been summarized by Sanders et al. (1979) and, most recently, by Doolittle (1990). Archaeological remains of Late

Aztec floodwater canal and terrace systems are abundant in the piedmont throughout the region, and all the sources for permanent irrigation were utilized in the 15th century (Palerm 1955). Localized zones of *chinampa* cultivation also occurred around the springs at Teotihuacan, in Lake Texcoco at the base of Cerro Chimalhuacan, and in Lake Xaltocan (Sanders et al. 1979:280). The recent archaeological investigations have provided additional details on the development of some of these systems.

The breakup of Teotihuacan ca. A. D. 750, which marks the start of the Postclassic period, was associated with important developments in hydraulic agriculture. In the southern Basin, Parsons (1991:37) sees for the first time a significant shift away from piedmont agriculture, to *chinampa* cultivation. In the northern Basin, the dispersal of population led to further development of irrigation systems, although the expansion of *chinampa* cultivation in the northern Basin seems to have taken place slightly later than in the southern Basin. We will begin our review of recent findings concerning the Postclassic period in the Teotihuacan Valley and then move westward.

Teotihuacan Valley

The existence of Early Postclassic irrigation systems in the Teotihuacan Valley was established nearly 40 years ago, when Pedro Armillas discovered the remains of a floodwater system on the piedmont in the northwestern part of the Valley (Armillas et al. 1956). Millon's (1957) excavations of the Maravilla system identified a small canal, three diversionary structures (one of which might actually have been constructed in the Colonial period (see Doolittle 1990:104), and a diverted stream that he dated to the Early Postclassic, Coyotlatelco phase (A.D. 750-1000), although Millon (1957:164) suggested that the stream might have been diverted during the Late Classic period. This was not a large system, and Millon estimated that it irrigated no more than 100 ha.

A larger Postclassic floodwater irrigation system is situated on the alluvial plain at the northern edge of the Aztec town of Otumba. The complex series of features investigated by Charlton (1990:201-202) include a main canal, distribution canals, and field canals that took water from the Barranca del Muerto and the ridgetop to irrigate the middle valley alluvial plain. Following the Spanish conquest, significant stream degradation took place, and both beds of the Barranca del Muerto are now entrenched 10m below the present ground surface. Charlton's excavations indicate, however, that erosion and sedimentation were on-going in prehispanic times, as well (see Doolittle 1990:102). An estimate of the size of the area irrigated from the canals is not available from the most recent work, but Doolittle (1990:103) suggests a minimum of 200 ha.

The majority of the excavated features date to the Late Aztec and Early Colonial phases, although water-rolled Mazapan phase (A.D. 1000-1150) pottery was recovered from the main canal. The Late Aztec period expansion of the irrigation system coincides with a marked increase in population, the appearance of elites, and the development of extensive craft specialization at Otumba, the capital of the city-state (Charlton et al. 1991).

To the southwest of Otumba, portions of the alluvial plain that were residential districts of Teotihuacan during the Classic Period were brought under irrigation using runoff from the Barranca de San Mateo, described earlier (Nichols 1988). A subsurface linear feature running east-west across the Tlajinga plain appears on both black-and-white and infrared aerial photographs. Excavations of the feature showed it to be an earthen ditch floodwater irrigation canal, 1.4-1.6m wide and 0.4-0.6m deep, filled with sandy deposits and located 0.30-0.50m below the present ground surface. Water-rolled pottery from the Late Aztec, Mazapan (A.D. 1000-1150), and Patlachique (150 B. C.-0) phases occurred in the fill—indicating, in conjunction with the stratigraphic data, that the canal functioned during the Late Aztec phase, although it might have been constructed during the earlier Late Toltec (Mazapan) phase. Since the canal crosses a Teotihuacan apartment compound, the Patlachique pottery is intrusive. This canal directed water from the Barranca de San Mateo to irrigate the Tlajinga plain, and water from this *barranca* and other nearby seasonal streams probably irrigated about 400-500 ha of land on the Tlajinga plain and the adjoining piedmont. As in the case of Otumba, the Tlajinga floodwater system reached its maximum extent during Late Aztec times.

Texcoco Region

Relatively little archaeological work has been done in recent years on hydraulic systems in the Texcoco region (Figure 1). During the Late Aztec period, water from a series of springs at the juncture of the upper piedmont and the sierra east of Texcoco was diverted into canals for a major irrigation system, and aqueducts were employed, apparently for the first time, to carry water between hills (Doolittle 1990:127). Based on survey data and other indications, Sanders suspected that, in earlier periods, the water from the Texcoco springs flowed through their natural drainages and that the major area of irrigation was land along the middle course of the Río de Papalotla (Sanders et al. n.d.:7). For that reason, infrared aerial photographs were taken of the middle Papalotla drainage. The photographs revealed linear features, possibly representing buried irrigation canals, but this has yet to be confirmed.

Williams' (1989) recent ethnohistoric studies have provided a detailed picture of agricultural landuse during the 15th century for portions of the Texcoco region that involved both permanent and floodwater irrigation of the plain and terraced piedmont slopes. Her analysis of data on landholdings suggests that, even with irrigation, some rural communities in the piedmont faced serious land pressure and that in some years they might not have been able to meet their own subsistence needs—which, as Williams (1989:730) points out, raises doubts about how much surplus production these communities could have contributed to the support of urban populations in Texcoco and Tenochtitlan (cf. Brumfiel 1980).

Tula

Archaeological work at Tula, the Toltec capital located just north of the Basin of Mexico, has documented the growth of permanent irrigation systems there during the Postclassic period. Mastache's (1976) surveys indicate that, during the Late Toltec phase, when Tula was at its height, water from springs and the Río de Tula was diverted to irrigate an area possibly as large as 10,000 ha. This was not an integrated system but consisted of a series of permanent irrigation networks on the alluvial plain, which is described in greater detail by Mastache (1976) and Sanders and Santley (1983:269).

Cuauhtitlan Valley

Two major developments in hydraulic agriculture during the Postclassic period took place in the northwestern Basin, namely, rerouting the Río de Cuauhtitlan and conversion of portions of Lake Xaltocan into *chinampas*. The well-known diversion of the Río de Cuauhtitlan has been examined by a number of scholars (e.g., Rojas 1974:85-96, Strauss K. 1974:147-154, Sanders et al. 1979:276-277, Doolittle 1990:115-120, Nichols 1987a:611-612). Accordingly, it will only be summarized here, although we will discuss the Xaltocan *chinampas* in greater detail, since they have been the subject of recent investigations by Brumfiel and Frederick.

The Cuauhtitlan Valley, drained by the Ríos de Tepotzotlan and Cuauhtitlan, was the largest single drainage in the Basin of Mexico (MOS 1975, I: 54-55). During the 15th century, the nobility of Cuauhtitlan rerouted the Río de Cuauhtitlan to join the Río de Tepotzotlan, ostensibly to reduce flooding in the town (Anales de Cuauhtitlan 1945:49). This was a large-scale project that took seven years to complete and entailed construction of an irrigation network northwest of the town (Doolittle 1990:118-119).

Political as well as economic motivations underlay this project. It created one of the largest irrigation systems in the Basin, capable of watering 8,000-10,000 ha (Nichols 1980:82-85, McBride 1974:42). Not only did canalizing the river enhance the area's agricultural potential, it also facilitated control of both labor and resources by concentrating population on the alluvial plain. Cuauhtitlan became one of the largest tributary domains under Aztec control in the Basin.

The second major change in hydraulic agriculture during the Postclassic period in the northwestern Basin was the development of *chinampas* southeast of the island of Xaltocan in the bed of former Lake Xaltocan (Figure 1). This *chinampa* zone was recently investigated as part of Brumfiel's project of excavations at the Postclassic site of Xaltocan. Xaltocan was at one time an island near the western margin of the former lake bearing the same name (Figure 1); it was linked to the western shore by means of a causeway (Díaz del Castillo 1956, López de Gómara 1943, Cortés 1960, and Palerm 1973). The island of Xaltocan presently rises 5-6m above the adjacent lake bed and exhibits irregular topography. Excavations during the summer of 1991 exposed more than 5m of cultural sediment near the center of the island, leading to the conclusion that the site is a tell constructed on the basin floor. Much of the relief of the island appears to have been created during the Early Aztec phase, which may date as early as A.D. 800 at this location (Brumfiel, pers. comm., 1992).

Lake Xaltocan was the middle of three cascading lakes that occupied the northern Basin of Mexico in the prehispanic period. Two of them, Lake Zumpango and Lake Xaltocan, were natural, while the third, Lake Ecatepec or San Cristóbal, was formed by a dike that extended from Ecatepec to Chiconautla. Lake Zumpango was the northernmost and highest of the three and was connected to Lake Xaltocan by means of a canal. Excess water from this basin drained into Lake Xaltocan, which in turn drained into Lake Ecatepec and eventually into Lake Texcoco. The popular image of the floor of the Basin of Mexico as a single sheet of water below the elevation of 2240m, however, has recently been contested by Hicks (n.d.), and it conflicts also with evidence of Postclassic relict shorelines and beaches, primarily preserved on the western margin of former Lake Xaltocan. Geologic evidence from this region (Brumfiel & Frederick n.d.) and elsewhere in the Basin of Mexico (Flores Díaz 1986, Bradbury 1989) indicates that, while higher lake stages occurred during the late Pleistocene, this was probably not the case during the Postclassic and Colonial periods in the northern basin.

The lakes of the northern Basin of Mexico have been described as saline (Sanders et al. 1979:84-85), leading some scholars to assume that these areas were of no agricultural use in prehispanic times (Donkin 1979:39). Others (e.g., Gibson 1964), however, have concluded that, as long as the water was not saturated with salts, then *chinampa* agriculture would not have been precluded. Ethnohistoric references suggest that *chinampa* agriculture occurred in Lake Xaltocan (Armillas 1971:661, Tezozomoc 1975, Boehm de Lameiras 1986:290; Colín 1967, Hicks n.d.), and fossil *chinampas* and associated canals are visible on aerial photos taken in 1955 by the Compañía Aerofoto Mexicana.

The center of the zone of *chinampas* lies approximately 1.7 km southeast of the town of Xaltocan and is estimated to have covered an area of at least 100 ha and perhaps even more than 200 ha (Figure 2). Features visible on the

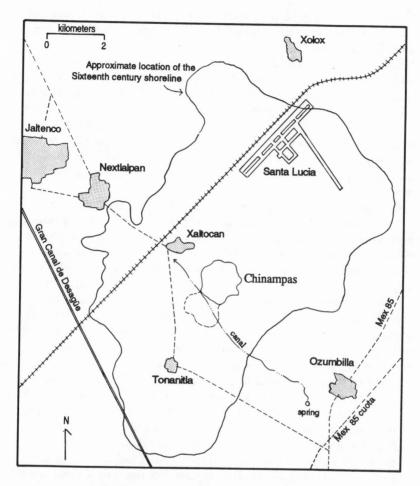

Figure 2. Location of the Xaltocan Chinampas with Respect to the Modern Landscape and the Approximate Location of the 16th-Century Shoreline

photographs include secondary and tertiary canals and several *camellones* (*chinampa* beds), but the largest feature on the photos—and the only one confirmed during a surface reconnaissance of the lake bed—was a canal extending about 5 km northwest across the basin floor from a spring at the base of Chiconautla (Ozumbilla). This feature appears to have been excavated into the lake bed, and extant vestiges are 50-100m wide and up to 1m deep, which, assuming modest enlargement and sedimentation through bank erosion and plowing, still leaves this as a significant canal. Presumably, this canal conveyed fresh water across the lake to the zone of *chinampas* and the island of Xaltocan, and may be the feature described by López de Gómara (1943: V. 2, 14) as "*acequias anchas, hondas y llenas de agua*" (wide, deep, irrigation canals filled with water).

Field inspection of the lake bed surface for the remains of the *camellones* and intermediate canals proved frustrating and largely unfruitful. Plowing of the lake bed soon after desiccation of the lake in 1945 and the subsequent dry season eolian mobilization of the basin floor sediment in the last 30 years have obliterated whatever surficial expression these features possessed in 1955 when the aerial photographs were taken. In spite of these disappointing results, the photographs were used to place two exploratory excavation trenches on the lake bed within the zone of *chinampas* to identify the physical remains of the fields.

Although minor differences were apparent, both trenches exhibited four general stratigraphic units: (1) lacustrine deposits; (2) a raised field surface, or chinampa bed; (3) a canal fill; and (4) a mantle of eolian sediment, presumably deposited after desiccation of the lake (see Figure 3). Prior to construction of the *chinampas*, the basin floor was underlain by multiple layers of very strongly calcareous, gray to light gray lacustrine sediment that ranged in texture from loam to clay loam. These deposits possessed a coarse prismatic structure that probably formed after desiccation of the lake and exhibited evidence of secondary salt deposits in the form of rhizoliths of tequesquite and fine crystals within pores. Up to four distinct zones of lacustrine sediment were recorded (Zones 6-9 in Trench 1; Zones 4 and 5 in Trench 2); the upper zone appeared to have been weakly modified by pedogenesis. This paleosol was less than 15 cm thick and was a gray to light gray silt loam to silty clay loam with subangular blocky structure. It was observed only in Trench 1. The apparent increase in organic matter indicative of a soil suggests that this surface probably experienced brief periods of subaerial exposure prior to construction of the *chinampas*.

The *chinampas* were excavated into the paleosol and underlying lacustrine sediment, and consisted of three distinct parts. The raised field planting surface possessed a fine-grained, dark-colored upper unit (Zone 3, Trench 1) that contained two distinct types of material mixed together and a lower, lighter colored zone (Zone 5, Trench 1) of loam to sandy loam that appeared to have accumulated some secondary salts. The upper layer (Zone 3 of Trench 1) was a clay loam to silty clay loam with blocky and subangular blocky structure and an irregular mixture of two sediments, one of which was gray and the other, light gray. An abrupt, irregular boundary separated the upper from the lower unit, and the undulatory boundary was consistent with that which might be caused by working with a *coa* or other form of digging stick. The light gray deposit upon which Zone 3 rested possessed weak prismatic to massive structure and included obvious secondary salt. The salt accumulation is probably associated with cultivation and may have contributed to abandonment of the features.

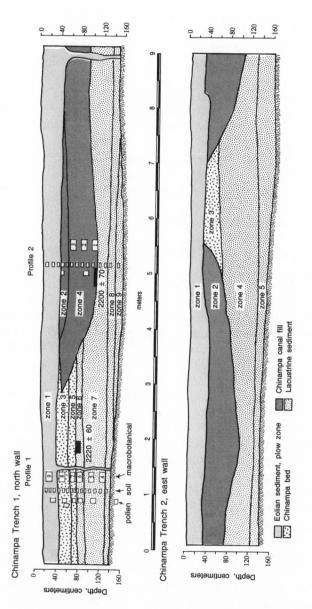

Figure 3. Profiles of the Two Trench Excavations from the Zone of Chinampas, Bed of Former Lake Xaltocan (Excavated and described by Charles Frederick and Jaime de la Cruz. Pollen samples are rank ordered from the bottom up in Profile 1 and from the top down in Profile 2. Soil samples are rank ordered from the top down. Macrobotanical samples are labelled as shown.)

139

The canals that once existed between the raised beds have filled in with sediment (Zone 4, Trench 1) to form semi-lenticular cross-sectional bodies of sediment that are inset into the *chinampa* bed and the underlying lacustrine strata. The deposits consisted of a massive silt loam and silty clay loam that ranged in color from light brownish-gray to light gray and grayish-brown. Like the lower parts of the *chinampa* bed, portions of the canal deposits exhibited obvious secondary salt accumulations, including subhorizontally-oriented, fragile, blade-like crystals (less than 2 cm wide and 5 cm long) possibly forming along visually imperceptible bedding planes. Molluscs such as snails and bivalves were also present within this deposit. Draping both the canal fill and the raised bed deposits was a dark gray to gray deposit of loam and silt loam that was inferred to be eolian sediment emplaced subsequent to desiccation of the lake (Zone 1 in both trenches). This deposit also filled cracks associated with large (up to 10m diameter) polygonal desiccation features, common on the unplowed portions of the basin floor, that cut across all the previously described deposits.

Analysis of the samples collected during 1991 is in progress, but some preliminary conclusions may be drawn. Perhaps most significant is the apparent age of the *chinampas*. Three lines of evidence are available to estimate the age and useful period of these fields: absolute age dating, ceramics collected from the excavation and surface within the zone of *chinampas*, and ethnohistorical documents.

Two radiocarbon ages were obtained from the *chinampas*, one was taken from the base of the canal fill and the other, from the top of the weak A horizon (a paleosol) formed in lacustrine sediments that were buried by the construction of the raised bed planting surface. Due to a lack of other materials suitable for dating, both ages were obtained from total organic matter of bulk sediment samples. The sample from the buried soil yielded a calibrated age between 388 and 196 B.C. (Tx-7395; ∂13C corrected age of 2220 ± 60 B.P.; ∂13C = −21.8) and was obtained from a depth of 60-70 cm. The second sample yielded a calibrated age between 383 and 177 B.C. (Tx-7394; ∂13C corrected age of 2200 ± 70; ∂13C = −20.4) and was taken from a depth of 90-100 cm near the base of the canal fill. Both these dates are considerably older than the associated ceramics (Table 2) and may reflect a hard water effect. Regardless of the validity of the ages, their similarity indicates either that (1) the canals began to fill relatively soon after construction or (2) the sediment that was deposited in the canals included organic matter recycled from the basin floor, with the addition of relatively little new organic matter.

Perhaps the best evidence for estimating the period of *chinampa* construction is provided by the ceramics found during excavation of the trenches and collected from the lake bed in the vicinity of the excavation (Table 2). In the small sample recovered from the excavation spoil dirt, the majority of diagnostic sherds were Early Aztec (Aztec I or II), but a glazed ware and an

Table 2. Ceramics Recovered from the Xaltocan Chinampas and Vicinity

Type	Surface Collection	Excavation
Aztec I	7	0
Aztec II (Black-on-Orange)	16	1
Huastec Tradeware	2	1
Glazed Ware	1	1
Red Ware Unidentified	1	0
Black-on-Red	4	0
Black-and-White-on-Red	9	2
Early Aztec Figurines	2	2
Early Aztec Comals	0	1
Chalco-Cholula Polychrome	1	0
Xochimilco Polychrome	1	0
Fabric Marked	2	0
Brown Incised	1	0
Texcoco Molded/Filleted	1	0
Misc. and Nondiagnostic sherds	22	3
Total Collected	70	11

Aztec III or IV black-and-white-on-red were also present. A nonrandomly selected sample of ceramics collected from the surface in the vicinity of the excavation also included a majority of Early Aztec (Aztec I and II) types. Although none of the material was recovered from primary context, the predominance of Early Aztec sherds in both collections arguably supports an Early Aztec construction age. This is coeval with the period of greatest construction on the island of Xaltocan, which occurred during the Early Aztec phase—specifically, Aztec I—that is associated with radiocarbon ages between A.D. 770 and 880 (Elizabeth Brumfiel, pers. comm., 1992).

Chinampa cultivation appears to have continued into the Colonial period, as indicated in documents reviewed by Palerm (1973) and Hicks (n.d.). Palerm describes a series of letters and instructions from Velasco el Viejo that refer to the flooding of A.D. 1553 and mention a protest by the community of Xaltocan regarding the high water levels caused by flooding (presumably, by the Río de Cuauhtitlan). In this protest, the community expressed concern that the rising waters might destroy their *chinampas*, as happened in the southern Lakes Xochimilco and Chalco (Carillo & Alvarez 1637). Further reference to *chinampa* farming in this portion of the Basin, cited by Hicks (n.d.:7; AGN Tierras 1584/1: f. 9v-13v), notes that Xaltocan and three other settlements (Tonanitlan, Nextlalpan, and Atenanco) cultivated *chinampas* in 1599. The latest reference to the *chinampas* at Xaltocan is dated 1636 and simply mentions their location (Colín 1967:590).

The preliminary results suggest that *chinampa* agriculture was not limited to the southern Basin of Mexico during the prehispanic period. Construction of the *chinampas* likely began in Early Aztec times, and *chinampa* cultivation continued into the Colonial period, perhaps as late as the middle 17th century. The system consisted of a large, broad primary canal that conveyed fresh water from a spring at the base of Chiconautla near Ozumbilla across the lake towards the island of Xaltocan. This canal was excavated into the lake bed and was probably intended to float the less dense fresh water upon the presumably more brackish lake water. This canal passed through the zone of *chinampas*, where fresh water was diverted into the fields and dispersed through secondary and tertiary canals to the *chinampas*. Specific figures on the cultivated area are difficult to compile, due to post-abandonment burial and disturbance, but conservative estimates based on air photo interpretation indicate that at least 100 ha and possibly more than 200 ha of *chinampas* existed at one time.

Although few vestiges of the system are visible upon the surface of the lake bed today, stratigraphic examination of two *camellones* demonstrates that *chinampa* width approached 1.5 m, suggesting wavelengths on the order of 3m, whereas the amplitudes (distance from field top to ditch bottom) varied between 70 and 80 cm. On the basis of this information, the lake depth in this area is estimated to have been less than 30 cm at the time of construction. If we assume that the small sample represented provides an accurate estimate of water depth, it suggests that inter-annual stage fluctuations were relatively small or controlled in some other manner. Presently, it is unclear if the prehispanic dike between Ecatepec and Chiconautla played a role in maintaining the level of Lake Xaltocan for *chinampa* agriculture. (See Palerm [1973] and Boehm de Lameiras [1986:257, 295] for a discussion of this feature.) The body of water created by this dike, often referred to as the Laguna de Ecatepec or San Cristóbal appears to have been physically separate from Lake Xaltocan at lower stages but connected by means of a sinuous canal. The structure reportedly served as a flood-control device during the Colonial period, but it may previously have served various functions.

The results of this study are insufficient to firmly establish the extent of the cultivated area and the precise date of construction of the *chinampas*. The morphology of the raised fields is similar to the "fossil" *chinampas* reported by Avila (1991) and those graphically depicted by Parsons et al. (n.d.: Photos 38-41), both of which are buried by larger, more recent, presumably post-conquest *chinampas*. The morphological similarity to prehispanic features and dissimilarity to the later *chinampas* in the southern Basin of Mexico further reinforces a prehistoric construction age for the Xaltocan *chinampas*. However, a larger sample is necessary to compile meaningful data on wavelength and the amplitude and length of the *chinampas*. In addition, stratigraphically controlled excavation of some of the features would provide better context for artifacts associated with *chinampa* cultivation. Closer, preferably subsurface, examination of the canal from the spring at Ozumbilla could provide clues to the exact dimensions and gradient, from which discharge estimates could be calculated.

These preliminary findings provide the first look at *chinampa* agriculture in the northern Basin of Mexico and provide a starting point for understanding the agricultural development and use of the basin floor. The complexity of this system would have required considerable centralized control of the lake bed and surrounding territory, most notably the lands east of the lake shore plain near Ozumbilla. If the radiocarbon analyses obtained by Brumfiel for the site of Xaltocan are correct, then the "Early Aztec" *chinampas* associated with the settlement of Xaltocan may not be much later than the Early Postclassic *chinampas* in the southern Basin (Parsons et al. 1985), suggesting a significant shift in land-use patterns beginning in the 9th century A.D.

According to Parsons (1992:34), *chinampa* development during the Postclassic period in the southern Basin took place in two phases. The first involved community-based systems constructed in piecemeal fashion by corporate peasant groups organized into *calpulli*, who cultivated the *chinampas* and provided labor and tribute to the ruler of their city-state in return for access to land. The second phase entailed large-scale development of *chinampas* during the Late Aztec period, which Parsons (1991:34) argues involved "direct state intervention," to create a predictable food supply in close proximity to Tenochtitlan. In this stage, Parsons suggests that the actual work of *chinampa* construction, maintenance, and cultivation was performed by dependent *mayeque* tenants. Brumfiel (1991) argues that little sociopolitical distinction existed between the estate-based *mayeque* cultivators and the *macehualtin* under the domain of local lords. The importance of the agricultural estates lay instead in the opportunity they provided for reorienting elite allegiances to consolidate the Aztec macro-state's power.

At this stage, we do not know the details of the organization of the Xaltocan *chinampa* system. While not as large as the Late Aztec chinampa system of the southern Basin, construction of the Xaltocan *chinampas* represented a significant undertaking, possibly greater than the piecemeal development of Early Aztec *chinampas* in the southern Basin. If the preliminary dating of the *chinampas* is correct, then the growth of this raised field system coincides with the development of Xaltocan as an important Early Aztec city-state capital.

From what is now known about the Late Postclassic period, increasing population, urbanization, and political considerations all played a role in the expansion of irrigation and *chinampa* systems. Given the limitations of the transportation system (Sanders & Santley 1983, Hassig 1985), elites promoted intensive and large-scale hydraulic agricultural systems in close proximity to urban centers as a way of securing urban food supplies and tribute and of consolidating their control over both regional elites and commoners. Commoners, in turn, received access to highly productive and relatively low-risk agricultural lands, which were in increasingly short supply (Williams 1989).

FUTURE DIRECTIONS

The research of the last 15 years that we have reviewed, in addition to providing important new details about prehispanic hydraulic agriculture in the Basin of Mexico, signals directions for future work, especially in three areas: environmental reconstruction, dating, and organization. Looking at this region today, with its ever-expanding urban population, it is difficult to envision how it appeared to prehispanic cultivators in the Formative, Classic, and Postclassic periods. Each excavation of prehispanic hydraulic features in the northern Basin has found indications of changes in hydrology and geomorphology—deposition in the Guadalupe Range, stream degradation at Otumba, and lake levels in the western Basin—significant for past agricultural utilization. We need to better understand, not just initial environmental conditions but how agricultural and other practices changed the landscape over both the short and long terms.

Dating the history of hydraulic agricultural systems in the Basin continues to be a problem. Brumfiel's recent work at Xaltocan suggests that the initial date for the Early Aztec phase, when *chinampa* construction probably began, may be earlier than indicated by the conventional chronology; however, this must still be confirmed. In terms of floodwater irrigation, all the recently discovered prehispanic irrigation networks have been floodwater systems, and we now have a reasonably good framework of the long history of this type of hydraulic agriculture in the northern Basin. Remains of floodwater systems have been *relatively* easier to locate than permanent irrigation features because many of the floodwater systems went out of use after the Spanish conquest and because the features themselves are recognizable when exposed on the alluvial plains: the sand, gravel, and cobble fill of the canals sharply contrasts with the soil matrix. As archaeologists become more familiar with what these remains look like, we suspect that more will be found; the discovery of buried irrigation canals in the Oaxaca Barrio at Teotihuacan should alert archaeologists to the possibility of other irrigation networks on the periphery of the ancient city. The history of permanent irrigation in the northern Basin remains elusive, and we can think of no easy solution. The possible canals visible on infrared photographs provide a starting point; if they are canals, then our experience suggests that large-scale excavations may be necessary to date them.

The foregoing raises another point about dating hydraulic agricultural remains. Even when irrigation canals, *chinampas*, and other hydraulic features have been found and excavated, their dating can still be ambiguous. The sample of datable materials may be small, and the materials are usually redeposited, so attention to site-formation processes is important for understanding both the chronology and the functioning of the agricultural system. Large-scale excavations would provide not only a larger sample of datable material but also a better basis on which to reconstruct the scale and organization of the system.

For archaeologists, the organization of hydraulic agriculture in the Basin remains an important theoretical issue. The recent investigations indicate that, beginning in the Formative period, agricultural intensification, population growth, stratification, and urbanization were interrelated processes. By the Classic period, the Teotihuacan state had become involved in manipulating hydraulic sources. The findings at Tlailotlacan provide some support for the view that Teotihuacan directly intervened in the allocation of economic resources. How this intervention was organized and whether it was short- or long-term is unclear at this point, although further work at Teotihuacan seems promising. The growth of the Late Postclassic city-states of Otumba, Cuauhtitlan, and Xaltocan in the northern Basin was in each case associated with the expansion of hydraulic agricultural systems directly adjacent to their urban cores.

Discussions of hydraulic agriculture have usually focused on managerial issues. As Parsons (1991:41) observes, however, the limitations of prehispanic political power in the Basin, even under the Aztec empire, favored population nucleation, which in turn stimulated agricultural intensification and the growth of hydraulic agriculture close to urban cores. Future research at sites such as Xaltocan needs to move beyond these broad correlations and undertake fine-grained studies of the organization of the *chinampa* and irrigation systems that became the agricultural foundations of Postclassic cities and states in the Basin of Mexico.

ACKNOWLEDGMENTS

The work at Xaltocan, under the direction of Elizabeth Brumfiel, was supported by a grant from the National Science Foundation to Albion College, and permission to conduct the excavations was granted by the Consejo de Arqueología, Instituto Nacional de Antropología e Historia. We thank Elizabeth M. Brumfiel for the opportunity to participate in the project and for identifying the ceramics listed on Table 2. Jaime de la Cruz coordinated the logistics of the field excavation and assisted with describing and sampling of the *chinampa* profiles. Deborah Hodges shared her editorial expertise with us. CDF greatly benefitted from numerous discussions with Karl W. Butzer, William E. Doolittle, and Greg Knapp. DLN extends her appreciation to Thomas H. Charlton, William T. Sanders, and Michael W. Spence.

REFERENCES

AGN Tierras (1584/1) Año de 1711. Testimonio de los autos de reducción que los naturales de los pueblos sujetos se hizo al de Xaltocan su cabezera, jur[on] de Sumpango de la Laguna, el año de 1599. (Testimony from the Reduction Order Made by the Natives of Xaltocan, Sworn at Zumpango in 1599.) Archivo General de la Nación (Mexico, DF), Ramo de Tierras Vol. 1584, No. 1.

Anales de Cuauhtitlan (1945) In *Códice Chimalpopoca*. (Primo Fleciano Velázquez, trans.). Mexico, DF: Universidad Nacional Autónoma de México.

Angulo, Jorge (1987) "El Sistema Otli-Apantli dentro del area urbana" ("The Otli-Apantli System within the Urban Area"). Pp. 399-416 in Emily McClung de Tapia & Evelyn C. Rattray (eds.) *Teotihuacán: Nuevos datos, nuevas síntesis, nuevos problemas (Teotihuacan: New Data, New Syntheses, New Problems)*. Mexico, DF: Universidad Nacional Autónoma de México, Instituto de Investigaciones Antropológicas, Arqueologíca Serie Antropológica 72.

Armillas, Pedro (1971) "Gardens on Swamps." *Science* 174:653-661.

Armillas, Pedro, Angel Palerm, and Eric R. Wolf (1956) "A Small Irrigation System in the Valley of Teotihuacán." *American Antiquity* 21:396-399.

Avila López, Raúl (1991) *Chinampas de Iztapalapa, D.F. (The Chinampas of Iztapalapa, Federal District)*. Mexico, DF: Instituto Nacional de Antropología e Historia.

Boehm de Lameiras, Brigitte (1986) *Formación del estado en el Mexico prehispánico (The Formation of the State in Prehispanic Mexico)*. Zamorra: Colegio de Michoacán.

Bradbury, J. P. (1989) "Late Quaternary Lacustrine Paleoenvironments in the Cuenca de México." *Quaternary Science Reviews* 8:75-100.

Brumfiel, Elizabeth M. (1980) "Specialization, Market Exchange, and the Aztec State: A View from Huexotla." *Current Anthropology* 21:459-478.

_____ (1991) "Agricultural Development and Class Stratification in the Southern Valley of Mexico." Pp. 43-62 in H. R. Harvey (ed.) *Land and Politics in the Valley of Mexico: A Two-Thousand Year Perspective*. Albuquerque: University of New Mexico Press.

Brumfiel, E. M., and C. D. Frederick (n.d.) "Xaltocan: Centro regional de la Cuenca de México" ("Xaltocan: A Regional Center in the Basin of Mexico"). *Consejo de Arquelogía, Boletín* (Bulletin of the Board of Archaeology), in press.

Cabrero, Teresa, G. (1980) *Entre chinampas y bosques: Arquelogía de Topilejo, D.F. (Between Chinampas and Forests: The Archaeology of Topilejo, D.F.)*. Mexico, DF: Universidad Nacional Autónoma de México, Instituto de Investigaciones Antropológicas, Arqueologíca Serie Antropológica 33.

Cancian, Frank (1980) "Risk and Uncertainty in Agricultural Decision Making." Pp. 161-176 in Peggy Bartlett (ed.) *Agricultural Decision Making*. New York: Academic Press.

Charlton, Thomas H. (1990) "Operation 12, Field 20, Irrigation System Excavations." Pp. 210-212 in Thomas H. Charlton & Deborah L. Nichols (eds.) *Preliminary Report on Recent Research in the Otumba City-State*. Iowa City: University of Iowa, Department of Anthropology, Mesoamerican Research Report 3.

_____ (n.d.a) Report on a Prehispanic Canal System, Otumba, Edo de Mexico Archaeological Investigations, August 10-19, 1977. Report submitted to the Instituto Nacional de Antropología e Historia. (MS, Department of Anthropology, University of Iowa.)

_____ (n.d.b) Investigaciones arqueolaogicas en el Municipio de Otumba, temporada de 1978. 1a Parte: Resultos preliminares de los trabajos de campo (Archaeological Investigations in the Town of Otumba, 1978, Part 1, Fieldwork). Report submitted to Instituto Nacional de Antropología e Historia. (MS, Department of Anthropology, University of Iowa.)

_____ (n.d.c) Investigaciones arqueológicas en el Municipio de Otumba, temporada de 1978. 5a Parte: el riego y el intercambio: la expansión de Tula (Archaeological Investigations in the Town of Otumba, 1978, Part 5a: Irrigation and Trade: The Expansion of Tula.) Report submitted to Instituto Nacional de Antropología e Historia. (MS, Department of Anthropology, University of Iowa.)

Charlton, Thomas H., Deborah L. Nichols, and Cynthia Otis Charlton (1991) "Aztec Craft Production and Specialization: Archaeological Evidence from the City-State of Otumba, Mexico." *World Archaeology* 23:98-114.

Charlton, Thomas H., and Deborah L. Nichols (1990) *Preliminary Report on Recent Research in the Otumba City-State*. Iowa City: University of Iowa, Department of Anthropology, Mesoamerican Research Report 3.

Cortés, Hernán (1960) *Cartas de Relación (Letters from Mexico)*. Mexico DF: Editorial Porrúa.

Cowgill, George (1974) "Quantitative Studies of Urbanization at Teotihuacán." Pp. 363-396 in Norman Hammond (ed.) *Mesoamerican Archaeology: New Approaches*. Austin: University of Texas Press.

Colín, Marío (1967) "Indicie de documentos relativos a los pueblos del estado de Mexico, Ramo de Mercedes" ("Catalogue of Documents on the Towns in the State of Mexico"). Pp.X, *Biblioteca Enciclopédica del Estado de Mexico, Vol. 1*.

Díaz del Castillo, Bernal (1956) *The Discovery and Conquest of Mexico*. (A. P. Maudslay, trans. & ed.) New York: Noonday Press.

Donkin, R. A. (1979) *Agricultural Terracing in the Aboriginal New World*. Tucson: University of Arizona Press.

Doolittle, William E. (1990) *Canal Irrigation in Prehistoric Mexico: The Sequence of Technological Change*. Austin: University of Texas Press.

Drewitt, Bruce (1967) "Planeación el la antigua ciudad de Teotihuacán" ("Plan of the Ancient City of Teotihuacan"). *Mesa Redonda* I:79-94. Mexico, DF: Sociedad Mexicana de Antropología.

Earle, Timothy K. (1987) "Chiefdoms in Archaeological and Ethnohistorical Perspective." *Annual Review of Anthropology* 16:279-308.

Feinman, Gary, and Linda Nicholas (1989) "The Role of Risk in Formative Period Agriculture: A Reconsideration." *American Anthropologist* 91:198-203.

Flores Díaz, Antonio (1986) "Fluctuaciones del Lago de Chalco desde hace 35 mil años al presente" ("Fluctuations in Lake Chalco from 35 Thousand Years Ago to the Present"). Pp. 109-156 in José Luis Lorenzo & Lorena Mirambell (eds.) *Tlapacoya: 35,000 Años de Historia del Lago de Chalco (Tlapacoya: 35,000 Years of History from Lake Chalco)*. Mexico, DF: Instituto Nacional de Antropología e Historia.

Gibson, Charles (1964) *The Aztecs Under Spanish Rule*. Stanford, CA: Stanford University Press.

Hassig, Ross (1985) *Trade, Tribute, and Transportation: The Sixteenth-Century Political Economy of the Valley of Mexico*. Norman: University of Oklahoma Press.

Hicks, Frederick (n.d.) "Xaltocan under Mexica Domination, 1435-1520." MS in the possession of the author.

Hunt, Robert C. (1988) "Size and Structure of Authority in Canal Irrigation Systems." *Journal of Anthropological Research* 44:335-355.

López de Gómara, Francisco (1943) *Historia de la Conquista de México. (History of the Conquest of Mexico)*, 2 vols. Mexico, DF: Editorial Robredo.

Mastache de Escobar, Alba Guadalupe (1976) "Sistemas de riego en el área de Tula, Hgo" ("Irrigation Systems around Tula, Hidalgo"). Pp. 49-70 in Eduardo Matos Moctezuma (ed.) *Proyecto Tula, Segunda Parte (The Tula Project, Part Two)*. Mexico, DF: Instituto Nacional de Antropología e Historia, Colección Científica No.33.

McBride, Harold W. (1974) *Formative Ceramics and Prehistoric Settlement Patterns in the Cuauhtitlan Region, Mexico*. Ph.D. diss., University of California at Los Angeles.

Miller, Arthur G. (1973) *The Mural Painting of Teotihuacan*. Washington, DC: Dumbarton Oaks.

Millon, René (1957) "Irrigation in the Valley of Teotihuacán." *American Antiquity* 23:160-166.

————— (1973) *The Teotihuacán Map, Part 1, Text*. Austin: University of Texas Press.

————— (1976) "Social Relations in Ancient Teotihuacán." Pp. 205-248 in Eric R. Wolf (ed.) *The Valley of Mexico*. Albuquerque: University of New Mexico Press.

————— (1981) "Teotihuacán: City, State, and Civilization." Pp. 198-243 in Jeremy Sabloff (ed.) *Supplement to the Handbook of Middle American Indians, Vol. 1, Archaeology*. Austin: University of Texas Press.

Millon, René, Bruce Drewitt, and George Cowgill (1973) *Urbanization at Teotihuacán, Mexico: The Teotihuacán Map.* Austin: University of Texas Press.

Monzón, Martha (1982) "El desague principal de la Calzada de los Muertos" ("The Principal Drainage of the Street of the Dead"). Pp. 101-111 in Rubén Cabrera, Ignacio Rodríguez, and Noel Morelos (eds.) *Teotihuacán 80-82: Primeros resultados (Teotihuacan: 80-82: First Results).* Mexico, DF: Instituto Nacional de Antropología e Historia.

MOS [*Memoria de las Obras del Sistema de Drenaje Profundo del Distrito Federal] (Report on the Works of the Final Drainage System of the Federal District),* I. (1975) Mexico, DF: Departmento del Distrito Federal.

Nell, Edward J. (1979) "Population Pressure and Methods of Cultivation: A Critique of Classless Theory." Pp. 497-468 in Stanley Diamond (ed.) *Toward a Marxist Anthropology: Problems and Perspectives.* The Hague: Mouton.

Netting, Robert McC (1990) "Population, Permanent Agriculture, and Polities: Unpacking the Evolutionary Portmanteau." Pp. 21-61 in Steadman Upham (ed.) *The Evolution of Political Systems: Sociopolitics in Small-Scale Sedentary Societies.* Cambridge, ENG: Cambridge University Press.

Nichols, Deborah L. (1980) *Prehispanic Settlement and Land Use in the Northwestern Basin of Mexico, the Cuautitlan Region.* Ph.D. diss., Pennsylvania State University.

_____ (1982) "A Middle Formative Irrigation System near Santa Clara Coatitlan in the Basin of Mexico." *American Antiquity* 47:133-144.

_____ (1987a) "Risk, Uncertainty, and Prehispanic Agricultural Intensification in the Northern Basin of Mexico." *American Anthropologist* 89:596-616.

_____ (1987b) "Prehispanic Irrigation Agriculture at Teotihuacan: New Evidence, the Tlajinga Canals." Pp. 133-160 in Emily McClung de Tapia & Evelyn C. Rattray (eds.) *Teotihuacán: Nuevos datos, nuevas síntesis, nuevos problemas (Teotihuacan: New Data, New Syntheses, New Problems).* Mexico, DF: Universidad Nacional Autónoma de México, Instituto de Investigaciones Antropológicas, Arqueologíca Serie Antropológica 72.

_____ (1988) "Infrared Aerial Photography and Prehispanic Irrigation at Teotihuacan: The Tlajinga Canals." *Journal of Field Archaeology* 15:17-27.

_____ (1989) "Reply to Feinman and Nicholas: There is No Frost in the Basin of Mexico." *American Anthropologist* 91:1023-1026.

Nichols, Deborah L., Michael W. Spence, and Mark D. Borland (1991) "Watering the Fields of Teotihuacan: Early Irrigation at the Ancient City." *Ancient Mesoamerica* 2:119-129.

Palerm, Angel (1955) "The Agricultural Basis of Urban Civilization in Mesoamerica." Pp. 28-42 in Julian H. Steward (ed.) *Irrigation and Civilization: A Comparative Study.* Washington, DC: Pan American Union, Social Science Monographs No. 1.

_____ (1973) *Obras hidráulicas prehispánicas en el sistema lacustre del Valle de México (Prehispanic Hydraulic Works in the Lake System of the Valley of Mexico).* Mexico, DF: Instituto Nacional de Antropología e Historia.

Parsons, Jeffrey R. (1991) "Political Implications of Prehispanic Chinampa Agriculture in the Valley of Mexico" Pp. 17-42 In H. R. Harvey (ed.) *Land and Politics in the Valley of Mexico: A Two-Thousand Year Perspective.* Albuquerque: University of New Mexico Press.

Parsons, J. R., M. H. Parsons, V. Popper, and M. Taft (n.d.) *La agricultura chinampera del periodo prehispánico tardío en el Lago Chalco-Xochimilco, México (Chinampa Agriculture during the Late Postclassic Period in Lake Chalco-Xochimilco).* Mexico, DF: Report submitted to the Instituto Nacional de Antropología e Historia, 1982.

Parsons, J. R., M. H. Parsons, V. Popper, and M. Taft (1985) "Chinampa Agriculture and Aztec Urbanization in the Valley of Mexico." Pp. 109-156 in Ian Farrington (ed.) *Prehistoric Intensive Agriculture in the Tropics.* Oxford: British Archaeological Report Series, No. 232.

Rattray, Evelyn C. (1987) "Los barrios forános de Teotihuacán" ("The Barrios of Foreigners in Teotihuacan"). Pp. 243-274 in Emily McClung de Tapia & Evelyn C. Rattray (eds.) *Teotihuacán: Nuevos datos, nuevas síntesis, nuevos problemas* (*Teotihuacan: New Data, New Syntheses, New Problems*). Mexico, DF: Universidad Nacional Autónoma de México, Instituto de Investigaciones Antropológicas, Arqueologíca Serie Antropológica 72.

Rojas Rabiela, Teresa (1974) "Aspectos tecnológicos de las obras hidráulics coloniales" ("The Technology of Colonial Hydraulic Works"). Pp. 19-133 in Teresa Rojas Rabiela, Rafael A. Strauss K., and José Lameiras (eds.) *Nuevas noticas sobre las obras hidráulicas pehispánicas y coloniales en el Valle de México* (*New Information on Prehispanic and Colonial Hydraulic Works in the Valley of Mexico*). Mexico, DF: Instituto Nacional de Antropología e Historia.

Sanders, William T. (1965) *Cultural Ecology of the Teotihuacán Valley*. University Park: Pennsylvania State University, Department of Sociology & Anthropology.

———— (1976) "The Agricultural History of the Basin of Mexico." Pp. 161-178 in Eric R. Wolf (ed.) *The Valley of Mexico*. Albuquerque: University of New Mexico Press.

———— (1981) "Ecological Adaptations in the Basin of Mexico: 23,00 B.C. to the Present." Pp.147-197 in Jeremy A. Sabloff (ed.) *Supplement to the Handbook of Middle American Indians, Vol. 1, Archaeology*. Austin: University of Texas Press.

Sanders, William T., Deborah L. Nichols, Rebecca Storey, and Randolf Widmer (n.d.) *A Reconstruction of a Classic Period Landscape in the Teotihuacán Valley*. Washington, DC: Final Report to the National Science Foundation, 1982.

Sanders, William T., Jeffrey R. Parsons, and Michael H. Logan (1976) "The Valley as an Ecological System: Summary and Conclusions." Pp. 161-178 in Eric R. Wolf (ed.) *The Valley of Mexico*. Albuquerque: University of New Mexico Press.

Sanders, William T., Jeffrey R. Parsons, and Robert S. Santley (1979) *The Basin of Mexico: Ecological Processes in the Evolution of a Civilization*. New York: Academic Press.

Sanders, William T., and Robert S. Santley (1983) "A Tale of Three Cities: Energetics and Urbanization in Pre-Hispanic Central Mexico." Pp. 243-291 in Evon Z. Vogt & Richard M. Levanthal (eds.) *Prehispanic Settlement Patterns: Essays in Honor of Gordon R. Willey*. Albuquerque & Cambridge, MA: University of New Mexico Press and Peabody Museum of Archaeology and Ethnology.

Sanders, William T., and David Webster (1978) "Unilinealism, Multilinealism, and the Evolution of Complex Societies." Pp. 249-302 in C. L. Redman, M. J. Berman, E. V, Curtin, W. T. Langhorne, N. M. Versaggi, & J. C. Warser (eds.) *Social Archaeology: Beyond Subsistence and Dating*. New York: Academic Press.

Santley, Robert S. (1977) *Intra-site Settlement Patterns in the Cuauhtitlan Region, State of Mexico*. Ph.D. diss., Pennsylvania State University.

Scarborough, Vernon L. (1991) "Water Management Adaptations in Non-Industrial Complex Societies: An Archaeological Perspective." Pp 101-154 in Michael B. Schiffer (ed.) *Archaeological Method and Theory, Vol. 3*. Tucson: University of Arizona Press.

Spence, Michael (1990) "Excavaciones en Tlailotlacan, Teotihuacán: Segunda Temporada" ("Excavations in Tlailotlacan, Teotihuacan: The Second Field Season"). *Consejo de Arquelogía, Boletín* 1989:128-130.

Strauss, K., Rafael A. (1974) "El area septentrional del Valle de México: Problemas agro-hidráulicas prehispánicas y coloniales en el Valle de México" ("The Northern Valley of Mexico: Prehispanic and Colonial Agro-hydraulic Problems in the Valley of Mexico"). Pp. 137-174 in Teresa Rojas Rabiela, Rafael A. Strauss K. & José Lameiras (eds.) *Nuevas noticas sobre las obras hidráulicas prehispánicas y coloniales en el Valle de México* (*New Information on Prehispanic and Colonial Hydraulic Works in the Valley of Mexico*). Mexico, DF: Instituto Nacional de Antropología e Historia.

150   DEBORAH L. NICHOLS and CHARLES D. FREDERICK

Tezozómoc, Hernando Alvarado (1975) *Crónica Mexicana* (*Mexican Chronicle*). Mexico, DF: Editorial Porrúa.

Tolstoy, Paul (1989) "Coapexco and Tlatilco: Sites with Olmec Materials in the Basin of Mexico." Pp. 85-121 in Robert J. Sharer & David C. Grove (eds.) *Regional Perspectives on the Olmec.* Cambridge, ENG: Cambridge University Press.

Williams, Barbara J. (1989) "Contact Period Rural Overpopulation in the Basin of Mexico: Carrying-Capacity Models Tested with Documentary Data." *American Antiquity* 54:715-732.

WATER CONTROL AND COMMUNAL LABOR DURING THE FORMATIVE AND CLASSIC PERIODS IN CENTRAL MEXICO (ca. 1000 B.C.-A.D. 650)

Jorge Angulo V.

(with illustrations by Chappie Angulo)

INTRODUCTION

Cultural anthropology is applied in archaeological research to understand forms of social organization reflected in the economic, political, and religious stage of development reached by the extinct culture under study. Although the search for past cultures is closely related to single evidences found in material remains, archaeological research relies on the assistance of other exact sciences to reconstruct the paleoecological ambiance, as well as on its own methods to classify technological advances. A solid aspect of archaeological research has been developed through the basic information given by physical

Research in Economic Anthropology, Suppl. 7, pages 151-220.
Copyright © 1993 by JAI Press Inc.
All rights of reproduction in any form reserved.
ISBN: 1-55938-646-0

and chemical analysis correlated to biological data and complemented by the study of natural resources utilized in a particular period of time by the settlements of the social group.

Evolutionary Stages in the Old and New Worlds

Through the lithic and ceramic typological seriations found in stratigraphic excavations, the archaeologist correlates the ranks of technological knowledge with the stage of cultural development. These methods have been borrowed from studies of the Old World, especially of Egypt, Mesopotamia, and the European Neolithic. Using these models as a base, Mesoamerican cultures have been classified, from their early beginning (2000 B.C.) to the time of their encounter with the Spanish conquerors (A.D. 1521), in an equivalent stage of development as the one reached by Neolithic European cultures in Lewis Henry Morgan's scheme of Savagery, Barbarism, and Civilization.

Some European scholars accept the concept that, only after the fall of the Classic (Theocratic) period or in the time of the Toltecs and beginning of the Postclassic era (A.D. 1000), did Mesoamerican cultures became "civilized," as the first works of metallurgy appear in excavations. In accordance with the model of development for the Old World, only when the copper stage began and metallurgy was mastered could groups be called "civilized," because only then would they configurate as organized sociopolitical states. A different approach was developed from the middle of the present century, as earlier works had demostrated that the models used by European archaeologists relied mainly on technological stages, the use of the wheel, and animal domestication—and did not fit the processes of economic organization, sociopolitical transformation, or religious achievements in the development of New World "High Cultures," such as the Mesoamerican and Andean cultures, as noted by Julian H. Steward (1948).

Perishable Infrastructural Works as Clues to Development

Since the time of the Hispanic conquest, Mesoamerican cultures have been known from descriptions by astonished friars and soldiers about the wonders of a city floating on a lake with wooden drawbridges to connect the sidewalks. Other Europeans were impressed by the few gold ornaments rescued from the melting pot before being transformed into ingots, as well as the garments and implements used by the Indians that were taken as trophies or souvenirs to show the "peculiarities" of the strange people subjugated by the sword and the Christian cross.

At present, archaeological classifications deal mainly with lithic and ceramic materials, whereas the arts and crafts manufactured from organic materials such as wood, basketry, and textiles have received only occasional mention.

Ethnohistoric references can explain some of the amazing engineering works made of wood on diverse types of structures or infrastructural works that characterized many of the cities destroyed by the Hispanic conquerors. Due to its easy degradation, ancient organic material has not been systematically classified in ethnographic collections and has rarely been found in archaeological excavations, but it is evident that these materials are important items in the so-called primitive economy.

During the early part of the 1960s, MacNeish (1967-72) found burials with ropes, sandals, basketry, and other items made of agave fibers as well as cotton textiles that belonged to the semi-sedentary groups of the Coxcatlán and El Riego phases (6500-3500 B.C.). Recent excavations by Serra Puche (1988) unearthed an Early Formative community on the shores of the Chalco-Xochimilco lakes, where a fishing village was found that manufactured basketry, ropes, and mats to complement their economy by trading them with other local and regional communities. This sort of new investigation amplifies the view of previously established statements, by assuming that the environment is related not only to the rate of technology applied but also to the form that the social organization assumed in such an environment.

METHODOLOGY

Archaeolgical Methods and Techniques

Archaeology has its own systems and techniques for recording human activities and social behavior to understand extinct cultures. Much has been said about the premise that archaeological research strives for a hypothetical reconstruction of the natural environment and its possible transformation through human presence in all its sequential settlements. The reconstruction of paleoecology includes the analysis of raw materials in an orderly stratigraphic sequence as evidence of natural and cultural changes detected by the eye of the specialist. This is why professionals in natural sciences, such as geologists, petrologists, mineralogists, pedologists, and experts in climatology, are required to understand the geomorphology of settlement. The study has to be complemented by paleobiological analysis of the flora and fauna to permit a hypothetical vision of the paleoecological ambience that characterized each of the cultural periods.

With this information as background, the archaeologist works with lithic and ceramic typologies, relating them to natural sources of raw materials in order to understand other aspects of their economy. Only then is it possible to apply different models of socioeconomic organization along with observations on political and religious behavior. Also, as in any other scientific discipline, archaeological research uses methods of analysis and observation to compare results to similar cases before drawing generalizations that can be established as rules or models.

We have to admit that there is very little information about the kind of social organization that made possible this sort of labor during the early stages of its development, although historical and ethnographic reference can be found, for the time of the Spanish conquest, to the practice of communal labor among indigenous communities that has survived until today in small towns. At any rate, according to lithic typology, only a few and insignificant changes in the shape of tools, implements, and labor technology have been detected from the Formative to Postclassic times and even after the Spanish conquest, when metal tools were introduced.

Cultural Anthropology Models

In anthropological sciences, one unconsciously has a global view of the economy of a town, city, or nation by looking at the architecture as well as other constructions, infrastructural works, communication systems, and endless types of material development used to satisfy social and psychological needs. Considering archaeology as one of the anthropological sciences, one assumes that the same kind of observations on material remains would be valid to understand the economy of extinct societies.

In order to achieve any understanding of the social history of ancient cultures, the archaeologist turns to sister disciplines in the social sciences, such as ethnology, ethnohistory, cultural anthropology, and even contemporary history. Among the materials of these disciplines, the archaeologist finds models described by chroniclers from the past who observed some "peculiar behaviors" during colonial times, by wanderers who related customs of cultural groups from different parts of the world in the last two centuries, and by anthropologists who recorded varied ways to resolve similar problems, according to the stage of development achieved by the group. These models could be used as alternatives to explain aspects of the culture of those who built the monumental works found in archaeological zones or ancient remains where other explanation has not been found.

This amounts to saying that these behaviors observed in ethnographic groups resemble the same stage of development that extinct groups from the past supposedly had. Comparisons could be utilized as models to understand aspects of archaeological cultures, even if separated in geographical space or living centuries apart, as long as they were in the same homotaxial stage of development. Therefore, analogies could be understood as forms suggesting that social groups have found equivalent solutions to resolve similar problems in different parts of the world, such as using caves as natural refuges, shaping stones into cutting tools, manufacturing organic material to protect their bodies, learning the medical properties of plants, discovering systems for growing crops, inventing irrigation, creating monumental constructions, sculpturing monolithic stones, modeling ceramics, weaving textiles, etc.

In the same way that analogies are applied to organic and inorganic material from ancient cultures, socioeconomic forms of organization from other cultures could be used as models dealing with production, distribution, division of labor, and ways of exchange inside as well as outside the group. These forms could include class stratification and gender differentiation, clan kinship, and the rest of the human aspects that constitute the formation of towns, trading centers, and urban areas. Consciously or unconsciously, these models have frequently been borrowed and compared with those found in ethnic groups that partially inherited the traditions from their ancestors, even when they were mixed, associated with, or controlled by the predominant culture that imposed new techniques and different cultural traits.

The information applied to this study has been compiled from ethnohistorical and anthropological reports, complemented by interviews with engineers, architects, and specialists in rural constructions who use both heavy machinery and human labor for digging, transporting, rearranging, and constructing roads, dams, and other infrastructural works that support modern field production and habitational settlement expansion. It has been amazing to see how many similarities still exist between present-day rural human labor and that recorded by the chroniclers during Colonial times. Some implements, tools, and techniques have barely changed over the last 500 years.

One important change that has occurred, though, is the introduction of metallurgy that substitutes an industrial iron point for the fire-hardened wooden point of the digging stick (*coa*). A significant change is the replacement of a type of *coa* by the pick and shovel. Technical innovations from the posthispanic past have cropped up in some places during the second half of the 20th century; for instance, wheelbarrows are now used instead of the traditional *chiquihuite*, or back-basket with shoulder straps, which was utilized in prehispanic cultures from their early beginning to carry dirt, stones, and other materials. There is no doubt that these ancient tools, implements, and techniques—utilized to extract dirt from the fields and to shape the structural core of pyramids, dams, and roads as well as to open water courses (*apantli*) and make different types of constructions—have been used from Formative times onward, through the Spanish invasion, the Colonial period, and even to the present.

A Combined Methodology

The present study involves two methodological approaches. One follows the rules of the natural sciences associated with archaeology to recover the paleoecological landscape in its natural ambience; the other, based on the social sciences, deals with the human presence that transformed the environment through simple technology, social organization, and other activities registered by cultural anthropological comparisons. The second approach, based on Steward's (1955) old model, establishes a strict interrelation among four elements (with some variants) that play an important role in the ongoing evolution or involution of all cultural groups at any particular historical moment. As explained below, the four elements are strongly interlocked and affect each other constantly in accordance with the variations to which each one is subjected: (1) Environment, (2) Demography, (3) Applied Technology, and (4) Social Organization.

1. *Environment* This element includes any ecological ambience in nature where human settlements have been found, from rich soils with water currents and abundant natural resources, to dry deserts with poor soils and scarce biological resources. There are all types of environments where cultures have flourished, containing rich fields provided with drinking water, good soils, and mild climate, that occasionally have been the cradle of many agricultural civilizations with monumental constructions known in world archaeology, such as the Nile basin with the Egyptian culture, the flooded land between the Tigris and Euphrates rivers where the Mesopotamian cultures flourished, and along the banks of the Yang-Tze and Yellow rivers, as well as the basins dispersed over the Yangshao region and the rivers that flow through the provinces of Henan, Shanxi, and Shandong, considered the cradle of Chinese civilization. In contrast, there are the environments composed of low-rated ecological features, wherein Andean and Mesoamerican cultures are held to be the main high cultures of the Americas, while the Orinoco and Amazon river basins in South America and the Mississippi basin in North America are considered areas of cultural development that did not achieve the standard of high cultures.

2. *Demography* It has been established that, when dealing with the economy of nomads and simple food gatherers, the quality of the habitat allows the presence of a certain number of people, requiring a minimum effort to collect foodstuffs freely obtained from the natural environment. This is only possible when the group maintains demographic stability. One example of this situation are the Yanomami groups living in the rain forest of one of the inflowing rivers that joins the Amazon—until the 1960s, when "civilization" began to destroy them.

Studies of these Yanomami groups show that, only in cases when the group multiples by natural reproduction or foreign in-migration, do alternative solutions have to be found: (a) The group separates into small sectors and settles in new areas within the same environment or expands the area of their settlement before it depletes the stock of natural resources; (b) the group changes its traditional methods of food gathering towards expending less effort to increase production, either by adopting more effective implements or exploiting areas not previously occupied; or (c) the group improves its methods and techniques of farming towards greater efficiency to take advantage of new natural resources.

3. *Applied Technology*   Perhaps this component of the model requires no explanation, due to the great abundance of examples of technological achievement in the transformation of ecological niches as well as of social groups. Examples can be found from the early prehistoric groups onward, of cultural transformation in which there have been periods or moments of rapid change. But from the beginning of the steamboats that bridged the continents of the world, the pace of change quickened and the long distances that had required months by sailboats were shortened by the speed of the 19th century. In no way was that change comparable, though, to the revolution caused by the discovery of electric energy, which created an authentic wave of inventions in different fields, such as the telegraph, telephone, radio, television, and FAX communication. The second part of this century has brought a wild stream of inventions and technical innovations that deserve the alternative names of New Age, Plastic Era, Atomic/Nuclear Age and (the beginning of) the Space Age in which we now live.

4. *Social Organization*   As stated earlier, the four components of the premise under discussion are closely interrelated, and there is no special hierarchy as between technological knowledge and social organization, for instance. There are some examples where technology has changed socioeconomic systems, while other examples show that new social organization can introduce technological changes.

One example goes back to the time when the Mesoamerican cultures from Remojadas, Veracruz, decorated the eyes and mouths of their clay figurines with *chapopote*, tar or raw petroleum, with the sole purpose of emphasizing their features and attributes or of marking the special filiations of these representations. The use of this type of black resin indicates that this group was familiar with this raw material even before the Christian era began. There are also references from Andrés de Tapia (writing in 1540), one of the Spanish conquerors, who said that "this black resin can be cooked and used for caulking or as glue," a concept probably learned by observing indigenous applications of the resin to organic and inorganic materials. Alfaro de Santa Cruz (writing in 1579), who subsequently colonized the same area "consideraba las 'chapopoteras' como tierras malditas y estériles." He explained by saying those "chapopoteras" were "un penoso estorbo para quienes las tenían en sus terrenos.... pues representaban una amenaza para el ganado." ("These raw petroleum sites were considered as damned sterile lands and a painful annoyance for those who have them in their property, because they represented a danger for the cattle.")

Although petroleum was used after the middle of the 19th century to light oil lamps, the industrialization of this raw material took place in Mexico a few years before the 20th century began, when foreign companies started experimenting to obtain a cheaper fuel for motor vehicles and, in less than two decades, the Standard Oil Co. invented a system to drill deep wells and refine the crude oil (Sánchez Flores 1980:334-336). It is amazing how this black resin, whose main use was for decoration nearly 2,000 years ago or a bothersome nuisance and peril for cattle during the Spanish colonial period, became the main fuel of the present era to move industry and power vehicles. After the second half of this century, petroleum became the basic source for plastics and the immense number of new products used in modern industry.

An inverse example of transformation of the environment through technology and social organization can be found in the desert lands of Palestine between the eastern shores of the Mediterranean and the Dead Sea. It is well-known that, for centuries, these sandy lands did not produce much agriculture. During the present century, however, another human group with a different mentality was settled in this same desert zone, where they began to use a different communal labor system and other techniques to control and utilize the scarce water supply to irrigate the desert. They also applied programs of reforestation and began to experiment in a new system to regenerate the sterile lands by creating artificial ponds filled with carp which reproduced abundantly. After a time, the fish changed the physical and chemical quality of the land, at one and the same time providing food and transforming the sterile land into fertile croplands. This is an example of how a sociopolitical system can transform a hostile environment into a garden by using the appropriate technology.

It is necessary to clarify that this binomial approach combining technology and social organization is only valid when dealing with an established demography. The socioeconomic situation related to political durability depends on production and distribution of goods and staples available in a particular area of its environment, and is directly related to the size of the existing population in a given historic moment. Otherwise, the balance of this relationship is placed in danger, as when a demographic increase requires more food or demographic decrease results in labor scarcity, if technology remains constant.

With the foregoing approach of combining two scientific methods, the archaeologist is able to make hypothetic reconstructions of life-styles of ancient cultures. The first approach, based on natural and exact sciences (geology, physicochemistry, and biology) aims at a broad view of the original environment in which the cultures were settled. The second approach applies models of ethnographic traits and solutions found in ethnic groups in a similar stage of development to archaeological remains that denote labor systems, building techniques, and the use of similar materials. Only in this way is it possible to hazard a hypothetical reconstruction of socioeconomic systems, with some probable inference about the political and religious organization.

Summary

The Tehuacán Archaeological-Botanical Project, directed by Richard MacNeish between 1960 and 1964, used both approaches, as can be seen in the several resulting volumes (1967-72) containing a detailed description of the process of change experienced by small tribal groups, starting from the beginning of their wanderings through hills and valleys during their search for food obtained through hunting and gathering. His explicit study shows the transformation sequence followed by the groups, who slowly replaced hunting with the collection of legumes. When this process was intensified, their temporary encampments became prolonged in time and the space was enlarged.

Similar investigations using both approaches, applied to all chronological periods, have been carried out in other Mesoamerican areas. One was directed by Kent Flannery (1976, 1985) in the Valley of Oaxaca, while in the Puebla-Tlaxcalan Valley the Fundación Alemana was exploring the macroarea (García Cook 1974, 1985). We have, as well, the intensive and extensive research of William Sanders et al. (1979) in the Basin of Mexico.

In all these studies, the authors agree that these early aggregates of semi-sedentary people always moved around permanent water sources. In the same way, the sedentary agricultural groups known as Preclásico Inferior or Early Formative are generally found near water sources such as rivers, lakes, *amanalli* (ponds), and springs. Examples of this observation are: Zacatenco and Ticomán, explored by Vaillant (1930, 1931); Tlatilco, studied by Piña Chan (1958) and Tolstoy (see Tolstoy & Guénette 1963); Zohapilco, by C. Niederberger (1976); and Terremoto-Tlatenco, by Serra Puche (1988), in the Basin of Mexico.

Archaeological research has revealed the existence of these early groups settled in dispersed or semi-concentrated villages without a predetermined plan, although in the following stage (Middle Formative) plazas are inserted among the main structures as congregation centers for civic or ceremonial activities, indicating the beginning of an incipient sociopolitical entity. Examples of these urban plans are found in San Lorenzo (Coe & Diehl 1980), La Venta (González L. 1989), and Chalcatzingo (Grove et al. 1987).

Since the 1930s, Gordon Childe (1946, 1950, 1951, 1956), Julian Steward (1936, 1938, 1948, 1953, 1955), Karl Wittfogel (1955, 1981), and other scholars have conducted studies on the evolution of urban societies that lack historic documentation. They focused their analysis on diverse systems of agricultural production found in the areas of so-called "High Culture." In the 1940s, this new approach to archaeology stimulated a favorable interest among Americanists such as Eric Wolf, Angel Palerm, and Pedro Armillas, followed by Pedro Carrasco, Teresa Rojas, and others who became interested in systems of Mesoamerican agricultural production correlated to the socioeconomic development and technical knowledge of the group under study.

THE CONCEPT OF CIVILIZATION
AND THE ROLE OF AGRICULTURE

The concept "civilized" automatically grouped together the Christian nations of Western culture whose advanced technical knowledge was directed toward the transformation of raw material from underdeveloped countries into fountains of energy that could be used in the creation of material benefits. The assurance of their power caused the destruction of the marginal groups with whom they had a socioeconomic treaty. Under this concept, the study of the development of marginal areas has been traditionally measured and classified by the appearance of similar achievements whose track seems to coincide with that experienced by the evolutionary route of Western culture.

A few investigators at the beginning of the 20th century classified these groups along still another parameter related to the evolutionist concept of "scientific and technological advancement" established in the 19th century. This premise was applied to a concept of lineal evolution, considered equivalent to "progress," that classified marginal groups as "primitive," ignorant, heretical, and backward, arguing that they lacked the technical advances found in "civilized" groups.

In contrast, many scholars have considered valid the term "civilization" where the natural environment was modified through human effort using different ingenious methods to expand cultivated fields, assuring agricultural production and distribution among large, organized groups found in Mesoamerica and the Andean region. The horizontal extension in the settlements and an increment in the height of monumental structures can be seen as by-products.

From its early beginning, agricultural production has been intimately related, first, to the foundation and development of concentrated villages and, later, to the establishment of urban and ceremonial centers. But once any given group achieved these attributes and entered the ranks of hydraulic societies, it could be considered a "civilized culture," as has been mentioned in the socioeconomic studies of historic materialism (Wittfogel 1981:203-207).

Under the anthropological focus that has flourished during the second half of this century, a new orientation began to spread slowly but steadily, possibly as a consequence of the intercommunication that developed after WWII. In this new conceptualization, diverse branches of anthropological investigation have contributed to a change in the established view of "lineal and progressive evolution" used for more than four centuries in the Western world. The new criteria as well as the "parallel achievement of development" were accepted in studies of different ethnic groups throughout the world in diverse stages of chronological development and geographical situations. Although these groups had no connection to one another, all attained the same technological achievements and a similar stage of social development, while they shared the same philosophic attitude of respect for the environment in which they lived.

In this way, economic production is related to an established social, political, and religious organization sharing its philosophical concept of total integration of human beings to their environment, making them part of a cosmic creation in which natural forces control all elements in nature. This is probably the basic reason why agricultural production and the other creative manifestations, such as architecture, urbanism, sculpture, painting, and other arts, did not transform, alter, or destroy the natural ambience where these groups created their cultural settlements. This mythical-philosophical concept probably made them aware that any abuse of their natural ambience was equivalent to an attempt against the existence of their own people and the generations to come, as modern Western cultures are beginning to realize.

During the Early and Middle Formative periods, Mesoamerican groups needed to increase their population by either "fusion" or "fission" (through group association or genetic reproduction), as Elman R. Service (1975/1984:82-84) implies, in order to control their environment and subsistence. In this historic moment, the purpose was to establish systems that would increase the utility of the occupied territories without altering natural resources or basic conditions by intensive or extensive cultivation methods. This same attitude has been observed in other cultures in distinct parts of the world in similar stages of cultural development.

Different authors have discussed distinct agriculture systems utilized by cultural groups in diverse periods of their socioeconomic development that applied intensive or extensive technology to all types of habitat. Examples of both systems, as found among the Mesoamerican and Andean cultures, are discussed below.

WATER CONTROL AS THE INTENSIVE SYSTEM

There has been disagreement for years about whether the origin and antiquity of the many hydraulic engineering manifestations shown on New World maps and documents of the 16th and 17th centuries correspond to the knowledge and organization of the European culture after the conquest of the American territories, or whether they were the result of traditional indigenous technology that continued in use even after the invaders became the new landowners. One group of scholars attribute the origin of the ideas and labor organization to the European conquerors and the physical work to the conquered, while others argue that prehispanic cultures based their socioeconomic development on diverse forms of intensive land cultivation that yielded two or three crops yearly while maintaining, at the same time, an internal balance between population and environment.

The aim of the present study is to clarify through archaeological explorations, plus ethnohistoric and ethnographic investigations, the locations and intensity of the systems of hydraulic cultivation that could be considered original to precolumbian cultures, as well as to clarify the chronological period in which the socioeconomic development and labor organization of those groups allowed that type of works. Fortunately, recent discussions of prehispanic agricultural systems have aroused sincere interest not only among anthropologists (archaeologists, cultural anthropologists, and ethnologists) but also among scholars in sister disciplines, such as ethnohistorians, historians, sociologists, economists, geologists, ecologists, biologists, agronomers, and others. All of these specialists have focused their studies from the standpoint of their own disciplines in a search—which hopefully will not remain simply a "curious" note of historic knowledge, but will serve for a possible reutilization of rejected and abandoned systems of the past—for ways to increase food production for the people and nations with less possibility of industrializing their agriculture.

Based on some observations by Rojas R. (1990:483-495), Denevan (1980:619-652), and other anthropologists, intensive cultivation can be described as any of the farming systems that produce more than two crops a year, especially when they are conditioned by an environment of prolonged humidity or supplied by some irrigation system. Within these conditions, the intensive method will be recorded as follows:

1. *Terraces* These constructions are built in slope areas delimited by *metepantles* (rows of maguey plants) or by retaining walls. Denevan (1980) notes that terraces are composed of diverse materials and construction techniques to modify the hillsides, reducing erosion and prolonging the humidity of accumulated land on a platform sustained by retaining walls. In accordance with the slope inclination, one can find long and large platforms or terraces of different widths, always preserving the humidity and slowing down run-off from the top of the hill to be drained from the upper terraces to the lower ones.

There has been disagreement for years about whether the remains of terraces found on hills near small towns of prehispanic origin correspond to an innovation introduced by the Spanish conquerors after they learned this technology in the Peruvian mountains or whether terracing was an authentic Mesoamerican practice during Postclassic times. R. A. Donkin (1979:17) finds that terraces in "the highlands of central and southern Mexico [Tehuacán Valley, Valley of Oaxaca, Mixteca Alta] and [in] the central Andes...commenced in the pre-classic period." The present essay makes clear that the system of terraces corresponds to a Mesoamerican technology from the Middle Formative. Special reference to the Late Postclassic was extracted by Rojas (1985:189) from 16th-century chronicles saying that "Todos los montes y barrancas están señalados de camellones...como escalones guarnecidos de piedra." ("All the mountains and ravines are covered with ridges...like steps protected by stones.") Quoting Burgoa (PNE,IV:141), she adds that "hay pueblos asentados en sierras y llanos hechos a mano" ("there are towns located in hills and plains made by hand").

Other terraces have been studied by Robert West (1970) under the name of "semi-terraces," or *metepantli* (deformed as *metepancle* in Spanish pronunciation). These terraces are not formed by stone walls but by rows of maguey plants whose strong roots extend over the soil, consolidating the piece of land (see Figure 1). The linguistic term is composed by the word *metl*, which refers to maguey (agave), and *pantli*, which signifies rows or a succession of something or aligned materials. There is another Nahuatl term, *tepemexcalli*, applied to the same type of structure. According to Rémi Siméon (1977:495), it is composed of the words *tepetl* = *cerro*, or hill, and *mexcal-metl*, in reference to a type of maguey (agave)

cuyas hojas son buenas para comer y se utiliza soazando las pencas centrales de la planta sobre el fuego, para atraer los jugos dulces que popularmente se conocen como mexcal.

(whose leaves are good to eat when the center leaves are lightly roasted to bring up the sweet juices popularly known as mexcal. [Not to be confused with the distilled liquor, mezcal.])

Apparently, this system fulfilled the double purpose of supplying this type of agave for food and consolidating and delimiting the cultivated areas in each terrace.

Many authors have described this system, presenting variations on the raw material used to build ridges with diverse construction techniques in Precolumbian cultures in the American hemisphere. They all agree, however, that the terrace system corresponds to the basic idea of utilizing the pronounced inclined scarpments, piedmont, and long slopes to halt or reduce natural erosion provoked by the removal of trees, bushes, and weeds that held the earth with their roots. It would have been a simple task to build the terraces with a row of maguey plants, an alignment of tree trunks, or a row of inclined stones forming a *talud* (wall) glued with mud. The main objective of this system would have been to retain the eroded material within a level plane, although in the beginning the dirt that filled the terrace might have been brought from other areas.

The horizontal plane created by terraces had a deep cultivatable soil in which humidity was preserved for a longer period and, in the structural succession of terraces, the lower ones utilized the drained water and dirt that came down from the upper levels. Denevan (1980:629-652) mentions several techniques for building terraces and more than four ways to detour and preserve water for agricultural use in Late Formative terraces (600 B.C.). Any doubt about whether the system started earlier than Postclassic times will be dispelled when the Middle Formative is discussed below.

Figure 1.   Transplanting Maguey (Agave) to Terrace Borders
(*Códice Florentino,* Vol. II, Libro 11, folio 200 r)

2. *Drained Fields*   These are found in swampy areas where farmers drag the mud from the bottom of inundated fields to deposit it along a long ridge protected by posts on both sides. The upper part of the ridge, kept constantly humid by capillarity from the water table below, allows two or three crops a year.

3. *Permanent Irrigation*   This entails the canalization of streams, brooks, and rivers to secure their natural course or to change it to protect dwelling settlements, as well as to detour them to distant localities for irrigating other areas. The system has been found in flat and large fields in valleys or basins with a mild slope where rivers can run through. The naturally irrigated land along the sides of the river was increased by artificial detours or the excavation of new branches of the same river, as well as by a series of new channels (*apantli*) to distribute small volumes of water to humidify areas untouched by the natural watercourse.

4. *Apantli, or Irrigation Channels* (*Acequias*)   *Apantli* is made up of two Nahuatl words: *atl* = water and *pantli* = duct or canal. There is much controversy on the origin and antiquity of this system of irrigation with channels. The *apantli* are formed by a network of canals in a hierarchal system according to their width and length. The larger canal distributes its waters to a system of smaller ones that move into an even narrower division to irrigate the cultivated parcels of diverse sizes. This network of canals must have been connected to a permanent or semi-permanent water supply—such as a spring, river, or natural or artificial lake or pond formed by small dams or boxes constructed specifically to retain water—to maintain a constant service (see Figure 2).

These large and permanent water resevoirs not only provided water for irrigation through the canals (*apantli*), but also supplied the population with fish, *ahuautli* (fish eggs), and larvaes and insects, as well as providing them with *tule* (reeds) to weave mats and baskets. Pictorial representations of this system can be found at the bottom of the mural paintings of Tepantitla, Teotihuacan (Angulo 1964, 1992).

Other works of infrastructure—such as terraces, dikes, dams, and similar types of simple hydraulic engineering works—were surely associated with this system of water storage and control. Recent excavations near archaeological sites have shown that the origin of this kind of construction can be dated as far back as Middle Formative (850-150 B.C.), according to MacNeish (in Denevan 1980:629), although it was more amply used during the Classic period (A.D. 150-750), as will be seen below.

5. *Transient Dams*   These dams were used to check the water course on seasonal creeks or semi-permanent brooks by piling stones in transversal form to the current or building shields of interwoven twigs supported by vertical posts set into the ground (see Figure 3). All the organic material hauled by the first rains was gathered on the retaining shield, covering more and more

tierra que se puede regar .

Figure 2. Opening Irrigation Canals (*Apantli*) with a
Coa (*Códice Florentino,* Vol. II, Libro 11, folio 228 r)

the tiny interstices between stones or twigs, although there was always a small seepage of water.

6. *Chultuns* These cysts are usually underground natural formations in karstic subsoils that are artificially conditioned or entail completely excavated tunnels ending in a spherical depository to store drinking water. Although they are frequently found in the Mayan area, as their name reveals—*chul* = concave space, and *tun* = stone—it is possible that the tronco-conic configurations found in Tlatilco and other Preclassic sites around the Basin of Mexico were likewise originally destined to store water but, after cracking, were used as granaries, cysts, or garbage deposits.

Figure 3. Transient Dam near Coatlán, Morelos

7. *Pocitos* This Spanish word means "small wells." They are usually dug in fields with a low water table to irrigate the land with hand-held vessels (*riego a mano*, in Spanish). The antiquity of this recourse is not known, although it was clearly used during the Postclassic in the area of Oaxaca, as Denevan (1980:638, citing A. Kirkby) states.

8. *Ameyalli, or Springs (Ojos de Agua)* It is difficult to say anything new about these recognized sources of life, except that, in almost every *ameyalli* found in the Mesoamerican area, there are evidences of structural remains that denote the construction of an altar, a temple, or a sanctuary related to the water and fertility deities that sprang up there. Archaeological materials related to *ameyalli* have been found at the top of mountains, in caves, on slopes, and in valleys that correspond to every chronological stage of Mesoamerican cultural development.

9. *Amanalli (Ponds or Small Lakes)* *Amanalli* are large natural ponds that retain water in shallow depressions. They are also called *aguadas* in Spanish, or *jaguey*, if we use the Tahino term learned by the Spaniards during their occupation of the Caribbean islands three decades before the conquest of Tenochtitlan. These open-air deposits differ in form, size, and depth, according to land irregularities, and they vary between 30m and 100m in diameter. It is possible that these ponds were used, as mentioned before, in the so-called *riego a mano* with a gourd (*xícara*) or a clay vessel to collect the water.

Remains of demolished structures and of preparatory works have been found around these natural ponds, indicating that, although the natural form for water deposits was respected, human labor placed a religious or civic structure there. M. Coe (1966:22) reports finding in San Lorenzo "artificial lakes or water deposits in which the majority do not have a clearly defined shape, although some of them are almost a perfect hexagon."

10. *Bajiales, or Humedales* These terms refer to the humid riverbanks, especially after the water overflows during the rainy season. The agricultural system utilizes the natural humidity of the riverbanks and lakeshores when the water level recedes once the rainy season is over. There is no way to know the antiquity of this system, for the lack of archaeological evidence, but there is an abundance of ethnohistoric and ethnographic references describing this practice.

This system has a variation called *tlaaquilia*, in which holes were bored to reach the water table to pull the water out in buckets or by the use a long wooden dipper called *t'aparatarácua* in P'urhepecha (Rojas 1985:205). This is also similar to the *campos de pocitos* (fields of small wells) that Kirkby (in Denevan 1980:638) describes as small wells close to ancient canals in Oaxaca. That author says that they have been used for watering the crops with vessels since 400 B.C. and observes that the same technique is still in use.

Another form of cultivation with the *bajiales* system has been practiced in some areas with rocky shores, where boxes filled with earth, in a similar way to the terraces, are constructed to retain the humidity after the flooded water recedes. A similar procedure is explained by Denevan (1980:633), in which rows of stones (like terraces) are used to retard the drainage water in long slopes but, because the original declination is not further modified, are not considered as terraces. These are similar to the ones "observed in various sites of the South West of the United States like those of Point of Pines...Mesa Verde, Río Grande Norte, Zuñi and Chaco Canyon" (op. cit.).

Similar examples are found on the shores covered with water during the rainy season, as Armillas (1949:83-113) reports at both shores in the Middle Balsas, especially in a section between Guerrero and Michoacán, where he found in *Suma de Visitas* and the *Relación de 1579* (PNE I:256, VI:135, I:34) a reference saying that

> en sus riberas siembran maíz, algodón, pepitas y melones, y ésto en los arenales que quedan sin agua cuando baja el río...[y] tienen algunas huertas de cacao que, con el agua que sacan de el [río] las riegan;... y así mismo...sacan agua para regar algunas sementeras.

> (on the shore they grow corn, cotton, seeds and melons and this in the sandbars that remain dry when the water recedes...[and] they have some cacao groves irrigated with the water they take from [the river] itself...and in the same fashion...they take water to irrigate some seedbeds.)

Further on he states (in free translation) that they had two crops yearly of maize, beans, *ají* (chile) and squash because, since it is *tierra caliente* (hot land), they planted all these seeds by the shores of the rivers and, with the humidity of the water, everything grew. Armillas (op. cit.:113) ends his observation by stating:

> los regadíos fueron abandonados después de la conquista española...[puesto que] la despoblación causada por las epidemias del siglo XVI, el interés de los españoles en la minería, que privó de muchos brazos al cultivo, y en la ganadería y la introducción...del sistema de cultivo extensivo con arado, deben haber sido factores que provocaron la decadencia de la horticultura indígena.

> (the irrigated lands were abandoned after the Spanish conquest...[because] the decrease in population caused by the epidemics of the 16th century, the interest of the Spaniards in mining, which deprived agriculture of many workers, and in cattle breeding and the introduction...of the extensive cultivation system with the plough, must have been factors that provoked the decadence of indigenous horticulture.)

11. *Xochimili (Almácigo) or Caanche*   Apparently, the Nahuatl term is related to the word *xochimilco—xochitl* = flower, *milli* = crops, and *co* = location—implying both the place where flowers are cultivated and a very well-known place on the south shores of the central Mexican lakes. The second term, *caanche*, is borrowed from the Yucatec Mayan language and refers to the system called *cultivo en cajones* (box crops or nursery beds), which has long been practiced in lake towns in Mexico and Guatemala (see Figure 4). Plastic bags are used nowadays as receptacles to hold the seeds in a bed of extremely good earth. Once the seed has sprouted and grown into a flower or fruit sapling, it is ready to be transplanted. Although this system is more prevalent in the lake towns of the Central Mexican Basin, it is not exclusive to this area. It has been found throughout the Mesoamerican region, probably because its easy technique permits the *almácigos* (box crops) to be watered by *riego a mano* (pot irrigation).

12. *Chinampas*   There is no doubt that the origin of the *chinampa* system was a prehispanic solution to growing crops on lakeshores and, in a way, related to *almácigo* or *xochimili*. In this system, as described in both archaeological and ethnographic reports, layers of mats were anchored by willow (*ahuejote*) posts and covered by silt obtained from the bottom of the lake. Although this system was well established during the Postclassic period on the Xochimilco-Chalco lakeshores as well as on Lake Amatitlán in Guatemala, it quite surprised the Europeans of the 16th century, who had no knowledge of such a system. According to Sanders and Price (1968:148):

> True chinampas are artificial islands constructed of alternate layers of vegetation and mud in shallow fresh water lakes. Special features include the use of seed beds to shorten the growing season (thus permitting a continuous succession of crops in a single year).... Chinampas were constructed in the form of narrow rectangles to facilitate bucket irrigation and natural seepage.

Figure 4.   Almácigo, or *Xochimilcalli:* Box Crops, or Nursery
Beds (*Códice Florentino,* Vol. III, Libro 11, folio 71 v)

There is no clear information on this amazing technique before the
Postclassic period, although Sanders and Price (1968:148), referring to Flannery
(1967), compare the *chinampas* with the *camellones* (elevated fields) found in
the Valley of Oaxaca, also with "pot irrigation," from Early Formative sites
(1500-900 B.C.). They (op. cit.) observe that

> A very similar system is found in the Teotihuacan Valley in the area of the springs, where
> the water table is less than a meter below the surface. Farmers dig trenches completely
> around their fields; seepage into the ditches produces a continuous water supply; and fields
> are irrigated by scoop from the water-filled ditches.

A similar configuration has been found by Serra Puche (1988) in the Early
Formative site of Terremote-Tlatenco, consisting of a few traces of posts
inserted into the shore to anchor a shield of twigs that formed a bed filled

with mud for gaining land from the lake. Still, it is not known whether its purpose was to grow crops, to expand the land for living quarters, or to serve as a kind of pier or embankment platform.

LAND EXPANSION AS AN EXTENSIVE AGRICULTURAL SYSTEM

As stated in the section on methodology, the main human transformations of the environment are due to either technical advances, a new form of social organization, or both interlaced factors working together. Another, even more impressive demographic explosion, similar to the one that occurred during the Middle Formative (1100-700 B.C.), took place when the cultural groups from the beginning and florescense of the Classic period (150 B.C.-A.D. 650) became associated into confederated states. Apparently, during that process the small cities and villages with similar economic, political, and religious systems were integrated into one important ceremonial center that amalgamated the multiethnic multitude, forming an independent regional state. The need to feed a constantly growing population required an even more intensive, as well as new and extensive way of agricultural production to satisfy the increasing demands from the dispersed towns surrounding the main city.

In this essay, I assume that the so-called extensive agricultural system of production did not start before the Late Formative period (500-150 B.C.), because no archaeological research has ever found Middle Formative (1100-700 B.C.) remains in valleys far away from water sources. Nevertheless, Hirth (1987:357—in his detailed study of Chalcatzingo's demography—considers this practice to have been earlier. He says that, during the Late Middle Formative or Cantera phase (700-500 B.C.),

> there are many indications to suggest the increasing use of temporal (rainy season) agriculture. New sites occur at great distances from areas with high subsurface water tables (springs or permanent rivers) than during the preceding phases. During the Cantera phase six permanent hamlet communities appear for the first time in areas where only temporal agriculture can be practiced.

Hirth's earlier date for the slash-and-burn technique is certainly disconcerting for the above theory and disagrees with the traces of dry streams around the site. Another slight disagreement is related to the amount of population that he calculates for the Barranca and Cantera phases (1100-500 B.C.), when all the monumental work of infrastructure was built, in which undoubtedly a huge amount of labor was needed, as will be discussed below. Extensive production probably occurred only when the Late Formative or Early Classic (500 B.C.-A.D. 300) cultures had to expand their territories to fulfill their increased demands on food supplies for the new affiliates, and when they had the possibility of organizing communal labor among the large and dispersed community that depended politically on a government settled in the ceremonial centers, as clearly happened in Teotihuacan, Cholula and, to a certain degree, in Monte Alban and some Mayan cities.

Only during this period and under a sociopolitical organization with strong religious ties would there have been sufficient power to organize labor that spread cultivation over the valleys by clearing off small sections of forest to be utilized during the rainy season for temporal crops. This practice, known as *tlacolol* among the indigenous people, is a variation of the similar European system of *roza*, or swidden agriculture, in which the land is used once a year during a period of four years, more or less. The two systems of cultivation under discussion differ in the extent of forest to be cleared and the frequency of its use, as explained below.

Roza, or Tumba y Quema (Slash-and-Burn)

These are Spanish names for the process better known in English as swidden or slash-and-burn agriculture. According to Palerm and Wolf's (1972:66) description, the system

> Consiste en talar una sección del bosque...a fin de quemarla. Después de la quema se siembra por medio de espeque (palo o bastón plantador) y se efectúan escardas periódicas. Trás un periodo...generalmente breve, el rendimiento disminuye. Entonces se abandona el terreno para permitir la regeneración del suelo y del bosque. Una nueva sección del bosque es talada a fin de continuar el ciclo agrícola.

> (It consists of cutting a section of forest...in order to burn it. After burning, the planting is done by *espeque* [planting stick], and periodic weedings are carried out. Generally, after a short period the yield lessens. Then the land is abandoned to permit the regeneration of the soil and the forest. A new section of the forest is cut to continue the agricultural cycle.)

Obviously, this system deals with rotating crops as defined above and depends totally on the rainy season. No irrigation is included. One might note that this system characterizes the European Neolithic period, in which the crops exhausted the nutrients in the fields after three or four years of monocultivation. When this happens, a new piece of forest has to be cleared while the old one rests. Most investigators have assumed without question that the system of slash-and-burn was used over large areas in prehispanic Mesoamerica. In fact, archaeological proof of this assumption is scarce, while ethnological information presents a variation of the system, called *tlacolol*, in which another type of plant is cultivated to restore the lost nutrients, and which fits better with anthropological information, as will be seen below.

The studies by Palerm and Wolf (1972) reveal that, in modern Mexico, fields that utilized this system attained the proportion of "twelve hectares of useful land for each hectare-and-a-half dedicated to crops." This system is used because all lands need to recover lost minerals and trophic elements. Recently, it was discovered that the rotation of different crops on the same land would replace the lost nutrients, which could shorten the cycle. This process increases production and also reduces the extent of forest land destined to be cultivated.

Something else to be considered is that systematic deforestation did not start in prehispanic times. Rather, it began during the 16th century, when colonial architecture used a great amount of large beams in the towns settled upon ancient prehispanic centers, when a completely new and intensive mining process that required large amounts of wood for melting minerals was introduced, and when the agricultural practice of roza was extended to new areas opened by the Spaniards to supply the nearby mining settlements—as 19th-century historians asserted (Paynó M. 1870, Peñafiel 1900).

Barbecho, o Tlacolol (Fallow)

Tlacolol or *tlacolloli* is an important variation of the slash-and-burn system and is called *barbecho* in Spanish. Rémi Siméon (1977:574-5) translates *tlacolli* as "waste, manure, garbage, squalor" and *tlacollolli* as a "curved or warped object." There is another translation for *tlacolol* or *tlacolloli*, by Cecilio Robelo (1912:483), as "a twisted crop or sowing on the sides of the hills... with grooves that follow the configuration of the land." Although this interpretation has to do more with the forms Robelo might have observed on the lower terraces that follow a twisted contour of the piedmont, the "twisting" of the crops could also have referred to the corn stalks after the ears of maize were pulled out.

As stated before, the slash-and-burn system requires a large area of reserve fields that are not used continuously because the land must be abandoned to its natural cycle of recovery. In the *tlacolol* system, smaller sections of forest are cleared and the land is simultaneously planted with two or more basic foods, combining grains with legumes and other plants that return to the earth the nitrates and other nutrients that have been absorbed by the basic crop. This combined form not only diminishes the cycle of recovery of the earth but, in the end, *tlacolol* serves to fertilize the land when the doubled and dry corn stalks are uprooted, leaving leaves and other vegetable waste half-covered by the turned earth. Since the land is also the repository for human feces, it attracts an abundance of insects, mice, reptiles, and small mammals whose presence accelerates the oxigenation and recovery of many nutrients, refertilizing the land.

Tlacolol was also used in what Palerm and Wolf (1972:68) describe as *calmil*, or *huerta de la casa* (kitchen/house garden) in their ethnographic research. They write that *calmil* is

> de cultivo permanente. Se abona con los desperdicios de la casa, con basura de animales dosmésticos y con hojas y ramas secas. El rendimiento... del calmil es doble del que se consigue con la milpa de roza....

(permanently cultivated. It is fertilized with the waste of the house, with the garbage of domestic animals, leaves and dry twigs. *Calmil* produces double the amount...that is obtained from a slash-and-burn field....)

Calmil is made up of the words *calli* = house and *milli* = cultivated field of maize (Sp. *milpa*). One can understand this concept better when thinking of house gardens for domestic use inside urban areas or cultivated areas interspersed among habitational quarters for family benefit. One can assume that *barbecho* and *tlacolol* are merely variations of the slash-and-burn extensive system of cultivating large open areas in valleys, while *calmil* can only refer to the small spaces around the houses or the empty lots dispersed within the urban setting, where human and animal waste was deposited and which received small amounts of daily irrigation from the living quarters.

AGRICULTURAL FIELD WORK

The processes used by field workers, or *tlapopoxoani* in Nahuatl, for both intensive and extensive systems of cultivation are described in the following sequence, in which male and female labor is combined. The words have been Hispanicized by common usage through the years, but in this essay they have been returned to the Nahuatl after consulting the Rémi Siméon (1977) dictionary.

(1) *Tlai*: "Labrar y preparar la tierra para la siembra" (Siméon 1977:17). ("To plow and prepare the land for sowing.") The Nahuatl term is composed of *tla(lli)* = earth, complemented by *aic(quen)* = untouched, fallow or not cultivated (see Figure 5).

(2) *Milchihuilli*: "Trabajar o cultivar el campo" ("To work or cultivate the land") (op.cit:276). The word is composed of *mil(li)* [Sp. *milpa*] = to cultivate maize fields, and *chihuil(lia)* = the act of creating or forming some important thing.

(3) *Xippopoa*: This word can be written and pronounced in several ways. Although it is a Nahuatl term, it has been deformed by indigenous linguistic influences from different regions. According to Siméon (1977:767), *xippopoa* is composed of *xi(huitl)* = fire, and *popoa* = act of cleaning, interpreted as "Arrazar, cortar y arrancar la mala hierba" ("To raze, cut and pull the weeds"). The Nahuatl term obviously describes the slash-and-burn system used in the *tlacolol* and *calmil* techniques, in which the act of opening and removing the earth to extract and burn roots and stalks of the previous cultivated plants is implied.

(4) *Tlalmananiztli*: "Aplanamiento del suelo, acción de nivelar la tierra" ("Planing the soil, the action of levelling the land"); or *tlalmoyaua*:

Figure 5.   Tlai: Preparing Land Parcels for Cultivation
(*Códice Florentino,* Vol. II, Libro 11, folio 228 r)

"Desmenuzar la tierra" (op. cit.:602). This act also turns the earth to bury ashes and dry leaves, thus promoting the absorption of gases and nutrients in the earth (see Figure 6).

(5) *Surcado:* Since Spanish colonization, this term has been used for ploughing the fields, although this system replaced the use of the ancient *coa,* or planting stick.

(6) *Tepehuar:* "Esparcir o desparramar (semillas) por el suelo" (ibid.:497). ("To broadcast [seeds] upon the ground"—although it is also used when the seeds are inserted in the earth with a planting stick; see Figure 7.)

(7) *Mimilpanoa:* "Recorrer y revisar los campos de cultivo" (ibid.:277). ("To walk around reviewing the crops"—a regular habit among farmers.)

(8) *Tl amatectli* and *Tlamatepualiztli:* "Podar, cortar y usar el espeque (coa) en la tierra" (ibid.:610). ("To prune, cut, and use the planting stick [now

o tupen amano, llamanla Hal uitectli
:que quiere dezir tierra asentada agol
pes.

¶ A la tierra estercolada, la lla
man Hal auiac, que quiere dezir tie
rra suaue: por que la an adouado cõ
nel estiercol.

¶ A las tierras donde se pudren los
magueies, y sean buelto estiercol di
zenla Mesталli tierra estercolada cõ
magueies.

¶ A la tierra de riego la llaman
A tlalli que quiere dezir de agua

Figure 6. *Tlalmanaliztli*: Levelling the Soil (top panel) and Breaking
Up Clods (bottom panel) (*Códice Florentino,* Vol. II, Libro 11, folio 227 v)

Figure 7. *Tepehuar*: Broadcast Seeding (*Códice Florentino,* Vol. II, Libro 4, folio 72 r [top panel], and Libro 11, folio 120 r [bottom panel])

Figure 8. *Tlamatectli*: Pruning and Cutting with the Planting
Stick (*Códice Florentino,* Vol. II, Libro 10, folio 28 r)

Figure 9. *Tlamatectli*: Eliminating Weeds Around the Shoots (*Códice
Florentino,* Vol. II, Libro 11, folio 133 v)

Figure 10. *Tlamatectli* (top panel): Breaking and Clearing the Ground Before the Maize is Mature and Piling the Earth into a Conical Mound; and *Tlapopoa* (bottom panel): Pulling out the Silk, Clearing the Stalk and Gathering the Corn (*Códice Florentino,* Vol. II, Libro 4, folio 72 r)

Figure 11. *Pixca*: Cutting and Gathering the Amaranth Crop
(top panel) and Sorting out Amaranth (bottom panel)
(*Códice Florentino,* Vol. II, Libro 4, folio 133 v)

pick and shovel] in the earth around the crops.") In other words, to eliminate the weeds around the shoots to let them grow stronger (see Figures 8 and 9). This labor is done several times and is combined with *tlapopoa*.

(9) *Tlapopoa:* "Acción de descubrir y limpiar la tierra antes de que el maíz esté completamente maduro" (ibid. 1977:640). ("The act of breaking and clearing the ground before the maize is completely mature.") The word is composed of *tla(lli]* = earth, and *popoa* = act. In practice, it means to unwrap the ear of maize, pull out the silk, and clear the stalk of weeds and reinforce it by gathering earth around it in a conical pile (see Figure 10).

(10) *Pixca:* "Recoger, segar, cosechar" ("To cut and gather in the crop") (see Figure 11). The term is widely used among Mexican field hands working in the U.S.

HYDROAGRICULTURE AND MASS PRODUCTION

Given the interrelation (discussed under Methodology) among demography, social organization, technology, and environment, it becomes obvious that any demographic explosion requires the creation of new tools and techniques or the extension of land cultivation. This is an invariable solution interrelated with different forms of social labor that produce better economic results. It is evident that this hypothesis requires statistical information to ascertain, in each case, which of the elements of the development formula is the cause and which ones are the consequences of these changes. However, it helps us to know that this is the product of a slow but continuous evolution of one process. In social sciences and technological inventions, most changes are the consequence of a slow transformation from previously established systems.

Apparently, in many places around the Central Mexican Highlands, Middle Formative settlement (1100-500 B.C.) indicates a clear increase of the population either by natural reproduction or by group association. It is reasonable to assume that the demographic explosion required an innovation in food producing techniques to supply the needs of a larger group that remained circumscribed to the same area, scarcely enlarged by new hydraulic works around nearby water sources.

With a larger water supply, ways were found to preserve its potability, to store it for a longer time, to channalize and utilize it in more ample forms of irrigation, and to drain it away from the living quarters to maintain urban sanitary conditions. According to the scarce archaeological information on this subject in the Highlands and the Basin of Mexico, this process began during the Middle and Late Formative (1100-500 B.C.) but flourished during the Early Classic (A.D. 0-150), when the large towns became incipient ceremonial and political centers. These centers enlarged their urban areas, establishing architectural structures in the conglomerated villages as seats of local government to organize economic, political, and religious activities related to water management. Then, through intensive and extensive agriculture, from the Early Classic a massive amount of diverse staples could be produced to fulfill the needs of the enlarged, multiethnic groups dispersed in a network of regional towns that depended on the ceremonial and political center. An example of this process can be found during pre-Teotihuacan times among the Cuanalán and Tezoyucan groups, long before they became affiliated during the Patlachique phase (150 B.C.) but immediatly before they initiated the ceremonial center, which was firmly established during the Tzacualli and Miccaotli phases (A.D. 0-150) of the Early Teotihuacan Classic. It is clear that, at this time, intensive and extensive agriculture was in full practice in all the Mesoamerican settlements, because traces of abandoned channels and terraces are found on almost every slope of the Central Highlands as part of the pan-Mesoamerican effort to increase the cultivated area.

It is inconceivable that this productive system, achieved by organized labor with only *coas* (planting sticks) to till the land, would have been abandoned and forgotten after the 16th century—except for the three following considerations: (1) The depletion of hand labor because workers were moved away from their natural ambience or destined to work in other activities, such as mining or building convents and mansions; (2) the introduction of the Egyptian ox-plough, which required long extensions of flat fields because it could not jump from terrace to terrace without destroying the stone borders of the platforms; and (3) the plea issued by Fray Juan de Zumárraga to the president of La Real Audiencia in 1537, for an edict to stop the Indians from using *coas* for working in the fields, because they were imbued with "diabolic" representations.

To understand the concern of the Spanish bishop in this seemingly small issue related to this common instrument, the *coa*, it is necessary to quote the descriptive references collected from diverse historical sources that Rojas R. (1985:212-225) has published, explaining the varied uses and applications of these tools, which were not only used in agriculture but in different tasks such as constructing buildings and houses, maintaining irrigation canals, conditioning the fields to be sown, making roads and other public works, and in crafts. Rojas classifies the *coas* into three large groups:

(1) *Palo Puntiagudo* (Sharpened Stick) or *Bastón Plantador* (Planting Stick) or *Uitzoctli*: "que se utilizó... para cavar los huecos en los que se depositarían las semillas o los esquejes de las plantas, y para resembrar.... [o] para remover las raíces de las hierbas y para desenterrar los tubérculos... " (Rojas 1985:216). ("which was used... to dig the holes in which seeds or shoots of plants were deposited, and for resowing.... [or] to remove the roots of weeds or to dig up tubers.... ")

Figure 12. Figure with a *Coa* (Planting Stick), Previously Interpreted as a Warrior with a Long Spear (Chalcatzingo Relief I B 2)

Figure 13. Cultivating Land (*Códice Nutall,* folio 44)

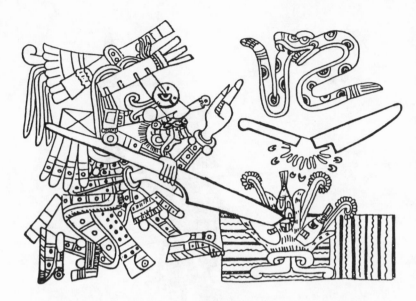

Figure 14.   The Rain God Tlaloc with a *Uictli* (so-called digging stick) in Irrigated Maize Fields—in Tlalocan (the Afterworld), According to E. Seler (*Códice Borgia*, Lámina 20)

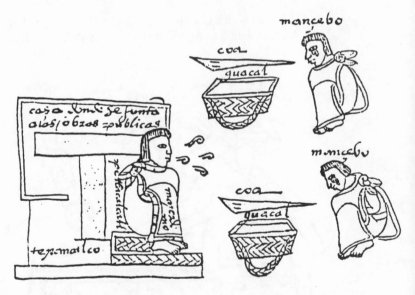

Figure 15.   Instructing the Youth to Participate in Public Works (Note that each youth [*mancebo*] has a *coa* [so-called digging stick] and a *guacal* [*huacal*, carrying basket]). (*Códice Mendocino*, folio 70)

(2) *Uictli* or *Verdadera Coa* (True Coa) or *Uictli de Hoja* (with Blade): "que cronistas e historiadores coloniales equipararon... [al] azadón, la azada y la pala.... [cuya] hoja era plana y se ensanchaba cerca de la punta para luego aguzarse formando una figura más o menos triangular..." (Rojas 1985:213, 218). ("which colonial chroniclers and historians equated with the hoe, the spade and the shovel.... [whose] blade was flat and it widened near the end and then came to a point, forming a more or less triangular shape...") (see Figures 12-15).

(3) *Uictli axoquen*, or *Coa con Mango Zoomorfo* (Coa with Zoomorphic Handle): "compuesta por dos piezas que se marraban con alguna fibra, cuero o bejuco.... El mango forma un ángulo recto y su remate es la cabeza de un animal..." (Rojas 1985:223). ("composed of two different pieces tied with some fiber, hide or cane.... The handle formed a right angle [with the shaft] and its top was an animal head...") (see Figure 16).

Rojas (ibid.:223-224) also cites strong opposition to the use of the *coa* by 16th-century Fray Diego Durán, who commented with much surprise:

Figure 16. Uictli-Axoquen, or *Coa* with Zoomorphic Handle (*Historia Tolteca-Chichimeca*, p. 35, folio 39 r)

Oh bestialidad extraña de esta gente, que en muchos casos tenían buen...entendimiento....
Advierto que hoy en día, en unas coas de hierro que para labrar la tierra usan, traen en
los palos, al cabo, unas caras de mono, otras de perros, otras, de diablos. Y no me ha
parecido bien, y es tan general que no hay indio que no traiga aquello. Y en particular
en Chalco y en la cordillera toda de la comarca.

(Oh, strange bestiality of these people, who in many cases had a good...understanding....
I warn that today, on some iron *coas* that they use to work the earth, they have at the
end of the sticks faces of monkeys, others of dogs, others of devils. And I don't think it
correct, and it is so general that there isn't an Indian who doesn't carry one. And especially
in Chalco and in the hills around this area.)

It is possible that this type of *coa* was the one that caused Zumárraga's
worries, enough to drive him to abolish their common use because it was not
only a technological instrument but was imbued with symbolic meanings. It
occurs as the sceptre in the hands of government leaders (see Figure 12), as
the rod associated with priests and vicars, or the cane that *pochteca* (traders)
had in their hands, according to several Postclassic codices as well as bas reliefs
and figurines from Classic and Formative times related to the higher echelons.
Zumárraga's struggle to forbid the use of the *coa* was in vain, as this ancient
instrument continued to be utilized in intensive and extensive agriculture even
until the 20th century, when it was replaced by metal utensils such as the
machete, pickaxe, pointed bar, and shovel.

As stated earlier, *tlacolol* (as part of the slash-and-burn technique) was
applied after the Late Formative or Early Classic (500 B.C.-A.D. 150) period,
when government leaders utilized intensive and extensive agricultural systems
to feed the increasing population that constantly settled around the ceremonial
and political centers, creating large suburban areas. That seems to be what
happened in Teotihuacan, where the city reached more than 22 km^2.

The constant demographic increment related to the enlargement of the living
quarters at the first Teotihuacan formation extended the cultivated lands
further out to surround the city, which expanded geographically and
demographically, as R. Millon (1973) shows in each of the chronological stages.
Apparently, the large population was concentrated around the naturally and
artificially irrigated lands. Other groups, established in new villages
interconnected with the city, cultivated the forest, slopes, and new sectors of
the valley cleared out by the slash-and-burn system only during the rainy
season, because they performed other activities in urban communal works
during the winter and spring to fulfill their *tequio*, or corvée, as citizens.

Slash-and-burn, then, was only applied in expanded areas where there was
no possible way of irrigation, while intensive agricultural production utilized
the extensive network of *apantli*, or water currents, for irrigation. An extra
benefit of the *apantli* system was its use for transporting heavy loads throughout
the natural and handmade water courses. As the *apantli* was described earlier,
just a brief quotation will be added to explain its importance.

Otli-apantli (*camino atarjea*), or road/dike-channels, is the form of irrigation by means of a canal system that deeply impressed the Spanish conquerors. T. Rojas (1974) has extracted the following description from *Cartas de Relación*, written by Hernán Cortés before his arrival in Tenochtitlan. He referred to

> puentes, acequias, caminos y calzadas que vieron al arribar al lago de Chalco de cuya orilla se vislumbraba una ciudad dentro de la laguna a la que llegaron por...una calzada tan ancha como una lanza jineta y por ella fuimos a una ciudad hermosa, aunque pequeña...de muy bien labradas casas y torres...que había sido armada sobre el agua...y la salida de la ciudad...es por otra calzada que tendrá una legua grande hasta llegar a la tierra firme.

> (bridges, canals, roads and avenues that they saw when they arrived at the Chalco lake shores, from which glimmered a city on the lake that they approached...by an avenue as wide as a knight's lance and on which we went into a small but beautiful city...of very well-constructed houses and towers...that had been built on the lake...and the exit from the city...is by another avenue that must be a league long to firm land.)

The reference is clearly to the dike-avenues that were used to separate the sweet and salt water and to communicate cities and islands inside the lake of Anahuac. These structures were widely described by historians from colonial times until the 19th century, when there were still visible remains of these structures, although altered through centuries of constant building and rebuilding. Archaeological excavations have found only small sections of these structures around the 16th-century city, although investigations in another area found the canal-road (*otli-apantli*) system among segments of the urban plan of Teotihuacan during Early Tlamimilolpa and Xolalpan phases (A.D. 300-650).

As noted in a previous work (Angulo 1987a), the *otli-apantli* system was used in a different way in urban areas than in the regular irrigation of large cultivated fields. Its function in cities such as Teotihuacan was to carry away the rain water, trapped in the "impluviums" of the apartment compounds, to join the running water that came from the north-south rivers crossing the urban plains. In this form, the drainage system installed in the city was used to irrigate the lands interspersed between apartment compounds utilizing the already described *calmil*. It is clear that cultivation of urban gardens or *calmil* lands is not strictly related to any particular method for growing crops, as different solutions were needed for each particular environment. The *calmil* system was included in the earlier description of *tlacolol* and *barbecho*, which used household waste as fertilizer. Here, suffice it to say that the city house gardens could also be irrigated by the apartment compound drainage or by the *otli-apantli* network of canals that carried water away from the urban areas.

The socioeconomic control exerted by the extensive city extended to the large population in the small and large villages of the region, becoming a unified goverment in the Early Tlamimilolpa period (A.D.150-350). Once the state was established, it began to absorb villages from long distances in an expansional movement that controlled the global economy (land and water) of the region through the political and religious organization that flourished during the Late Tlamimilolpa and Xolalpan period (A.D. 350-650), as various scholars have concluded (Millon 1973, Cowgill 1973, Angulo 1987a, n.d.).

A late reference to the *otli-apantli* system used to transport merchandise was found by R. Strauss (1974:155-158) in a 1542 edict by Virrey D. Antonio de Mendoza (A.G.N.M. Mercedes Vol.2 exp 309), in which he ordered ancient channels reopened when he realized that

en tiempos de Moctezuma había ciertas acequias y calles de agua que venían de las alagunas [sic] de Citlaltepeque y Saltocan a la laguna de esta ciudad [México] en las que traían...en canoas todos los mantenimientos y proveimientos necesarios...y que ahora no se hace, a causa de estar 'ciegas'...[por lo] que convendría y sería necesario al bien y provecho que se abriesen...[para que] todos los indios de los dichos pueblos y comarca traían [sic] los dichos bastimentos por agua y no se vengan cargados como vienen.

(During Moctezuma's time there were channels and streets of water that came from the lakes of Citlatepec and Xaltocan to the lake of this city [Mexico], where canoes were used to bring all the goods and necessary staples...although this is no longer done because the channels are 'blind'...[for which reason] it would be convenient and necessary to [re]open them in benefit of all the Indians from these towns and surroundings to bring the merchandise by water instead of carrying it as they do.)

Strauss (op. cit.) assumes that the "blind," or filled-up condition of the water courses was due to the lack of labor for maintenance because of "the social disorganization of the prehispanic systems caused by the Spanish conquest." It is evident that more archaeological and ethnohistorical investigation is required to find old water trajectories, such as the Cuautitlan River and other natural avenues that were used to navigate north-south and probably vice versa between the intercommunicated lakes.

SYSTEMS THAT BEGAN DURING THE MIDDLE FORMATIVE (1000-700 B.C.)

Although the origin of the irrigation of agricultural systems is clearly prehispanic, some archaeologists still refuse to accept that this practice existed before the Classic period (A.D.150-750). In fact, sherds and structural remains found in archaeological excavations confirm that irrigation with the *apantli* system can be dated as far back as the Middle and Late Formative period (1200-200 B.C.), which corresponds to the Olmec Horizon, according to some scholars.

In this regard, Woodbury and Neely (1972) published a profound study of the *apantli* system of irrigation channels found in Mixteca lands during their

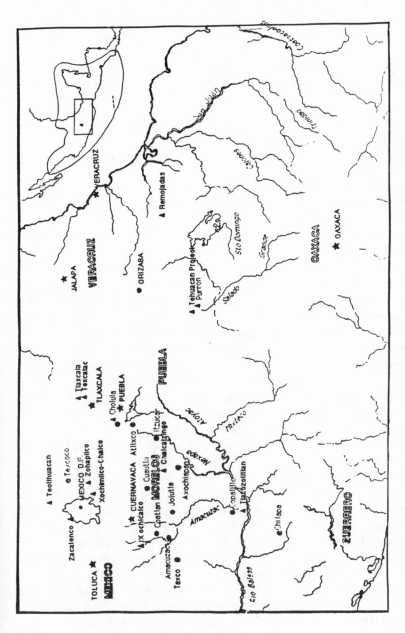

Figure 17. Archaeological Sites Mentioned in the Text (Inset shows both the area enlarged here [box] and the Mesoamerican Culture Area.)

189

participation in the Archaeological-Botanical Project conducted by R. S. MacNeish during the 1960s. Furthermore, the Fundación Alemana surveyed and explored the Puebla-Tlaxcala Valley (see Figure 17), where—as García Cook (1989:169) reports for the Tlatempa phase (1200-800 B.C.)—they found

> canales, al parecer para controlar el agua de lluvia...que se fabricaban en la parte superior o inicial de la terraza....También están presentes los depósitos excavados en el *tepetate* o bien se construyen represas a manera de 'jagueyes' en las barrancas que cruzaban los sitios.
>
> (channels, to control rain water, apparently...which were made in the upper or initial part of the terrace.... Excavated deposits in the *tepetate* [porous bedrock] are also present or else dams similar to ponds were built in the ravines that run through the sites.)

In search of early forms of social life, Kent Flannery and his group (1967, 1976) gathered basic information about village settlements from diverse Mesoamerican sites for the Early and Middle Formative period. Also, many authors dealt with prehispanic agriculture in Volume XL of *América Indígena* (see Denevan 1980).

The multidisciplinary work realized by a large group of scholars from diverse scientific disciplines, led by R. S. MacNeish in an archaeological-botanical project in the Tehuacán Valley (see Figure 17), discovered a complex of several dikes constructed to create a large water depository in a gorge that was previously formed by the ancient Lencho-Diego stream, a short distance before its waters joined the Río Salado, which runs through the southern part of Mequitongo valley. According to the reports of geologist J. Brunnet (1967) and archaeologists R. Woodbury and J. Neely (1972,IV:81-153), the dikes were built in several construction periods. They explained that, due to "the heavy subsequent erosion in the canyon," it was neccesary to raise the height of the dikes to increase the volume of the water carried.

Following is a condensed account of the Tehuacán Valley Project's reports on the Purron Dam (see Figure 17). The first construction was formed by a large dome-like shape nearly 6m wide, 3m high, and almost 175m long, which closed almost half of the canyon. The structure that served as a dike was similar to a *momoxtli* made of large and small rocks mixed with earth. The second construction reached a level of 5m over the silt deposits accumulated by the first dam and was 100m wide, this time covering the 400m width of the canyon. According to excavation data, the large platform was composed of large igneous rocks carried by the stream and metamorphic slabs and sedimentary rocks that are abundant in the area. Sixteeen complete walls and more than three incomplete ones were distributed in an irregular form between 4m and 8m along the exploratory trench that crossed the 100m width of the structure.

To ascertain age, carbon-14 dating was applied to organic material related to the ceramic sherds found in the silt of the dam of the first construction phase.

A comparison of these sherds with the others obtained from the stratigraphic pits excavated in Purron and Abejas caves dated the first structure between 1200 and 800 B.C. The accumulated material of the second dam revealed a date between 800 and 550 B.C., or the end of the Ajalpan phase and the beginning of the Sta. María. The materials found in the silt of the third period corresponded to the late Sta. María phase and early Palo Blanco phase (150 B.C.-A.D. 150). This phase was constructed while the dam of the second phase was still in use, since the modification was only an addition or repair of the upper part of the structure that did not alter or reinforce the retaining walls.

The construction of the fourth level was apparently carried out with the following technology. A floor of stone was consolidated to serve as a base for the walls of large stone placed 3-5m apart to contain a fill of earth, sand, gravel, and small stones of 4m height, forming a large platform on which another structure was built, with previously described technique, which reached the height of nearly 18m. According to calculations by Woodbury and Neely (1972,IV:98), the platform contained a fill of stones and dirt of 37,000 m^3 that were extracted, accumulated, and carried, using only stone, wood, and rope implements. It seems that a fifth construction phase lasted until the time of the Spanish Conquest, when it was abandoned to the erosional processes that finally destroyed it.

Other excavations of the same project performed in the Tehuacán Valley also found smaller dams in diverse sections of the study area. One of them had walls closing the El Tecorral canyon near the town of San Marcos (6.5 km south of Tehuacán), and another dam was found in the extreme southwest of the Zapotitlán Valley, nearly 11 km south of Santa Ana Texoloc.

Complementing the water control system was an aqueduct more than 6 km long, constructed with three distinct methods. It incorporated the waters of the Xiquila river and other springs into the main channel, where some sections were excavated into rocks, while others were trenches reinforced by slabs of rock with deposits of alluvial land and still others were built with rows of stones consolidated with mud. These three techniques were used to build the aqueducts to irrigate cultivated lands in La Mixteca Alta. Similar systems were found in Chalcatzingo, Morelos, in 1972-74 (Grove et al. 1976, 1987), in which the Middle Formative people struggled to keep their field crops irrigated as well as to preserve humidity on slopes and hills somewhat separated from water sources (Angulo 1987b-c).

THE TLALNAHUAC VALLEY 3,000 YEARS AGO

A good attempt at paleoecological reconstruction was made in the small area of Tlalnahuac, the eastern valley of the state of Morelos (see Figure 18), by David Bugé, Kenneth Hirth, and David Grove as part of the Chalcatzingo

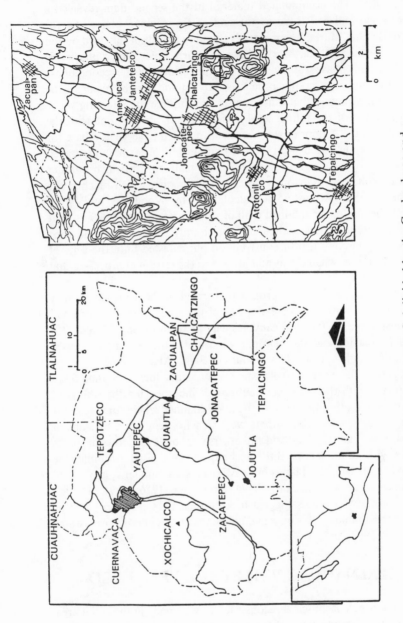

Figure 18. State of Morelos, Subdivided by the Cuahnahuac and Tlalnahuac Valleys, and a Section of the Chalcatzingo Survey Area

192

project (Grove et al. 1987:6-13). The study area included the whole basin of the Amatzicnac River, from which geological and physiographic information was previously gathered by Hirth (1973). A topographic plan of the archaeological site was surveyed using photogrammetry with leveled curves at each meter. Information was collected from geologic and climatic maps of the area to make a correlation and analysis of the new information in the microarea being investigated. A hydrologic study was included as well as the analysis of soils and types of vegetation, which were compared with pollen and spore analyses from different laboratories. With this information, it was possible to reconstruct paleosoils and paleoclimates for the different periods in which the Formative cultures flourished (2000-0 B.C.).

The Tlalnahuac Valley is composed basically of alluvial materials. It is located south of the "cold hills" of the Ajusco-Chichinautzin and Popocatepetl mountain chain (with heights of over 2,000m above sea level) and the row of mountains that cross the southeast end of the state of Puebla and continue through the state of Guerrero, where the *tierra caliente* (hot land) begins. The Popocateptl glaciers abruptly cut the slopes made up of alluvial deposits to the south of the volcano, forming deep ravines that descend in a winding path to form the Amatzinac River, which runs through a subtropical climate with abundant precipitation in the summer but which is quite dry during winter and spring.

The basins of the Amatzicnac-Tenango and Cuautla rivers form part of the Amilpas Valley, which divides the state of Morelos. The altitude of the slopes of this valley varies between 2,500m in the north (in Hueyapán) and 1,000m above sea level in the extreme south (in Axochiapán). It has been considered a temperate-hot area with summer showers (900mm) situated between Cw and Aw climates in the classification of Köeppens (D. Diez 1969).

The southern part of the central portion of the valley is abruptly interrupted by enormous rock formations caused by volcanic intrusions not completely erupted as igneous material. These intrusions transformed the Tertiary sedimentary deposits into mountains of metamorphic rocks of the "Inselberg" type, which is an isolated formation that juts out of the valley floor, exactly as an iceberg juts up from the sea. Because of the heat and pressure of the underground igneous current in search of an exit, this mass of sedimentary material erupted as a compact horizontal stratum that became mountains with cliffs of sharp vertical cuts and indications of the flaking off of metamorphized material, which can be found for several hundred meters around the mountain. It is important to note that a climatic change is recorded between the Early and Middle Formative (Bugé 1987:20) and that it is coincident with technological and cultural changes, as is the case in the great majority of Mesoamerican sites.

It is evident that, between the Early and Middle Formative (1500-800 B.C.), there was no significant change in the typology of lithic artifacts, although there was a noticeable change in the sequential forms of vessels and ceramic figurines. Another change is seen in the incipient constructions and works of infrastructure for production and habitation, which included terraces, plazas, platforms, and other works of proto-urban character that transformed the main characteristics of dispersed towns into concentrated villages with space for civil and religious activities. These places fulfilled the internal requisites of the community as well as the needs of smaller and friendly neighboring towns. Perhaps the greatest change in this period (also called Olmec horizon) was the intensification of agricultural production through the construction of terraces for planting crops—with living quarters, retention and distribution of water for both irrigation and domestic use, and control of food and labor redistribution as part of the socialpolitical organization.

At the time of this development, new techniques and new knowledge arose in many aspects of culture. Of these, the first stages of pictographic and symbolic writing should be mentioned, as well as the beginning of a written numeration and a knowledge of the movement of the sun, moon, and stars. David Bugé (1987:418) believes that calendric knowledge and associated rituals were basic in planning agricultural activities and in determining the area to be cultivated and the distribution of the land, the types of plants to be farmed, and the appropriate time for planting. He states that those who had the knowledge to predict the timing of the rainy season also had the power to control the social stratum that performed elaborate rituals and built monumental works during the time not dedicated to farming.

One could easily assume that, in this period (Olmec horizon), a new social and labor organization was achieved which constructed agricultural terraces and built dams and channeled waters for irrigation and drainage, as discussed elsewhere (Angulo 1987c). People of this period also worked the huge monolithic boulders that are found in many Mesoamerican sites of this horizon, among which are the engraved reliefs on the cliffs of Chalcatzingo and the colossal heads of San Lorenzo, Tres Zapotes, and La Venta.

Despite the many concepts of "the Olmec" that have been put forth and the diverse theories explaining its presence, this horizon in fact corresponds to a period of change in various Mesoamerican sites. The most important point is that a different type of control utilized by an administrative organization was created, bringing together groups of people from dispersed and nucleated towns into the main village to organize various types of labor to benefit the community.

Even if this system had its roots in earlier phases, it could not have been developed on a local or regional level until it became part of an extensive, interrelated movement that would last for a long time and affect a great number of sites that were in a similar state of cultural development. This cultural movement, independent of the great distances that separate the sites distributed throughout the Mesoamerican area, could be called "Olmecization," as others have done with reference to many of its aspects and cultural traits (see Clark 1990). This Olmecization seem to be homogenous in relation to the characteristics that define this period, such as sculpture, pictographic and ceramics styles, canalization, or infrastructural works and other archaeological remains.

Much archaeological material of this period has been classified as Olmec, basing the analysis mostly on artistic characteristics. The result has been somewhat controversial, although interesting to art historians and the many archaeologists given to deciphering iconography. This theme is not included in this study because its focus is the process of socioeconomic change and the analysis of social organization related to human and technological resources.

NEW CONSIDERATIONS ON CHALCATZINGO'S MIDDLE FORMATIVE

Although the earliest human presence in the Chalcatzingo area goes back as far as Early Formative (1800 B.C.), there are clues to indicate an almost continuous human occupation in different sectors of the once prehispanic site. This occupation continued until the Spanish conquest and has been restructured through Colonial times to the present.

The most recent period of excavations (INAH-University of Illinois) at Chalcatzingo took place in 1972-1974 (Grove et al. 1987), when an accurate chronological study of ceramics established three main phases of development: Amate (1500-1100 B.C.), Barranca (1100-700 B.C.) and Cantera (700-500 B.C.). Apparently during the Barranca and Cantera phase of the Olmec Horizon, monumental bas reliefs were carved on boulders at the foot of the cliffs. These reliefs have given fame to the site since its discovery by Eulalia Guzmán (1934).

It is evident that Chalcatzingo was not the first or the only site at which Middle Formative people struggled to preserve humidity on the slopes of the hill used as settlement and to control the natural courses opened by rainwater along the slanted lands that form ravines. At the northern part of the main plaza in this archaeological site, the sides of two small brooks have traces of being excavated in order to conduct the water in a particular route. Extensive clearing of the brush and excavations around the site brought out aspects that were lost by natural erosion and growth of vegetation through the centuries. The landscape now found is not related to the one created by the groups that settled there during the several periods of prehispanic occupation. The main features that modified the archaeological area can be perceived on the retaining walls of the large platforms and the terraces of different sizes distributed along the piedmont to the north of Cerro La Cantera and northwest of Cerro Delgado, although these constructions have been destroyed by several decades of constant use of the ox-plough and by natural erosion (see Figure 19).

Figure 19. Chalcatzingo's Cerro Delgado, Showing Terraces

196

The systems to preserve and control the water of this dry area, discussed below, were partially discovered years later, after several visits to the site and a review of the field notes and individual reports presented by each of the participants in the excavation. During the four seasons of archaeological research in Chalcatzingo, more than 40 terraces were found and partially explored in the 15,000 m^2 covered by the project. The upper levels of these abandoned terraces, which resembled a stepped profile on Cerro La Cantera and Cerro Delgado during precolumbian times, became an almost continuous inclined plane through the destruction of ridges of the ancient terraces by the dual intervention of humans and time.

The struggle to obtain and preserve water resources in a hot and dry place like Chalcatzingo was probably one of the most time- and energy-consuming activities in the community that consolidated the site as one of the most important regional centers of that epoch. Archaeological evidence exists of ingenious works of engineering to resolve the problems of scarcity and sudden abundance of water during the extremely dry and rainy seasons, as the inhabitants endeavored to ensure their village and the growth of their society. Good examples of terrace construction were found during the exploration of the two highest structures on the slopes of Cerro Delgado. Hirth (1987:343-367) states that these terraces existed during the Cantera phase (700-500 B.C.).

It should be emphasized that the Chalcatzingo people of Barranca times (1100-700 B.C.) designed the shape of the terraces according to the natural locations of big boulders that weigh more than 20 tons. The cutting and placement of big rocks to complement the shape of retaining walls on each terrace could only have been possible with a team of workers in which 8-10 men participated in aligning the rocks (carried by another 2-3 men) to the natural contour of the slope. Another team would have transported small rocks while others would have piled them and glued them together with mud to form a retaining wall in the shape of a talus slope. This process seems to have been used in Terrace 4, although just a few remains inside the wall have preserved indications of rocks covered with a fine coat of mud.

During her explorations of Terrace 4, Teresita Majewski (1972-73) found a solid structure formed of a double wall, 6m long and 0.7m thick, which was partially destroyed and reused as the base of a later wall built during the next period to enlarge the size and height of the same terrace. At the bottom of this modification, Majewski found an offering to the structure; it corresponds to Late Barranca and Early Cantera periods (900-600 B.C.), when the site flourished.

Water Storage in Caves

Because Cerros Cantera and Delgado, and the small hill between them, are composed of a metamorphic rock known as granodiorite, there is no possibility of finding natural caves, caverns, or long grottos—although, among the cracks, fissures, and conglomerated boulders, there are many natural shelters that vary from 1-2m to nearly 18m deep and which are classified under the generic name of caves. After a general survey in more than 25 caves in Cerro Cantera and Cerro Delgado, Burton (1973) reported traces of occupation in the majority of them, with painting and other remains dating from prehispanic times to recent vandalisms.

When the term "occupation" is used in reference to the caves, it is not limited to a strictly habitational sense, but includes a general utilization of the cave for ritual and practical reasons such as storing edible plants, seeds, fibers for weaving, basketry or textiles because the humidity helped to preserve these various organic materials. In some of the caves, it was observed that the walls had an eroded horizontal line caused by the constant or prolonged presence of water, as if the place had been used to store water. In the great majority of these caves or shelters with traces of water deposits, monochromatic and polychromatic paintings were found expressing motifs related to rituals or acts of magical/religious ceremonies. A great percentage of these paintings correspond to the Middle Formative (Barranca and Cantera phases, 1100-500 B.C.), although there is one with designs similar to the Teotihuacan murals (A.D. 450-650), as well as others associated to the Toltec Horizon (A.D. 950-1250) and still others to the final stage of Postclassic times (A.D. 1250-1521).

The most important cave for this study was called Shaman Cave by the archaelogical crew. It has one of the largest interior spaces of all the caves and has a depression in the middle, apparently lined with a stucco coating to keep the water clean and to avoid seepage. From the exterior south end of the shelter, a channel was carved into the rock to bring rain water to the depression, which might have been used as a sacred water depository. This probably was the case, because a pile of standing stones was found, reminiscent of an altar (Grove et al. 1987:53-54, Angulo 1987c), at the end of the pool.

Modifying the Natural Course and Canalization

At the northern part of the main plaza of the archaeological site, the walls of two small brooks have traces of being enlarged by digging sticks (similar to the *uictli coa*) to change the course of the water (see Figure 2). In different sections of some creeks, one can observe traces of modifications on the natural walls of the water channel to widen or deepen it or change its direction. In some other creeks, there are traces of cuts made by a stick 8-12 cm (3"-4") wide, similar to the width of the *coa* referred to as *uictli de hoja* (plain digging stick) and which historians and colonial writers compare with the hoe and shovel for maintaining irrigation works and land conditioning (Rojas 1985:217-218). This type of slash tracks have been found in a brook that runs along the 980m contour line in the archaeological zone of Chalcatzingo as well as in the water course that comes down from Cerro Portezuelo, located between Cerro La Cantera and Cerro Delgado.

A more sophisticated kind of channel from the same period drained the artificial pond explored by M. Coe (1966:23) in San Lorenzo, Veracruz. It was formed by a long succession of "U"-shaped stones, with the same kind of rocks used as cover slabs, suggesting that it was a drain. In a second report of his excavations, Coe (1967:10), observed that water flows through this channel once the lakes are filled with rain water. He also found a complicated system of other drainages distributed around the area.

In Tlacozotitlán, Guerrero, also called Teopantecuanitlán, similar channels were found that run "around 200m to the NE of the precinct... [the channel was] built with limestone blocks...of different sizes that varied from 120 to 190 cm long, 50 to 75 cm wide and 20 to 40 cm thick....The channel was covered with slabs of the same material used in the walls and just a few were found in situ" (Martínez D. 1986:55-80). Apparently, the channels in both sites (San Lorenzo and Tlacozotitlán) were built during the Middle Formative (1100-850 B.C.), although they are quite similar to the smaller ones that drained the apartment compounds located in Classic period Teotihuacan (Acosta 1971, Angulo 1987a).

El Ojito de Agua

One water hole at Chalcatzingo was described as an "ojito de agua (small spring) where sherds were washed during the archaeological excavations" (Angulo 1987b:58). In reality, this formation is not a spring but a natural drainage system that slowly gathers the filtrations from higher slopes of the hill in an artificial shallow deposit formed by a wall of rocks (see Figure 20).

Ameyalli, Ojos de Agua or Springs

There is an *ameyalli*, now dry, that formed the creek that used to run over the 980m level (*cota*) separating Terrace 45 from the lower cultivated lands to the north, located at the southern part of the present town of Chalcatzingo. Apparently, it comes from the upper terraces, where the water flowed freely until the 1970s. Although this creek delineated the archaeological exploration, sherds and other cultural materials were also found in the fields as well as in the *calmil* (house gardens) that formed part of the house lots in town.

At the entrance of the archaeological zone, there is a colonial stone wall smoothed with mortar that used to retain water from the creek. The location of the wall in relation to the surveyed prehispanic terraces with sparce houses among the cultivated lands, strongly suggests that this colonial dam replaced a previous wall of stones smoothed with mud that could have been built during the Middle Formative. Apparently, it was enlarged during colonial times and

Figure 20. The So-Called *Ojito de Agua,* or Small Spring at Chalcatzingo (Right: David C. Grove, Center: Jorge Angulo V.)

could easily have contained 50-100 m^3 or one million liters (250,000 gal), or even more water if the space in the ravine is also considered.

Sadly, this ancient dam, which stored water during prehispanic and colonial times, was transformed into a garbage dump during the present century. "Civilization" and "progress" introduced the electricity and modern technology that drilled private wells to pump water from lower water tables, consuming the supply for the *ameyalli* (springs) that fed this and other old dams (see Figure 21).

Figure 21. Remains of an Abandoned Colonial Dam near Chalcatzingo

Axayotl, or Atecochtli (Tanks or Water Depositories)

This system was not included in the earlier descriptions of hydraulic techniques because the only example found to date was in Chalcatzingo and because its use has not been confirmed as yet by archaeological excavation in this site or in other ancient cultural centers. It has been described in previous works (Angulo 1987c, 1990) as a simple but ingenious system that used the natural orohydraulic form to install a series of water depositories along the ravine that drains rain water from the cliff (see Figures 22-24). One can surmise that this system for storing water was built simultaneously with the terrace's walls, because the tanks are part of those same structures. These deposits could have been used for drinking water or for pot irrigation (*riego a mano*), described above. An important point to be considered is that, during the Middle Formative, not only were the great hydraulic systems invented but other ingenious devices were used locally or regionally to stimulate hydroagriculture techniques in all Mesoamerican areas where Olmec-type material has been found.

Most archaeologists and art historians have been concerned with the symbolic and religious connotations attributed to El Rey and other bas reliefs.

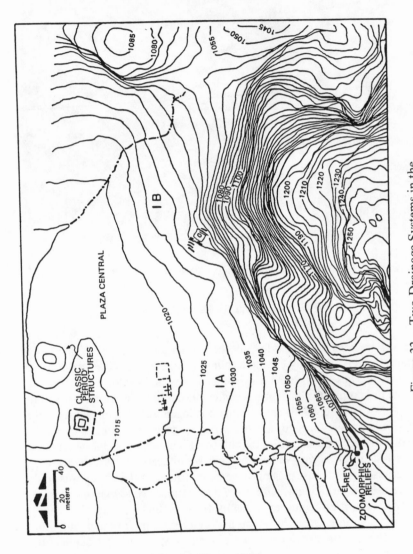

Figure 22. Two Drainage Systems in the
Chalcatzingo Hills, with El Rey Drainage at Left

Figure 23. El Rey Drainage at Chalcatzingo, Showing
Axayotl (Tank, or Water Depository) System (in black)

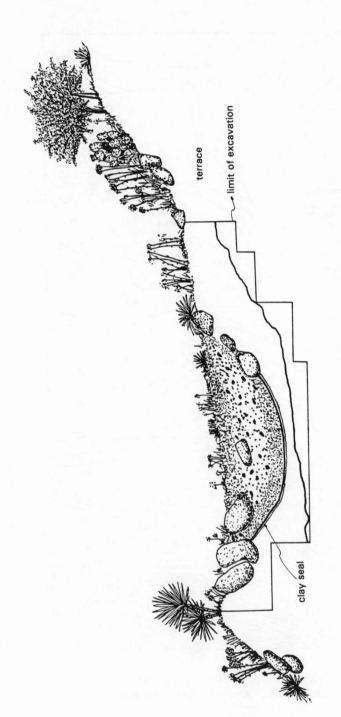

terrace

limit of excavation

clay seal

sand

sand and gravel

fine sand

0 1 2 3 4

meters

Figure 24. Profile of an Axayotl (Tank, or Water Depository)

However, since the publication of the excavations (Grove et al. 1987; Angulo 1987b-c, 1990), El Rey cannot be seen as an isolated figure but as the final element of a series of zoomorphic over phytomorphic figures performing ceremonies to bring the heavy clouds, pregnant with rain, to shower the cultivated areas. In the carving preceding El Rey, the cloud is replaced by a 10 cm (4″) chiseled groove in the upper boulder located directly above 11 conical perforations or "cup mark holes," at the beginning of the abrupt ravine (*barranquilla*) at the foot of El Rey. In the lower part of the ravine, a sand pit was found and later explored. After reviewing field notes and making new observations at the site, it was possible to understand the sand pit as part of a series of tanks, called *axayotl*, and also as being related to "the more symbolic than utilitarian canal" in the upper part of the boulder, before El Rey and the 11 conical perforations.

Gay and Pratt (1972:73-84) and Grove et al. (1987:159-170) have discussed the boulders dispersed in the lower piedmont of the site, with conical perforations or cup mark holes that are larger but otherwise similar to the group found at the foot of El Rey (see Figures 25 and 26). They classified them as either altars or places to hold holy water. In a recent work (Angulo 1990), these perforated boulders were considered as markers of a series of *axayotl* (tanks) distributed in the piedmont where Barranca and Cantera phase houses were located. A project for the careful exploration and reconstruction of several of these tanks has been delayed by bureaucratic procedures, but the idea was to rehabilitate them for use by the guards at the site and to measure how long it would take before they filled with silt, as well as to figure out their capacity and the duration that rainwater remained in them. If future excavation and restoration of the *axayotl* indicate that their rational use has practical results, the project could serve as a model to search for similar systems undetected in the ravines and along the banks of rivers, creeks, or other water sources near archaeological zones.

The *axayotl* system has been described earlier and its technological structure is reported elsewhere (Angulo 1987b-c). Suffice it here to analyze the origin of the word. *Ayotl* in Nahuatl means "turtle" as well as "gourd (*calabazo*)," while *a(tl)* means "water." The "a" is used as a prefix, while the "x" is inserted in the middle to break the cacophonic sound. Because the concavity of the tank resembles an inverted turtle shell or gigantic gourd cut in half as a vessel to hold water, the term for this tank is *axayotl* or *atecochtli* (see Siméon 1977:36).

A Dam-like Structure

A dam-like structure, part of Terrace 15 at Chalcatzingo, partially blocks or at least detours the seasonal rainwaters that run down (south-north) from Cerro Portezuelo, located between Cerro Cantera and Cerro Delgado.

Figure 25.   Conical Perforated Boulder
Marking a Water Depository, at Chalcatzingo

Figure 26.   Perforated Boulder Classified as Altar at Chalcatzingo

According to Grove and Cyphers (1987:41), "The structure is about 35m long and 7m high. It is constructed primarily of earthen fill, although lines of stones were found along its south side, apparently to resist the erosive force of the water being diverted eastward." To understand its chronology and construction system, four trenches were excavated in this monticule, revealing that it

> had been built of basketloads of fill over a small stone core. The construction had been done in one operation and was an integral part of terrace 15... [during the] Early Barranca subphase. One of the trenches was run along the structure's south side to discover... [that] the original natural drainage... was covered by the structure (ibid.:42).

The great majority of ceramic sherds among the earthen fill were of the Amate phase (1500-1100 B.C.), with some from the Barranca period (1100-900 B.C.), although "a minor amount of Cantera phase sherds occur within the surface level, suggesting a possible Cantera phase resurfacing" (ibid.). This amount of Cantera (700 B.C.) sherds could also be explained as cultural material that slipped down from the top of the structure to rest on the slope's surface.

It was disconcerting not to find a corresponding structure on the east side (Terraces 6 and 12) to complement this dam-like structure, as expected. Nor did we ever consider that Structure 3, partially explored on Terrace 6, might have been constructed with the intention of retaining rainwater during that same Amate phase.

Two monumental stone structures were found from this Amate phase. One was located at the northern end of Terrace 1, better known as Plaza Central. The second, named Structure 3, was on Terrace 6, which was partially explored with two perpendicular trenches that uncovered a heavy stone structure facing the watercourse under discussion (Prindiville & Grove 1987:78). It is difficult to know if this structure was in reality a dam or if it was an unsuccesful construction damaged by the yearly torrential drainage. Another possibility is that the function of the structure was completely irrelevant to this subject.

There might have been a new attempt to retain these waters during the Early Barranca period (1100-900 B.C.), when terraces were begun on the slopes of both *cerros* (hills) in Chalcatzingo, including the large Terrace 15 with its additional appendage, like a monticule, that extends eastward, covering the original drainage course. This same technique of piling stones to retain water during the Amate phase (1250-1100 B.C.) was used in the core of the Early Barranca dam-like structure, but this time it was covered with earth framed by a grid of stones glued with mud and protected by a surface of rocks. It is impossible to know how long this structure served its purpose, if it ever did, because it seems that the waters found a weak point at the eastern extreme of the construction, near Terrace 12, where it ran down the hill, recovering its original watercourse. This failure might be due to the increased humidity that occurred during the Barranca phase, detected by Bugé (1987:20) through pollen analysis. It was probably produced by a period of heavy rains that also increased the destructive power of the torrential waters.

The lack of evidence to sustain the position that the Early Barranca phase structure functioned as a dam convinced Grove and Cyphers (1987:42) that it was only a device to break the power of the strong temporal water course: "Diverting the water flow sharply twice, serves to slow it down and alleviates the dangers of washouts further down the hill." Curiously enough, Terraces 25, 29, and 18, located in the areas "down the hill" that were meant to be protected, have archaeological materials indicating that they were used as residential, ceremonial, and farming spaces during the Cantera phase, centuries after the dam-like structure was built. Whatever its purpose, this structure was placed in front of the watercourse either to retain the waters of the swift current or to detour them and mitigate the constant erosion of the terraces down below.

Monumental Constructions and Labor Requirements

The structure under discussion is located in the northeast extreme of Terrace 15, which is more than 200m wide and nearly 240m long. This appendage was constructed, as stated earlier, "in one operation...[as] an integral part of Terrace 15." The 35m long, 7m high appendage has an almost triangular form of nearly 30m wide at the base with a vertex that could have extended to 40-42m but which was truncated at 35m by the watercourse. This cut enclosed the triangular base, converting it into a trapezoid form with a smaller side of 3m width. The volume of this monticule is 3,430 m^3 of earthen fill combined with rows of stones that might have been carried from the nearby slopes and valley lands where Amate phase houses were distributed, covering a distance that surpassed 200m. The most important consideration is that the structure must have been completed during one dry season, when construction was not threatened by torrential waters that could carry off the materials, damaging the structure. As the dry season is from October to May, there were 210-240 possible working days during which well-organized groups of 4-10 people would have had to move this volume of earth and rocks in back-baskets (*chiquihuitl*) to form the monticule, while other workers shaped and framed the volume before covering it with rows of stones to protect the surface from an onslaught of sudden seasonal rains.

After consulting architects, engineers, and building contractors, we arrived at the conclusion that removing a volume of 2 m^3 of earth from its natural context, using only picks and shovels and transporting it by wheelbarrow a distance of 100m, would require the labor of 4 men during 8 hours of heavy work. Considering that the same kind of work had to be done in prehispanic times with digging sticks instead of picks and shovels and that the carrying had to be in back-baskets instead of wheelbarrows, the results could be reduced to half the volume of earth (1 m^3) or else the time and/or number of participants would have to be doubled.

Erasmus (1965), analyzing various forms of communal labor in several parts of the world, in different cultures with diverse socioeconomic types of organization, tabulated the number of workdays per year donated to the polity among the following social groups:

(1) In a clan organization or a "chiefdom" in New Guinea having an agricultural economy complemented by gathering, fishing, and hunting, 40-45 days of free labor were given yearly to the polity.

(2) In Feudal England, "from a third to half of a man's year could be demanded for service on his Lord's demesne" among peasants or town workmen—meaning 120-180 days yearly.

(3) Bolivian peons before the Agrarian Revolution of 1952 also had to contribute 120-180 days in benefit of the haciendas.

(4) In Ukranian Kolkhozes after World War II, "the entire family had to work at least part of the time on the Kolkhoz demesne." This figures out to 500 days of labor service for each household, estimated at 5 or 6 members on average.

(5) The idea of donating working days as a contribution to the state is firmly rejected in U.S., although Erasmus estimates that "20 to 25 percent of the average wage-earner's salary goes into taxes...giving only 52 to 65 work days per annum to the state." Recent commentaries in newspapers and other media, however, calculate the average taxation to be 25-35 percent, equivalent to 90-120 days of "donated" labor, almost equal to the feudal cases.

In his analysis of physical labor with primitive tools, Erasmus (1965) calculated that four men can move 1 m^3 of earth a day, while 5.5 men are needed to excavate rocks. Woodbury and Neely (1972:101) modified these figures, estimating for the Middle Formative constructions in the Tehuacan Valley that 5 men could move 1 m^3 per day over a 50m distance. However, when the distance is doubled, the volume of dirt is automatically diminished.

To calculate the dam-like structure of Chalcatzingo, we have to think of working teams for excavating earth with digging sticks (*uictli coa*), collecting broken stones, and carrying the stones and earth in back-baskets (*chiquihuitl*) to be piled, leveled, and framed into the monticule with stones lined in a grid to hold the earthen fill before covering the surface with rocks. This type of work would require the participation of a large number of people, considering the suggested distance of 200m or more from the lower terraces and valley lands, where the Amate sherds were found, to the construction of the upper terraces. Nevertheless, if we simplify the modified Erasmus formula to its minimum level, carrying 3,430 m^3 of fill to the dam-like structure would have required 17,150 (5 x 3,430) workmen for one day, 171.5 if done in 100 days, or 86 laborers working constantly during the 200 dry days left in the year after eliminating festivity days.

As Middle Formative societies have been considered "chiefdoms" by Sanders and Price (1968:115-128), the problem is to ascertain the population size that would be needed to provide 40 labor days of communal work during 200 calendar days. The number 40 is drawn from the New Guinea "chiefdom" case discussed by Erasmus (1965) and referred to in (1), above. Then, the equation would be set as follows: If one group of 86 people have to work 40 continuous days, five groups of 86 people would have to work continuously to accomplish 200 workdays. This operation would need 430 (5 x 86) people working simultaneously during the 200 days to build the dam-like structure.

The problem of figuring out the Barranca phase population is greater considering that more than 7 wide terraces and 5 large architectural structures were constructed during that same period. Prindiville and Grove (1987:79) figure that there were 130-325 people living in small, dispersed villages spread over 13 ha. They use Hirth's (1987:343-367) data from the studies in which he states that "8 small hamlets and isolated residences are found within a 5 km radius of the site" (60-75 minutes' walk). Hirth adds a conglomeration of large houses at the center of the site and other hamlets distributed on the recently constructed terraces at the piedmont of the sacred mountain. Even for the Amate phase, demographic estimation at Chalcatzingo involves misleading numbers when Prindiville and Grove (1987:78), based on structural remains, figure a population of 66 inhabitants living in isolated hamlets dispersed over 4-6 ha. Grove and Cyphers (1987:25), reassured by these data and by the count of sherd distribution, suggest "that the Amate phase occupation occurred on the unterraced hillslopes." Such a low estimation is incongruous with Prindiville and Grove's (1987:78) own description, in which they attribute to this early phase the two monumental architectural features classified as Structure 4 on Plaza Central and Structure 3 on Terrace 6, because these large structures could not have been constructed by 10-12 families of 5-6 members. The enormous amount of earthen fill saturated with Amate sherds found in all trenches exploring the upper Barranca terraces, as well as the dam-like structure, were not included when the low demographic estimation was calculated.

It is evident that, to date, not one of the archaeological methods for calculating population in a particular period has been completely appropriate, although the count of sherd density by square meter and the consideration of different types of architectural remains, correlated to the quality of the land settlement, have been good bases for any estimation in demography. Nevertheless, as mentioned in the Methodology section, the interrelationship of technology with social and labor organization (which plays an important role in economy) is still missing.

Woodbury and Neely (1972:98) observed in their study of the Tehuacán Valley that "[t]he magnitude of this [amount of] construction...suggests a sufficient complex social organization to secure and control such a large body of laborers." It is undeniable that all these monumental constructions and infrastructure works were the result of an affluent economy based on a demographic increment of multiethnic elements dispersed in neighborhood villages that assured the chain of production, storage, and distribution of food and other staples.

The same monumental constructions and infrastructure works serve as a mirror reflecting the existence of a well-established group that commanded a large population concentrated in a central town, or *altepetl*. They organized internal services as well as communal labor among their neighborhood protégés living in dispersed hamlets within a radius of 1-2 hours' walk (4-10 km), who periodically came to the civic-ceremonial centers from the nearby villages. These centers included a marketplace for trade and exchange of raw materials, fruits, food, arts, crafts, and other types of goods.

Social Stratification

Drawing on Wittfogel's ideas, as followed, developed, and applied to Mesoamerica by various anthropologists, Santley (1984:44-48) states that, in "Central Mexico, a principal factor affecting the rise of highly stratified societies is the control of water by a small group." However, Santley casts serious doubt upon this opinion when it comes to matters such as water abundance in the environment, the length, extension, and complexity of the hydraulic system, the social organization, and the chronological period when this type of control is considered as part of the material production. Another sociological point to clarify is why trade and exchange are considered a form of redistribution within the chiefdom dominion, when these activities could have been managed by an incipient stratified society to improve their economy. It has been found that, most of the time, this latter situation precedes any type of state organization, especially the one that apparently began during the Late Formative period.

TEQUIO, OR OBLIGATORY COMMUNAL LABOR

The concern of this essay is to hypothesize the forms of social organization that might have been used during the beginning of the Olmec horizon, coincident with the Early Barranca phase (1100-900 B.C.), when the aforementioned monumental structures were built in benefit of a large community. In this regard, there is an abundance of slight references to "obligatory communal labor," better known as *tequio*, which impressed the

Spanish chroniclers of the 16th century, a system that still can be found among small and semi-isolated indigenous communities.

Tequitl, tequiotl, or *tequio,* is defined by Siméon (1977:511-512) as "tributo, impuesto, tarea, función, responsabilidad y deber" ("tribute, taxation, task, function, responsibility and duty"). According to popular and ethnographic knowledge, *tequio* can be understood as "trabajo comunal obligatorio en beneficio del grupo social" ("obligatory communal work [done as taxation] in benefit of the social group"). It is surprising that *tequio* can still be found in small towns where people substitute communal duties for monetary taxation or contribute several days of free labor in benefit of the community. In the present-day town of Chalcatzingo, with little more than 1,000 inhabitants, a communal duty system has been in operation for centuries, according to oral testimony. Men aged 18-50 are responsible for patrolling the town at night, forming teams of two that interchange partners (in alternative roles) until they fulfill their yearly time of service. During the time of the archaeological excavations, the federal goverment provided the community with materials to open and pave a road from the highway to town. The town population contributed several weeks of free labor and complementary tasks to connect the town with the outside world. A similar system was carried out by the townspeople who dug long trenches to place pipes for water and electricity.

There is another type of *tequio,* observed in Chalcatzingo and in many small communities throughout the world, which promotes closer relations among group members. This communal service is performed by organized teams of townspeople and craftsmen who contribute raw or manufactured materials, food, or free labor during the construction of the new house that many couples receive after their marriage.

In reality, this is an ample subject that has been studied by historians, ethnographers, and cultural anthropologists, who have found remains of this practice among many different groups living today. It would be fair to point out that this system, bearing different names and found less often in large cities, can be detected in urban communities among small groups that are closely related by kinship, guild associations, ideologies, or other affinities that bind them together. The system might be seen as a form of interchange of goods, welfare, or services in which a similar kind of human reciprocity performed as personal favors persists, such as alternating invitations to dinner, interchange of gifts among the Haida (potlatch), reciprocal field labor and house construction among the Mennonites, plus many other reciprocated activities still found in social groups.

Among the Zapotecs of Oaxaca, *tequio* and *gozona* are found in the whole area, as L. Nader (1969:345) reports when she says that "gozona" is an established system of mutual aid, usually called *a mano vuelta* and *dar la mano,* translated as "a hand back" and "give a hand," respectively. In the same volume, G. DeCicco (1969:363) wrote about the Chatino and observed, "Kinship solidarity and neighborhood interdependence are further enforced by the system *dar la mano*, in which relatives, neighbors, and those who owe favors are expected to give a helping hand in house construction, feast preparations, agricultural labor, etc."

R. Wietlaner and W. Hoppe (1969:520) found in their research among the Mazatecs that

> Communal work (*tequio*) takes on exceptional importance here and is performed with the compulsory assistance of officials and citizens alike.
>
> An important detail is the custom of the municipal president of Huatla, at the busiest hour of the weekly market day, to inform the inhabitants, in the Mazatec language, about the most important events in the municipality...[as] an important aid to the formation of group spirit.

The same Weitlaner, in his study with Cline on the Chinantecs (Weitlaner & Cline 1969:549), found that

> The [municipal] president sets the communal work projects...to be accomplished during his term. Road building, maintenance of bridges, reconstruction of chapels, erection of a school, weeding the cementery, are types of tequios. All males...[except the following] are subject to such communal work. Elders or ancients are exempted, as are the officially named village musicians, who form a band. It has religious and political obligations. Some males, denominated 'intelectuals' as distinct from the general body of 'workers,' also are extempted; their public service lies in copying papers, and performing 'intelectual' duties, at the demand of the municipal goverment.

Tequio is an ancient labor enterprise that unified the economy of neighborhood groups into one collective effort, in which extra-polarity resources located at different places were utilized to obtain communal benefits. *Tequio* also has been understood as a concentration and distribution of collective labor organized by the administrators to accomplish a general service to benefit the townspeople.

A few anthropogists connect the origin of this labor system to hunting and gathering societies, as they consider that their prey was the result of a communal effort shared by a group which was part of an egalitarian society or in the stage of chiefdom. Clearly, this communal labor is not exclusive to egalitarian tribes or the type of sophisticated chiefdom attributed to Teotihuacan by several archaeologists, even when they admit that this huge city was in the stage of amalgamating clanic and large tribal groups dispersed in the hinderlands, into a confederated state by "fusion and fission," as E. Service (1975/1984:82-84) visualizes it. The present essay proposes that *tequio* might have started as early as the Middle Formative (1100-850 B.C.), when the great amount of human labor began to produce in abundance. *Tequio* and much of the obligatory communal labor existent in the world have been an important part of the basic socioeconomic systems that have achieved amazing infrastructural works among modern societies, often concealed behind the credits to municipal, state, or federal institutions.

There is no doubt that the erection of those monumental structures that are found in prehispanic archaeological zones, such as the pyramids of the Sun and the Moon, the so-called Quetzalcoatl Temple, and others that were built by early Teotihuacans during the Tzacualli and Miccaotli periods (A.D. 0-200), required a communal effort, as Millon (1973) states. Rubén Cabrera (pers. comm.), who has been in charge of the excavations in Teotihuacan from 1980 until today, is also completely convinced that the nearby towns contributed communal labor to construct those monumental pyramids. To figure the volume of earth and chiseled stone contained in these huge structures is a matter for another study, which could be correlated to the demographic estimations calculated by Millon (op. cit.) and G. Cowgill (1973) for each chronological period.

In conclusion, the present study clearly proposes that the *tequio* system might have started as early as the Middle Preclassic period. It was then that the great amount of human labor began to produce food in abundance and large infrastructural works were constructed with communal labor, such as the Chalcatzingo terraces, structures, and hydraulic works discussed earlier, as well as other infrastructure constructed by Middle Formative groups.

ACKNOWLEDGMENTS

There would not be enough space in this book for the long list of scholars, teachers, colleagues, and friends from other disciplines whom I would like to thank—apart from those mentioned in the bibliographic references who, through their observations on national and international affairs, have stimulated my interest in diverse forms of socioeconomic organization found in extinct and modern groups studied by cultural anthropology. This essay has been sponsored by Mexico's Instituto Nacional de Antropología e Historia (INAH), in which I have participated since 1955, and the Sistema Nacional de Investigadores, with which I have been associated since 1986. The four years of research in Chalcatzingo, Morelos, have been fully credited earlier in *Ancient Chalcatzingo* (Grove et al. 1987:vii-viii). The drawings and photographs included here owe to the participation of artist Chappie Angulo, who has been my life companion. I also thank Barry Isaac for his patience and dedication in helping to make this essay more readable.

REFERENCES

Acosta, Jorge R. (1971) *El Palacio del Quetzalpapalotl* (*The Palace of Quetzalpapalotl*). Mexico, DF: Instituto Nacional de Antropología e Historia, Memorias, No. 10.

Angulo V., Jorge (1964) *Teotihuacan: Un autoretrato cultural* (*Teotihuacan: A Cultural Self-Portrait*). Tesis de Maestría en Arqueología, Escuela Nacional de Antropología, Mexico, DF.

_____ (1987a) "Sistema otli-apantli dentro del área urbana" ("The Otli-Apantli System within the Urban Area"). Pp. 399-416 in Emily McClung de Tapia & Evelyn Ch. Rattray (eds.) *Teotihuacan: Nuevos datos, nuevas síntesis, nuevos problemas* (*Teotihuacan: New Data, New Syntheses, New Problems*). Mexico, DF: Universidad Nacional Autónoma de México, Instituto de Investigaciones Antropológicas, Serie Antropologícas, 72.

_____ (1987b) "The Chalcatzingo Reliefs: An Iconographic Analysis." Pp. 132-158 in David C. Grove (ed.), *infra.*

_____ (1987c) "Siete sistemas de aprovechamiento agrohidráulico localizados en Chalcatzingo" ("Seven Hydraulic Systems Found in Chalcatzingo"). *Arqueología* 2:37-75 (Mexico, DF: INAH-SEP.).

_____ (1989) "Aprovechamiento agrohidráulico en el Preclásico Medio y Superior" ("Agrohydraulic Utilization in the Middle and Upper Preclassic"). Pp. 223-236 in Marta Carmona [Museo National de Antropología] (ed.) *El Preclásico o Formativo: Avances y Perspectivas* (*The Preclassic or Formative: Advances and Perspectives*). Mexico, DF: Instituto Nacional de Antropología e Historia/Secretaría de Educación Pública.

_____ (1990) "El Axayotl: Un sistema de drenaje-aljibe localizado en Chalcatzingo" ("Axayotl: A System of Localized Drainage-Aljibe in Chalcatzingo"). Pp.89-108 in Teresa Rojas R. (ed.), 1990, *infra.*

_____ (n.d.) "Aspectos de la cultura a través de su expresión pictórica" ("Aspects of Culture through Pictorial Expression"). Forthcoming in *La pintura mural prehispánica de México: Teotihuacan* (*Prehispanic Mural Painting of Mexico: Teotihuacan*). Mexico, DF: Universidad Nacional Autónoma de México, Instituto de Investigaciones Estéticas.

Armillas, Pedro (1949) "Notas sobre sistemas de cultivo en Mesoamérica: Cultivo de riego y humedal en Cuenca del Balsas" ("Notes on Systems of Cultivation in Mesoamerica: Irrigation and Humid-lands Cultivation in the Balsas Basin"). *Anales del Instituto Nacional de Antropología e Historia* 3:86-113 (Mexico, DF).

Armillas, Pedro, Angel Palerm, and Eric Wolf (1956) "A Small Irrigation System in the Valley of Teotihuacan, Mexico." *American Antiquity* 21:396-399.

Brunnet, Jan (1967) "Geologic Studies." Pp. 66-90 in Douglas S. Byers (vol. ed.) [R. S. MacNeish, gen. ed.] *Prehistory of the Tehuacan Valley, Vol. l, Environment and Subsistence.* Austin: University of Texas Press.

Bugé, David E. (1987) "Contemporary Agriculture at Chalcatzingo." Pp. 409-419 in David C. Grove (ed.), *infra.*

_____ (n.d.) "The Paleoecology of Chalcatzingo." Paper presented at the 73rd Meeting of the American Anthropological Association, Mexico City, 1974.

Burton, Robert J. (1973) "Excavations on the Cerro Delgado," in David Grove et al., *Progress Report on Archaeological Investigations at Chalcatzingo, Morelos, 1972.* Mexico, DF: Instituto Nacional de Antropología e Historia, Archivo Arquelogía.

Cabrera Castro, Rubén, Ignacio Rodríguez, and Noel Morelos (1991) *Teotihuacan 1980-1982, nuevas interpretaciones* (*Teotihuacan 1980-1982, New Interpretations*). Mexico, DF: Instituto Nacional de Antropología e Historia.

Carrasco, Pedro, and Johanna Broda (1976) *Estratificación social en Mesoamérica prehispánica* (*Social Stratification in Prehispanic Mesoamerica*). Mexico, DF: Instituto Nacional de Antropología e Historia.

Clark, John E. (l990) "Olmecas, olmequismo y olmequizacion en Mesoamerica" ("Olmecs, Olmecism, and Olmecization in Mesoamerica"). *Arqueología* 3:49-55. (Mexico, DF: INAH)

Coe, Michael (1966) "Exploraciones arqueológicas en San Lorenzo Tenochtitlan, Ver." ("Archaeological Explorations in San Lorenzo Tenochtitlan, Veracruz"). *Boletín del Instituto Nacional de Antropología e Historia* 24:21-25 (Mexico, DF).

_____ (1967) "Segunda temporada en San Lorenzo Tenochtitlan" ("Second Season in San Lorenzo Tenochtitlan"). *Boletín del Instituto Nacional de Antropología e Historia* 24:1-10 (Mexico, DF).

Coe, Michael, and Richard Diehl (1980) *In the Land of the Olmec, Vol. 1, The Archaeology of San Lorenzo Tenochtitlan.* Austin: University of Texas Press.

Childe, V. Gordon (1946) *What Happened in History.* Harmondsworth, ENG: Penguin Books Ltd., Pelican A-108.

_____ (1950) *Social Evolution.* New York: H. Schuman.

_____ (1951) *Man Makes Himself.* New York: New American Library, Mentor Book.

_____ (1956) *Piecing Together the Past: The Interpretation of Archaelogical Data.* London: Routledge & Kegan Paul.

Cowgill, George L. (1966) "Evaluación preliminar de la aplicación de métodos de máquinas computadoras a los datos del mapa de Teotihuacan" ("Preliminary Evaluation of the Application of Computer Methods to the Data of the Map of Teotihuacan"). Pp. 95-112 in *Teotihuacan, Onceava Mesa Redonda (Teotihuacan, 11th Round Table).* Mexico, DF: Sociedad Mexicana de Antropología.

_____ (1974) "Quantitative Studies of Ubanization at Teotihuacan." Pp. 363-396 in Norman T. Hammond (ed.) *Mesoamerican Archaeology, New Approches.* Austin: University of Texas Press.

Cyphers, Ann, and David C. Grove (1987) "Chronology and Cultural Phases of Chalcatzingo." Pp. 56-62 in David C. Grove (ed.), *infra.*

DeCicco, Gabriel (1969) "The Chatino." Pp. 360-366 in Robert Wauchope (gen. ed.) & Evon Z. Vogt (vol. ed.), *infra.*

Denevan, William M. (1980) "Tipología de configuraciones agrícolas prehispánicas" ("Typology of Prehispanic Agricultural Configurations"). *América Indígena* XL:4:619-652.

Diez, Domingo (1969) *Bosquejo histórico-geográfico de Morelos, Summa Morelense (Historical-Geographical Sketch of Morelos, Summa Morelense).* (Centenary Ed., with Prologue & Notes by Valentín López González) Cuernavaca, Morelos.

Donkin, R. A. (1979) *Agricultural Terracing in the Aboriginal New World.* Tucson, AZ: Viking Fund Publications in Anthropology, No. 56.

Erasmus, Charles J. (1965) "Monument Building: Some Field Experiments." *Southwestern Journal of Anthropology* 21:277-301.

Flannery, Kent V. (1967) "The Olmec and the Valley of Oaxaca: A Model for Interregional Interaction in Formative Times." Pp. 79-110 in E. P. Benson (ed.) *Dumbarton Oaks Conference on the Olmecs.* Washington, DC: Dumbarton Oaks Research Library and Collection.

_____ (1985) "Los orígenes de la agricultura en México: Las teorías y la evidencia" ("The Origins of Agriculture in Mexico: The Theories and the Evidence"). Pp. 237-266 in Teresa Rojas R. & William T. Sanders (eds.), Vol. 2, *infra.*

_____, ed. (1976) *The Early Mesoamerican Village.* New York: Academic Press.

Flannery, Kent, Anne Kirkby, Michael Kirkby, and Aubrey Williams (1967) "Farming Systems and Political Growth in Ancient Oaxaca." *Science* 158(3800):445-454.

García Cook, Angel (1974) "Una secuencia cultural para Tlaxcala" ("A Cultural Sequence for Tlaxcala"). *Comunicaciones, Proyecto Tlaxcala-Puebla* 10:5-22 (Puebla: Fundación Alemana para la Investigación Científica).

_____ (1985) "Historia de la tecnología agrícola en el Altiplano Central, desde el principio de la agricultura hasta el siglo XIII" ("History of Agricultural Technology in the Central Highlands, from the Beginnings of Agriculture until the 13th Century"). Pp. 7-76 in Teresa Rojas & William Sanders (eds.), Vol. 2, *infra.*

_____ (1989) "El Formativo en Tlaxcala-Puebla" ("The Formative in Tlaxcala-Puebla"). Pp. 161-193 in Marta Carmona [Museo Nacional de Antropología] (ed.) *Preclásico o*

Formativo: Avances y Perspectivas (Preclassic or Formative: Advances and Perspectives). Mexico, DF: Instituto Nacional de Antropología e Historia.

García Cubas, Antonio (1888) *Diccionario geográfico, histórico y biográfico de los E.U. Mexicanos, 5 Vols.* (*Geographical, Historical and Biographical Dictionary of the United States of Mexico, 5 Vols.*). Mexico, DF: Antigua Imprenta Munguía.

Gay, Carlo T., and Frances Pratt (1972). *Chalcacingo.* Portland, OR: International Scholarly Book Services Inc.

Grove, David C., ed. (1987) *Ancient Chalcatzingo.* Austin: University of Texas Press.

Grove, David C., and Ann Cyphers G. (1987) "The Excavations." Pp. 21-55 in David C. Grove (ed.), *supra.*

Grove, David, Kenneth Hirth, David Bugé, and Ann Cyphers (1976) "Settlement and Cultural Development at Chalcatzingo." *Science* 192(4245):1203-1210.

Grove, David, Kenneth Hirth, and David Bugé (1987) "The Physical and Cultural Setting." Pp. 6-13 in David C. Grove (ed.), *supra.*

González Lauck, Rebecca (1989). "Recientes investigaciones en La Venta, Tabasco" ("Recent Investigations in La Venta, Tabasco"). Pp. 81-97 in Martha Carmona [Museo Nacional de Antropología] (ed.) *El Preclásico o Formativo: Avances y perspectivas (The Preclassic or Formative: Advances and Perspectives).* Mexico, DF: Instituto Nacional de Antropología e Historia.

Guzmán, Eulalia (1934) "Los relieves de las rocas del Cerro de la Cantera, Jonacatepec, Morelos" ("The Reliefs on the Rocks of Cantera Hill, Jonacatepec, Morelos"). *Anales del Museo Nacional de Arqueología, Historia y Etnografía, Epoca* 5:11:2:237-251 (Mexico, DF).

Hirth, Kenneth G. (1973) "Soil and Settlement at Chalcatzingo, Morelos." Report submitted to the "Proyecto Chalcatzingo" of the Centro Regional del Instituto Nacional de Antropologia e Historia (INAH), Morelos.

———— (1984) "Trade and Society in Late Formative Morelos." Pp. 125-146 in Kenneth Hirth (ed.) *Trade and Exchange in Early Mesoamerica.* Albuquerque: University of New Mexico Press.

———— (1987) "Formative Period Settlement Patterns in the Río Amatzicnac Valley." Pp. 343-367 in David C. Grove (ed.), *supra.*

Kirchhoff, Paul (1943/1960) "Mesoamérica: sus límites geográficos, composición étnica y características culturales" ("Mesoamerica: Its Geographical Limits, Ethnic Composition, and Cultural Characteristics"). Mexico, DF: Escuela Nacional de Antropología e Historia, Suplemento de la Revista *Tlatoani* (2nd ed., pamphlet).

MacNeish, Richard S. (1961) *First Annual Report of the Tehuacan Archaeological-Botanical Project.* Andover, MA: R. S. Peabody Foundation for Archaeology.

———— (1966) "The Domestication of Agriculture and the Origin of Sedentary Life." Pp.39-45 in John Graham (ed) *Ancient Mesoamerica.* Berkeley: University of California Press.

————, gen. ed. (1967-1972) *The Prehistory of the Tehuacan Valley, 4 Vols.* Austin: University of Texas Press.

Majewski, Teresita (1973) "Terrace Excavations," in David C. Grove et al., *Informe preliminar excavaciones arqueológicas en Chalcatzingo, 1973* Preliminary Report, Archaeological Exlavations in Chalcatzingo, 1973. Mexico, DF: Instituto Nacional de Antropología e Historia, Archivo Arqueologia.

Martínez DonJuan, Guadalupe (1986) "Teopantecuanitlan." Pp. 53-80 in *Arqueología y etnología del estado de Guerrero (Archaeology and Ethnology of the State of Guerrero).* Mexico, DF: Instituto Nacional de Antropología e Historia/Estado de Guerrero.

Millon, René (1973) *Urbanization at Teotihuacan: The Teotihuacan Map, Vol. 1.* Austin: University of Texas Press.

Morgan, Lewis Henry (1877) *Ancient Society.* Chicago: Charles Kerr & Co.

Nader, Laura (1969) "The Zapotec of Oaxaca." Pp. 329-359 in Robert Wauchope (gen. ed.) & Evon Z. Vogt (vol. ed.), *infra*.

Niederberger B., Christine (1976) *Zohapilco*. Mexico, DF: Instituto Nacional de Antropología e Historia/Secretaría de Educación Pública, Colección Científica, No. 30.

————— (1986) "Excavación en una área habitacional doméstica en la capital Olmeca de Tlacozotitlan" ("Excavation in a Domestic Habitation Area in the Olmec Capital of Tlacozotitlan"). Pp. 83-103 in *Arqueología y etnología del estado de Guerrero (Archaeology and Ethnology of the State of Guerrero)*. Mexico, DF: Instituto Nacional de Antropología e Historia/Estado de Guerrero.

————— (1987) *Paleopaysages et archaeologie pre-urbain du Bassin de Mexico, 2 Vols. (Paleolandscape and Pre-Urban Archaeology of the Basin of Mexico, 2 Vols.)*. Mexico, DF: Centre d'Etudes Mexicaines et Centramericaines, Collection Etudes Mesoamericaines, I-11.

Palerm, Angel (1972) *Agricultura y sociedad en Mesoamérica (Agriculture and Society in Mesoamerica)*. Mexico, DF: Secretaría de Educación Pública, SEP-SETENTAS, No. 55.

Palerm, Angel, and Eric Wolf (1972) *Agricultura y civilización en Mesoamérica (Agriculture and Civilization in Mesoamerica)*. Mexico, DF: Secretaría de Educación Pública, SEP-SETENTAS, No 32.

PNE [*Papeles de Nueva España/ Papers of New Spain*] (1905-1906) Francisco del Paso y Troncoso, ed., 6 vols. (2nd series). Madrid: Est. Tip. Sucesores de Rivadeneyra.

Paynó, Manuel (1870) "Estudios sobre la historia antigua de México" ("Studies of the Ancient History of Mexico"). *Boletín de la Sociedad Mexicana de Geografía y Estadística, Epoca* II:117-140.

Peñafiel, Antonio (1900) *Teotihuacan: Estudio histórico y arqueológico (Teotihuacan: Historical and Archaeological Study)*. Mexico, DF: Secretaría de Fomento.

Piña Chan, Román (1955) *Las culturas preclásicas de la Cuenca de México (The Preclassic Cultures of the Basin of Mexico)*. Mexico, DF: Fondo de Cultura Económica.

————— (1958) *Tlatilco*. Mexico, DF: Instituto Nacional de Antropología e Historia, Serie Investigaciones.

————— (1960) *Mesoamérica*. Mexico, DF: Institutio Nacional de Antropología e Historia, Memorias, No. 6.

Prindiville, Mary, and David Grove (1987) "The Settlements and Its Architecture." Pp. 63-81 in David C. Grove (ed.), *supra*.

Robelo, Cecilio (1912) *Diccionario de aztequismos (Dictionary of Aztec-isms)*. Mexico, DF: Editorial Fuente de Cultura.

Rojas Rabiela, Teresa (1974). *Aspectos tecnológicos de las obras hidráulicas coloniales en el Valle de México* (Technological Aspects of the Colonial Hydraulic Works in the Valley of Mexico). Tesis de Maestría, Escuela Nacional de Antropologia e Historia, Mexico, DF.

—————, ed. (1983) *La agricultura chinampera: Compilación histórica (Chinampa Agriculture: Historical Compilation)*. Mexico, DF: Universidad Autónoma de Chapingo.

————— (1985) "La tecnología agrícola mesoamericana en el siglo XVI" ("Mesoamerican Agricultural Technology in the 16th Century") . Pp. 129-231 in Teresa Rojas & William Sanders (eds.), Vol. 1, *infra*.

—————, ed. (1990) *Agricultura indígena, pasado y presente (Indian Agriculture, Past and Present)*. Mexico, DF: Ediciones Casa Chata, No. 27.

Rojas R., Teresa, and William T. Sanders, eds. (1985) *Historia de la agricultura, epoca prehispanica–siglo XVI, 2 vols. (History of Agriculture, Prehispanic Epoch–16th Century, 2 vols.)*. Mexico, DF: Instituto Nacional de Antropología e Historia, Colección Biblioteca del INAH.

Sahlins, Marshall, and Elmer R. Service (1960) *Evolution and Culture*. Ann Arbor: University of Michigan Press.

Sánchez Flores, Ramón (1980) *Historia de la tecnología y la investigación en México* (*History of Technology and Research in Mexico*). Mexico, DF: Salvat Mexicana, F. C. Banamex.

Sanders, William T. (1965) *The Cultural Ecology of the Teotihuacan Valley, Preliminary Report.* University Park, PA: Pennsylvania State University.

Sanders, William, and Barbara Price (1968) *Mesoamerica: The Role of a Civilization.* New York: Random House.

Sanders, William, Jeffrey Parsons, and Robert Santley (1979) *The Basin of Mexico: Ecological Processes in the Evolution of Civilization.* New York: Academic Press.

Santley, Robert S. (1984) "Obsidian Exchange, Economic Stratification and Evolution of a Complex Society in the Basin of Mexico." Pp. 43-86 in Kenneth Hirth (ed.) *Trade and Exchange in Mesoamerica.* Albuquerque: University of New Mexico Press.

Serra Puche, MariCarmen (1988) *Los recursos lacustres de la Cuenca de México durante el Formativo* (*Lacustrine Resources in the Basin of Mexico during the Formative*). Mexico, DF: Universidad Nacional Autónoma de México, Instituto de Investigaciones Antropológicas, Colección Posgrado, No. 3.

Service, Elman R. (1975/1984) *Los orígenes del estado y de la civilización* (*The Origins of the State and Civilization*). Madrid: Alianza Editorial.

Siméon, Rémi (1977) *Diccionario de la lengua náhuatl o mexicana* (*Dictionary of the Nahuatl or Mexican Language*). Mexico, DF: Siglo XXI, Colección América Nuestra.

Steward, Julian H. (1936) "The Economic and Social Basis of Primitive Bands." Pp. 331-345 in Robert Lowie (ed.) *Essays in Honor of Alfred L. Kroeber.* Berkeley: University of California Press.

———— (1938) *Basin-Plateau: Aboriginal Sociopolitical Groups.* Washington, DC: Bureau of American Ethnology, Bulletin 120.

———— (1948) "A Functional Development Classification of American High Cultures." Pp. 103-104 in Wendell Bennett (ed.) *A Reappraisal of Peruvian Archaeology.* Menasha, WI: Society for American Archaeology, Memoir No. 4.

———— (1953) "Evolution and Process." Pp. 313-326 in Alfred L. Kroeber (ed.) *Anthropology Today: An Encyclopedia Inventory.* Chicago: University of Chicago Press.

Steward, Julian (1955) *Theory of Culture Change.* Urbana: University of Illinois Press.

Strauss, Rafael A. (1974) "El área septentrional del Valle de México: Problemas agrohidráulicos prehispánicos y coloniales" ("The Northern Area of the Valley of Mexico: Prehispanic and Colonial Agrohydraulic Problems"). Pp. 135-17 in *Nuevas noticias sobre obras hidráulicas prehispánicas y coloniales en el Valle de México* (*New Findings about Prehispanic and Colonial Hydraulic Works in the Valley of Mexico*). Mexico, DF: Secretaría de Educación Pública/Instituto Nacional de Antropología e Historia, Centro de Investigaciones Superiores.

Tolstoy, Paul, and André Guénette (1963) *Le placement de Tlatilco dans le cadre du Pre-Classic du Bassin de Mexico* (*The Site of Tlatilco within the Framework of the Pre-Classic of the Basin of Mexico*). Montreal: Conseil des Arts du Canada.

Vaillant, George C. (1930) *Excavations at Zacatenco.* New York: American Museum of Natural History, Anthropological Papers, Vol. 32, Pt. 1.

———— (1931) *Excavations at Ticoman.* New York: American Museum of Natural History, Anthropological Papers, Vol. 32, Pt. 2.

Wauchope, Robert, gen. ed., and Evon Z. Vogt, vol. ed. (1969) *Handbook of Middle American Indians, Vol. 7, Ethnology, Part One.* Austin: University of Texas Press.

Weitlaner, Roberto, and Walter Hoppe (1969) "The Mazatec." Pp. 516-522 in Robert Wauchope (gen. ed.) & Evon Z. Vogt (vol. ed.), *supra.*

Weitlaner, Roberto, and Howard Cline (1969) "The Chinantec." Pp. 523-552 in Robert Wauchope (gen. ed.) & Evon Z. Vogt (vol. ed.), *supra.*

West, Robert (1970) "Population Densities and Agricultural Practices in Precolumbian Mexico, with Special Emphasis on Semi-terracing." *XXXVIII Internationalen Amerikanisten Kongresses, Vol. 2*:361-369. (Munich)

West, Robert, and Pedro Armillas (1950) "Las chinampas de México" ("The Chinampas of Mexico"). *Cuadernos Americanos* 50:165-182.

Wittfogel, Karl A. (1955) "Aspectos del desarrollo de las sociedades hidraulicas" ("Aspects of the Development of Hydraulic Societies"). Pp. 43-52 in *Las civilizaciones antiguas del Viejo Mundo y de América* (*The Ancient Civilizations of the Old World and of America*). Washington, DC: Pan American Union, Social Science Monographs, No. 1.

———— (1981) *Oriental Despotism*. New York: Vintage Books. (Originally published in 1957.)

Woodbury, Richard, and James A. Neely (1972) "Water Control Systems of the Tehuacan Valley." Pp. 81-153 in Frederick Johnson & Richard MacNeish (eds.) *The Prehistory of the Tehuacan Valley, Vol. 4, Chronology and Irrigation*. Austin: University of Texas Press.

PART III

WEST MEXICO AND THE U.S. SOUTHWEST

LARGE-SCALE HYDRAULIC WORKS IN PREHISTORIC WESTERN MESOAMERICA

Phil C. Weigand

INTRODUCTION

Angel Palerm, in his classic studies of the evolution of prehispanic agricultural systems (Palerm & Wolf 1972; Palerm 1973, 1990), thought that the concentration of irrigation activities that the Spanish encountered in western Mesoamerica indicated the existence of an ancient hearth of irrigation development: "This [concentration] might indicate the existence of two centers of diffusion, perhaps [one] in Central Mexico and the other in the West" (1972:63; translation mine). Palerm arrived at this preliminary observation by the examination of early Colonial documents that mentioned "hydraulic complexes," by which he meant the terraces, springs, rivers, arroyos, checkdams, swamps (*ciénagas*), irrigated fields, and raised marsh gardens (*chinampas*) in various combinations or all taken together (see Table 1). For ancient Mesoamerica above the Isthmus of Tehuantepec, he found a total of

Research in Economic Anthropology, Suppl. 7, pages 223-262.
Copyright © 1993 by JAI Press Inc.
All rights of reproduction in any form reserved.
ISBN: 1-55938-646-0

Table 1. Irrigation Systems in Western Mesoamnerica, Mentioned in
Early Colonial Documents (tabulated from Palerm 1972, 1990)

Modern State	Type of Agricultural System	Number of Mentions	Percentage of Total
Colima	field	10	78 of 294 mentions, or 27 percent
Jalisco	field	50	
Nayarit	field	18	
Colima	gardens/orchards	17	27 of 40 mentions, or 68 percent
Jalisco	gardens/orchards	9	
Nayarit	gardens/orchards	1	
Colima	cacao plantations	7	23 of 42 mentions, or 55 percent
Jalisco	cacao plantations	9	
Nayarit	cacao plantations	7	
TOTALS			128 of 376 mentions, or 34 percent

382 mentions of irrigation, in the broadest sense of that term, i.e., *regadío*. There were 294 mentions of fields, 40 mentions of gardens/orchards, and 42 mentions of cacao (plantations). The states of Jalisco, Nayarit, and Colima comprise about 20 percent of the surface of this overall unit; however, these states had 34 percent of the mentions of prehispanic *regadío*, as recorded in the early Colonial Record.

The problem with this tabulation is that it does not consider scale and/or intensity of the system, no matter what type it may have been. In fact, there is very little in the primary Colonial documentation that discusses scale or extent of the systems mentioned. Indeed, a mention is about all that occurs in most documents. For example, the *Relaciones Geográficas de Nueva Galicia* (Acuña 1988) at times note the lack of irrigation. In the "Relación de Amula: Tuscacuesco" therein (p. 74), we find that "there is no irrigation [*regadío*]...." At times, irrigation is mentioned but not described, for example, in the "Relación de Amula: Zapotitlan" (p. 67): "And they have [in] all of the aforementioned meadow an irrigation system from an arroyo that brings water down from the aforementioned volcano, with which they presently irrigate their fields of maize...." At other times, there is a description of the extent of the system, with some indication of its carrying capacity, for example, in the "Relación de la Provincia de Tenamaztlan" (p. 285):

> [A]fter it [the river] enters the valley of Teculutlán, it is used to irrigate all of the valley (which is a league long, with a width, at its widest, of a shot from an arquebuse, and, in other parts, the width of a shot from a crossbow) in which they sow wheat and maize. It renders magnificently. In this valley, they harvest maize twice each year....

Very few are mentions as detailed as the one encountered in the "Relación de Ameca" (p. 43), wherein the productive potential of an irrigation system actually is given in some detail:[1]

> [N]ear to the aforementioned pueblo [town], a large river runs....Its source is five leagues from this pueblo; it comes from several black rock outcrops with great force. The river has other springs, which join this outflow; it is such a quantity of water that with it one could irrigate more than 1500 *fanegas* of agricultural lands. At river's edge there are 10 or 12 wheat fields, in which are sown more than 500 *fanegas* of seed, which are irrigated from the river. At the river's edge, they sowed much more wheat in years past, and they have abandoned [some] for the lack of people,...; and as the Indians of this area are disappearing, hence the fields are abandoned and given up, leaving this area depopulated.

Sources later than the *Relaciones Geográficas....* (i.e., after the late 16th century) are not much better when it comes to quantification. For example, in the *Descripción de la Nueva Galicia*, written in 1621 by Domingo Lázaro de Arregui, the word *despoblado*—ostensibly meaning "depopulated"—occurs very frequently. In fact, Spanish *despoblado* most often meant "underpopulated" in comparison to prior levels. The most detailed description of irrigation is a very generalized one: "those that use irrigation sow in August and September, and harvest in March and April" (p. 82). In the documentation supplied in the González Navarro (1977) collection of *repartimientos* (partitions), which largely date to the late 1600s, phrases such as: "to construct canals in his hacienda at Copala" (p. 41), "to make drains, canals, fields, and the rest." (p. 57), or "to open canals and clean drains. . ." (p. 23) occur 10 times out of 250 documents. In these documents, obviously oriented toward Native American service within the Spanish haciendas, irrigation systems seem neither large-scale nor very important. For the same area, the classic statistical study by Bárcena (1983), first published in 1888, irrigation obviously is of little importance; typical are phrases such as, "...they use [arroyos] to irrigate on a small scale" (p. 460), and "There exists an arroyo and various permanent springs...that they use to irrigate over 16 *fanegas*" (p. 501). (All of the foregoing translations are mine.)

What obviously is lacking from these historical descriptions is their contextualization in field surveys and on-the-ground inspections for evidences of ancient irrigation systems. For our study area in the basins of Etzatlán-Magdalena and Teuchitlán-Ahualulco-Tala, Jalisco (see Figure 1), we have provided precisely that contextualization. Our results, which are very preliminary, are a surprize to us, as we did not anticipate the large scale of ancient irrigation that we encountered. We have found both dense settlement systems and well-developed, contemporaneous hydraulic systems. Elsewhere, research has shown an intimate social relationship between the two systems, which indeed must be viewed as complementary (Armillas 1971, 1987; Adams 1965, 1966, 1974; Adams & Nissen 1972; Boehm de Lameiras 1986; Butzer

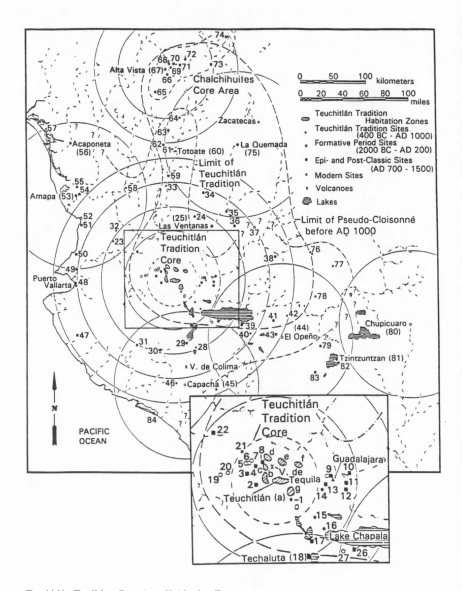

Teuchitlán Tradition Core Area Habitation Zones

a. Teuchitlán/El Refugio   e. Las Pilas
b. Ahualulco   f. Sta. Quiteria
c. La Providencia   g. San Juan de los Arcos
d. Huitzilapa

Figure 1.   The Teuchitlán Tradition of Western Mexico and Related Sites

Teuchitlán Tradition and Other West Mexico Sites

1.	Sta. María de las Navajas	43.	Jacona
2.	Sta. Cruz de Bárcenas	43.	El Opeño
3.	Etzatlán	45.	Capacha
4.	Las Cuevas	46.	Comala
5.	El Arenal	47.	Tomatlán
6.	Sta. Rosalia	48.	Ixtapa
7.	San Pedro	49.	San Juan de Abajo
8.	La Joya	50.	La Penita
9.	Tabachines/El Grillo	51.	Sta. Cruz
10.	Matatlán	52.	Matanchen
11.	Coyula	53.	Amapa
12.	Tonalá	54.	Ixcuintla
13.	Ixtepete	55.	Coamiles
14.	Bugambilias	56.	Acaponeta
15.	El Molino	57.	El Calón
16.	Jocotepec	58.	Guaynamota
17.	Zacoalco	59.	Las Juntas
18.	Techaluta	60.	Totoate
19.	Pipiole	61.	Cerro Prieto
20.	San Felipe	62.	Tenzompan
21.	Llano Grande	63.	Huejuquilla
22.	Ixtlán del Río	64.	La Florida
23.	San Pedro Langunillas	65.	San Andés de Teul
24.	Teul	66.	El Chapín
25.	Juchipila/Las Ventanas	67.	Alta Vista
26.	Tizapan	68.	Pedragoso
27.	Citala	69.	Calichal
28.	Gómez Farias	70.	Gualterio
29.	Sayula	71.	Moctezuma
30.	Tuxcacuezco	72.	Cruz de la Boca
31.	Autlán	73.	Sain Alto
32.	Sta. María del Oro	74.	Río Grande
33.	Cerro Cototlán	75.	La Quemada
34.	Tlaltenango	76.	San Francisco del Rincón
35.	Jalpa	77.	La Gloria
36.	Nochistlán	78.	El Cobre
37.	Teocaltiche	79.	Zacapu
38.	San Miguel el Alto	80.	Chupicuaro
39.	Cojumatlán	81.	Tzintzuntzán
40.	Jiquilpán	82.	Ihuatzio
41.	Ixtlán/El Salitre	83.	Tingambato
42.	Ecuandureo	84.	Cuyutlán

1976; Chi 1936; Doolittle 1990; Farrington 1974; Harrison & Turner 1978; Jacobsen & Adams 1958; Kolata 1991; Kosok 1965; Masse 1981; Neely 1974; Parsons 1976; Puleston 1977; Sanders et al. 1979; Turner & Harrison 1983; etc.). This essay, however, does not enter into the "Oriental Despotism" discussion (cf. Wittfogel 1957, Mitchell 1973), but rather presents our field results concerning large-scale hydraulic works in the aforementioned basins in Jalisco.

THE SETTING

Both the Etzatlán-Magdalena and Teuchitlán-Ahualulco-Tala valleys were closed basins; both are drained by canal and river systems today. The latter valley's drainage is very old and was a natural process, while the former's is new and was accomplished by canal digging during the 1950s (Orive Alba 1970, Weigand & Ron 1987). The historically known lake in the Etzatlán-Magdalena basin covered about 12,000 ha at maximum, as evidenced by its highest beaches (*playas*), but far more frequently only about 7,000 ha. The Spanish encountered the lake at its latter size. Both basins are surrounded by high mountains, most of which are of volcanic origin. These volcanos produced large amounts of ash. The alluvial bottom soils, when combined with this ash, have very high agricultural potential if properly drained. More detailed descriptions of the natural regime can be found in Weigand (1985), Comisión Nacional del Agua (n.d.), and the Secretaría de Agricultura y Recursos Hidráulicos (n.d.).

The strategic profile for this zone is superior, but the low areas, or *vasos reducidos*, required management for full exploitation, both anciently and today. The *lagos, lagunas*, and *ciénagas* (lakes, lagoons, and swamps) were far too soggy to support agriculture without some sort of modification and water management. The 7,000 ha Laguna de Etzatlán-Magdalena had an average depth of 3m and an average capacity of 210,000,000 m^3 of water. The lake of the Teuchitlán-Ahualulco-Tala basin was gone before humans tried to alter it for agricultural purposes, having been captured by the Río Ameca and hence drained by that river into the Pacific Ocean at the Valle de las Banderas. At Spanish contact, however, it had many low areas, which were called *ciénagas* or, at times, *lagunas*. These low areas have been calculated at 7,000-9,500 ha of swampy zones and standing water, therefore containing ca. 225-270,000,000 m^3 of water.

THE ARCHAEOLOGICAL BACKGROUND

More comprehensive materials may be found in Weigand (1985, 1989, 1990a, 1990b, 1993), Soto de Arechavaleta (n.d.), and Galván (1984). The first evidences for hydraulic works in our study zone are from the Classic period (ca. A.D. 200-900). Complexity in the settlement systems and the cultural realm precede that period by at least 1,500 years. The El Opeño phase (ca. 1500-1000 B.C.) in the study area is characterized by complex shaft-tombs, which marked high status for the upper elements of a settled series of societies heavily involved in rare resource procurement and trade. These crypts contain jade, turquoise, imported ceramics, and many other status-marking elements. Olmec influences are notable for their lack of any importance, though the blue-gray jade must have passed through zones influenced by them. By the San Felipe phase (ca. 1000-300 B.C.), the tombs become slightly simpler, but surface architecture occurs. Most preserved buildings are circular platforms that average 25-30m in diameter and 2m high. These platforms served as burial mounds—shaft-tombs for the elites and simple pits for the rest. These sites are located on the uppermost beaches of the lakes and lagoons of the zone, obviously well situated for the exploitation of the waters and their shores as well as the lower terraces of the hills, which then were quite well-watered by streams. Certainly, at this time the present-day rainfall patterns and soil regimes were firmly in place, and they probably remained little modified until the massive deforestation of recent years.[2]

The late Formative record is far more complete. The El Arenal phase (ca. 300 B.C.-A.D. 200) is characterized by the appearance of the unique and quite unusual architectural style of concentric circles. These circular buildings were laid out from radial centers and are remarkably symmetrical (Figure 2). They serve as a signature for the Teuchitlán Tradition from this time period until the tradition collapsed between A.D. 700 and 900. (Weigand 1990b). The El Arenal phase sites, too, contain the monumental shaft-tombs and extremely rich figurine offerings for which West Mexico is so well-known in the art history-oriented literature.

The Ahualulco phase (ca. A.D. 200-400) marks the beginning of monumental surface architecture of five-element circles (Figure 2). Florance (1992) has suggested a 200-year downward revision of the chronology of the El Arenal and Ahualulco phases for a better fit with the Chupicuaro ceramic styles of the middle Lerma Valley (Figure 1). At this date, the disagreement about the chronology cannot be resolved. Nonetheless, it is clear that the population implosion into the two study basins and the resulting very large settlement, as well as in the valleys of Amititán and Tequila, began during the Ahualulco phase.

Whatever the causes for this rapid demographic intensification, the result was the impressive settlement hierarchy of the Teuchitlán I phase (ca. A.D. 400-700), in which we have sites where the processes of urbanization are underway, represented by craft specialization, an ideographic writing system, monumental architecture, etc. The largest settlement is near the modern town of Teuchitlán: ca. 3,000 ha of circular ceremonial buildings and ballcourts (both in 4 tiers and represented in 18 ancient precincts), palace-like structures and

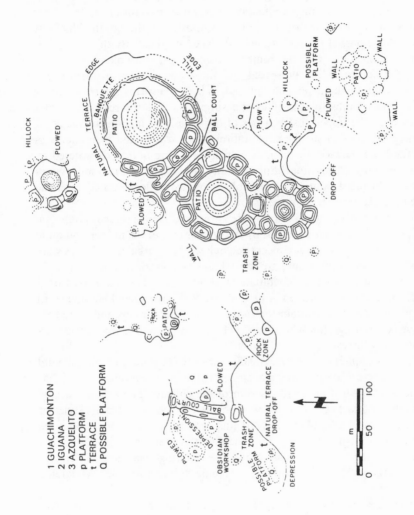

1 GUACHIMONTON
2 IGUANA
3 AZQUELITO
p PLATFORM
t TERRACE
Q POSSIBLE PLATFORM

Figure 2. The Guachimontó Complex at Teuchitlán, Jalisco, One of 18 Precincts within the Habitation Zone

other residential areas clearly meant for an elite, massive obsidian workshops which supplied cores and large blade blanks to more numerous other workshops, highly terraced garden areas, more open in-field terraces, and an extensive habitation zone with some 1,000 platform-court complexes of varying degrees of complexity (though mostly poorly preserved). We have estimated, based on 60 percent coevality, a population of 20-25,000 inhabitants for the habitation zone, though this calculation does not take into account the large number of ceremonial complexes and habitations located in the present-day sugarcane fields just below the foothill component of this site, from which the estimate was made. In addition, from this time period comes the first firm evidence for the hydraulic systems that we have been able to document, in a preliminary fashion, from the sugarcane fields.

Other sites, such as the Ahualulco, San Juan de los Arcos, Huitzilapa, Las Pilas, and Santa Quitería habitation zones, also were quite large and well-developed. These habitation zones were considerably smaller: 300-500 ha each. For all of the habitation zones, suggested population densities are about 600-800/km^2, thus falling short of what Sanders et al. (1979) think appropriate for an urban classification. Whether or not there existed actual cities in these sections of West Mexico during the Classic period cannot be resolved here, but we can certainly demonstrate that the processes of urbanization were underway.

Very likely, the societies of the Teuchitlán I phase were organized as states, as well. The interest in rare resource procurement and trade over long distances for status markers is very well-developed. One export was highly processed prismatic blades; another was carefully ground obsidian eccentrics and jewelry; a third valuable export was the codical-style pseudo-cloisonné ceramic vessels (Holien 1977, Weigand 1992b). Infrequent Thin Orange vessels are represented from sherd collections, but there are very few other imports of obvious Teotihuacan manufacture. Teotihuacan seemed to have had no major stylistic impact in this area at all (Weigand 1992a). Chemical turquoise exists in small quantities from the status burials of this period, and marine shell from the Pacific coast is frequent, as are semiprecious stones from the northern canyons and possibly the Chalchihuites area of Zacatecas (Figure 1).

The frequent ballcourts may have served as the locations (and institution) for the distribution of such exotica, as well as the organization for the regional social integration of the societies of the Teuchitlán I phase (Weigand 1991). Such a model has been proposed for another hydraulically-oriented society in the New World, the Hohokam (Wilcox 1991). The hydraulic system of this phase, to be discussed in more detail below, was complex: terraces, canals, spring management, and *chinampas* (raised marsh or lagoon fields) were all in place by ca. A.D. 500 and integrated into an interdependent unit in selected zones.

The Teuchitlán II phase (ca. A.D. 700-900) represents the period of collapse and reorganization of the settlement system and culture of the entire region.

The parallel at the other extreme of Mesoamerica was the period of decline and reorganization that the Maya underwent at approximately the same time. Everything changed. The unique and symetrical architectural style, based upon concentric circles, disappeared, and rectangular/square buildings took their place. Changes are noted also in burial practices, culinary and decorated ceramics, figurine types, etc. The settlement system was completely reorganized, in addition, and new sites, such as Santa Cruz de Bárcenas, Techaluta, and Coyula, grew up to replace the older settlements. These sites are impressive, too, but their elite architecture had neither the grace nor formality of the prior tradition. In the Teuchitlán-Ahualulco-Tala basin, many of these new settlements are located at some distance from the lake/marsh shores, away from the area that had been so intensely developed as *chinampas*. These sites are terraced, but their inhabitants apparently were not as involved in marsh agriculture as was the case during the Teuchitlán Tradition.

The Santa Cruz de Bárcenas phase (ca. A.D. 900-1250) is not well understood, but its inspiration certainly came from the outside. For example, the palace-like buildings found at Tabacal (also called Tabaquero), within the Santa Cruz de Bárcenas habitation zone, are close copies of the open "U" buildings found by Muller and Lizardi (1959) at Tulancingo, Hidalgo (Figure 3). The great stelae that were looted from Tabacal resembled the "Atlantean" figures found at Tula, Hidalgo, the postulated capital of the Toltec polity for the early Postclassic period in Central Mexico. Without doubt, outside influences in the study area are from the northern sectors of Central Mexico and the Bajío (eastern-most Jalisco, northern Michoacán, Guanajuato, and Querétaro). We are not able to identify a single lakeside hydraulic feature from this phase, though it is very probable that many of the terraces adjoining then active streams were irrigated. Some of these terraces have associated early Postclassic remains and are still irrigated today.

The late Postclassic, or Etzatlán phase (ca. A.D. 1250 to Spanish contact), witnessed still another reorganization within the study zone. Possibly in response to the first stirrings of the rise of the Purépecha (Tarascan) state in the lake districts of Michoacán and the expansion out of the north of the Caxcan states, the settlements of the early Postclassic were mostly abandoned. Tala (Tlala) and Etzatlán began their rise to prominence. Both became capitals of extensive settlement hierarchies by ca. A.D. 1400.

When the Spanish entered in force in this area with the Guzmán expedition (1530), they arrived during or just after the arrival of the first epidemiological front of European diseases. As with the Purépecha state, there was little initial military resistance, perhaps due to demoralization and/or shock (Weigand 1992c). Active and violent political resistance began by the mid-1530s and was finally suppressed in 1542. The famed "Guerra de Mixtón" was in reality the last phase of this conflict; this long war cost the Spanish as many casualties as they suffered in the conquest of Central Mexico. In short, it is not true that

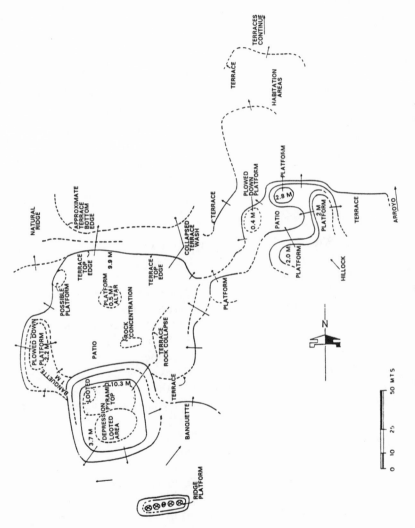

Figure 3. Santa Cruz de Bárcenas, Tabacal Complex, Jalisco

233

Table 2. Chronology of the Teuchitlán Region[a]

Date	Phase Name	Reference
1500-1000 B.,C. (Early Formative)	El Opeño	Oliveros (1974), Weigand (1985)
1000-300 B.C. (Middle Formative)	San Felipe	Weigand (1985)
300 B.C.-200 A.D. (Late Formative)	El Arenal	Long (1966), Weigand (1985)
200-400 A.D. (Early Classic)	Ahualulco	Weigand (1985)
400-700 A.D. (Middle Classic)	Teuchitlán I	Weigand (1985), Galván (1984), Soto de A. (n.d.)
700-900 A.D. (Epiclassic)	Teuchitlán II	Weigand (1985), Galván (1984)
900-1250 A.D. (Early Postclassic)	Bárcenas	Weigand (1990b), Galván (1984)
1250 to Spanish Contact (Late Postlassic)	Etzatlán	Weigand (1990b, 1991)

[a] Florance (1992) suggests a downward revision by 200 years of lthe El Arenal and Ahualulco phases.

the conquest of West Mexico was pacific; the resistance was belated rather than immediate, but nonetheless strong and well-organized.

The Spanish did not comment about hydraulic systems in West Mexico until the aforementioned *Relaciones Geográficas....* of the 1580s. The documents from Guzmán and Cortés de San Buenaventura (1937) have very little sociological depth; the demographic materials, while probably accurate in general terms, are not always specific, either. Pedro Armillas (pers. comm.) warned me about drawing strong conclusions about this type of data. He reminded me that the first Spanish in the Basin of Mexico walked over the causeways that went through the middle of the great Chalco-Xochimilco *chinampa* systems but did not comment on them, either, because they had another more immediate agenda. In our study area, we do not have good descriptive documents of the countryside between those of Guzmán and Cortés (1937) for the 1520-30s and the *Relaciones Geográficas....* (1988) some 50 years later.

The hydraulic systems that were reported by the Spanish, as outlined above, do not appear to have had the scale or intensity of development that we see for those of the Teuchitlán Tradition. Contrary to the Central Mexico situation, where the maximum development of the *chinampa* systems apparently took place during the late Postclassic, under the sponsorship of the Culhua Mexica (Aztec) and the rulers of Texcoco (Armillas 1971, 1987; Sanders 1971; Boehm de Lameiras 1986; Hicks 1991; Palerm 1972, 1973, 1990), the maximum period of hydraulic development in the study area apparently took place during the

KEY:

▲ Sites ⟵ Invasion Route or Thrust

● Battle Sites ⊜ Lake

(Territorial limits are approximate)

TEULES CHICHIMECS CAXCAN STATES	MARCH STATES	Tonalá's fortifications
1 Tuitlán	1 Etzatlán	a Las Paredes
2 Tlatenango	2 Tonalá	b Coyula
3 Teul	3 Zacoalco	c Atenco
4 Juchipila	4 Sayula	d Huentitan
5 Jalpa	5 Autlán	e Mesa Colorada
6 Nochistlán	6 Acolimán	

Figure 4. The Trans-Tarascan Double Military Frontier
on the Eve of the Spanish Conquest: A.D. 1460s-1521

Classic period and then tapered off significantly during the Postclassic. During the late Postclassic, this zone was a double frontier wedged between the Purépecha and Caxcan expansive military activities. This zone, having become a military march between two systems bent on raiding and conquest, may not have had the stability to maintain complex and large hydraulic systems. The fall off of hydraulic activity continued during the Colonial and Republican periods, as mentioned. It revived only after the 1920s, when the demographic recovery of this zone was well underway (see Figure 4 and Table 2).[3]

THE CLASSIC PERIOD HYDRAULIC SYSTEM

At the outset, we should deal with how we know that the particular systems to be discussed are actually from the Classic period (A.D. 200-900). The most obvious answer is that the very light artifact cover found within the *chinampa* zone is by far mostly from the Classic period. In the lake soil low areas, any rock that is found is cultural. There are scatters of obsidian, including infrequent workshops dedicated to touch-up activities. Sherds are not frequent, and most are culinary wares and thus not always easy to date. There are finds of the Oconahua and Teuchitlán series of Red-on-White ceramics, however, and these are definitely Classic period in date. But the firmest evidence is to be seen in the interrelationships between the low, lake-oriented settlement and ceremonial system and the canals and *chinampas*. This association is especially notable in the swamp areas most intensively surveyed, such as the area of confluence of the Arroyo las Animas and the Río Mezquite just north of San Juan de los Arcos, in the heart of the present-day sugarcane field systems of the Municipio de Tala. In this area, which today is still a poorly drained sub-basin, comprising what remains of the Ciénaga de Tala (see the Ortelius map, which was first published in 1579), there are 15 ceremonial circles within the 6×3 km area of the Ciénaga, countless habitations, and the badly destroyed remains of a *chinampa* district. Few of these features per se are preserved, but they remain as soil stains, areas of differential plant growth and, most importantly, in the memories of the informants whom we used as guides in order to survey in such dramatically altered field systems. The interlacing of settlement and hydraulic features is a strong affirmation of the coevality of both systems. Some of the ceremonial centers and most of these habitations literally must have been islands within the overall Ciénaga.

The evidence for coevality of settlement and *chinampas* exists in the Magdalena area, too, though not as strongly or with such numbers of ceremonial circles. The third area where evidence of coevality of Teuchitlán period architecture and *chinampas* occurs is the zone just south of Estanzuela. Estanzuela has three ceremonial precincts in the foothills just above the lake's ancient shore. The Potrero Abajo (or Loma Baja) precinct has two circles,

Estanzuela per se has two more, and the Arroyo de los Lobos has three circles in its precinct. The latter two precincts have medium-sized ballcourts; the first precinct is so plowed over that the ballcourt cannot be identified, if it existed at all. There is very little Postclassic material hereabouts, and that which does exist consists of widely scattered *ranchos*, each having one or two platforms without any ceremonial components. The few artifacts found within the Estanzuela *chinampa* zone are not really conclusive, though Teuchitlán Red-on-White is in the local collections from the *chinampa* area. Proxemics and the general outlay of the *chinampa* zone at Estanzuela strongly suggest a Classic period association. The three aforementioned precincts all belong to the greater Teuchitlán habitation zone.

The terrace systems that exist in the area are indeed both Classic and Postclassic in date, but those that exist within the Classic period habitation zones are without doubt from that same time. They, too, are integrated into the settlement systems, often involving ceremonial buildings and/or ballcourts in their overall configuration. While these terraces were mostly unirrigated, their functions as checkdams and general erosional and runoff control factors meant that they played an important role within the hydraulic system. Indeed, there is every reason to believe that the system was quite interdependent and interrelated, possibly so even by design, but certainly so in fact of utility. The spring areas and terraces at the lower edges of the foothills, often very close to the upper beaches of the swamps, certainly were irrigated, as some of them still are today. It is tempting to see these as the earliest hydraulic features in the study zone, but no real evidence yet exists to substantiate that idea. A few of these spring irrigation features may comprise some of the mentions numbered by Palerm (Palerm & Wolf 1972), cited above.

What remains impressive is that the great number of systems documented in the early Colonial records have such prominent roots in the Classic period. Also impressive is that the quantity of Postclassic and early Colonial *regadío* systems apparently represent a decline from the complexity (if not scale) of the systems we are beginning to document for the Classic.

To date, we have documented, using the methodology of the archaeology-in-the-field approach (see Note 3), four definite zones of *chinampas* and two other zones as strong possibilities. Taken together, the four definite zones constitute a little over 30 km² (3,250 ha). Due to the nature of present-day agricultural practices for sugarcane, I believe that this surface is just a fraction of what once existed; that a far greater area was involved in marsh gardens is extremely likely, given the distribution of architecture (and even burial areas) within or adjoining the swampy areas. In the discussion that follows, however, I will restrict my comments only to the zones where *chinampas* can be proven (though to differing degrees) to exist. With the likelihood of vastly understating the area dedicated to *chinampas* will come, logically, an understatement of the productive benefits to the Teuchitlán system. At this point in our study, it is best to keep the argument as conservative as possible, and this will be my intention throughout the rest of the text.

The two aforementioned lake basins are ideal for *chinampa* development. Palerm (1990:456) defined a *chinampa* as "a small artificial island constructed in shallow places of a sweet water lake or swamp" (translation mine). Both of the basins in the study area are shallow yet very well and consistently watered. An abundant shoreside spring and stream system existed. The upper shores, without this exterior source of water, would have been left vulnerable to drying. Obviously, in very dry years the upper shore area would have suffered the most, just as in very wet years the lower shore area would have been flooded out. It seems no mistake, then, when we find most of the *chinampas* in this area located in the middle shore areas of the basins, an ample zone in which sub-irrigation (the penetration of canal water through the soil to the root levels) was always possible no matter how wet or dry the year and/or season.

THE LAGUNA DE MAGDALENA SYSTEM

By far best preserved is the *chinampa* area found in the Magdalena sub-basin of the Etzatlán-Magdalena lake. Most of this lake has been drained (see Note 3; also, Weigand & Ron 1987), but the Laguna de Magdalena (a term which refers only to this sub-basin in the Recursos Hidráulicos and Reforma Agraria archives) was left preserved to serve as a reservoir for the irrigation systems just to its south. The Dren Norte (see Figure 5) controls the level of this Laguna, plus the amount of water available to the south. This sub-basin is about 1,000 ha in extent, and much of it has never been plowed, subjected to land leveling projects, or modified in any major manner since the building of the *chinampas* there during prehispanic times. A series of small ridge dams keep the sub-basin's water at a regulated depth, though most often it is deeply drained for the southern sugarcane fields. The two dams, called the Presa del Trigo and the Presa del Llano, scraped away a section of the *chinampa* zone but also guaranteed that much of the land surface was never dramatically altered.

Not since the ridge dams were finished in the late 1950s has the Laguna completely dried out, though during the middle 1970s it was so low that cattle could wade across it easily. The rains of the following season were torrential and sustained. Not only did the Laguna de Magdalena fill backup, but so did another 3,500 ha of the Laguna de Etzatlán-Magdalena. As the sub-basin at Magdalena was refilling, we noticed that the *chinampas* were outlined in detail we had never before seen (see Figure 6). The rising water settled into the looser soil of the canals and ditches first, permitting that soil to settle further and leaving the *chinampa* islands very well defined. The elevation of the top edge of the upper shore (and above which no *chinampa* remains are found) is 1,360m above sea level. The lower edge of the lower shore is 1,356m, and apparently

Figure 5. The Dren Notre, Which Regulates the Outflow of Irrigation Waters from the Laguna de Magdalena and Its Zone, Jalisco

this zone was too soggy to permit utilization, as there are no *chinampa* remains that deep. The *chinampa* remains are between the top edge of the upper shore (1,360m) and the 1,358m elevation contour. More than 50 percent of the Laguna de Etzatlán-Magdalena falls within this elevation range, so there is a strong possibility that far more *chinampa* areas exist, beyond those at the Laguna de Magdalena. Indeed, at La Joya (see below) there is another such zone.

Firmly dating the Laguna de Magdalena systems has proved to be a challenge. There was never any doubt at all that the system is prehispanic. The Recursos Hidráulicos personnel to whom we showed the *chinampas*, and Ing. Francisco Ron Siordia, who was studying the basin as a project for the Universidad de Guadalajara's School of Engineering, all agreed that it was not recent. Since both the dams contain waters with raw sewage from the city of Magdalena, the detailed survey following the summer rains of 1976 proved to be an ambivalent experience, but the excitement of discovery won out over the odors.

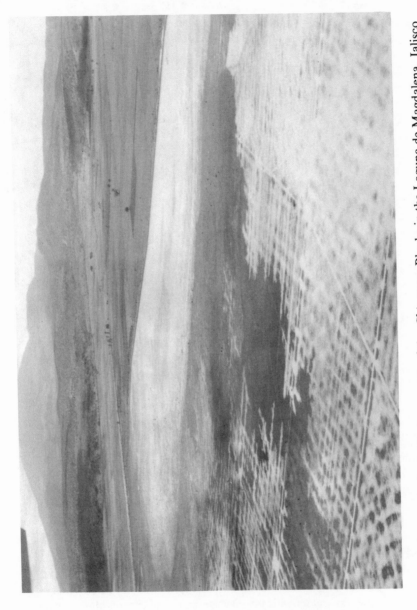

Figure 6. Oblique Aerial-photograph of the *Chinampa* Blocks in the Laguna de Magdalena, Jalisco

We found no Postclassic ceramic material within the *chinampa* zone. Postclassic ceramics, however, are found on the southwestern outskirts of the current city of Magdalena, where a small irrigated garden system still functions. This system is watered by springs, which helped keep the *chinampa* system maintained as well. Traces of ditches between the springs and the upper shore still can be seen. The infrequent and small habitation areas within these *chinampas* are composed of rock alignments, very occasional *metates* (grinding stones), and obsidian blades and flakes. Two exploratory looters' pits showed sherds of Classic period Red-on-White and polished red ceramics, though the sherds were too small to actually type.

Just above the *chinampa* area, however, is the extensive Huitzilapa habitation zone, with four known ceremonial precincts featuring the circular architecture of the Classic period, along with ballcourts, high-status burials, high-status residential compounds, and obsidian workshops. The habitation area covers around 500 ha, and the western-most components of this zone overlook the Magdalena basin. The Postclassic settlement of Xochitepec, which was relocated to the site of the contemporary city of Magdalena, is located still further away. Thus, site proxemics, in addition to the light artifact cover, argues strongly for a Classic period assignation for the *chinampa* zone. These *chinampas* had small but regularly situated habitation areas within them. The rock alignments mentioned above are seldom more than several meters long and only a few centimeters above the surface.

As Figure 7 shows, the *chinampas* here are well organized into blocks that average ca. 300m × 150m. These blocks are surrounded by the major canals so visible in the aerial photographs (Figure 6). These canals average about 4m wide but can be up to 6m. Their depths are unknown, but they most likely were deep enough to allow canoe-borne traffic within the *chinampas*. A consistent feature of the largest canals appears to be regularly spaced access to all types of other canals and ditches. Separating the large blocks are either these canals or those just slightly smaller (which average about 3m wide). Within each large block is an access canal that runs its length.

The *chinampa* islets are laid out to conform to the rectangular or square format of the canals and larger ditches. In overall perspective, the layout is regular and highly uniform, though some islets are larger than others. The largest islets are 20m × 10m, but most are ca. 10m × 15m. This morphology makes them look more like the raised fields of the Llanos de Mojos of Bolivia (Denevan 1966, Parsons & Denevan 1967) or those of Pulltrouser Swamp of Belize (Turner & Harrison 1983) than those of Central Mexico (Armillas 1971), except that they are far more geometrical than the former two examples. The surface of each individual *chinampa* could range from about 150 m^2 to 200 m^2, or about 0.02 ha. Using the Central Mexico calculations found in Sanders (1971), Sanders et al. (1979), Parsons (1976), and Hicks (n.d.), about which more will follow, it would take about 15 of these *chinampa* islets to support

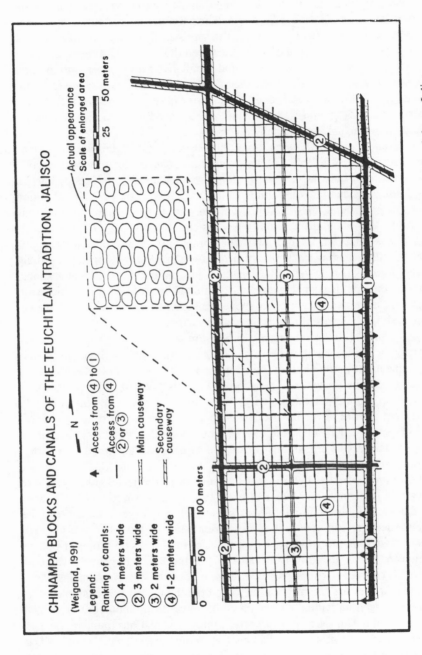

Figure 7. Plan of the *Chinampa* Blocks and Canals in the Laguna de Magdalena, Jalisco

a household of 5-7 members. We can calculate, in addition, that about 25-30 percent of the surface of this *chinampa* zone was covered by water, as canals, pools, and ditches, thus leaving 70-75 percent for the cultivation surface. Habitation areas within the *chinampa* blocks did not noticeably subtract from the amount of surface that could have been cultivated.

Elevated areas on the edges of the largest canals may be the remains of causeways through the *chinampa* districts. If so, they appear to have been breached frequently and at regular intervals. Major canals are oriented along north-south or east-west axes, which bend at times to conform with the upper shore topography. Dikes would have proved necessary to have kept water in the upper part of the system. The canals classified as numbers 1 and 2 in Figure 7 would have functioned as the systems of delivery and drainage. The ditches classified as numbers 3 and 4 in Figure 7 would have served as the system of distribution within the blocks. Each large block covers 3-5 ha, though the higher figure is more common. Within each block, therefore, 12-18 households could have been supported.

While only about 40 blocks like those illustrated in Figures 6 and 7 can be seen in such good detail, based on the visibility of the larger canals, we have calculated over 200 such blocks for this one particular area. The Laguna de Magdalena *chinampa* system, therefore, could have supported 2,400-3,600 households (or 12,000-18,000 people, figured at 5 per household). This calculation is considerably higher than that which we had calculated for the entire area of the Huitzilapa settlement system, and it obviously does not take into account the productive potential (and, thus, population) that could have been supported from the dry terraces and fields. At this point in our study, we cannot resolve this discrepancy. Even if only half of the *chinampas* were in production at any one time, this is still a higher demographic figure than we had calculated based just on what is visible within the Huitzilapa system.

THE LAGUNA DE ETZATLAN SYSTEM

The other *chinampa* system within the Etzatlán-Magdalena basin that we have been able to partially document is located in front of the small present-day village of La Joya. The closest ceremonial centers are located near the Laguna Colorada: La Providencia is composed of two small precincts with two ballcourts (see Figure 8), and Laguna Colorada is a single precinct apparently without a ballcourt. Neither of these small habitation zones has monumental architecture and, since they are located about half-way between Huitzilapa and Ahualulco, they likely were dependent centers. At La Joya, we have mapped 1,264 obsidian mines (Weigand & Spence 1982), which makes this mining area comparable to that of the Sierra de las Navajas in the state of Hidalgo (Charlton & Spence 1982). While we feel that most of this mining was Postclassic, it probably was underway in Classic times.

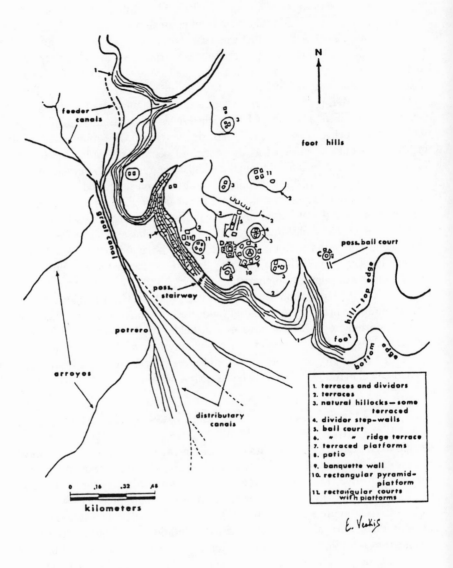

Figure 8. The La Providencia Ceremonial Circles, in the Laguna Colorada Basin, with the Great Canal and Its Distributaries, Jalisco

The *chinampa* zone in front of La Joya has about the same elevational configuration as that at the Laguna de Magdalena, except that the former is situated slightly more deeply into the middle and lower shore zone. While this zone appears quite clearly on the early aerial photographs taken by the Compañía Aereofoto Mexicana during the 1930s and 1940s, it is not preserved today. Land leveling equipment and deep disk plowing for sugarcane cultivation have eliminated the surface vestiges of this area. In field survey, we could find an occasional lineal pattern of differential growth or crop color, but usually no more. Since these crop and color markers coincide with the traces of canals on the aerial photographs, we feel certain that the system can still be documented, even if only in a superficial fashion. The area visible on the aerial photographs covers about 175 ha, with another 125 ha as strong possibilities. As at the Laguna de Magdalena, the major canals are over 100m apart, and those that run parallel with the shore topography also are straight. The individual *chinampa* plots seem quite small, too, as at the Laguna de Magdalena.

SUMMARY OF THE ETZATLAN- MAGDALENA SYSTEMS

In summary, concerning the Etzatlán-Magdalena basin, we can document only a portion of the system that once existed. Elsewhere in this valley, at the same elevations (1,358-1,360m), there are many other areas with very suggestive traces—straight lines through sugarcane fields that do not follow either the directionality of the plowing pattern or the field dividers; evenly spaced but very vague light squares grouped in rectilinear patterns, often in different alignments than the field dividers; and so on. These traces are too illusive to be recorded as *chinampa* zones, though we feel that a percentage of them are just that. What can be documented is around 1,200 ha of *chinampas* in this basin, with the very high probability that they date from the Classic period. If 70-75 percent of this zone was the cultivation surface, then around 840-900 ha of actual marsh garden fields are represented. Given the proven productive profile of *chinampa* agriculture, this system constituted a major economic asset for the settlements within this basin.

THE TEUCHITLAN-AHUALULCO- TALA HYDRAULIC SYSTEM

The topographic situation in the Teuchitlán-Ahualulco-Tala basin is considerably more complex, due mostly to the fact that the valley was naturally drained thousands of years prior to the development of any agricultural interest in the zone. Thus, a great deal more topographic relief exists within this basin between the upper (and fossil) shore and the point of drainage to the Ameca basin at La Vega. The upper-most shore's elevation is at 1,300m, while the breach of the basin at La Vega is at 1,260m. This 40m difference is considerable, but it obscures two important points: (1) the slope toward La Vega is not even and regular, and (2) the basin is full of many sub-basins that are either not drained at all or only poorly so. Locally, these are called *ciénagas* (swamps), and they were/are fed by springs (at the shore edges and within the sub-basins) and by streams in huge, meandering multichanneled drainages that have been greatly altered by the land leveling and canalization projects of the sugarcane irrigation system. The aerial photographs of the Compañía Aereofoto Mexicana show the drainage system and the swamps before they were heavily altered; the 1973 CETENAL maps show what little is left of them. Only the two largest swamps were shown on the 1579 map of Ortelius (the Ciénaga de Teuchitlán and the Ciénaga de Tala). The soils within this basin are far more sandy than the soils in the Etzatlán-Magdalena basin, thus making them easier to drain without much noticeable difference in fertility.

The largest extant (though mostly poorly preserved) swamps are:

(1)   the general confluence area of the Arroyos Ahuijotel, El Sexto, and Ahuisculco (the first and third being called *riachuelos*, or small rivers) near the town of Cuisillos;

(2)   the area between the Arroyos Gacho (also called Mezquite) and Las Animas near San Juan de los Arcos, which is the Ciénaga de Tala and is still poorly drained;

(3)   the swamp at the foot of the Potrero Grande, half-way between the towns of Teuchitlán and El Refugio, where the Arroyos Tabaquera, Chivas, and Los Lobos discharge (see Figure 9);

(4)   the large marshy area just south of Estanzuela, formed mostly by the great spring system at El Rincón and Los Baños, which constitutes part of the Ciénaga de Teuchitlán (the rest being covered over by the La Vega reservoir); at the northern edge of the Ciénega, nearest to the El Rincón springs, is the largest extant system of *chinampas* in the study area (see Figures 9 and 10);

(5)   the large marsh area due north of Pacana, formed by the distributaries of the Río Salado, the largest river of the entire zone, just before its confluence with the Río Ameca (see Figure 9);

(6)   the small but well-preserved swamp at the Hacienda Labor de Rivera, west of Teuchitlán;

(7)   the swamp at El Bajío (near Los Hervores), where hot water geysers of very high mineral content are active; and,

(8)   the swamp at the Hacienda el Carmen, which has been largely drained.

The extant swamps cover ca. 20-22 km^2, though they vary dramatically in their states of preservation. As mentioned, the damage has resulted mostly from

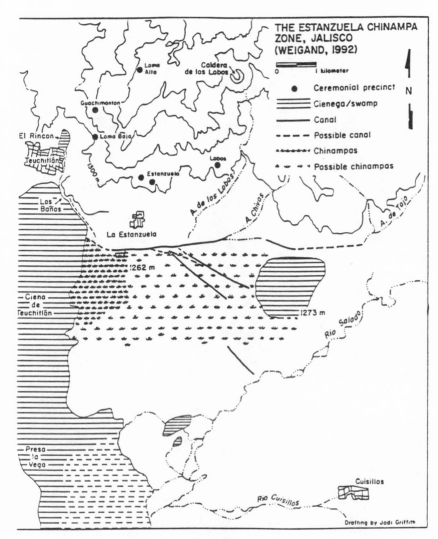

Figure 9. The Estanzuela-Potrero Grande-Río Salada
Chinampa and Canal Zone, Teuchitlán, Jalisco

post-World War II land leveling and deep disk plowing programs for sugarcane cultivation (see Note 3). From informants come descriptions of still other swamps, and the larger sizes of those, mentioned above, that have been modified. Our survey is still underway in the sugarcane fields around and between the Ciénaga de Teuchitlán and the Ciénaga de Tala, so the following comments are but preliminary.

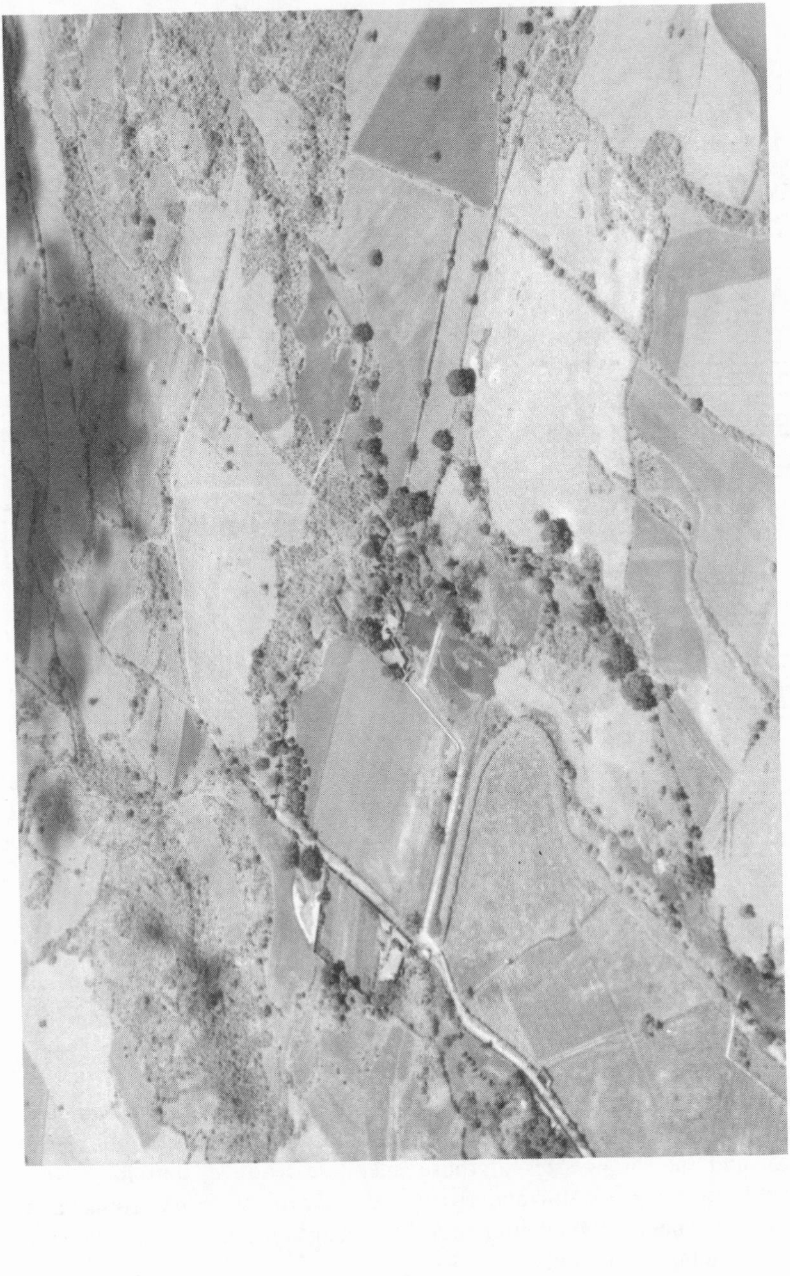

Figure 10. The Contemporary *Chinampas* at El Rincón, Jalisco, with Adjacent Terracing

THE ESTANZUELA SUB-BASIN SYSTEM

In many ways, the areas discussed in points 3 and 4, above, are the most fascinating because two sub-basins were linked by a large canal in order to regulate the flow of water into the Ciénaga de Teuchitlán area near Estanzuela. At the edge of the low hills at Los Baños are a strong series of springs, which were apparently canalized through a network of small ditches into the upper shore area of the sub-basin. This year-round water source, however, could not begin to supply the overall *chinampa* zone. The Presa de la Vega has covered approximately 18,000 ha of land to the west and south of these springs, but during the early 1980s, this reservoir all but dried up, and the complete area of the Ciénaga de Teuchitlán was briefly exposed to view. The streams that come from El Rincón (where the extant *chinampas* are located) and Los Baños wound their ways through the sub-basin with chronic meanders and semistagnate swamps. The dead water lily cover and alluviation within the reservoir prevented a detailed look at the surface of this area, but it did show the traces of the major artificial drainage features and how they articulated with those near the upper shore above the reservoir's level. Unfortunately, the area briefly described under point 5 (above) was not examined during this dry spell; however, since it is watered by the Río Salado, there is a high probability of *chinampas* in this zone, too.

South of Estanzuela (see Figure 9), the aerial photographs show a well-developed pattern of small squares and straight lines almost exactly like those of the Laguna de Magdalena in size and block organization. Ground survey cannot locate these squares, however, except in the most elusive and problematic manner. There has been just enough plow and disk agriculture, coupled with heavy cattle grazing, to have highly altered these features to the point of their obliteration. What can be traced by ground survey are sections of the larger canals that serviced this *chinampa* zone. This zone had at least 1,000 ha of marsh gardens, though only about 200 ha are fairly visible as squares in the aerial photographs. The rest are more problematic, though many of the largest canals can still be partially traced.

As mentioned, two and possibly three sub-basins and drainages were interlocked into a common system. The most problematic of these great canals is that which comes north from the Río Salado into the southern sector of the Estanzuela *chinampa* zone. This canal can be traced for about 1 km without much trouble just north of the Rio Salado. It was obviously taking water from this river, given its directionality, but the off-take point cannot be located, having been obliterated by the river's frequent meanderings. The canal disappears from sight at the southern edge of where the traces of *chinampa* squares can just barely be seen on the aerial photographs (but not on the ground). Its function must have been to carry water from the Río Salado into the southern area of this *chinampa* zone.

The Potrero Grande sub-basin is located to the east of this *chinampa* zone (point 3, above; see Figure 9). Traces of the small squares exist to the west, southwest, and south of this sub-basin on the aerial photographs, also, but they are likewise not visible on the ground. From the western edges of this sub-basin come the traces of 2 large canals, which carried water toward the west and the heart of the *chinampa* district. These canals are visible as very modest soil stains and lines of differential plant growth, both on the ground and on the aerial photographs. At their northwestern terminus, they become very hard to see, but most probably they joined the east-to-west canal that ran ca. 4 km and which served to canalize the run-off from the general Arroyo de los Lobos zone.

The Arroyo el Tajo, a canalized run-off from still further east, empties into this general area, too, but we have not yet surveyed the critical points of intersection of these systems. The middle course of the Arroyo el Tajo has been excavated several times in recent decades, but informants agree that the overall system was already in place before their projects were initiated. Both the Potrero Grande canals and that which canalized the Arroyo de los Lobos and Arroyo de las Chivas drop 10m over a distance of just at 4 km. This means that for every 1 km there is a 2.5m decline, or a drainage declivity of 0.25 percent. Since more than 0.5 percent means erosion within the canal, and less than 0.15 percent means siltation, the 0.25 percent declivity may indicate another element of engineering in the overall design of the system. William Doolittle (pers. comm., 1992) has cautioned me against taking this figure too literally, and perhaps indeed it is coincidence.

The interweaving of two (and possibly three) sub-basins into a common hydraulic system maximized the utility of areas of standing water (the Potrero Grande swamp) and of the drainages of running water (the Arroyos de los Lobos and de las Chivas), in addition to the spring system at Los Baños. It is possible that this system tapped into the Río Salado, in addition. Within the best preserved section, just south of Estanzuela, other, smaller canals and ditches are visible by ground inspection (as well as in the aerial photographs). As mentioned, the actual layout of the *chinampa* squares has proved very difficult to document, especially when compared to the really pristine character of those in the Laguna de Magdalena. In the aerial photographs, these squares appear to be about the same size as those in the Laguna de Magdalena zone. This area is still under field study, and these observations are still very preliminary and subject to revision as our survey progresses.

The spring systems at Los Baños and El Rincón are high water producers year after year, never having in memory dried up or even lessened in volume. This means that a large section of the upper shore system could have been dependably irrigated even during the worst of years when the swamps all but dried up or the Río Salado and the aforementioned arroyos failed, too. The El Rincón springs still supply an area of about 25 ha for sub-irrigation (as well as the drinking water for the town of Teuchitlán, with its 3,500 inhabitants). It could supply 5-6 times that surface if actually managed for that purpose. The springs at Los Baños are smaller in individual sizes but more numerous than those at El Rincón. If tapped for sub-irrigation, they could easily supply another 150-175 ha. Thus, even in the worst of times, the Estanzuela area could have kept around 300 ha under sub-irrigation production (see Figure 10).

THE CIENAGA DE TALA SYSTEM

The second area where we have evidences for a major *chinampa* zone within the Teuchitlán-Ahualulco-Tala basin is the area between the Río Salado in the north and the Río Cuisillos in the south. This region, point 2 above, is the zone where the Arroyos Gacho (Mezquite) and Animas have their confluence, and the area for several kilometers to the east (upstream) of that confluence. The overall area is ca. 22 km² just below the 1,290m elevation. Much of this area is still very marshy during the rainy season, depending upon the amount and timing of the rains. If the rainy season is front-loaded and heavy, there will be standing water in the lowest areas, though usually no more than 1 km² or so. Even during the dry season, there are swampy areas that do not give good sugarcane harvests. Crop damage or loss is a frequent occurrence in the heart of this area, despite sustained efforts at drainage ditch building and maintenance.

Indeed, it was one of these drainage projects that recently gave us the empirical data to postulate the existence of *chinampas* in this zone. We had known from survey, using guides to take us where they remembered ancient architectural features or burial areas, that this area had a great number of circular ceremonial buildings and habitation areas, which I briefly discussed above. We saw the suggestions of long lineal features on the aerial photographs, especially those taken by the Companía Aereofoto Mexicana. We could not locate these features precisely on the ground, however. A color aerial photographic flight which we took in the late 1970s confirmed the existence of these features, but added little else. These lineal features run at odd angles to the current field boundaries and often roughly parallel the meandering courses of the arroyos that drain the area. The circular architecture that we had located with informants seems well integrated with these lineal features.

As the modern ditches were being reworked, we found quite by chance a 200m exposure which, as a profile, had sectioned a buried *chinampa* block. The clearest section of this profile is presented in Figure 11. The profile is located near the Arroyo Gacho. None of the features in the profile, with the possible exception of the major canal near the "A" section, are visible on the surface or from the air. The land leveling and deep-disk plowing for sugarcane had homogenized the top 1.5m of soil and left the ancient hydraulic features

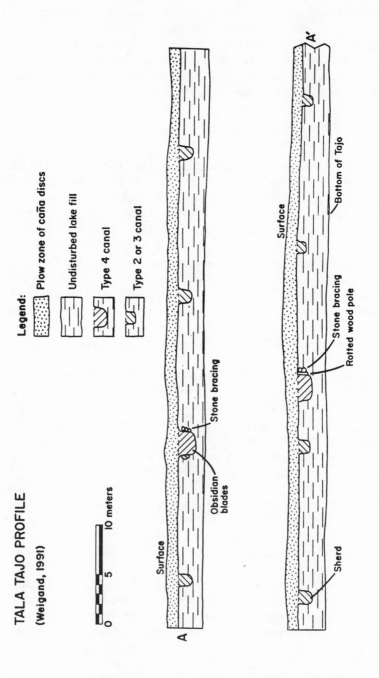

Figure 11. The Canal/*Chinampa* Profile from the Ciénaga de Tala, Jalisco

completely obscured. This was our first and, to date, our only *chinampa* profile. The profile seems to represent a section within a *chinampa* block, as no truly large-scale canal was sectioned. The distances between the smaller ditches are compatible with those measurable from the better preserved *chinampas* at the Laguna de Magdalena. The larger canals have some stone for side bracing. Two and three courses are preserved under the plow zone. The sectioned canal near the "A" section has a possible highly rotted pole as part of the bracing. Otherwise, there seems to have been no surfacing of the ditches. Artifacts were found in the profiles within the sectioned ditches. The single sherd is so nondescript and tiny that it defies classification, though it is clearly prehispanic. Two obsidian prismatic blades, both large and heavily used, were located on the bottom of the sectioned canal near the "A" section.

The fill of all of the ditches was noticeably different than the plow zone materials, indicating very probably that this area had silted up or had been flood-filled long before the modern land modification projects. The fill, while much looser than the undisturbed lake deposit, is far more compact than the plow zone. The ditch fill is of relatively uniform quality, in addition, though we could not see internal differences or bands within it. The character of the ditch fill probably indicates that the ditches were filled slowly but in a relatively brief time period. This is the same sequence of fill events for the contemporary ditches in this area. Informants state that, if the ditches are left alone for several years, without cleaning, they will begin to choke with weeds and fill in very rapidly thereafter.

Though the evidence for estimating the overall size of this *chinampa* zone is slight, the faint lineal features in an area we know to have *chinampas*, because of the profile seen in Figure 11, probably indicate a zone of about 800-1,000 ha at the least, though I feel that this zone could be double or even triple that very preliminary estimate. As with the Estanzuela zone, this area is still being surveyed, and new finds of architecture continue to turn up, especially to the north and west of the confluence area. What is obvious now is that the *chinampas* and architectural complexes are interlaced, and thus not only coeval but complementary in function.

OTHER POSSIBLE CHINAMPA SYSTEMS

Air survey and the study of older aerial photographs shows that this system of lineal features, at times associated with the faint indications of squares, continues into the Ameca basin. It is important to note that these features occur away from the Rio Ameca's edges, where the irrigation system described in the "Relación de Ameca" (Acuña 1988) was located. No ground survey of any consequence has been accomplished in the Ameca basin to date, but we do know that the circular ceremonial architecture, marking participation in the Classic period Teuchitlán Tradition, is found there.

In other zones within the Teuchitlán-Ahualulco-Tala basin, we also have very preliminary evidence for hydraulic features. In the Cocoliso drainage, southeast of Ahualulco (see Figure 1), beginning at the Ahualulco ceremonial circles and extending 5 km east-southeast toward the Hacienda el Carmen (and its swamp), is a poorly defined lineal feature that may be a major canal. It parallels the aforementioned arroyo but has a different alignment from the contemporary field patterns. This area today is drained by using the arroyo rather than a specialized ditch. Still more elusive lineal features both parallel this possible ditch and run at angles from it. We regard this zone, which constitutes about 450 ha, as a zone of probable *chinampas*. The major feature becomes visible just at the 1,300m elevation and disappears completely from sight at the 1,275m elevation, a decline of 25m over 5 km, or a gradient of 0.5 percent. This gradient would probably be erosion prone unless there were occasional dikes to control the speed of flow.

THE LA PROVIDENCIA CANAL SYSTEM

At La Providencia, in the tiny Laguna Colorada basin (wedged between the Etzatlán-Magdalena basin to the west and the Teuchitlán-Ahualulco-Tala basin to the southeast), there is a large ditch feature that is not associated with lakeshores or swamps (see Figure 8). This ditch runs in front of the La Providencia ceremonial area and its habitation zone, draining toward the south. To the ditch's east is a small system of tightly organized terraces. The ditch captured the runoff from at least two arroyos (perhaps year-round streams during the Classic periods) and canalized that runoff into a system of feeder canals and smaller ditches, which are poorly preserved and quickly fade from view. This system may have irrigated 50 ha or more.

When we first discovered this ditch, our inclination was to attribute it to the ruined 19th-century hacienda at La Providencia. However, none of the several very old individuals still resident there remember an irrigation system in this locality. The historian Antonio Domínguez Ocampo, who has specialized in the Colonial and modern history of the Municipio de San Juanito, in which La Providencia is located, could find no reference to an irrigation feature above the hacienda, either (pers. comm., 1992).

THE TERRACE SYSTEMS

Within the Etzatlán-Magdalena and Teuchitlán-Ahualulco-Tala basins, we have discovered extensive systems of terracing for dry field farming. Most of these terraces are prehispanic; contemporary farmers are actively tearing down many of them to consolidate fields and be able to run tractors unimpeded over larger surfaces. This program of terrace destruction has given us the opportunities to study prehispanic terrace building technologies and to actually date several complexes. In most areas, it is not possible to determine whether a terrace or terrace system is Classic or Postclassic in date. The best kinds of evidence for dating usually are proxemics and/or integration of the terraces into either Classic or Postclassic period ceremonial and/or residential architecture. Very few areas are tightly terraced, though this does occur within the hearts of the habitation zones of both Classic and Postclassic settlements (for an example, see Figure 8). Most terraces are rather open and restricted to the flatter uplands rather than the higher and steeper hills. We estimate ca. 350 km^2 terraced in this open fashion and less than 1 km^2 terraced in tight configurations.

Terraces were built by using 1-3 foundation courses of very large rock. From this course(s), progressively smaller rock was stacked atop the foundation, leaning into the uphill side of the building site. The result was a near vertical back side and a front side at a 10-30° angle. Terraces are seldom higher than 2m, and most are 1m or slightly more. The fill behind the terraces is often rather rough next to the actual wall, indicating that, at times, fill was purposefully brought in to start the consolidation process. The upper courses of the fill are usually composed of fairly evenly textured soils, without as much rock, indicating that natural processes were meant to complete the building projects. As mentioned, these terraces are mostly unirrigated. Nonetheless, they helped to control runoff and, thus, erosion and alluviation in the swamp and shore-side hydraulic systems, and to regulate the water supply to those downhill areas. This was especially important in the great habitations zones, such as that at Teuchitlán, where deforestation must have been severe. Thus, terrace building was an integrated part in the construction of the Classic period Key Economic Area (cf. Chi 1936) which, accompanied by a population implosion, saw the differential development of these basins compared to the rest of West Mexico.

CONCLUSIONS

The hydraulic system in the highland lake zone of Jalisco appears to have been relatively short-lived when compared to some of the very long-lasting systems of the Near East (Adams 1965, 1974, Adams & Nissen 1972, Jacobsen & Adams 1958), Egypt (Butzer 1976), and Peru (Kosok 1965). It was more long-lived than that reported for the southern sectors of the Basin of Mexico (Armillas 1971, Boehm de Lameiras 1986), however, and in this sense was much more like the Mayan marsh garden system (Harrison & Turner 1978, Puleston 1977, Siemans & Puleston 1972, Pohl 1990) or the ditch-field system reported for the Hohokam (Haury 1976, Masse 1981).

The hydraulic system of this study area is very poorly understood, in part due to the state of preservation but in part due also to the lack of comprehensive field work, oriented toward landscape studies, in West Mexico. The zone is still dominated by ceramocentric studies—"ceramic provinces" that have become "cultures"—and other art historical considerations. The hydraulic system, though, can be shown to have existed, as Palerm (Palerm & Wolf 1972) suspected would be the case. In addition, the system has strong indications of complex engineering. Some of the best evidence for complexity within the system, aside from its scale, is the geometry applied to the *chinampa* zones. This formal planning is a strong indication of careful engineering to maximize the potential of these fields. It is likely, though, that some of these systems may have been first independent irrigation areas that were later woven into larger agglomerations. Often, as both Palerm (1990, Palerm & Wolf 1972) and Wittfogel (1957) point out, this pattern results in more efficient systems than those planned from the outset on a grand scale. Doolittle (1984) actually has documented this process. The Estanzuela-Potrero Grande system may be an example of the former, though the Laguna de Magdalena system may be an example of the latter. By whichever formative process, once established they became prime economic resources.

The *chinampa* zones may have become objects of contention between polities or separate groups within the same polity, a point made by Boehm de Lameiras (1986) and Palerm (1973) for the Basin of Mexico. For that same area, Boehm de Lameiras (1986) also notes that *chinampas* had a role in key and strategic political decision making. We still do not know enough about the hydraulic systems (including the terraces) in the Etzatlán-Magdalena, Teuchitlán-Ahualulco-Tala, and Ameca basins to decide whether the systems were entirely local or had regional aspects. Certainly, the major basins were not connected in the fashions that have been demonstrated for Peru. However, within the same basin selected systems may have been interconnected, as mentioned.

We must consider the scale of these hydraulic systems, plus their engineering, as we continue to evaluate the nature of the settlement system, the demographic implosion and concentration, the monumentality and sophistication of the circular architecture, the pseudo-cloisonné codical materials, the mining and workshop activities, etc. It was in the interest of the elites of the Teuchitlán Tradition to maximize agricultural productivity, given the large concentration of population within the core. Obviously, there were projects to accomplish that maximalization, or ones that were at least supported through the political system(s).

A great variety of traditional maize types exist in this area or in zones fairly close by. There are 90-day and 100/120-day maize types, the former among the Huicholes (Weigand 1972) and the latter within the present study area. With the 90-day types, three harvests per year could have been possible. Certainly, two harvests were possible, as they still are today in the small areas of these basins that are not dedicated to sugarcane, especially in the Etzatlán-Magdalena Unidad de Riego (Weigand & Ron 1987). However, we should be aware of the strong possibility that not all, or even a major percentage, of the *chinampas* were dedicated to maize cultivation. In these types of fields, the amaranths could render three harvests per year. Beans, squash, tomatoes, jitomates, and many other cultigens must have formed part of the inventory, as well. Within the swamps and canals per se would have been a wealth of foods: algae, fish, ducks, turtles, frogs, etc.

Using the figure of 3,000 ha, or 30 km^2, of *chinampa* surface for the study area (understanding that this is just a fraction of the probable hydraulic field system), and 70 percent field surfaces within the field system, then around 40,000 individuals could have been supported by *chinampas*, figured at 0.3 ha per household. Hicks (n.d.) calculated the range at 0.25-0.35 ha per household and Sanders (1971) at 18 people per ha, both for the Basin of Mexico. Armillas (1971, 1987) felt that only about 10 percent of the society's food needs in the Basin of Mexico were met by *chinampa* production. These figures, derived from the Basin of Mexico as guides in understanding our study area's productive potential, must be used with caution. However, until we have paleo-environmental studies of our own, these figures are the best we have.

We have no way at present of calculating the *chinampa*:dry field production ratio in our study basins. Certainly, the dry field system, improved through terracing and check dams, was very important. We had previously estimated a total population of 40-60,000 inhabitants for the entire Key Economic Area of the Teuchitlán Tradition, more or less marked by the first circle around the Volcán de Tequila in Figure 1. In the light of the *chinampa* data, it is very probable that this estimate is far too low.

ACKNOWLEDGMENTS

This work has been accomplished under permit from the Instituto Nacional de Antropología e Historia. My special thanks to Dra. Brigitte Boehm de Lameiras for the encouragement and support that she has given this project in recent years. The collaboration of Ing. Jesús Lomelí of the Secretaría de Recursos Hidráulicos and Ing. Francisco Ron Siordia was invaluable. The field training and aid so unselfishly given me by Dr. J. Charles Kelley and Prof. Pedro Armillas were invaluable. My thanks go to Dra. Dolores Soto de Arechavaleta, Lic. Acelia García de Weigand, Dr. Michael Spence, Dr. Joseph Mountjoy, Lic. Luis Arias, Ing. Francisco Francillard, Arqlgo. Javier Galván, Arqlgo. Otto Schondube, and many others for their field aid, encouragement, and support; and to Jodi Griffith of the Museum of Northern Arizona, who prepared Figures 1, 4, 7, 9, and 10. Thanks to Dr. David Wilcox, Dr. William Doolittle, Dra. Brigitte Boehm, Dr. Barry Isaac, and Dr. Michael Foster for their invaluable comments on the first draft of this study.

NOTES

1. The measurements included in the "Relación de Ameca" (Acuña 1988) are: 1,500 *fanegas de tierra de sembradura*, or 940 ha (9.4 km^2); and 500 *fanegas de sembradura*, or 313 ha (3.13 km^2).

2. The lake bottom soils are classified as Vertisol Pelico (VP) by the Secretaria de Agricultura y Recursos Hidraulicos, CETENAL, and the Comision Nacional del Agua. They are widely recognized as having high fertility limited only by their texture (in the cases when there is not enough ash silica) or poor drainage. If they do not have sufficient ash, then they are very "sticky" and difficult to work. A second bottom land soil is the Fluvisol Eutrico (FE), which is found primarily along the lower streams and in places that are continuously flooded. Their textures are fine and they are highly fertile. The VP soils and FE ribbons are actually a lattice work of interwoven types. The *chinampa* systems crossed through some of these lattices. These classifications, while general, are being revised by more detailed field studies by the government agencies named above. To date, however, there is only one neutron activation study of trace element compositions of these soils. That study was made at the San Isidro clay beds, on the upper shore of the San Marcos basin, just west of the Etzatlán-Magdalena valley (Weigand & García de Weigand 1989; Weigand et al. 1981). Rainfall in this area is largely governed by a summer monsoon season in which ca. 80 percent of the yearly rains usually occur. Some years, such as the 1991/ 92 winter season, have very heavy rains. When winter rains are heavy, the annual precipitation can be as high as 1,300mm. Far more frequently, the annual precipitation range is 900-1,100mm.

3. The following material concerning the modern irrigation developments in the Etzatlán-Magdalena and Teuchitlán-Ahualulco-Tala basins was taken from Orive Alba (1970) and Hewitt de Alcántara (1976). The contemporary strategy in opening up new irrigation districts is to provide "irrigated emporia" operating in the benefit of banks and middlemen in the handling of agricultural produce (sugarcane, in our study area). These are high technology islands, and they usually result in an exodus of rural peoples to near-by cities, such as Guadalajara. Currently, Jalisco is among the four largest irrigation agricultural states; Jalisco, Sonora, Sinaloa, and Guanajuato account for 42 percent of all of the irrigated land in Mexico, or ca. 2,000,000 ha. The contemporary irrigation districts in the study area represent about 25,000 ha of that 2 million. The first modern project, the Proyecto Canales de Magdalena y Ahualulco, sponsored by the federal government, between 1935 and 1940, was a drainage endeavor. By 1946, around 13,000 ha in the area had been drained. By the late 1950s, another 6,000 ha had been drained and a system of reservoirs was started. The largest one, La Vega, was operating fully in the early 1960s. By 1966, at the conclusion of Díaz Ordaz's presidency, the formal total was 22,000 ha reclaimed. Since that date, much smaller projects have raised the total slightly (Weigand & Ron 1987). Also, see Kroeber (1983) for additional contextual material for irrigation policy during the P. Díaz de la Cruz period.

4. My interest in the interface of planned, large-scale irrigation systems and social organization comes directly from two members of my Ph.D. candidacy committee, Prof. Pedro Armillas and Dr. Robert McC. Adams. In 1965, I had the opportunity to work with Prof. Armillas, examining the *chinampas* of the Basin of Mexico. That survey, plus work that I did concerning ancient mining for Dr. J. Charles Kelley that same year, introduced me to the concepts behind the landscape archaeological approach (cf. Crawford 1953). Armillas viewed ancient landscapes processually, looking for the social dimensions that led to their evolution. He strongly felt that archaeology without that dimension was not anthropological. Armillas coined the term "social archaeology" in the 1960s, though others have taken credit for it. To obtain this social perspective requires a specific series of methodologies. One of the first steps is to understand a region and its cultural/ natural resources, i.e., the landscape.

REFERENCES

Acuña, René (ed.) (1988) *Relaciones geográficas del Siglo XVI: Nueva Galicia* (*Geographical Relations of the 16th Century: Nueva Galicia*). Mexico, DF: Universidad Nacional Autónoma de México.

Adams, Robert McC. (1965) *Land Behind Baghdad*. Chicago: University of Chicago Press.

―――― (1966) *The Evolution of Urban Society: Early Mesopotamia and Prehispanic Mexico*. Chicago: Aldine.

―――― (1974) "Historic Patterns of Mesopotamian Irrigation Agriculture." Pp. 1-6 in T. E. Downing & M. Gibson (eds.) *Irrigation's Impact on Society*. Tucson: University of Arizona Anthropological Papers, No. 25.

Adams, Robert McC., and Hans Nissen (1972) *The Uruk Countryside*. Chicago: University of Chicago Press.

Armillas, Pedro (1971) "Gardens on Swamps." *Science* 174(4010): 653-661.

―――― (1987) "El paisaje agrario azteca" ("The Aztec Agrarian Landscape"). Pp. 67-107 in *La aventura intelectual de Pedro Armillas* (*The Intellectual Adventure of Pedro Armillas*). Zamora: Colegio de Michoacán.

de Arregui, Domingo Lázaro (1980) *Descripción de la Nueva Galicia* (*Description of Nueva Galicia*). Guadalajara: Gobierno de Jalisco.

Bárcena, Mariano (1983) *Ensayo estadístico del Estado de Jalisco* (*Statistical Essay on the State of Jalisco*). Guadalajara: Gobierno de Jalisco.

Boehm de Lameiras, Brigitte (1986) *Formación del estado en México prehispánico* (*Formation of the State in Prehispanic Mexico*). Zamora: Colegio de Michoacán.

Butzer, Karl (1976) *Early Hydraulic Civilization in Egypt*. Chicago: University of Chicago Press.

Charlton, Thomas, and Michael Spence (1982): "Obsidian Exploitation and Civilization in the Basin of Mexico." Pp. 7-86 in P. Weigand & G. Gywnne (eds.) *Mining and Mining Techniques in Ancient Mesoamerica*. Stony Brook, NY: Special issue of *Anthropology*, Vol. VI (State University of New York at Stony Brook).

Chi, Ch'ao-ting (1936) *Economic Areas in Chinese History, as Revealed in the Development of Public Works for Water Control*. London.

Comisión Nacional del Agua (n.d.) Various MMS and archives in the Guadalajara office, Gerencia Estatal de la Comisión Nacional del Agua.

Crawford, O. G. S. (1953) *Archaeology in the Field*. London: Phoenix House.

Denevan, William (1966) *The Aboriginal Cultural Geography of the Llanos de Mojos of Bolivia*. Berkeley, CA: Ibero-Americana 48.

Doolittle, William (1984) "Agricultural Change as an Incremental Process." *Annals of the American Association of Geographers* 74(1):124-137.

―――― (1990) *Canal Irrigation in Prehispanic Mexico*. Austin: University of Texas Press.

Farrington, Ian (1974) "Irrigation and Settlement Pattern: Preliminary Research Results from the North Coast of Peru." Pp. 83-94 in T. E. Downing & M. Gibson (eds.) *Irrigation's Impact on Society*. Tucson: University of Arizona Anthropological Papers, No. 25.

Florance, Charles (n.d.) "The Late and Terminal Preclassic in Southeast Guanajuato: Heartland or Periphery." Paper presented to the seminar "Cultural Dynamics of Precolumbian West and Northwest Mesoamerica," organized by Shirley Gorenstein & Michael Foster, Center for Indigenous Studies in the Americas, Phoenix, 1992.

Galván, Javier (1984) *Las tumbas de tiro del Valle de Atemejac, Jalisco* (*Shaft Tombs of the Atemejac Valley, Jalisco*), 2 vols. Guadalajara: Instituto Nacional de Antropología e Historia (on file at the Centro Regional de Jalisco).

Glassow, Michael (1967) "The Ceramics of Huistla, a West Mexican Site in the Municipality of Etzatlán, Jalisco." *American Antiquity* 32:64-83.

Gonzáles Navarro, Moisés (1977) *Repartimientos de indios en Nueva Galicia* (*Partitions of the Indians of Nueva Galicia*). Mexico, DF: Instituto Nacional de Antropología e Historia/ Museo Nacional de Historia.

Guzmán, Nuño de, and Hernán Cortés (1937) *Nuño de Guzmán contra Hernán Cortés* (*Nuño de Guzmán vs. Hernán Cortés*). Mexico, DF: Boletín del Archivo General de la Nación, Vol. VIII (4 & 5).

Harrison, P. D., & B. L. Turner, eds. (1978) *Prehispanic Maya Agriculture*. Albuquerque: University of New Mexico Press.

Haury, Emil (1976) *The Hohokam: Desert Farmers and Craftmen*. Tucson: University of Arizona Press.

Hewitt de Alcántara, Cynthia (1976) *Modernizing Mexican Agriculture: Socioeconomic Implications of Technological Change 1940-1970*. Geneva: United Nations Research Institute for Social Development, No. 76.5.

Hicks, Frederic (n.d.) "Large Estates and Peasant Plots: The Production of Food in Aztec Times." Paper given to the Chicago meeting of the American Anthropological Association, 1991.

Holien, Thomas (1977) *Mesoamerican Pseudo-Cloisonné and Other Decorative Investments*. Ph.D. dissertation, Southern Illinois University at Carbondale.

Jacobsen, T., and R. McC. Adams (1958) "Salt and Silt in Mesopotamian Agriculture." *Science* 128:1251-1258.

Kolata, Alan L. (1991) "The Technology and Organization of Agricultural Production in the Tiwanaku State." *Latin American Antiquity* 2:99-125.

Kosok, Paul (1965) *Life, Land, and Water in Ancient Peru*. Long Island, NY: Long Island University Press.

Kroeber, Clifton B. (1983) *Life, Land, and Water: Mexico's Farmlands Irrigation Policies 1885-1911*. Berkeley: University of California Press.

Long, Stanley (1966) *Archaeology of the Municipio of Etzatlan, Jalisco*. Ph.D. dissertation, University of California at Los Angeles.

Masse, W. Bruce (1981) "Prehistoric Irrigation Systems in the Salt River Valley, Arizona." *Science* 214:408-415.

Mitchell, W. P. (1973) "The Hydraulic Hypothesis: A Reappraisal." *Current Anthropology* 14:532-534.

Müller, Florencia, and César Lizardi Ramos (1959) "La Pirámide 6 de Huapalcalco, Hidalgo, México" ("Pyramid 6 at Huapalcalco, Hidalgo, Mexico"). *Cuadernos Americanos* 33:146-157.

Neely, James (1974) "Sassanian and Early Islamic Water Control and Irrigation Systems on the Deh Luran Plain, Iran." Pp. 2142 in T. E. Downing & M. Gibson (eds.) *Irrigation's Impact on Society*. Tucson: University of Arizona Anthropological Papers, No. 25.

Oliveros, Arturo (1974) "Nuevas exploraciones en El Opeño, Michoacán" ("New Explorations at El Opeño, Michoacán"). Pp. 182-201 in Betty Bell (ed.) *The Archaeology of West Mexico*. Ajijic, Jalisco: West Mexican Society for Advanced Study.

Orive Alba, Adolfo (1970) *La irrigación en México* (*Irrigation in Mexico*). Mexico, DF: Editorial Grijalbo.

Palerm, Angel (1973) *Obras hidráulicas prehispánicas en el sistema lacustre del Valle de México* (*Prehispanic Hydraulic Works in the Lake System of the Valley of Mexico*). Mexico, DF: Secretaría de Educación Pública/ Instituto Nacional de Antropología e Historia.

———— (1990) *México prehispánico: Evolución ecológica del Valle de México* (*Prehispanic Mexico: Ecological Evolution of the Valley of Mexico*). Mexico, DF: Consejo Nacional para la Cultura y las Artes.

Palerm, Angel, and Eric Wolf (1972) *Agricultura y civilización en Mesoamérica* (*Agriculture and Civilization in Mesoamerica*). Mexico, DF: Editorial Grijalbo.

Parsons, James, and William Denevan (1967) "Pre-Columbian Ridged Fields." *Scientific American* 217:92-100.

Parsons, Jeffery (1976) "The Role of Chinampa Agriculture in the Food Supply of Aztec Tenochtlan." Pp. 233-257 in C. E. Cleland (ed.) *Cultural Change and Continuity*. New York: Academic Press.

Pohl, Mary, ed. (1990) *Ancient Maya Wetland Agriculture*. Boulder, CO: Westview Press.

Puleston, D.E. (1977) "The Art and Archaeology of Hydraulic Agriculture in the Maya Lowlands." Pp. 449-467 in N. Hammond (ed.) *Social Process in Maya Archaeology: Studies in Memory of Sir Eric Thompson*. New York: Academic Press.

Sanders, William (1971) "Settlement Patterns in Central Mexico." Pp. 3-44 in *Handbook of Middle American Indians, Vol. 10*. Austin: University of Texas Press.

Sanders, William, Jeffery Parsons, and Robert Santley (1979) *The Basin of Mexico: Ecological Processes in the Evolution of a Civilization*. New York: Academic Press.

Secretaría de Agricultura y Recursos Hidráulicos (n.d.) Various MSS, maps, and archives in the San Juanito, Ameca, and Guadalajara (Jalisco) offices.

Siemans, A. D., and D. E. Puleston (1972) "Ridged Fields and Associated Features in Southern Campeche: New Perspectives on the Lowland Maya." *American Antiquity* 37:228-240.

Soto de Arechavaleta, Dolores (n.d.) *Análisis de la tecnología de producción del taller de obsidiana de Guachimontón, Teuchitlán, Jalisco* (*Analysis of the Technology of Production of the Guachimontón Obsidian Workshop, Teuchitlán, Jalisco*). Mexico, DF: Instituto de Investigaciones Antropológicas, Universidad Nacional Autónoma de México. (forthcoming)

Turner, B. L., and P.D. Harrison, eds. (1983) *Pulltrouser Swamp: Ancient Maya Habitat, Agriculture, and Settlement in Northern Belize*. Austin: University of Texas Press.

Weigand, Phil C. (1972) *Co-operative Labor Groups in Subsistence Activities Among the Huichol Indians*. Carbondale: Southern Illinois University Museum, Mesoamerican Studies, No. 7.

———— (1985) "Evidence for Complex Societies During the Western Mesoamerican Classic Period." Pp. 47-91 in M. Foster & P. Weigand (eds.) *The Archaeology of West and Northwest Mesoamerica*. Boulder, CO: Westview Press.

———— (1989) "Architecture and Settlement Patterns Within the Western Mesoamerican Formative Tradition." Pp. 39-64 in Marta Carmona Macías (ed.) *El preclásico o formativo: Avances y perspectivas* (*The Preclassic or Formative: Advances and Perspectives*). Mexico, DF: Museo Nacional de Antropología/Instituto Nacional de Antropología e Historia.

———— (1990a) "The Teuchitlán Tradition of Western Mesoamerica." Pp. 25-54 in Amalia Cardós de Méndez (ed.) *La época clásica: Nuevos hallazgo, nuevas ideas* (*The Classic Period: New Finds, New Ideas*). Mexico, DF: Museo Nacional de Antropología/Instituto Nacional de Antropología e Historia.

———— (1990b) "Discontinuity: The Collapse of the Teuchitlán Tradition and the Early Postclassic Cultures of Western Mesoamerica." Pp. 215-222 in Federica Sodi Miranda (ed.) *Mesoamérica y Norte de México, siglos IX-XII* (*Mesoamerica and Northern Mexico, 9th-11th Centuries*). Mexico, DF: Museo Nacional de Antropología/Instituto Nacional de Antropología e Historia.

———— (1991) "The Western Mesoamerican Tlacho: A Two-Thousand Year Perspective." Pp. 73-86 in V. Scarborough & D. Wilcox (eds.) *The Mesoamerican Ballgame*. Tucson: University of Arizona Press.

———— (1992a) "Central Mexico's Influence in Jalisco and Nayarit during the Classic Period." Pp. 221-232 in E. M. Schortman & P. A. Urban (eds.) *Resources, Power, and Interregional Interaction*. New York: Plenum Press.

———— (1992b) "Ehecatl: ¿Primer dios supremo del occidente?" ("Ehecatl: First Supreme God in the West [of Mexico]?"). Pp. 205-237 in B. Boehm & P. Weigand (eds.) *Origen y desarrollo de la civilización en el occidente de México: IV Mesa de Trabajo, Homenaje a Pedro Armillas y Angel Palerm (Origin and Evolution of Civilization in Western Mexico: IV Workshop, In Honor to Pedro Armillas and Angel Palerm)*. Zamora: Colegio de Michoacan.

_____ (1992c) "The Political Organization of the Trans-Tarascan Zone of Western Mesoamerica on the Eve of Spanish Contact." Pp. 191-217 in A. Woosley & J. Ravesloot (eds.) *Culture and Contact: Charles Di Peso's Gran Chichimeca*. Albuquerque: University of New Mexico Press.

_____ (1993) *Evolución de una civilización: Arqueología de Jalisco, Nayarit, y Zacatecas (Evolution of a Civilization: Archaeology of Jalisco, Nayarit, and Zacatecas)*. Zamora: Colegio de Michoacán.

Weigand, Phil C., Garman Harbottle, and Sue Ward (1981) "Mexican Sherds Recovered from the Archaeological Excavations at Yuquot, British Columbia." Pp. 171-178 in W. Folan & J. Dewhirst (eds.) *The Yuquot Project, Vol. 3*. Quebec: Canadian National Parks and Sites Branch, History and Archaeology, 44.

Weigand, Phil C., and Michael Spence (1982) "The Obsidian Mining Complex at La Joya, Jalisco." Pp. 175-188 in P. Weigand & G. Gywnne (eds.) *Mining and Mining Techniques in Ancient Mesoamerica*. Stony Brook, NY: Special issue of Anthropology, Vol. VI (State University of New York-Stony Brook).

Weigand, Phil C., and Francisco Ron Siordia (1987) "The Marginalization of the Ejidos of the Magdalena-Etzatlán Unidad de Riego, Jalisco." Pp. 46-55 in N. R. Crumrine & P. Weigand (eds.) *Ejidos and Regions of Refuge in Northwest Mexico*. Tucson: University of Arizona Anthropological Papers, #46.

Weigand, Phil C., and Celía García de Weigand (1989) "An Ethnographic Consideration of an Archaeological Problem: Ceramic Production in Western Mexico. A Case Study." Pp. 175-185 Yólotl González (ed.) *Homenaje a Isabel Kelly (In Honor of Isabel Kelly)*. Mexico, DF: Instituto Nacional de Antropología e Historia, Colección Científica.

Wilcox, David (1991) "The Mesoamerican Ballgame in the American Southwest." Pp. 101-125 in V. Scarborough & D. Wilcox (eds.) *The Mesoamerican Ballgame*. Tucson: University of Arizona Press.

Wittfogel, Karl (1957) *Oriental Despotism*. New Haven: Yale University Press.

A PALEOHYDRAULIC APPROACH TO EXAMINING AGRICULTURAL INTENSIFICATION IN HOHOKAM IRRIGATION SYSTEMS

Jerry B. Howard

INTRODUCTION

Understanding the impact of the introduction of irrigation technology on human society has long been a goal of anthropological research. The adoption of irrigation agriculture represents a major change in subsistence technology that can produce dramatic changes in human lifestyles. Irrigation systems are a direct interface between cultural systems and their environments. In most cases, irrigation systems significantly increase the short-term dependability of agricultural water supplies and the constancy of crop yields. While reducing short-term risk, irrigation systems are vulnerable to catastrophic flooding and a loss of labor investment. The introduction of irrigation technology represents a major process of agricultural intensification, simultaneously increasing both

Research in Economic Anthropology, Suppl. 7, pages 263-324.
Copyright © 1993 by JAI Press Inc.
All rights of reproduction in any form reserved.
ISBN: 1-55938-646-0

labor expenditures and crop yields. Theoretically, the adoption of irrigation technology has long been tied to processes of intensification, the production of surplus, population growth and aggregation, circumscription and warfare, increased sociopolitical complexity the and promotion of urbanization (Carniero 1970, Childe 1936, Wittfogel 1957).

Anthropological studies of irrigation societies have focused on the larger issues engendered by the Wittfogel debates (Carniero 1970, Millon 1962, Mitchell 1973, Netting 1974, Wittfogel 1957). Wittfogel's argument that the logistical and administrative needs of "hydraulic societies" led to increased sociopolitical complexity were quickly attacked. Many researchers argued that irrigation systems do not require special administrative or sociopolitical needs, pointing to "non-complex" (i.e., non-state-level) societies having large, complex irrigation systems (Netting 1974, Millon 1962).

Archaeological studies of irrigation agriculturalists have focused primarily on the Old World, with a secondary concentration on Mesoamerican and Peruvian groups. Less attention has been paid to the Hohokam, the only prehispanic group in present-day United States to construct monumental irrigation works. Within the Salt and Gila river valleys and the Sonoran Desert environment of south-central Arizona, the Hohokam constructed large, integrated irrigation systems containing multiple, parallel main canals with multiple villages spaced at intervals of 5 km (Figure 1). The main canals were often in excess of 24 km in length. These efficient and well-engineered systems were highly stable, persisting in operation between A.D. 600 and 1450.

While it is not generally recognized, the study of Hohokam irrigation has played a prominent role in anthropological debates concerning the relationships between irrigation technology and sociopolitical complexity. The significant contribution of Hohokam studies to these debates lay in the availability of an archaeological explanation of processes of agricultural intensification within irrigation systems. This explanation was a model of "accretionary growth" presented by Richard Woodbury (1961). Woodbury's model of the accretionary growth of canal systems held that large canal systems could be expanded through an incremental, additive process, with small segments being periodically added to the end of individual canals. He argued that the monumental Hohokam irrigation works could have been constructed through very small, periodic labor investments. Given the size and periodicity of construction requirements under the accretionary growth model, it was argued that noncomplex and even acephalous social organizations could easily construct large irrigation systems (Service 1975, Steward 1955b, Woodbury 1961). The Hohokam, viewed at that time as a noncomplex society provided an important archaeological example with which to counter the arguments of Wittfogel (Haury 1962:121-125, Service 1975:273; Steward 1955a, 1955b:71-72; Woodbury 1961).

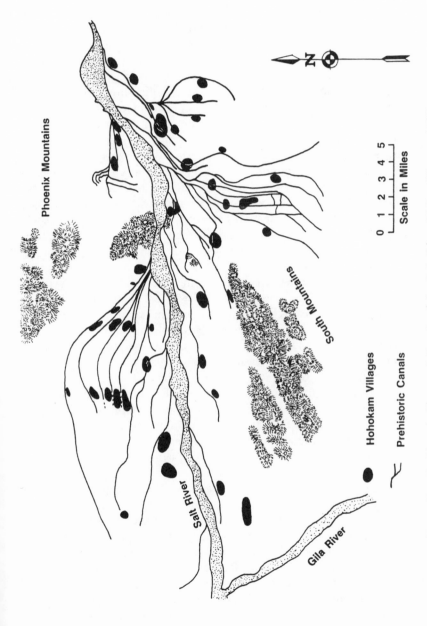

Figure 1. Prehistoric Sites and Canals of the Salt River Valley (Turney 1929)

Transpositions of this argument have also been employed to explore sociopolitical complexity of the Hohokam heartland in the Salt and Gila River valleys (Howard 1990a, n.d.b.; Neitzel 1987, 1991; Nicholas 1981, Nicholas & Feinman 1989, Nicholas & Neitzel 1984, Upham & Rice 1980). It has been argued that the logistical requirements of irrigation technology, including labor investment in construction, maintenance, water allocation, water scheduling, and conflict resolution, can require the development of some level of sociopolitical complexity at specific thresholds of scale. Conceptually, most of these researchers have viewed agricultural intensification in the large Hohokam irrigation systems from an accretionary viewpoint. Crop yields, surpluses, and demographic growth accompany the continuous and almost exponential expansion of the irrigation systems through time, often with concomitant increase in system complexity (Nicholas & Feinman 1989). It is generally argued that, during the Classic period (A.D. 1100-1450), the final stage of Hohokam development (see Table 1), the logistical needs of irrigation exceeded an organizational threshold requiring an increase in sociopolitical complexity. In most cases, some form of hierarchical, ranked, or "chiefdom" organization is proposed for the Classic period Hohokam.

The major focus of these arguments is the size and complexity of the irrigation systems or measures of system structure and scale. The most prominent question concerns the processes of system expansion, an important variable in the study of agricultural intensification. Unfortunately, past reconstructions of system growth have been based on inaccurate assumptions concerning the processes of expansion. Chronological reconstructions, often based on cross-dating between canals and associated village sites, must be revised. System structure—how the basic components of the irrigation system are designed and how they interface with the basic economic and agricultural task groups—has received little attention. Yet, an understanding of the basic units of agricultural production and how they are embedded in higher levels of system organization is critical to reconstructions of sociopolitical complexity.

The question of processes of intensification in Hohokam irrigation is not only critical to issues of sociopolitical complexity, but it continues to have ramifications for general anthropological studies of irrigation societies. Recent, more empirically-based studies of Hohokam irrigation have resulted in the development of new methodological approaches for modeling the operation and capacities of prehistoric canals. Paleohydraulic reconstructions (Howard 1990a), combined with newly developed dating techniques (Eighmy & Howard 1991), have provided a dramatically different view of the processes of system expansion and canal use-life. An improved understanding of the engineering and structure of the irrigation systems provides archaeological correlates for task group organization.

Table 1. The Hohokam Chronology, by Period and Phase

Time	Period	Phase
1500		
1400	Classic (A.D. 1100-1450)	Polvorón (A.D. 1350-1400)
1300		Civano (A.D. 1300-1400)
1200		Soho (A.D. 1100-1300)
1100		
1000	Sedentary (A.D. 900-1100)	Sacaton (A.D. 900-1100)
900		
800	Colonial (A.D. 600-900)	Santa Cruz (A.D. 700-900)
700		Gila Butte (A.D. 600-700)
600		
500	Pioneer (A.D. 0-600)	Snaketown
400		Sweetwater/Estrella
300		Vahki
200		Red Mountain
100		
A.D.		
0		

This essay reviews past models of irrigation system expansion and provides an alternative view based on more recent paleohydraulic and chronological reconstructions. I then discuss processes of agricultural intensification (such as shortening fallow systems) that do not rely on the expansion of the irrigation system. The structure of Hohokam irrigation systems is used to examine how task groups are organized and integrated at various levels of organization. Finally, I discuss the implications of our current understanding of processes of agricultural intensification and canal system expansion for changing sociopolitical organization from the household, irrigation community, and regional levels.

MODELS OF AGRICULTURAL INTENSIFICATION IN HOHOKAM IRRIGATION

Questions concerning the development of the canal systems within the Salt River Valley have long been a focus of Hohokam research. In *Prehistoric Irrigation in Arizona*, Omar Turney (1929) was the first to propose a chronological sequence to describe the development of the canal systems in the Salt River Valley. Turney numbered the canals and canal systems on his map of the prehistoric remains of the Phoenix basin according to the order of their construction. The chronology was based on Turney's informal understanding of ceramic change, probably based at least partly, on the early stratigraphic work of Schmidt (1928). Turney was the first researcher to postulate a process of growth in which earlier canals were constructed near the river, followed by an expansion away from the river onto the pediment. Turney characterized this process as a movement from the areas of more optimal gradients to areas of less optimal gradients. The gradients close to and paralleling the river were indeed steeper than those located higher on the pediment; however, this does not necessarily mean they were more optimal, since they often created velocities in excess of the erosional threshold of local soils.

Recent research within Turney's Canal System Two, a large, integrated canal system on the north side of the Salt River underlying modern-day Phoenix, has confirmed this sequence of growth. Main canals were first constructed near the margin of the Salt River (Cable & Doyel 1987, Greenwald & Ciolek-Torrello 1989) in the Late Pioneer and Colonial periods (beginning circa A.D. 550-700). Canal construction then moved progressively higher, onto the second terrace of the Salt River, with those canals farthest from the river becoming fully developed later in time.

Woodbury's Model of Accretionary Growth

As noted above, Richard Woodbury (1961) influenced not only Hohokam archaeology but general anthropological studies of irrigation societies by introducing the concept of accretionary growth of canal systems. Working with the Arid Lands Department of the University of Arizona, Woodbury conducted several canal excavations, including those at Pueblo Grande and Snaketown (Woodbury 1960, Haury 1976). His investigations highlight the distinctive approach of archaeological research and its contribution to anthropological studies of irrigation. Cultural anthropologists usually approach irrigation studies with informant testimony and focus primarily on social organization, with only secondary consideration of the mechanics of canal engineering and operation. The archaeological perspective examines the physical remains of the irrigation systems, focusing on a more basic set of functional questions concerning hydraulic engineering, discharge, velocity, water quality, soil edaphic factors, and crop yields. Archaeologists start with a more detailed view of the physical operation of the canal system and attempt social, political, and economic reconstructions from a more basic set of data. When a diachronic perspective is added, archaeologists are in a position to discuss processes of canal system expansion.

The concept of accretionary growth held that the construction of canal systems proceeded intermittently, beginning with the addition of a short canal and followed by the addition of subsequent canal segments as additional area was required. Woodbury argued that small, periodic labor investments over several hundred years resulted in the monumental Hohokam irrigation works (Woodbury 1961). Emphasizing canal construction as the major logistical challenge for sociopolitical control in irrigation societies, he concluded that irrigation technology does not require sociopolitical complexity. Given that small, incremental labor investments can result in the construction of very large systems, even egalitarian groups (such as the Hohokam were assumed to be by Woodbury and others) could organize such efforts.

Continued research and a more detailed examination of the engineering of irrigation systems in the Hohokam area have resulted in the identification of two basic factors that make Woodbury's assumed process of accretionary growth untenable. First, the extension of the length of a canal increases the total discharge needed for its operation. The construction of additional segments would quickly exceed the discharge capacity of the original canal head. Extending the operational length of a canal requires an enlargement of the existing canal segment. Thus, the small labor investments envisioned by Woodbury cannot significantly extend a canal system (cf. Doolittle 1989).

Secondly, Woodbury, along with several subsequent researchers, did not recognize the limited use-life of the Hohokam canals and the need for the constant rebuilding of canal features. In its wider applications, the accretionary model assumes that, once constructed, Hohokam canals (or canal segments) remain in use. Nicholas and Neitzel (1984) explicitly argue that the configuration of the Hohokam systems do not change and that the canals are maintained but are not periodically rebuilt. Recent research (Ackerly et al. 1987, Ackerly & Henderson 1989, Greenwald & Ciolek-Torrello 1989, Howard 1990a) has demonstrated that Hohokam main canals had a relatively short use-life (approximately 50-100 years) and that they were constantly rebuilt, often in response to damage inflicted by catastrophic flooding on the Salt River (Nials et al. 1989).

The Settlement and Demographic Growth Model (Upham & Rice 1980)

Given these recent findings, the model of accretionary growth does not represent a significant process of expansion for Hohokam canal systems. While small extensions may be viable in some cases, such a process could not be sustained. Woodbury's model of accretionary growth is not only technically incorrect, it dramatically underestimates the amount of labor required for canal construction.

Approaching agricultural intensification from another viewpoint, Upham and Rice (1980) conducted an examination of changing settlement throughout the Salt River Valley. Their study suggested a continuous process of demographic growth with corresponding expansion and addition of canal systems in the Salt River Valley. Intensification of agricultural production was suggested by changing settlement location, differentiation in settlement function, and specialization of production. Following Turney (1929) and

Woodbury (1961), they viewed processes of internal canal system growth as being both (1) accretionary, expanding the length of existing canals, and (2) additive, constructing new canals upslope along "less optimal gradients" (Upham & Rice 1980:81). While suggesting continuous growth, they failed to provide quantified data on canal systems and settlement size for each period. They saw differentiation and exploitation of different resources as occurring when site locations shifted away from the riparian environment into environmental zones along the pediments. Thus, differentiation of the subsistence base is seen as being a function of the processes of canal expansion into more diverse environmental zones. Upham and Rice also explored several aspects of settlement pattern structure based on a rank-size curve, SYMAP distributions, and linear nearest-neighbor analysis.

While providing some useful insights, the study by Upham and Rice (1980) suffered from several problems related to their data base. Their primary variable, that of site size, was measured as the maximum recorded extent of each site. They then used this measure to represent the size of the site throughout its occupation. It has now been demonstrated that Hohokam sites display significant horizontal stratigraphy, shifting spatially through time (Howard 1990b). Maximum site size, as measured simply by defining site boundaries, provides a measure of the maximum area covered by the horizontally shifting occupations. Even given a stable population, the maximum horizontal extent of the archaeological deposits would be expected to increase as greater lateral shifting occurs though time. The use of maximum site extent to measure population size for all time periods masks the variability Upham and Rice wished to study. An accurate measure of site size requires comprehensive data to document site boundary shifts through time. Currently, data of this type are available only from a few sites in the valley (Howard 1990b), and even in these cases the level of resolution in the data needs improvement.

Recent research also shows that the chronological and site-size data available at the time of the Upham and Rice (1980) study were often incorrect. Upham and Rice argued, for example, that the sites of Los Muertos and Cashion are the two primary sites of the Classic period. Cashion actually became much reduced in size in the Classic period, and Los Muertos covers 0.5 mi^2, not the 12 mi^2 figure used in their study (see Wilcox & Howard n.d.).

The Application of Remote Sensing Techniques

Nicholas (1981, Nicholas & Feinman 1989, Nicholas & Neitzel 1984) presented the most comprehensive and innovative studies of canal system expansion. She combined the use of a detailed map of the prehistoric canals of the Salt River, produced from aerial photographs and the cross-dating of sites and canals, to produce a diachronic reconstruction of system growth

(Nicholas 1981). This reconstruction suggested a process of dramatic growth in the canal systems through time (see Nicholas & Feinman 1989). Nicholas postulated that the canal systems at least doubled in size during each chronological period (Table 2). This model again follows Woodbury's (1961) concept of accretionary growth. Different segments of the same main canal were often dated to different chronological periods, based on known dates of occupation for associated sites. The Nicholas reconstruction often suggests continual expansion of main canals, increasingly farther from their heads on the river.

The Nicholas (1981) reconstruction suffered from both methodological problems and data-base problems that could not be resolved at the time. By using the chronological data provided by Upham and Rice (1980), several significant inaccuracies were perpetuated. For example, the Mesa-Lehi system, operational only in the very late Sedentary and the Classic period (Howard 1987), is shown by Nicholas (1981) as being fully operational in the Colonial period; this error is apparently based on a single date from survey notes for the site of La Casa de Mesa.

Three major methodological and conceptual problems can also be noted. First, Nicholas used the chronological assignments of sites (primarily village sites) along the canals to date the canals themselves. While these data can provide rough chronological parameters, they are poor indicators of canal construction dates. Recent research has demonstrated a budding process for site establishment and growth within Turney's (1929) Canal System 2 (Howard & Wilcox 1988). When new canals are constructed, fieldhouses represent the first type of land use established. Later, as the canal system expands, small but more permanent farmsteads and hamlets are established by populations budding off villages within an expanding "occupation zone" that cross-cuts a set of parallel main canals (Howard & Wilcox 1988). Within Canal System 2, larger village sites may be established more than 100 years after initial canal construction. Given the limited archaeological visibility of fieldhouses and small hamlets, the dates for initial expansion into specific areas are not generally available in the existing survey data. The use of problematic dates from outdated survey information has led to inaccurate diachronic reconstructions.

Additional problems in the Nicholas reconstruction involve assumptions concerning the engineering and operation of Hohokam irrigation systems which must now be revised. First, the reconstruction is based on an acceptance of Woodbury's (1961) concepts of accretionary growth and indefinite canal use-life. Recent large-scale subsurface investigations have identified non-contemporaneous sets of main canals that represent the continual rebuilding of canals servicing the same area. The use-life of the canals appears to be limited, with abandonment and rebuilding being the norm.

The third problem is that the Nicholas reconstruction, along with other early projections, is predicated on the assumption that all canals are equal in terms

Table 2.   Reconstruction of the Growth of Canal System 2
as Suggested by Nicholas (1981) and Howard (1990a)

	Nicholas (1981)	Howard (1990)	Howard (1990)
Period and Dates	Number of Acres	Number of Acres	M₃ per second
Pioneer (A.D. ? - 600)	5,120	2,354	7
Colonial (A.D. 600 - 900)	11,040	20,936	59
Sedentary (A.D. 900 - 1100)	24,620	16,579	46
Classic (A.D. 1100 - 1450)	44,740	18,814	53

of their size and capacity (cf. Neitzel 1991). However, subsurface investigations have demonstrated significant variability in canal morphology and capacity between individual main canals. If the expansion of the canal system capacity is to be demonstrated, adequate measures of the discharge carried by individual canals must be developed. Total canal length is not an adequate measure; canals of similar length can irrigate areas of dramatically different sizes, depending on how far the fields extend laterally away from the canal.

In a more recent but related paper, Nicholas and Feinman (1989) suggest that increasing organizational complexity and integration in the Hohokam canal systems reflects increasing managerial and sociopolitical complexity. They argue that branch canals represent distinct organizational units (also see Howard n.d.a). Through time, branches are added onto the canal system, increasing the need for communication and sociopolitical integration. Nicholas and Feinman (1989) further argue that "cross-cut" canals, operating to divert water from one main canal to another, were added to the system in the Classic period. They suggest that the interconnection of the main canals reflects a higher level of integration, uniting the operation of the individual main canals in the canal system. They note that, at this level of system integration, water allocation and scheduling may be coordinated not only within a single main canal but within the entire canal network. Nicholas and Feinman (1989) suggest that the increased level of integration in the Classic period probably reflects an increased level of sociopolitical complexity at that time. They do caution, however, that these results are tentative and could change as more detailed excavation data become available (Nicholas & Feinman 1989:230).

Excavation data are now suggesting that the majority of the branch and cross-cut canals identified in aerial photos and older maps are actually separate, non-contemporaneous canal features. When a main canal is abandoned, a new canal may be constructed using portions of the old channel, but at some point it diverges along a new route (Greenwald & Ciolek-Torrello 1989, Howard 1990a). Distribution canals often ran downslope from a new main canal and turned into the alignment of an abandoned, parallel main canal, creating the impression of a "cross-cut" canal. The use of aerial photographs to identify canal alignments is a powerful tool; alternative methods are needed, however, to determine the contemporaneity and continuity of overlapping alignments. Without these methods, aerial photographic interpretations can be very inaccurate in their portrayal of system structure and growth.

Summary

Past studies of canal system expansion and agricultural intensification within the large Hohokam irrigation systems have relied on surface data to identify the locations of canals and sites. These data are supplied by early maps (primarily, Turney 1929 and Midvale 1968), aerial photographic interpretation, and recent archaeological survey data. These sources have not provided the empirical data base necessary for the detailed, quantified diachronic reconstructions of system expansion that have been attempted. They have suffered from three major deficiencies:

1. *Lack of chronological control:* Chronological control is often provided through an argument of association, cross-dating canals with often poorly derived (surface ceramic) dates for sites.
2. *Rough estimations of canal capacity:* Canal capacities were not previously quantified, or even considered. Only rough estimates of canal length have been employed.
3. *Lack of understanding of canal system structure:* The engineering of the canal systems—including canal morphology, longitudinal change of the canals from their head to terminus, the operation of distribution systems, the manipulation of water levels and hydraulic heads, and the nature and use of water control features—has not been considered. This deficiency has led to misconceptions concerning the structure and operation of the canal systems.

While past studies, and particularly those of Nicholas, have pioneered innovative techniques and concepts, they were necessarily limited by the nature of the available data. Subsurface data, derived from the excavation of canal channels, were only slowly accumulating (Masse 1981). More accurate and detailed studies required larger, more systematic subsurface investigations and the development of new techniques and methodologies.

PALEOHYDRAULIC RECONSTRUCTIONS

Urban expansion in the Phoenix metropolitan area over the last decade has resulted in numerous excavation projects through cultural resource management studies. Several researchers have used this opportunity to continue and refine irrigation studies and develop new methodologies and techniques (Ackerly et al. 1987, Ackerly & Henderson 1989, Eighmy & Howard 1991, Howard 1990a, Howard & Breternitz 1989, Huckleberry 1992). Subsurface excavations of irrigation features have facilitated the reconstruction of the engineering principles and the designs of canal systems. The application of open channel equations and the retrodiction of the critical velocities needed to move and deposit canal sediments have provided a means to quantify channel discharge and water velocity from canal profiles. The development of improved dating methods that can be directly applied to canal contexts (Eighmy & Howard 1991) provides a greatly revised view of system development. Drawing on an improved knowledge of canal engineering, canal use-life and canal dating, this view departs from the accretionary growth model: canal systems are perceived as more dynamic entities undergoing a process of continual rebuilding and re-engineering. This process appears to be punctuated by catastrophic flood events that can require major rebuilding episodes.

Much of the data on prehistoric Hohokam irrigation have appeared in individual project and site reports. In most cases, the analytical breadth has not extended much beyond the confines of the project area. Questions concerning canal engineering and capacity are usually addressed within a limited contextual frame, calculating canal capacity at single spatial points along the canal system. System capacity, the total discharge passing through the canal headgate, cannot be determined from a single segment or profile. Recently, an overview of system operation, capacity, and diachronic change has been presented (Howard 1990a). Excavation data, geomorphological analysis, improved chronological control, and engineering designs were incorporated into a synthesis of system expansion to provide a more detailed view of agricultural intensification in Canal System 2.

Two major conceptual concerns distinguish the current study from past reconstructions of irrigation systems. The first is the concern with paleohydraulic variables, the calculation of cross-sectional area, hydraulic radius, water velocity, and discharge, and their interpretation within the context of hydraulic engineering. The focus of this research is on water flow characteristics of the canals rather than simply the location and length of the canals. The second major focus lies in the modeling of the longitudinal section of the canal: how the canal changes from its head at the river to its terminus. The longitudinal section provides a holistic, or three-dimensional view of canal operation, permitting investigations of changing channel morphology, velocity, and discharge through the system. Canals do change as they progress from the head to the terminus, reducing in size in response to water loss through seepage and evaporation as well as through discharge into distribution canals and onto fields. By modeling longitudinal change, it is possible to project the size of the channel at any point along the canal, to reconstruct water availability in different areas, and to calculate both the total discharge capacity and the amount of soil removed for initial canal construction (Howard 1990a). The major techniques, methodologies, results and implications of this study are presented below.

Canal System 2 Data Base

This analyses of the processes of canal expansion focuses on a detailed study of Turney's Second Canal System (Canal System 2), a large integrated canal system located on the north side of the Salt River and underlying Phoenix, Arizona (Figure 1). Approximately 50 main canals were constructed within this system from the late Pioneer period through the Classic period of Hohokam development, circa A.D. 550 to 1450 (see Table 1). Approximately nine large main canals were active at any one time, fanning out in a series of parallel canals closely following the topographic contour of the valley. The canal heads for Canal System 2 all clustered along a reasonably short stretch of river. The heads met the Salt River just below the point where a granitic dike crossing the river forced the underground flow to the surface, creating a substantial increase in local streamflow and a hydrographic boundary (Howard 1990a).

Pueblo Grande, the largest site within the canal system and the location of one of the two largest platform mounds, is placed in the headgate area. This large administrative site was in direct control of water flow in the canal system. While the lengths of individual canals varied, the majority extended 12-16 miles from their head. A minimum of 15 village sites and numerous smaller occupation areas were located within the canal system. The larger village sites (containing a minimum of nine platform mounds during the Classic period) were clustered in three occupation zones arrayed perpendicular to, and located at intervals of 5 km along, the canals (Figure 1).

Hundreds of cross-sectional profiles have been secured from the canals in this system by various archaeological projects. The sample is largely opportunistic, with data being retrieved from randomly spaced construction projects; it is also clustered, with multiple samples being secured from a linearly restricted segment of a canal as it passed through a project area. Freeway project right-of-ways have provided several comprehensive transects through portions of the system (Figure 2).

All available profiles were carefully examined to determine how representative they were of the segment of the canal they represented. Localized processes of channel erosion can exaggerate cross-sectional area of channels in an archaeological context, while the degree of historic truncation can underestimate channel size. In most cases, multiple, closely spaced cross-sections were recorded as a canal passed through a project area. From the hundreds of available profiles, a sample of 176 of the most representative profiles were selected for this study. Paleohydraulic variables were calculated for each profile in the sample (Howard 1990a).

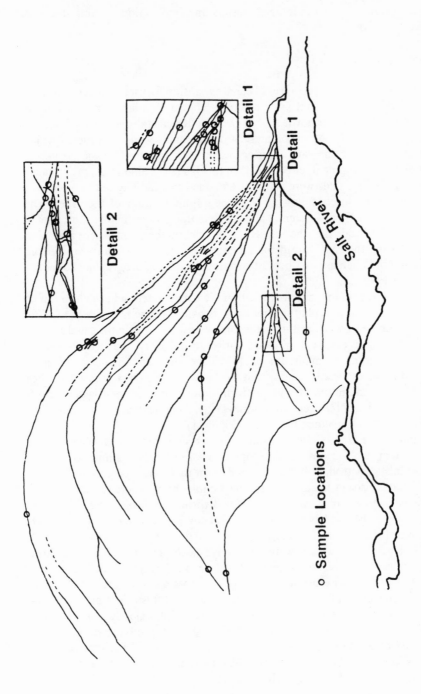

Detail 1

Detail 2

Detail 1

Detail 2

Salt River

o Sample Locations

Figure 2. The Data Points and Freeway Transects through Canal System 2

276

Paleohydraulic Variables

Analysis of the paleohydraulics of Hohokam canals involves a series of variables and concepts that can be expressed mathematically. The major variables of interest in system reconstruction are discharge and velocity. Discharge is a good relative measure of system capacity: how much water an open channel can transport. This measure can be used in comparative studies to examine the relative capacity of different canals. Further, this measure can be transformed into absolute measures, such as the total area that can be irrigated. The accuracy of absolute measures, however, can be affected by many different variables and often have high error factors.

Estimates of water velocity are necessary for the calculation of discharge and are critical to an understanding of flow regimes and their impact on canal maintenance. Next to discharge, channel velocity is the most important concern in canal engineering and design. Velocity must be balanced between two thresholds, the erosion threshold and the siltation threshold. If the velocity is excessive, channel erosion will occur until the increase in cross-sectional area reduces the velocity, bringing it below the erosional threshold. If the velocity falls below the siltation level, the canal will rapidly silt up, requiring frequent cleaning. The retrodictions of discharge and velocity in modern as well as archaeological channels have been calculated from open channel equations. Manning's formula (Chow 1959:98) is employed in almost all cases (Chow 1959, Busch et al. 1976, Masse 1981, Huckleberry & Howard n.d.). The Manning equation calculates maximum channel velocity and is defined as:

$$V = n^{-1} * R^{2/3} * S^{1/2}$$

Where: V = water velocity (m/s)
R = hydraulic radius (m)
S = hydraulic gradient
n = coefficient of roughness

Discharge (Q) can then be calculated using the continuity equation:

$$Q = A * V$$

Where: Q = discharge (m^3/s)
A = cross-sectional area (m^2)
V = water velocity (m/s)

Several variables must be calculated to solve these equations. Cross-sectional area must be calculated from trench profiles, with different equations being used for different channel shapes (Chow 1959). The two common morphological shapes for Hohokam canals are parabolic (characteristic of the greatest percentage of the sample) and trapezoidal. Cross-sectional area is calculated for a parabolic channel with the equation:

$$A = 2/3\,Ty$$

Where: $T =$ top width
$y =$ channel depth
$A =$ cross-sectional area

Cross-sectional area is calculated for a trapezoidal channel with the equation:

$$(b + zy)y$$

Where: $b =$ width of the channel base
$y =$ channel depth
$z =$ slope of the sidewall

Hydraulic radius (R) is solved to calculate the Manning equation. R is calculated for a parabolic channel using the equation:

$$R = A/P$$

Where: $R =$ hydraulic radius
$P =$ wetted perimeter
$A =$ cross-sectional area

Wetted perimeter is calculated from the equation:

$$P = (T/2)[1+x2 + 1/x \ln (x + 1+x2)]$$

Where: $P =$ wetted perimeter
$T =$ top width
$\ln =$ log normal
$x = (4 *$ channel depth$)/$channel width

R is calculated for a trapezoidal channel using the equation:

$$R = ((b + zy)y)/(b + 2y\, 1 + z2)$$

Where: $b =$ width of the channel base
$y =$ channel depth
$z =$ slope of the sidewall

The measurement of several variables for the calculation of open channel equations can be problematic. These variables include hydraulic gradient, operative water levels, cross-sectional area, and Manning's *n* (a coefficient of channel roughness). Hydraulic gradient is the slope of the *water level* within the channel.

In an archaeological context, the hydraulic gradient cannot be directly identified in most Hohokam canals. Measurements of the slope of the base of prehistoric canals do not provide the true hydraulic gradient, only an approximation. Often, the slope of the canal base can only be recorded over a short horizontal segment due to the restricted nature of arbitrary archaeological project boundaries. The calculation of hydraulic gradient (the slope of the surface of the water) over short distances has been found to be susceptible to substantial error when the slope of the base of a prehistoric channel is used. Substantial error can be created by localized fluctuations along the base of the canal as noted by Ackerly et al. (1987).

Despite claims to the contrary (Ackerly & Henderson 1988), canal gradients should not be expected to display substantial deviation from local topographic slope. Gradients exceeding local slope would quickly entrench the canal, lowering the command (the elevational difference between the water level and the adjacent ground surface) to unusable levels. Gradients shallower than the local slope would raise the command, a positive accomplishment, but one that could not continue over a large distance without creating too great a command. Topographic gradient was selected in this study as being most representative of the true hydraulic gradient. The gradients of local historic canals were also examined and found to be isomorphic with, and representative of, local topographic slope (Huckleberry 1989).

Determining the cross-sectional area involves a series of variables that must be measured. A primary concern has been establishing prehistoric water levels. The water levels for Canal System 2 were identified by examining the dynamic interaction between the topographic slope and distribution canal gradients (Howard 1990a). Water levels must be high enough in the main canal to enter the shallower distribution canal. The water level in the distribution canal must ultimately be higher than the surface of the field so that water can be released onto this surface. Finally, the water levels in the distribution canals cannot exceed the berm of the distribution canal, or it will be breached. Using an analytical procedure that examines these parameters provided the first empirical evidence of water levels in the Hohokam main canals. In most cases, the calculations suggested that the water levels in the main canals were 30-40 cm below the surrounding ground surface. Manning's *n* is a coefficient of roughness and is used to determine the effects of sidewall friction on channel velocity. Friction results from the regularity or irregularity of the canal sidewall, channel sinuosity, and the amount of phreatophytic (aquatic plant) growth in the canal. Israelsen and Hansen (1962) provide *n* values corresponding to different channel conditions. A roughness coefficient (Manning's n) of 0.030 is viewed as the most likely value for most Hohokam canals (Huckleberry 1988).

Manning's Equation and the continuity equation were applied to field data from Canal System 2, using basic channel shape along with depth and width measurements taken from trench profiles. This step permitted the calculation of a series of hydraulic variables for each specific cross-section, including wetted perimeter, hydraulic radius, velocity, and discharge. This information (Howard 1990a:Appendix B) forms a substantial data base for understanding changes in the hydraulic variables throughout the system. The next major goal was to refine the data base by understanding localized variability in associated cross-sections and to remove anomalous measures.

The set of profile records from a single canal within a project area represents a sample of the morphological and sedimentological variation for a restricted segment of that canal. For purposes of modeling longitudinal change through the system, each aggregate sample was carefully examined and characterized by a single set of dimensions which best represented the canal channel at that point from the headgate. A comparative examination of a larger aggregate sample allows the researcher to factor out problems created by erosion and historic disturbance, thus creating a higher quality data base.

A data base was assembled, consisting of the hydraulic variables for 57 individual data points, one for each of the major sampling locations along the main canals in Canal System 2. The majority of these data points are characterized from aggregate samples, multiple cross-sections along a restricted portion of a main canal. The attributes included within this data base include channel chronology, distance from the projected canal head, cross-sectional area, discharge retrodiction, and velocity.

The Linking Analysis

To examine longitudinal change in paleohydraulic variables, canal size, velocity, and discharge must be compared between widely spaced points along the same, contemporaneous canal channels. The analytical challenge was to "link" up cross-sections of contemporary canal profiles from complex sets of prehistoric channels. A set of linking criteria was established to accomplish this task:

1. *Contemporaneity:* Individual canals must be contemporaneous to be linked. Given the difficulties in assigning dates to canal features, the reliability of assigned dates must be carefully examined and the degree of certainty assessed. Sorting the total sample by chronological placement significantly reduces the number of possible matches.

2. *Elevation, Contour, and Gradient:* The position and elevation of a canal on the Salt River terrace system was used to project the general location of a canal alignment. The canal should follow a reasonable gradient to avoid siltation and erosion. Alignments of canals climbing higher up on the contour create a negative gradient and, except in very localized situations, can be ruled out. The drop of the canal downslope should not be so great as to create velocities substantially above the erosion threshold. If canals diverge and follow slightly different alignments or gradients, an increase in gradient should be apparent in an increase in the projected critical velocity for the canal sediments.

3. *Mapped Alignments:* Early maps of the canal alignments (Midvale 1968, Turney 1929) provide information on the patterned relationships between topography, canal gradient, and probable alignment. These maps often have variable levels of resolution, however. The overview maps of the valley exhibit low resolution; they show the approximate placement of single canals but cannot be used to distinguish between non-contemporaneous canals closely following the same alignment. Midvale's notes often provide more precise locational information that distinguishes between individual canals, but such information is limited. Maps based on surficial evidence are strongly biased toward the last canal constructed along an alignment. Given demonstrable contemporaneity, cross-sections along a mapped alignment provide strong evidence for linkage. However, it must be recognized that not all canals will necessarily follow the mapped alignments. Earlier canals in particular may display different head locations and may turn downslope or terminate sooner than the Classic period canals.

4. *Aerial Maps:* The exact alignment of a canal identified by subsurface information can often be tracked using aerial photo- interpretation. The maps generated by Nicholas (Nicholas 1981) and Masse (1981, 1987) provide information on alignments that can be seen on early aerial photographs. It is often necessary to examine the primary data to determine the usefulness of aerial photo-interpretation to a specific canal or set of canals. Tracing the signature of a prehistoric canal between profile cross-sections provides significant evidence for linkage.

5. *Channel Morphology:* Channel morphology can be variable, even over short distances. Channel shape is particularly variable and should not be employed as a basis for comparison. Channel size as represented by cross-sectional area is variable but should diminish with distance. A matching profile several kilometers down-canal should exhibit a reduction in cross-sectional area. Enlargements in the hydraulic radius, wetted perimeter, and cross- sectional area should result in substantially lowered velocities and suspended load deposition.

Table 3. Data Used in the Linking Analysis

Data Point	Feature[a]	Km from Headgate	Date Assigned	A^b	Q^c	V^d
Appropriator's Canal						
Section 1	Historic	0.00	Historic	18.85	15.15	0.82
Section 2	Historic	7.00	Historic	9.29	7.33	0.79
Section 3	Historic	14.00	Historic	6.19	3.20	0.52
Section 4a	Historic	15.00	Historic	3.87	2.55	0.66
Section 4b	Historic	16.75	Historic	3.10	1.57	0.51
Section 5	Historic	21.00	Historic	2.32	1.15	0.50
Section 7	Historic	28.00	Historic	1.55	0.73	0.47
Canal Grande						
2	Bradley; F19	1.68	Classic	5.10	4.77	0.93
22	EP; F3	3.50	Classic	3.40	2.87	0.87
35	GC; 124	8.85	Classic	1.65	0.83	0.51
39	Camelback	13.90	Classic	1.04	0.92	0.41
Canal Ciudad						
Early 9	Masse; F7a; C1	0.55	Sedentary	12.75	16.76	1.31
33	Ciudad; 1310	5.50	Colonial	7.47	8.16	1.09
Late 10	Masse; F7a; C2	0.55	Sedentary	8.87	9.95	1.11
34	Ciudad; 1311	5.50	Sedentary	2.99	2.53	0.85
Canal Grande Alignment F5						
3	Masse; F14	1.59	Sedentary-Classic	6.49	6.68	1.03
23	EP; F5	3.50	Classic	3.63	3.13	0.86
38	GC; F22	7.40	Classic	2.80	2.58	0.92
Woodbury North						
19	Woodbury North	0.33	Classic	18.33	25.99	1.42
6	Masse; F11	0.61	Classic	10.13	11.71	1.16
25	EP; F30	4.30	Classic	6.75	5.56	0.82
49	Los Colinas; F1	14.00	Sedentary-Classic	5.67	5.44	0.88
Woodbury South						
20	Woodbury South	0.30	Classic	6.42	6.50	1.10
14	Masse; F3	0.47	Classic	5.58	5.32	0.95
East Papago (EP) Feature 1						
21	EP; F1	3.40	Sedentary-Classic	1.20	0.72	0.60
54	PG; F794	0.31	Classic (?)	18.04	23.32	1.29
Los Colinas						
50	Las Colinas; F5	6.60	Sedentary-Classic	12.67	14.76	1.17
51	Los Aumentos; C1	18.10	Classic	1.20	1.49	1.24
52	Los Aumentos; C2	18.10	Classic	0.90	1.01	1.12

Notes: EP = East Papago Project, PG = Pueblo Grande Project, GC = Grand Canal Ruins.

   a. A = Canal cross-sectional area, in cubic meters.

   b. Q = Maximum discharge capacity, in cubic meters per second.

   c. V = Velocity in meters per second.

These criteria provided a framework for evaluating proposed linkages and for setting confidence levels (Howard 1990a). Six prehistoric canals having linked sets of profiles were identified in this study (Table 3). The most comprehensive data set was derived from two chronologically distinct canals within the alignment for Canal Grande, representing the northernmost canals in the system. Four linked cross-sections were identified for the northernmost canal (Canal Grande proper) and three for an earlier canal (Feature 5). A patterned reduction in cross-sectional area (A), discharge (Q), and velocity (V) with distance from the canal head can be seen in Table 3 and is portrayed graphically in Figure 3. Eight additional linked pairs of cross-sections were also identified.

Cross-sectional figures for the longitudinal section of the historic Appropriator's Canal have been included here for comparative purposes. This canal was constructed prior to the damming of the Salt River and thus was operating under environmental conditions similar to those of the prehistoric canals. It also parallels the course of the prehistoric Canal Grande, crossing the same topography and soils. Given the similarity of their operational parameters, the Appropriator's Canal and Canal Grande provide an excellent comparative case study for examining the differences between prehistoric and historic irrigation engineering using archaeological data.

Regression Modeling of the Longitudinal Section

The degree of cross-sectional reduction through the longitudinal section should vary in relationship to a series of variables. The major variable of water loss, the rate of discharge per linear measure (such as water use per km), will vary with the size of the fields being supplied, the continuity or regularity in the distribution of fields along the canal, and water duty per unit of farmland. In some cases, canal function may affect water use. Transport sections, those segments of canals that carry water from a source to the vicinity of fields without discharging water for use, should display minimal reduction in cross-sectional area. It is expected, then, that the ratio of water use to linear distance and the resulting cross-sectional reduction curve will show significant variation between canals traversing different terrain. However, canals following similar topography and having similar field systems may produce comparable reduction curves (see Howard 1990a).

To examine variability in water use in the Salt River Valley on both an inter- and intra-canal system basis, data on water use from historic canals were examined (Howard 1990a). A ratio of water use, defined as m^3/second divided by km of canal length, was calculated for historic canals in the valley. Variability was high on an intrasystem basis, when canals traversing different topographic situations were compared. In this case, water use varied from 0.08 to 2.73 m^3/second/km of canal length. However, the historic canals traversing

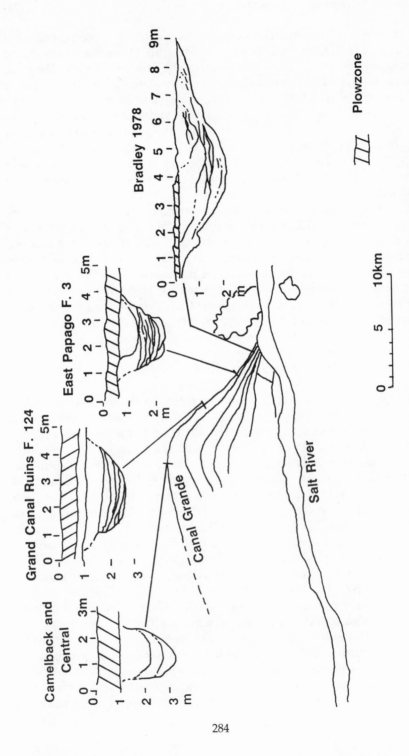

Figure 3. The Linked Cross-Sections Identified along Prehistoric Canal Grande

284

the Canal System 2 area displayed extremely low variability, ranging between 0.22 and 0.37 m^3/second/km of canal length.

Historic analogs display little variation in the Canal System 2 area; the canals followed nearly identical contours and gradients, and traversed similar sediments. The uniformity in water use per km for unlined historic canals suggests that the pattern of reduction in cross-sectional area through the longitudinal section would be similar for all of the prehistoric canals in Canal System 2. Furthermore, the variability between the historic canals from Canal System 2 and other canal systems suggests that greater variability might be present on an intersystem basis. These results provided support for the contention that change in the longitudinal section was uniform for all of the prehistoric canals in Canal System 2. Given such uniformity, it should be possible to develop techniques for predictive modeling. Once developed, the predictive model could then be tested against the actual archaeological data base for Canal System 2. If the model predicted cross-sectional change within an acceptable range of error, it could then be used to characterize or model the longitudinal section for all canals that have at least one acceptable data point (i.e., adequate characterization of cross-sectional area at one point along their alignment).

To examine patterns of longitudinal change in the prehistoric canals, channel reduction was graphed by comparing cross-sectional area and distance from the head (Figure 4). The Appropriator's Canal, Canal Grande, and other known paired sections of other canals follow a concave reduction curve. The reduction curve indicates that cross-sectional area is very large at the canal head but rapidly reduces in size in the head area and then smooths out as the canal progresses toward its terminus. The prehistoric and historic channels appear to follow the same reduction curve, regardless of the overall size of the canal. The regularity in the reduction curves suggests that mathematical or predictive modeling of morphological change through the longitudinal section was possible.

To model the reduction curve, a simple regression analysis was conducted, based on the variables of cross-sectional area and distance of the profile cut from the canal head (Howard 1990a). A curvilinear regression analysis can be more problematic than simple linear functions. Given a curvilinear regression line, the most robust analytical approach is to seek a data transformation that will convert the curvilinear relationship into a linear one. Following the data transformation, standard linear models can then be applied (Thomas 1976:427). One standard technique for data transformation is logarithmic transformation.

A logarithmic transformation using the standard logarithmic formula $\hat{y} = \log(X + 1)$ is appropriate for the concave reduction curve for the cross-sectional area. To meet the needs of the current regression analysis, two additional variables—an additive constant (the y intercept) and a multiplicative constant

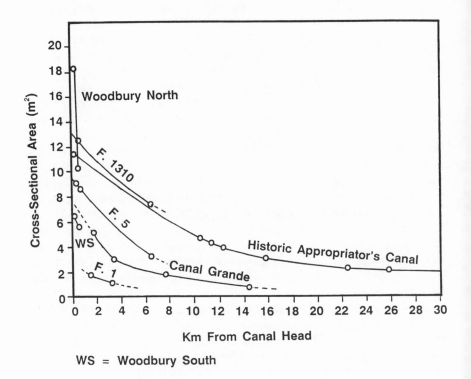

Figure 4.   Cross-sectional Reduction Curves for Linked Points along the Prehistoric Canals in Canal System 2 and the Historic Appropriator's Canal

(z)—are added to the formula. The additive constant, or *y* intercept, calibrates the overall size and length of the canal. The multiplicative constant determines the slope (i.e., the curve as transformed by the log function) of the line and will remain constant for all canals in the Canal System 2 analysis. While the regression line for the cross-sectional reduction curve will maintain its reduction rate as determined by the multiplicative constant, the curve will move up and down the graph in response to the variables of overall size and length. Again, while the size and length of the canals will vary, the pattern of reduction will remain constant. The resulting regression formula is:

$$\hat{y} = z(\log(x+1)) + y \text{ intercept}$$

Where: $\hat{y}$ = dependent variable (cross-sectional area)
         x = independent variable (distance from head)
         z = multiplicative constant (slope [curve] of the line)

To calculate the multiplicative constant and establish the predictive regression formula, I used the two known variables x (distance from head) and y (cross-sectional area) for the data points from the two most comprehensive samples, the historic Appropriators' Canal and prehistoric Canal Grande. Additional linked samples were not included in the generation of the predictive model but were employed for the subsequent testing of it.

The x and y values for the Appropriators' Canal were initially used to solve for z. The simple regression procedure of SYSTAT (1985) was employed for the regression analysis. Standard linear correlation statistics were also generated by SYSTAT. Pearson's correlation coefficient was generated to determine the linearity of the relationship between x and y (i.e., the fit of the regression line to the actual data points). The squared r denotes the proportion of the total variance of y (cross-sectional area) that is accounted for by the independent predictor x (distance from headgate).

For both the Appropriator's Canal and Canal Grande, Pearson's correlation coefficient reveals a strong fit between the regression line and the actual data points, with correlations of .998 and .991, respectively. The squared r indicates that a very high proportion of the variability in cross-sectional area (y) is predicted by distance from the river (x). The squared r for the Appropriator's Canal and prehistoric Canal Grande are very high, accounting for almost 100 percent of the observed variability (99.7% and 98.2%, respectively). The adjusted multiple r for all runs is also very high, suggesting that, for both canals, over 97 percent of the known variability can be predicted using additional data points drawn from the same population. Such high correspondence in the predictive regression line is unusual in archaeological research, and it may be largely attributed here to the natural processes that help to ameliorate the variability created by human error during canal construction.

The curvilinear regression analysis resulted in the generation of a predictive model of cross-sectional reduction for all prehistoric canals in Canal System 2 from our historic analog, where:

$$\hat{y} = -2.215(\log(x + 1) + (y \text{ intercept})$$

To operationalize the predictive model for a particular canal, a single data point with known cross-sectional area (y) and distance from the canal head (x) must be used to solve for the y intercept. This calculation provides a calibration for the overall size, or magnitude, of the canal. When operationalized, a cross-section of a canal in Canal System 2 can be used to predict the size and general length of the canal when the location of the head is determined. Once the y intercept is determined, the model can then be used to predict points beginning at the head and projecting toward the terminus. Predictions were generated for every 2 km increment, and the points were then plotted to predict the cross-section reduction curve for each canal (Howard 1990a).

The sample of prehistoric canals identified in the linking analysis as having more than one recorded cross-section were used to test the predictive model. A single data point from each linked canal sample was used to solve for the y intercept and to calibrate canal size. Using the y intercept provided by the first cross-section, the regression formula generated the predicted cross-sectional area ($\hat{y}$) for the distance (x) of the second recorded cross-section or data point. The predicted cross-sectional area was then compared with the recorded cross-section for the second data point.

I conducted comparative testing of the regression analysis on seven linked canal features, including Canal Grande. A total of 17 linked data points were compared; seven functioned as calibration points for the y intercept with 10 functioning as predictive tests. Table 4 presents the comparisons between $\hat{y}$

Table 4. Testing the Predictive Model Against Known Data Points

Canal	Data Point	CP^a	X^b	Distance CP^c	$\hat{y}^d$	$\hat{y}^e$	Error^f
Canal Grande	1		1.68	1.82	4.55	5.10	-0.55
	2	CP	3.50	—	3.40	3.40	—
	3		7.70	4.20	1.94	1.87	0.07
	4		13.90	10.40	0.75	1.04	-0.29
La Ciudad F.1310	1		0.55	4.95	10.6	12.7	2.10
	2	CP	5.50	—	7.47	7.47	—
La Ciudad F.1311	1		0.55	4.95	6.17	8.87	2.70
	2	CP	5.50	—	2.99	2.99	—
East Papago F.1	1	CP	3.40	—	1.20	1.20	—
	2		1.63	1.77	2.34	1.80	0.54
East Papago F.5	1		1.59	—	4.85	6.49	-1.64
	2	CP	3.50	1.91	3.63	3.63	—
	3		7.40	3.90	2.25	2.80	-0.55
Woodbury North	1		0.33	0.28	10.5	18.3	-7.78
	2	CP	0.61	—	10.1	10.1	—
Woodbury South	1		0.30	0.17	5.85	6.50	-0.65
	2	CP	0.47	—	5.58	5.58	—

Notes: a. The Calibration Point: The variables of distance from the river and cross-sectional area from this point were entered into the regression formula to model the changing longitudinal section.

b. Distance in Km of each point from its head on the river.

c. The distance of the secondary points (the points to be modeled by the regression formula) from the calibration point.

d. The predicted cross-sectional area ($y\pi$) of the secondary points as modeled by the regression formula using the calibration point.

e. The actual cross-sectional area (y) of the canal.

f. The error, in cubic meters, of the predicted cross-sectional area ($y\pi$) when compared to the documented cross-sectional area (y).

and observed y for all linked points. The distance over which the prediction is made ($x_1 - x_2$) is given (i.e., distance from calibration point), as are $\hat{y}$, y, ($\hat{y} - y$), and the error rate per kilometer ($\hat{y} - y$)/($x_1 - x_2$). As would be expected, given the quality of the data points, the results for the four data points from Canal Grande are very good. The error for the three data points predicted by the regression model ($\hat{y} - y$) varies between 0.07m and 0.55m, with error per kilometer values of 0.017-0.302.

Using the regression modelling developed above, cross-sectional area, discharge, and velocity were projected for the 57 data points developed for Canal System 2. Using the regression modeling technique, even individual profiles, those not linked to any other available cross-sections, could be used both to calibrate the curve (using cross-sectional area and distance from head) and to model the capacity of all of the known canals within Canal System 2. The modeling procedure provided a good reconstruction of water flow and availability throughout individual canals. The regression model calculates the discharge available at the headgate, providing a good relative measure of the total capacity of individual canals. The maximum discharge at the headgate can then be used as a measure of the relative size of individual canals and, when combined with chronological information, the size of the system through time.

I should stress, however, that the paleohydraulic reconstruction of discharge is often a poor absolute calculation of the actual water use from a canal. Discharge calculations represent the maximum amount of water that can be transported down a canal at the time of its construction. In-filling from siltation will quickly restrict channel size, reducing cross-sectional area. Seasonal variability and the use of headgates will control the amount of water introduced at the canal head. Ackerly (1989) has demonstrated that the discharge capacity, as represented by the morphology and gradient at historic canal headgates, significantly overestimates actual discharge used. The relationship between mean and maximum discharge for the historic Salt River Valley canals is plotted in Figure 5. Ackerly's (1989) use of historic analogs suggests that actual mean discharge typically represents only 25-30 percent of the maximum discharge calculated from open channel equations.

Calculating Total Canal Volume and Labor Investments

The measure of canal volume, as defined here, is the total cubic meters of soil that must be removed in the excavation of the canal channel. While the excavation of a canal channel does not represent the entire labor expended in canal construction, it provides a good relative measure of labor input (Howard 1990a:130-136). To calculate volume, the regression modeling was employed to estimate the cross-sectional area for each canal at 2 km intervals. Projections for volume were made between 2 km cross-sectional area points

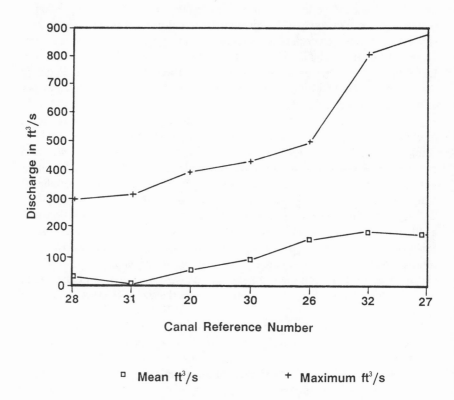

Figure 5.   Mean Water Use versus Maximum Discharge Calculated
from Open Channel Equations for Historic Salt River Valley Canals

by adding the cross-sectional area of the first point (A_1) to the cross-sectional
area of the second point (A_2), dividing by 2 for a mean cross-sectional area,
and multiplying by distance in meters ($x = 2,000m$). The formula, similar to
all volumetric formulas, multiplies the area by the third dimension, length, to
calculate volume between each data point:

$$\text{Volume} = [(A_1 + A_2)/2] * x$$

Where: $A_1 =$ cross-sectional area of point 1
$A_2 =$ cross-sectional area of point 2
$x =$ linear distance between points 1 and 2

This calculation provided the volume of soil removed within the canal channel
as it is defined archaeologically. Formation processes must be taken into

account in the case of Canal System 2, where the upper portion of the channel (a portion above the water line and not included in cross-sectional area and discharge calculations) is not defined, due to truncation by the plowzone. The portion removed by the plowzone was estimated after conducting a series of empirical tests. The tests suggested that the portion removed was approximate 30 percent of the existing channel (Howard 1990a).

The calculation of canal volume, like discharge, provides a good relative measure of labor input. However, converting canal volume to absolute measures of labor expenditure and total construction time is difficult. The first problem lies in estimating the mean cubic meters of soil that can be moved in a person-day of effort. Estimates abound in both the archaeological and planning literature (Ashbee & Cornwall 1961, Doolittle 1984, Erasmus 1965). Such estimates vary from 12 m^3 per person-day in the construction of field bunds using a shovel (Doolittle 1984), to 2.6 m^3 a day (5 hours) using a digging stick (Erasmus 1965:285). The average cubic meters of soil a man can move per day will vary with many factors, including soil type, compaction, and moisture, the tools used, the distance the soil being removed is transported, excavation technique, weather conditions, and the length of the work day. Following Erasmus (1965), an average of 3 m^3 per person-day is employed as a standard here, with the explicit understanding that it be used as a heuristic device and that it is purely an estimate.

To estimate the duration of a canal construction project, factors of seasonality of work (winter? spring? all year?), the number of consecutive days worked (i.e., the periodicity of work: every day? every other day?), and the number of workers must be taken into account. Conservative estimates are obtained by assuming full-time, continuous effort, as opposed to seasonal or periodic work.

CHRONOLOGY BUILDING AND SYSTEM RECONSTRUCTION

The dating of prehistoric irrigation features has been a challenging and often difficult proposition. In the Hohokam area, canal contexts have not provided the types of archaeological materials generally used for dating. Ceramic dating, the cornerstone of chronological analysis in the American Southwest, is ineffective in most cases due to low sample sizes and questions concerning formation processes. Ceramics are rare in canal contexts, except in those cases with an adjacent occupation area. Methods for documenting stratigraphic relationships between parallel main canal alignments have not been sought. Materials amenable to traditional absolute dating techniques, such as wood charcoal for radiocarbon dating and burned sediments for archaeomagnetic dating, do not generally occur in canal contexts.

Developing Chronological Techniques

The difficulty of securing reliable relative and absolute dates for irrigation features in the Hohokam area required new approaches to chronology building. The approach taken here focused on two principal objectives: the development of new absolute dating techniques applicable to materials found in canal contexts and the use of multiple lines of evidence to produce more reliable chronological assessments. A full discussion of chronology building for Canal System 2 is beyond the scope of this essay (see Howard & Eighmy n.d.), but the general approaches and techniques can be presented. The application of relative dating techniques is discussed first, followed by a brief discussion of the development of absolute dating techniques. The relative dating techniques employed in canal studies focus on ceramic dating and stratigraphic relationships. As noted above, the ceramic dating of irrigation features encounters several problems. Securing adequate ceramic samples is difficult except in canal segments lying adjacent to habitation areas. Once the samples are secured, it is necessary to determine the types of formation processes responsible for the deposition of the ceramics in the canal.

Ceramics can be introduced in several ways but almost always as secondary trash deposits and not primary or de facto refuse. Canals often intrude through earlier archaeological deposits, and early ceramics can be introduced into the canal through the erosion of the walls of the channel. Noncontemporaneous ceramics can also be discarded into abandoned channels. In the case of Canal System 2, the stratigraphic context for ceramic samples can be divided into active (fluvial) and post-abandonment (eolian) sediments. Ceramics incorporated in post-abandonment trash can also be separated from water-worn ceramics deposited in the active canal (Ackerly et al. 1987). Given the degree of mixing that might be predicted in secondary trash deposits, ceramic assemblages are often quite homogeneous. In some cases, consecutive periods of use and abandonment can be discerned (see Ackerly et al. 1987). Small sample sizes frequently create interpretive problems, often exacerbated by temporal mixing.

When available, stratigraphic relationships can provide excellent relative dating sequences. Within site areas, canals may intrude or be intruded by a wide variety of features, such as pithouses and earth ovens. Direct stratigraphic relationships can also occur between main canals and/or distribution canals. In Canal System 2, non-contemporaneous main canals often run parallel to local contours and to each other. Distribution canals carry water downslope, at right angles to the main canals, and can intersect adjacent main canal alignments, providing detailed stratigraphic sequences.

Recent research has also focused on the development of new absolute dating techniques. Radiocarbon dating of organic humates extracted from canal clays was repeatedly attempted (Howard & Eighmy n.d.). Unfortunately, in the sediments of the Salt River Valley, humates in canal clays appear to be contaminated through processes that have not as yet been fully explained. Samples tend to be hundreds and often thousands of years too early.

Wood cellulose samples from canal contexts can produce dates that correlate with other lines of chronological evidence (Masse 1987). In such cases, the formation processes responsible for the deposition of the wood sample in the context of the canal may create problems between the target date and the actual date (Dean 1978). In situ burned lenses do occur within canal sediments and appear to represent the periodic burning off of vegetation to maintain water flow. Wood samples from in situ burning provide an improved sampling context.

The most significant advance in dating canal samples has been the application of archaeomagnetic dating to canal sediments (Eighmy & Howard 1991). This technique relies on Thermal Remnant Magnetism (TRM), a magnetic signal created by the application of heat and which records a paleopole position. A recent experimental program, carried out by the Archaeometry Laboratory of Colorado State University and the author, explored the use of Post-Depositional Remnant Magnetism (PDRM) of canal sediments and Chemical Remnant Magnetism (CRM) of ferromanganese deposits that form in waterlogged soils under the canals. The PDRM samples provided the best results and have been developed as a useful tool for chronological interpretation (Eighmy & Howard 1991).

The complexity of the chronological analysis of Canal System 2 is illustrated by the data for three non-contemporaneous main canals and a series of related distribution canals near the site of La Lomita, presented by Eighmy and Howard (1991). While the main canals run parallel to each other, a stratigraphic sequence was determined by examining the intersections between main and distribution canals. Ceramic dates provide another relative sequence, and both archaeomagnetic and radiocarbon dates are then used to assign a calendrical date range.

The temporal resolution that can be achieved using current techniques for canal dating are a significant improvement over past chronological reconstructions. Subsurface investigations allow for the direct application of a series of chronological techniques. In most cases, complex and overlapping series of main and distribution canals do occur. When multiple lines of evidence are examined, the sequencing and calenderical dates can be assigned within a reasonable range of error. Using these techniques, the canals within Canal System 2 can be assigned to their period of use (see Table 3).

A Diachronic Analysis of Canal System 2

Utilizing the paleohydraulic and chronological analysis summarized above (also see Howard 1990a), data relevant to a diachronic examination of system expansion and system capacity are presented in Table 5. This table summarizes the key variables of the analysis, including total canal volume, retrodicted discharge at the canal head, calculated length of the canal, and irrigated acreage. The calculation of irrigated acreage from available discharge is a complex multivariate problem that has not been adequately addressed in Hohokam irrigation studies. An in-depth discussion of the problems and the methods of calculation used here is presented in Howard (1990a). The calculation of total irrigated acres figures are based on a historic standard of 40 acres for each cubic foot per second of discharge (Haury 1976). As discussed above, this figure dramatically overestimates irrigated acres, due to the use of maximum discharge based on open channel equations. Ackerly (1989) suggests that maximum discharge figures derived from open channel equations are four times the actual average flow. A rough estimate of actual discharge is 25 percent of the maximum discharge figures. Finally, a 10 percent correction factor for water loss through evaporation and seepage is presented in Table 5. Again, figures used here are for comparative and heuristic purposes and should not be used as absolute measures. For ease of diachronic analysis, the data have been sorted by period and, when available, phase designations are provided (see Table 1).

Two major groupings have also been provided for each period: a "calculation grouping" (CG) and a "rebuilding event" (RE). The "calculation groups" represent groupings of features believed to be relatively contemporaneous, in operation at approximately the same time, and representative of the canal system during that particular period. "Rebuilding events" consist of canal rebuilding along the same alignment during a single period. When two non-contemporaneous features occur in the same alignment but date to the same period, the rebuilding episode (or the smaller of the two features) is placed in the RE category.

The data necessary for an accurate characterization of the nature of early Pioneer period (A.D. 1-500) irrigation have long eluded Hohokam archaeologists. Haury (1976:120-125) believed that he had located a Vahki phase irrigation canal at Snaketown. However, as Wilcox has pointed out (Wilcox & Shenk 1977:180), there are several indications, including the presence of Snaketown Red-on-buff ceramics in the canal fill, that this feature was not used until the late Pioneer period (Snaketown phase). It has often been suggested (Cable & Doyel 1987, Wilcox & Shenk 1977) that the early Pioneer populations practiced floodwater farming and possibly the use of small irrigation ditches near the active Salt River floodplain. A small irrigation channel near the floodplain in the Price Road project area (Ackerly & Henderson 1988), dated to A.D. 50, provides the first evidence in support of this hypothesized early agricultural pattern. In the Snaketown phase (circa A.D. 500-700), large-scale canals appeared on the first and second terraces of the Salt and Gila rivers. At least two such features have been documented

Table 5. Reconstructions of System Capacities and Labor Estimates[a]

Periods and Features	Phase	Contemporaneity Group[b]	Total m³ of Soil Removed[c]	Person-Days of Labor	Discharge at Head m³/sec	Canal Length Km	Irrigated Acres	Irrigated Acres (25%)	Water Loss[d]
PIONEER PERIOD (A.D. 0-600)									
Dutch Canal Ruins SM1	Snktn	CG	47,286	15,762	6.59	14.0	9,414	2,354	2,118
COLONIAL PERIOD (A.D. 600-900)									
Hohokam Expressway F.2b	Col	CG	5,558	1,853	2.67	3.0	3,814	954	858
Dutch Canal Ruins F.8537	Col	CG	106,347	35,449	10.26	22.0	14,657	3,664	3,298
Dutch Canal Ruins F.8555	Col	CG	101,771	33,924	8.94	22.0	12,771	3,193	2,874
East Papago F.7a	GB	CG	22,341	7,447	4.38	7.0	6,257	1,564	1,408
Dutch Canal Ruins NM1	GB	CG	20,157	6,719	4.78	8.0	6,829	1,707	1,536
East Papago F.57	GB-SC	CG	18,805	6,268	4.17	6.0	5,957	1,489	1,340
La Ciudad F.247.01	GB-SC	CG	222,624	74,208	8.95	34.0	12,786	3,196	2,877
La Ciudad F.1310	GB-SC	CG	253,122	84,374	12.10	34.0	17,286	4,321	3,889
Hohokam Expressway F.4a	Col-Sed	CG	5,040	1,680	2.37	2.0	3,386	846	762
Hohokam Expressway F.2a	Col	RE	1,872	624	1.55	1.5	2,214	554	498
Dutch Canal Ruins NM3	SC	RE	15,577	5,192	4.33	6.0	6,186	1,546	1,392
East Papago F.7b	SC	RE	17,973	5,991	4.12	7.0	5,886	1,471	1,324
Dutch Canal Ruins NM2	SC	RE	18,805	6,268	4.62	7.5	6,600	1,650	1,485
Hohokam Expressway F.4b	Col	RE	1,788	596	1.57	1.5	2,243	561	505
Total Contemporaneity Group			755,765	251,922	58.62	138.0	83,743	20,936	18,842
Total of all Colonial Canals			811,780	270,592	74.81	161.5	106,871	26,718	24,046
SEDENTARY PERIOD (A.D. 900-1100)									
Hayden 1938	Sac	CG	33,922	11,307	5.74	10.0	8,200	2,050	1,845
Hohokam Expressway F.5	Sac	CG	8,524	2,841	3.11	3.5	4,443	1,111	1,000
East Papago F.26	Sac	CG	52,200	17,400	5.59	13.0	7,986	1,996	1,797

(continued)

Table 5. (Continued)

Periods and Features	Phase	Contemporaneity Group[b]	Total m³ of Soil Removed[c]	Person-Days of Labor	Discharge at Head m³/sec	Canal Length Km	Irrigated Acres	Irrigated Acres (25%)	Water Loss[d]
La Ciudad 247.02	Sac	CG	44,010	14,670	5.17	14.0	7,386	1,846	1,662
La Ciudad F.1311	Sac	CG	53,838	17,946	6.47	14.0	9,243	2,311	2,080
Hohokam Expressway F.10	Sac	CG	18,642	6,214	4.29	6.0	6,129	1,532	1,379
East Papago F.5	Sed-Cl	CG	52,703	17,568	6.25	16.0	8,929	2,232	2,009
Los Colinas F.5Los Aumentos	Sed-Cl	CG	77,336	25,779	7.81	32.0	11,157	2,789	2,510
Hohokam Expressway F.1, C1	Sac	CG	2,282	761	1.99	1.0	2,843	711	640
Hohokam Expressway F.7a, C3	Sac	RE	24,128	8,043	5.01	8.0	7,157	1,789	1,610
Hohokam Expressway F.7b	Sac	RE	23,296	7,765	4.69	8.0	6,700	1,675	1,508
East Papago F.1	Sed-Cl	RE	13,486	4,495	3.34	3.0	4,771	1,193	1,074
Total Contemporaneity Group			343,457	114,486	46.42	109.5	66,314	16,579	14,921
Total Sedentary Canals			404,368	134,789	59.46	128.5	84,943	21,236	19,112
CLASSIC PERIOD (A.D. 1100-1450)									
Hohokam Expressway F.13	Cl	CG	3,224	1,075	1.48	1.0	2,114	529	476
Grand Canal Ruins f.22-16	Cl	CG	69,312	23,104	7.08	20.0	10,114	2,529	2,276
Woodbury South	Cl	CG	39,382	13,127	5.96	12.0	8,514	2,129	1,916
Woodbury North	Cl	CG	233,674	77,891	12.55	34.0	17,929	4,482	4,034
Casa Buena F.79, C1	Soho	CG	86,632	28,877	6.45	14.0	9,214	2,304	2,073
East Papago F.3	Soho-Ci	CG	46,413	15,471	5.99	14.0	8,557	2,139	1,925
East Papago F.30	Ci	CG	223,066	74,355	9.04	34.0	12,914	3,229	2,906
AZ T:12:47(ASM)	Ci	CG	16,513	5,504	4.13	6.0	5,900	1,475	1,328
Grand Canal Ruins F.3-14	Cl	RE	45,102	15,034	5.57	12.0	7,957	1,989	1,790
Casa Buena F.79, C1	Ci	RE	42,757	14,252	5.38	14.0	7,686	1,921	1,729
Grand Canal Ruins F.121	Cl	RE	40,162	13,387	5.53	12.0	7,900	1,975	1,778
Total Contemporaneity Group			718,216	239,404	52.68	135.0	75,257	18,814	16,933
Total Classic Canals			846,236	282,079	69.16	173.0	98,800	24,700	22,230

Notes: [a] CG = Contemporaneity Group, RE = Rebuilding Event, Snktn = Snaketown phase, Col = Colonial period, no phase assignment, GB = Gila Butte phase, SC = Santa Cruz phase, Sac = Sacaton phase, Sed-Cl = Sedentary and Classic period use, Cl = Classic period, no phase assignment, Soho = Soho phase, Ci = Civano Phase.
[b] The Contemporaneity Group is the set of features that appear to be contemporaneous, with non-contemporaneous rebuilding episodes being removed from the sample. This provides the best estimate of system size during each chronological period.
[c] Total m³ of Soil represents the amount of soil removed in the construction of the canal.
[d] Estimated water loss through evaporation and seepage, based on data concerning water loss from unlined historic canals.

296

archaeologically (Haury 1976, Greenwald & Ciolek-Torrello 1989). Additional alignments dating to the Snaketown phase in Canal System 2 are suggested by the presence of Snaketown phase sites up on the first and second terrace. Figure 6 presents the known Snaketown phase settlements and possible canal alignments for Canal System 2. The identified Snaketown phase main canal in Canal System 2 suggests that large main canals exhibiting reasonably good engineering principles (although in this case located along steep topographic slopes) were operating at this time. A maximum length of 14 km and a maximum headgate discharge of 6.59 m^3/s are projected. This canal was capable of irrigating an impressive area covering over 7 km^2. At a point 4.5 km from its head, this canal had a cross-sectional area of 3 m^2 and carried a discharge of 3.02 m^3/s.

The most startling result of the detailed reevaluation of the growth of Canal System 2 was the intensity of growth suggested for the Colonial period (A.D. 600-900). Instead of intensive growth occurring during the Sedentary (A.D. 900-1100) and Classic periods (A.D. 1100-1450), as most developmental models have suggested, the most explosive period of growth occurred early in the sequence. During the Gila Butte phase, the system expanded intensively to cover the southern portion of the system, and two of the largest canals (as measured by discharge) were constructed. In the Santa Cruz phase, the northernmost recorded alignment (the Canal Grande alignment) was in use. Figure 7 presents the reconstruction of Canal System 2 for the Colonial period (A.D. 600-900).

Rebuilding episodes occurred regularly in the southern area of the system, near the geomorphically active floodplain. Nials et al. (1989), examining the reconstructions of Salt River streamflow, have identified two separate intervals within the Colonial period that are characterized by different Salt River streamflow regimes. The period A.D. 740-798 was characterized by a low mean annual flow and low variability, creating favorable conditions for irrigation. The period A.D. 798-899 reflects high variability punctuated by periods of extremely high discharge. The streamflow during this interval would have had devastating effects on Hohokam irrigation, causing the abandonment of canals damaged by high-magnitude flood events. The southern portion of the system, having higher gradients and long headward segments within the active floodplain, would have been more susceptible to flood events, since they could be damaged by lower-magnitude floods. By the end of the Colonial period, the southern canals close to the floodplain were abandoned and new canals were constructed higher on the contour, away from the river.

The modeling of the Colonial period canals suggests a dramatic and early expansion into much of the area eventually covered by Canal System 2, with the exception of the far northern and western reaches. This can be seen in the "calculation group" measure (see Table 5). This measure is obtained by summing the discharge for a contemporaneous set of canals for each period.

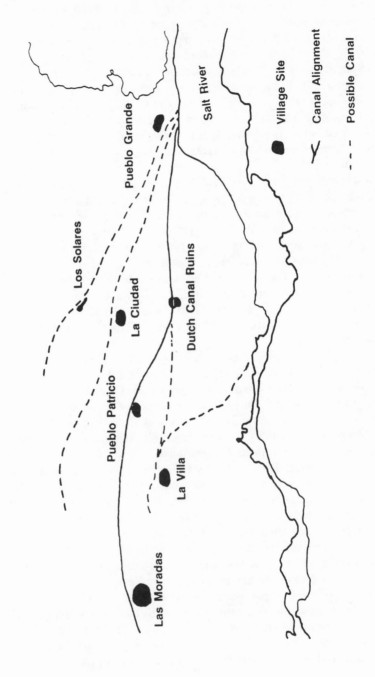

Figure 6. Reconstruction of the Pioneer Period Configuration of Canal System 2

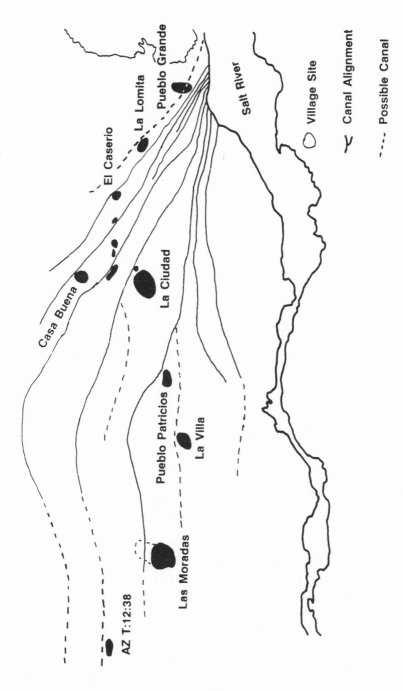

Figure 7. Reconstruction of the Colonial Period Configuration of Canal System 2

Casa Buena

El Caserio

La Lomita

Pueblo Grande

Salt River

○ Village Site

⋎ Canal Alignment

--- Possible Canal

La Ciudad

Pueblo Patricios

La Villa

Las Moradas

AZ T:12:38

299

Subsequent rebuilding episodes occurring within the same period are examined, and only the most representative is used.

A maximum discharge of 58.62 m^3/s is derived for the Colonial period calculation group (Table 5), having a combined maximum length of 138 km for the system. Advanced hydraulic engineering principles, including those used in the distribution system, were being employed. Population increase is suggested by the establishment and growth of a series of new villages. Numerous fieldhouse and farmstead sites were developed in the northern and possibly in the western portions of the system (Howard & Wilcox 1988). The organization of labor must have presented numerous challenges by this time, particularly to mobilize the population for repairing canals subjected to frequent flooding in the southern portion of the system. The total volume estimate for canals constructed during the Colonial period is 755,765 m^3, with a corollary estimate of 251,922 person-days of labor investment.

The steamflow variability and high-magnitude discharge on the Salt River during A.D. 798-899 created a change in the configuration of Canal System 2 by the beginning of the Sedentary period (A.D. 900-1100). The southern portion of the system was abandoned, shifting both settlements and canals to the north (Figure 8). Occupation along Canal System 2 suggests a moderate population expansion. Streamflow retrodictions and the character of the reconstruction of the building activity in Canal System 2 during the Sedentary period suggest a period of relative calm for the Salt River Hohokam. The period during A.D. 900-1051 is characterized by few high-magnitude flows (only three widely separated years having above mean annual discharge) creating conditions favorable to canal operation with minimal flood damage (Nials et al. 1989). The displacement of canals and population movement from the Salt River floodplain and lower terrace areas to higher ground during the latter half of the Colonial period, combined with improved streamflow conditions, appear to have minimized the need for canal rebuilding. Throughout the Sedentary period, a calculated volume of only 404,368 m^3 of soil was moved in construction activities, requiring a projected 114,486 person-days of effort, approximately half of the labor investment calculated for the Colonial period. Yet, in both periods nine major alignments were active in the calculation group, with similar total discharge capacities: 58.62 m^3/s in the Colonial period and 46.42 m^3/s in the Sedentary period. However, the two extremely large volume estimates for the two large Colonial period canals located near La Ciudad account for much of this variation. Further, if a fine-grained construction and abandonment sequence were available, we would probably discover that the southernmost canals in the floodplain were abandoned prior to the construction of the northernmost canals.

The maximum calculated canal length figures—138 km in the Colonial versus 109.5 km in the Sedentary period—follow the same pattern. The major difference between the Colonial and Sedentary periods is the number of rebuilding events. Two minor and three major rebuilding events occurred in the Colonial period, but only three minor rebuilding events occurred during the Sedentary period (Table 5).

The Classic period system reconstruction (Figure 9) again suggests structural changes punctuated by the abandonment of the large canal alignments in the central area of the system. A hypothesis of general abandonment of canals in this area during the Classic period is supported by the concurrent abandonment of the sites in this area, including the site of Los Solares. Only two canals were in operation in the central portion of the system, near the site of La Ciudad. The major Classic period concentration of sites and canals occurred in the northern portion of the Canal System 2.

The Classic period appears to have been a time of shifting settlements, with the movement of the population and expansion of canals into the northern portion of the system. In the northwestern area of the system, a series of small sites occur. Given the current data, population increase appears to have been occurring, but certainly not in the intensity suggested by most models. The key difference in viewpoint is the recognition here that the current data suggest that a large central section of the system was abandoned. Previous researchers, usually adhering to the concept of continued accretionary growth, have noted only the increase in the northern portion of the system.

Graybill (Nials et al. 1989) divided the Classic period into three intervals marked by increasing variability in streamflow conditions on the Salt River. The interval A.D. 1052-1196, spanning the Sedentary to Classic period transition, was similar to the preceding Sedentary period. It did, however, reflect an increase in streamflow variability, with an increase in high-magnitude flows periodically causing major damage to the canal system. However, high flows were spaced at wide intervals, and generally favorable conditions prevailed. Increased variability characterized the next interval, A.D. 1197-1355, with periods of low mean flow punctuated by high-magnitude events and deepening of the Salt River channel. Increased variability and increased high-magnitude flows would present a periodic need for large-scale labor to repair headgates, weirs, and the headward canal segments. Low flows may have caused water shortages. Although these events were not as destructive as the flood sequences observed in the Colonial period, the Classic period may have presented greater challenges in the administration of the system. The final period of streamflow reconstruction, A.D. 1356 to 1370, Nials et al. (1989) consider to be a unique event. In A.D. 1358, following 33 years of low flow, the largest discharge in the Graybill reconstruction in 450 years is noted. Nials et al. (1989:69-70) have suggested that this "catastrophic event" resulted in severe channel widening and deepening, and that the occurrence of upstream bedrock "may have precluded reclamation of the system." They appear to suggest the intriguing hypothesis that the canal systems could not be reactivated, resulting in the emergence of the Polvorón phase and, ultimately, the Hohokam collapse.

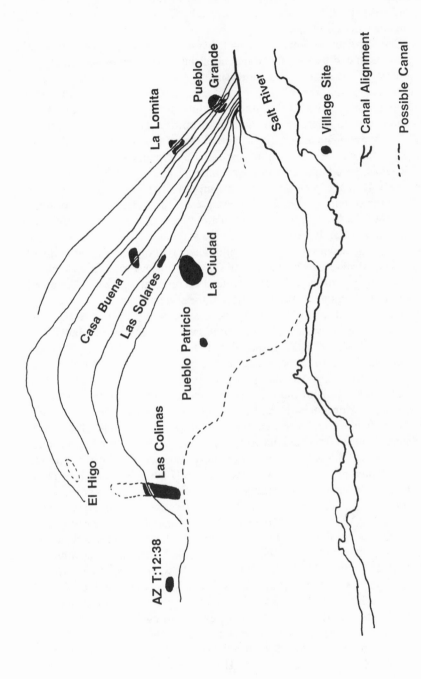

Figure 8. Reconstruction of the Sedentary Period Configuration of Canal System 2

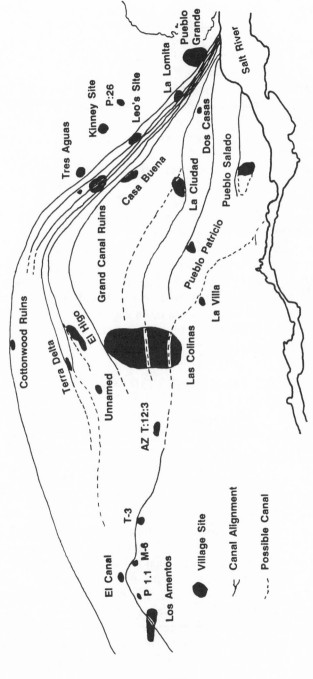

Figure 9. Reconstruction of the Classic Period Configuration of Canal System 2

Total system discharge indicates a capacity of 52.68 m³/sec for the calculation group, which contained eight main canal alignments. This figure is again very close to the discharge capacity suggested in both the Colonial (58.62 m³/s) and the Sedentary period (46.42 m³/s). Total maximum length of canals is also similar to the Colonial period, but represents an increase over the Sedentary period reconstruction.

The system reconstruction generated from the paleohydraulic approach appears to present a pattern of expansion that is different from those of previous researchers. Patterns of abandonment of both canals and areas previously under irrigation have been recognized for the first time. Incorporating sequences of abandonment into the system reconstruction, along with the use of discharge as a measure of system capacity, alters the process of change from one of continuing expansion and growth to one of shifting land use.

Covariation between environmental perturbations in streamflow and the development of the system have also been suggested by this reconstruction. Frequent high-magnitude flows during the middle to late Colonial period do appear to correlate with the abandonment of the first terrace—an area that was heavily exploited in the earliest building stages. I suggest that placement of the canals higher on the contour would have reduced the impact of floods on the canal system, although to an unknown degree. The placement of main canals higher on the contour appears to have been a cultural response or strategy to minimize risk posed by the environment.

ALTERNATIVE PROCESSES OF INTENSIFICATION

The reconstruction of system expansion, summarized above, is derived from a different analytical approach and presents dramatically different results than previous studies. Figure 10 presents growth curves for Canal System 2 to compare the Nicholas (1981) and Howard (1990a) models. The reconstructions presented here are based on both the total amount of water capture by the canal heads and projected acreage irrigated (also see Table 2).

The model of the expansion of Canal System 2 is quite divergent from earlier reconstructions in several regards. In the reconstruction presented here, the system reaches its maximum capacity early in the sequence (Colonial period) and then stabilizes. The continuous internal growth suggested by past studies does not occur. Rebuilding of canal features is found to occur through time, however, with new canals being constructed and old ones abandoned during each chronological phase. Labor inputs for canal construction and maintenance are much higher than suggested by both Woodbury (1960) and Nicholas (1981). Significant agricultural intensification does not appear to occur through the physical expansion of individual canal systems, as has been

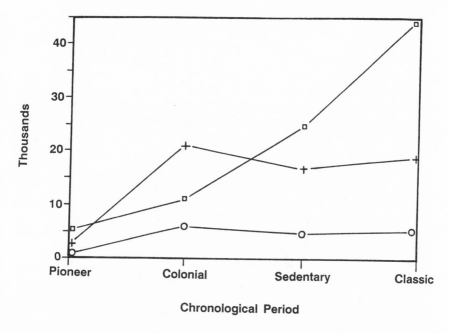

□ Acres, Nicholas   + Acres, Howard   o m³/s * 100, Howard

Figure 10.   A Comparison of the Growth Curves for
Canal System 2 for Nicholas (1981) and Howard (1990a)

previously suggested (Nicholas 1981, Nicholas & Feinman, Turney 1929, Woodbury 1961).

The small extent of physical expansion of Canal System 2 beyond the Colonial period raises a series of questions concerning population growth and agricultural intensification. Does the relative lack of growth within this canal system suggest stable population and production? Did intensification and increased production occur through processes other than the physical expansion of individual canal systems? Several processes of intensification could have been operating, including changes in organization of the basic economic units, changes in the units of production and consumption, manipulation of crop yields through increased fertilization, changes in fallow systems, and the innovation of double- or multi-cropping. Unfortunately, the destruction of Hohokam fields by modern agriculture limits the types of archaeological data available. Thus, quantitative approaches that can characterize the size and use of fields have not been developed. Historic and ethnographic analogs are the best source of models currently available to investigate questions of processes of agricultural intensification employed by the Hohokam.

Organization of Production

One possible process of agricultural intensification consists of changes in the organization of production, creating more efficient strategies of resource exploitation. Two types of archaeological data that can be useful in defining the primary units of agricultural production and consumption are examined here. The first is the architectural evidence of Hohokam corporate household groups and the second is the size and configuration of fields.

Two types of architectural arrangements, pre-Classic courtyard groups (Wilcox et al. 1981, Howard 1985) and Classic period compounds (Sires n.d.), have been interpreted as prehistoric households. Courtyard groups typically consist of 1-6 pithouses arranged around a rectangular open space. Classic period compounds consist of rooms and plazas in a rectangular space that is enclosed within massive walls. These units typically included several (2-6) residential structures, apparently representing related nuclear families that operated as a productive unit. While Hohokam architectural styles change from the pre-Classic to the Classic period, it has generally been assumed that the size and composition of these groups show no appreciable change. Recent research has suggested a trend toward increasing group size in courtyard groups (David Gregory, pers. comm.) through time, as well as an increase in household size between courtyard groups and compounds (David Abbott, pers. comm.). It can be shown that Classic period compounds can have more rooms than courtyard groups. However, larger compounds are usually partitioned into smaller groups of rooms (1-5) surrounding a plaza that may be comparable to earlier courtyard groups. More detailed and comprehensive studies are needed to adequately address the issue of changing household size. Increases in group size may represent significant changes in the household labor force and efficiency that would increase the productive capabilities of these units.

While the pitfalls of ethnographic analogy are well known, data on early Pima household composition can provide insight into, if not testable models, for the prehistoric Hohokam. In the 1700s and 1800s, the Pima occupied a small stretch of the Gila River south of its confluence with the Salt. They resided in a small district within the Hohokam "core" area. Although executed on a much smaller scale, the Pima constructed canals along the terraces of the Salt River using an irrigation technology similar to that of the Hohokam. They had to contend with the same set of environmental variables, including streamflow regimes, rainfall, sediment loads, water quality, topographic slope, soils, drainage, and salinity. Avoiding environmental determinism, it is recognized that the Pima could have responded in different ways to these same set of environmental variables. However, Pima ethnography can provide both parameters for what is possible and models that can eventually be tested against the archaeological record.

In 1697, Manje (Karns 1954) reported both population size and the number of houses for three Pima villages, each producing a ratio of approximately four individuals per house. This type of village-wide estimate based on a count of houses to people is very crude, but it may bypass some problems that have been encountered in projections using floor space as a demographic measure. To contrast architectural styles, the traditional Pima structure, or "ki," is similar in size and construction to Hohokam pithouses. If kis and pithouses house similar group sizes, it would suggest a very rough estimate for an economic group size of 8-20 for Hohokam courtyard groups. The size of the extended-family unit appears to be similar to that found in the patrilineal-patrilocal organization of the Pima. Historic and ethnographic data provide some further insight into the organization of cultivated plots and economic group composition, as detailed below.

In the Pima case, irrigated farmlands were divided into "small parcels and cultivated by families related to each other in marriage" (Karns 1954:28; also see Ezell 1961, Hackenberg 1974). In the later historic period, each family group is said to have farmed an area of approximately 2-5 acres (Castetter & Bell 1942). Early reports consistently describe clearly bounded and even fenced field areas. As early as 1796, Friar Bringas (Matson & Fontana 1977) noted for the Gila Pimas: "Their fields are solidly and cleverly fenced and diligently worked." Emery, in 1848 (see Hackenberg 1974: IV-50), noted: "The fields are sub-divided by ridges of earth, into rectangles of about 200×100 feet for the convenience of irrigating." Curiously, Ezell (1961:39) reproduced the same quote from Emory's military reconnaissance document but gave measurements of 200×300 feet. Many of these accounts record the use of fences but do not state the type of construction. However, in 1849, Charles Pancoast observed: "They had enclosures made by so planting cactus as to form a solid hedge six feet through, so impenetrable that not even a rabbit could get through it...." (Hackenberg 1974:IV-97). Also in 1849, A. B. Clark stated that their fields were "...formed by driving stakes into the ground...." (Hackenberg 1974:IV-97). In 1852, Bartlett bridged these two accounts by noting the use of both cactus and stakes: "Their cultivated fields are generally fenced with crooked stakes, wattled with brush, the thorny mezquit predominating...." (Hackenberg 1974:IV-121).

There is good correspondence between the size ranges suggested for Pima fenced fields. In 1857, Antisell (Hackenberg 1974:IV-148) noted that the fenced fields were "small," being 150 feet "each way" (square?). J.C. Reid, in his 1858 journal (Hackenberg 1974:IV-155), reiterated the 100×200 foot measure. The recorded sizes suggest plots in the range of 20,000 ft^2 (1858 m^2), or approximately 0.5 acre (0.2 ha). This figure suggests that a smaller size plot supported an extended-family group. Ezell's (1961) reading of Emory suggests

60,000 ft^2 (5574 m^2), producing a figure of 1.5 acres (0.6 ha) that is more in line with Russell's estimates of 2-5 acres (0.81-2.0 ha). The larger figures probably represent the area used to produce surplus for the vigorous historic Pima trade with Anglo populations. Unfortunately, the connections between the Pima fenced fields and social or economic groups is not discussed in detail in the historic records.

A census of both population and the number of Pima "farms" was taken by the U.S. Deputy Marshal ca. 1860. Table 6 presents this information for eight Pima and two Maricopa villages, as well as a ratio of people to "farms." This census suggests that each farm supported 5.4-7.5 individuals for the Pima and 4.6-5.0 individuals for the Maricopa. While the number of fields shows a regular linear increase with population, the ratio of individuals to farms does not appear to correlate with either total population or total number of fields. This ratio may correlate with other environmental or social factors. The general regularity of the figures does suggest, however, that the "farms" support group sizes reflective of nuclear families as opposed to larger groupings (unless the census included only adult individuals). The undefined "farms" likely would have been the fenced fields mentioned by 19th-century observers, since no other physical division of farmland is mentioned in the historic records. However, this conclusion does not correspond well to the smaller (0.5 acre, 0.2 ha) plots. If each of the 604 "farms" measured 0.5 acre (0.2 ha), the total cultivated area would have been 302 acres (122.2 ha). This is far short of the 15,000 acres (6,070.5 hectares) that St. Johns reported in cultivation in 1859, supplying both the local population of 4,242 and an impressive food surplus (Hackenberg 1974:IV-167 to IV-168). St. John's figures would suggest an average "farm" size of 24.8 acres (10 ha) and 2.8 (in 1858) to 3.5 (in 1859) acres (1.1-1.4 ha) in cultivation per person. While the total population figures between these two censuses are close (3,697 to 4,242), they are difficult to reconcile with fenced plot size and general figures recorded for the areas farmed by extended-family groups (Russell 1905).

The size and organization of Hohokam irrigated fields is unknown, and direct archaeological correlates for basic plot sizes have yet to be identified. The nature of the architectural organization of courtyard groups suggests basic economic and agricultural units comparable to those described for the Pima— multiple, related nuclear families that form cooperative units. Future testing of this hypothesis, possibly by examining the spatial patterning of fields, is necessary.

Modern engineers have recognized the importance of designing the various elements of irrigation systems to accommodate patterns of social organization (Uphoff 1988). Fields and distribution systems must be organized to conform to the size and structure of the social and economic groups that operate them. The spatial structure of prehistoric irrigation systems arguably can provide direct archaeological correlates reflecting the organization of task groups

Table 6. Circa 1860 Census, Showing Population Size and the Number of Farms for Both the Pima and Maricopa Villages

Village	Population	Number of Farms	Persons/Farms Ratio
Pima Villages	533	99	5.4
Aqua Raiz	257	45	5.7
Cerrita	616	104	5.9
Arenal	438	70	6.3
Cachanillo	315	51	6.2
Casa Blanca	514	81	6.3
Horniquero	232	33	7.0
Llano	392	52	7.5
Total	3,297	535	Mean 6.3
Maricopa Villages			
Huesco Parrado	232	46	5.0
Sacaton	106	23	4.6
Total	338	69	Mean 4.8

operating them. Physical elements of irrigation systems, such as branch canals, often require the formation of cooperative task groups, which must collaborate in order to maintain and operate portions of the system. Such task groups are often embedded sets, with lower-level task groups combining into larger cooperative entities. Measures of system structure, the number of sets within the system, can be used to evaluate the operational complexity of irrigation systems.

In the Hohokam area, an archaeological correlate for a production group above the household level is the "Unit Command Area" (Howard n.d.a, Uphoff 1988). The Unit Command Area was the group of farmers who formed a cooperative productive unit along a single distribution canal. Members of the Unit Area Command would have had to cooperate in water allocation, water scheduling, and local ditch maintenance and construction. Distribution canals have been recorded within Canal System 2, although variation in the size of these features has not been determined (Ackerly et al. 1987, Howard 1990b). The size and discharge capacity of several recorded distribution canals suggests that a single Unit Area Command would have minimally included several extended family groups.

Branch canals are physical elements of the system that would have drawn together sets of distribution canals and, concomitantly, Unit Area Command groups. Each group would have had to coordinate water scheduling and use along the branch canal. Several early researchers identified branch canals and even water control gates at branch heads (Hodge 1893, Woodbury 1976), although modern excavations of these features are now needed. Individual canals (including all branches) form the next level of organization. Farmers along individual canals may have been required to contribute corvée labor for main-canal maintenance.

In the Salt River Valley, the village appears to have been the next level of agricultural cooperation and production. The patterned regularity in the spacing of major villages along series of parallel canals at 5 km intervals appears to reflect territorial spacing (Howard & Wilcox 1988). The territorial spacing appears to cross-cut individual canal alignments, with villages located between parallel canal alignments. Each village territory could have several main canals running through it. Having the village as a major organizational unit is again in accordance with Pima ethnography. The Pima village was the major unit of organization for canal construction and maintenance operations (Castetter & Bell 1942, Ezell 1961, Hackenberg 1974).

When multiple villages occur along a single canal or canal system, the village near the canal head takes the lead in organizing the system as a whole (Howard n.d.b). In the Salt River Valley, the largest villages—often those containing the largest platform mounds—are located adjacent to the canal heads. These villages probably took the lead administrative roles, controlling flow within the canals and organizing annual maintenance of the headgates and weirs.

Current data suggest that the hierarchy of task groups postulated above and the organization of production did not display major temporal changes through the Hohokam sequence. Community patterns, the size of corporate groups, and settlement patterns within the large canal systems remained constant through time (Howard n.d.a, Howard & Wilcox 1988).

Land Tenure, Soil Fertility, and Fallow Cycles

Boserup (1965), in the process of presenting her model suggesting that population pressure is the causal element in agricultural intensification, provides a good discussion of land tenure patterns and their relationship to agricultural technologies. She notes that low-intensity land use patterns, such as slash-and-burn agriculture, usually employ long fallow periods. The labor investments in clearing forest land, as opposed to using previously cleared land under fallow, often are not great. In such cases, families often do not exercise strict ownership rights to agricultural lands. In contrast, land tenure patterns that have inheritable ownership or stringent use-rights usually arise in those cases where (1) land use is more frequent (short or no fallow system), and (2) labor expenditures for land improvement and field maintenance are great. Boserup (1965:26) notes that "the use of irrigation techniques and other capital investment is related to the fallow system. Irrigation facilities and other land improvements, for instance terracing, are never used with long fallow and rarely with short fallow."

The use of irrigation technology dramatically increases the ratio of labor to crop yield. Labor expenditure is increased for the construction and maintenance of distribution systems, the preparation of field systems (land leveling, plowing, construction of bunds), increased weeding (which increases with length of fallow), and increased harvest time. Boserup (1965:41) suggests that intensification (culminating in the use of irrigation facilities) will occur only when population reaches a certain density; this does not appear to be true in the Hohokam case, where irrigation appears to have been necessary for agricultural production. The annual precipitation is exceedingly low, averaging only 7.27 inches (181.75mm). Rainfall patterns are winter dominant, with summer thunderstorms providing poor coverage and low overall infiltration. Of the staple crops of the Hohokam, it is likely that only agave could have been successfully cultivated without irrigation. It is possible that some combination of floodwater farming, runoff systems, and gathering wide resources could support small populations. However, further work is needed to define the subsistence practices of the early Hohokam before this issue can be adequately addressed.

The question of fallow systems and the permanency of land use are major issues in land tenure patterns. Concomitantly, soil fertility and resulting crop yields are the primary variables that determine the need and frequency of fallow. Archaeological evidence relevant to systems of fallow employed by the Hohokam has not been identified at this time. However, three types of information—soil fertility under irrigation, ethnographic analogy, and historic data—can be used to address this question.

Forbes (1902) presents information concerning the chemical constituents found in the water transported by the Salt and Gila rivers. A complete review of this work and of the soil edaphic factors in the Salt and Gila river valleys is beyond the scope of this essay, but we can note that the silt loads carried by these rivers and deposited on irrigated fields contain sufficient quantities of silt and nutrients to maintain soil fertility under prehistoric agricultural operations. The most important element, nitrogen, is plentiful, with 29-69 lbs being supplied per acre-foot of water in the Salt River in 1899 (Forbes 1902:160). The Gila River delivers even higher amounts of nitrogen, supplying up to 173 lbs/acre-foot. Potash and phosphoric acid are also present in abundance.

Early historic and ethnographic accounts consistently note that the Pima, irrigating the terraces of the Gila River, did not employ a fallow system, but cultivated fields year after year (Ezell 1961, Hackenberg 1974). Even the earliest observers describing the Salt and Gila rivers commented on the high fertility of their irrigating waters. As early as 1796, Friar Bringas (Matson & Fontana 1977:90) observed: "The river can fertilize these beautiful tracts of land with its waters." Bartlett noted, in 1853, "soil of great fertility...." along the Gila River (Hackenberg 1974:IV-135). In 1857, geologist Thomas Antisell recognized the beneficial impact of irrigation on soil fertility when he observed that the soils of the Gila floodplain were "a fine sandy (granitic) clay, very light in color, and only fertile where watered by the acequias [canals] of the Pimos, when it produced abundantly" (Hackenberg 1974:IV-148). Passing through the Gila Valley in 1858, Lieutenant Chapman commented that he had never seen "richer soil or more beautiful fields...." (Hackenberg 1974:IV-160).

Another set of observations relevant to Pima fallow systems concerns the continuity of field use. If fields are placed under fallow, a patchwork of cultivated fields should be present. Under a system of continuous cultivation, fields may be more spatially continuous. Historic accounts of Pima fields do suggest a spatial continuity of fields, with no accounts of land lying in fallow. In 1774, Anza wrote of Pima fields: "The fields of wheat that they now possess are so large that, standing in the middle of them, one cannot see the ends, because of their great length. They are very wide, too, embracing the whole width of the valley on both sides...." (Bolton 1930,II:127). Such accounts again suggest that the majority of the land under the irrigation systems was under cultivation and that little if any fallow was being employed.

Like the Pima, early historic farmers in the Salt and Gila river valleys practiced a system of continuous cultivation. Only later in the historic period, after the construction of the dam systems (resulting in lower silt loads and decreased fertility of irrigating waters), was the use of nitrogen-fixing plants recommended.

Historic patterns suggest that Hohokam irrigated agriculture did not require a fallow system. Given the labor intensive nature of canal expansion, it is likely that all available land was used intensively before the alternative of new canal construction was selected (cf. Boserup 1965). Field preparation would have been labor intensive, with farming groups investing heavily in the field systems. This suggests that Hohokam land tenure probably was similar to that of the Pima, who had strong property rights (Hill 1936). Once assigned, the land and its attendant water rights became the property of the individual Pima household group and could be inherited. It appears unlikely that manipulation (shortening) of fallow would have been used by the Hohokam as a method of agricultural intensification.

Double- and Multi-cropping

Double-cropping, the planting of two crops per season, was possible, given the environment of the Salt River Valley (Bohrer 1970). Multi-cropping, the process of planting multiple crops to intensify yields, is also possible in the Salt River Valley. Monocropping does not appear to have been practiced by any prehistoric or aboriginal groups in the New World. In this discussion, intensification through multi-cropping refers to increasing diversification of cultivated species. Intensification can also be achieved through the introduction of new species that can be double-cropped or which produce higher yields.

Many historic and ethnographic accounts demonstrate that the Pima double-cropped (Bohrer 1970, Hackenberg 1974, Russell 1905). The second crop, planted in the summer months during the time of low river flow, faced greater risk of failure than did the earlier planting (Masse 1987). While it is extremely likely that the Hohokam did practice double-cropping, archaeological evidence for this strategy is difficult to identify. Nevertheless, several studies (Gasser & Kwiatkowski 1991, Mitchell 1989) suggest a lack of intensification through a diversification of species. The archaeobotanical evidence does not show dramatic shifts in the types, ubiquity, or frequency of cultivated species. To again employ a logical argument, given the labor intensive nature of canal expansion, it is likely that the prehistoric inhabitants would intensify production under an operating canal system before constructing more elaborate systems. Thus, it is unlikely that diversification of cultigens is a strategy that would only be employed after the maximum size of Canal System 2 was reached.

Significant changes in multiple-cropping, or a diversification of the crops being grown in irrigated fields, does not appear to have occurred in the Hohokam area. In a recent review of the expanding Hohokam archaeobotanical data base, Gasser and Kwiatkowski (1991) show that regional variability is far greater than temporal variability in the Hohokam area. Diversification of crops through time does not currently appear to have been a significant process of intensification, since most species were in production by the Colonial period (A.D. 600).

Tests of the long-held hypothesis that Classic period populations significantly increased their exploitation of available wild resources (Doyel 1981:46) have also failed to demonstrate great temporal diversity (Gasser & Kwiatkowski 1991, Mitchell 1989). Furthermore, the increased use of new technologies to exploit marginal environments through time has not been demonstrated. In the Phoenix Basin, large terraced gardens have been identified. If these features are late in time, they could represent the exploitation of more marginal environments by introducing new technological approaches (Wilcox 1979). Dating these features, believed to represent the cultivation of agave in more marginal agricultural zones, is difficult. Classic period structures (A.D. 1100-1450) often occur in proximity to the terrace gardens, but contemporaneity between the structures and terrace gardens has not been demonstrated. The suggestion that the use of floodwater or runoff irrigation to exploit new water and land resources was introduced in the Classic period is speculative. Runoff technology was in use early in the Hohokam sequence, and the terraces could date to the pre-Classic. Further, the degree of intensification would not have been significant when contrasted with the increases in cultivated acreage suggested by previous models of canal system expansion (Nicholas 1981).

AGRICULTURAL INTENSIFICATION
AND SOCIOPOLITICAL COMPLEXITY

In this essay, potential processes of agricultural intensification in Hohokam irrigated agriculture have been explored. I have proposed a paleohydraulic approach, the formation of a series of techniques for measuring discharge in prehistoric canal systems. The resulting paleohydraulic reconstruction of the growth of Turney's Canal System 2 suggests that, contrary to earlier models, the system underwent its most dramatic growth during the Snaketown and Gila Butte phases, essentially attaining its large spatial extent early in the sequence. By the Santa Cruz phase, the system shows relative stability; water capture at the headgate area may have been the limiting parameter in system growth. The implication is that, once the maximum water capture was attained, total system discharge stabilized (Howard 1990a). Population growth may have continued within Canal System 2, but probably at a reduced pace.

Researchers have proposed that sociopolitical complexity developed among the Hohokam in the Classic period (A.D. 1100-1450). The increase in complexity is viewed as a response to expanded organizational needs created by the dramatic growth of the canal systems. Eliminating the argument for continued and dramatic increase in overall size of Canal System 2 does not invalidate the argument for sociopolitical complexity among the Hohokam. While the size and capacity of Canal System 2 has been found to stabilize early in time, our understanding of labor investment has changed. Following the model of accretionary growth, Woodbury (1961) argued that the expenditure of labor for canal construction was low. However, recent research has demonstrated a need for continual rebuilding of the system through time. Further, canal construction is a periodic, labor intensive effort and not the gradual and accretionary process envisioned by Woodbury (1961). The need to construct large canals as complete operational units creates higher but more periodic labor needs. New evidence has also shown canal use-life to be much more restricted than previously believed. The need to rebuild entire canals and canal systems following high-magnitude flood events argues for a dramatically increase need for labor expenditure than has been previously suggested. Our current understanding of canal construction and use-life suggests high labor needs on a more periodic basis. Following major flood events, the mobilization of large numbers of people would have been necessary and the organization of labor would probably have been a difficult and complex undertaking.

Measures of scale (discharge capacity, irrigated acreage, and labor requirements) and system complexity suggest that the administrative requirements for Canal System 2 were extremely high. Further, this analysis suggests that a complex system was in place by the Colonial period. It can be argued that large irrigation systems with the labor demands for the construction and maintenance calculated for Canal System 2 would arguably require a complex, centralized administration on an intrasystem level. The diachronic reconstruction of system growth suggests that this type of organization was required by the Colonial period.

Following the argument that the physical elements of the irrigation system represent specific task groups and levels of organization, a model of the intrasystem organizational hierarchy can be suggested for Canal System 2. At the lowest level, the distribution canals represent the Command Area Unit: farmers, probably residing in the same village, who must cooperate in local water allocation and in scheduling and maintenance activities. Local main canal segments, primarily territorial segments divided along large villages and occupation zones, represent the next level of administration. Local leaders within these villages would be responsible for controlling land tenure, dividing water allocated to the village by higher level administrators, resolving conflicts arising within their territorial units, and organizing corvée labor and meeting demands for goods and materials from higher organizational levels. The uniform spacing of villages at 3-mile intervals suggests the occurrence of localized administrative units having limited autonomy from the centralized authority. The centralized authority, probably residing at the site of Pueblo Grande, would organize water allocation and scheduling to the segmented units along the main canals. The current evidence from archaeological settlement patterns and modelled labor requirements, along with the argument presented here concerning a direct correlation between the physical elements of an irrigation system and task groups, suggests the emplacement of a hierarchically organized authority structure by the Colonial period.

The hierarchical organization in settlement structure and the physical elements of the irrigation systems appear to reflect a hierarchy of task groups and sociopolitical organization on an irrigation community level. It has been suggested that the Hohokam achieved a ranked or stratified society, often subsumed under the general typological category of "chiefdom" (Schroeder 1966, Haury 1956, Grebinger 1971, 1976; Rice 1987, Wilcox & Shenk 1977). The occurrence of administrative sites, primarily located at system headgates (including Pueblo Grande, Mesa Grande, Plaza Tempe, and Tres Pueblos), secondary administrative sites along the canal system, and smaller tertiary villages and hamlets suggest a well-defined settlement hierarchy.

It can further be argued that these site types are units that reflect functional and sociopolitical differentiation. The fundamental organizational level of irrigation societies is the irrigation community—the set of related sites and canals having a common headgate area (Howard & Wilcox 1988). The administrative needs of irrigation technology—including canal construction, maintenance, water allocation, water scheduling, and conflict resolution—are often linked to causal arguments concerning the rise of sociopolitical complexity. In the Hohokam case, these needs are postulated to have been met on the level of the irrigation community. Given the complexity of the

Hohokam irrigation systems, each irrigation community probably represents a largely autonomous sociopolitical unit by the Colonial period (Howard n.d.a). I suggest that sociopolitical integration between irrigation communities provides no tangible benefit unless conflicts arise over allocations of water taken from a common source. When competition for limited water resources occurs, cooperation and sociopolitical integration provide a mechanism for water allocation and conflict resolution.

This analysis has suggested that significant intrasystem expansion of Canal System 2 stopped early, possibly after reaching the limits of intake efficiency. What does this mean in regards to demographics and population growth for the Salt River Valley through time? While significant agricultural intensification does not appear to continue for Canal System 2 following the Colonial period, the expansion of irrigated acreage and of population probably occurred in adjacent areas along the Salt River. Despite data problems, the diachronic increase in site areas suggested by Upham and Rice (1980) does appear to have some validity (also see Wilcox 1979).

Although reconstructions of population and settlement growth on a valley-wide basis need to be examined in greater detail, the construction of new irrigation systems on the Salt River appears to take place though time (Howard 1990, n.d.a). New construction appears to be a function of agricultural intensification within the Salt River Valley. This process also appears to reach a peak and possibly a critical threshold at the end of the Sedentary period (ca. A.D. 1000-1100) (Howard n.d.a). At this time, the Lehi canal system (Figure 1), the third largest in the valley, appears to have been constructed (Howard 1987). The construction of the eastern portion of Canal System 1 (Figure 1) also appears to have taken place primarily in the late Sedentary period. The Scottsdale system may also expand at this time, and it is possible that the Coyote Ruin canal system dates primarily to the Classic period (A.D. 1100-1450) (Midvale n.d.). However, as this study shows, chronological reconstructions are often complex. A much more comprehensive chronological database is needed before questions concerning the overall development of the valley can be adequately addressed.

It is possible that the construction of most of the canal systems along the Salt River reached a peak during or shortly before the Sedentary to Classic period transition (ca. A.D. 1000-1100). Demand for water resources would increase with the addition of new canal systems along the Salt River. Conflicts over water use and water rights may have occurred, particularly during summer months in years when the streamflow fell below average. If conflicts over water did occur, they may have begun in the late the Sedentary period (A.D. 1000-1050), when the Lehi canal system became operational.

The many changes in Hohokam society, correlated with the Sedentary to Classic transition, may be primarily a reflection of sociopolitical integration on an inter-irrigation-community level. To alleviate conflict and possibly warfare between communities and to regulate water capture (particularly in times of low flow) in ways that would be economically beneficial, irrigation communities in the valley may have been integrated at a higher level of sociopolitical organization.

This suggestion is supported by the wide-scale abandonment of irrigation systems downstream from the central portion of the Phoenix Basin. The Cashion and Gila Bend areas, well-populated in pre-Classic times, show dramatic population drops in the Classic period. Perhaps political unification in the upstream systems allowed the Phoenix Basin populations to successfully appropriate most of the discharge of the Salt River at critical times. During summer months, in the peak of the irrigating season, the river is at its lowest streamflow. In low flow years, streamflow may not have been adequate to supply all of the canal systems extant by the Classic period. Historic records clearly indicate that the Pima utilized the entire flow of the Gila River during the summer months (Ezell 1961, Hackenberg 1974). Similar water shortages were also experienced by Anglo farmers on the Salt River prior to the construction of Roosevelt Dam (Merrill 1972). Given the comparable size of the Hohokam irrigation systems by the Classic period, similar water shortages may have occurred.

A similar process of unification and aggregation of population in upstream areas may also have occurred along the Gila River. During the Sedentary to Classic transition (A.D. 1000-1100), portions of the Gila River showed a pattern of abandonment or population decline in downstream areas. In the Snaketown area, settlement shifts led to the abandonment of the site of Snaketown, with the population shifting into much smaller site areas than is typical of the Colonial (A.D. 600-900) and Sedentary period (A.D. 900-1100) occupation of the area (Haury 1976, Rice et al. 1979). Large sites, such as the platform mound site of Casa Blanca, still occur in this area, but population may have actually declined. A large gap in settlement distribution also occurred at this time between the Sacaton-Olberg area and settlements in the Casa Grande area (also see Wilcox n.d.). Populations appear to have been aggregating in the Casa Grande area, where large canal systems do occur in the Classic period. Further investigation of the processes of system expansion and shifts in settlement patterns is needed in this area. While similar processes of agricultural intensification appear to be operative, differences in environment may have influenced patterns of subsistence change. The floodplain of the Gila River is narrower than that of the Salt River, while pediment areas useful for agave cultivation and other types of resources may be more prevalent (John Andresen, pers. comm.).

Political integration between the irrigation communities in the Salt and Gila river valleys may have occurred during the Sedentary to Classic transition, representing the establishment of a higher level of sociopolitical control. This higher administrative level and the establishment of a centralized authority over the Salt River Valley would suggest the attainment of a level of political control and integration rarely suggested in the Hohokam literature (but see Wilcox 1988). If this level of integration did occur, it would suggest the attainment of a level of complexity above simple rank or hierarchical societies and implies a range of complexity usually attributed to the formative states of Mesoamerica. While the attainment of this level of integration cannot currently be demonstrated, future research can address the question of sociopolitical integration between individual irrigation communities.

In this essay, I have examined previous models of irrigation system expansion and agricultural intensification. Paleohydraulics, methods for reconstructing engineering techniques and measuring discharge within prehistoric canal systems, were employed to explore diachronic change in irrigation system capacity. Models of Hohokam sociopolitical complexity were also reviewed in light of new data concerning the evolution, complexity, and economics of the irrigation system. While some of the interpretations presented here are tentative, they provide new models that can be subjected to future testing. Further, I hope that the methods of paleohydraulic reconstruction can provide useful quantitative approaches to the study of prehistoric irrigation systems in other areas. If the relationships of sociopolitical organization and the needs of irrigation technology are to be examined in detail, quantitative methods for measuring system structure and scale are needed.

ACKNOWLEDGMENTS

The study of prehistoric irrigation requires a multidisciplinary approach and interaction with a diverse group of scholars. It has been my privilege to work with and learn from many outstanding researchers. I thank my long-time friend and mentor, David Wilcox, and volume co-editor Vernon Scarborough for making it possible for me to publish this essay. Barry Isaac not only improved the quality of the essay but also taught me valuable lessons in clarity of presentation. I thank the members of my graduate committees at Arizona State University for their ongoing support and guidance, including Sylvia Gaines, Keith Kintigh, Charles Redman, Patricia Crown, Barbara Stark, and David Wilcox. Keith Kintigh, George Cowgill, Chris Carr, David Abbott, Gary Huckleberry, and John Cable have all added to my knowledge of open channel equations and statistical analysis. Portions of this essay were prepared for a seminar with Katherine Spielmann, and her guidance in economic anthropology is gratefully acknowledged. William Doolittle has continually provided significant insights into Hohokam irrigation from his wider geographic perspective. Jeffrey Eighmy has played a leading role in developing dating techniques applicable to canal contexts. Robert Gasser provided comments concerning the current archaeobotanical information and interpretations. Geoarchaeology plays an important role in paleohydraulic research. My close colleague, Gary Huckleberry, provided much of the geoarchaeological expertise in the field. Michael Waters, Fred Nials, and Karl Butzer also provided significant observations in the field. A large number of scholars have contributed to my understanding of Hohokam irrigation. Conversations with Bruce Masse, David Wilcox, David Gregory, David Abbott, Neal Ackerly, Paul Fish, Suzanne Fish, Ann Howard, Todd Bostwick, Randell McGuire, Adrianne Rankin, Kathleen Henderson, Sam Baar, Mike Gregory, and Chuck Hoffman have influenced my thinking and helped to resolve many issues. Portions of the research reported here was supported by funding from the State of Arizona through the Arizona Department of Transportation. The City of Mesa, the Mesa Southwest Museum, and Tray C. Mead provided the support necessary for the preparation of this paper.

REFERENCES

Abbott, David R., and Jerry B. Howard (n.d.) "Paleohydraulics and Ceramic Exchange: Structure and Interaction in Hohokam Irrigation Communities." Paper presented before the Society for American Archaeology, New Orleans, 1991.

Ackerly, Neal W. (1982) "Irrigation, Water Allocation Strategies, and the Hohokam Collapse." *Kiva* 47:91-106.

———— (1989) "Constructing Analog Models of Hohokam Irrigation." Pp. 159-178 in Jerry B. Howard & Cory D. Breternitz (eds.), *infra*.

Ackerly, Neal, and K. Henderson, eds. (1988) *Prehistoric Agricultural Activities: Hohokam Irrigation Cycles A.D. 700-1100.* Flagstaff, AZ: Northland Research.

Ackerly, Neal W., Jerry B. Howard, and Randall H. McGuire (1987) *La Ciudad Canals: A Study of Hohokam Irrigation Systems at the Community Level.* Tempe: Arizona State University Anthropological Field Studies, No. 17.

Ashbee, P., and I. W. Cornwall (1961) "An Experiment in Field Archaeology." *Antiquity* 35:129-134.

Bohrer, Vorsila L. (1970) "Ethnobotanical Aspects of Snaketown, a Hohokam Village in Southern Arizona." *American Antiquity* 35:413-430.

Bolton, Herbert E. (1930) *Anza's California Expedition's* (2 vols.). Berkeley: University of California Press.

Boserup, Ester (1965) *The Conditions of Agricultural Growth.* Chicago: Aldine.

Busch, C., M. Raab, and R. Busch (1976) "Q=AV: Prehistoric Water Canals in Southern Arizona." *American Antiquity* 41:531-534.

Cable, John, and David Doyel (1987) "Pioneer Period Village Structure and Settlement Pattern in the Phoenix Basin." Pp. 21-70 in David E. Doyel (ed.) *The Hohokam Village.* Glenwood Springs, CO: Southeastern and Rocky Mountain Division, American Association for the Advancement of Science.

Carneiro, Robert L. (1970) "Theory of the Origin of the State." *Science* 169:733-738.

———— (1988) "The Circumscription Theory: Challenge and Response." *American Behavioral Scientist* 31(4):497-511.

Castetter, Edward F., and Willis H. Bell(1942) "Pima and Papago Indian Agriculture." Albuquerque: University of New Mexico Press, Inter-Americana Studies I.

Childe, V. Gordon (1936) *Man Makes Himself.* New York: Mentor Books.

Chow, Ven Te (1959) *Open Channel Hydraulics.* New York: McGraw-Hill.

Crown, Patricia L. (1991) "The Role of Exchange and Interaction in Salt-Gila Basin Hohokam Prehistory." Pp. 383-416 in George Gumerman (ed.) *Exploring the Hohokam: Prehistoric Desert Peoples of the American Southwest.* Albuquerque: University of New Mexico Press.

Dean, Jeffrey S. (1978) "Independent Dating in Archaeological Analysis." Pp. 223-255 in Michael B. Schiffer (ed.) *Advances in Archaeological Method and Theory, Vol. 1.* New York: Academic Press.

Dittert, A. E., Jr., and D. E. Dove, eds. (1985) *Proceedings of the 1983 Hohokam Symposium.* Phoenix: Arizona Archaeological Society.

Doolittle, William (1984) "Agricultural Change as an Incremental Process." *Annals of the Association of American Geographers* 74:124-138.

———— (1989) "Finger on the Hohokam Pulse." Pp. 245-276 in Jerry B. Howard & Cory D. Breternitz (eds.), *infra.*

Downing, Theodore E., and Gibson McGuire, eds. (1974) *Irrigation's Impact on Society.* Tucson: Anthropological Papers of the University of Arizona.

Doyel, David (1981) *Late Hohokam Prehistory in Southern Arizona.* Scottsdale, AZ: Gila Press, Contributions to Archaeology, No. 2.

———— (1991) "Hohokam Exchange and Interaction." Pp. 225-251 in Patricia Crown & William Judge (eds.) *Chaco and Hohokam: Prehistoric Regional Systems in the American Southwest.* Santa Fe, NM: School of American Research.

Eighmy, Jeffrey L., and Jerry B. Howard (1991) "Direct Dating of Prehistoric Canal Sediments Using Archaeomagnetism." *American Antiquity* 56:88-102.

Erasmus, Charles (1965) "Monument Building: Some Field Experiments." *Southwest Journal of Anthropology* 21:277-301.

Ezell, Paul H. (1961) *The Hispanic Acculturation of the Gila River Pimas.* Menasha, WI: American Anthropological Association, Memoir No. 90.

Forbes, R. H.(1902) *The River-Irrigating Waters of Arizona-Their Character and Effects.* Tucson: University of Arizona Agricultural Experimental Station Bulletin No. 44.

Gasser, Robert E., and Scott M. Kwiatkowski (1991) "Food for Thought: Recognizing Patterns in Hohokam Subsistence." Pp. 417-459 in G. Gumerman (ed.) *Exploring the Hohokam: Prehistoric Peoples of the American Southwest.* Albuquerque: University of New Mexico Press.

Grady, Mark A. (1976) *Aboriginal Agrarian Adaptation to the Sonoran Desert: A Regional Synthesis and Research Design.* Ph.D. diss., University of Arizona.

Grebinger, Paul (1971) *Hohokam Cultural Development in the Middle Santa Cruz River Valley, Arizona.* Ph.D. diss., University of Arizona.

———— (1976) "Salado—Perspectives from the Middle Santa Cruz Valley." *Kiva* 42:39-46.

Greenwald, David H., and Richard Ciolek-Torrello, eds. (1989) *Archaeological Investigations at the Dutch Canal Ruins, Phoenix, Arizona.* Flagstaff: Museum of Northern Arizona.

Gregory, David A., and Fred Nials (1985) "Observations Concerning the Distribution of Classic Period Hohokam Platform Mounds." Pp. 373-388 in Alfred E. Dittert, Jr. & Donald E. Dove (eds.), *Supra, Part I.*

Grossman, Frederick E. (1873) "The Pima Indians of Arizona." Pp. 407-1119 in *Annual Report of the Smithsonian Institution 1871.* Washington, DC: Government Printing Office.

Hackenberg, Robert A. (1974) *Pima-Maricopa Indians: Aboriginal Land Use and Occupancy of the Pima-Maricopa Indians.* New York: Garland Publishing, Inc.

Haury, Emil W. (1945) *The Excavation of Los Muertos and Neighboring Ruins in the Salt River Valley, Southern Arizona.* Cambridge, MA: Papers of the Peabody Museum of American Archaeology and Ethnology 24(1).

———— (1956) "Speculations on Prehistoric Settlement Patterns in the Southwest." Pp. 3-10 in G. R. Willey (ed.) *Prehistoric Settlement Patterns in the New World.* New York: Wenner-Gren Foundation for Anthropological Research.

———— (1962) "The Greater Southwest." Pp. 106-146 in Robert J. Braidwood & Gordon R. Willey (eds.) *Courses Toward Urban Life.* Chicago: Aldine.

———— (1976) *The Hohokam, Desert Farmers and Craftsmen: Excavations at Snaketown, 1967-1965.* Tucson: University of Arizona Press.

Hill, W. W. (1936) "Notes on Pima Land Law and Tenure." *American Anthropologist* 38:586-589.

Hodge, Frederick (1893) "Prehistoric Irrigation in Arizona." *American Anthropologist* 6:232-240.

Howard, Ann V. (1983) *The Organization of Interregional Shell Production and Exchange within Southwestern Arizona.* M.A. Thesis, Arizona State University.

_____ (1985) "A Reconstruction of Hohokam Interregional Shell Production and Exchange within Southwestern Arizona." Pp. 459-472 in A. E. Dittert, Jr. & D. E. Dove (eds.), *Supra.*

Howard, Jerry B. (1985) "Courtyard Groups and Domestic Cycling: A Hypothetical Model of Growth." Pp. 311-326 in A. E. Dittert, Jr. & D. E. Dove (eds.), *Supra.*

_____ (1987) "The Lehi Canal System: Organization of a Classic Period Irrigation Community." Pp. 211-222 in David E. Doyel (ed.) *The Hohokam Village: Site Structure and Organization.* Glenwood Springs, CO: American Association for the Advancement of Science.

_____, ed. (1988) *Excavations at Casa Buena: Changing Hohokam Land Use along the Squaw Peak Parkway.* Phoenix, AZ: Soil Systems Publications in Archaeology, No. 11.

_____ (1990a) *Paleohydraulics: Techniques for Modeling the Operation and Growth of Prehistoric Canal Systems.* M.A. Thesis, Arizona State University.

_____ (1990b) "Los Hornos: Site Structure and Community Patterning at a Large Hohokam Village." Pp. 73-110 in David Wilcox, Jerry Howard & Rueben Nelson, *One Hundred Years of Archaeology at La Ciudad de Los Hornos.* Phoenix: Soil Systems Publications in Archaeology, No. 16.

_____ (n.d.a) "Sociopolitical Integration in Irrigation Societies: Measures of Structure and Scale." Pp. 9.1-9.53 in Jerry B. Howard, *The Operation and Evolution of an Irrigation Society: The East Papago Canal Study.* MS on file, Arizona Department of Transportation, Phoenix, 1989.

_____ (n.d.b) "The Effects of Irrigation Systems on Settlement Patterns." MS on file, Department of Anthropology, Arizona State University.

Howard, Jerry B., and Cory D. Breternitz, eds (1989) *Prehistoric Irrigation in Arizona: Symposium 1988.* Phoenix: Soil Systems Publications in Archaeology, in preparation.

Howard, Jerry B., and Jeffrey Eighmy (n.d.) "Chronology Building and Hohokam Canal Systems: The Development of Absolute Dating Techniques." Pp. 5.1-5.113 in Jerry B. Howard, *The Operation and Evolution of an Irrigation Society: The East Papago Canal Study.* MS on file, Arizona Department of Transportation, Phoenix, 1989.

Howard, Jerry B., and David R. Wilcox (1988) "The Place of Casa Buena and Locus 2 in the Evolution of Canal System 2." Pp. 903-939 in Jerry Howard (ed.) *Excavations at Casa Buena: Changing Hohokam Land Use Along the Squaw Peak Parkway, Vol. 2.* Phoenix: Soil Systems Publications in Archaeology, No. 11.

Huckleberry, Gary (1988) "Relict Irrigation Canals in the East Papago Freeway Corridor." Pp. 109-167 in Daniel G. Landis (ed.) *Arizona Department of Transportation Archaeological Testing Program: Part 2, East Papago Freeway.* Phoenix: Soil Systems Publications in Archaeology, No. 13.

_____ (1989) "Reconstructing Hohokam Canal Hydrodynamics." Pp. 13.1-13.14 in Jerry B. Howard & Cory D. Breternitz (eds.) *Supra.*

_____ (1992) "Soil Evidence of Hohokam Irrigation in the Salt River Valley, Arizona." *Kiva* 57(3):237-250.

Huckleberry, Gary, and Jerry B. Howard (n.d.) "The Value of Particle-Size Analysis in Prehistoric Canal Studies." Paper presented before the Society for American Archaeology, Phoenix, AZ, 1988.

Israelsen, Orson W., and Vaughn Hansen (1962) *Irrigation Principles and Practices* (3rd ed.). New York: John Willey & Sons.

Kappel, Wayne (1974) "Irrigation Development and Population Pressure." Pp. 159-168 in T.E. Downing & M. Gibson (eds.) *Irrigation's Impact on Society.* Tucson: University of Arizona Anthropological Papers, No. 25.

Karns, Harry J., trans. (1954) *Captain Juan Mateo Manje Unknown Arizona and Sonora, 1693-1721; Luz de Tierra Incognita.* Tucson, Arizona Silhouettes.

Katzer, Keith (1989) "The Hydrologic Characteristics of the Las Acequias Canals." Pp. 222-234 in Neal Ackerly & Kathleen Henderson (eds.) *Prehistoric Agricultural Activities: Hohokam Irrigation Cycles A.D. 700-1100.* Flagstaff, AZ: Northland Research, Inc.

Kelly, William W. (1983) "Concepts in the Anthropological Study of Irrigation." *American Anthropologist* 85:880-886.

Lindauer, Owen (1988) *A Study of Vessel Form and Painted Designs to Explore Regional Interaction of the Sedentary Period Hohokam.* Ph.D. diss., Arizona State University.

Midvale, Frank (1968) "Prehistoric Irrigation in the Salt River Valley." *The Arizona Archaeologist* 8:37-39.

———— (n.d.) Notes of Frank Midvale. On file, Department of Anthropology, Arizona State University, Tempe.

Masse, Bruce (1981) "Prehistoric Irrigation Systems in the Salt River Valley, Arizona." *Science* 214:408-415.

————, ed. (1987) *Archaeological Investigation of Portions of the Las Acequias-Los Muertos Irrigation System: Testing and Partial Data Recovery within the Tempe Section of the Outer Loop Freeway System, Maricopa County, Arizona.* Tucson: Arizona State Museum Archaeological Series No. 176.

Matson, Daniel S., and Bernard L. Fontana (1977) *Friar Bringas Reports to the King.* Tucson: University of Arizona.

McAllister, Martin E. (1980) *Hohokam Social Organization: A Reconstruction.* Phoenix: Arizona Archaeological Society, *Arizona Archaeologist, No. 14.*

Merrill, W. Earl (1972) *One Hundred Yesterdays.* Mesa, AZ: Lufgreen Printing Co.

Millon, René (1962) "Variations in Social Responses to the Practice of Irrigation Agriculture." Pp. 56-88 in Richard Woodbury (ed.) *Civilizations in Desert Lands.* Salt Lake City: University of Utah, Anthropological Papers, No. 62.

Mitchell, Douglas R. (1989) "Settlement Patterns and Social Organization for the Phoenix Area Classic Period." Pp. 859-878 in D. Mitchell (ed.) *Archaeological Investigations at the Grand Canal Ruins: A Classic Period Site in Phoenix.* Phoenix, AZ: Soil Systems Publications in Archaeology, No. 12.

Mitchell, William P. (1973) "The Hydraulic Hypothesis: A Reappraisal." *Current Anthropology* 14:532-534.

Neitzel, Jill E. (1984) *The Regional Organization of the Hohokam in the American Southwest: A Stylistic Analysis of Red-on-buff Pottery.* Ph.D. diss., Arizona State University.

———— (1987) "The Sociopolitical Implications of Canal Irrigation: A Reconsideration of the Hohokam." Pp. 205-212 in Sylvia W. Gaines (ed.) *Coasts, Plains and Deserts: Essays in Honor of Reynold J. Rupp.* Tempe: Arizona State University, Anthropological Research Papers, No. 38.

———— (1991) "Hohokam Material Culture and Behavior: The Dimensions of Organizational Change." Pp 177-229 in George Gumerman (ed.) *Exploring the Hohokam: Prehistoric Desert Peoples of the American Southwest.* Albuquerque: University of New Mexico Press.

Netting, Robert McC. (1974) "The System Nobody Knows: Village Irrigation in the Swiss Alps." Pp. 67-76 in T.E. Downing & M. Gibson (eds.) *Irrigation's Impact on Society.* Tucson: University of Arizona, Anthropological Papers, No. 25.

Nials, Fred L., and David A. Gregory (1989) "Irrigation Agriculture in the Lower Salt River Valley." Pp. 39-58 in Donald A. Graybill, David A. Gregory, Fred L. Nials, Suzanne K. Fish, Robert E. Gasser, Charles H. Miksicek & Christine R. Szuter, *The 1982-1984 Excavations at Las Colinas: Studies of the Prehistoric Environment and Subsistence.* Tucson: Arizona State Museum Archaeological Series, No. 162, Vol. 5.

Nials, Fred L., David A. Gregory, and Donald A. Graybill (1989) "Salt River Streamflow and Hohokam Irrigation Systems." Pp. 59-76 in Donald A. Graybill, David A. Gregory, Fred L. Nials, Suzanne K. Fish, Robert E. Gasser, Charles H. Miksicek & Christine R. Szuter, *The 1982-1984 Excavations at Las Colinas: Studies of Prehistoric Environment and Subsistence.* Tucson: Arizona State Museum Archaeological Series, No. 162, Vol. 5.

Nicholas, Linda (1981) *Irrigation and Sociopolitical Development in the Salt River Valley, Arizona: An Examination of Three Prehistoric Canal Systems.* M.A. Thesis, Arizona State University.

Nicholas, Linda, and Gary Feinman (1989) "A Regional Perspective on Hohokam Irrigation in the Lower Salt River Valley, Arizona." Pp. 199-235 in S. Upham, K. Lightfoot & R. Jewett (eds.) *The Sociopolitical Structure of Prehistoric Southwestern Societies.* Boulder, CO: Westview Press.

Nicholas, Linda, and Jill Neitzel (1984) "Canal Irrigation and Sociopolitical Organization in the Lower Salt River Valley: A Diachronic View." Pp. 161-178 in S. Fish & P. Fish (eds.) *Prehistoric Agricultural Strategies of the Southwest.* Tempe: Arizona State University Anthropological Papers, 33.

Rice, Glen E., ed. (1987) *The Hohokam Community of La Ciudad.* Tempe: Arizona State University, Archaeological Field Studies, No. 69.

Rice, Glen E., David R. Wilcox, Kevin Rafferty, and James Schoenwetter (1979) *An Archaeological Test of Sites in the Gila Butte-Santan Region, South-Central Arizona.* Tempe: Arizona State University, Anthropological Research Papers, No. 18.

Russell, Frank (1905) *The Pima Indians.* Washington DC: Smithsonian Institution, Twenty-sixth Annual Report of the Bureau of American Ethnology, 1904-1905. (Reprinted 1975, University of Arizona Press)

Schmidt, Eric (1928) *Time Relations of Prehistoric Pottery Types in Southern Arizona.* New York: American Museum of Natural History, Anthropological Papers XXX(V).

Schroeder, Albert (1966) "Pattern Diffusion from Mexico into the Southwest after A.D. 600." *American Antiquity* 31:683-704.

Service, Elman R. (1975) *Origins of the State and Civilization: The Process of Cultural Evolution.* New York: W. W. Norton & Co.

Sires, Earl W., Jr. (n.d.) "Hohokam Architectural Variability and Site Structure in Southern Arizona." Paper presented before the 47th Annual meeting of the Society for American Archaeology, Minneapolis, MN, 1982.

Steward, Julian H. (1955a) "Some Implications of the Symposium." Pp. 58-78 in Julian H. Stewart (ed.) *Irrigation Civilizations: A Comparative Study.* Washington, DC: Pan American Union of Social Sciences, Monograph 1.

———— (1955b) *A Theory of Culture Change.* Chicago: University of Illinois Press.

SYSTAT (1985) *The System for Statistics.* Evanston, IL: Systat Corporation, Systat Statistical Programs and Documentation.

Teague, Lynn S. (1984) "The Organization of Hohokam Economy." Pp. 187-250 in Lynn Teague & Patricia Crown (eds.) *Hohokam Archaeology Along the Salt-Gila Aqueduct, Central Arizona Project, Vol. 9, Synthesis and Conclusions.* Tucson: Arizona State Museum Archaeological Series, 150.

Thomas, David Hurst (1976) *Figuring Anthropology, First Principles of Probability and Statistics.* New York: Holt, Rinehart & Winston.

Turney, Omar (1929) *Prehistoric Irrigation in Arizona.* Phoenix, AZ: Office of the State Historian.

Upham, Steadman, and Glen Rice (1980) "Up the Canal Without a Pattern: Modelling Hohokam Interaction and Exchange." Pp. 78-105 in David Doyel & Fred Plog (eds.) *Current Issues in Hohokam Prehistory: Proceedings of a Symposium.* Tempe: Arizona State University Anthropological Papers, No. 23.

Uphoff, Norman (1988) *Improving International Irrigation Management with Farmer*

Participation: Getting the Process Right. Boulder, CO: Westview Press, Studies in Water Policy and Management, No. 11.

Wilcox, David R. (1979) "The Hohokam Regional System." Pp. 77-116 in Glen Rice (ed.) *An Archaeological Test of Sites in the Gila Butte-Santan Region, South-Central Arizona.* Tempe: Arizona State University Anthropological Papers, No. 18.

———— (1988) "The Regional Context of the Brady Wash and Picacho Area Sites." Pp. 244-267 in David Wilcox & Richard Ciolek-Torrello (eds.) *Hohokam Settlement Along the Slopes of the Picacho Mountains: Volume 6, Synthesis and Conclusions.* Flagstaff: Museum of Northern Arizona, Research Paper 35.

———— (n.d.) *The Changing Structure of Macroregional Organization in the American Southwest.* MS on file, Museum of Northern Arizona.

Wilcox, David R., and Jerry B. Howard (n.d.) "The Contributions of the Hemenway Southwestern Archaeological Expedition to Hohokam Archaeology." Paper presented before the Annual Meetings of the American Anthropological Association, Phoenix, 1988.

Wilcox, David R., Thomas McGuire, and Charles Sternberg (1981) *Snaketown Revisited.* Tucson: Arizona State Museum Archaeological Series, No. 155.

Wilcox, David R., and Lynnette O. Shenk (1977) *The Architecture of Casa Grande and Its Interpretation.* Tucson: Arizona State Museum Archaeological Series, No. 115.

Wittfogel, Karl A. (1957) *Oriental Despotism: A Comparative Study of Total Power.* New Haven, CT: Yale University Press.

Woodbury, Richard (1960) "The Hohokam Canals at Pueblo Grande, Arizona." *American Antiquity* 26:267-270.

———— (1961) "A Reappraisal of Hohokam Irrigation." *American Anthropologist* 63:550-560.

———— (1976) "The Canal Fork West of Snaketown." Pp. 141-142 in Emil Haury, *The Hohokam: Desert Farmers and Craftsmen.* Tucson: The University of Arizona.

PART IV

THE CENTRAL ANDES

CHIMU HYDRAULICS TECHNOLOGY AND STATECRAFT ON THE NORTH COAST OF PERU, A.D. 1000-1470

C. R. Ortloff

INTRODUCTION

Within the river valleys and desert margins of the north Peruvian coast lie vast networks of irrigation canals that have sustained the agricultural base of pre-Columbian civilizations for millennia. The major north coast rivers that supplied the canal networks originate from seasonal rain runoff west of the Andean continental divide. These rivers begin their westward journey through deeply entrenched mountain canyons that broaden into fertile river valleys on the Pacific coast margin. It is here, within these valleys, that ancient civilizations mastered the principles of irrigation technology.

Vital to irrigation agriculture is knowledge of the principles of open channel flow hydraulics, together with canal surveying and construction techniques. These engineering disciplines, applied within a framework mindful of the successes and failures of previous canal designs and future requirements of

Research in Economic Anthropology, Suppl. 7, pages 327-367.
Copyright © 1993 by JAI Press Inc.
All rights of reproduction in any form reserved.
ISBN: 1-55938-646-0

replacement systems, led to technical innovations among early coastal civilizations. These innovations evolved from the need to maximize agricultural land area and canalized river water available for irrigation while minimizing construction time and labor, subject to the constraints of the available technology base. The economic decisions involved in this process therefore reveal aspects and insights of the water management philosophy and political structure of a civilization insofar as archaeological synthesis permits.

This essay discusses technical, historical, ecological, economic, and political aspects of water management policies of the coastal civilizations of Peru in pre-Inca times, to establish the delicate interplay of all factors in the decisions that evidence themselves in the archaeological remnants observed in present times. Within these ruins of irrigation networks and canal systems lie the solutions to optimization problems in terms of the technical and economic variables that are the subject of the present essay.

HISTORICAL SETTING

This section examines the achievements in hydraulics technology and water management originating from Chimu occupation of the Moche and Chicama Valleys of Peru during the Late Intermediate Period (A.D. 1000-1470). The Chimu empire in the 15th century included the coastal valleys extending from Supe northward to Tumbes (Figure 1). Each of the major valleys of the Chimu empire contains an aggregation of many kilometers of ancient canals that were used, modified, and abandoned by pre-Chimu cultures. Excavations performed in the Moche and Chicama Valleys under the auspices of the Field Museum's Programa Riego Antiguo have revealed insights into Chimu hydraulic practice as well as stimuli of technical progress.

Figures 2 to 5 show the multiplicity of Late Intermediate Period intravalley Moche Valley canals that supplied water to field systems surrounding Chan Chan, capital city of the Chimu empire. The 74 km Intervalley Canal (Figure 3) was designed to lead water from the Chicama River south to an intersection point with the Moche River-sourced Vichansao Canal (Figure 2) located northeast of Chan Chan. Some canals in the Three Pampa field system area (Figure 5) are thus designed to be supplied from two independent rivers in adjacent valleys. The canals shown were not all contemporary but rather represent all known Chimu systems existing after hundreds of years of use, modification, reconstruction, and abandonment.

Upon excavation, each major canal exhibits sequential stratigraphic phases of construction within the earliest canal bed and occasional relocation and placement excursions of certain branches associated with different temporal phases. These phases are characterized by differences in lining material, usage indications (silt layers, oxidation lines) and/or basic changes in cross-sectional

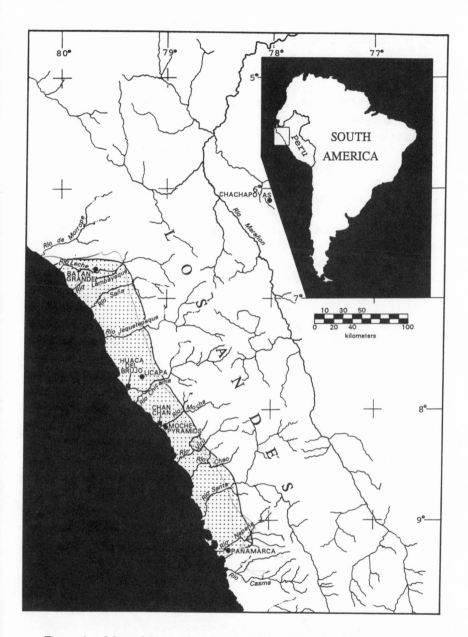

Figure 1. Map of Peru, Showing the Chimu Heartland between the
Moche and Chicama Valleys and the Capital City of Chan Chan
(The maximum extent of the empire stretched from the Lambeyeque
Valley in the north to valleys some 200 km south of the Casma Valley.)

geometry. Sorting out the temporal sequence of the many canal phases and branches in the excavation data is key to understanding the reasons for sequential abandonment of major canal systems and the economic and technical strategy behind construction of differently placed new designs incorporating advances in technology.

To understand the reasons for the canal sequence, it is necessary to consider first the geodynamic forces acting to slowly distort the coastal landscape. As a result of the steady subduction of the Nazca Plate under the South American Plate, the Peruvian coastal environment is continually subject to tectonically driven uplift and seismic disturbances (Barazangi et al. 1976) as primary effects inducing topographic landscape distortions over time (Cobbing 1972). Secondary changes result over long time periods as natural weathering processes establish new equilibrium topographies (Moseley et al. 1983).

Tectonically induced displacements acting on the coastal zones alter the canal slopes (Sandweiss et al. 1981), causing their flow characteristics to change. Typically, Chimu canal slopes are less than half a degree. Thus, minor tectonically induced ground slope distortions over time can easily render canal systems disfunctional and require new replacement systems to be constructed. Further, seismic events combined with pre- and post-seismic dilatational distortions (Wyss 1978) and ground settling can lead to patterns of local subsidence or elevation imposed upon the gradually uplifting coastal margin containing the entire network of Chimu canal systems.

Numerous examples exist of silt-lined canals that functioned before and/ or during Late Intermediate Period times but which now point uphill or have sinusoidal beds attesting these cumulative distortions. Other evidence of tectonic distorition exists in the form of entire sites that have been differentially tilted within the same time frame. Tectonic forces driving coastal and valley landscape changes cause rejuvenation effects on step gradient river valleys (Whitten et al. 1972), resulting in river downcutting effects. The presence of raised and angled beach areas subject to strong onshore winds leads to travelling sand dune formation in some areas, while winds can deflate other areas, producing sequences of site burial and exposure.

Further geomorphological effects are induced by the infrequent El Niño rains and flash floods acting on a nonequilibrium landscape. Runoff leads to large-scale mass wasting by erosional carving of a new local equilibrium landscape. Redisposition of flood-transported sediments within valleys leads to a further landscape nonequilibrium configuration to be acted upon by prevailing winds, while sediments carried by flood swollen rivers mix with the offshore northward oceanic currents to cause coastal beach depositions marking the passage of major El Niño events.

Coastal valley topography has therefore been dynamically changing throughout time from a combination of interdependent sources and accordingly has presented challenges to coastal civilizations to develop strategies of canal design and water management policies to maintain and expand the irrigation agriculture base over time. The enginering changes in canal system design over the millennia in the coastal valleys of Peru reflect these and other influences.

Early in the history of the Moche Valley, "great trench" canals many meters in width and depth led from the Moche River across intervalley desert regions to join together adjacent river drainages (see Figures 2 and 3). This early environment (estimated to have occurred in the early part of the Early Intermediate Period, 200 B.C.-A.D. 600) was characterized by inflationary sand accumulations evidenced by sand banked against the Andean foothills and large stretches of exposed beach sands. This topography facilitated the construction of long, low-slope canals extending into wide expanses of coastal sands (Figures 2 and 3).

As environmental changes altered and eroded the landscape upon which great trench systems were constructed, new irrigation strategies were required. As uplift and river downcutting proceeded, trench canal inlets became standed by the deepening river beds, necessitating enlargement of the trenches in the original bed until the canal inlets could once again accept river water. As river downcutting proceeded in the presence of coastal uplift, inlets were cut deeper to accept river flow. An enlargement of the downstream canal was therefore required. As each deepening episode essentially led to a slope decrease throughout the entire canal length, the canals were made wider to support the required flow rate. Since the canal water velocity then became very low, clearly the limits to this construction strategy were encountered. Adding to the problem of canal deepening was the presence of bedrock underlying the infilled sand overburden, limiting the practicality of further deepening operations.

As river downcutting proceeded further and as river erosion cut away old canal inlets, a new strategy of canal design was required, since each successive canal deepening made it more difficult to get water onto field surfaces. Because the field systems where irrigation can begin must be at a slightly lower level than the water level at the canal inlet, progressive riverbed and canal deepening gradually removes land from cultivation, as the feeder systems from the main canal must be cut at shallower angles than the canal bedslope to approach usable field systems. Each successive deepening therefore causes a progressive loss of downslope land reachable by canal water.

While the great trenches were in existence, subtle design changes were introduced as precursors of things to come. Where trenches crossed *quebradas* (erosional gulleys), flood erosion from El Niño events caused washouts, requiring canal reconstruction at near original slope but now through the eroded, flood-deepened *quebrada*. Reconstruction took place with an up-*quebrada* contour—the only possible path on the altered topography permitting the same slope. Contour canals were thus probably introduced in an evolutionary manner in response to a flood-altered landscape. In order to

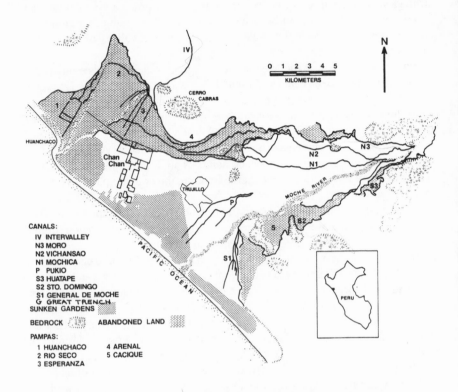

Figure 2. Detail of the Moche Valley Canal Systems on the
North and South Sides of the Moche River, and Two Spring-Supplied
Canals (P) as well as Sunken Gardens Near the Coast.

maintain the maximum size of an irrigated area, placement of supply canals
must be upstream of river downcut knick point, as the river is deeply entrenched
downstream of this point. (The knick point is the intersection point in a river
between old and new bed slope profiles arising from a tectonically-induced
ground slope change.) The new profile is established by means of erosive bed
slope cutting until an equilibrium profile is established. From field
observations, it appears that a tectonically-induced coastal plate slope change
occurred in early Chimu times, changing surface topography and initiating a
rejuvenation episode. In this environment, post-trench contour canals were
located in an old river profile zone upstream of the knick. Low-slope contour
canals of great length then evolved and originated from far up-valley river
locations; this led to canal paths through rugged Andean foothill terrain and
required precise surveying skills to implement.

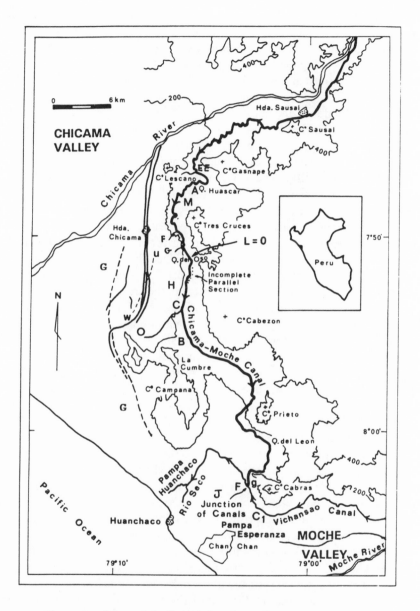

Figure 3. Map of the Intervalley Canal from the Chicama
to the Moche Valley (Branch EE from the Main Canal supplies
extensive field systems in the Lescano area; Branches F, G, and H
lead to smaller field systems. At Point J, the Intervalley Canal
intersects the Vichansao Canal within the Moche Valley.)

The next step in the evolutionary process was the "highest inlet" contour canal designed to incorporate the maximum arable land area. This design implies a river inlet as far up-valley as is feasible. (See, for example, the contour canal networks in Figures 2 to 5.) These systems are typical of Middle Horizon and Late Intermediate Period times (A.D. 800-1400). As ongoing river downcutting ultimately stranded the highest inlets, these systems were ultimately abandoned and new canals cut at downstream points along the river at lower slope. The key point is that, with further river downcutting, leadoff canal segments riding up the river banks to field systems must have progressively shallower slopes to emerge onto the land area adjacent to the river. Therefore, as the river deepens in its banks, the shallower lead-off feeder canals lead to progressively less downslope land. In this description, the highest elevation canal is backed up against valley neck bedrock obstacles, limiting further upstream extension. When these canals fail from river downcutting effects, then only new systems cut far downriver can replace them due to the concave nature of the valley topography. Thus, the progression from initial large trenches (in a sand inflated environment) to high level contour canals, then to far downvalley, late canals appears in the archaeological record.

Deeper river trenching originating from rejuvenation effects then gradually leads to loss of arable land and abandonment of high contour canals, forcing a new strategy for recapture of arable land. The new strategy of canal building is therefore consistent with the need to maintain agricultural production levels required by increasing population size from early to late Late Intermediate Period times in the Chimu empire. The final strategy is construction of downvalley canals originating from regions downstream of the knick point; this strategy results in further decrease in irrigated land, as only near-river downslope agricultural land is used. These two canal strategies may coexist for a while with the near-river canals the ultimate survivor. The canals shown in Figures 2 to 5 represent the collection of all system types over 1,000-year period; further details of their origins and function are presented below.

With this introduction, Moche Valley canal development can be further detailed. Starting with Early Horizon/Early Intermediate Period (c. 500 B.C.-A.D. 800) trenches originating from the Pampa Cacique (Figure 2) region of the Moche Valley (in a sand-filled, inflationary environment), land between the Moche and Viru Valleys was utilized for agricultural purposes and was irrigated by great trench systems. In the northside of the Moche Valley, great trenches originated from the Chicama River to irrigate the south side of this valley and Pampa Huanchaco zones (Figures 2 and 3). Trench deepening occurred as a response to river downcutting, pushing agriculture out of the Pampa Cacique region. Uplift-caused river downcutting was complicated by differential tilting of land areas on the north and south sides of the Moche and Chicama rivers. The net result was the erosion of trench inlets by river

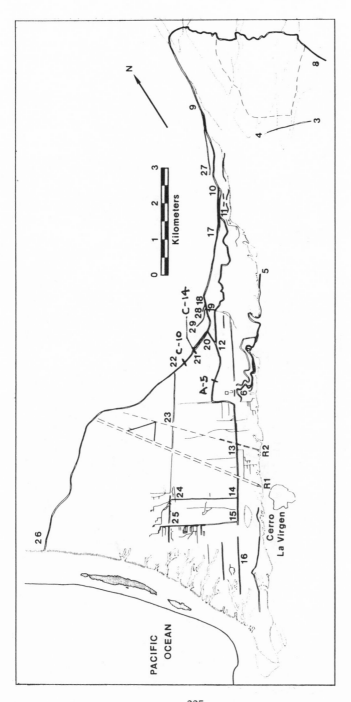

Figure 4. Detail of the Pampa Huanchaco Canal System (Lines R1 and R2 indicate roads leading from Chan Chan into the agricultural field systems.)

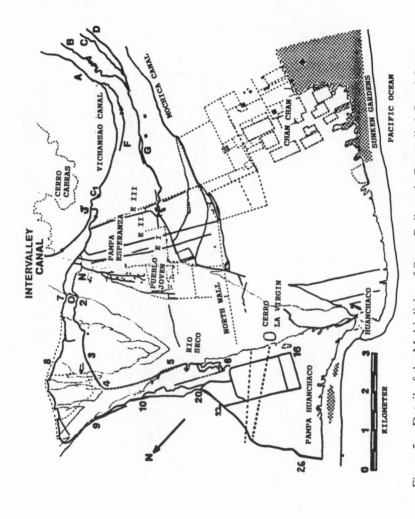

Figure 5. Detail of the Multiplicity of State-Built and -Controlled Canal Systems Surrounding Chan Chan in the Three-Pampa (Río Seco, Huanchaco and Esperanza) Area

action, despite further trenching efforts. Thus, the stranding of river southside systems required a new canal design strategy.

The latter half of the Late Intermediate Period appears to be deflationary, with sand shifting from zones previously banked against mountain ridges. Easy traverse of the previously gently-sloping, sand-filled environment by large, low-slope trenches was no longer viable as the old environment became erased. Emphasis then shifted to contour canals. The S2 southside canal (Figure 2) exemplifies a canal where the highest possible river inlet elevation was chosen to recapture agricultural lands within the Pampa Cacique region and to gain extension to the site of Moche (the capital of the pre-Chimu Mochica empire, A.D. 200-700); collapse of this system from downcutting effects led to the far downriver S3 system. The Intervalley Canal between the Chicama and Moche valleys (Figure 3) was another example of a contour canal built on the deflated environment with a high Chicama up-valley intake. On the north side of the Moche Valley, the highest N3 (Moro) canal ultimately was replaced by the longer Vichansao Canal (N3), opening new lands for agriculture; the far downriver, late N1 system was built with concomitant agricultural land loss when the Vichansao system failed.

The gradual decline of irrigated agricultural land manifested throughout the centuries of coastal occupation (as observed in the archaeological record) is thus explained by the dynamic model. Each successive canal type is optimum for maximum land usage on the contemporary land environment. Each successive canal phase, however, has associated with it significant loss in agricultural land reachable by irrigation waters.

El Niño rains and consequent floods (discussed in detail in a subsequent section) appear several times in each century, and there is evidence for infrequent massive flooding events in the archaeological and geomorphological record. These major events leave traces in the form of beach ridges created by sedimentary outwash from coastal rivers interacting with northward flowing ocean currents in conjunction with the uplifting coastal margin. In the archaeological record, preservation patterns in architectural and field system remains indicate that many such El Niño events (Figure 6) occurred in the Late Intermediate Period.

Thus, against the backdrop of a dynamically changing environment, Chimu engineers had to originate design strategies to deal with current and anticipated water supply problems. To add to the complexity of interpretation, analysis of canal system slopes built centuries ago must take into account changes that occurred over the active period of these systems as well as geomorphic changes that have occurred in the intervening centuries to the present.

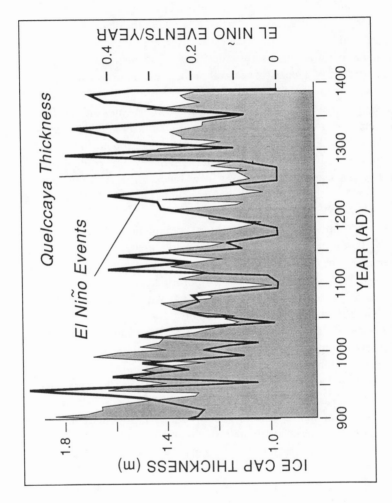

Figure 6 Summary of Quelccaya Ice Cap Thickness Records and El Niño Events, A.D. 900-1400 (Pers. comm., L. Thompson, Byrd Polar Research Center, Ohio State University)

THE INTERVALLEY CANAL SYSTEM SEQUENCE

The irrigation system of the lower Moche Valley is based on three sequential major canal systems on each side of the Moche River. The Moro Canal (N3) is the highest elevation canal on the north side and could potentially water the greatest area, but it carried the smallest percentage of the Moche River source. This canal is the earliest preserved channel built on the north side of the valley. During Moche III-IV times (ca. A.D. 400-600) an early version of the Moro most probably supplied canal B-G on the Pampa Esperanza (Figure 5). The Moro Canal slope averages 0.003 radians, and excavated profiles reveal two usage phases. The earlier phase was in use during Moche IV and early Chimu times (A.D. 500-950), while the second phase is a Chimu construction built after El Niño derived flooding about A.D. 1000-1100 (to be subsequently discussed). This canal served the up-valley area and was largely abandoned in early Chimu times.

The 30 km replacement Vichansao Canal consisted of a number of unlined channel segments connected to segment A (Figure 5), which were dug through stabilized sand drifts banked against Cerro Cabras (Figure 2). This canal is intersected by the Intervalley Canal, and the downstream channel led to canals on the Three Pampa area (Pampas Huanchaco, Río Seco and Esperanza; see Figure 3). Since the intake of the Vichansao was at lower elevation than the Moro, a low slope was needed to intersect the later reused distal end of the Moro. As the Vichansao slope averages 0.0003 radians, a large channel cross-sectional area was required to obtain the calculated 65 percent flow rate increase over the last phase Moro flow rate. The Vichansao-Huanchaco-Esperanza system represents both peak land usage and peak percentage of Moche River water flow utilized for irrigation.

The Vichansao exhibits four major usage phases, reflecting declining flow rate, and was abandoned during the last phase owing to river entrenching effects. A contraction sequence of five phases in the Huanchaco system (see Figure 4) mirrors the decline in the main Vichansao supply canal. While the early Vichansao and Huanchaco canal phases had large flow rates, later Huanchaco phases show deliberate filling-in of older canals (see Figure 7) within the same bed and construction of later phases supporting lesser flow rates. The canal usage configurations are determined by computer search through hundreds of Vichansao-Huanchaco-Esperanza excavated canal phase cross-section geometries for flow paths supporting a common flow rate. Measured wall roughness factors and local slopes permit subcritical flow rate calculations to be performed and matched to Vichansao flow rates associated with its various phases. By this process, the functioning and abandonment of various temporal usage configurations is established. The Vichansao Canal in its last phase was severely contracted and served only up-valley feeder canals close to its inlet, with the loss of large tracts of land once reached by irrigation

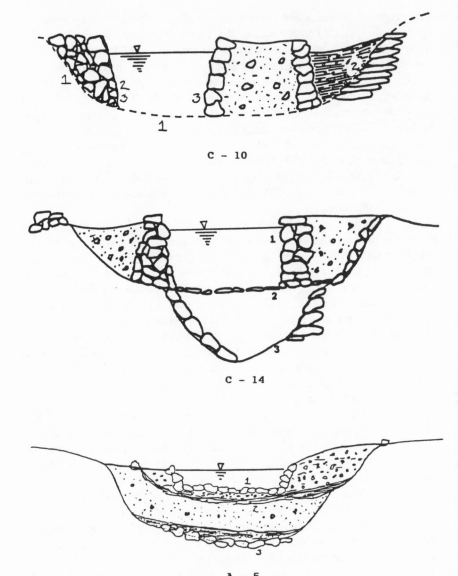

Figure 7. Canal Cross-Section Phases 1, 2, and 3, Reflecting
Various Construction Stages Indicative of Decreased Water Supply
at Locations Shown in Figure 4 for the Huanchaco Canal Systems

canals in the Pampa Huanchaco and Esperanza field system. With abandonment of the Vichansao, the N3 Canal was emplaced, resulting in loss of downslope irrigable land between these canals. The N3 flow rate matched that of the Vichansao Phase 1; its placement downstream of the Vichansao inlet signals the final abandonment of most of the Three Pampa fields.

A similar situation existed on the south side of the Moche Valley for successive S3, S2, and S1 systems. By recutting new upstream lead-off canal segments that roughly parallel the entrenched river, some extension of canal life was obtained under the penalty of a lower intake flow rate and greater transport loss through seepage and evaporation. Extensions of the intake further upstream were finally limited by bedrock obstacles near the valley neck and lead to the end to canal reworking. New canals could only be built leading off the stabilized river bed downstream of the active downcutting zone. This process accounts for the canal retraction and abandonment sequence observed in the Moche and similarly affected north and south coast valleys in this time period. Large Moche River downcut areas exhibiting nearly vertical banks have exposed strata containing Chimu and pre-Chimu cultural remains that attest an acceleration of the downcutting in early Chimu times.

During the many years of operation of the Vichansao Canal, it was apparent to Chimu engineers that a gradual decrease in water supply was occurring. This realization led to action in anticipation of the time when the major intravalley system would fall from use. The solution to this problem was the Intervalley Canal (Figure 3). By a junction of the Intervalley Canal was a point (J) sufficiently far upstream along the Vichansao Canal, the canals and lands of the Three Pampa region could be reactivated and agricultural production restored. A calculation of the theoretical Intervalley flow rate reveals parity with the Vichansao Phase 2 flow rate. Intervalley Canal flow could have been added to existing Vicahnsao flow to obtain the original Phase 1 flow rate and further expand land area under cultivation by means of activating the specially constructed 20-26 branch of the Huanchaco system (Figure 4). This Phase 3 branch shows similarity of construction techniques with the last Intervalley phase. The sum of Intervalley and Vichansao Phase 2 flow rates was nearly equal to the Vichansao Phase 3 flow rate; this fact could represent a strategy of widening the Vichansao upon the realization that the Intervalley Canal experienced distortions during its long construction time and would require continual redesign before completion.

The Intervalley Canal was constructed on terraces up to 30m high along much of its 74 km length. Many large and small aqueducts cross the numerous small *quebradas* (erosion gullies), while contour canals skirt larger *quebradas*. Intervalley Canal construction was initiated from the Chicama inlet; its route south passed by many large field areas suitable for cultivation by means of feeder canals leading off from the main canal. Large field systems at Lescano and Quebrada del Oso (Figure 3) attest to this feature; south of

Oso, partially completed lead-off canals exist but no preserved field systems are evident.

The Intervalley was conceived from necessity; its scope and design required a leap forward in technical innovation. The urgency of constructing an alternate supply canal to the failing Vichansao and Three Pampa system necessitated that the Intervalley Canal be quickly constructed to match the Huanchaco Phase 3 flow rate, while requiring that its flow rate be the maximum possible for the least inlet to outlet height difference. The problem of finding the shortest canal path requiring the minimum construction labor and time while providing safeguards against flood damage led to many technical and economic innovations (as discussed in the next section). The passage of El Niño floods between Huanchaco Phases 2 and 3 undoubtedly reinforced the need for an alternate intervalley water supply, while the reconstruction of the Huanchaco and Esperanza Canals after the A.D. 1000-1200 El Niño events bears evidence of built-in hydraulic control features that served to protect the canals from flooding conditions. However, the many construction phases of the Intervalley Canal attest that the same distortion effects acting to disable the Vichansao system were at work over the Intervalley's great length. Since it is doubtful that the last Intervalley phase worked south of the Quebrada del Oso area, its failure to supply fields surrounding Chan Chan with water finalized the loss of agricultural land on the Three Pampa area. The final N3 and S3 canals are of simple design requiring minimal engineering skills and labor input.

TECHNICAL INNOVATIONS AND WATER MANAGEMENT STRATEGIES

The earliest usage phases of the Pampa Huanchaco canal system (Figures 2 to 5) exhibit cross-sectional profiles characteristic of water erosion of sandy soils. Later post-Phase 2 profiles, which reflect increasingly smaller cross sections (Figure 7) indicative of lower flow rates, are stone-lined and are mostly built within beds of earlier canal phases. This construction technique takes advantage of thick silt deposits within earlier beds, which significantly reduce canal water seepage. Phase 3 post-flood reconstruction canals present opportunity for major design innovations. In these later Huanchaco system constructions (branch 22-26) and reconstructions (branch 9-20), Chimu engineers give considerable effort to increasing design flow rate by means of increasing the hydraulic radius and decreasing the roughness factor for the contour canal system, which can be seen in the post-Phase 2 use of low-wetted-perimeter masonry-lined channels as opposed to earlier, wide base channels with a large-wetter-perimeter and unlined earth banks (Ortloff 1988).

There is a trend toward canals of higher hydraulic efficiency by use of new cross-section geometry in the post-Phase 2 stoned-lined canals. For these canals, the channel geometry is close to the optimal half-hexagon trapezoidal profile required to maximize flow rate for the minimum wetted perimeter for fixed slope and cross-sectional area (Morris & Wiggert 1973). Calculation of critical and normal depths, slopes, and roughness factors for excavated channel profiles indicate subcritical flow for all phases. Thus, constrictions or obstacles placed downstream in the canal would raise the water height upstream and provide a method for diverting water into feeder canals. All drop structure inlets thus far excavated are raised some distance above the canal floor, requiring a water level rise to activate; the changes in cross-sectional area seen from phase to phase kept the water level high enough to permit activation of the drop structures, even when the canal flow rate decreased.

Another change designed to increase canal efficiency was the reduction in channel sinuosity; for example, the Huanchaco Phase 3 9-10-17-20-22 system was far less sinuous than the earlier Phase 2 9-11-12 channel. This change permitted a greater flow rate through the channel for the same hydraulic head. Thus, it appears that the post-flood reconstruction Huanchaco Phase 3 canals were attempts to make the reduced flow from the Vichansao supply the maximum flow rate by reduction of downstream flow resistance and to keep the water level sufficiently high to activate drop structures. Vichansao Phase 4, which appears to be associated with the Huanchaco Phase 4 canals, indicates that the water supply decrease was felt back to the Vichansao intake, implying supply difficulties over the entire valley. Pampa Huanchaco bed slopes are on the order of 0.009 radians for most of the system, which implies a technology to measure these slopes and an appropriate route selection based on alternate canal paths with different slopes.

The presence of complex hydraulic works requiring knowledge of civil engineering skills to design, execute, modify, and maintain over hundreds of years of operation implies a considerable technological base, yet the archaeological record has not yielded evidence of a written Chimu language or mathematical notation. Nevertheless, a hint of how the surveying may have been performed (Ortloff 1988) comes from a Late Intermediate Period ceramic in the Archaeological Museum in Huaraz (see Figure 8). It consists of a vertical hollow cylinder about 18 cm in height, capped by a shallow bowl. The cylinder has level, cruciform opposing cutouts along one transverse axis and vertically staggered, cruciform cutouts on the perpendicular in-plane axis. The bowl rim is parallel to the sight line from the center points of the opposing cruciform openings, so that when the bowl is brimmed with water, the cylinder is held vertically. A hollow sighting tube inserted through the vertical parts of the opposing cruciform openings at the maximum obtainable angular position allows a known angle to be sighted with respect to an artificial horizon created by the water surface.

For a polar angle Θ, $\Theta = h/R$ radians, where R is the radius of a circle and h is a circumferential arc length. With this relationship, a constant slope

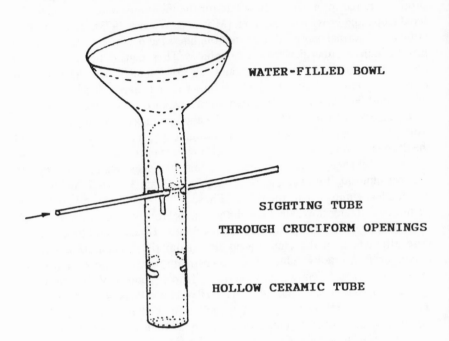

WATER-FILLED BOWL

SIGHTING TUBE

THROUGH CRUCIFORM OPENINGS

HOLLOW CERAMIC TUBE

Figure 8. Sketch of the Surveying Device Located in the Huaraz
Museum (Approximate height of the device is about 12 cm.)

can be surveyed approximately by measuring a ground length R and then a
horizontal line to a rod top at height h above the ground at distance R, assuming
the sight tube-ground level distance negligible. The division of h by R may
then be performed by counting the number of times (n) the rod height h "fits"
into the distance R. If the sighting bowl is next placed at point A and the top
of the rod sighted when the rod is located at point B, then the A-B distance
is $R = nh$, where $\Theta = 1/n$ for large n. To continue surveying the slope Θ to
point C, it is necessary to lay out a distance nh along various trial paths. The
path for which the rod's top is at the horizontal line sighted from B continues
the constant Θ path from A to B to C. Paths of different Θ angles can be
surveyed to determine the downslope land area adjacent to the canal path. Once
the angle is surveyed, hydraulic calculations proceed in parallel to confirm the
engineering basis for the selected canal system design. Figure 9 illustrates the
methodogy utilized to perform field survey with the survey instrument.

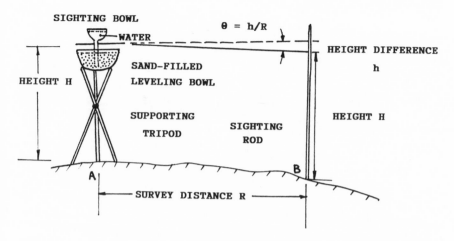

Figure 9. Spatial and Angular Relationships Employed for the Surveying Device (A tripod supports a sand-filled bowl into which the surveying device is inserted for leveling purposes. When the water is flush with the bowl rim, the sighting tube is parallel to the water surface when inserted through the cruciform centers. An artificial horizon is established by the water surface.)

TECHNICAL INNOVATIONS WITHIN THE INTERVALLEY CANAL

Because of the technical problems inherent in designing a canal through mountain and sand dune terrain, the Intervalley Canal contains the most information about Chimu ideas on optimal canal design and water management techniques. One feature of the Intervalley Canal (Figure 3) is the appearance of many canal lengths exhibiting wide variations in streamwise cross-sectional geometry. Two such lengths are found north of Quebrada del Oso and at point C. Each of these canal segments also exhibits local streamwise variations in opposing sidewall slopes, masonry wall roughness, and bed slope. As both sections lie upstream of large aqueducts, their function appears to be related to control of the water flow entering the aqueducts.

To test this hypothesis, a scale model of channel section C was made, instrumented with velocity measuring devices and tested in a hydraulic flume over a Froude number range characteristic of typical design and off-design conditions. (Froude number = square root of the flow velocity divided by the flow depth times the gravitational constant.) Observed streamline patterns and velocity profile surveys were used to interpret the function of the channel section. At low inlet Froude numbers (Figure 10), the subcritical flow experiences a net velocity decrease through the section from expansion effects

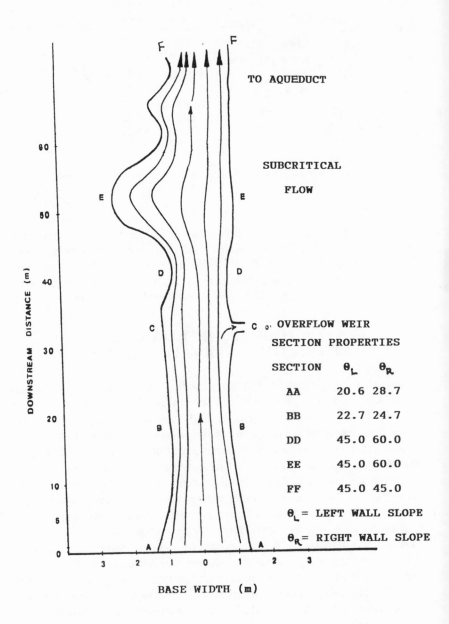

Figure 10. Intervalley Canal Segment at Location C in Figure 3:
Surface Streamline Pattern for Low Speed (FR < 1) Subcritical Flow

related to the larger exit than inlet area. At higher subcritical inlet Froude numbers, a standing vortex appears in the concave hollow (Figures 11 and 12); this closed streamline pattern acts to reduce the channel width in this area, creating and "effective wall" bounded by the outer vortex streamline. Downstream subcritical expansion further lowers water velocity. For supercritical inlet flow, the "effective wall" created by the standing vortex acts as a supercritical choke and creates a hydraulic jump at the throat section (Figure 12). The presence of the turbulent water zone downstream of the jump is effective in transferring energy to the recirculation zone. As the post-jump flow is subcritical, downstream expansion results in a velocity decrease. At high supercritical inlet Froude numbers, a complex interaction of the strong oblique hydraulic jump (Figure 13) with the recirculation zone results in a subcritical downstream zone which experiences velocity reduction due to expansion.

A plot of the ratio of the measured outlet (FR-OUT) to inlet (FR-IN) Froude number reveals (Figure 14) that, the higher the inlet Froude number, the lower is the outlet Froude number. Thus, this unusually shaped section is effective in reducing the outlet Froude number by employing a sophisticated mix of sub- and super-critical hydraulic phenomena operational in different Froude number ranges. In practical terms, the canal shaping is effective in lowering the outlet flow velocity, no matter the velocity of the inlet flow. Since erosion of the aqueduct sidewall lining increases for high flow velocities, the velocity decrease is effective in preserving the aqueduct lining over a range of high inlet Froude numbers. Such high Froude numbers could result from El Niño rain runoff into the channel along its length. An overflow weir built into the channel sidewall (Figures 10 to 13) with a spill height from the bottom that may be adjusted by inserting stones, may have served to drain off water under heavy rainfall conditions.

For the channel bed width distribution upstream of the aqueduct at Quebrada del Oso (Figure 15), the bed slope undergoes minor changes every 5m or so, and the asymmetric sidewall angles and wall roughness change radically along this length. The situation is further complicated by the fact that cumulative distortions acting during the approximately 900 years since construction have altered the bed slope, so that the original slope must be estimated. A computer solution of the local streamwise Froude number distribution can be made (Ortloff et al. 1982) under the assumption that the original slope will yield flow heights safely contained within the channel walls at the flow rate equal to that of the destination Huanchaco Phase 3 system. Since wall heights frequently vary from 0.3m to 3.0m, some 500 checkpoints in the computer calculation test the validity of the assumed slope. Results for the local Froude number distribution (Figure 15) indicate that values between 0.6 and 1.8 are maintained; large deviations from critical flow ($FR = 1.0$) are corrected by deliberate channel shaping and wall roughness changes in both sub- and super-critical flow regimes. Hydraulic jumps created by super-critical

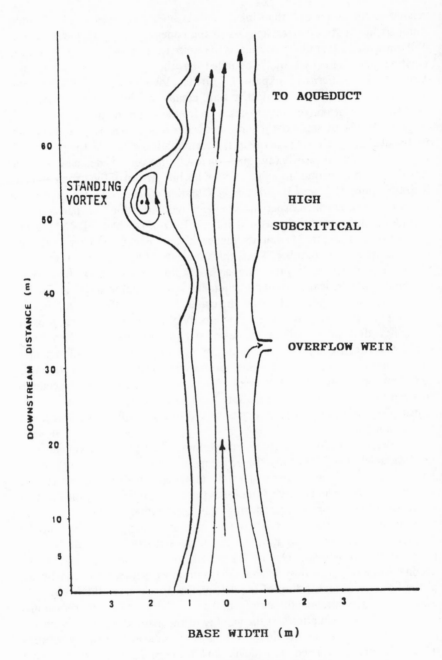

Figure 11. Intervalley Canal Segment at C: Surface Streamline
Pattern for High Speed Subcritical (FR $\widetilde{<}$ 1) Flow

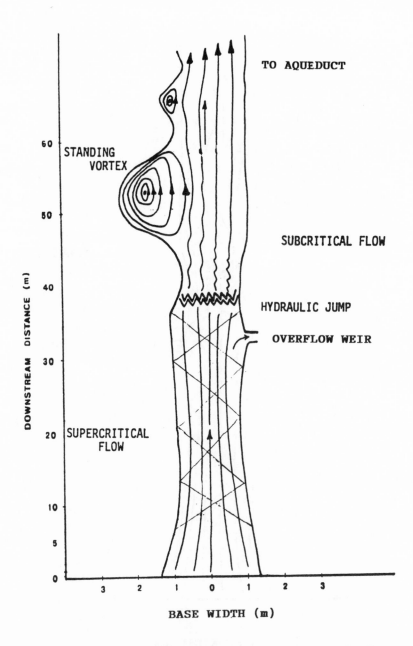

Figure 12. Intervalley Canal Segment at C: Surface Streamline Pattern for Supercritical (FR > 1) Flow (Note the weak hydraulic jump transforming the incoming supercritical flow to subcritical.)

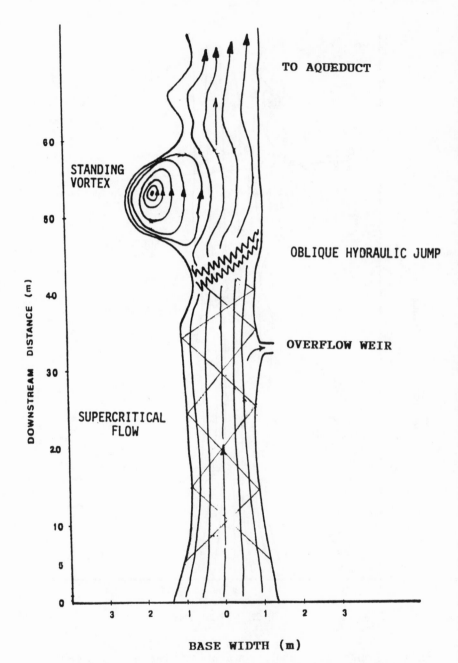

Figure 13. Intervalley Canal Segment at C: Supercritical
Inlet Flow (FR ≫ 1) (Note the Oblique Hydraulic Jump.)

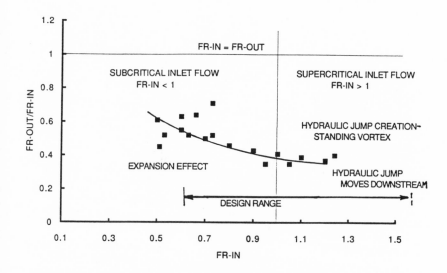

Figure 14. Results of Hydraulic Flume Tests (performed by the author at San Jose State University, Santa Clara, CA), Showing the Ratio of Outlet (FR-OUT) to Inlet (FR-IN) Froude Number Plotted Against the Inlet Froude Number (Froude Number = Square Root of Mean Flow Velocity ÷ Water Depth × the Gravitational Constant; see Morris & Wiggert 1972.)

choke sections are used to change to subcritical flow; use of contraction sections to induce hydraulic jumps is frequent along this section.

The section flow again shows a subcritical flow before entry onto the aqueduct structure, leading to low velocity flow that limits sidewall erosion. This segment of channel indicates many phases of construction in response to distortions experienced over the long time period of canal construction. Apparently, a high-subcritical design Froude number was intended for the canal, with local use of channel shaping to produce subcritical flow before aqueducts to limit erosion. This section's design is close to the FR = 1.0 optimum for transport at a given flow rate for given hydraulic head (Morris & Wiggert 1972).

If, from among the numerous placement and design options, a very low-slope, subcritical design were selected for the given flow rate, a large cross-section area canal with an inlet far downstream in the Chicama River would be needed. This design would exclude valuable arable land and would not be able to join the Vichansao to reopen the Three Pampa area to irrigation, and would be more subject to disfunction by small land slope changes. Additionally, because of the large cross-sectional area and concomitant large width and depth, the canal would need to be excavated to great depth through

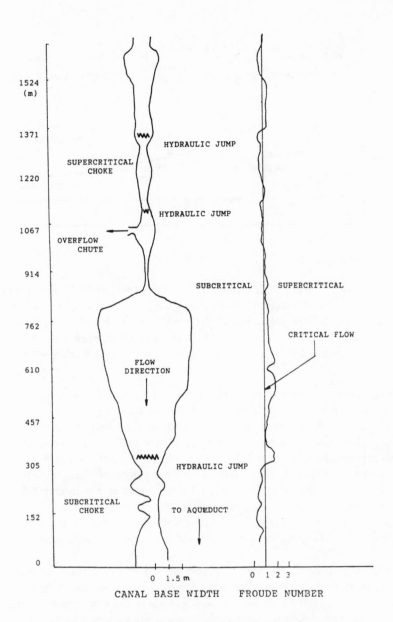

Figure 15.   Top View of the Bed Width Distribution of a 1.4 km
Canal Segment Immediately North of the Quebrada del Oso, and the
Calculated Froude Number Distribution Within the Canal Reach (Note that
the Froude number is designed to be within the range 0.6 < FR < 1.8.)

bedrock. If a supercritical Intervalley design were alternatively selected, a long canal path would need to start from an entrenched, up-valley Chicama River intake and traverse the rugged interior mountain range; this would require long terrace and aqueduct structures subject to major sidewall erosion problems and would require a large construction labor force in areas remote to supply. The actual canal path chosen is consistent with the urgency to rapidly complete the canal with minimum labor. Thus, the chosen canal design is the best possible from a labor minimization and hydraulic efficiency point of view, while permitting the maximum adjacent arable land en route as well as the vital hookup with the Vichansao to restore the Three Pampa area.

The economic advantage of the canal can be seen by examining Figure 16, which shows the seasonal river hydrographs (river flow rate during a yearly cycle). Since the Intervalley Canal in pratice subtracts water from the Chicama River and adds it to the Moche River, the adjusted hydrographs of the Chicama minus the Moche River flow and Moche plus Chicama River flow are shown. Since Intervalley Canal supply was to be input into the Vichansao Canal, the maximum Intervalley Canal input flow onto Phase 1 systems would supply water 1-1/2 months beyond that from the Moche River alone. Based on the diminished Vichansao Phase 2 flow rate, an extra six month's watering is possible. Part of the economic strategy to maintain agricultural output in the face of declining Vichansao flow rate was, then, to use the lower flow rate Huanchaco post-2 phases, with their smaller adjacent land areas, for longer periods of time, with the help of the Intervalley to Vichansao linkup. The computed maximum flow rate of the Intervalley Canal is matched closely to the Phase 2 Huanchaco system (see Figure 17), indicating a strategy of water resupply to this area.

The five usage phases of the Huanchaco system (Figures 2 and 4) are shown in Figure 17. Phase 1 indicates supply through the Moro Canal into the lower N-6 branch (Figure 5). Phase 2 represents the maximum extent phase. Vichansao phases indicate that the use of upvalley canals somewhat diminishes water supply to Phase 2 systems. With the advent of a major El Niño event, Phase 3 reconstruction canals emphasize northwest branches as the 20-15 branch is abandoned. Phase 4 indicates further construction and that the lower N-6 branch may be activated to serve field plots of the 5-6 region. Final Phase 5 serves limited Río Seco field plots and signals the near abandonment of the Huanchaco system. The Intervalley Canal contribution to the Three Pampa area was meant to augment Vichansao flow rate and return the area to productivity. Phase 3 of the Vichansao shows a widening effort to increase flow rate. This attempt may have been successful in supplying some upvalley systems, but Huanchaco Phase 4 clearly indicates the decline of water supply to this region and the final necessity for installation of the near-river, short-length N1 Mochica Canal (Figure 2), with a large agricultural land area loss.

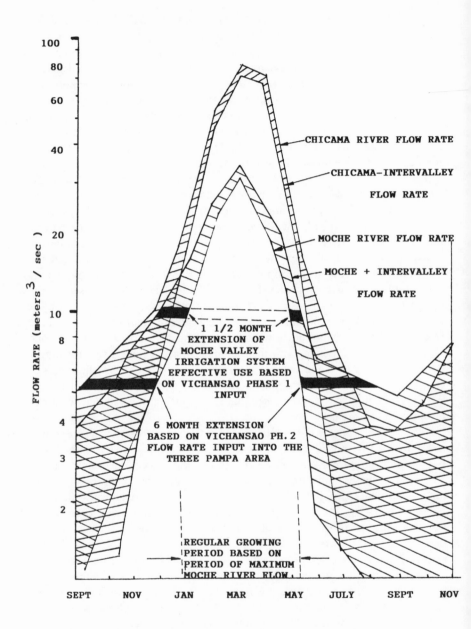

Figure 16. Hydrographs (river flow rate during a yearly
cycle) of the Moche and Chicama Rivers, Showing the Theoretical
Extension of the Watering Season Made Possible by the Addition
of Intervalley Waters to the Moche Valley

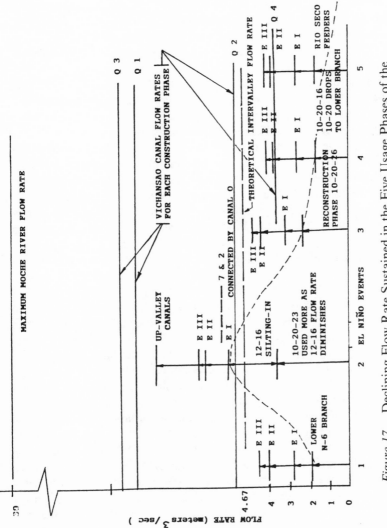

Figure 17. Declining Flow Rate Sustained in the Five Usage Phases of the Huanchaco Canal Systems (See Figure 5 for canal numbering system. The I, E II and E III Canals are located on the Pampa Esperanza, Figure 5.)

355

The decision to divert excess Chicama River flow to supply Moche Valley lands may have been influenced by the presence of Chimu nobility in Chan Chan and the special status of the adjacent field systems. The desire not to have lands surrounding the city barren may have provided the political rationale for extraordinary state-directed efforts to reopen the Three Pampa area by use of the Intervalley Canal. Since Chan Chan had a large population of artisans producing high-status trade goods for the ruling class of the city, the local fields served to produce crops (largely cotton) for those purposes as well as for the sustenance of the residents of the large agricultural zone adjacent to the main royal compounds of the city.

A further reason for bringing water back to the Three Pampa area was that Chan Chan derived its water supply largely from deep wells within the city. Water draining into the aquifer from the field systems recharged the city wells. In the presence of coastal uplift, however, the land slowly rises above the water table. The recharge effect was therefore important to raise well water levels to limit the amount of well redigging over time. Since there were scores of very large and deep walk-in wells throughout the city, it was more economical in the long run to resupply the field systems and wells at the same time.

Although the calculated original slope of the Intervalley Canal is higher than that of the Vichansao Canal, the difficult intervalley terrain requires precision surveying to produce a workable canal. The multiple canal phases within the earliest canal bed and canals adjacent to the last Intervalley phase represent efforts (over more than 100 years, according to C-14 dates taken from organic debris recovered from the Intervalley Canal) to obtain a workable canal in the presence of ground distortions. The fact that corrections to the slope in one part of the system require a reconstruction extending over many kilometers up- and down-stream complicates the modification process. The use of canal cross section shaping, wall roughness, and local bed slope changes to modulate flow to remain between definite Froude number limits were the major innovations of the Intervalley Canal. The bed slope may have been limited by hard-to-excavate bedrock patches, but the remaining parameters were skillfully varied to control water velocity within given limits. While the canal functioned optimally at a Froude number of unity, practical necessity dictated only piecewise satisfaction of this criterion by near critical flow zones.

Along the Intervalley Canal, early canal segments contouring inside deep *quebradas* (erosion gullies) were replaced by later aqueducts across *quebrada* mouths, thus saving several kilometers of canal path and reducing seepage rates. In other locations, multiple trial canal paths were laid out and partially dug to explore bedrock depth and construction options to reduce labor input. Large boulders were used for the construction of porous culverts that underlay the base of the aqueducts spanning the mouths of large *quebradas*. When El Niño rains collected to form torrents flowing down *quebradas* blocked by aqueducts, the stacked boulders forming the base allowed the flow to pass through and prevented water entrapment behind the fill structure—which could have led to washout and destruction of aqueducts.

With the abandonment of the segment of the Intervalley Canal from the Quebrada del Oso to the Vichansao linkup, the N3 canal, as the last resort, was extended toward Chan Chan. Compound walls within the city were breached, and irrigation agriculture occurred within city walls in the final stages. This collapse of the Moche Valley agricultural base was near completion in the 15th century, despite heroic efforts to extend its lifetime.

CLIMATE CORRELATIONS

To further set the stage for an economic analysis of water management practices of the Chimu, it is necessary to describe further the environment in which strategies necessitating technical innovations were required. The innovations described were the solutions to problems deriving from excessive El Niño flooding and ground distortions, but there was yet a further climate problem facing Chimu agriculturalists that influenced their water management strategies.

With recent advances in the reconstruction of the Andean paleoclimate through ice core analysis (Thompson et al. 1979, 1982, 1985, 1987; Shimada et al. 1991), it is now possible to estimate periods of drought and excessive rainfall over many centuries of importance to the present study. In particular, the period A.D. 800-1450 is characterized by many significant climate changes that affect agriculture. The Quelccaya Icecap is located in southern Peru (13°56′S, 70°50′W) and is the source of climate data obtained from analysis of snow layer thicknesses related to yearly cycles of rainfall intensity. Analysis performed by Thompson and co-workers has shown that climate trends obtained from this source apply throughout Peru and are relevant to this study.

From current work (Ortloff & Kolata 1992), Figure 18 indicates the nine-year moving average of ice layer thickness over the period A.D. 800-1400. Periods characterized by large layer thickness are generally wet periods with sequential years of above average rainfall; small layer thicknesses are typical of extended drought periods. As seen from Figure 18, a decrease in the mean rainfall level from pre- to post-A.D. 1000 is statistically significant, indicating that a climate change occurs at this time. In addition to the rainfall decrease in the post-A.D. 1000 environment, a second drought occurs from A.D. 1250 to 1320, within the already reduced rainfall period extending from A.D. 1000 to 1400. If this curve is integrated, the effect of the mean level change is more evident (Figure 19); areas above the mean are positive while those below are negative. Given these changes and the trends described in the previous sections, it is now possible to piece together the environmental change and societal response of the Chimu in some detail.

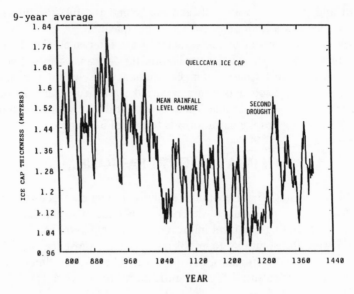

Figure 18.   Nine-Year Moving Average of Adjusted Quelccaya
Ice Cap Thickness, A.D. 800-1400 (Pers. comm., L. Thompson,
Byrd Polar Research Center, Ohio State University.)

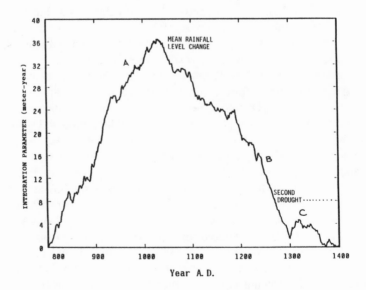

Figure 19.   Integrated Quelccaya Ice Cap Thickness, A.D.
800-1400, Indicative of Change in Mean Levels of Rainfall.

WATER MANAGEMENT STRATEGIES OF THE CHIMU

Given the descriptive material thus far presented, the water management strategy of the Chimu can be graphically represented as in Figure 20. This figure represents the history of various key parameters governing irrigation agriculture in the Moche Valley during the Chimu occupation. The curves shown represent land area under cultivation (A), total flow rate of all supply canals (Q), construction labor input (Ψ), and engineering sophistication index (Φ). These curves and the calculations to derive specific values originate from data analysis performed previously (Ortloff et al. 1982, 1985; Ortloff 1988).

As can be seen from Figure 20, a steady increase in land area, water supplied, input labor, and technical sophistication characterized pre-A.D. 1000 times. With the advent of the shift in rainfall level in the post-A.D. 1000 environment, the canal supply rivers underwent a decline in flow rate, affecting the water supply. Both Moche Valley north- and south-side canals (Figure 2) dropped out in sequence, gradually eliminating the Pampa Huanchaco and Esperanza canals (Figures 4 and 5) from use and lowering the available land area for cultivation (Figure 20). The gradual decline in canal flow rate was addressed by redesign of the cross sections (Figure 7) to improve their hydraulic efficiency. The cross-section contraction phases reflect decreased water supply to the Pampa Huanchaco area. This system was sourced by the Vichansao Canal, which also exhibits a corresponding set of contraction profiles. Phase 3 profiles indicate that about a third of the Phase 2 flow rate is available for field watering. Although most of the smaller reconstruction profiles have stone linings, the C-10 profile shows a stack of "pancake" adobes used to narrow the channel for the smaller flow rate.

Frequent El Niño flooding, distortion introduced by coastal uplift, and shifts toward drier climate drove the rebuilding and modification efforts in the proximity of Chan Chan. After many years of decline, new water sources were sought to revitalize this area by means of the Intervalley Canal linkage. This massive construction project required labor resources from throughout the empire as well as new technologies. With a design flow rate of 4.67 m^3/second (Ortloff et al. 1982), the Three Pampa systems could theoretically be revitalized through the N3 system since the Intervalley Canal had the same design flow rate. As the Intervalley Canal was functional only as far south as the Quebrada del Oso, the restoration of the Three Pampa area was never realized from Chicama River water. As the drought period extended over many decades, the water supply to canals declined gradually (Figures 17 and 20) and land area under cultivation declined precipitously. The city of Chan Chan was not without recourse, however, as valleys to the north containing large flow rate rivers were next subject to conquest and consolidation within the expanding empire.

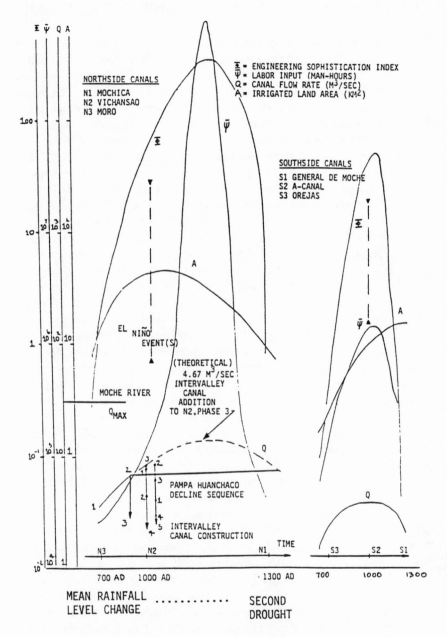

Figure 20. Moche Valley Canal System Diagnostics: Engineering Sophistication Index, Labor Input, Total Canal Flow Rate, and Irrigated Land Area Distributions over the Chimu Period, A.D. 800-1400

ECONOMIC ANALYSIS

Having outlined the development and decline of Moche Valley canal systems, we can now turn to water management strategies and service sector aspects. From calculations (Ortloff et al. 1985) of the technical sophistication index (Φ) and the labor index (Ψ) for certain key canals (Figure 21), estimates of construction manpower were obtained. For most of the intervalley canals, it appears that a crew of specialists directing a labor force of perhaps 300 men for several months would have sufficed to build the major canals, based on man-hour estimates.

Major projects such as the Intervalley Canal and S-2 canals clearly would have required the recruitment of labor from outside of Chan Chan's labor resource pool. Since time was of the essence for incorporation of Intervalley waters into the Moche Valley, large numbers of workers were necessary for completion of the system to replace the declining intravalley systems. C-14 dates for the Intervalley show perhaps 50-100 years of construction. Based on the man-hour estimate, 1,000 men working 10 hrs/day for 150 days/year for 50 years could have completed the Intervalley Canal system down to Quebrada del Oso. Additional workers used to convey supplies to construction workers would have increased the toal numbers required to undertake major projects. Since agriculture was in decline in the Moche Valley at the time of construction, importation of food from other parts of the empire and harvest time synchronization must have played a part in the labor supply totals.

The total infrastructure necessary for the project therefore consisted of several thousand workers under the direction of a central administration in the capital city. Since the city was mostly populated by royalty, retainers, and artisans (Moseley & Day 1988), and since agricultural workers were largely located in outlying communities adjacent to the cultivated areas but distant from the capital city, clearly the labor pool of thousands of workers must have been drawn from the non-elite classes of the empire by mandate of the rulers of the empire. The establishment of an optimal system design in terms of maximum canal flow rate for the minimum construction labor expenditure required that the labor expenditure remain small while completing the project as rapidly as possible.

Since the technical sophistication of the Intervalley Canal was maximal (Figure 20), we can assume that a team of water management specialists were directing the project and applying accumulated knowledge in hydraulics and systems management expertise. Thus, to the craft specialists involved in metal working, ceramics, textile production, and architectural design, there must be added a specialty group involved in the design and direction of large hydraulics and irrigation projects under the command of Chimu royalty. In the absence of major emergency projects, this group easily could have directed the maintenance and elaboration of relatively low sophistication intravalley canals;

Canal Name	"Engineering" Index Φ	Labor Index Ψ (man-hours)	Cultural Affiliation
Moro (N3)	0.18	26,000	Moche/Earlier
Canal G (distal)	0.34	17,000	Moche/Earlier
Vichansao Q-1 (N2)	64.4	140,000	Chimu
Intervalley Canal	320	<760,000,000	Chimu
Esperanza			
EI	0.34	1,500	Chimu
EII	0.05	2,600	Chimu
EIII	0.03	410	Chimu
Lower Milagro			
(2-4-5-6)	0.20	25,000	Chimu
Huanchaco Segment:			
22-26	0.90	33,000	Chimu
10-11-12	0.40	5,200	Chimu
10-20	0.25	2,400	Chimu
13-16	0.02	130	Chimu
22-25	0.02	130	Chimu
Canal A			
(S2-Southside)	52.0	1,500,000	Chimu
Pukio Canals	0.04	15,000	Chimu
Mochica (N1)	1.02	96,000	Chimu
General de Moche			
(S1-Southside)	0.19	51,000	Chimu/Modern

Figure 21. Compilation of the Calculated Technical Sophistication Index (Engineering Index), Labor Index (Man-Hours of Canal Construction Time), and Cultural Affiliation for Various Canals Shown in Figures 2 to 5 (from Ortloff et al. 1985)

for major systems, years of route surveying, labor estimation, supply planning, and hydraulic calculation probably preceeded the initiation of work.

In this sense, the methods applied to major hydraulic works are not dissimilar to those involved in massive city building efforts continually carried out during the enlargement and expansion of royal and workers' quarters for several centuries. Since the population of Chan Chan has been estimated at 20,000-40,000 persons (Moseley & Day 1988), part of the construction labor force could have been recruited by a labor tax upon worker communities dedicated to agricultural and non-specialized (i.e., non-craft) labor. Such communities were largely self-sustaining and directed produce to supporting the bureaucratic and craft specialists of the city. Comparison of elite burial goods and practices within Chan Chan and those in agricultural communities supporting the capital city indicates that the agriculturalist's lot was one of low status.

Water management policy was most probably dictated from the central authority of the Chimu state. Rural administrative centers at Quebrada del Oso, Cerro de la Virgin (northwest of Chan Chan near the Huanchaco system) and Pueblo Joven (Figure 5) probably served as the main outposts to house and administer workers connected with nearby agricultural field systems. The land surrounding Chan Chan was used in conjunction with up-valley field systems irrigated by feeder canals tapped from the highest elevation canal in use. Most of the arable land of the Moche Valley was reachable by canals during the maximum extent of the systems in the A.D. 1000-2000 period. The agricultural policy appears to have been one of maximum utilization of land area; this policy was supported by improvements in surveying technology of low slope canals, which extended the reach of canals to include more downslope area.

Ideally, ground porosity is adequate to support drainage of irrigation water into the deep aquifer; this feature limited the build-up of accumulated salts in the fields. Since rainfall is usually limited to a few millimeters per year (except during El Niño events), the possibility of groundwater excursions to reintroduce salts to the farming landscape was remote. Earlier canal versions dug into the sands were allowed to form thick silt layers; these layers limited seepage from canals during transport. Water draining into the aquifer from the fields was tapped by means of numerous deep, walk-in wells to provide the capital with a dependable water supply. Since the climate is temperate, multiple cropping was limited only by the intermittent water supply of the Moche River. The nearby, high flow rate Chicama River and large arable land area provided a further resource base for multiple cropping (and the possibility of water transport to the nearby Moche Valley through the Intervalley Canal connection).

The successful integration of technical innovation to extend, modify, and repair canal systems in the presence of tectonically induced ground distortions and El Niño flooding led to three centuries of successful operation of the total system; only extended drought caused a decline of the system's productive capacity. The presence of northern frontier polities with rich agricultural potential but limited defensive capability allowed yet another "extension" of the agricultural system in the 15th century, when the conquest of these northern territories was begun.

At present, the ten large compounds within Chan Chan are characterized as the seats of royal dynasties of successive eras (Moseley & Day 1988). It appears that the water management system was centrally controlled, due to its vast scope and complexity, using command labor and produce redistribution as its basis. While many types of food crops were grown, a sizeable component of production was in the form of fiber crops (cotton, for the most part) for textile manufacture. The presence of vast storage areas within the royal compounds may be evidence of the collection and redistribution system.

Clearly, status within the system regulated the degree of reward; the impression is that all were provided for adequately, although agricultural workers were clearly at the bottom of the economic scale, as evidenced by the quality of grave goods from rural centers.

Within the capital city, vast compounds of living quarters, workshops, kitchens, livestock pens, and storage rooms adjoin royal private compounds. These areas were apparently for the retainers, artisans, and support laborers necessary for the daily operation of the city. The success of the agricultural system over centuries is what drove the increasing growth and prosperity of the city. Conquest added further prosperity as the metalworking resources of the northern polities were absorbed into the empire, together with their agricultural resource base and population available for labor. Since labor tax was apparently state practice (Moseley & Day 1988), vast city building and hydraulic works (such as the Intervalley Canal) were well within the capability of the state, due to the large population of the empire.

The drought period beginning in the 13th century required further acquisition of lands associated with large-flow-rate rivers to support royal privilege. Since these rivers were some distance from Chan Chan, the implication is that tribute, trade, and redistribution of land area under irrigation were required to balance the productive capacity of the empire. In short, the empire moved from an intravalley perspective to one of intervalley scope by focusing on central control of the agricultural resources of the empire-wide regions. In drought times, the contraction of Moche Valley irrigation systems had to be countered by expansion into well-watered northern valley agricultural systems to increase production (Eling 1986, Keatinge 1977).

Thus, state control probably expanded as the complexity of directing resources forced an empire-wide perspective onto the ruling class of Chan Chan through consideration of water management and agricultural policy. Centers of provincial administration in the northern valleys (such as Farfan in the Jequetepeque Valley and Chuquitoy Viejo in the Chicama Valley) appear to mimic some features of Chan Chan architecture and are most likely manifestations of a centrally controlled agricultural strategy (Keatinge 1988). Older regional cities in conquered valleys appear not to be used in this fashion, as new administrative centers are built there in central locations to effectively manage hydraulic works installed (or taken over) by Chimu engineers.

Following Wittfogel's (1957) characterization of hydraulic societies as "large-scale and government managed works of irrigation and flood control," there is now significant evidence that the Chimu can be classified as a hydraulic society. For Chimu society, there are several special features in place to drive water management policy. The foremost is the ability to devise technical solutions to water supply problems at a faster rate than they occur. This procedure assumes the ability to observe problems in their early stages, project the consequences, and then derive a solution to counter the worst-case scenario.

Therefore, an observational science oriented to geophysical and climate-related problems must be in place with a transferable knowledge base that anticipates future problems.

Chimu engineers successfully designed flood control mechanisms into major canals (Ortloff et al. 1982, 1985) that would protect them against all but the worst flooding; this is an example of observational science in action. Similarly, tectonic distortion could be observed by resurvey of canal slopes on a regular basis; the fact that new canals were cut or modified after older ones proved untenable shows a flexible technical approach designed to maintain continuity of agricultural production (although perhaps in reduced form). The presence of drought signaled the start of the Intervalley Canal, which required a long lead time to design and build, so that its completion would not come too late to be useful. Hydraulic modifications of intravalley canals to decrease flow resistance are yet another example of the technical base present to maintain agricultural production in the presence of drought conditions.

Faced with the prospect of failing agricultural resources, the military option could be employed as an extension of political policy to capture and incorporate new agricultural lands into the empire. Since the Chimu state successfully managed all aspects of state survival for almost 500 years, and since at least some aspects of their technology base are now known, Chimu dominance of the Peruvian north coast is now, in part, understandable on this basis. The Chimu state used a modern-day approach, to develop and apply new technology to solve tomorrow's problems by first understanding the nature of the problems and then devising necessary technology for their resolution over time. The Chimu state therefore serves as a model of efficiency in anticipating and solving problems by application of appropriate technology. Wittfogel's question of whether "the technical problems create the bureaucracy to solve them" seems to be answered affirmatively, as efficient problem-solving institutions were evolved to maintain the productive agricultural capacity of the empire despite threats from many quarters.

Characteristic of successful hydraulic societies, then, is a technical base responsive to present and anticipated problems affecting agricultural production; this base is manifested by demonstrated technical innovation and introduction of new design philosophies to counter problems in water supply. Additionally, technical strategies to minimized labor input and maximize flow rate while building in damage-limiting hydraulic controls are indicative of the strong technical, pragmatic component of Chimu society. The ability to direct labor resources and manage complex water supply systems provided Chimu society with a secure agricultural base for several centuries.

Although many aspects of Chimu cultural and administrative life are known (Moseley & Day 1988, Kolata 1990, Lumbreras 1986), the present study adds new elements by presenting aspects of Chimu water management policy, historical development, and technical base. The final picture is one of a dynamic, innovative society meeting technical challenges by an integrated approach based on past observations of climate and geomorphic change, and a measured response utilizing a sound engineering and systems approach. The net result was a largely successful agricultural program over many centuries, despite a climate-driven decline in the water supply to agricultural field systems in the later periods of empire.

REFERENCES

Barazani, M., and B. Isacks (1976) "Spatial Distribution of Earthquakes and Subduction of the Nazca Plate Beneath South America." *Geology* 4:688-692.

Cobbing, E. (1972) "Tectonic Elements of Peru and the Evolution of the Andes." *Proceedings of the 24th International Geological Congress, Section 3, Montreal, Canada*:306-315.

Eling, H. (1986) "Pre-Hispanic Irrigation Sources and Systems in the Jequetepeque Valley, Northern Peru." Pp. 130-149 in R. Matos, S. Turpin & H. Eling (eds.) *Andean Archaeology*. Los Angeles: University of California, Institute of Archaeology, Monograph 27.

Keatinge, R. (1988) *Peruvian Prehistory*. Cambridge, ENG: Cambridge University Press.

Kolata, A. (1990) "The Urban Concept of Chan Chan." Pp. 107-144 in M. Moseley (ed.) *The Northern Dynasties: Kinship and Statecraft in Chimor*. Washington, DC: Dumbarton Oaks Press.

Lumbreras, L. (1974) *The Peoples and Cultures of Ancient Peru*. Washington, DC: Smithsonian Institution Press.

Morris, H., and J. Wiggert (1972) *Applied Hydraulics in Engineering*. New York: Ronald Press.

Moseley, M., and K. Day (1982) *Chan Chan: Andean Desert City*. Albuquerque: University of New Mexico Press.

Moseley, M., R. Feldman, C. Ortloff, and A. Narvaez (1983) "Principles of Agrarian Collapse in the Cordillera Negra, Peru." *Annals of Carnegie Museum* 52:229-327.

Ortloff, C., M. Moseley, and R. Feldman (1982) "Hydraulic Engineering Aspects of the Chicama-Moche Intervalley Canal." *American Antiquity* 48:572-595.

Ortloff, C., R. Feldman, and M. Moseley (1985) "Hydraulic Engineering and Historical Aspects of the PreColumbian Intravalley Canal Systems of the Moche Valley, Peru." *Journal of Field Archaeology* 12:77-98.

Ortloff, C. (1988) "Canal Builders of Ancient Peru." *Scientific American* 256 (No. 12):67-74.

Ortloff, C., and A. Kolata (1992) "Climate-Driven Collapse of the Agricultural Base of the Tiwanaku Empire and other Middle Horizon Societies and the Period 800-1100 AD in Peru and Bolivia." *Journal of Archaeological Science*, December Issue.

Sandweiss, D., H. Rollins. and T. Anderson (1981) "A Single Large Magnitude Uplift in the Holocene Record of the Peruvian North Coast." *Geological Society of America* 13:545-553.

Shimada, I., C. Schaff, L. Thompson, and E. Moseley-Thompson (1991) "Cultural Impacts of Severe Droughts in the Prehistoric Andes: Applications of a 1500 Year Ice Core Precipitation Record." *World Archaeology* 22:247-269.

Thompson, L., L. Hastenrath, and B. Arnao (1979) "Climate Ice Core Records from the Tropical Quelccaya Ice Cap." *Science* 203:1240-1243.

Thompson, L., E. Moseley-Thompson, J. Bolzan, and B. Koci (1985) "A 1500 Year Record of Tropical Precipitation Records in Ice Cores from the Quelccaya Ice Cap." *Science* 229:971-973.

Thompson, L., and E. Moseley-Thompson (1987) "Evidence of an Abrupt Climate Change During the Last 1500 Years Recorded in Ice Cores from the Tropical Quelccaya Ice Cap." Pp.

99-110 in W. Berger & L. Labeyrie (eds.) *Abrupt Climate Change Evidence and Implications*. New York: D. Reidel Publishing Co.

Whitten, D., and J. Brooks (1972) *A Dictionary of Geology*, pp. 383-384. Middlesex, ENG: Penguin Books.

Wyss, M. (1978) "Sea Level Change Before Large Earthquakes." *U.S. Geological Survey, Earthquake Information Bulletin* 10:165-168.

THE SOCIAL ORGANIZATION OF PREHISPANIC RAISED FIELD AGRICULTURE IN THE LAKE TITICACA BASIN

Clark L. Erickson

INTRODUCTION

When flying or walking over the vast plains (*pampas*) of the high Andean plateau (*altiplano*) of the northern Lake Titicaca basin, one is impressed by the immensity of landscape modification undertaken by pre-Columbian farmers.[1] Hundreds of thousands of raised field platforms that extend in every direction are a stunning testimony, even in their eroded state, to Andean institutions for the sociopolitical organization of labor and land (see Figure 1). The highly structured patterning of the landscape reflects an explicit concern with order, both of land and society. The scope of the sophisticated engineering of water management is truly monumental. It would be easy to interpret these earthworks as the enterprise of a highly centralized state. After extensive

Research in Economic Anthropology, Suppl. 7, pages 369-426.
ISBN: 1-55938-646-0

Figure 1. Pampa Landscape near Huatta, Peru, Showing Prehispanic and Rehabilitated Raised Fields (Lighter areas are field platforms; darker areas are canals between fields.)

archaeological survey and excavation of raised fields and associated settlements, and after working with contemporary Andean farmers on rehabilitating the ancient raised fields, I have become convinced otherwise. I argue here that various sources of evidence strongly indicate that raised field farming was organized, at least initially and probably throughout its history, at the local level. These precolumbian agricultural works are the accumulation of the activities of many generations of farmers, producing a totally human-made landscape.

Two major theoretical issues have been continually addressed in studies of the evolution of intensive agricultural systems, but only recently in terms of raised fields. The most conspicuous has been the relationship between social organization and agriculture, in particular, the amount of centralization necessary to carry out intensive agriculture. If raised fields require administration, coordination and planning, and massive amounts of labor, one would expect to find them inevitably associated with centralized bureaucratic government. The other issue involves the causes of agricultural evolution and agricultural intensification. If raised fields were labor intensive, they would not have been adopted unless the farmers were forced to do so by population pressure (according to the Boserup [1965] model) or by state demands for surplus production. These two issues are interrelated, although rarely discussed as such.

Traditionally, archaeologists have closely associated intensive agricultural systems with highly centralized political control. In the case of raised field agriculture, an analogy is often made to large irrigation systems, assumed to be associated with centralization and bureaucracy in the planning and operation of such systems, as argued by Karl Wittfogel (1957) many years ago. To the contrary, I have found that prehispanic raised field agriculture in the Lake Titicaca Basin developed early (ca. 1000 B.C.), apparently in the absence of population stress and state organization. I argue that, even during the various periods when state polities were present in the zone, raised fields were built and managed by local communities. Ethnographic analogy, experimental archaeology, ground survey, aerial photographic interpretation, and excavation provide evidence that raised field technology was well within the means of small-scale organizations.

A useful classification for the analysis of social organization associated with water management has been presented by Scarborough (1991:120), based on Chambers (1980). He contrasts the "top down view" with the "bottom up view." The top down view is in many ways similar to the elite-focused perspective taken by Wittfogel (1957) regarding irrigation systems. The bottom-up view takes the perspective of the farmer and the community-level institutions which make irrigation systems work. In discussing the case of the Lake Titicaca raised fields, Kolata (1991:100, 112-113) uses the terms, "bottom up perspective" (or "the *ayllu*/local level organization hypothesis") and "top down perspective."[2]

A similar perspective is used here to contrast archaeological interpretations of the social organization of prehispanic raised field agriculture in the Lake Titicaca Basin. I would also like to show that a synthesis of these opposing approaches is possible.

THE TOP-DOWN APPROACH
TO INTENSIVE AGRICULTURE

The Wittfogel Hypothesis and Its Critique

The relationship between sociopolitical organization and intensive agriculture has long been an important topic in anthropology, history, and geography. The most important treatment of the subject was Wittfogel's *Oriental Despotism: A Comparative Study of Total Power* (1957; also see Wittfogel 1955, 1972) and the subsequent critical response by scholars from many disciplines. Wittfogel (1955, 1957) argued that large-scale hydraulic agriculture required a high degree of administrative centralization in order to mobilize and coordinate labor for irrigation activities, to plan hydraulic engineering, and to provide capital. Over time, the need for centralized administration gave rise to the stagnant "despotic societies" or "agro-managerial despotism" (adapted from Marx's concept of the Asiatic Mode of Production) found historically in many parts of the world. Wittfogel saw inevitable deterministic links between water management and centralized social systems. In his comparative studies, he argued that centralized despotic societies arising out of a reliance on irrigation agriculture could be documented in the prehistoric record.

Wittfogel's hypothesis had wide ranging implications for comparative studies of the origins of the state and has had a lasting impact on archaeological and ethnological interpretation (e.g., Steward 1955). Ethnographers provided richly detailed studies of the social and technical elements of contemporary irrigation systems (Leach 1959, Fernea 1970, Gray 1963, Geertz 1980, Palerm 1955, 1973; Hunt & Hunt 1974, 1976; Hunt 1988; Mitchell 1973, 1976, 1977, 1991; Guillet 1987, 1992; Gelles 1986, 1990, n.d.a-b; Lewis 1991; Kelly 1983, Spooner 1974, Netting 1974) and archaeologists provided cases with time depth to test the hypothesis (Woodbury 1961, Earle 1978; Hunt & Hunt 1974, 1976; Price 1971, Steward 1955, Sanders & Price 1968, Doolittle 1990, Adams 1966, Butzer 1977, Millon 1962, Wheatley 1971, Downing & Gibson 1974b, Park 1992, Sanders et al. 1979, and others). These studies are generally critical of Wittfogel's deterministic, unilineal model of causality and the necessary relationship between despotic societies and irrigation. Instead, they argue that communities have traditional informal means of dispute resolution and cooperation that permit large-scale irrigation outside of a state apparatus. This position does not deny that the state can be directly involved in intensive agriculture, but rather claims that there have been some instances in which the state was clearly not involved.

Neo-Wittfogelian Thinking Applied to Prehispanic Raised Fields

Although most scholars focusing on agricultural systems have rejected the causal relationship between hydraulic agriculture and the rise of the state, certain archaeologists and geographers still support the assumption that intensive agriculture, such as raised fields (Kolata 1983, 1986:759, 1987, 1991; Wilkerson 1983:64; Matheny 1978:206-210; Darch 1983:2; Turner 1983:15; Armillas 1971:660; Doolittle 1990:115-135, 149, 154; Moore 1988; Stanish n.d.; Boehm de Lameiras 1988; Palerm 1955:37-39, 1973; Matheny & Garr 1983; Parsons 1991; Brumfiel 1991; Sanders et al. 1979:280-281), terraces (Sanders et al. 1979, Conrad & Demarest 1984), and large irrigation systems (Kus 1980, Matheny 1978:209, Matheny & Garr 1983, Sanders & Price 1968, Ortloff et al. 1982) are, by necessity, associated with centralized forms of sociopolitical organization, if not states. This perspective could be considered typical of the "top-down approach" to prehispanic agriculture.

Many scholars cited above would deny that they are following Wittfogel's claims, agreeing, at least theoretically, that major agricultural landscapes could have been created by non-state organizations. However, except for Kolata (1986, 1991), their use of terms such as "centralization," "centralized direction," "centralized administration," and "centrally organized" in describing raised field agriculture is vague and imprecise (for examples, see Wilkerson 1983:64, Boehm de Lameiras 1988:92; Parsons 1991:22, 34; Brumfiel 1991:44, Moore 1988:274, Armillas 1971:660, Darch 1983:2, Matheny & Garr 1983:99). As a result, the critical question of causality and necessity is avoided, but customary assumptions about intensive agriculture can still be embraced comfortably. In the case of raised field agriculture, many of these scholars accept the assumptions that (1) raised fields are a labor intensive form of agriculture, (2) raised field planning, construction, and maintenance require a certain degree of centralized bureaucratic management, and (3) as a result, farmers would not (and could not) adopt the raised field agricultural system unless forced to and directed by authoritative centralized polities (e.g., states).

Much of the classical debate involving Wittfogel's hydraulic hypothesis revolves around the problem of terminology. What do we mean by "centralization"? Can non-states be "centralized"? Can irrigation and social organization be quantified and compared cross-culturally? Several scholars have attempted to grapple with these issues (Millon 1962, Leach 1959, Kelly 1983, Hunt & Hunt 1974, Hunt 1988, Geertz 1980, Gelles 1990), but it is beyond the scope of this paper to fully address these questions. I recognize that the various degrees of centralization fall along a continuum, but for the purposes of this paper, I use Gelles's (1990:20) definition of "centralization":

> Centralization...generally refers to complex and stratified political systems which are characterized by an administrative machinery, judicial institutions, and specialists. The term serves to differentiate these from evolutionary or structurally (diachronically or synchronically) more 'simple' ones. Centralized systems...are seen as 'growing out of' other simpler systems which are kinship based, examples of which are often found in the nearby vicinity. Evolutionists point to the state and centralization as responses to the need for increasing and higher levels of integration and organization, or more cynically, as an instrument of domination of the ruling class.

Centralization, according to Flannery (1972:417), "represents a 'linearization' of the linkage between the special-purpose arm of a higher-order system (the federal government) and an important variable (water) in a lower-order system (the local village ecosystem); response is now direct, rather than buffered by the village government." Throughout this essay, I refer to centralized political system, centralized bureaucracy, centralized social organization, and the centralized state. These terms are used interchangeably with the concept of the state (see Flannery 1972:403-404).

Intensive agriculture is commonly associated with dense and urban populations, often within state societies (Boserup 1965, Sanders et al. 1979, Denevan & Turner 1985, Parsons 1991, and others). Economic models of preindustrial societies used by archaeologists generally stress the need for nonagricultural urban populations, especially an elite group, to develop efficient means to extract surplus agricultural production from the rural hinterlands (Parsons 1991). Common means of extracting such surpluses are tribute payments, markets, exchange, trade and, more rarely, the direct control of agricultural production.

The common association between intensive agriculture and centralized bureaucracy does not imply a relationship of causality or necessity. Many Mayanists have discussed the intensive nature of raised field farming and its apparently inherent relationship to centralized authority (Pohl 1990a:2, 12 & her concluding chapter; Scarborough 1991, Matheny 1978:206-210, Matheny & Garr 1983:99; several chapters in Harrison & Turner 1978). Present-day Maya farmers are viewed as practicing "devolved" or "extensive" agriculture in the form of slash-and-burn, or swidden, whereas their distant ancestors practiced "evolutionarily advanced" forms of agriculture such as terracing, raised fields, and irrigation (e.g., Harrison & Turner 1978).[3] Population pressure and/or complex sociopolitical organization is generally believed to have been responsible for the development of these intensive systems. Early radiocarbon dates on raised field agriculture in the Americas, such as those presented by Puleston (1977b) for Albion Island in Belize, are often dismissed as improbable because of the lack of population pressure and state organization at those dates (e.g., Pohl 1990b; Turner & Harrison 1978:358-359, 1983:253, 255, 270; and others).[4] The Maya may have directly controlled the agricultural production of raised fields, as many scholars have argued, but this does *not* mean that earlier raised fields in a non-state context could not have also existed.

Through our raised field agricultural experiments, stratigraphic excavations, radiocarbon and thermoluminescence dating, survey, ethnobotany, soil studies, and aerial photographic interpretation, I likewise hope to demonstrate that small groups of prehispanic farmers constructed and maintained raised fields in the Lake Titicaca Basin. I argue that these independent, experimentally-derived data provide a better "fit" with the ethnographic, historical, and experimental case studies of the sociopolitical organization of raised field agriculture than do the archaeological scenarios mentioned above (excluding Puleston's work [1977a, 1977b]). This position does not deny the possibility that raised fields were on occasion constructed and managed directly by the state, but rather stresses that small-scale farming communities are capable of producing the productive landscapes we see in the archaeological record.

The scale of the irrigation system has always been a key problem in the Wittfogel thesis.[5] Prehistoric, ethnohistoric, and ethnographic cases of irrigation societies demonstrate the diversity of alternatives of social organizational from simple to complex and the ranges of scale from small to large regional systems (see Spooner 1974, Hunt & Hunt 1974, Hunt 1988, Price 1971, Scarborough 1991). Robert Hunt's (1988) detailed comparative study of irrigation agriculture and social organization concluded that many large irrigation systems (ranging from 700 to 458,000 ha) operate without any centralized authority. The implications of this scale problem have been generally neglected by archaeologists. Only a small minority of the archaeologists and geographers who have done research on raised fields have urged caution with regard to the assumption that raised field agriculture must be associated with large-scale, centralized organization (see Bronson 1978, Harris 1978:310-318, Siemans 1983:50; also see Turner & Harrison 1978:361-368, Denevan 1970:653, and Denevan 1982:186).

Local communities have developed complex means for managing large regional irrigation systems that do not always rely on the development of hierarchical and centralizing institutions (for the Andean region, see Mitchell 1973, 1976, 1977; Guillet 1987, 1992; Treacy 1989a-b; Gelles 1986, 1990; n.d.a-c; Seligmann & Bunker 1986; and Sherbondy 1982, 1987, 1992; for Mesoamerica, see Hunt 1988, Hunt & Hunt 1974, Doolittle 1984, 1990). The local institutions developed for insuring the smooth functioning of hydraulic agriculture could be considered a form of "heterarchy," or complex sociopolitical institutions which rely on nonhierarchical, horizontal, cross-cutting infrastructure (Crumley 1987). This is a powerful, alternative way of viewing the concept of social complexity, while many traditional classifications deny complexity to societies or groups that are not centralized and/or hierarchical. These alternative, heterarchical principles can been seen in Andean communities where ritual-symbolic traditions of water, earth and mountain worship, reciprocal labor exchange, rotating offices of water mayors, the *ayllu*, and dual organization provide the basis for water management (e.g., Gelles 1986, 1990; n.d.a-c; Zuidema 1986; Sherbondy 1982, 1987, 1992; Guillet 1992; and others; for Bali, see Lansing 1987, 1991, and Geertz 1980). Present-day raised field management in highland New Guinea (discussed below) also provides a good example of the noncentralized community form of organization.

Top-down bureaucratic meddling in local community-based farming systems may actually be a detrimental and inefficient strategy (Treacy 1989a, Montmollin 1987, Netting 1990, Leaf 1992, Lansing 1991, Guillet 1992; Gelles 1990, n.d.a-b; Lees 1986). As Leaf (1992:116) notes, "Social scientists with practical involvements in irrigation management uniformly reject the idea that authoritarian control is natural or inevitable—or even workable." The nearly complete failure of the "Green Revolution" in the Andean region during the 1960s/70s is a prime example of the problems of a highly technical, top-down approach. In the case of raised field rehabilitation in the Lake Titicaca Basin, top-down approaches have been less successful than more grassroots approaches (Erickson & Brinkmeier n.d., Erickson & Candler 1989).

One could question whether the prehispanic elite of the Americas would be interested in local-level decisions regarding mundane agricultural production. Montmollin (1987) has provided an interesting critique of the "managerialist thesis" in archaeological interpretation. He considers these perspectives to be based in an "etic," rational, maximizing, adaptationist interpretation (one which equates better managed with better adapted for long-term survival). In his "emic" approach to management by the prehispanic Mesoamerican elites, Montmollin notes that (1) the day-to-day production is managed at lower social levels, (2) the Mesoamerican elite were not professional bureaucrats, and (3) the concern for political resources, not economic rulership, was most prominent. According to Montmollin (1987:56), rulers were more interested in "being custodians of relations between polity and cosmos, cosmic balance" and "interactions between and within polities, heirs, successionship, usurpation, rotation, dynastic politics." One could argue that this emic approach could be extrapolated to the prehistoric elite of most of nuclear America. This would not be to claim that elites were never concerned about tribute flow, intensification of agriculture, and the co-opting of labor which sustained their position and the state, but rather that they were often disassociated from the tedious and routine management of local production. At the very least, Montmollin's argument requires a re-examination of the nature of centralized control.

Several studies support a model of local, not state, control of Andean agriculture. A major goal of Inka elite expansionist policy was to extend irrigation and terracing for the generation of state surplus (Conrad & Demarest 1984:129-130). Despite the overt interest of the Inka elite in irrigated terracing, local systems appear to have been managed by local community groups. Even within the Inka capital of Cuzco, terraces were constructed and managed by local *ayllus*, not the state (Zuidema 1986, Sherbondy 1982, 1987, 1992). Nor does the ethnographic record for terrace water management in the South Central Andes support a model of direct control by the Inka state (Treacy 1989b, Guillet 1987, 1992). On the North Coast, the large, intervalley La Cumbre canal constructed during the Late Intermediate Period has been attributed to the Chimu state (Kus 1980, Ortloff et al. 1982). However, Netherly (1984) has demonstrated that the regional irrigation networks of the north coast of Peru were locally managed systems and that the intervalley canal was probably a rare case of state intervention in local agriculture. The state's role in irrigation was probably limited to providing the capital and *mit'a* labor for rebuilding canal networks after natural disasters such as El Niño flooding (Moseley et al. 1981, Netherly 1984).

Gelles (1990, n.d.a-b; also see Treacy 1989a-b, Guillet 1992) has discussed the dialectic between state and local organization of irrigation water in the community of Cabanaconde in the Colca Valley of Peru. The local system is based on the Andean dual organization model—the division of the community into "upper" and "lower" halves—and sacred water, mountain, and earth worship. It combines complex ritual and social mechanisms that have traditionally controlled the hydraulic resources. The local model, of which dual organization is a fundamental component, provides a form of cultural resistance to the secularization of water management and other modern state interferences and is intimately tied to ethnic identity. In contrast, the recently introduced Peruvian state system uses appointed managers as "water controllers" and stresses civic duty and the "rational," sequential distribution of water. The intrusion of the state system into the traditional local system has had a disorganizing effect on the distribution of water and tends to favor local elites, resulting in rising tensions and local resistance.[6] These studies show that the relationship between state and local systems can be complex, and the issue of control cannot be assumed to have a simple answer. For example, it cannot be assumed that Tiwanaku elites managed the raised fields in the southern Lake Titicaca Basin.

THE BOTTOM-UP APPROACH
TO INTENSIVE AGRICULTURE

In response to the influential theory proposed by Wittfogel (1957) and Steward (1955) regarding the relationship between bureaucratic central organization (in particular, the despotic state) and intensive agriculture, anthropologists produced a wide range of ethnographic case studies of irrigation societies of different scales (e.g., Fernea 1970, Millon 1962, Woodbury 1961, Leach 1959, Mitchell 1976, Hunt & Hunt 1976, Gray 1963, Price 1971, Downing & Gibson 1974b, and others). The general consensus of these studies is that some level of coordination is necessary for the proper functioning of irrigation societies, but that the locally-based sociopolitical organization available to farmers in "traditional" peasant societies is sufficient for planning, construction, maintenance, distribution of water resource, and resolution of conflicts over water and land.

Stephen Lansing's *Priests and Programmers: Technologies of Power in the Engineered Landscape of Bali* (1991) provides an excellent example of how sophisticated farming systems involving a network of tens of thousands of hectares of irrigated terraced rice padi fields can be constructed, managed, and maintained independently of state control or interference, although they operate within the bounds of a modern state society. In Bali, kin-based cooperative groups of farmers are bound with other groups over wide areas through a hierarchical system of "water temples," where necessary complex scheduling, decision making, and cooperation is accomplished in a ritual context. Lansing demonstrates that tightly ordered, technologically sophisticated "engineered agricultural landscapes" of regional proportions can be efficiently managed by local groups and local ceremonial centers. Although the irrigation system exists within the boundaries of a modern state, the farming activities are under local control. In the words of Valeri (1991:136), "this *centered* (rather than *centralized*) system of coordination is independent of the state and, in fact, somewhat in conflict with it."

Ethnographic and contemporary raised field practices in New Guinea and Irian Jaya of Indonesia provide another possible analogy for examining the social organization of agriculture (see Heider 1970 for the Dani, Pospisil 1963 for the Kapauku, Serpenti 1965 for the Kiman, and Golson 1977 and Gorecki 1982 for the Kuk). Very dense populations are supported by a combination of raised field and swidden agriculture. Raised field systems, including some very large regional complexes, exhibit an impressive organization of raised field platforms and canals, field boundaries, fence lines, and drainage canals. These agricultural earthworks appear similar to those of the Lake Titicaca basin in terms of structural complexity and integration. Despite the high degree of landscape order, many of the basins where raised fields are used today have been farmed only for a short time (a relatively recent reintroduction of raised fields). Although a wide range of sociopolitical organization is found within these societies, the raised field farming is a noncentralized, nonhierarchical, and relatively "egalitarian" kin-based activity.

Ethnographic analogy and cross-cultural comparison must be used cautiously. New Guinea raised field agriculture is practiced in a different environmental and cultural context from that of the Lake Titicaca Basin and should not be taken as a model of the Andean case. However, at a very general level, the New Guinea analogy demonstrates that sophisticated raised field farming sustaining large populations can be organized within family and localized sociopolitical units. The raised fields of New Guinea do not provide any evidence that Andean fields were associated with one type of sociopolitical organization or another. They do, however, prove that it is possible to practice raised field agriculture within a noncentralized organization, and this possibility must not be automatically discounted for the Andean case.

RAISED FIELD AGRICULTURE

Raised field agriculture is a remarkably efficient, sustainable, and productive technology. Raised fields are large, elevated platforms constructed to improve agricultural production by removal of soil from adjacent canals. Morphology of fields varies greatly, but the platforms in the Lake Titicaca basin (see Figure 2) tend to be rectangular, 0.2-1.0m tall, 5-10m wide and up to 50m long. Remains of prehispanic raised fields are found throughout the Americas in a wide range of environment and temporal contexts (Parsons & Denevan 1967; Denevan 1970, 1982; Siemans 1989; and others). There is a large literature on prehistoric, ethnographic, and contemporary forms of raised field agriculture in various parts of the Old World (Farrington 1985, Denevan & Turner 1974). The most common context of raised field farming is permanent or seasonal wetlands, in particular, areas near rivers, lakes, poorly drained soils, or permanent swamps and marshes. The widespread distribution of the technology in time and space in both the Old and New Worlds suggests that it was adopted independently in most cases by farmers seeking to exploit wetland ecosystems. A number of archaeological, agronomic, and ethnographic studies have defined the function of raised field farming as improving soil conditions through increasing topsoil depth, providing aeration, mixing and burying organic matter by turning over soils, locally draining waterlogged soils, and ameliorating the effects of adverse agro-climates such as frosts, droughts, and flooding. Canals or ditches adjacent to the field platforms conserve water, act as a heat sink for storage of solar energy, collect and produce organic sediments, and provide a habitat for economically important species of plants and animals and possible aquaculture. Periodic "mucking," or removal of organic sediments collected and/or produced in the canals for placement on the cropping platforms, provides soil renewal and sustainable high production (Denevan & Turner 1974; Denevan 1970, 1982; Erickson 1985, 1988a-b, 1992a; Garaycochea 1986a-b, 1987; Kolata 1991; Kolata & Ortloff 1989; and others).

Even as eroded archaeological remains, a raised field system spread out over the Andean landscape is an impressive sight. The orderliness of the patterning,

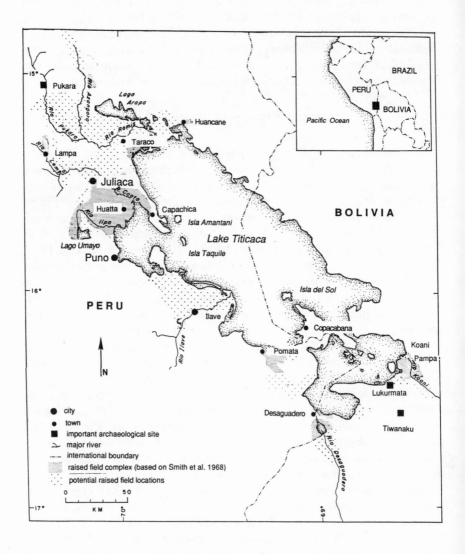

Figure 2.   Location Map of Prehispanic Raised
Field Systems, Major Archaeological Sites, and
Modern Population Centers in the Lake Titicaca Basin

usually a highly structured, rectilinear grid of blocks or bundles of raised fields, is stunning. This vast anthropogenic landscape seems to have been associated with centralized bureaucratic states simply because of its massive scale and structural integration. When viewed with the commonly unspoken, unanalyzed Wittfogelian assumptions, it seems that these structured and orderly remains could not have been constructed by the local social organization of Andean farmers.[7] I argue here that this reasoning is based on unsound assumptions. These landscapes represent the results of thousands of years of evolving local and regional farming systems and the gradual accumulation of landscape capital or landscape infrastructure by both communities and states.

THE IRRIGATION MODEL AND RAISED FIELD AGRICULTURE

Many researchers have supposed that raised fields are similar or identical to large-scale irrigation systems and have the same or similar requirements (Scarborough 1991, Matheny & Garr 1983, various chapters of Harrison & Turner 1978; Kolata 1986, 1991; Ortloff & Kolata 1989). This "irrigation model" of raised field agriculture has led to confusion about the functions and organization of the system. A strong hydraulic element has been documented for raised field farming (Lennon 1982, 1983; Erickson 1988a, Kolata 1991, Scarborough 1991, Ortloff & Kolata 1989, Denevan & Turner 1974, and others), but the specific needs and goals of raised field farmers are very different from those of farmers relying on irrigation.

Raised field agriculture can be considered a form of hydraulic agriculture. In both irrigation and raised field agriculture, water resources are managed through complex engineering constructions enabling the manipulation and conservation of water. Despite this similarity, raised fields differ from irrigation systems in several important ways. Irrigation systems are commonly found in arid areas, while raised field systems are most common in areas of seasonally high rainfall, waterlogging of soils and standing water, and/or high humidity (e.g., the tropical savannas of Ecuador, Colombia, Venezuela, and Bolivia, the highland basin of Lake Titicaca; and the highland regions of the Valley of Mexico). While water scarcity is a limiting factor in irrigation systems, an *excess* of water is commonly the problem in areas where raised fields are found.[8] The removal of water from the raised planting surfaces never poses the kinds of problems that the distribution of water, as a scarce resource, presents in irrigation systems. Accordingly, scheduling and equitable distribution of water resources is of minimal importance in raised field agriculture. Irrigation systems require that water be transported and distributed over wide areas of cropland, potentially crossing political, social, and ethnic boundaries in the longer canal systems. Raised fields, on the other hand, do not require the movement of large amounts of water across territorial boundaries.[9]

Although we lack detailed comparative data, raised fields appear to be less
labor intensive than irrigation systems in terms of construction and general
maintenance (at least in comparisons with Andean terrace irrigation farming;
see Treacy 1989a-b, Erickson & Candler 1989, Erickson 1988a). For example,
sedimentation of canals is a factor in both systems but, in contrast to irrigation,
raised field functioning depends on the capture, removal, and recycling of
sediments, which is considered to be a positive feature, not a detrimental
drawback. It was probably advantageous to fill the canals with water as soon
as possible at the beginning of the rainy season and to conserve the water in
them as long as possible into the dry season, in order to extend the cropping
period. The transport of water to achieve this goal is part of the hydraulic
function of raised fields, but it bears little resemblance to the coordination of
regional irrigation systems. Scarborough (1991:113) has referred to the hydraulic
management of raised fields as "still water canalization," whereby water is not
transported long distances from source to destination in areas with little
topographic relief. Hydraulic features also might have included eliminating
encroachment of salt water into field canals (Ortloff & Kolata 1989, Erickson
1988a, Palerm 1955), although this has not been adequately demonstrated.

Because of these differences, raised fields do not require the same amount
of coordination and cooperation as irrigation systems. I will also argue that
the small, modular blocks of raised field systems can function successfully
without the coordination of regional systems, in contrast to most medium and
large-scale irrigation systems. In other words, one does not have to rely on
close coordination with one's neighbors in order to farm raised fields. This
point has been clearly demonstrated in our experimental raised fields in Peru,
where only small, isolated parts of the total system have been reconstructed,
and in the ethnographic record of raised field farming in non-Western societies.

A STATE MODEL OF RAISED FIELD
ORGANIZATION IN THE ANDES

Kolata (1983, 1986, 1987, 1989, 1991) has argued that the raised fields of Koani
Pampa, the Tiwanaku Valley, and Desaguadero floodplain of Bolivia were
"Tiwanaku estates" of the elite. He (1991:120) contends that "Tiwanaku
established proprietary agricultural estates in which ownership and usufruct
rights were vested directly in state institutions, or perhaps more precisely in
the hands of the elite, dominant classes." Kolata (1991:100) believes that "the
organization of agricultural production in this core entailed structured,
hierarchical interaction between urban and rural settlements, characterized by
a substantial degree of political centralization and the mobilization of labor
by social principles that reached beyond simple kinship relations." Kolata goes
beyond most archaeologists in arguing for the need for centralization and

bureaucracy to do raised field agriculture, and he believes that the state was *directly* involved in the production system. Kolata (1991:119) states that "archaeological instances of capital investments in expanding reclamation of potentially arable land and in altering and controlling the hydraulic regime of the raised field systems *directly implies* the action of a regional political authority" (my emphasis). He (1991:120) believes that "periodic mobilization and coordination of a substantial non-resident labor force demanded a political order with powerful regional authority to alienate land and co-opt labor, and at least a rudimentary bureaucratic system to track the extraction of labor service from subject communities and the subsequent flow of produce from state-operated fields." Although he specifically states that this system of "centralized state action" is not "despotic" in the Wittfogelian sense, Kolata speaks of "mass alienation of land and labor by elite" with "ruthless efficiency" (ibid.: 121), an apparent contradiction. A detailed argument has been presented for this hypothesis (see Kolata 1986, 1991), but the basic, underlying theme is that raised fields and the associated agricultural infrastructure are too complex for common farmers to plan, construct, and manage and, thus, had to be "designed by the agroengineers of Tiwanaku" (1991:101).[10]

The argument provided by Kolata (1986:760, 1991:115) to support this thesis is (1) the apparent hierarchical structure of settlements associated with raised field in Koani Pampa, Bolivia, with evidence of elite administrators' and common farmers' residences, (2) the need for a highly organized labor force directed by a technically sophisticated administration to construct and maintain fields and the agricultural hydraulic infrastructure, and (3) the relatively close correlation between the chronology of raised field use/abandonment and the origin/collapse of the Tiwanaku state.

Settlements range from small house mounds of farmers and field guardians to larger, "monumental" platform mounds attributed to elite state administrators. According to Kolata, residential settlements within the raised field area are not numerous enough to account for the labor necessary for construction and maintenance; thus, corvée labor had to be brought in by the Tiwanaku state from the outside. Structures such as "river-by-pass systems" or "river shunts" with artificial earthen levees, aqueducts associated with irrigation and drainage, river canalization and diversion, causeways, and dikes are examples of earthmoving projects believed to have been undertaken by Tiwanaku (Kolata 1991:101, 104; Ortloff & Kolata 1989).[11] Kolata and colleagues have argued that these engineering elements are part of a complex agricultural infrastructure constructed by Tiwanaku "agroengineers" (Kolata 1991:101), and that this infrastructure was beyond the capabilities of locally autonomous village level organization (1991:115).[12] The dating of these infrastructural features has been difficult (Kolata 1986, 1991; Ortloff & Kolata 1989), although indirect association with urban settlements suggests to them a Tiwanaku IV and Tiwanaku V construction and use (A.D. 400-1100) (see Figure 3).

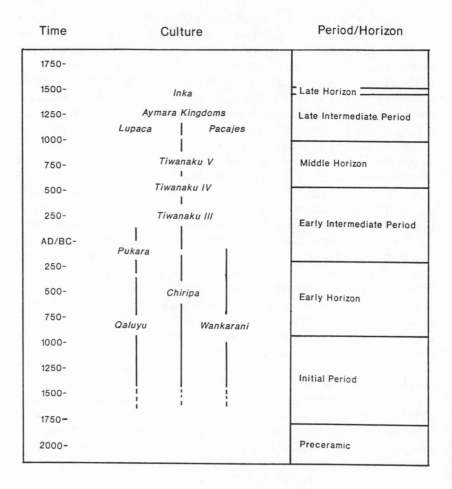

Figure 3. Chronology of the Lake Titicaca Region

Improved dikes and artificial levees on rivers to prevent flooding of the pampa lands are still constructed in the northern Lake Titicaca Basin. For instance, community projects have been undertaken for many years to prevent flooding of the Río Coata (see Figure 4) and Río Illpa. Here, huge embankments up to 2.5m tall and 3m wide at the base are constructed of sod cut from the pampa. Some of these massive dikes run for kilometers on both sides of the rivers. Similar in terms of labor investment are the programs to construct raised roads within the pampa, using the same methods as those now used to reconstruct raised fields. These projects are undertaken by small local groups, under their own incentive and without external coordination.

Figure 4. Modern Canalization and Artificial Levees Constructed of Sod Blocks by the Community of Coata, along the Río Coata

Kolata (1991:120) sees a pattern of "state action at a distance" in the settlement distribution, in contrast to what he hypothesizes is the model of local control of raised fields (e.g., key sites at critical infrastructural points in the water control system). As I argue below, local control at the household or *ayllu* level would produce a dispersed pattern of settlement within field systems (identical to what is found in Koani Pampa), and there would be no need for hierarchical "control points" of the raised field water management system.

Some raised fields may have been associated and contemporaneous with the Tiwanaku state, but the total distribution of these fields is unknown. Kolata (1991:124, n. 1) has calculated that Tiwanaku engineers constructed 150 km^2, or 15,000 ha, of raised fields, based on study of aerial photographs, ground survey, and conjecture. Smith et al.'s (1968) figures are conservative (see Erickson 1988a), but those calculated by Kolata and colleagues for Tiwanaku should be considered with caution. For instance, there are 30 km^2 of preserved fields in the Middle and Lower Tiwanaku Valley, and another 60-65 km^2 of fields are projected to account for those that may have been destroyed through erosion (Kolata 1991:124, Albarracín & Mathews 1990:117). Many of these features are more similar to large lazy beds (*wachos*, or narrow sod platforms for potatoes) than to true raised fields (Mathews n.d.a).[13] In addition, neither the Koani Pampa nor the Desaguadero Valley has been adequately surveyed. These estimates for Tiwanaku raised field distribution remain uncertain until detailed photographic interpretation, excavation, and ground survey are completed.

The areal extent of the fields is not the only problem. The affiliation of the Tiwanaku Valley raised fields to Tiwanaku IV and Tiwanaku V periods is based on the dating of raised fields in Koani Pampa (Kolata 1983, 1986, 1989, 1991; Kolata & Graffam 1989) primarily using field associations with occupation sites (Albarracín & Mathews 1990:117). Recent excavations of raised fields in the Middle Tiwanaku Valley by Mathews (n.d.b) have demonstrated that some fields were constructed and used very late in the Tiwanaku sequence and well into the post-Tiwanaku period. According to the spatial and temporal distribution of rural occupation sites as presented in site survey maps (Mathews n.d.b:Maps 2-7), the raised fields could just as easily be attributed through site association dating to the whole spectrum of prehispanic cultures occupying the immediate area. For instance, fields near the urban center of Tiwanaku could be affiliated with any of the pre-Tiwanaku cultures, the mature Tiwanaku Phases (A.D. 375 1000/1100)[14] or with the post-Tiwanaku presence on the site and vicinity. The only direct contexts for dating raised fields to Tiwanaku were three excavations in fields near Luqurmata within a very small (6.5 ha) block of raised fields where diagnostic sherds were recovered in field fill dating to Tiwanaku IV and Tiwanaku V (A.D. 400-1000/1100) (Kolata & Graffam 1989, Graffam 1990:122-135, 243). Graffam's (1990:133-135) ceramic analysis indicates that the fields were constructed and used between A.D. 400 and A.D.

1100. A corrected radiocarbon date of 1085 ± 90 BP (A.D. 865, ETH 3178) from a hearth stratigraphically above the fields provides a *terminus ante quem* for use (Graffam 1990:135). A radiocarbon date of A.D. 950 ± 100 is given for a "raised field complex," although no archaeological context is described (Ortloff & Kolata 1989:517). Graffam (1990:153) has dated an aqueduct structure associated with a small raised field block near the type site of Chiripa to Tiwanaku III-V through ceramics. An aqueduct at Lukurmata was dated to Tiwanaku IV-V by diagnostic sherds (Ortloff & Kolata 1989). The river channelization structures in Koani Pampa and the river by-pass shunts of the Tiwanaku Valley have not been adequately dated. There is evidence that the canalization may be relatively modern and that it relates to pastoral use of the pampa (Graffam 1990:43, 172). The most serious problem is Kolata's extrapolation of the Tiwanaku IV-V dates from only three excavation trenches in raised fields and a single excavation in an aqueduct structure at a single site (Lukurmata) to an area of 150 km^2 of raised fields in the assumed "Tiwanaku heartland."

Critical to Kolata's state administration argument is that the field system was abandoned with the collapse of the Tiwanaku bureaucracy (e.g., Kolata 1983:262, 1986:753, 1987:41). Graffam (1989, 1990, 1992) presents archaeological evidence, based on survey and excavation of both occupation sites and fields, that raised field construction and use continued in the Koani Pampa long after the collapse of the Tiwanaku state. He estimates that the majority (68%) of the fields visible on the surface in Koani Pampa were constructed and used in the Late Intermediate Period (A.D. 1000-1476). Mathews' (n.d.b) excavations of raised fields near Tiwanaku also demonstrate post-Tiwanaku construction and use. There is also a possibility that raised fields predate the Tiwanaku state (before A.D. 375). Graffam recovered limited evidence that Chiripa farmers (800-400 B.C.) may have been involved in raised field construction (Graffam 1990:242; also see Kolata 1986, 1991). Stanish (n.d.) has found that fields in Moyopampa, near Juli, were constructed from the early part of the Early Intermediate Period (200 B.C.-A.D. 600) through the Late Intermediate Period. This evidence highlights the problems of dating fields and the extrapolation of this dating over such large areas.

When Koani Pampa is compared to other raised field contexts in the Lake Titicaca Basin, an interesting observation can be made, namely, that the patterning of fields in Koani Pampa appears relatively less structured than that of Huatta pampa or other raised field areas presented in Smith et al. (1968). The predominant form of field, "the combed field" type (Smith et al. 1968, Kolata 1986, Graffam 1990) is analogous to natural levee geomorphological features of abandoned and active rivers within the pampa.[15] These are in striking contrast to the more orderly, structured form of fields in most of the large blocks in the northern Lake Titicaca Basin and the smaller blocks along the western edge of the lake (Smith et al. 1968; Erickson 1985, 1988a; Lennon

1982, 1983). It could be argued, based on patterning, that the raised fields in Koani Pampa are "more primitive," or less structured, having started out as early farming on natural river levees to prevent flooding. Later farmers may have copied the natural form artificially with the construction of raised fields as more land was needed. The combed fields may represent an old pattern, which established the model for rebuilding and reconstruction throughout the farming history of Koani Pampa.

Much of Kolata's original formulation of the idea of Tiwanaku state control of the raised fields relies on the ability to identify "elite" and "commoner" settlements in the archaeological record (Kolata 1986). According to his model, the elite administrative sites should be larger, more centrally located, and have a material culture distinct from that of the smaller, rural farmsteads within Koani Pampa. Kolata (1983:260-261) argues that the elite sites within the raised field blocks are monumental platforms of "enormous proportions" with "large scale corporate construction" (his hierarchical level 3) built of fill by the Tiwanaku state. Ceramic inventories suggest a higher number of "elite" wares on the larger sites than on the small farming sites, but this argument is not very convincing after considering that sites of Kolata's "administrative" category are found by the hundreds in the Huatta plain in Peru. Today, many of these mounds are densely occupied by small hamlets of non-elite farmers and fishermen. In regard to the "elite" ceramics, so little useful work has been done on Tiwanaku ceramics that it is difficult to argue for diagnostics of "elite" versus "commoner" pottery. Fancy Tiwanaku keros, a hallmark of the Tiwanaku urban center and large satellite sites, are also regularly found in small farming settlements in the southern Lake Titicaca Basin. This same problem of identifying state presence within zones of raised fields applies to interpretations made for *chinampa* agriculture under the Aztecs (Parsons 1991, Sanders et al. 1979, Brumfiel 1991, and others).

EVIDENCE FOR A LOCAL MODEL OF RAISED FIELD ORGANIZATION

Do traditional agricultural systems of a large regional scale require state "agro-engineers" and elite managers in order to be planned, constructed, used, and maintained? The immense literature of cross-cultural case studies of water management mentioned above presents a strong case that the answer is "not necessarily." Very few traditional irrigation systems are under state control, even those that exist within modern state boundaries. The same can be said for other forms of intensive agriculture, such as terracing. Then, what about the massive and extensive raised field system constructed before the arrival of the Spanish in the Lake Titicaca Basin of Peru and Bolivia? Were the pre-Tiwanaku and Tiwanaku fields organized and run by the state?

In this section, data on field chronology, field patterning, settlements and settlement survey, experimental archaeology, and abandonment are presented from fieldwork studies undertaken by the Raised Field Agricultural Project between 1981 and 1986 (Erickson 1985, 1987, 1988a-b, 1992a). These data provide indices for addressing issues regarding the social organization of raised field agriculture in the northern Lake Titicaca Basin. In addition, they may have wide-reaching implications for raised fields in other areas of the Andean highlands and elsewhere.

The Dating of Raised Field Agriculture

Raised fields appear to have been established at a relatively early date and have a long history in the northern Lake Titicaca Basin. The direct dating of ceramics recovered from excavations of 11 raised field locations by thermoluninescence (TL) has provided data on the chronology and evolution of raised field agriculture. The TL-based chronology is internally consistent with raised field stratigraphy. Diagnostic ceramics from several contexts within raised fields also provide support. Radiocarbon dates and ceramic dates from excavations in occupation mounds within the raised field blocks provide indirect evidence to support this chronology. Two phases of construction and use have been documented. Phase I is characterized by small wavelength fields,[16] dating to ca. 1000 B.C.-A.D. 300, stratigraphically buried under later large Phase II fields that probably date to the Late Intermediate period (A.D. 1000-1476). Blocks of fields in the northern basin were partially abandoned or "deintensified" during the Tiwanaku Middle Horizon and the Inka Late Horizon (Erickson 1987, 1988a).

It is clear that widespread raised field construction began long before the appearance of the state and continued during the periods of state collapse in the Lake Titicaca Basin. I have argued (Erickson 1987, 1988a) that this farming system evolved out of an early lacustrine and riverine wetland economy based on agriculture, hunting, fishing, and gathering. Because of the high yields to labor ratio and the simple organizational requirements, raised field agriculture would have been an efficient alternative to other agricultural technologies (discussed below). Sometime during the Initial Period (1800-900 B.C.), raised fields were firmly established in the northern lake plains around Huatta and possibly in the southern basin, as well.[17] The system gradually expanded to include over 82,000 ha of fields and became more sophisticated through time.

Field Patterning

The argument is commonly made that, if raised fields (or other forms of intensive agriculture) show patterning, planning, and formal structure, the construction must have been centrally planned and organized. All prehispanic and modern raised fields found in the Americas and elsewhere demonstrate formal structure, as do most agricultural systems. Since scholars disagree on their subjective evaluations of how to classify the continuous variation between unstructured and structured landscapes, this issue may never be resolved.

Raised fields in the Huatta pampa and elsewhere demonstrate clear structural patterning. This patterning has two very distinct levels. The most basic structure is one of individual bundles or blocks of 5-7 parallel fields (Lennon 1982, 1983; Smith et al. 1968) (see Figures 5 and 6) bounded by canals or encircling embankments (see Figures 7 and 8). In addition, these individual bundle units are prominent because of the alternating directions of field orientation between blocks. This has been called the "checkerboard pattern" (see Figure 5) the most common form of raised fields (Smith et al. 1968).[18] All of the field types in the northern Lake Titicaca basin have a general orientation towards the cardinal directions. The regularity of wavelength within and between field blocks indicates careful planning and suggests that there was a possible prehispanic measurement system for field layout. Nevertheless, our experiments demonstrate that raised fields are simple to plan and lay out using string and stakes.

In their discussion of field form and its potential relationship to social organization, Smith et al. (1968:357-359) interpret the general irregularity of overall field patterning and the lack of major irrigation canals as the work of small groups of cooperating individual farmers. Lennon (1982) disagrees with regard to field patterning, arguing that there is a strong indication that fields were constructed for relatively complex hydraulic functions; in terms of social organization necessary for construction, however, he concedes that these fields could have been built by individual farmers (ibid.:227, 189).

Lennon's (1982) detailed analysis of these individual bundles of raised fields (normally rectangular or square) is very important for my interpretation of the land tenure and social organization of raised field agriculture. He found that the average block size of fields (including canals) sampled in the riverine area was 2,300 m². This figure correlates closely with my calculations of the area of raised fields (2,665 m²) that a single household of 5 could construct and manage in a year, according to our experimental labor figures discussed below (Erickson 1988a). This basic unit could be a prehispanic expression of the basic Andean *topo* measurement used in the Colonial period and in some communities today. The crop production from such a unit would also provide the necessary caloric values to sustain that household for a year (based on potato production). In addition, I found that a family of 5 could easily construct a block this size in a season. This evidence strongly suggests a local organization of field tenure organized among family and local communities.

A second level of organization can be seen in larger divisions of complexes of raised fields into irregular polygons, the most common form being a narrow pie-shaped wedge. These complexes of fields are bounded by large straight canals (of greater length, depth, and width than the common raised field canals) (see Figure 7). These canals routinely radiate from "centers" (on low hills overlooking the plain, on mounds, and sometimes from no visible topographic feature) (see Figure 9). The arrangement of these canals is strikingly similar to the structure of the *ceques* described by Inka Cuzco, a system of sociopolitical and ceremonial organization (Zuidema 1990, Bauer 1992).[19] I argue that, in the case of raised fields in Huatta, these canals probably reflect *ayllu* divisions or subdivision of the community of raised field farmers. These radial systems are also a key feature of the rotational fallow systems and sectorial farming, described for contemporary Andean farmers (Orlove & Godoy 1986, Guillet 1981), which may have also been used by raised field farmers to organize planting schedules, crop rotation, and land tenure.[20] The patterning that occurs in the prehispanic raised fields is that which would be expected in an Andean farming community where parcels of land (in this case, raised fields) are divided according to traditional Andean structures of family and communal land distribution, probably at the level of *ayllu* or *saya*.

These agricultural earthwork structures in the raised field landscape of the Lake Titicaca region exhibit remarkable formal traits of symmetry, modularity, and hierarchy over a wide area. Within the 52,000 ha block of fields in the Huatta pampa, there is much regional diversity in field form (Erickson 1985, 1988a; Lennon 1982, 1983). These morphological distinctions probably represent different local community expressions of ethnicity or style, or possibly temporal differences in field construction and use. Despite these differences, there is a certain generic level of similarity of raised field morphology over time and space that suggests a shared regional tradition of a proper underlying structural principle of raised field layout and construction.

The raised fields of Koani Pampa, Lukurmata (Kolata & Graffam 1989, Graffam 1990, Kolata 1986, 1991), and the Valley of Tiwanaku (Albarracín & Mathews 1990, Kolata 1991, Mathews n.d.b), assumed by Kolata to be contemporaneous with Tiwanaku IV and Tiwanaku V (A.D. 375-1000/1100), also show considerable variation in morphology. The aerial photographs and illustrations indicate that there are a remarkable variety of sizes and forms in a small, concentrated area of raised fields. Albarracín and Mathews (1990:37) note differences between the Tiwanaku Valley fields and Koani Pampa fields, suggesting that the contrasts are due to different ecological adaptations or different construction periods. The variety of field forms could also be related to noncentralized construction, as well as ecological and chronological factors. Following Kolata's state model for raised field agricultural organization, one might expect that field patterns would be more regular and uniform, dictated by centralized bureaucratic planning. This is certainly not the case, even in the Tiwanaku heartland.

Figure 5. Aerial Photograph of Raised Fields of the "Checkerboard Pattern," near Huatta

392

Figure 6. Aerial Photograph of Large Raised Fields of the "Ladder Pattern," near Pomata

Figure 7. Aerial Photograph of Raised Fields of the "Checkerboard Pattern" and "Embanked Pattern," near Huatta (Several major canals divide the field blocks into sectors.)

0 meters 100

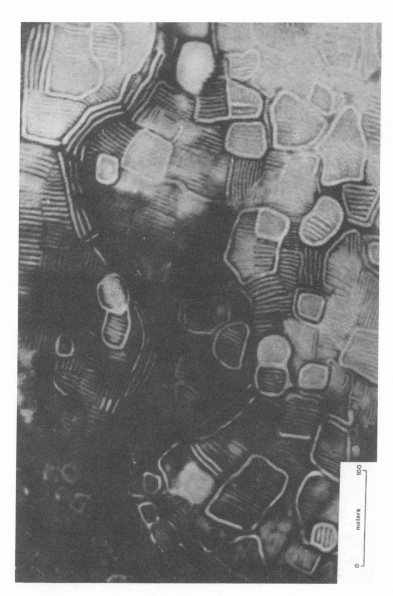

Figure 8. Aerial Photograph of Raised Fields of the "Embanked Pattern" at the Edge of Lake Titicaca, Huatta

395

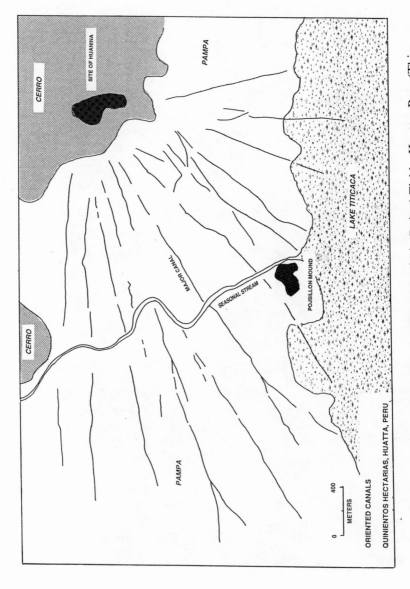

Figure 9. Section of Radial Canal Network within Raised Fields, Huatta, Peru (This feature possibly represents an ancient form of land tenure based on the *ceque* system.)

Settlements and Settlement Survey

The density of residential sites associated with raised field farming is remarkable. In the contiguous block of 52,000 ha of raised fields around Huatta, I estimate that there are some 1,000 mounds larger than single-house mounds. If single-house mounds are added to this list, the figure would be many times greater. Most of these mounds are relatively evenly distributed on the pampa, but the largest concentrations are near the lake edge or are islands within the lake shallows (see Figure 10). Dense concentrations of sites are also found on the hillslopes and valleys that ring the raised field-covered plains. Occupation mounds are easy to locate on the ground in the flat terrain of the lake plain. They also are easy to distinguish on aerial photographs using stereo pairs to discern the low relief. Mounds range in size from individual house mounds or temporary field camps of several square meters to huge earthen structures covering many hectares and rising up to 15 meters above the natural surface of the pampa.

The dating of these mounds is difficult without excavation. Surface collections made during 1981-1986 indicate that most, if not all, of the larger mounds are multicomponent sites, spanning the Initial Period to the present. This situation appears to be similar to that of Koani Pampa (Kolata 1986; Graffam 1989, 1990), the Taraco peninsula, and Juli Pampa (Stanish n.d.).[21] Albarracín and Mathews (1990) had similar problems providing convincing associations of sites to raised field complexes in their Tiwanaku Valley survey.[22]

Limited excavations in three prehispanic residential sites were made in 1983.[23] The excavations confirmed that the sites were occupied primarily by farmers. Common artifacts included thousands of basalt flakes from the sharpening of stone hoes, as well as numerous ceramics (from both well-made serving vessels and common utilitarian wares). Organic remains included fish, bird, and camelid bone, as well as carbonized plants such as chenopods, shrubs used for cooking, and tuber fragments. The mounds are clearly the result of "tell-like" accumulations of adobe and sod structures that had been occasionally leveled and constructed upon at later periods. The profiles of the excavations showed several meters of stratigraphically superimposed house floors. Excavations indicated that some areas had received quantities of fill to raise the occupation platform. A number of sites have cut stones on the surface, and one site, Pancha, may have held a platform with a stone retaining wall dating to the early Pukara (200 B.C.-A.D. 600) or possibly pre-Pukara (before 200 B.C.) occupation of the site. Other than this, there is no evidence of any administrative or bureaucratic "centers" identified with any known prehispanic state society within the farming settlements of the pampa. Evidence of a state administrative presence has not been found within the raised field blocks.

Figure 10. Prehispanic and Modern Settlements on the Flooded Pampa, near Huatta (Contemporary farmers use ancient mounds for dry house sites.)

Many of these mounds are still occupied today, some seasonally and some permanently. There is no reason to expect that the use of these mounds was much different in the past, except that the population living on the pampa was probably much greater. Housemounds near the lakeshore or within the lake (which become small islands during the rainy season) are occupied by fishermen or farmers who use these locations to gain access to the dense mats of aquatic plants for animal forage. These pampa sites were settlements of raised field farmers, not elite managers or bureaucrats. The distribution of small to large mounds is what would be expected in a rural landscape of farming communities exploiting the natural and agricultural resources of the lake and pampa. Locally produced fine Inka ceramics occur on many of the larger mounds, but these appear to have been occupations that post-date the use of the raised fields.

EXPERIMENTAL ARCHAEOLOGY: LABOR AND PRODUCTION

Between 1981 and 1986, the Raised Field Agricultural Project worked with local Quechua-speaking communities in a small-scale experimental program of raised field agriculture (Erickson 1985, 1988a-b; Erickson & Candler 1989, Erickson & Brinkmeier n.d.; Garaycochea 1986a-b, 1987). In addition, several other related development projects promoting raised field rehabilitation were inspired by this work, on both the Peruvian and Bolivian sides of the Lake Titicaca basin (Ramos 1986, 1990; Rivera 1989, Kolata 1991). Much of the work has been continued by governmental and nongovernmental institutions.

Experimental raised fields were modelled on archaeological data recovered from topographic mapping, survey, and excavation of prehistoric fields. Experimental fields were rehabilitated or reconstructed eroded prehispanic fields. Raised fields blocks of up to 10 ha in area were constructed in the communities of Huatta, Coata, and Capachica, Department of Puno, within the *pampas* on the edges of Lake Titicaca. Communities (*parcialidades*, possibly descendants of the original *ayllus*) were approached by the research team and meetings were organized to discuss raised fields with members (*comuneros*). Participants were offered free potato seed as an incentive in return for the use of the individual's or community's land, the labor of the community for the construction, maintenance, and harvest of the fields, and the recording of labor and production data involved in raised field farming. The participants also received all the harvest, which was divided amongst the community group or families.

Andean Social Organization and Labor Mobilization

The household and the supra-household *ayllu* have been considered the basic social, political and economic units in the rural Central Andes. These institutions—combined with the dual organization of communities or *sayas*, culturally defined land divisions such as *suyu, chuta*, and *ceques*, and reciprocal labor relationships—are very powerful and resistant structural forces for mobilizing labor, coordinating large public projects, resolving disputes, controlling land tenure, and spatially organizing populations.

Although believed to be widespread and of considerable time depth, the *ayllu* is difficult to define precisely (see Zuidema 1990, Allen 1988, Isbell 1985, Conrad & Demarest 1984:97-98, 105). In an excellent survey of the concept, Urton describes *ayllus* as "particular units of social organization," and states (1992:230):

> In general terms, *ayllus* are named, clanlike groupings of people whose internal unity and differentiation from each other are based on a variety of factors, including landholding, kinship, festival sponsorship, and the performance of public labor projects. *Ayllus* have been central institutions in community organizations from pre-Hispanic times to the present day in the Andean nation-states of Peru, Bolivia, and Ecuador.

As Urton stresses, it is not an inflexible or static institution and "the persistent nature of the *ayllus* as a central institution of social organization in Pacariqtambo is linked to the support and services that certain members of the community are constantly in need of, and by the recurring demands associated with building and maintaining community facilities" (Urton 1992:235) and is "continually reproduced and transformed" (ibid.:235). In some cases, there appears to be a certain hierarchical nature to the *ayllus*, which can be formed at various levels, depending on local contexts and needs.[24] In many cases, *ayllus* are ranked. Higher levels of community organization are the *sayas*, or asymmetrical moieties made up of numerous *ayllus*. Most scholars agree that the *ayllu* has a long history and certainly is responsible for many of the monumental works constructed before the Spanish conquest of the Andes. Because of the material manifestations of the *ayllu* and its works, it should be possible to archaeologically document the *ayllu*. Urton points to the segmental maintenance of the church plaza by the eight *ayllu* groups of the town, the territoriality of *ayllu* residence, and the land tenure organization of the agricultural landscape surrounding the town as examples.

As Urton (1992) notes, the ayllu's existence is centered around the need for organizing local services and labor. Institutions of Andean labor reciprocity are an efficient means of mobilizing work forces of various sizes to complete suprafamily projects, ranging from individual agricultural fieldwork to sponsorship of public rituals and community construction projects. At the lowest level, work is shared through *ayni*, a symmetrically balanced form of labor between individuals who are equals. Labor performed by one individual is repaid at a later date. For larger projects, work is commonly done through *minka* or *faena*, other forms of reciprocal labor. *Minka*, organized at the group level, is asymmetrical and includes the exchange of goods for short-term labor or services mobilized for an individual's or community's benefit. *Faena*, also asymmetrical, is often a form of labor tax imposed by communities on their individual members for construction and maintenance of local infrastructure (roads, schools, canals) and has a coercive element (Gelles 1986:138). The *mit'a*, or state system of mass mobilization of rotational corvée labor practiced by the Inka, is—at least functionally and symbolically—a form of *minka* or *faena* writ large.[25]

Dual organization is ubiquitous in the ethnographic literature on communities in the Central Andes. It is characterized as asymmetrical moieties, or *sayas*, usually referred to as *anansaya* ("upper" half) and *urinsaya* ("lower" half) in the Quechua-speaking zones. Traditional irrigation management, or "the local model of irrigation," revolves around dual organization of communities under "water mayors," and earth and mountain worship (Gelles 1990:154-156). Besides the spatial and social components of the system, this dual organization is also important in ritual. The organization of Andean irrigation is tightly tied to calendrical rituals, which are an integral part of local water management (Zuidema 1990, Sherbondy 1982, 1987, 1992; Gelles 1990, n.d.b; Treacy 1989b, and others). Most scholars agree that the institutions of dual organization, earth and mountain worship, *ayllu*, and reciprocal labor relationships have deep historical roots in the Andes, although these institutions have certainly been transformed over time.[26] Working with ethnohistorical documents in the north coast of Peru, Netherly (1984) has identified a local segmentary system of ranked dual organization and hierarchically nested community groups, which were in charge of hierarchical levels of the irrigation system.

In our experimental fields, labor was organized by the community groups or individual households. Specified workdays of 5 hours each were called on by the community for the communal work project (*faena*). Adult male heads of family (or designated adult substitutes) were responsible for showing up for the days of work. Communal work groups ranged from 5 to 60 individuals, depending upon interest and community membership. If additional days were required to complete the preplanned work, they were added to the community work schedule. Participation of the communal groups was continued over many years, with field blocks becoming larger and more dispersed over time. Some groups utilized another traditional form of labor mobilization, referred to as *tarea*. Here, each *comunero* is assigned a set area of raised fields to reconstruct at his/her own pace. This segmental organization for construction for public works has been documented in Andean prehistory (Hastings & Moseley 1975).

The tools used to construct the fields were those available to all farmers in the area—the Andean footplow (*chakitaqlla*), hoe (*rawkana*), wooden clod-breaker (*waqtana*), shovel, and pick (see Figure 11). Large woolen cloths were also used to transport loose soil from canal to field surface. Field and canal boundaries were marked by string, using the old abandoned field and canal surfaces as models. The rich organic soil of the A horizon from the sediment-filled canals was cut into sod blocks using the footplow and placed as a retaining wall and fill for the raised field platform. The platforms were built up to a height of 20-50 cm and were bordered with correspondingly deep adjacent canals (see Figure 12). Sod blocks and clods were broken up with picks and clod-breakers, and field surfaces were formed into a cambered shape for drainage.

Fields were planted in local crops—potatoes, oca, ulluco, isañu, quinua, cañihua, maize, winter wheat, peas, broad beans, tarwi, and various garden vegetables. Fields received no fertilizers. Maintenance activities such as weeding and banking of tuber crops were done in the same manner as in traditional fields.

The research team also worked with some individual farmers (*parceleros*) and non-community groups of farmers. These farmers tended to construct small blocks of rehabilitated raised fields adjacent to households, taking on the form of house gardens. Labor was commonly mobilized using *ayni*, symmetrical reciprocal labor exchange between neighbors and extended-family members. These fields generally were better constructed and better maintained than the community fields. In 1989, individual farmers were adopting raised fields faster than community groups. Ground and aerial survey demonstrated that hundreds of families in the pampa of Huatta, Coata, and Caracoto had begun to construct small plots near their houses.

Several assumptions about the way raised fields work were shown to be erroneous in our experimental research. One erroneous assumption is that raised fields need a high level of centralized organization for construction and maintenance. The raised fields were constructed by communal groups and individual families using the traditional Andean labor reciprocity, *ayni, minka*, and *faena*. Piecemeal construction of raised fields over 10 years by individual households and communities has resulted in over 100 ha of rehabilitated fields in the Huatta area (Juan Palao, pers. com.) and 150 ha in the Koani Pampa/ Valley of Tiwanaku (Oswaldo Rivera S. and Enrique González A., pers. comm.). Several blocks of communal fields in Huatta and Coata belonging to small communities have grown to over 15 ha by accretion over an 8-year period. The traditional reciprocal labor institutions, *ayni* and *minka*, proved an efficient means of mobilizing labor for raised field farming. Clearly, small groups of farmers are capable over time of creating a large-scale, heavily modified, regional landscape.

Figure 11. Cutting Sod Blocks with the Andean Footplow (*chakitaqlla*) for the Construction of Raised Fields, Community of Yasin, Huatta

Figure 12. Manual Reconstruction of Raised Fields by the Community of Yasin, Huatta, for Experiments

Raised Fields, Labor Investment, and Production

Raised fields are not necessarily labor intensive. Because few experiments constructing raised fields with manual labor had been conducted (e.g., Puleston 1977a, Gómez-Pompa et al. 1982, Muse & Quintero 1987), previous labor estimates were based on simplistic comparisons with other forms of traditional agriculture or, more commonly, with labor estimates for moving earth (e.g., Erasmus 1965). According to the Boserup (1965) hypothesis on agricultural intensification and the "Law of Least Effort" (Zipf 1949), intensive forms of agriculture requiring large inputs of labor and energy for construction and maintenance will be adopted by traditional farmers only if population stress becomes too great or, according to the Wittfogelian counterpart to the theory, if the centralized political state forces local farmers to adopt the technology.

Our experimental data indicate otherwise. The initial construction of raised fields—digging canals and transferring soil to construct the platforms—involves a relatively large input of labor (in comparison to traditional *wacho* lazy bed construction). From several years of controlled experimental construction using manual labor in diverse locations in the Huatta pampa, we estimate that 200-1,000 person-days of labor are necessary to construct 1 ha of raised fields and canals (Erickson 1988a, Erickson & Candler 1989, Garaycochea 1986a, 1987). These figures have been duplicated experimentally in other areas (Ramos 1986). The work is considerably faster than estimates previously calculated using earthmoving figures (Erasmus 1965) for prehispanic raised field construction (Denevan 1982, Turner 1983). This lower calculation for construction is probably due to the different techniques used in earthmoving and the advantages of working in the grasslands, where large sod blocks can be easily cut and moved using the Andean footplow. In addition, the traditional labor mobilization institutions of the Andean community and family groups are an efficient means of providing the necessary work force.

Labor input on raised fields becomes almost negligible when labor and production are considered over the long term. Raised field agriculture is efficient and sustainable because fields can be farmed continuously with high productivity for many years. Many raised field platforms in Viscachani Pampa in the Huatta area have been farmed for over 10 years without a significant decline in productivity. Raised field maintenance requirements are low (occasional weeding, irrigation, and banking tubers). Harvest takes longer than on regular potato fields[27] because the production is so much higher (see Figure 13). The fertility of raised fields is maintained through the periodic re-excavation of sod in dry canals or organic mucks and sediments in wet canals and the placing of these materials on the field platforms. Estimates of 270-person days/ha [$\alpha 5$ hour/day] have been calculated for raised field construction and necessary maintenance (annual and periodic) over the long

Figure 13. Potato Harvest from Raised Fields by the Community of Primera Collana, Huatta

run (a 10-year period), based on experimental results (Erickson 1988a, Erickson & Candler 1989). The figures are even more impressive in terms of the agricultural production returns on labor input. Production data from several years of experimental raised field potato harvests range from 8 to 16 metric tons of potatoes per hectare, or 2-3 times that of regular potato farming.[28] This yield converts to 37 kg of potatoes per person-day of work, in sharp contrast to the 19 kg per person-day of work for regular fields in the Andean region (Erickson 1988a). Given such a reliable, sustainable production, farmers may have adopted raised field farming early in Andean prehistory without having been forced to do so by population pressure or other stresses such as state imperatives.

Another premise that the experimental fields showed to be incorrect was that the fields would not function without the rehabilitation of the complete regional hydraulic system as envisioned by Kolata (1991). Small, isolated blocks of rehabilitated raised fields did produce remarkable harvests, despite being surrounded by eroded, unreconstructed, abandoned raised fields. It is clear that larger, contiguous blocks of fields would produce the desired microclimate effects better than small, isolated blocks (Erickson 1988a, Grace 1983), but the individual components of regional raised field systems do not require the rehabilitation of the whole system to function (see Figure 1). There is no need to invoke large-scale hydraulic integration and a state-level organizational apparatus for raised fields to function properly.

COLLAPSE AND ABANDONMENT

In discussing the Tiwanaku raised fields of the Koani Pampa, Kolata (1983:262, 1986:753, 1987:41) suggests that one of the potential causes of the collapse of raised field farming was the disintegration of the Tiwanaku state after the Tiwanaku V Phase.[29] He assumes that, without the bureaucratic organization of the state, raised field farming would break down. His evidence for the co-occurrence of the Tiwanaku collapse and raised field abandonment comes from early excavations of a limited number of occupation mounds within Koani Pampa (Kolata 1986, 1987). Graffam (1989, 1990, 1992) has recently demonstrated that raised field construction continued in Koani Pampa and the Taraco Peninsula after the fall of Tiwanaku during the Late Intermediate Period. According to Graffam's investigation of house mounds and associated fields, the majority of visible raised fields in the best-preserved section of Koani Pampa are post-Tiwanaku. Survey work in the Tiwanaku Valley itself demonstrates that raised fields, terraces and *qochas* (sunken gardens) continued to be constructed during the post-Tiwanaku period (Albarracín & Mathews 1990:146-147, Mathews n.d.b). There is considerable debate regarding the level of political organization present during the Late Intermediate Period in the

Lake basin, but most agree that it was less centralized than during the Middle Horizon (Stanish n.d., Graffam 1992:885). Thus, raised field production appears to have continued under local sociopolitical organization, independent of state administration.[30]

Our investigations in the Huatta pampa indicate that the rise and fall of local states had little to do with the success or failure of raised field systems. Field blocks may have been abandoned periodically as part of a rotational fallow system or because of low demand. Two climaxes of raised field construction and use appear to have been before Pukara developed into a major center (and possible state) and during the Late Intermediate Period in the Huatta pampa (Erickson 1987, 1988a). Raised fields in the northern basin may have been abandoned for a time during the Middle Horizon (A.D. 600-1000) and Late Horizon (A.D. 1476 1534), the periods of state (Tiwanaku and Inca) presence in the region. Raised fields under community control were apparently resilient and functioned independently of centralized state control, which waxed and waned in the region.

INFRASTRUCTURE, CAPITAL, AND EVOLUTION OF REGIONAL LANDSCAPES

The vast Huatta pampa is covered with earthworks that could represent elements of agricultural infrastructure of a level beyond the basic organization of raised field blocks and bundles of fields. The most impressive are the extensive canal networks, discussed above, which divide and interconnect raised field blocks into social and functional units, and which may have also had a hydraulic function (Lennon 1982, 1983; Erickson 1988a). In addition, there are artificial levees associated with most, if not all, active and nonactive river and stream channels crossing the pampa. Smith et al. (1968) reported large causeways from Machacmarca associated with raised fields. Do these earthworks necessarily represent the work of supralocal bureaucratic organizations that controlled the labor of local farming communities? Are they beyond the scale of engineering ability of small social units?

Kolata (1991) has argued that the "regional" infrastructure of earthworks— including artificial canalized sections of the Rio Catari, the river by-pass systems or river shunts in Koani pampa and the Tiwanaku Valley, causeways/ dikes, and aqueducts—are definitely projects of a state because they would have been far beyond the labor and organizational capability of local groups of farmers. Admittedly, these constructions are impressive engineering accomplishments, but it is premature to deny the possibility of local level construction.

What is often forgotten by scholars studying agricultural infrastructure is the considerable time depth of the evolution of cultural landscapes in the

Americas. What we see today in the form of massive infrastructural modifications of the slopes, deserts, and *pampas* is the gradual accumulation of constructions produced by hundreds of generations of farmers. Archaeological evidence indicates that the raised fields of the Lake Titicaca Basin have a long evolutionary history and that they certainly were not all constructed at a single point in time. Agricultural landscapes take on a high degree of engineering complexity, or "integrativeness," over time. Several scholars have referred to this phenomena as the accumulation of "landscape capital" by traditional farmers (Brookfield 1986, Bronson 1972, 1975). This capital includes infrastructures such as terraces, irrigation systems, dikes, fences, ponds, reservoirs, aqueducts, road networks, and raised fields. As Doolittle (1984) has noted, these complex systems evolve over long periods of time, through what could be considered a piecemeal accretion process, the day-to-day activities "that take place in the normal course of cultivation and maintenance" (Doolittle 1990:151; also see Downing & Gibson 1974a:x, Donkin 1979:120, 133).[31] Much of the early construction of fields, boundaries, canals, and settlements of any system is relatively haphazard and unstructured. The process involves working out the kinks of the production system through experimentation and fine tuning. This process is not necessarily a conscious, intentional effort, or part of a long-term plan on the part of the farmers, but rather results from the simple annual rebuilding or maintenance activities which altered and improved elements of the infrastructure. Over time, as a result of these activities, the system may take on a high degree of formal structural patterning. What we see today as archaeologists is a complex, sophisticated, and once highly productive system spread over a regional cultural landscape. This landscape is a result of the gradual accumulation of landscape capital. I would argue that the raised field systems and the associated irrigation, *qocha*, terracing complex are the result of a similar process of accumulation of landscape capital over a long period of time by small-scale farmers organized in traditional community structures such as the *ayllu*. As Glick (1970:173-174) notes, "The physical aspects of a system can be deceiving and Wittfogel...seems to say that an impressive irrigation system must be the work of an impressive government, an agromanagerial despotism commanding an unpaid labor force."

Leach's (1959) warning about scale, sociopolitical organization, and chronology is relevant here. He states that the 55 km Kalawewa canal network in Ceylon "looks like a colossal and highly organized piece of bureaucratic planning, the work of one of Wittfogel's idealized Oriental Despots. But if so, the planning must have been done by a kind of Durkheimian group mind! The system took about 1400 years to build"(Leach 1959:13). In addition, Leach (1959:14) states that, "although the Ceylon irrigation works and the associated palace and temple construction works do represent a gigantic accumulation of capital resulting from an enormous number of man-hours of labour, this fact does not *in itself* imply any massive control over labour resources by the 'bureaucratic rulers.'" If Tiwanaku IV and Tiwanaku V represent the period of the Tiwanaku state and the period of raised field construction, the creation of the now abandoned landscapes could have been spread over a 600-year period. An even longer period of 2,000 years of construction is suggested by dates for raised fields in the northern basin (Erickson 1987, 1988a; Stanish n.d.). This is more than enough time for small-scale organizations to produce these highly structured and productive agricultural landscapes. There is no need to invoke the state to explain the origin of all these works.

Over the years of experimental construction of raised fields in the communities around Huatta between 1981 and the present, farmers have altered and improved the methods of construction and maintenance of the plots to increase labor efficiency and production and to reduce risk. This fine-tuning of the system involves primarily trial and error procedures. Raising the elevation of platforms after problems of flooding and using living sod walls to protect field edges from erosion are some examples of such changes. These alterations are conducted seasonally or when maintenance is necessary. This form of landscape capital improvement can also be seen in the larger, regional hydraulic and transportation works such as the river canalization and dike program (discussed above), where dikes are periodically repaired and improved after serious flooding problems to prevent future inundation. This accretion process can also be seen in the construction and maintenance of community road causeways in the *pampas*, which are continually rebuilt and modified to provide the necessary drainage to use the *pampas* for farming and grazing. This is the gentle process of incremental change in action.

ALTERNATIVE SYSTEMS OF AGRICULTURAL PRODUCTION

Because raised field agriculture is such an impressive production system, a major misconception is the implication that raised fields were the main or only economic system available to farmers during the Middle Horizon (A.D. 600-1000) in the Tiwanaku core area, as implied by Kolata (1986:748, 760; 1991; Ortloff & Kolata 1989). The new survey work in the Tiwanaku Valley undertaken by Albarracín and Mathews (1990; also see Albarracín 1992) demonstrates that Tiwanaku peoples used multiple systems of production. Their work provides evidence of extensive terracing and *qochas*, in addition to raised fields.

Terracing has not been investigated in much detail, but the technology had been mastered by the Early Intermediate Period (200 B.C.-A.D. 600). The ceremonial precinct at Pukara was placed on monumental terraces. During the Middle Horizon, large areas of residential zones of Lukurmata and Pajchiri were located on artificial terraces (Kolata 1986, 1987). Many of the terrace systems in the Lake Titicaca Basin are integrated into raised field systems through continuation of boundary walls that extend from the hillslopes into the *pampas* (Erickson 1988a). If terraces were constructed for occupation, they may also have been in use for agricultural production at a very early time. The advantages of favorable lakeshore microclimates, higher rainfall, better soils, and longer growing seasons made labor-intensive terracing a practical option for lake edge farmers. The archaeological record indicates that pre-Tiwanaku farmers, and colonial and contemporary farmers (Aymara, Quechua, and Uru-Puquina), also relied heavily on lacustrine and aquatic resources such as fish and gathered plants, as well as camelid herding (Erickson 1988a).

These diverse production strategies available to Tiwanaku, in addition to long-distance trade and establishment of production colonies in multiple resource zones (Browman 1981), suggest that the central resource base for Tiwanaku was much broader than the limited raised field model presented by Kolata (1986, 1991). We should also note that these multiple resource production systems were in place long before the establishment of Andean states in the Lake Titicaca Basin.

THE RELATIONSHIP OF RAISED FIELD AGRICULTURE TO THE STATE

If the success of raised field agriculture does not rely on state bureaucratic management, then what is the relation between the prehispanic state and raised fields? Raised fields did not "cause" the first state in the Lake Titicaca Basin, but this impressive agricultural system is certainly indirectly related to the development of the state. Raised fields farming preceded the state by possibly 500-1000 years (Erickson 1987, 1988a; Stanish n.d.). Because raised field agriculture is an intensive and effective form of production technology, it is usually discussed in the context of surplus production, not subsistence production. Inherent in discussions of the state's relationship to raised fields is the state's need to produce large quantities of surplus to sustain urban populations, craftspersons, the elite, and state activities and enterprises. There is no doubt that the state would have a strong interest in raised field agriculture, appropriating this surplus through taxation, expropriation of peasant labor for construction and maintenance of new fields, establishment of colonies of state agriculturalists, and/or direct government control of fields.

Kolata, Graffam, and I have argued that the vast extension of raised fields represent much more than a subsistence economy. The highly productive regional landscape was definitely important in setting the stage for state development. The fields were effective means of generating huge surpluses and sustaining large nonfarming populations. But, while the state may have had a strong influence over raised field production through taxation, it does not follow that the state necessarily had a direct hand in the planning, construction, and administration of raised fields. There is no need to invoke direct Tiwanaku state control over raised field farming, the "top-down" approach. Indirect demands and pressures such as taxation, co-option of labor, and tribute demands can induce farmers to intensify and boost levels of surplus production. The Tiwanaku state may even have expanded the agricultural frontier into marginal zones. This still does not mean that the Tiwanaku elites necessarily planned and managed all of the fields in the Lake Titicaca Basin, or that raised field agriculture did not exist or was not productive before the Tiwanaku state.

What raised fields and other landscape capital systems did was to tie farmers to the land, making them relatively immobile and subject to labor taxes and tribute. Such a situation is beneficial to the state in that such farmers can easily be controlled and labor and goods can easily be expropriated for the elite's purposes. As in the Inka case of terracing (Conrad & Demarest 1984, Sherbondy 1982, Murra 1980), the state may have encouraged the expansion of raised fields at the community level in order to create a more favorable economic environment. As long as the tribute flowed from the local communities, it would not be in the state's best interest to meddle with well-established and efficiently functioning raised field agriculture.

Raised fields have a long history in the Lake Titicaca Basin, much longer than that of the Tiwanaku state, which may have lasted less than 600 years. Why would early farmers adopt raised field agriculture at a time when there was no demand for surplus from urban populations and the state? Because raised field farming is more labor efficient, more productive, and less risky than alternative technologies, it would have been one of the best choices for early farmers in the Lake Titicaca basin making the transition from lacustrine-based hunting and gathering economies (Erickson 1987, 1988a). Raised fields evolved from a subsistence to a surplus production system as local demands and population grew. By the Initial Period and Early Horizon, these demands could have included: taxation and tribute to local *ayllu* and supra-*ayllu* lords and temples; support of a nonfarming population, including craft specialists and such other specialists as warriors, religious officials, pastoralists, fishermen, hunters, and collectors; local reciprocity, gift giving, and barter; long-distance exchange of resources between ethnic groups of different environmental zones; procurement of exotic goods as part of a prestige good economy; support of pilgrimage activities of important regional shrines; underwriting ritual and ceremony; and the stockpiling of production for adverse times. The combined demands of subsistence and social production were continuously high. All of these activities are documented in the archaeological record for pre-Tiwanaku cultures of the Lake Titicaca Basin (Kolata 1983, Erickson 1988a, Bermann 1990, Albarracín 1992, Browman 1981, Moseley 1992). Archaeological survey has demonstrated that populations around the lakeshore were dense and that many of the pre-state and post-state settlements are located within or near remains of raised fields (Erickson 1988a, Albarracín & Mathews 1990, Stanish n.d.). Raised fields must have supplied the needs of many different types of sociopolitical organizations, both state-level and non-state, throughout prehistory.

In summary, raised field were developed, constructed, and maintained by farmers organized in localized *ayllus* and communities. The Andean states of the region developed and collapsed with regularity, but the agricultural systems organized at lower levels continued relatively unaffected and perhaps thrived. To suppose that raised field farming could only be planned, executed, and maintained by the highly centralized state is to disregard the rich agricultural knowledge and organizational potential of the Andean farmer, both past and present. This is not a stale academic issue to be debated by scholars, but has very specific implications in regard to whether or not raised field farming can be reintroduced at the local level in the Andes and elsewhere. The evidence strongly indicates that the assumption that raised field agriculture requires state administration is incorrect.

CONCLUSIONS

Most discussions of raised fields have focused on the technology and the environmental and evolutionary context of raised field farming (Denevan 1970, 1982; Denevan & Turner 1974; and others). The cultural materialism and cultural ecology perspectives tend to dominate this literature. Little emphasis has been placed on the sociopolitical context of raised field agriculture, in contrast to the rich discussion regarding the organization of prehistoric irrigation systems. Kolata and others have presented a provocative hypothesis regarding the relationship of raised fields and the state. The primary assumption is that, because raised fields are an intensive form of agriculture, they must have been constructed and controlled by centralized bureaucratic institutions. I have reviewed these perspectives and presented an alternative model, that they were developed and managed by local household and community organizations.

Hierarchically organized, highly centralized, complex state-level society was probably never the norm in Andean prehistory. Widespread "horizon styles," commonly assumed to be associated with the expansion of state organizations, appear and disappear throughout the Andean chronological sequence (Moseley 1992). Class struggle, ethnic unrest, and peasant rebellion date to at least the Late Horizon and possibly earlier (Patterson 1992). Documentary data for the Lake Titicaca Basin indicate widespread warfare and interethnic unrest during the post-Tiwanaku Late Intermediate Period and Late Horizon

(Julien 1983). The most enduring Andean organizational structures over these long periods of time appear to have been the household and supra-household community level *ayllu* organizations (Alberti & Mayer 1974a; Mayer 1974, 1976; Stanish 1992, Isbell 1985, Urton 1992). Despite these long periods of unrest and lack of strong state presence, intensive raised field agriculture flourished in the northern Lake Titicaca Basin under local control. The raised field system did not need the state.

Archaeological, ethnohistorical, and ethnographic case studies document that large-scale regional, intensive forms of agriculture are associated with a wide range of social systems. To automatically assume that the sociopolitical organization associated with these systems has to be centralized and directed by bureaucracies would be a mistake. It is clear that raised field agriculture is highly sustainable and efficient for the production of subsistence and surplus foodstuffs. At times, large and dense populations must have been sustained by raised field agriculture. But it is important to remember that raised fields were used in the Titicaca Basin before, during, and after the Tiwanaku phenomena. There is no necessary relationship between the Tiwanaku state and the construction and management of raised field systems.

The implications of the debate among scholars regarding the social organization of prehistoric raised field agriculture are potentially far reaching. Both the Peruvian and Bolivian governments, in addition to numerous governmental and nongovernmental organizations, have adopted raised field technology to certain degrees as part of development programs for the rural *altiplano* (Erickson & Candler 1989, Kolata 1991; Rivera 1989, Erickson & Brinkmeier n.d., Brinkmeier 1985, Erickson 1992b, Garaycochea 1988). Much of the planning and organization for the diffusion of this technology has been haphazard—some groups favoring a heavy-handed "top-down approach," others focusing on a more grassroots development, or a "bottom-up approach" (for details, see Erickson & Brinkmeier n.d.). The future and success of raised field agriculture may depend heavily on what prehistoric archaeology can tell these development institutions about the optimal level of social organization for the reintroduction of raised field farming in the Andes.

ACKNOWLEDGMENTS

This essay has benefitted greatly from comments, discussions, and interactions with many individuals interested in intensive agricultural systems over the past 10 years. I thank Kay Candler, Dan Brinkmeier, Alan Kolata, Charles Stanish, William Denevan, Kent Mathewson, John Treacy, Jeffrey Parsons, Donald Lathrap, Thomas Lynch, Paul Gelles, William Isbell, Michel Muse, Paul Goldstein, Michael Moseley, Ignacio Garaycochea, Gray Graffam, and Jim Mathews. Kay Candler, Dan Brinkmeier, and Ignacio Garaycochea aided in the archaeological and experimental fieldwork in Huatta between 1981 and 1986. Various field seasons of research were conducted with generous grants from the Social Science Research Council, the National Science Foundation, and the Interamerican Foundation. Gray Graffam, Charles Stanish, Barry Isaac, Paul Gelles, Kay Candler, and Jim Mathews provided detailed criticism at various stages of the manuscript. We strongly disagree on many key points and their critique made me rethink several issues. I especially thank the people of Huatta and Coata who participated wholeheartedly in the archaeological and experimental project and personally taught me about the "bottom-up" approach to the social organization of agriculture and what dedicated communities could do for and by themselves.

NOTES

1. An early version of this essay was presented in the Symposium, "The Emergence of the Andean State in the Circum-Titicaca Basin," organized by Charles Stanish, Alan Kolata, and Mario Rivera at the 47th International Congress of Americanists, New Orleans, Louisiana, June 7-11, 1992.

2. Kolata (1991:112) has referred to the Ayllu/Local Level Organization Hypothesis as the "new orthodoxy." I would argue that the bottom-up approach has not been considered or accepted by most archaeologists writing about intensive agriculture.

3. Wittfogel (1957:184-188) used the prehispanic Maya as a case of "marginal agromanagerial society." According to him, they did not practice irrigation agriculture *per se*, but rather used hyraulic works for accumulating and storing water (the *cenotes, chultuns,* and *aguadas*). These systems were believed to have been derived from highland Mesoamerican sources. Marcus (1983) is one of the few Mayanists writing about prehispanic Maya fields who has stressed caution regarding the automatic association of raised fields with centralized authority.

4. This is ironic, considering that Puleston's (1977a, 1977b) pioneering experimental work with raised fields clearly demonstrated that small groups of farmers could easily construct blocks of raised fields.

5. Wittfogel (1957) was careful to distinguish between "hydroagriculture," in which farmers use small-scale traditional irrigation systems, and "hydraulic agriculture," in which the government controls large-scale irrigation networks and flood control structures. The literature on prehispanic intensive agriculture, in particular that written by archaeologists, tends to neglect this scale problem. In addition, Wittfogel did not argue that all large-scale irrigation systems necessarily will result in the despotic state.

6. Additonal commentary regarding the problems of compatibility of centralized state bureaucracy and local organization of irrigation agriculture can be found in Coward (1976, 1979, 1980a-b), Chambers (1980), Lees (1986), Lewis (1991), and Lansing (1991).

7. The construction and maintenance of terracing and irrigation systems throughout the Andes are commonly attributed to Inca state policy imposed on local communities through *mit'a* labor and land tenure changes (e.g., Conrad & Demarest 1984). This Inca analogy has been used by archaeologists to interpret the organization of raised field agriculture. Much of the terracing in the Andes is referred to by scholars as "Inca terracing," although there is a near complete lack of archaeological study of these features. Although the Inca were responsible for large tracts of terracing, it is clear that terracing as an Andean agricultural technology does not have its origins with the Inca state and that pre-Inca terracing is widespread (Denevan et al. 1987, Treacy 1989b, Malpass 1987, Donkin 1979). The irrigated terraces of the Inca capital of Cuzco were constructed and operated at the *ayllu* level, not by the state (Sherbondy 1982, 1987; Zuidema 1986). As Leach has noted in regard to Ceylon, the attribution of hydraulic works to historical individuals or states is often unfounded: "Might it not be that the 'greatness' of the hydraulic monarch is itself a product of propaganda myth?"; and, "While myth invariably attributes their construction to the initiative

of a single outstanding monarch, archaeology shows each has been slowly developed over a long period of time" (Leach 1959:13).

8.   I have argued that many of the large canals that bisect raised field blocks may have been used to create and maintain artificial wetlands environments instead of "draining" these areas (Erickson 1988a). Much of the structure of fields, canals, and embankments would have actually *impeded* the drainage of water.

9.   Several scholars have hypothesized that salinization of raised field surfaces was prevented by moving and distributing fresh water to field canals from aqueduct structures (Stanish, pers. comm.; Kolta & Ortloff 1989). It has not been demonstrated that salinization was a problem facing raised field farmers. Our experiments have shown that rehabilitated fields in areas with extensive surface salt accumulation produced as well as those in areas without salts.

10.   In the 1991 article, Kolata appears to equate the sophisticated nature of the raised field *technology* (waterlogging protection, management of hydraulic resources, high sustainable production, elevated carrying capacity, production and recycling of nutrients, and micro-climate improvements) with the need for a sophisticated and complex system to permit it to operate. I have argued that the two concepts are distinct and have no necessary relationship (Erickson 1988a). Also implicit in Kolata's and other work is the assumption that raised fields are necessarily "intensive" and, following the "Law of Least Effort," that farmers will not adopt this system unless forced to by the state or by environmental stress such as population pressure. The high productivity documented in the Bolivian experiments demonstrates that raised field farmers are capable of producing large surpluses. This does not necessarily mean that the impetus for the generation of these surpluses was state policy.

11.   Stanish (n.d.) also argues that, in the case of Moyopampa, Peru, the larger, more integrated raised field complexes associated with hydraulic structures (aqueducts and canals) must have been state controlled, while smaller blocks without these features may have been organized at a lower level by *ayllus*.

12.   If the aqueducts and river channelization found within the Tiwanaku field blocks functioned, as Kolata and Ortloff (1989) have argued, to prevent flooding and lower water tables within the pampa by diverting water directly into Lake Titicaca, the optimal hydraulic conditions within field canals may have been disputed. Graffam (1990:43, 172) has argued that these hydraulic modifications are more appropriate for pastoral use of the pampa during later prehistory or the historical period. The recent artificial tampering with the annual flooding of the Huatta pampa, a necessary factor in prehispanic and contemporary raised field farming, has been detrimental to the raised field agriculture being reintroduced in the area (Erickson & Brinkmeier n.d, Erickson & Chandler 1989).

13.   Mathews (n.d.b) reports on excavations of several raised fields near the urban center of Tiwanaku. Although small, these fields are larger than *wachos* commonly used by farmers today.

14.   I follow the chronology presented in Keatinge (1988:xv) for the Central Andes. The Tiwanaku phase sequence is based on Kolata (1983, 1986, 1991).

15.   It should be noted that the raised fields of the Koani Pampa are highly variable according to the published maps (Kolata 1986:Figure 4; also see Graffam 1990) and aerial photographs that I have studied from the Instituto Geográfico Militar archive. Fields within the Valley of Tiwanaku near the site of Tiwanaku appear to be very different, smaller with the more orderly checkerboard and ladder forms (Mathews n.d.a:4-5, n.d.b). Mathews (n.d.a) suggests that these differences may be due to the Tiwanaku Valley fields being older than those of Koani Pampa or to the different ecological context (riverine vs. lacustrine).

16.   Wavelength is the distance from canal center to adjacent canal center (passing over a raised field platform). More accurate measurements can be made by averaging many measurements. It provides an important and accurate measurement with which raised fields can be compared (Erickson 1988a).

17.   Kolata (1986, 1987) and Graffam (1990) report finding Chiripa ceramics (which span that Initial Period and Early Horizon) within the fill of Middle Horizon and Late Intermediate Period

occupation mounds in the pampa of Koani. These sherds possibly represent earlier occupations by raised field farmers in the pampa, but this has not been firmly established (Kolata 1986, 1991; Graffam 1990). There is also Early Horizon material at the site of Luqurmata (Bermann 1990). A short survey I conducted in 1975 along the northern shoreline of the Taraco Peninsula delineated numerous Early Horizon settlements adjacent to prime raised field land. This has also been addressed by Graffam (1990). At the beginning of the Tiwanaku state, the raised field zones were already being occupied and utilized by farmers.

18. Long "linear" raised fields extending several kilometers are commonly found in the Capachica region north of Huatta (Smith et al. 1968). They extend perpendicularly from the base of the slopes and cross the pampa to the lake shallows. Another rare form is the "ladder" field pattern, a bundle of short fields between two parallel canals, found in the Pomata region. These also probably represent a social structure of land tenure similar to the more common "checkerboard" pattern (Erickson 1988a). These systems resemble the present-day land tenure that is commonly organized as long, thin strips of land extending from hillcrests across the pampas to the lake edge, sometimes extending out from the lake edge into the *totorales* (cattails).

19. There is evidence that the local *ayllu* organization of irrigation agriculture in Cuzco was based on the form of the *ceque* model (Sherbondy 1982, 1987, 1992; Zuidema 1986).

20. This radial system of organization has been discussed for various pre-Columbian cultures, such as its presence in the Nasca lines (Aveni 1990), Inka irrigation (Sherbondy 1982, 1987, 1992; Zuidema 1986), and Inka settlement patterning (Hyslop 1990). Other, related but non-radial forms, have been documented (Urton 1992).

21. Dating of occupation mounds by surface collections is inadquate. There tends to be an overabundance of diagnostic late prehistoric ceramics on the surface, which masks the presence of occupation at earlier periods. Relating these mounds to the construction and use of the raised fields is even more difficult. Kolata (1986) has attempted to relate mounds and fields by associations of proximity in Koani Pampa. I have argued elsewhere (Erickson 1987, 1988a, 1992, n.d.b) that mounds and fields should be dated independently to establish contemporaneity. Kolata (1986, 1991) and Graffam (1989, 1990, 1992) have also used mounds that they argue are integrated into field systems for dating, although their interpretations often differ. Stanish (n.d.) has recently argued that mounds within the Juli Pampa may have been occupied only when the raised fields were in a state of abandonment.

22. Even though the raised fields were not directly dated during survey, Mathews and Albarracín (1990) assume that most of the fields are associated with, and thus are contemporaneous with, Tiwanaku IV and Tiwanaku V period sites. It is interesting that their maps (Mapas 2-7) show that the numbers of settlements increase in the raised field zones after Tiwanaku collapses. They note (1990:146) that some of the fields continued to be in use during the post-Tiwanaku, period but the map shows a much reduced area under cultivation. How they determined this reduction of field use from surface evidence is not clear.

23. A monograph presenting these excavation results is currently in preparation. Preliminary analysis is briefly summarized in Erickson (1988a-b).

24. Bertonio's 16th-century terms and Platt's (1987) study of the Aymara *ayllu* have been used by Graffam (1992:886) and Albarracín (n.d.) to support the presence of hierarchy in traditional *ayllu* organization.

25. There are many terms used in the literature for a variety of Andean institutions of labor mobilization. Some additional examples include *chuqu* (Graffam 1990:72), *washka-washka, tuma, uyari, rantin, turnapeón* (Fonseca 1974:87), and *voluntad, waje-waje, yanapi,* and *ayuda* (Mayer 1974:47). There is little agreement on precise definitions of these terms, and their use is highly variable in the Andean region.

26. Gelles (n.d.c) has recently argued that certain elements of the system of dual organization were imposed by the Inka on the farming populations of the Colca Valley as a means of organizing production, taxation, and expropriation of labor. According to Gelles, this system, combining

elements of both Inka and Spanish Colonial political economy, has been transformed over time into a local model of water management.

27. By "regular fields," I mean the fields currently used by Quechua and Aymara farmers in the Lake Titicaca Basin. These include dry fields on slopes and hills ringing the pampa and the *wachos*, or narrow sod lazy beds constructed for potato cultivation. These fields are prepared by wooden scratch plows pulled by teams of oxen, tractors, or the *chakitaqlla*. The use of irrigation is rare in Huatta.

28. Raised field experiments conducted in the southern Lake Titicaca Basin have recorded even high estimates of potato production using fertilizers (Kolata 1991).

29. Kolata states that "there seems to have been a massive agricultural collapse, probably brought on by the political disintegration of the Tiwanaku empire. After this time, the drained fields of the Pampa Koani were never reutilized" (1983:262), and that "the evident decline in human activity on the Pampa Koani after Tiwanaku V times was related to the disintegration of the Tiwanaku state, with the collapse of strong central authority inducing disruption of the formidable seasonal maintenance requirements of the field systems" (1986:753).

30. In a recent article, Graffam (1992) argues that the post-Tiwanaku, *ayllu*-based Pacajes polity relied on raised field agriculture as a means of subsidizing a large, pastoral herding component.

31. Doolittle (1990:3) has recognized that, "Studies that either compare ancient irrigation systems in their temporal contexts or emphasize the environmental factors responsible for the use of different systems fail to recognize the long-term and cumulative nature of technological changes. Carl O. Sauer's (1952:9) observation that 'Ideas must build upon ideas' seems to have been lost. For the most part, technological change involves degree rather than kind. Although changes in types of technology have never been uncommon, change in the nature of a particular kind of technology have been more typical."

This process is obvious in the evolution of raised fields in the Northern Titicaca basin, where earlier Initial Period and Early Horizon fields have wavelengths of 5m, whereby the later Late Intermediate Period fields have wavelengths of over 10m (Erickson 1987, 1988a). The fields are morphologically and structurally the same; the scale has simply changed over time. I do not mean to suggest here that agricultural landscapes were never formed rapidly or that states are incapable of implementing or drastically altering large scale production systems. Inka agricultural policies, such as that practiced for the establishment of agricultural colonies in Cochabamba (Wachtel 1982) or the reworking of production systems in the Mantaro Valley (D'Altroy 1992, Hastorf 1992), are prime examples of the state's role in redefining the Andean landscape.

REFERENCES

Adams, Robert McC. (1966) *The Evolution of Urban Society*. Chicago: Aldine.

Albarracín-Jordan, Juan V. (1992) *Prehispanic and Early Colonial Settlement in the Lower Tiwanaku Valley, Bolivia*. Ph.D. Dissertation, Southern Methodist University.

———— (n.d.) "The Tiwanaku Settlement System: The Integration of Ayllu-like Nested Hierarchies in the Lower Tiwanaku Valley." Manuscript.

Albarracín-Jordan, Juan V., and James E. Mathews (1990) *Asentamientos prehispánicos del Valle de Tiwanaku, Vol. 1 (Prehispanic Settlements in the Tiwanaku Valley, Vol. 1)*. La Paz: Producciones CIMA.

Alberti, Giorgio, and Enrique Mayer (1974a) "Reciprocidad andina: ayer y hoy" ("Andean Reciprocity: Yesterday and Today"). Pp. 13-38 in G. Alberti and E. Mayer (eds.), 1974b, *infra*.

———— (1974b) *Reciprocidad e intercambio en los Andes peruanos (Reciprocity and Exchange in the Peruvian Andes)*. Lima: Instituto de Estudios Peruanos.

Allen, Catherine (1988) *The Hold Life Has: Coca and the Cultural Identity of an Andean Community*. Washington, DC: Smithsonian Institute Press.

Armillas, Pedro (1971) "Gardens on Swamps." *Science* 174:653-661.

Aveni, Anthony, ed. (1990) *The Lines of Nasca*. Philadelphia: American Philosophical Society.

Bauer, Brian (1992) "The Royal Roads of the Incas: An Analysis of the *ceques* of Collasuyu, Cuzco." *Latin American Antiquity* 3:183-205.

Bermann, Marc P. (1990) *Prehispanic Household and Empire at Lukurmata, Bolivia*. Ph.D. dissertation, University of Michigan.

Boehm de Lameiras, Brigitte (1988) "Subsistence, Social Control of Resources, and the Development of Complex Society in the Valley of Mexico." Pp. 91-102 in John Gledhill, Barbara Bender & Mogens Trolle Larson (eds.) *State and Society: The Emergence and Development of Social Hierarchy and Political Centralization*. London: Unwin Hyman.

Boserup, Ester (1965) *The Conditions of Agricultural Growth: The Economics of Population Pressure*. Chicago: Aldine.

Brinkmeier, Daniel A. (1985) *A Plan for Disseminating Information about Traditional Agriculture to Indigenous Farmers in the Department of Puno, Peru*. M.A. Thesis, Iowa State University, Ames.

Bronson, Bennett (1972) "Farm Labor and the Evolution of Food Production." Pp. 190-218 in Brian Spooner (ed.) *Population Growth: Anthropological Implications*. Cambridge, MA: M.I.T. Press.

_____ (1975) "The Earliest Farming: Demography as Cause and Consequence." Pp. 52-78 in Stephen Polgar (ed.) *Population Ecology and Social Evolution*. The Hague: Mouton.

_____ (1978) "Angkor, Anuradhapura, Prambanan, Tikal: Maya Subsistence in an Asian Perspective." Pp. 255-300 in Peter Harrison & B. L. Turner II (eds.), 1978, *infra*.

Brookfield, Harold C. (1986) "Intensification Revisited." *Pacific Viewpoint* 25:15-44. Wellington.

Browman, David L. (1981) "New Light on Andean Tiwanaku." *American Scientist* 64(4): 408-419.

Brumfiel, Elizabeth M. (1991) "Agricultural Development and Class Stratification in the Southern Valley of Mexico." Pp. 43-62 in H. Harvey (ed.) *Land and Politics in the Valley of Mexico*. Albuquerque: University of New Mexico Press.

Butzer, Karl (1977) *Early Hydraulic Civilization in Egypt: A Study in Cultural Ecology*. Chicago: University of Chicago Press.

Chambers, Robert (1980) "Basic Concepts in the Organization of Irrigation." Pp. 28-50 in E. Walter Coward (ed.), 1980b, *infra*.

Conrad, Geoffry, and Arthur Demarest (1984) *Religion and Empire: The Dynamics of Aztec and Inca Expansionism*. Cambridge, ENG: Cambridge University Press.

Coward, E. Walter, Jr. (1976) "Indigenous Organization, Bureaucracy, and Development: The Case of Irrigation." *Journal of Development Studies* 13:92-105.

_____ (1979) "Principles of Social Organization in an Indigenous Irrigation System." *Human Organization* 38:28-36.

_____ (1980a) "Irrigation Development: Institutional and Organizational Issues." Pp. 15-27 in E. Walter Coward, Jr. (ed.), 1980b, *infra*.

_____, ed. (1980b) *Irrigation and Agricultural Development in Asia: Perspectives from the Social Sciences*. Ithaca, NY: Cornell University Press.

Crumley, Carole L. (1987) "A Dialectical Critique of Hierarchy." Pp. 155-169 in Thomas C. Patterson & Christine W. Gailey (eds.) *Power Relations and State Formation*. Washington, DC: American Anthropological Association.

D'Altroy, Terence N. (1992) *Provincial Power of the Inka Empire*. Washington, DC: Smithsonian Institute Press.

Darch, J. P., ed. (1983) *Drained Field Agriculture in Central and South America*. Oxford: British Archaeological Reports, International Series, No. 189.

Denevan, William M. (1970) "Aboriginal Drained-Field Cultivation in the Americas." *Science* 169:647-654.

———— (1982) "Hydraulic Agriculture in the American Tropics: Forms, Measures, and Recent Research." Pp. 181-203 in Kent V. Flannery (ed.) *Maya Subsistence*. New York: Academic Press.

Denevan, William M., Kent Mathewson, and Gregory Knapp, eds. (1987) *Pre-Hispanic Agricultural Fields in the Andean Region*. Oxford: British Archaeological Reports, International Series, No. 359, Parts i and ii.

Denevan, William M., and B. L. Turner II (1974) "Forms, Functions, and Associations of Raised Fields in the Old World Tropics." *Journal of Tropical Geography* 39:24-33.

———— (1985) "Prehistoric Manipulation of Wetlands in the Americas: A Raised Field Perspective." Pp. 11-30 in Ian Farrington (ed.), 1985, *infra*.

Donkin, R. A. (1979) *Agricultural Terracing in the Aboriginal New World*. Tucson: University of Arizona Press.

Doolittle, William (1984) "Agricultural Change as Incremental Process." *Annals of the Association of American Geographers* 74:124-137.

———— (1990) *Canal Irrigation in Prehistoric Mexico: The Sequence of Technological Change*. Austin: University of Texas Press.

Downing, T. and M. Gibson (1974a) "Preface." Pp. ix-xi in T. Downing & M. Gibson (eds.), 1974b, *infra*.

————, eds. (1974b) *Irrigation's Impact on Society*. Tucson: University of Arizona Press.

Earle, Timothy (1978) *Economic and Social Organization of a Complex Chiefdom: The Halelea District, Kaua'i, Hawaii*. Ann Arbor: University of Michigan, Museum of Anthropology.

Erasmus, Charles J. (1965) "Monument Building: Some Field Experiments." *Southwestern Journal of Anthropology* 21:277-301.

Erickson, Clark L. (1985) "Applications of Prehistoric Andean Technology: Experiments in Raised Field Agriculture, Huatta, Lake Titicaca, Peru, 1981-1983." Pp. 209-232 in Ian Farrington (ed.), 1985, *infra*.

———— (1987) "The Dating of Raised Field Agriculture in the Lake Titicaca Basin of Peru." Pp. 373-383 in William M. Denevan, Kent Mathewson & Gregory Knapp (eds.), 1987, *supra*.

———— (1988a) *An Archaeological Investigation of Raised Field Agriculture in the Lake Titicaca Basin of Peru*. Ph.D. dissertation, University of Illinois, Urbana-Champaign.

———— (1988b) "Raised Field Agriculture in the Lake Titicaca Basin: Putting Ancient Andean Agriculture Back to Work." *Expedition* 30(2):8-16.

———— (1992a) "Prehistoric Landscape Management in the Andean Highlands: Raised Field Agriculture and Its Environmental Impact." *Population and Environment* 13(4):285-300.

———— (1992b) "Applied Archaeology and Rural Development: Archaeology's Potential Contribution to the Future." *Journal of the Steward Anthropological Society* 20:1/2: 1-16.

———— (n.d) "Methodological Considerations in the Study of Ancient Andean Field Systems." Forthcoming in Kathryn L. Gleason & Naomi Miller (eds.) *The Archaeology of Garden and Field*. Philadelphia: University of Pennsylvania Press.

Erickson, Clark L., and Daniel A. Brinkmeier (n.d.) *Raised Field Rehabilitation Projects in the Northern Lake Titicaca Basin*. Manuscript, 1991.

Erickson, Clark L., and Kay L. Candler (1989) "Raised Fields and Sustainable Agriculture in the Lake Titicaca Basin." Pp. 230-248 in John Browder (ed.) *Fragile Lands of Latin America: Strategies for Sustainable Development*. Boulder, CO: Westview Press.

Farrington, Ian, ed. (1985) *Prehistoric Intensive Agriculture in the Tropics*. Oxford: British Archaeological Reports, International Series, No. 232, Part i and ii.

Fernea, R. A. (1970) *Shaykh and Effendi: Changing Patterns of Authority among the El Shabana of Southern Iraq.* Cambridge, MA: Harvard University Press.

Flannery, Kent V. (1972) "The Cultural Evolution of Civilizations." *Annual Review of Ecology and Systematics* 4:399-426.

Fonseca Martel, César (1974) "Modalidades de la minka" ("Types of Minka"). Pp. 86-109 in Giorgio Alberti & Enrique Mayer (eds.), 1974b, *supra.*

Garaycochea Z., Ignacio (1986a) *Rehabilitación de camellones en la comunidad campesina de Huatta, Puno (Rehabilitation of Raised Fields in the Peasant Community of Huatta, Puno).* Agricultural Engineering thesis, Department of Agronomy, Universidad Nacional del Altiplano, Puno, Peru.

_____ (1986b) "Potencial agrícola de los camellones en el *altiplano* Puneño" ("Agricultural Potential of the Raised Fields in the Puno Plateau"). Pp. 241-251 in Carlos de la Torre & Manuel Burga (eds.) *Andenes y camellones en el Perú andino: Historia, presente y futuro (Terraces and Raised Fields in Andean Peru: History, Present and Future).* Lima: Consejo Nacional de Ciencia y Tecnología.

_____ (1987) "Agricultural Experiments in Raised Fields in the Titicaca Basin, Peru: Preliminary Considerations." Pp. 385-398 in William M. Denevan, Kent Mathewson & Gregory Knapp (eds.), 1987, *supra.*

_____ (1988) *Community Based Organisations and Rural Development with a Particular Reference to Andean Peasant Communities.* M.A. Thesis, Agricultural Extension and Rural Development Centre, Reading University, Reading, England.

Geertz, Clifford (1980) *Negara.* Princeton, NJ: Princeton University Press.

Gelles, Paul H. (1986) "Sociedades hidráulicas en los Andes: Algunas perspectivas desde Huarochirí" ("Hydraulic Societies in the Andes: Some Perspectives from Huarochirí"). Allpanchis 27 (año 18):99-148 (Cuzco).

_____ (1990) *Channels of Power, Fields of Contention: The Politics and Ideology of Irrigation in an Andean Peasant Community.* Ph.D. dissertation, Harvard University.

_____ (n.d.a) "Ecology and Ritual: The Cultural Construction of Water Availability in Cabanaconde (Caylloma, Arequipa), Peru." Paper presented before the 47th International Congress of Americanists, New Orleans, 1991.

_____ (n.d.b) "Channels of Power, Fields of Contention: The Politics of Irrigation and Land Recovery in an Andean Peasant Community." Forthcoming in David Guillet & William P. Mitchell (eds.) *Irrigation at High Altitudes: Socio-political Aspects of Water Control in the Andes.* Washington, DC: American Anthropological Association.

_____ (n.d.c) "Equilibrium and Extraction: Dual Organization in the Andes." Manuscript.

Glick, Thomas F. (1970) *Irrigation and Society in Medieval Valencia.* Cambridge, MA: Harvard University Press.

Golson, Jack (1977) "No Room at the Top: Agricultural Intensification in the New Guinea Highlands." Pp. 602-638 in J. Allen, J. Golson & Rhys Jones (eds.) *Sunda and Sahul.* New York: Academic Press.

Gómez-Pompa, Arturo, Héctor Luis Morales, Epifanio Jiménez Avila, and Julio Jiménez Avila (1982) "Experiences in Traditional Hydraulic Agriculture." Pp. 327-342 in Kent V. Flannery (ed.) *Maya Subsistence.* New York: Academic Press.

Gorecki, Pawel P. (1982) *Ethnoarchaeology at Kuk: Problems in Site Formation Processes.* Ph.D. dissertation, Department of Anthropology, University of Sydney.

Grace, Barry (1983) *The Climate of the Altiplano, Department of Puno.* Puno: Canadian International Development Agency.

Graffam, Gray (1989) "Back across the Great Divide: The Pakaq Señorio and Raised Field Agriculture." Pp. 33-50 in Virginia J. Vitzthum (ed.) *Multidisciplinary Studies in Andean Anthropology.* Ann Arbor: Michigan Discussions in Anthropology, 8 (Fall 1988).

———— (1990) *Raised Fields without Bureaucracy: An Archaeological Examination of Intensive Wetland Cultivation in the Pampa Koani Zone, Lake Titicaca, Bolivia.* Ph.D. dissertation, University of Toronto.

———— (1992) "Beyond State Collapse: Raised Fields and Pastoral Finance in the South Andes." *American Anthropologist* 94:882-904.

Gray, Robert F. (1963) *The Sonjo of Tanganyika: An Anthropological Study of an Irrigation-Based Society.* London: Oxford University Press.

Guillet, David (1981) "Land Tenure, Agricultural Regime, and Ecological Zone in the Central Andes." *American Ethnologist* 8:139-156.

———— (1987) "Terracing and Irrigation in the Peruvian Highlands." *Current Anthropology* 28:331-348.

———— (1992) *Covering Ground: Communal Water Management and the State in the Peruvian Highlands.* Ann Arbor: University of Michigan Press.

Harris, David (1978) "The Agricultural Foundations of the Lowland Maya Civilization: A Critique." Pp. 301-324 in Peter Harrison & B. L. Turner II (eds.), 1978, *infra.*

Harrison, Peter D., and B. L. Turner II, eds. (1978) *Pre-Hispanic Maya Agriculture.* Albuquerque: University of New Mexico Press.

Hastings, Charles, and Michael Moseley (1975) "The Adobes of Huaca del Sol and Huaca de la Luna." *American Antiquity* 40:196-203.

Hastorf, Christine (1992) *Agriculture at the Onset of Political Inequality.* Cambridge, ENG: Cambridge University Press.

Heider, Karl (1970) *The Dugam Dani: A Papuan Culture in the Highlands of West New Guinea.* New York: Wenner-Gren Foundation, Viking Fund Publications in Anthropology, No. 49.

Hunt, Robert C. (1988) "Size and the Structure of Authority in Canal Irrigation Systems." *Journal of Anthropological Research* 44:325-355.

Hunt, Eva, and Robert Hunt (1974) "Irrigation, Conflict and Politics: A Mexican Case." Pp. 127-158 in T. Downing & M. Gibson (eds.), 1974b, *supra.*

Hunt, Robert, and Eva Hunt (1976) "Canal Irrigation and Local Social Organization." *Current Anthropology* 17:389-411.

Hyslop, John (1990) *Inka Settlement Planning.* Austin: University of Texas Press.

Isbell, Billie Jean (1985) *To Defend Ourselves: Ecology and Ritual in an Andean Village* (2nd ed.). Propect Heights, IL: Waveland Press.

Julien, Catherine J. (1983) *Hatuncolla: A View of Inca Rule from the Lake Titicaca Region.* Berkeley: University of California Press.

Keatinge, Richard (1988) "Preface." Pp. xii-xvii in his (ed.) *Peruvian Prehistory.* Cambridge, ENG: Cambridge University Press.

Kelly, William W. (1983) "Concepts in the Anthropological Study of Irrigation." *American Anthropologist* 85:880-886.

Kolata, Alan L. (1983) "The South Andes." Pp. 241-286 in Jesse D. Jennings (ed.) *Ancient South Americans.* San Francisco: W. H. Freeman.

———— (1986) "The Agricultural Foundations of the Tiwanaku State: A View from the Heartland." *American Antiquity* 51:748-762.

———— (1987) "Tiwanaku and Its Hinterland." *Archaeology* 40(1):36-41.

————, ed. (1989) *Arqueología de Luqurmata, T. 2, La tecnología y organización de la producción agrícola en el estado de Tiwanaku (Archaeology of Luqurmata, Vol. 2, The Technology and Organization of Agricultural Production in the State of Tiwanaku).* La Paz: Instituto Nacional de Arqueología and Ediciones Puna Punku.

———— (1991) "The Technology and Organization of Agricultural Production in the Tiwanaku State." *Latin American Antiquity* 2:99-125.

Kolata, Alan, and Gray Graffam (1989) "Los campos elevados de Lukurmata, Bolivia" ("The Raised Fields of Lukurmata, Bolivia"). Pp. 173-212 in Alan Kolata (ed.), 1989, *supra.*

Kolata, Alan L., and Charles Ortloff (1989) "Thermal Analysis of Tiwanaku Raised Field Systems in the Lake Titicaca Basin of Bolivia." *Journal of Archaeological Science* 16:233-262.

Kus, James (1980) "La agricultura estatal en la costa norte del Perú" ("State Agriculture on the North Coast of Peru"). *América Indígena* 40:713-729 (Mexico).

Lansing, J. Stephen (1987) "Balinese 'Water Temples' and the Management of Irrigation." *American Anthropologist* 89:326-341.

_____ (1991) *Priests and Programmers: Technologies of Power in the Engineered Landscape of Bali.* Princeton, NJ: Princeton University Press.

Leach, Edmund (1959) "Hydraulic Society in Ceylon." *Past and Present* 15:2-26.

Leaf, Murray J. (1992) "Irrigation and Authority in Rajasthan." *Ethnology* 31:115-132.

Lees, Susan (1986) "Coping with Bureaucracy: Survival Strategies in Irrigated Agriculture." *American Anthropologist* 88:611-622.

Lennon, Thomas J. (1982) *Raised Fields of Lake Titicaca, Peru: A Pre-Hispanic Water Management System.* Ph.D. dissertation, University of Colorado, Boulder.

_____ (1983) "Pattern Analysis of Prehispanic Raised Fields of Lake Titicaca, Peru." Pp. 183-200 in J. P. Darch (ed.), 1983, *supra.*

Lewis, Henry T. (1991) *Ilocano Irrigation: The Corporate Resolution.* Honolulu: University of Hawaii Press.

Malpass, Michael (1987) "Prehistoric Agricultural Terracing at Chijra in the Colca Valley, Peru." Pp. 45-66 in William M. Denevan, Kent Mathewson & Gregory Knapp (eds.), 1987, *supra.*

Marcus, Joyce (1983) "Lowland Maya Archaeology at the Crossroads." *American Antiquity* 48:454-488.

Matheny, Ray T. (1978) "Northern Maya Lowland Water-Control Systems." Pp. 185-210 in Peter Harrison & B. L. Turner (eds.), 1987, *supra.*

Matheny, Ray T., and Denise Garr (1983) "Variation in Prehispanic Agricultural Systems of the New World." *Annual Review of Anthropology* 12:79-103.

Mathews, James E. (n.d.a) "Preliminary Investigations of Prehistoric Raised Fields in the Tiwanaku Mid-Valley, Tiwanaku, Bolivia." Paper presented before the 17th Annual Midwest Conference on Andean and Amazonian Archaeology and Ethnohistory, Mount Pleasant, MI, 1991.

_____ (n.d.b) "Raised Field Excavations in the Middle Tiwanaku Valley, Bolivia: Implications for Chronology of Raised Field Agriculture." Manuscript.

Mayer, Enrique (1974) "Las reglas del juego en la reciprocidad andina" ("The Rules of the Game in Andean Reciprocity"). Pp. 37-65 in Giorgio Alberti & Enrique Mayer (eds.), 1974b, *supra.*

_____ (1977) "Beyond the Nuclear Family." Pp. 67-80 in Ralph Bolton & Enrique Mayer (eds.) *Andean Marriage and Kinship.* Washington, DC: American Anthropological Association, Special Publication No. 7.

Millon, Rene (1962) "Variations in Social Response to the Practice of Irrigation Agriculture." Pp. 56-88 in Richard Woodbury (ed.) *Civilizations in Desert Lands.* Salt Lake City: University of Utah Anthropological Papers, No. 62.

Mitchell, William P. (1973) "The Hydraulic Hypothesis: A Reappraisal." *Current Anthropology* 14:532-534.

_____ (1976) "Irrigation and Community in the Central Peruvian Highlands." *American Anthropologist* 78:25-44.

_____ (1977) "Irrigation Farming in the Andes: Evolutionary Implications." Pp. 36-59 in Rhoda Halperin & James Dow (eds.) *Peasant Livelihood: Studies in Economic Anthropology and Cultural Ecology.* New York: St. Martin's Press.

————— (1991) *Peasants on the Edge: The Struggle for Survival and the Transformation of Social and Religious Organization in the Andes.* Austin: University of Texas Press.

Montmollin, Oliver de (1987) "Temporal and Social Scales in Prehispanic Mesoamerica." *Archaeological Review from Cambridge* 6(1):51-61.

Moore, Jerry D. (1988) "Prehistoric Raised Field Agriculture in the Casma Valley, Peru." *Journal of Field Archaeology* 15:265-276.

Moseley, Michael (1992) *The Incas and Their Ancestors: The Archaeology of Peru.* London: Thames & Hudson.

Moseley, M. E., R. A. Feldman, and C. R. Ortloff (1981) "Living with Crisis: Human Perception of Process and Time." Pp. 231-267 in M. Nitecki (ed.) *Biotic Crisis in Ecological and Evolutionary Time.* New York: Academic Press.

Murra, John V. (1980) *The Economic Organization of the Inca State, Suppl. 1, Research in Economic Anthropology.* Greenwich, CT: JAI Press.

Muse, Michael, and Fausto Quintero (1987) "Experimentos de reactivación de campos elevados del Peñón del Río, Guayas, Ecuador" ("Experiments in Reactivating the Raised Fields of Peñón del Río, Guayas, Ecuador"). Pp. 249-266 in W. M. Denevan, K. Mathewson & G. Knapp (eds.), 1987, *supra.*

Netherly, Patricia (1984) "The Management of Late Andean Irrigation Systems on the North Coast of Peru." *American Antiquity* 49:227 254.

Netting, Robert McC. (1974) "The System Nobody Knows: Village Irrigation in the Swiss Alps." Pp. 67-76 in T. Downing & M. Gibson (eds.), 1974b, *supra.*

————— (1990) "Population, Permanent Agriculture, and Polities: Unpacking the Evolutionary Portmanteau." Pp. 21-61 in Steadman Upham (ed.) *The Evolution of Political Systems: Sociopolitics in Small-Scale Sedentary Societies.* Cambridge, ENG: Cambridge University Press.

Orlove, Benjamen, and Ricardo Godoy (1986) "Sectorial Fallowing Systems in the Central Andes." *Journal of Ethnobiology* 6:269-304.

Ortloff, C., and A. Kolata (1989) "Hydraulic Analysis of Tiwanaku Aqueduct Structures at Lukurmata and Pajchiri, Bolivia." *Journal of Archaeological Science* 16:513-535.

Ortloff, C. R., M. E. Moseley, and R. A. Feldman (1982) "Hydraulic Engineering Aspects of the Chimu Chicama-Moche Intervalley Canal." *American Antiquity* 47:572-595.

Palerm, Angel (1955) "The Agricultural Basis of Urban Civilizations in Mesoamerica." Pp. 28-42 in Julian Steward (ed.), 1955, *infra.*

————— (1973) *Obras hidráulicas prehispánicas en el sistema lacustre del Valle de México (Prehispanic Hydraulic Works in the Lake System of the Valley of Mexico).* Mexico, DF: Instituto Nacional de Antropología e Historia.

Park, Thomas (1992) "Early Trends towards Class Stratication: Chaos, Common Property, and Flood Recession Agriculture." *American Anthropologist* 94:90-117.

Parsons, James, and William Denevan (1967) "Pre-Columbian Ridged Fields in New World Archaeology." *Scientific American* 217(1):92-100.

Parsons, Jeffrey (1991) "Political Implications of Prehispanic Chinampa Agriculture in the Valley of Mexico." Pp. 17-41 in H. Harvey (ed.) *Land and Politics in the Valley of Mexico.* Albuquerque: University of New Mexico Press.

Patterson, Thomas (1992) *The Inca Empire: The Formation and Disintegration of a Pre-Capitalist State.* Oxford, ENG: Berg.

Platt, Tristan (1987) "Of Mirrors and Maize: The Concept of *yanantin* among the Macha of Bolivia." pp. 228-259 in John Murra, Nathan Wachtel & Jacques Revel (eds.) *Anthropological History of Andean Polities.* Cambridge, ENG: Cambridge University Press.

Pohl, Mary D. (1990a) "The Rio Hondo Project in Northern Belize." Pp. 1-19 in Mary Pohl (ed.), 1990b, *infra.*

_____, ed. (1990b) *Ancient Maya Agriculture: Excavations on Albion Island, Northern Belize.* Boulder, CO: Westview Press.

Pospisil, Leopold (1963) *Kapauku Papuan Economy.* New Haven, CT: Yale Publications in Anthropology, No. 67.

Price, Barbara (1971) "Prehispanic Irrigation Agriculture in Nuclear America." *Latin American Research Review* 6:3-60.

Puleston, Dennis E. (1977a) "Experiments in Prehistoric Raised Field Agriculture: Learning from the Past." *Journal of Belizan Affairs* 5:36-43.

_____ (1977b) "The Art and Archaeology of Hydraulic Agriculture in the Maya Lowlands." Pp. 449-467 in Norman Hammond (ed.) *Social Processes in Maya Prehistory.* New York: Academic Press.

Ramos, Claudio (1986) "Evaluación y rehabilitación de camellones o 'kurus' en Asillo" ("Evaluation and Rehabilitation of Raised Fields, or 'kurus,' in Asillo"). *Allpanchis* 27(año 18):239-284 (Cuzco).

_____ (1990) *Rehabilitación, uso y manejo de camellones: propuesta técnica (Rehabilitation, Use and Management of Raised Fields: Technical Proposal).* Lima: Programa de Rehabilitación y Uso de Waru-Waru, Centro Canadiense de Estudios y Cooperación Internacional-Centro de Communicación Audiovisual para la Educación Popular.

Rivera Sundt, Oswaldo (1989) "Una tecnología que viene del pasado" ("A Technology That Comes from the Past"). *Anales del Seminario de Desarollo Rural*, Serie Documentos 4-1-119-90:60-91 (La Paz).

Sanders, William T., and Barbara Price (1968) *Mesoamerica: The Evolution of a Civilization.* New York: Random House.

Sanders, William T., Jeffrey R. Parsons, and Robert Santley (1979) *The Basin of Mexico: The Cultural Ecology of a Civilization.* New York: Academic Press.

Sauer, Carl (1952) *Agricultural Origins and Dispersals: The Domestication of Animals and Foodstuffs.* New York: American Geographical Society.

Scarborough, Vernon L. (1991) "Water Managment Adaptations in Non-Industrial Complex Societies: An Archaeological Perspective." Pp. 101-145 in Michael Schiffer (ed.) *Archaeological Method and Theory, Vol. 3.* Tucson: University of Arizona Press.

Seligmann, Linda, and Stephen Bunker (1986) "Organización social y visión ecológica de un sistema de riego andino" ("Social Organization and Ecological View of an Andean Irrigation System"). *Allpanchis* 27(año 18):149-179 (Cuzco).

Serpenti, L. M. (1965) *Cultivators of the Swamps: Social Structure and Horticulture in a New Guinea Society.* Assen: Royal van Gorlum.

Sherbondy, Jeanette (1982) *The Canal Systems of Hanan Cuzco.* Ph.D. dissertation, University of Illinois, Champaign-Urbana.

_____ (1987) "Organización hidráulica y poder en el Cuzco de los Incas" ("Hydraulic Organization and Power in Inca Cuzco"). *Revista Española de Antropología Americana* 17:1117-153.

_____ (1992) "Water Ideology in Inca Ethnogenesis." Pp. 47-66 in Robert Dover, Katherine Seibold & John McDowell (eds.) *Andean Cosmologies through Time: Persistence and Emergence.* Bloomington: Indiana University Press.

Siemans, Alfred H. (1983) "Modelling Pre-Hispanic Hydroagriculture on Levee Backslopes in Northern Veracruz, Mexico." Pp. 27-54 in Janice Darch (ed.), 1983, *supra.*

_____ (1989) *Tierra Configurada (Configurated Land).* Mexico, DF: Consejo para la Cultura y las Artes.

Smith, Clifford T., William M. Denevan, and Patrick Hamilton (1968) "Ancient Ridged Fields in the Region of Lake Titicaca." *The Geographical Journal* 134:353-367.

Spooner, Brian (1974) "Irrigation and Society: The Iranian Plateau." Pp. 43-57 in T. Downing & M. Gibson (eds.), 1974b, *supra.*

Stanish, Charles (1992) *Ancient Andean Political Economy*. Austin: University of Texas Press.
———— (n.d.) "A Regional Settlement Perspective on Prehispanic Raised Field Agriculture in the Titicaca Basin." Manuscript.
Steward, J., ed. (1955) *Irrigation Civilizations: A Comparative Study*. Washington DC: Pan American Union, Social Science Monograph No. 1.
Treacy, John M. (1989a) "Agricultural Terracing in the Colca Valley: The Promises and Problems on an Ancient Technology." Pp. 209-229 in John Browder (ed.) *Fragile Lands of Latin America: Strategies for Sustainable Development*. Boulder, CO: Westview Press.
———— (1989b) *The Fields of Corporaque: Agricultural Terracing and Water Management in the Colca Valley, Arequipa, Peru*. Ph.D. dissertation, University of Wisconsin, Madison.
Turner, B. L. II (1983) "Constructional Inputs for Major Agrosystems of the Ancient Maya." Pp. 11-26 in J. P. Darch (ed.), 1983, *supra*.
Turner, B. L. II, and Peter D. Harrison (1978) "Implications from Agriculture for Maya Prehistory." Pp. 337-374 in Peter Harrison & B. L. Turner II (eds.), 1978, *supra*.
————, eds. (1983) *Pulltrouser Swamp: Ancient Maya Habitat, Agriculture, and Settlement in Northern Belize*. Austin: University of Texas Press.
Urton, Gary (1992) "Communalism and Differentiation in an Andean Community." Pp. 229-266 in Robert Dover, Katherine Seibold & John McDowell (eds.) *Andean Cosmologies through Time*. Bloomington: Indiana University Press.
Valeri, Valerio (1991) "Afterword." Pp. 134-144 in Stephen Lansing *Priests and Programmers: Technologies of Power in the Engineered Landscape of Bali*. Princeton, NJ: Princeton University Press.
Wachtel, Nathan (1982) "The *Mitimas* of the Cochabamba Valley: The Colonization Policy of Huayna Capac." Pp. 199-235 in George A. Collier, Renato I. Rosaldo & John D. Wirth (eds.) *The Inca and Aztec States, 1400-1800: Anthropology and History*. New York: Academic Press.
Wheatley, Paul (1971) *The Pivot of the Four Corners*. Chicago: Aldine.
Wilkerson, Jeffrey K. (1983) "So Green Like a Garden: Intensive Agriculture in Ancient Veracruz." Pp. 55-90 in Janice Darch (ed.), 1983, *supra*.
Wittfogel, Karl A. (1955) "Developmental Aspects of Hydraulic Societies." pp. 43-52 in Julian Steward (ed.), 1955, *supra*.
———— (1957) *Oriental Despotism*. New Haven, CT: Yale University Press.
———— (1972) "The Hydraulic Approach to Pre-Spanish Mesoamerica." Pp. 59-80 in Frederick Johnson (ed.) *The Prehistory of the Tehuacan Valley, Vol. 4, Chronology and Irrigation*. Austin: University of Texas Press.
Woodbury, Richard B. (1961) "A Re-Appraisal of Hohokam Irrigation." *American Anthropologist* 63:550-560.
Zipf, George K. (1949) *Human Behavior and the Principle of Least Effort*. Reading, MA: Addison-Wesley.
Zuidema, R. Tom (1986) "Inca Dynasty and Irrigation: Another Look at Andean Concepts of History." Pp. 177-200 in John Murra, Nathan Wachtel & Jacques Revel (eds.) *Anthropological History of Andean Polities*. Cambridge, ENG: Cambridge University Press.
———— (1990) *Inca Civilization in Cuzco*. Austin: University of Texas Press.

PART V

DISCUSSION

AMP, HH & OD: SOME COMMENTS

Barry L. Isaac

The interest of U.S. and Mexican anthropologists in the political-economic implications of prehistoric water management was largely stimulated by the work of Karl Wittfogel. In the U.S., this interest dates mostly from the publication of *Oriental Despotism* in 1957, although Julian Steward (1955a) had made important use of Wittfogel's earlier writings before then. In Mexico, considerable interest was awakened during the 1940s by Wittfogel's early work, which was disseminated there by Paul Kirchhoff and Pablo Martínez del Río (see Armillas 1987:150-151, Boehm de Lameiras 1986a:152; Palerm 1972:165-166). In U.S. anthropology, the resulting discussion centered around the politically safe question of the role of irrigation in the rise of the archaic state. Almost no one had the stomach for pursuing the larger Marxian tradition, and specifically the Asiatic Mode of Production (AMP), that was the springboard for Wittfogel's strictly intellectual concerns as well for as his anti-Communist/ anti-U.S.S.R. rantings. In contrast, Mexican anthropologists enjoyed greater intellectual freedom with respect to Marxism—living under a government that not long before had endorsed "socialist education"—although their energies were largely "absorbed by pragmatism: *indigenismo*, on the one hand, [and] reconstruction of archaeological sites for tourism and the pursuit of spectacular finds for the museums, on the other" (Boehm de Lameiras 1986a:153).

Research in Economic Anthropology, Suppl. 7, pages 429-471.
Copyright © 1993 by JAI Press Inc.
All rights of reproduction in any form reserved.
ISBN: 1-55938-646-0

In U.S. anthropology, interest in prehistoric water management waned once archaeologists succeeded in calling into question Wittfogel's specific linkage of irrigation and state origins, which also linked his ideas to Marxism. By the 1970s, when U.S. anthropologists at last became free to discuss Marx without fearing for their jobs or reputations, few were interested in exploring Wittfogel and prehistoric irrigation in the Marxian framework. Thus, while "mode of production" (including the "Asiatic" variety) became a tiresome cliché of the Marxian fad in both U.S. and Mexican anthropology during the late 1970s (see Palerm 1980:67ff.), its usage in the U.S. was largely ethnographic-synchronic; it was not widely reconnected there to the great evolutionary questions (including that of state origins) that had moved U.S. anthropology during the 1960s. In Mexico, in contrast, that reconnection was a salient aspect of archaeology and ethnology in the 1970s and 1980s (see, e.g., Medina et al. 1986; Bartra 1975, 1986; Palerm 1976)—probably because of the greater continuity of the Marxian scholarly tradition there.

The essays in the present volume attest a renewed interest, within U.S. archaeology, in the evolutionary implications of water management systems and in their relationship to the emergence and development of the state. The volume reflects our editorial preference for empirically-based studies instead of abstract theoretical treatises. Nevertheless, we feel that some discussion must be offered concerning the intellectual bases of the Hydraulic Hypothesis (HH), the Oriental Despotism (OD) idea, and the inextricably related matter of the Asiatic Mode of Production (AMP)—and that is the purpose of the following comments.

My comments are necessarily incomplete; I have not even attempted to compile a full or representative bibliography on the HH or the AMP, although the reader could easily do so for the European and U.S. literature by pursuing the citations in the sources indicated herein. The history and currency of these ideas in Mexico—where they perhaps have had greater anthropological impact than anywhere else in recent years—are covered by Brigitte Boehm de Lameiras (1985, 1986a, 1987:243ff., 1988:540ff.), Pedro Carrasco (1988:502-504), Andrés Fábregas (1987), and Angel Palerm (1972:164ff., 1973:9-11). Elsewhere, Vernon Scarborough (1991) has provided a comprehensive conceptual framework for the study of water management and an overview of archaeological work on it (also see his "Introduction" in this volume). Roger Bartra's (1986:53-78) compilation (with commentaries) of Marx and Engels' writings on the AMP was an important touchstone to keep this essay on track. My debt to Perry Anderson's (1974) essay is especially great; before discovering it, however, I had been inclined in its direction by Angel Palerm's essays (Palerm 1972, Palerm & Wolf 1972), although Palerm would not have endorsed many of the conclusions I drew from them. While drafting these remarks, I reread Manuel Gándara's (1986) brilliant essay; it presents the best short discussion of the AMP's theoretical adequacy that I have encountered to date.

Brendan O'Leary (1989) provides the most incisive critique of Karl Wittfogel's work. Some opposing views of the AMP are easily available in Bartra (1986), Dunn (1982), Krader (1975, 1987), and Medina (1986). The monumental books by Immanuel Wallerstein (1974) and Eric Wolf (1982) present or suggest some interesting alternative formulations.

ROOTS OF THE ASIATIC MODE OF PRODUCTION (AMP) IDEA

The general intellectual context of Karl Wittfogel's "Oriental Despotism" (OD) idea and his discussion of the evolutionary role of irrigation is Karl Marx's idea of the Asiatic Mode of Production (AMP) as a societal type or stage in socioeconomic evolution. In the 1859 "Preface" to his *A Contribution to the Critique of Political Economy*, Marx wrote: "In broad outline, the Asiatic, ancient, feudal and modern bourgeois modes of production may be designated as epochs marking progress in the economic development of society" (Marx 1977:21). As Timothy Brook (1989a:3) points out, "Marx never provided a definition of the [AMP] concept." Indeed, the notion of "mode of production" itself—quite apart from its Asiatic variety—has always presented difficulties of both definition and operationalization (see Palerm 1980:69-75, Gándara 1986:44-47). Most generally speaking, "mode of production" refers to "the relationships between people which arise in the course of the production of material goods" (Dunn 1982:5). In class-stratified societies, the mode of production includes such matters as the legal aspects of the ownership of productive property and the means of elite appropriation of "surplus product" from the immediate producers (ibid.). The definition of the AMP itself will emerge in the following discussion.

The European idea that Asian societies are fundamentally different from (and politically inferior to) anything found in Europe goes back to classical Greek times. As Brook (1989a:4) writes, "For Hippocrates [born 460 B.C.] and Aristotle [born 384 B.C.], the world divided at the Dardanelles: civilization lay to the west, and barbarism, a world of despotic potentates and servile subjects languishing in tropical lassitude, lay to the east." In more sophisticated or intellectualized form, this notion persists down to the present day in both the popular and intellectual subcultures of Europe and the Americas. It was very much part of the 19th-century European milieu in which Marx lived.

The intellectual lineage of the "Oriental Despotism" (OD) and AMP ideas is spelled out by Bartra (1986:21-42), Krader (1975), and Anderson (1974:462-472). This latter specifies 10 components to the AMP/OD constellation inherited by Marx from his predecessors of the 17th-19th centuries. With the exception of the ninth trait (torrid climatic environment), they are still represented—in various combinations and magnitudes or priorities—in our contemporary models of the AMP (see Palerm 1972:97-98, Brook 1989a:10-11; cf. Bartra 1975:87-89). The 10 components (Anderson 1974:472) are:

(1)   State property [ownership] of land
(2)   Lack of juridical restraints
(3)   Religious substitution for law
(4)   Absence of hereditary [landowning] nobility
(5)   Servile social equality
(6)   Isolated village communities
(7)   Agrarian predominance over industry
(8)   Public hydraulic works
(9)   Torrid climatic environment
(10) Historical immutability

Montesquieu (1689-1755) had formulated the only general theory of OD as such, in his *De l'Espirit des Lois* (published in 1748), in which he included traits 1-5 and 9-10 (Anderson 1974:472; cf. Bartres 1986:24-25). Trait 7 was formulated by François Bernier (1625-1688), whose memoir on Mughal India greatly interested Marx. Trait 8 (public hydraulic works) was inserted by Adam Smith (1723-1790) and John Stuart Mill (1806-1873).

Georg Hegel (1770-1831), whose profound influence upon Marx is common knowledge, was responsible for Trait 6 (isolated village communities). Hegel also subscribed to Traits 5 (servile social equality) and 10 (historical immutability) (after Anderson 1974:472). These three traits were causally interrelated in both Hegel's and Marx's models of Oriental society, although for Marx "the absence of private property in land...was the first 'key' to the whole structure of the Asiatic mode of production"(Anderson 1974:482). Later, both Marx and Engels "reverted to the idea that the social basis of Oriental despotism was the self-sufficient [i.e., isolated] village community, with communal agrarian property" (Anderson 1974:483).

Owing to such "oscillations" in Marx's and Engels' writings, "no wholly consistent or systematic account of the 'Asiatic mode of production' can be derived from [them]...."(Anderson 1974:483). Gándara (1986:44) refers to this situation as the "exegesis problem": "it is unclear what would constitute...the 'official version' of the theory, or which are the texts that would be considered definitive...." The practical consequences are twofold: (1) each investigator must decide which of the attributes variously mentioned by Marx or Engels are crucial and assess their relative weights within the model, and (2) any other investigator can make an arguable case that the wrong attributes were chosen or their priorities were wrongly assigned. In short, it's rather like trying to interpret the Bible!

Nevertheless, Anderson (1974) is able to offer some general statements about Marx's views of Asian society (and OD) and the AMP. The first is that Marx's ideas about Asia remained "very close to the themes of traditional European commentary...." The continuity "is especially striking in Marx's repeated assertion of the stagnation and immutability of the Oriental world" (p. 476). The distinctive aspects of Marx's formulation involved novelties of synthesis and emphasis (cf. Bartra 1986:34). In this regard, Anderson (ibid.:476-477) writes:

> The first [innovation] was the notion that public irrigation works, necessitated by climatic aridity, were a basic determinant of centralized despotic states, with a monopoly of land, in Asia. This was, in effect, a fusion of three themes that had hitherto been relatively distinct—hydraulic agriculture (Smith), geographical destiny (Montesquieu), and state agrarian property (Bernier). [The] second [innovation]...was...the claim that the basic social cells on which oriental despotism was superimposed were self-sufficient village communities, embodying a union of domestic crafts and cultivation [from Hegel].... Marx...gave it a new and more prominent position within the general schema he had inherited.

Elsewhere, Anderson (ibid.:483) distills the following "fundamental elements" of "the archetypal Asian social formation" (i.e., the AMP) in Marx's thinking:

> the absence of private property in land, the presence of large-scale irrigation systems in agriculture, the existence of autarchic village communities combining crafts with tillage and communal ownership of the soil, the stagnation of passively rentier or bureaucratic cities, and the domination of a despotic state machine.... Between the self-reproducing villages 'below' and the hypertrophied state 'above', dwelt no intermediate forces. The impact of the State on the mosaic of villages beneath it was purely external and tributary; its consolidation or destruction alike left rural society untouched. The political history of the Orient was thus essentially cyclical: it contained no dynamic or cumulative development. The result was...secular inertia and immutability....

From Montesquieu's day onward, the OD idea was used polemically (cf. Bartra 1986:26). For more than two centuries, it served to argue the superiority of European society and culture (including its economy), and to rationalize European colonialism in Asia. In our own time, Wittfogel (1957, 1963) used it to argue against Communism. In all such polemical uses, the concept's ethnocentrism is palpable—even in the great Marx's own hands. Regarding Marx's "The British Rule in India" (in Feuer 1959:474-481, Marx 1951:21-29), Angel Palerm (1972:94) anguished:

> I wish I were capable of communicating the stupefaction I felt upon reading this article.... I came to doubt that Marx could have written such things. The article struck me as a defense of capitalist imperialism, made by a European chauvinist who with grave injustice attacked a great Oriental civilization. Later I was to encounter similar opinions in Marx, expressed with the same violent vigor and eloquence of a Biblical prophet, with reference to the conquest of Algeria by the French and the possibility of a German-Russian war. The majority of our New World [*criollo*] Marxists would feel very uncomfortable reading Marx

and Engels' searing opinions about Latin America with regard to the wars of the United States against Mexico.

The passages in Marx's "The British Rule in India" which probably elicited the most visceral reactions in Palerm are worth quoting. First, with respect to irrigation works in the East and the West, Marx wrote (in Feuer 1959:476, Marx 1951:24; emphasis mine):

> Climate and territorial conditions...constituted artificial irrigation by canals and waterworks the basis of Oriental agriculture.... This prime necessity of an economical and common use of water, which, in the Occident, drove private enterprise to voluntary association, as in Flanders and Italy, necessitated *in the Orient, where civilization was too low* and the territorial extent too vast to call into life voluntary association,... the centralizing power of government. Hence an economic function devolved upon all Asiatic government: the function of providing public works.

Of the relatively isolated and self-sufficient villages (the "village system"), Marx wrote (in Feuer 1959:480-481, Marx 1951:28-29):

> [W]e must not forget that these idyllic village communities...had always been the solid foundation of Oriental despotism, that they restrained the human mind within the smallest possible compass, making it the unresisting tool of superstition, enslaving it beneath traditional rules, depriving it of all grandeur and historical energies. We must not forget the barbarian egotism which, concentrating on some miserable patch of land, had quietly witnessed the ruin of empires, the perpetration of unspeakable cruelties, the massacre of the population of large towns.... We must not forget that this undignified, stagnatory, and vegetative life, that this passive sort of existence evoked on the other part, in contradistinction, wild, aimless, unbounded forces of destruction and rendered murder itself a religious rite in Hindustan. We must not forget that these little communities were contaminated by distinctions of caste, and by slavery, that they subjugated man to external circumstances instead of elevating man into the sovereign of circumstances, that they transformed a self-developing social state into never changing natural destiny, and thus brought about the brutalizing worship of nature, exhibiting its degradation in the fact that man, the sovereign of nature, fell down on his knees in adoration of Hanuman, the monkey, and Sabbala, the cow.... Can mankind fulfill its destiny without a fundamental revolution in the social state of Asia? If not, whatever may have been the crimes of England [in colonizing India], she was the unconscious tool of history in bringing about that revolution.

The fact that Marx also railed against the wars, class stratification, mind-numbing religion, etc., of Europe does not negate Palerm's accusation of ethnocentrism. Marx clearly regarded capitalism, with all the evils he perceived in it, as a higher evolutionary stage. After all, Marx was a Modern Man, an Urban-Industrial Man, who believed in Progress—"economic development," as it is known today. To him, Asia represented "stagnation" and resistance to industrially-based Progress; if it took British conquest and colonialism to bring Asia into the mainstream of historical Progress, so be it.

With the foregoing as background, we can now turn our attention to some concrete aspects of the AMP model. Specifically, we will examine the "village system," the nature of land tenure, the importance of hydraulic works, and the supposed cultural (including economic) stagnation. In each instance, I concentrate on the AMP's *empirical* rather than its *theoretical* adequacy (see Gándara 1986:42f.). In the more complicated matters, I have let Anderson (1974) be my guide, although this choice of counsel will be viewed through narrowed eyes by the AMP's firm adherents.

THE "VILLAGE SYSTEM"

India

Bartra (1986:61) includes "self-sufficient communities or villages" among the "three important aspects of the structure" of the AMP (also see Gellner 1988). More specifically, he delineates the following "internal characteristics" of the "village system": "collective ownership of the land, traditional union of agriculture and artisanry, isolation, relatively autonomous political organization and economic self-sufficiency." The combination of these traits causes "another of the characteristic traits of the Asiatic mode of production: stagnation or, rather, the great slowness of its evolution." To these traits, we should add "egalitarianism" (after Anderson 1974).

Anderson (1974:487-488) points out that Marx's model of the "village system" was founded "virtually entirely on his study of India" a century after the British conquest. Marx's model now seems highly inadequate for the historical Indian village, with regard to land ownership (see Neale 1957, 1973), internal stratification, and external contacts (see O'Leary 1989:299-302). Anderson (p. 488) writes:

> [T]here is no historical evidence that communal property ever existed in either Mughal or post-Mughal India. The English accounts on which Marx relied were the product of colonial mistakes and misinterpretations. Likewise, cultivation in common by villagers was a legend: tillage was always individual in the early modern epoch. Far from the Indian villages being egalitarian, moreover, they were always sharply divided into castes, and what co-possession of landed property did exist was confined to superior castes who exploited lower castes as tenant cultivators on it.

Naturally, Marx was aware of the hierarchical caste system in the Indian village and the general social and economic disabilities of the lower castes. We have seen that Marx (quoted above) once lamented the "distinctions of caste" in the Asiatic village. Elsewhere, however, "he virtually ignored the... Hindu caste system... altogether" (Anderson 1974:488). In fact, Marx could hardly have picked a worse example than rural India to represent the egalitarian production-consumption unit of the AMP.

Nor is the picture any better with reference to village isolation and political autonomy. Anderson (ibid.:489) is again unequivocal:

> [T]he rural villages of India were never in any real sense 'detached' from the State above them, or 'isolated' from its control.... Administratively..., Indian villages were always subordinated to the central State through its appointment of their headmen.

Furthermore, taxation was "mostly payable in cash or in commercial crops subsequently re-sold by the State" and was so heavy that it severely limited "even the 'economic' autarky of the humblest rural communities" (ibid.:489). We should note that Marx pictured the rural village as lacking in horizontal as well as vertical integration: "These small communities may vegetate independently, side by side, and within each the individual labors independently with his family...." (Marx 1964:70).

What about the "traditional union of agriculture and artisanry" (Bartra 1986:61) aimed at local consumption, a feature that Marx saw as providing a great measure of village economic self-sufficiency? Anderson (1974:489, n.11) writes:

> [I]t could be said that the only accurate element in Marx's image of Indian villages was their union of crafts and cultivation: but this trait was common to virtually any pre-industrial rural community in the world, whatever its mode of production. It revealed nothing specific about the Asian countryside. In India, moreover, it did not exclude considerable commodity exchange beyond the village, in addition to the domestic pattern of labour.

Anderson (ibid.:489-499) summarizes:

> The self-sufficiency, equality and isolation of the Indian village communities was thus always a myth; both the caste system within them and the State above them precluded either. The empirical falsity of Marx's image of the Indian village communities...could have been guessed from the theoretical contradiction which they introduced into the whole notion of the Asiatic mode of production. For the presence of a powerful, centralized State presupposes a developed class stratification [structure].... The combination of a strong, despotic state and egalitarian village communes is thus intrinsically improbable; politically, socially and economically they virtually exclude one another.

If the contradiction that Anderson points to were the only major weakness in the AMP concept, we could mitigate it simply by minimizing or abandoning the "village system" idea and, instead, emphasizing its counterpoint, as Krader (1987) has done. The result would be a very different concept from the one that has moved scholars and (in the U.S.S.R.) politicians in the key debates on the AMP concept, however. For it is the combination of these two traits, the village system and the state, that is "the heart of the matter. The...[associated] traits...—despotism, absence of private ownership in land, irrigation, etc.—are indeed connected with these two central features, as either their precondition or their consequence" (Gellner 1988:49).

Furthermore, we cannot get off the hook simply by retreating to a position of *relative* isolation and *relative* self-sufficiency for the AMP village. Modern studies of "peasant resistance to the state" would suggest that the AMP model stood causality on its head in this regard. In a nutshell, the suggestion would be that the extent of village striving for relative isolation and self-sufficiency is inversely related to the strength of the state. Where the state is strong and rapacious, the wise peasant (being essentially powerless against it under ordinary circumstances) withdraws into the greatest possible village self-sufficiency and, thus, the lowest possible chance of coming to the attention of the state's official agents or protected elites (see Colburn 1989; Isaac 1991:2-11; Scott 1985, 1989, 1990; Wolf 1957). A present-day example is afforded by parts of Africa in which peasants have withdrawn from cash-cropping and other outside involvements in order to escape the predations of state agents (see Azarya & Chazan 1987).

Of course, to the developmentalist who is out to promote Progress, such resistance to the state can be seen as rural stultification. In the writings of Marx and Engels (see Bartra 1986:53-78) there are hints of an idea that was certainly implicit in the thinking of their intellectual predecessors (see Anderson 1974:467ff.), namely, that horizontal and vertical social-political-economic integration was a positive feature facilitating (even denoting) Progress. Present-day U.S. "economic development" policy (and "development anthropology") is still founded on this notion (see Escobar 1991); in Mexico, regional (horizontal) and national (vertical) integration was official policy, unquestioned even (especially?) by anthropologists, until the 1970s (see Medina & García 1983/1986). With reference to the AMP, the implication is that village "isolation"—both horizontal (from other villages) and vertical (from higher administrative levels)—not only allowed but virtually necessitated the formation of a "despotic" state as the bearer of "civilization." In that framework, the Occident did not suffer such despotism because it had the advantage of a landed nobility to both buffer the power of the state and promote Progress (resulting in Capitalism). Of course, the root idea is that social stratification is "beneficial" or "functional" to society. This idea has had amazing resiliency in Western social science, even in anthropology, as Coupland (1988) and Gilman (1981) point out.

China

Perry Anderson (1974:520-549) handles the Chinese case in considerable detail, whereas I shall give it cursory treatment here because India, rather than China, was the inspiration for Marx and Engels' "village system" ideas. Like pre-British India, though, historical China violates several major features of the AMP model. In the first place, private rather than collective or state ownership of land was the norm—despite clan control in some times and places, and episodic state control or intervention in others (P. Anderson 1974:526-527, 539-540, 543, 546; also see Ke Changji 1989:51-54, 57-60; cf. Brook 1989a:18-20). Even if we accept that there was some kind of "communal" landownership during the first state period (Shang, 1750-1122 B.C.), it was simply a carryover from pre-state times; in fact, "in the process of the rise of the first Shang state there are detected no significant qualitative changes in its mode of subsistence or in its technology" (Sugiura 1986:65). Although the succeeding Zhou Dynasty (1122-221 B.C.) apparently instituted state control ("ownership") over farming land, the Warring States period thereof (450-221 B.C.) saw a "growing tendency towards [private] property in land" (ibid.:71; also see Ke Changji 1989)—at the very time, we should note, of the first great state-sponsored hydraulic works (Sugiura 1986:69). During the succeeding Han Dynasty (207 B.C.-A.D. 220), "China became a land of small, independent peasant farms"; despite occasional experiments with "socialism, landlordism, and communism," China subsequently (after Emperor Wu's time, 140-87 B.C.) "always returned fairly quickly to the small independent farm as the backbone of the rural economy" (E. Anderson 1989:141-142).

Second, the emergence of a landed gentry fairly early in Chinese state history meant both that the countryside was sharply stratified and that agrarian villages were not isolated from the hierarchy above them (P. Anderson 1974:525-527, 546). At least as early as the Warring States period (450-221 B.C.), there was "a growing inequality within the agrarian communities" which, along with "the growing tendency towards [private] property in land...led to a clear antagonism in relation to the means of production...." (Sugiura 1986:70, 71). Indeed, "from Wu's time [140-87 B.C.] on the rise of latifundia and landlordism became increasingly a problem" (E. Anderson 1989:141).

Third, during major sweeps of Chinese state history peasants were heavily taxed in money rather than in kind, which implies considerable market involvement (ibid.:525, 534). In fact, as long as 2,000 years ago, "the rural economy was so market-driven" that farmers "chose to live on small farms near cities, rather than getting more land in isolated regions" (E. Anderson 1989:137). By the early 20th century, and doubtless much earlier, the settlement pattern of rural China conformed to the market-determined, hexagonal lattice of Christallerian central-place theory (Skinner 1964/65).

Finally, village agricultural economy was highly dynamic, not "stagnant," over the centuries; sometimes the state promoted major agricultural change (E. Anderson 1989) but the "great advances in agricultural productivity...typically occurred from below, in phases of lessened fiscal and political pressure by the State on the peasantry...." (P. Anderson 1974:546; cf. E. Anderson 1989). Later, I will return to the issue of stagnation and will take up the hydraulic component of Chinese agriculture.

The Basin of Mexico

The earliest state formation in the Basin of Mexico, ca. 200 B.C.-0 at Teotihuacan, almost certainly entailed the obliteration or, at least, the severe reduction of the villages in the capital city's effective hinterland (see Parsons 1987:47-53, Kurtz 1987)—a phenomenon apparently present in some early Mesopotamian states, also (see Adams 1972:739). This means that "one of the central principles of the [AMP] theory falls: the relative persistence and immobility of the village communities that Marx mentions" (Gándara 1986:55). Furthermore, as Gándara (loc. cit.) points out, if the AMP is applicable to the 16th-century Aztec case (about which there is still much debate) but not to Teotihuacan, "this means that we are speaking of an historical moment 1,500 years after the moment of the rise of the state" as the starting point for the AMP in Central Mexico!

The 16th-century Aztec case is problematical with respect to the "village system" component of the AMP, though, for the settlement pattern of the Aztec heartland unmistakably exhibits a central-place hierarchy, which we would not find if rural communities were relatively self-sufficient or autonomous. There is disagreement about the nature or mechanism of interconnectedness of these Aztec communities—whether the integration was predominantly horizontal (Smith 1979), predominantly vertical (Santley 1986), or something in between (Evans 1980)—but not about whether strong interconnectedness existed.

Once again, if this were the only difficulty with the AMP idea, we could salvage a version of it by downplaying or eliminating the idea of village autonomy, self-sufficiency, and isolation, as Krader (1987) has attempted to do. There are a host of other empirical (and conceptual) problems, though, as we shall see below. Furthermore, what we salvaged would not be the historical AMP concept that has entered the major debates over the years; that concept is defined by "the formula well known to us: primitive community plus government" (V. N. Nikiforov, quoted in Gellner 1988:49), i.e., the village system *as well as* the state.

France

No one ever claimed to have found the AMP in France. Nevertheless, there is a passage in Marx's *The 18th Brumaire of Louis Bonaparte* (written in 1852, republished in 1869) that is unsettling if we read it with the AMP in mind. In the famous passage that contains Marx's definition of "class," he describes French peasants as being isolated and self-sufficient *in the very same senses*, apparently, that he and Engels wrote of isolated and self-sufficient "Asian" peasants. Marx (1969:123-124) says:

Their mode of production isolates them from one another.... Each individual peasant family is almost self-sufficient; it itself directly produces the major part of its consumption.... A small holding, a peasant and his family; alongside them another small holding.... A few score of these make up a village, and a few score of villages make up a Department. In this way, the great mass of the French nation is formed by simple addition of homologous magnitudes, much as potatoes in a sack form a sack of potatoes.

If this passage, which makes French peasants seem identical to the AMP peasants of India, represents Marx's enduring outlook, then for him the distinctiveness of the AMP would have to rest entirely on its *supra*-village and *supra*-regional qualities, that is, on the structure or actions of the State. In short, the Asiatic "village system," unless further defined, would *not* be diagnostic of the AMP at all. If so, this adds appreciably to what Manuel Gándara (1986) generously calls "the exegesis problem."

STATE OWNERSHIP OF LAND

On June 2, 1853, Marx wrote to Engels, with reference to François Bernier's 1670 memoir of his 12 years in Hindostan: "Bernier rightly considered the basis of all phenomena in the East—he refers to Turkey, Persia, Hindustan—to be the *absence of private property in land*." For good measure, Marx added, "This is the real key, even to the Oriental heaven" (in Feuer 1959:456, also Marx & Engels 1975:66; see Bernier 1826:247-248). Four days later, Engels replied that "Old Bernier's things are really very fine" and then called him "a sober old clear-headed Frenchman, who keeps hitting the nail on the head...." (in Marx & Engels 1975:68). Just why they placed so much faith in the likes of Bernier, whom Marx called "brilliant, graphic, and striking" (loc. cit.), is something of a mystery. Krader (1987:118-119) points out that the Marx who "skillfully detected the interests and prejudices of Adam Smith, Ricardo, Bismarck, [and] Proudhon, did not do likewise in the case of the travellers and administrators" upon whose accounts he relied for his knowledge of Mughal India—even though the materials to assess them critically were available in the very British Museum Library where Marx labored so famously (also see O'Leary 1989:264-266). Among other things, Bernier's memoir was an impassioned plea for private property and laissez faire.

Following are some passages that show Bernier's political motivation, which was, as Krader (1987:124) notes, to assert that the king's ownership of all the land in Mughal India "had turned it into a desert." Bernier (1826:263) wrote of Turkey, Persia, and India (Hindostan):

[H]aving lost that respect for the right of [private] property, which is the basis of all that is good and useful in the world...they fall into the same pernicious errors, and must, sooner or later, experience the natural consequences of those errors—tyranny, ruin, and misery.

How happy and thankful should we feel...that in our quarter of the globe, kings are not the sole proprietors of the soil.... If this exclusive and baneful right prevailed...the sovereigns of Europe.... would soon reign over solitudes and deserts, over mendicants and barbarians.

And lest the good French king get any ideas about taking over existing private property, let him be warned (p. 264):

Our large towns would become uninhabitable in consequence of the unwholesome air, and fall into ruins...; our fertile hills would be abandoned, and the plains would be overrun with thorns and weeds, or covered with pestilential morasses. The excellent accommodations for travellers would disappear; the good inns...between Paris and Lyons, would dwindle into ten or twelve wretched caravansaries....

The foregoing sounds like something from one of Ronald Reagan's index cards—but there's more (pp. 270-271):

Yes, my lord, I must repeat it; take away the right of private property in lands, and you introduce, as a sure and necessary consequence, tyranny, injustice, beggary and barbarism: the ground will cease to be cultivated and become a dreary wilderness; in a word, the road will be opened to the ruin of kings and the destruction of nations. It is the hope by which a man is animated, that he shall retain the fruits of his industry and transmit them to his descendants...; and...the different kingdoms in the world...prosper or decline according as this principle is acknowledged or contemned....

Of course, Marx was not about to use Bernier's memoir to justify capitalism or laissez faire! Its utility for Marx was simply to show that the Orient had a political economy very different from that of the Western European feudal period.

Marx's fullest statement on state ownership of land under the AMP was actually very restrained; it appears in the draft manuscript, usually known as the *Grundrisse*, written in 1857/58 but never intended for publication. The passage below (Marx 1964:69-70; emphasis his) follows several paragraphs devoted to pre-state communal ownership:

[I]n most Asiatic fundamental forms it [communal ownership] is quite compatible with the fact that the *all-embracing unity* [i.e., the State] which stands above all these small common bodies may appear as the higher or *sole proprietor*, the real communities only as *hereditary* possessors. Since the *unity* is the real owner, and the real precondition of common ownership, it is perfectly possible for it to appear as something separate and superior to the numerous real, particular communities. The individual is then in fact propertyless, or property.... appears to be mediated by means of a grant (*Ablassen*) from the total unity to the individual through the intermediary of the particular community. The despot here appears as the father of all the numerous lesser communities, thus realising the common unity of all. It therefore follows that the surplus product...belongs to this highest unity. Oriental despotism therefore appears to lead to a legal absence of property. In fact, however, its foundation is tribal or common property, in most cases created through a combination of manufacture and agriculture within the small community which thus

becomes entirely self-sustaining.... Part of its surplus labour belongs to the higher
community, which ultimately appears as a *person*. This surplus labour is rendered both
as tribute and as common labour for the glory of the unity, in part that of the despot,
in part that of the imagined tribal entity of the god.

Got that? Marx was being so cautious—even in a manuscript that he said he
intended "for my own clarification and not for publication" (quoted in
Hobsbawm 1964:10)—that we remain in doubt: Did he believe that the state's
ownership of land under the AMP is merely symbolic (*de jure*) or that it is
vital (*de facto*)? Or was Marx *unsure which it is*? Whatever it was that Marx
believed to be the nature of landownership under the AMP, he was willing,
in the *Grundrisse* manuscript, to extend the notion to cover certain non-Asian
cases: "[T]he unity can involve a common organization of labor itself...as in
[Aztec] Mexico, and especially [Inca] Peru, [and] among the ancient
[European] Celts...." (Marx 1964:70). Indeed, if we accept that the essence
of the AMP is "primitive community plus government" (Nikiforov, in Gellner
1988:49), then we can generalize the AMP quite widely, to cover most or even
all early states, as some modern scholars have done. (More on that later.)

The empirical adequacy of the position that the state was the landowner
under the AMP must still be addressed. Did this condition exist in the AMP?
If so, is it confined to Asia? or to the cases mentioned by Marx? or is it more
widespread? With this problematic in mind, one of my students, David
Sherman, recently examined the question of landownership in the 16 Sub-
Saharan African chiefdoms and states that appear in the Standard Cross-
Cultural Sample (Murdock & White 1969). Including only African cases
allowed an independent check on the claims about Asian cases; examining all
the appropriate (chiefdom/state) African cases in the SCCS avoided the daisy-
picking bias of many other studies.

The results (Sherman n.d.) are partially reported here in Table 1. In three
cases, Sherman found no statement on landownership. In one other case, he
found that the village owned the land. In the other 12 of these 16 cases, he
found that the highest ruler (chief/king) was considered to be the owner of
the land. (By the way, in only one of these cases, Hausa, was agriculture
dependent upon irrigation.) In most of the 12, land allocation (usufruct)
ultimately resided in polity officials; in only 4 cases could an individual claim
use-right simply in virtue of his having cleared virgin or unused land. Claims
of chiefly/kingly ownership of the land were typically explicit in the
ethnographic sources. "The chief...is referred to, sometimes, as...'land man',
or 'owner of land', in the sense of his being the ultimate owner of all lands
in his chiefdom," Kenneth Little (1967:89-90) wrote of the Mende. "[A]ll the
land belonged to the King alone," wrote John Roscoe (1965:268) of the Ganda.
"[T]he Chief was looked on as the owner of his land.... Headmen might buy
the right of ruling over an area from the Chief..., but the actual land did not

Table 1.   Land Tenure in 16 Sub-Saharan African
Chiefdom/State Societies (from Sherman n.d.) [a]

SCCS Name and Number [b]	Type of Agriculture [c]	Extent of Political Hierarchy [d]	Land "Owner"	Allocation (Usufruct) [e]	Inheritability (Usufruct)
Shilluk (31)	E	1	Highest Ruler	A	yes (?)
Lozi (4)	I	3	Highest Ruler	A	yes
Ganda (12)	I	3	Highest Ruler	A	yes (semi-)
Hausa (26)	J	3	Highest Ruler	A	yes (some)
Fon (18)	E	3	Highest Ruler	A	yes (?)
Mende (20)	E	1	Highest Ruler	A	yes (in time)
Thonga (30)	E	2	Highest Ruler	A	yes
Bemba (7)	E	2	Highest Ruler	SA	yes
Mbundu (5)	E	2	Highest Ruler	A	yes
Azande (28)	E	2	Highest Ruler	SA	yes
Bambara (22)	I	1	Highest Ruler	A	yes
Ashanti (19)	E	2	Highest Ruler	A	yes
Suku (6)	E	3	?	SA	yes
Wolof (21)	E	2	?	A/SA	yes
Nyakyusa (8)	I	2	Village	A	yes (some)
Nkundo (14)	E	2	?	?	?

Notes: [a] In selecting these units, Sherman followed the lead of another student, Rex Jungerberg (1990), who
had conducted an earlier study using all the hierarchical societies in Sub-Saharan Africa (two of which
units actually fall into Murdock's "Circum-Mediterranean" area).
[b] SCCS = Standard Cross-Cultural Sample (Murdock & White 1969).
[c] From Murdock (1967:Col. 28): E = Extensive or shifting cultivation (long-fallow), I = Intensive
agriculture on permanent fields (at most, short-fallow), J = Intensive agriculture largely dependent
upon irrigation.
[d] From Murdock (1967:Col. 32): 1 or 2 = "petty and large paramount chiefdoms or their equivalent,"
3 or 4 = "large states."
[e] SA = right of usufruct is obtained by the act of clearing the land; A = right of usufruct is allocated
by a ruler or his representative or "by the village."

[thereby] become theirs...," wrote G. M. Larken (1930:423) of the Azande. Max Gluckman (1941:26) wrote, "According to Lozi law, all land in Barotseland is vested in the king." Audrey Richards (1939:245) wrote of the Bemba: "[A]ny chief will...[say] that the whole territory belongs to him, together with the food that is produced in it, its game and fish, and the labour of its people." At the same time, Sherman's (n.d.) study revealed that commoners typically had legal rights of inheritance of usufruct (Table 1).

How do we reconcile this seeming paradox of royal ownership, on the one hand, and inheritable tenure, on the other? The ethnographic sources were typically loquacious on this point, in recognition of the potential for cross-cultural misunderstanding. I shall illustrate by quoting a fragment of Gluckman's (1959:61-62) rich account of Lozi landownership:

All Loziland and all its products belong to the nation through the king. Though one right of Lozi citizenship is a right to building and arable land and the use of public lands, it is by the king's bounty that his subjects live on and by the land. Commoners think of themselves as permanently indebted to the king for the land on which they live and its wild and domesticated products which sustain them. The Lozi say this is why they gave tribute and service to the king.... The king thus is the owner...in the sense that ultimately he has a right in every piece of Lozi land. Though he owns the land, the king is obliged to give every subject land to live on and land to cultivate, and to protect him against trespassers; and he must allow every subject to fish in public waters, to hunt ..., to gather..., and to use [other natural resources].... The king's rights are to claim the allegiance of everyone living on his land, to demand (in the past) tribute from their produce, to control the building of villages, and to pass laws about the holding and use of land. He may make treaties affecting the land. He also holds...land which has not been allocated to any subject, he takes over land to which an heir cannot be found, and he has a 'potential right' to unused land, i.e., he can beg it from the holder [but not confiscate it outright] in order to give it to a landless person or use it himself or for public works.... In exercising his rights to land the king must bear in mind the interests of his subjects: for example, if he moves a man he must give him land elsewhere. The king thus owns the land as trustee for his people.

Each ethnographic case is distinctive, of course, but the lengthy ethnographic commentaries might be distilled as follows. First, royal ownership entailed the right and *duty* to allocate usage. Second, from the standpoint of commoners, access to land was a function of politics ("citizenship," as it were, which established eligibility for an allotment) and kinship (which established eligibility to inherit an allotment). Third, in pre-colonial times, land was not (ordinarily) a marketable commodity—for any stratum. Note that these three points are logically intertwined. Fourth, the ideological claim of royal ownership of land (and often, other resources) established a corollary claim to tax the users of the land. Fifth, as trustee for the people—and typically also for gods or ancestors or spirits—the ruler had certain pre-eminent claims upon the land; the important variation in this regard is that such claims (i.e., the exercise of eminent domain) were strongly enforceable in some cases but only weakly in others.

Thus, Asia—homeland of the AMP—was not unique in having rulers who "owned" all the land. Nor, for that matter, are Europe and its offshoots different from Asian and African states in this regard. What Bernier and the other writers who inspired Marx about the AMP seem to have discovered in the Orient was a principle that also obtained in their own countries, namely, the state's right of eminent domain. In fact, there are probably few exceptions to the existence of this right—the polity's "real" or "ultimate" ownership of productive resources—in chiefdoms and states in any part of the world, although the scope or limits of the right would vary from one case to the next.

Through ignorance, state-sponsored mystification, and ethnocentrism, we can easily mislead ourselves about property rights in our own Western tradition. In this regard, many U.S. college students would probably be surprised to learn that their government is the ultimate owner of all land and other property in its territory. Furthermore, the U.S. government does not have to "beg" it from the holder, as was the case of the Lozi king, according to Gluckman (above). In my native Kansas, where we agrarians had a nearly spiritual attachment to the land, the clearest civics lesson of my childhood was taught by the U.S. Army Corps of Engineers. When there was no real war to absorb their destructive power, these bulldozing bureaucrats razed houses, uprooted precious trees, destroyed landmarks, transplanted cemeteries, moved villages—all against the angry protests of the affected persons. The purpose was to build dams that would flood much of the best farming land but which would provide irrigation water to the large-scale farmers who could afford it, recreational opportunities (boating, fishing) for townfolks, and, of course, jobs for the Corps. Although the expropriations were reimbursed at "fair market value" (determined by those same bureaucrats), the fact remains that the affected (and distraught) property holders were not given the choice of whether to vacate their houses and homesteads or to remain. They, who thought of themselves as sovereign owners—"Every man's home is his castle!"—were up against the "real" owner, the state. Where's François Bernier when you really need him?

Let's return briefly to the Lozi and view the situation at the village level (Gluckman 1959:64-65):

> The king may give a piece of land to an individual, but in practice all land is held by villages in the name of their headmen.... The land of a village is distributed by a headman among his villagers, or had been distributed thus in the past; for each heir to a headmanship inherits the obligations of his predecessor. Once a member of a family homestead by right of blood or adoption...has been granted land, he retains the right to use that land, and to transmit it to his own heirs.... The holder cannot give the land to anyone, and if he leaves the homestead the land reverts to the headman.... Thus the village is the group in which political and kinship ties...are intertwined.... In landholding, a villager here has rights because he is attached in a political sense to the headman, and because he is kin to the headman.

Think back to the quotation from Marx's *Grundrisse*, in which he was trying to depict both the state's right of eminent domain and village communalism. He began with the point of village ownership of land; he then said that the state "may appear as the...sole proprietor" and the villagers "only as hereditary possessors"; he ended by saying that, despite the appearance of "a legal absence of property," the actual "foundation" of the political-economic system he was modelling is "tribal or common property" (Marx 1964:69-70). Could we not describe the Lozi thusly?

Indeed, the Lozi would seem to conform to V. Nikiforov's "formula" for the AMP: "primitive community plus government" (quoted in Gellner 1988:49). By "primitive community," Nikiforov of course denotes communal ownership of land and the egalitarianism that this feature implies, conditions that seem to be met in Lozi but which were not met in India, Marx's type case, or in China. Have we rejected the *Asiatic* Mode of Production in Asia only to discover it in Africa? Not exactly. If we insist on stripping the AMP model to Nikiforov's basic "formula," allowing no other traits to be specified, then we may simply be describing the early state fairly generally (cf. Krader 1987). If so, there's no reason whatsoever to speak of an *Asiatic* Mode of Production; even if the stripped-down model applied to the earliest state formations in Asia, it would not differentiate them from the earliest states elsewhere in the world.

   If, on the other hand, we include the other traits of the AMP, i.e., the model as it has entered the AMP debates in this century, we begin running into problems. The Lozi king could hardly be described as a "despot"; even his right of eminent domain extended only to "begging" (with all the pressure that may be implied, of course) but not to the confiscations that we find in stronger governments, e.g., that of the U.S. Furthermore, Lozi agriculture did not entail irrigation works. Although each Lozi king directed the construction of a canal, he did so "to make easy the travels of his people" and to leave "his distinguishing mark...on the land itself" (Gluckman 1959:63), with no apparent reference to agriculture. The Lozi simply were not water managers; for about five months each year, the entire population abandoned their (preferred) homes on the floodplain and moved to high ground to escape the annual inundation.

   The general question is this: Is the AMP a coherent and useful social science model? or is it instead a list of traits that occur in varying combinations or even separately through time and space? As we have seen, this latter seems to be the case. Such empirical volatility inevitably raises grave questions about a model's theoretical adequacy (see Gándara 1986). We shall return to these matters.

ASIAN STAGNATION

Of all the components of the AMP model, the one that is least acceptable today is Asian historical immutability, or stagnation. This component actually has two aspects. The first is that the AMP rested upon the "village system" with its self-sufficing mix of subsistence agriculture and local-service artisanry, and a stable, tributary relationship to the state above it. Marx (1967:357-358) wrote:

> Those small and extremely ancient Indian communities...are based on possession in common of the land, on the blending of agriculture and handicrafts, and on an unalterable division of labour, which serves, whenever a new community is started, as a plan and scheme ready cut and dried.... The simplicity of the organisation for production in these self-sufficing communities that constantly reproduce themselves in the same form, and when accidentally destroyed, spring up again on the same spot and with the same name—this

simplicity supplies the key to the secret of the unchangeableness of Asiatic societies, an unchangeableness in such striking contrast with the constant dissolution and refounding of Asiatic States, and the never-ceasing changes of dynasty. The structure of the economic elements of society remains untouched by the storm-clouds of the political sky.

Karl Wittfogel (1955:43; emphasis mine) expressed this idea very succinctly: "In contrast to the stratified agrarian societies of Medieval Europe, they [hydraulic or "Oriental" societies] failed, *of their own inner forces*, to evolve beyond their general pattern" (also see pp. 49-50).

The second aspect of the stagnation idea was that external force was needed to break AMP societies out of their vegetative condition. And the external force was provided by Western society under capitalism. Shades of Kipling!—as Gellner (1988:42) points out. We saw earlier that Marx (1951:29; also in Feuer 1959:480-481) posed the question, "Can mankind fulfill its destiny without a fundamental revolution in the social state of Asia?"; and answered it, "If not, whatever the crimes of England [in colonizing India], she was the unconscious tool of history in bringing about that revolution." More recently, Karl Wittfogel (1963:8) expressed similar notions about what he called, interchangeably, Asiatic society and hydraulic society: "Nowhere...did hydraulic society, without outside aid, make a similar advance," as feudal Europe and Japan did, to "commercial and industrial society"; this is why, he added with apparent approval, "Marx called Asiatic society stationary and expected British rule in India to accomplish 'the only social revolution every heard of in Asia' by establishing there a property-based non-Asiatic society." Wittfogel (ibid.:420; emphasis his) also wrote: "Hydraulic society is the outstanding case of societal stagnation.... [H]ydraulic society did not abandon its basic structures except under the impact of *external* forces."

We have seen that Marx and Engels did not originate this feature of the model; the Baron de Montesquieu, John Stuart Mill, and (most importantly) Georg Hegel all subscribed to it. At the same time, Marx and Engels were neither fools nor passive slaves to tradition; to the contrary, they (especially Marx) made penetrating, often biting criticisms—many of which strike us still as witty and incisive—of most of their intellectual predecessors and contemporaries. This is why we are shocked or embarrassed today, as was Angel Palerm (quoted earlier), upon reading Marx's commentaries on Asia: How *could he* have said those things?

Our reaction is actually based on a misplaced projection: In awe of the enormous scholarly prowess that makes Marx still a major player in world political and intellectual circles over a century after his death, we tend to forget the limitations of time and place to which he, too, was subject. Most of our present knowledge of world history has accumulated since Marx's death. There was no Immanuel Wallerstein or Eric Wolf in Marx and Engels' day to put

Europe into perspective. Hobsbawm (1964:26) characterizes the state of Marx
and Engels' historical knowledge as

> thin on prehistory, on primitive communal societies and on pre-Columbian America, and
> virtually non-existent on Africa. It was not impressive on the ancient or medieval Middle
> East, but markedly better on certain parts of Asia, notably India, but not on Japan. It
> was good on classical antiquity and the European middle ages.... It was, for the times,
> outstandingly good on the [European] period of rising capitalism.

We should also guard against losing sight of the Big Question that
preoccupied Marx in terms of global history: Why had capitalism emerged
in Europe, rather than in Asia? In contemplating this question, Marx (and
Hegel before him) assumed (1) that "civilization" began in Asia and (2) that
19th-century European capitalism represented a "higher stage" of civilization
than Asia had reached. Against that backdrop, the question easily became one
of why Asia had stopped developing and was lagging behind Europe.

Stripped of its ethnocentric components, the question still interests us today.
We don't have to read far in world history to be impelled to ask, with Immanuel
Wallerstein (1974:52-63), "Why not China?" This is not the place to sing the
paeans of Chinese civilization, but I do want to point to some salient features
and to linger a moment over the foregoing question.

In the 2,000 years or so preceding the 16th-century dawn (according to Marx
1967:715) of European capitalism, Chinese civilization not only had been
dynamic but was also the source of key inventions for eventual European
"development"—especially for warfare (gunpowder, firearms, bombs) and
sailing (magnetic compass, axial rudder). China also pioneered in such
important inventions as cast iron, steel, paper, printing (and moveable type),
paper money backed by metals, and so forth (see P. Anderson 1974:521ff.,
E. Anderson 1989, Gernet 1970, Wallerstein 1974:52-63). In agriculture, China
experienced its first Green Revolution in 400-100 B.C. This major agrarian
reform saw the innovation of such things as "farm price supports, agricultural
extension, and government-sponsored controlled experimentation" (E.
Anderson 1989:135); it also resulted in the widespread diffusion of the
moldboard plow, "supplemented by advanced harrows, seed drills, and oil and
flour milling machinery," as well as "pretreatment of seed with fertilizer and
insecticide" (ibid.:136). This early Green Revolution was the model for a second
one in A.D. 900-1100 (ibid.:135).

Furthermore, China was for long the world's leader in ocean sailing. By
about A.D. 600, its naval architects were "already building long-haul vessels
with as many as five decks, and measuring more than a hundred feet from
truck to keel...." (Davidson 1959:183). Her ships were sighted and admired
by Arab sailors (no slouches at sea travel themselves) in the Indian Ocean at
least as early as the 9th century A.D. After a lull in the 10th century, China

became "a maritime nation" during the Song Dynasty (A.D. 1127-1279). Philip Snow (1988:8-9) writes:

> Chinese merchants travelled in ships 'like houses', with five to six decks, provisioned for ocean voyages with a year's grain supply, herds of pigs and jars of fermenting wine. Their navigators possessed the world's most advanced seafaring technology in the form of magnetic compasses, water-tight bulkheads, axial rudders, floating anchors and sounding lines.

The first "ambassadors" (probably traders) from East Africa reached the Chinese court in A.D. 1071 and 1081, almost certainly travelling in Arab as well as Chinese vessels. But the first giraffe arrived directly, by Chinese ship, in 1415. It was delivered by admiral Cheng Ho, who conducted seven expeditions westward from 1405 to 1433. Philip Snow calls him "the Chinese Columbus." Snow (ibid.:21) writes of Cheng Ho's fourth voyage:

> [T]his Ming dynasty admiral had at his disposal resources which make the Genoese explorer [Columbus] look like an amateur. Columbus had three ships. They had one deck apiece, and together weighed a total of 415 tons. Zheng He [Cheng Ho] had sixty-two galleons, and more than a hundred auxiliary vessels. The largest galleons had three decks on the poop alone, and each of them weighed about 1,500 tons. They had nine masts and twelve sails, and are said to have measured 440 feet long by 180 feet wide.

Furthermore, Columbus had a force of a few hundred, whereas Cheng Ho's retinue included 26,800 soldiers and over 1,500 officers of various ranks.

Thus, we can stand amazed that Europe, not China, ended up dominating the world. What happened to China? Saying that China "stagnated" just boots the question around without answering it. We should begin, rather, by asking why the Chinese government disallowed the great voyages of exploration after 1433. And why, by 1450, the "inland party" of Confucian mandarins at the Chinese court had defeated its rival "ocean party," which had sponsored the great eunuch admirals. We cannot know for certain, but it doubtless involved the events to which Wallerstein (1974:56-58) points: (1) threats from their inland enemies to the north, the Mongols; (2) a policy decision to devote resources to infrastructure for wet rice development in the southeast; and (3) the vastness of the inland empire, which forestalled any "necessity" for external empire. At any rate, "by 1500 the great shipyards were all closed down; the building of a sea-going junk with more than two masts became a capital offense" (Davidson 1959:190).

The poignancy of the matter is that "Chinese and Portuguese overseas exploration began virtually simultaneously, but that after a mere 28 years [1405-1433] the Chinese pulled back into a continental shell" (Wallerstein 1974:54)—even though they clearly had the initial advantage. The great irony, of course, is that the Chinese dismantled their ocean-going fleet at the most fateful moment: By 1487, the Portuguese finally were able to round the Cape of Good Hope at the southern tip of Africa and, in 1497, Vasco da Gama's fleet burst into the Indian Ocean with guns blazing. Da Gama met no effective rival there, and by 1502 he was "Admiral of India." The Chinese had stopped innovating at the very time that the Europeans were on the verge of "a crucial technological innovation—the cutting of ports for guns in the actual hulls of the ships as opposed to the superstructure—[which] had been achieved in 1501" (Wallerstein 1974:326). In its heyday, of course, the Chinese navy would have had no trouble in adapting this innovation to their own, vastly superior ships; after all, they had pioneered firearms and bombs as well as the compass, the axial rudder, and the art of sailing into the wind.

Modern history might have been very different had the "ocean party" and its maritime eunuchs not lost the day at the Chinese court ca. 1450. If China had been able to mount an effective opposition in the Indian Ocean, it might not have "stagnated" and Europe might never have "developed" at all. Significantly, early 16th-century Europe's "advantage was only at sea. On land she was still retreating in the face of Ottoman attack, and this military balance would only change with the Industrial Revolution" (Wallerstein 1974:332). Whether Europe would nevertheless have beat the Chinese to the conquest of the Western Hemisphere is beyond speculation, but we can say that the Chinese would have been in a position to try to wrest it away if Europe had reached it first and started pouring its metallic wealth—a major ingredient of the eventual European industrial revolution—into the Eastern Hemisphere.

Almost certainly, the history of modern India would have been vastly different had the Chinese been able to keep the European powers from dominating the Indian Ocean. We think of India today as a poor and "stagnant" land, but it was once a rich and fabled land that excited the European imagination. India became the crown jewel of English colonialism, a source of wealth (raw materials and market for manufactures) in her own right and the staging area for the English domination of the economy of China. The English words "mogul" and "nabob," denoting rich and powerful persons, are colonial neologisms that reflect India's former splendor. Wolf (1982:244-245) tells us that, following its takeover of Bengal in 1757, the East India Company plundered "over 5 million pounds sterling" from the Bengali state treasury and later realized "another 5 million pounds sterling in profit" in the years 1775-1780. Imagine how many zeros it would take to convert that wealth into 1993 dollars! Furthermore, the company gained control over the output of 10,000 Bengali weavers, "whose contracts forced them to deal exclusively with the Company" (loc cit.).

The underdevelopment of the Indian subcontinent through the application of colonial policy had begun; India became mainly an exporter of raw materials rather than of manufactures, as England tightened her grip on the Indian economy (cf. Marx 1967:752-753). "The bones of the cotton-weavers are bleaching the plains of India," the British Governor-General of India reported in 1834/35 (quoted in Marx 1967:432). Wolf (1982:251) depicts the late-18th/ early-19th century thusly:

> Indian textiles, until the end of the eighteenth century a major export, were banned from British markets, while India was required to admit the entry of English manufactures duty free. This led to the rapid destruction of specialized Indian textile handicraft production. The spread of machine-made goods disrupted village crafts, reducing the number of artisans who derived their living from producing pottery, tanned skins, dyed cloth, oil, and jewelry. Shipbuilding and railroad construction in the 1840s and 1850s...promot[ed] exports of wheat..., cotton..., and jute..., as well as a shift from the production of food crops to industrial crops such as cotton, peanuts, sugarcane, and tobacco. Moneylending at high interest rates expanded steadily as peasants began to buy foodstuffs on the market, as money was needed to spur cash-crop production, and as land prices rose after mid-century. There was a rising tide of dissatisfaction....

Regarding agriculture, we have nothing for India equivalent to the Chinese written agrarian history reported earlier. Furthermore, as Christopher Baker (1984:38) points out, European scholars have always taken a "hovercraft view" of historical rural India, rather than a close inspection—on the assumption that the dynamic of Indian history is to be found exclusively in the state apparatus and the cities. The result is that we can actually say very little about long-term agricultural change. We do know, though, that Indian tillers were quick to adopt new crops and new techniques and to respond to new market incentives during the 19th century. Furthermore, the English agronomists who studied Indian agriculture for the colonial government in the late-19th and early-20th centuries "all reported their appreciation (and indeed surprise) at the complexity of technical change and adaptation in Indian agriculture" (ibid.:44). In summary, "The argument for a general condition of torpidity (whether attributed to the climate, the capacity of the people, the social structure, or the state) is continually cut short by examples of specific dynamism" (ibid.:40).

WITTFOGEL: HH & OD

We have already seen that European interest in the developmental significance of Asian public hydraulic works goes back more than two centuries. As a trait of the AMP, hydraulic works were mentioned here and there by Marx and Engels in their correspondence and publications. Contemporary anthropological interest in the topic stems neither from their musings nor from those of their predecessors, however, but from the work of Karl Wittfogel, especially his *Oriental Despotism* (1957, 1963). I will not attempt a full exegesis of *OD* or even of the many twists and turns of the HH therein; these tasks are accomplished fully by O'Leary (1989:235-250) and Palerm (1972:Ch. 5). My aim, rather, is simply to provide enough background and excerpted material in each of the following sections to carry the reader through them with understanding

Irrigation and the Rise of the State

The possibility that Wittfogel had hit upon a universal theory or mechanism of the origin of the state was what excited the greatest anthropological interest in his writings. Wittfogel postulated clearly that the requirements for large-scale irrigation constituted the causal component of the formula for "Oriental Despotism" (= hydraulic society = Asiatic/Oriental society) under specific environmental circumstances. "Of all the tasks imposed by the natural environment," Wittfogel (1963:13) wrote, "it was the task imposed by a precarious water situation that stimulated man to develop hydraulic methods of social control." Controlling and channelling "a large quantity of water" required "the use of mass labor," which had to be "coordinated, disciplined, and led"; accordingly, farmers wishing to manage water on a large scale had to "work in cooperation with their fellows and *subordinate themselves to a directing authority*" (Wittfogel 1963:18; emphasis mine). Once these farmers' agricultural production was dependent upon this new irrigation system, the "directing authority" was "uniquely prepared to wield supreme political power" (ibid.:27). Now, it is not simply, as Lord Acton said, that "power tends to corrupt and absolute power corrupts absolutely" (ibid.:133); there's a prior circumstance: "[H]uman nature is the same everywhere and...man succumbs to the corrupting influence of power *whenever circumstances permit*" (ibid.:145; emphasis mine).

Given the clear causal chain that Wittfogel laid out, it is definitely not a "misunderstanding" or a basic "ambiguity" in our thinking (*contra* Mitchell 1973:533) to expect that large-scale irrigation works—the kind that require the "use of mass labor" and, thus, subordination of masses to a "directing authority"—should *predate* rather than postdate the state. And that expectation is most definitely *not* met in at least several (perhaps all!) of the major areas of primary state origin (see Carneiro 1970, Mitchell 1973, O'Leary 1989:270ff., Schaedel 1987, Sugiura 1986). Even if we were to demonstrate that the proposed causal sequence indeed occurred in *some* place(s), we still would not have the *general* theory of state origin that Wittfogel's formulation once seemed to hold out.

Sadly enough, the emergence of the state in China—Wittfogel's type case of Hydraulic Society—seems to contradict the HH. Sugiura (1986:63) summarizes the evidence with respect to the first Chinese states (Shang, 1750-1122 B.C.): "The documentary as well as archaeological studies support the thesis that the society of those times was sustained by a rainfall agrarian economy with a Neolithic instrumental technology." Even as late as 700 B.C., i.e., a millennium after the appearance of the first state, agricultural technology showed "no notable changes since Neolithic times"; only towards the end of the Warring States Period (450-221 B.C.) were "great construction works realized in various states" (ibid.: 62, 69; also see E. Anderson 1989:135). Of the regions that gave rise to the earliest states, in the 2nd and 1st millennia B.C., Zhao Lisheng (1989:69) writes: "The people in this area relied on natural rainfall, and their fear was of floods caused by excessive rainfall, not drought. Ancient China had irrigation [sic!] ditches, but they served primarily to drain flood waters." Finally, let us permit Perry Anderson (1974:521) to weigh in: "The cradle of Sinic civilization was North-West China, whose economy was based on a dry cereal agriculture... millet, wheat and barley." Even during Han Dynasty times (207 B.C.-A.D. 220), when great hydraulic works were indeed constructed, "dry cereal cultivation of millet and wheat was still overwhelmingly predominant in the rural economy" (ibid.:521). Citing the great Sinologist Joseph Needham, Anderson (loc. cit.) alludes to the Han Dynasty's "imposing transport canals for the swift shipment of grain-taxes to their treasuries," and then says: "[T]hroughout Chinese history, in fact, the State was always to give priority to transport waterways, with their fiscal and military (logistic) functions, over irrigation systems proper, for agricultural purposes"!

Let us now look briefly at Mexico and Peru in terms of a possible causal role for irrigation in the birth of the state. Schaedel (1987) has weighed the Peruvian evidence and found it wanting in this regard. During the "chiefdom" period (1500 B.C.-A.D. 500) in Peru, the manipulation of water seems to have concerned the capture and storage of rainwater in small tanks or cisterns (p. 130); there is no evidence that water management was causal in either sedentarization (which occurred before agriculture) or the emergence of the earliest stratified polities ("chiefdoms"). Regarding the earliest state period (A.D. 500-750) in Peru, problems of dating the water works lead Schaedel to hedge his bets—"[I] believe that I should leave open the question of whether hydraulic controls were a determinant of the Mochica expansion" (p. 131)— but the settlement pattern, for both "hegemonic centers" and peasant communities, is "out of focus" for either "hydraulic hegemony" or "hydraulic control" (pp. 131-134). In fact, this is so not only of coastal Mochica (A.D. 500-750) but also of Huari (ca. A.D. 700-1100), the first highland state. Schaedel concludes that John Murra's "archipelago model" of multi-stranded control over localized, microniche economic-ecological specialization "satisfactorily explains the socioeconomic formation of the first Andean state, the Huari, as well as the initial redistributive phase of the Inca state" (p. 139). Going back to the earlier transition from "small chiefdoms...to large chiefdoms" in the highlands, Schaedel postulates that "the expansion...was related to...the concentration of surplus from a plurality of microniches via a network of roads, rather than to the intensification of production in a large, cultivable, contiguous macroniche" (p. 139). Schaedel's assessment brings to mind Clark Erickson's essay in the present volume, which argues that strictly local (village-level) water management (in the form of raised fields) was both feasible and highly productive in the Andes.

Highland Mexico gave rise not only to the so-called Aztec Empire but to the earlier Teotihuacan polity (ca. 100 B.C.-A.D. 750). With reference to the question at hand, Scarborough (1991:128) sums up the evidence: "Although canalization has been reported as early as 700 B.C..., clear associations between the state and the construction and maintenance of water systems are not apparent until the Aztec Postclassic period (A.D. 1350-1520)." As Schaedel (1987:137) puts it, the many "detailed and exhaustive studies" here have "been able to confirm only a juxtapositional role of irrigation in the earlier states and cities"; in other words, the features co-occur but causality has yet to be demonstrated. In the Aztec period, there is little evidence for regional hydraulic control and, where we find irrigation works, "generally speaking, organization of irrigation was villagewide and sometimes drainagewide" but not interdrainage in scale (Scarborough 1991:130).

The Aztecs were noted for their water management works around the lake system where their capital cities were located, but the causal role of these works in state formation is unresolved. Although saying anything at all about this controversial subject—on which the data are at once excitingly rich and riddled with distressing lacunae—is like waltzing across a minefield, I shall venture the following. First, if I have indeed found the telling passage in Boehm de Lameiras' (1986b:254) frighteningly detailed and lengthy book, her position is that it was military control of the economically and logistically strategic lakes as a geographical area, rather than any attempt to exercise control of the area by means of integrated hydraulic systems, that got the state-building process re-started in the early 13th century. Second, after the rise of the Aztec state in 1428/31, raised-field (*chinampa*) production seems to have remained mostly under local community control, although state (central) planning may well have been crucial in establishing and maintaining proper water levels for the important raised-field zone at the southern end of the lake system. Third, the most famous Aztec hydraulic accomplishment, Nezahualcoyotl's dike separating the sweet and briny portions of the lake system, obviously postdates the founding of the Aztec Triple Alliance; earlier diking systems having this function very probably existed, but their scale and management remain to be determined (see Boehm de Lameiras 1986b; Palerm 1973, 1990). Fourth, knowledge of hydraulic techniques in the central lakes area is of "considerable antiquity," having been "in use at least in the period that followed the fall of [Toltec] Tula" (Palerm 1973:173, 1990:363), i.e., in the late-12th/early-13th centuries (see Boehm de Lameiras 1986b:237-238, 275ff.). Fifth, hydraulic-political causality is extremely difficult to determine in the lacustrine system of the Aztec core; witness this statement by Angel Palerm (1973:181, 1990:372-373):

The enormity and complexity of the [hydraulic] works realized in the Lake of Mexico is [sic] related to the ascension of the Mexica to political-military hegemony. Hydraulic technology was very advanced....But even more advanced was the technology which we could call social; or rather, the capacity to obtain materiel and to organize the labor of large masses of people originating from all parts of the Valley.

On the other hand, it seems clear that the [hydraulic] works could not have been realized in benefit of some areas without harming others and without stripping them of particular and important human and material resources. This means conquest before political-military supremacy.

Palerm himself, the most "wittfogellian" of his contemporaries (Boehm de Lameiras 1986b:245), had to wonder if state power over conquered peoples were not what made possible the extraction of the resources needed to build the great hydraulic works of the Aztec heartland.

HH and OD

There is no easy way to summarize Wittfogel's enormous book, *Oriental Despotism* (1957, 1963). Even the HH *per se* developed therein becomes so convoluted with qualifying conditions, typological exercises, and geographical-historical excursions that it is difficult to present succinctly. Some general statement is necessary here, however, and I offer the following excerpt, necessarily incomplete, from Brendan O'Leary (1989:238-244):

Wittfogel argued that there were two types of irrigation in agrarian societies: *hydro-agriculture*, or small-scale irrigation farming, and *hydraulic agriculture*, or large-scale and state-directed farming.... The latter created the opportunity for despotism to emerge.... where rainfall farming was problematic. Arid and semi-arid regions were [thus] more likely to develop stratified and civilized but despotic and state-dominated societies.... Hydraulic agriculture was the agrarian analogue of the socialist command economy of the modern world....Making fields cultivable and protecting them against...flooding necessitated corvée labour, and therefore...a centralized despotism.... The technologies of hydraulic society produced, as by-products, all of the major construction achievements of agrarian empires.... huge defense structures.... the great roads...and the major palaces, capital cities, tombs, monuments and temples.... Hydraulic regimes were...antonyms of pluralist agrarian regimes.... [H]ydraulic states prevented non-state actors...from acquiring sufficient autonomy to act as countervailing powers. The sheer organizational power of the hydraulic state apparatus..., was reinforced by its hydraulic management capabilities, its organization of roads and its surveillance resources.... The organizational power of the hydraulic state was mirrored by the weak property rights of its subjects.... The hydraulic state's power was also buttressed ideologically.... [Most] hydraulic civilizations had large and influential priesthoods.... many hydraulic societies were theocratic. Secular and religious authority was fused.... This fusion of functions was the source of the despotic power of the hydraulic regime, which was 'total and not benevolent'.... Hydraulic regimes lacked not only legal but also social pluralism. There were no independent intermediary powers.... [H]ydraulic regimes also practised 'total terror', producing 'total submission' and 'total loneliness'.... This portrait of unpredictable and capricious use of force by the despot...implemented through terror...was sharply contrasted with occidental forms of rule.

Clearly, *Oriental Despotism: A Comparative Study in Total Power* is not primarily about forms of water management or economic production—as archaeologists or ethnologists would have liked and Marxian scholars might have expected (cf. Bartra 1975:27-29). Rather, the book focusses precisely upon what the title suggests, Asian despotic ("total") state power.

It was, moreover, a "comparative study" of the conditions that give rise to despotic state power, and a "comparative study" is clearly one that leads to (follows from?) a *general* theory. Therein lies the book's greatest weakness as well as its greatest strength: the latter, because it excited great interest; the former, because it led to typological and conceptual excesses. In the "core" area, the rise of "despotic" governments rested upon the base of hydraulic agriculture. But what about the many autocratic governments outside of the "core"? When Wittfogel encountered these extra-core cases, he either stretched his theory around them (by proliferating subtypes that pulled apart the causal nexus of the constellation), attributed them to diffusion from the "core," or denied that the autocratic government in question was "despotic."

The theory-stretching solution began at the "margin" and continued into the "sub-margin." Of the "margin," Wittfogel (1963:191-192) wrote: "Along the moderately humid periphery of the arid and semi-arid world.... Oriental despotism may prevail with little or no dependence upon hydraulic activities." He had in mind such cases as "the Hopi Pueblos, the kingdoms of ancient Asia Minor, Middle Byzantium, Tibet, Liao, and the Maya," as well as Muscovite Russia. (Politics makes for strange bedfellows, eh?) Their common characteristics, according to Wittfogel (ibid.:188), were "organizational and acquisitive methods of despotic statecraft." These "methods of social control place all of them definitely in the 'Oriental' world," no matter how "marginal they may be hydraulically." Most such "marginal agromanagerial states" postdated "the[ir] area's oldest hydraulic civilizations." Although "it is entirely possible that some agrodespotic societies emerged independently," we should accede such independent origin of the marginal cases—despotism without hydraulic agriculture—"only when... institutional diffusion can be excluded as *altogether unlikely*" (ibid.:192-193; emphasis mine). "Virtually all historically significant agrodespotisms that fulfill no hydraulic functions seem to have been derived from hydraulic societies" (ibid.:193-194), i.e., by institutional diffusion. The case of Russia, which "had no close hydraulic neighbors," shows just how far such things can diffuse (ibid.:191-192). The Russian case is also the only one that could be argued on historical grounds, i.e., that the Mongols had introduced OD in the 13th century.

The other cases are empirically or conceptually problematical. In particular, Wittfogel's two "particularly significant" examples of "supplementary data to strengthen our basic classification" (p. 188)—bilateral inheritance and state "dependence on religious authority"—are outrageous in this context. For instance, he writes (pp. 188-189) of Byzantium, "The Justinian

Code...prescribes the equal division of property among the children of a deceased person. This provision, whatever its origin, fits to perfection the needs of agrarian despotism." The outlandishness of this trait as supporting evidence for OD is that it is also the basic inheritance rule of the U.S. and of many other areas of the world, both East and West. The other example, state-controlled religion (p. 190), is simply a widespread trait of the state, and has nothing to do with hydraulics *or* despotism. Let us not forget that the English monarch is still head of the state church (Anglican), and that this was the case with occidental monarchs generally until recent centuries. In short, we are dealing with spurious correlation, as O'Leary (1989:252, 259) points out.

The sub-marginal stretch is a full-throated groaner. The sub-marginal "civilizations" lack "the effective coordination of absolutist methods of organization and acquisition [that] is the minimum requirement for the maintenance of a genuine agrarian despotism" (ibid.:195). These cases nevertheless "exhibit stray features of hydraulic statecraft" (loc. cit.). They include the Minoan, Mycenean and Etruscan cases, as well as Japan, early Rome, and pre-Mongol Russia. Their "stray" oriental features reflect either their past incorporation into an hydraulic order (e.g., post-Moorish Spain) or their "voluntary adoption of desirable 'Oriental' features...." (e.g., Japan) (ibid.:203). I agree with O'Leary's (1989:259) assessment that "sub-marginal" was an ad hoc, residual category designed "to sweep up regimes which were neither oriental despotisms nor occidental feudalisms" and that it represents "a clear example of what philosophers of science describe as an effort to 'save the phenomenon'." I also agree with him that the entire classification scheme— core, marginal, sub-marginal—is extremely difficult to operationalize (also see Bartra 1975:32-33). "There were many ancient empires with so much internal regional variation within their frontiers that they could be classified under each of the three headings" (O'Leary 1989:259)—and reclassified for each dynasty or century!

There is a further problem, alluded to earlier. Remember that Wittfogel was mostly interested in explaining "despotism"—"total power," he also called it. In Asia, he tied it to state-directed hydraulic agriculture. Where it suited his purpose, though, Wittfogel seemed willing to give up almost any diagnostic feature or component of his theory/model to encompass a "despotic" regime within his schema. At the "margin," for instance, Wittfogel freely spoke of "despotisms" in the absence of the very hydraulic base that in the "core" area was causal to the rise to "hydraulic society" or to "despotism" itself. Given this flexibility, why do we not hear more about Medieval and modern Western Europe? What about the Inquisition? the Tower of London and all that? the genocidal policies of Charles I and Cromwell against Ireland? Negro slavery? European colonialism in Africa? Nazi Germany? Francisco Franco and Spanish fascism? O'Leary (1989:245) has discerned four alternative strategies by which Wittfogel overcame such occidental embarrassments:

First, he would contend that the appearance of equivalence was deceptive. Second,... that while the trait was systemic in the Orient, it was not an intrinsic feature of the Occident. Third,... that the Occident had experienced the trait in question in a 'weaker', more 'benign' or 'balanced' form. Finally,... despotic traits in the Occident could... be attributed to the diffusion of the political technologies... [originated] by hydraulic despots. The Orient remained the font of original sin.

In this manner, O'Leary (loc. cit.) continues, "The contrast between the angelic Occident and the devilish Orient, between the non-hydraulic and the hydraulic, was thus made more immune to falsification." Like Marx's AMP before it, Wittfogel's OD "fuses Marx and Kipling" (Gellner 1988:42).

Why was it important for Wittfogel to maintain such an East-West dichotomy? The answer is that his book was about much more than an ancient form of despotism; it was also (mainly?) about the 20th century and the Cold War. The U.S.S.R. had resuscitated OD—without hydraulic agriculture, to be sure, but in the form of "a society whose leaders are the holders of despotic state power and not private owners and entrepreneurs" (Wittfogel 1963:4). Furthermore, "Total power... is spreading like a virulent and aggressive disease" (ibid.:2). China had succumbed. We might be next. Already, intellectual dupes in our midst had infected us with "the belief that practically any form of avowedly benevolent state planning is preferable to the predominance of private property,... which modern sociological folklore deems most abhorrent" (ibid.:4). The West must wake up and "take the calculated risk of alliance against the total enemy...," because there are just "two simple issues: slavery and freedom" (ibid.:448). "There is no excuse for letting the enemy have things his way when our side possesses infinite reserves of superior strength" (ibid.:10). But, "You cannot fight something with nothing. In a crisis situation, any theoretical vacuum... invites disaster" (loc. cit.). *Oriental Despotism* would fill that vacuum with weapon-grade ideas for our side. "My book, *Oriental Despotism*, is the greatest blow against Communism in this century," Wittfogel said emphatically in a public lecture I attended at the University of Kansas in 1963 or 1964.

Brendan O'Leary's (1989:261) summary assessment is perhaps a bit too rough: "*Oriental Despotism* was the consequence of hydrophobia and hydrocephalus in a Cold War warrior." Nevertheless, Wittfogel clearly (and mainly, I think) was politically motivated on the side of laissez faire capitalism, and this motivation led him into historical simplifications and ethnocentric East-West stereotypes. Despite its evident garb of erudition, at bottom *Oriental Despotism* is not much more sophisticated or any freer of ethnocentrism than François Bernier's *Travels in the Mogul Empire*.

Wittfogel vs. Marx on the AMP

In Chapter 9 of *Oriental Despotism*, Wittfogel accuses Marx, Engels, and Lenin of intellectual dishonesty. Their "sin against science" consisted of suppressing the AMP. They did so because they came to realize that their Communist programme contained the AMP germ: absence of private ownership of the means of production coupled with centralized, bureaucratic, state control of the economy. In short, they saw that Communism would lead not to freedom but to slavery, to OD. As a cover-up, Marx, Engels, and Lenin began writing of Asia as having a "feudal" rather than an "Asiatic" or "Oriental" mode of production—or simply avoided the topic. Later, Stalin banned the AMP concept and made the primitive communal-slave-feudal-capitalist-socialist sequence official.

We see here the worst side of Wittfogel as scholar and as human being, because he used against living people the same shoddy technique by which he detected the "sin against science" of the dead Marx and Engels. The basic technique is spelled out in the title of the book (*Ordeal by Slander*) by Owen Lattimore, one of Wittfogel's victims. It consists of finding inconsistencies in an author's writings over time and attributing the changes to the worst possible political motives. The technique is devastating because it is virtually impossible to defend against; the smaller the inconsistencies, the more damning they are made to seem, because sham and subversion have to be practiced with the greatest subtlety.

Let us look at only one of the instances in which Wittfogel used this technique against his rival scholar, Owen Lattimore, whose career was totally ruined by the U.S. Senate's McCarran Committee (Subcommittee on Internal Security), before which Wittfogel had testified against him. In 1936, *Pacific Affairs*, of which Owen Lattimore was editor, published a bibliography in which the staff authors acknowledged that the AMP idea had been influential among Soviet scholars even though the official viewpoint by then was that China was "semi-feudal" (Wittfogel 1963:410n.). In 1940, in his own book, Lattimore "upheld the 'bureaucratic' against the feudal interpretation of imperial Chinese society" (loc. cit.). As late as March 1944, Lattimore "still classed Stalin's concept of 'feudal survivals' among the 'paramount Communist theses' that 'a Communist writer has...to maintain' when he discusses Chinese society" (loc. cit.). Lattimore's suspicious behavior apparently did not begin until 1948. I'll let Wittfogel sleuth it out: "In 1948 members of a research group directed by Lattimore published a survey of Sinkiang which applied to the typically hydraulic conditions of that area a variety of 'feudal' terms..." (loc. cit.). And there's more! "And in 1949 Lattimore himself spoke of Asia's 'feudal land tenure'..." (loc. cit.). Did Lattimore gradually—subtly, sneakily, subversively—change his ideas to bring them into line with the post-1934 official view of the Communist Party of the Soviet Union? "Of course, Lattimore is free to hold whatever sociohistorical ideas he wants and to change them in whatever way he deems fit," Wittfogel (loc. cit.) granted magnanimously, but "he may legitimately be asked to explain his recent position in light of his earlier appraisal." Unable to come up with an explanation that would satisfy the U.S.

Senate's star-chamber Internal Security Subcommittee, before which Wittfogel had testified, Lattimore was ruined.

Wittfogel's case against Marx, Engels, and Lenin was not one whit better. His arguments are "both tendentious and false" (O'Leary 1989:140), lacking in material evidence and resting upon debatable and largely *ex silentio* circumstantial evidence (also see Dunn 1982:12-17, Krader 1975:115-117). For instance, the main case against Engels is this: While he was still mentioning OD in his "anti-Dühring" essays (written in 1877/78), by the time he wrote *The Origin of the Family, Private Property, and the State* in 1884, "Asiatic society as a major societal order has altogether disappeared" (Wittfogel 1963:385). The fact that Engels' *Origin* was an exegesis of Lewis Henry Morgan's *Ancient Society*, and not a work about modes of production, seems lost on Wittfogel (see Bartra 1975:34-35, Krader 1975:301-302). Curiously enough, a few pages earlier Wittfogel (1963:282) says that "from 1853 until his death in 1895 Engels upheld, in largest part, the theory of Oriental society." I guess we are supposed to think that this makes the omission of the theory from the 1884 work all the more sinister!

In the case of Marx, as O'Leary (1989:141-142) points out, wherever his views correspond to Wittfogel's own conclusions, Marx is an honest man; but wherever he disagrees with Wittfogel, Marx is engaged in a "retreat from truth" (see Wittfogel 1963:380, heading "C"). According to Wittfogel (ibid.:381), "Marx should have designated the functional bureaucracy as the ruling class of Oriental despotism." The fact that "Marx did nothing of the kind" shows his attempt to "obscure" or "mystify" the true nature of Oriental society (loc. cit.). Similarly, Marx's *lack of elaboration* becomes "his *reluctance to discuss* the managerial aspect of Oriental despotism" (loc. cit.; emphasis mine). Wittfogel also plays off Early Marx against Late Marx (loc. cit.), an ever popular academic game.

In playing sly games with the Marxian source materials on the AMP, Wittfogel quite unwittingly leads us back onto the track of a major scholarly concern, namely, "the exegesis problem" (after Gándara 1986:44) referred to earlier in this essay. The reader will recall that, in constructing the AMP model, 20th-century scholars have drawn upon Marx and Engels' personal letters, Marx's newspaper articles, a paragraph here and there in their published scholarly works, and the draft manuscript (*Grundrisse*) that Marx said he wrote "for my own clarification and not for publication" (quoted in Hobsbawm 1964:10). The best comment on this matter is by O'Leary (1989:23), who decries "writers on the AMP, like Wittfogel, who treat all of Marx and Engels's views and writings as if they have identical theoretical stature...." He continues (loc. cit.): "Simply to sew together a theory from journalism, letters and incidental remarks is unsubtle."

Extensions and Comparisons

The problem with "sewing together" a theory from disparate sources of differing extents of authorization is that we have to use so broad a stitch that our theoretical fabric will easily rip apart. Thus, the components of the AMP model/theory not only are combined with differing emphases by different commentators, but they are also used disparately, i.e., the components included by one writer may be excluded or de-emphasized by the next. It is this very disparateness, or volatility, of the elements of the AMP model that have allowed its overextension in recent decades. Earlier in this essay, I commented on the temptation to strip the AMP to Nikiforov's basic elements of "primitive community plus government" (quoted in Gellner 1988:49). If we do so, then we are simply describing the early state fairly generally (cf. Krader 1987)— and there is no reason to speak of an *Asiatic* Mode of Production at all, let alone, to attempt to trace an *Asiatic* mode diachronically and synchronically.

Along this line, Perry Anderson (1974:485-487) has written a pithy commentary on the latter-day "minting of Asianisms." He notes two directions of overextension, which I shall call prehistoric and ethnographic. The prehistoric extensions generally retain the features of "a powerful centralized state, and often hydraulic agriculture" as well as corvée levies for public works. Ethnographic extensions (especially popular among French anthropologists) generally discard or de-emphasize hydraulic works or even the despotic state in favor of focussing "essentially on the survival of kin relationships, communal rural property and cohesively self-sufficient villages." The result is "an enormous inflation of the scope" of the AMP, a "supra-historical melange." He (1974:487) continues:

> To mix such immensely disparate historical forms and epochs under a single rubric is to end with the same *reductio ad absurdum* produced by an indefinite extension of feudalism: if so many different socio-economic formations, of such contrasting levels of civilization, are all contracted to one mode of production, the fundamental divisions and changes of history must derive from another source altogether.... The inflation of ideas, like [that of] coins, merely leads to their devaluation.

Ironically enough, it was Wittfogel himself who similarly inflated OD. We have seen that Wittfogel was willing to dismantle the constellation of traits of the OD model to hoop in the "margin" and "sub-margin." We have also seen that his typological categories contained peculiar "melanges" (after Anderson, above) of societies. Within the "core" cases, for instance, "Compact 1" societies included "most Rio Grande Pueblos, the small city states of ancient coastal Peru, Pharaonic Egypt"! "Loose 2" societies included both "Tribal civilizations: The Suk of East Africa, the Zuni of New Mexico" and "State centered civilizations: indigenous Hawaii, many territorial states of ancient

Mexico" (Wittfogel 1963:166). Geographical-temporal extension came at the expense of cross-cultural sensitivity to major differences in organizational scale and complexity.

Furthermore, the traits that Wittfogel enumerated as correlative features of "core" hydraulic states—e.g., cities, palaces, armies, infrastructural works, theocratic religion, corvée labor levies, taxation, noble estates, judicial torture or ordeal, surveillance of citizens, and the like—are not exclusive to "agrodespotisms" and have no necessary connection with centralized water management. Even Wittfogel's occasional disclaimer to the effect that his is not a theory of necessary causality does not overcome this difficulty, because the traits—at the gross feature level of his theory, at any rate—would seem to have neither necessary nor sufficient causal connection to each other or with hydraulic agriculture. Indeed, they would seem to be fairly general features of the pre-/non-industrial state.

NEW DIRECTIONS

Nearly 20 years ago, Perry Anderson (1974:548) proposed that the AMP "be given the decent burial that it deserves." I think we ought to inter the HH, OD, "Irrigation Civilization," and the like right alongside it. Yes, I know the old saw about not throwing the baby out with the bathwater. But what if the bathwater is stagnant and the baby is possessed by political demons? I will grant, of course, that the AMP-HH-OD complex stimulated much useful research. More importantly, the parent Marxian heritage, with its economic production (supply-side) emphasis, recently has had a largely healthy impact upon anthropology (see Palerm 1980). Also, we must not lose sight that Marx is properly a victim, not a villain, in the AMP matter; later scholars have taken scraps of his writings and sewn them into fabrics of their own designs, not his. We need not accept their limitations.

In the same year that Perry Anderson was proposing "a decent burial" for the AMP, Eva and Robert Hunt (1974:131) laid out "three major tasks" to be accomplished if progress was to be made in the study of the "many varieties of society practicing irrigation": (1) to define our terms precisely, (2) to specify our research variables in theoretically adequate ways, and (3) to "test the propositions about relationships between variables in the only valid way, with a large-sample comparative study." Our excursion through the AMP-HH-OD thicket shows the urgency of the first two of these tasks when the Hunts specified them. A look through the many books and articles published within the AMP framework during the 1970s and 1980s, or even a general ruffling of current social science journals, shows that we still have far to go.

Some significant movement has occurred on the third front, however. While the "large-scale" study that the Hunts had in mind has not (to my knowledge) been carried out yet, we do now have some good comparative studies of the state—which is, after all, the social formation about which almost all "hydraulic" arguments have revolved to date. The collections edited by Claessen and Skalník (1978, 1981) and by Claessen and van de Velde (1987, 1991) equip us with a cross-cultural/cross-temporal comparative framework that our predecessors so sorely lacked. For instance, Claessen's (1978) essay alone would have shown Wittfogel at the outset of his study that many of the traits that he thought were peculiarly or especially connected with hydraulic agriculture or early Asian states or "agrodespotisms" were in fact very common among early (and later) states worldwide. On the other hand, much that we need to know about state-level economy per se is still treated in gross or nonoperationalized ways in the comparative works available to us at this time. The topics of land tenure and taxation (see Jungerbérg 1990) come readily to mind.

The aforementioned cross-cultural/cross-temporal studies of the state ought also to help us assess more realistically the extent of power in the hands of ancient or non-/pre-industrial state rulers. Sometimes, we seem to underestimate that power (see Cohen 1991). Most usually, though, we overestimate it, often by assuming that massive ancient constructions reflect massive ancient state power. As Leach (1959) points out, massive power would have been required only if the great public works had been constructed very quickly; instead, many—probably most—ancient monumental constructions seem to have grown by accretion over years or decades. I hedge my bets ("many—probably most") because the essays in this volume show that the matter is by no means simple. Logically speaking, certain *kinds* of constructions (e.g., palaces or temples) could always be built by accretion, but certain other kinds (e.g., some kinds of fortifications) most probably would be built or refurbished quickly. Regarding hydraulic works specifically, certain construction *scales* or *scopes* or *environments* would seem to permit accretionary growth (e.g., see Scarborough, this volume), whereas others would not (e.g., see Ortloff or Howard in this volume). The interesting future task, of course, will be to define which kinds, scales, and scopes of public construction reflect strong and which reflect weak state power—or even (shudder!) no state or centralized power at all. More than political organization is to be discerned, of course; the economy—everything from the differential (private vs. public) allocation and scheduling of labor to the collection and redistribution of the required raw construction materials and foodstuffs—must also be accounted for empirically and conceptually.

The AMP-HH-OD framework not only predisposes us towards a certain view of the state ("despotism"), it also encourages our predilection for viewing the New World through Old World lenses, a bad habit pointed out by Jorge Angulo in this volume. We have not only *Oriental* despotism but also the *Asiatic* mode of production etched onto our mental template. (As Brook

[1989a:7] points out, the AMP is the only one of Marx's own "modes" that bore a specific geographic identity—and, at that, a name "freighted...with pejorative meanings.") These Old World (Asian) models have predisposed us to think in terms of canal irrigation at the expense of other forms of water management, as Scarborough (1991 and "Introduction" here) has pointed out. Several of the essays in this volume show the greater importance of still-water management in major areas of the New World.

Implied above is that the AMP-HH-OD template encourages a "top-down" approach to water management even where a "bottom-up" approach is called for (after Erickson, this volume). The Olympian viewpoint leads us to look specifically for centrally-directed, monumental transformations of the landscape and to overlook or underestimate the significance of less spectacular means of water management. In this sense, as noted, the old template is an especially poor guide to empirical research in parts of the New World.

The combined Wittfogel-Steward (OD-HH) impact upon U.S. anthropology also directed attention towards ecology and away from economy in the research and theorizing about water management and the broader questions to which that topic became attached. Wittfogel's interest in promoting a "multilinear" alternative to Stalinism (i.e., to primitive communal-slave-feudal-capitalist-socialist evolutionism) dovetailed with Steward's interest in constructing a "multilinear" alternative to Michiganism (i.e., to Leslie White's general-stage evolutionism). Steward was also a developer of "cultural ecology," an adaptive-radiation/local-ecology viewpoint that fits nicely with the local-variation focus of multilinear evolutionism (cf. Bartra 1975:21). The outcome was that the very topic of water management and its evolutionary implications was captured by the ecological paradigm in U.S. archaeology, as Donald Kurtz (1987) has protested. That situation, in turn, reflects the ecological reductionism of U.S. anthropology more generally speaking (see Halperin 1989, Isaac 1990, Tankersley & Isaac 1990). In Mexican anthropology, where the Marxian heritage has enjoyed greater continuity, the AMP itself got more attention than the offshoot HH-OD combine and, thus, the economic component of the total research situation seems to have received greater emphasis (for example, see Bartra 1975, Carrasco 1978, Medina et al. 1986, Palerm 1973, 1980). Nevertheless, economy and political economy have been slighted relative to other sociocultural dimensions in both ethnology and archaeology in Mexico, too (see Boehm de Lameiras 1987:239ff.).

I am not proposing to bash ecological studies, of course. Without doubt, ecology is a broader conceptual umbrella than economy. Indeed, human adaptation—the processes by which humans articulate with their environments—is the dominant framework or background for both archaeology and ethnology in general. At the same time, though, the most basic mechanisms of human adaptation are *economic*, involving the processes of *production* (extraction, transformation, elaboration), *consumption* (use, whether instrumental or final), *distribution* (movement from one social node to another), and *exchange* (two-way transfers) of goods (materials) and services that sustain or reproduce material livelihood. If we do not take these basic mechanisms specifically into account in both the design and analysis stages of our research, we risk falling into functionalist tautologies (see Tankersley & Isaac 1990:343-344) or biologistical reductionism (see Isaac 1990:331-333).

Turning to another matter, anthropological interest in prehistoric water management has focussed overwhelmingly upon the large state or "civilization." There is nothing wrong here but, from time to time, we ought to think about the broader context of the cultural manipulation of water. Everywhere, not just in states or civilizations, water is a critical resource, i.e., one that must be present if humans are to inhabit the setting. Water's quanta and distribution everywhere affect the quanta and distribution of the human population—whether we are talking about a simple hunting-gathering band (e.g., the !Kung San) or a great empire—and thus, if for no other reason, have implications for the entire sociocultural system (see Isaac 1992). Everywhere, water is a *cultural* as well as a natural phenomenon for humans, that is, it always enters the symbolic repertoire. Nowhere do humans simply accept their surroundings unthinkingly, nonsymbolically, or strictly ecologically (like blackbirds or deer); instead, they always project themselves symbolically onto the landscape, culturally appropriating its features through mythology, magic, religion, rational discussion and planning, and so forth. In these ways, humans culturally *manipulate* the features (including water) of their environments, trying to harness or manage or predict them. Where these cultural (symbolic) means convert mere environment into human resources for material livelihood, they and the concomitant transformations, uses, or transfers are quite properly "economic."

There is great cross-cultural disparity in the empirical efficacy of this manipulation, of course. Hunter-gatherers such as the !Kung San or the Great Basin Shoshoni (to take two time-honored examples) have but puny means of material resource management when compared with nonindustrial (e.g., historical Chinese) or postindustrial (e.g., present-day USA) state-level peoples. But no matter how "ineffectual" a culture's symbolic projections and machinations may appear to us as means of harnessing their setting for material livelihood, they do establish certain cultural claims that we should treat analytically as economic rights of appropriation (extraction, distribution, consumption). Whether these rights are conceived as obtaining in nature spirits, ancestors, gods, living elders, extended families, whole settlements, or individuals, they are cultural (human symbolic creations) and they are economic (i.e., factors in human material livelihood). That they are also "religious" or "familial" in non-/pre-industrial societies shows only that those economies are typically "embedded in" (to use Karl Polanyi's term), culturally packaged with, noneconomic features.

This is the cross-cultural scope of context in which, eventually, we will have to decide such matters as land "ownership" among the Lozi (of whom we heard earlier) or in the historical cases that have bedeviled social theorists from Montesquieu to the present day. The broader context will show that the sticky wickets in state-level cases are not unique in their occurrence or in the kinds of analysis required. Allow me to illustrate by alluding to a "simple" case involving the ownership of waterholes. Each hunting-gathering !Kung San band has some members, usually siblings, who "own" the band's customary waterhole and its adjoining territory, and this "ownership" is "inherited." Yet, neither the water nor the surrounding resources are reserved for the "owners"; indeed, residence is highly fluid, and anyone with "elementary good manners" who has a relative in any band may use that band's resources. And, within the band, "food is shared in such a way that everyone—residents and visitors alike—receives an equitable share..." (Lee 1976:77-78).

What, pray tell, does resource "ownership" mean to the !Kung San? Finding the answer would involve a very fine-grained, context-sensitive analysis of that particular case, of course. But that strategy could not lead us to theoretical elegance unless it was informed by the broader knowledge that "ownership" can mean something quite different to hunter-gatherers *generally* (see Dowling 1968) *and* to nonindustrial state-level peoples (as we have seen in this essay) than it means in our own culture. In this as in other matters, the wider our purview, the greater the variety of contexts in which we can view a construction as subtle as "ownership," the better the possibility that we will be able to analyze it in such a way as to contribute to productive theory.

One other matter deserves mention before I bring these comments to a close. We cannot successfully theorize about a phenomenon unless we know its empirical range or scope. If we insist on proceeding to general theory when our database is fragmentary, as Wittfogel did, we may do more harm than good. Premature theorizing "lays down the lines for our thinking to follow when we do not know enough to say whether one direction or another is the more promising" (Kaplan 1964:279). It leads to a premature closure that makes alternative ideas very difficult to originate and often even difficult to get published (see Kurtz 1987:340). We hope that this volume's essays, which report the fruits of exploratory field studies, will help to keep the theoretical door open.

ACKNOWLEDGMENTS

This essay was written during Winter Quarter 1993, while I was on academic leave provided by the University of Cincinnati; without that leave of absence, it could not have been written. I am also grateful to Mr. David Sherman for his intelligent labor in preparing the "Graduate Paper" on African land tenure, which is the basis for Table

1. My colleagues, Vernon Scarborough and Rhoda Halperin, tolerated my grumbling and offered support and suggestions during the writing.

REFERENCES

Adams, Robert McC. (1972) "Patterns of Urbanization in Early Southern Mesopotamia." Pp. 735-749 in P. J. Ucko, Ruth Tringham & G. W. Dimbley (eds.) *Man, Settlement and Urbanism*. Cambridge, MA: Schenkman.

Anderson, E. N. (1989) "The First Green Revolution: Chinese Agriculture in the Han Dynasty." Pp. 135-151 in Christina Gladwin & Kathleen Truman (eds.) *Food and Farm: Current Debates and Policies*. Lanham, MD: University Press of America, Monographs in Economic Anthropology, No. 7.

Anderson, Perry (1974) "The 'Asiatic Mode of Production.'" Pp. 462-549 in his *Lineages of the Absolutist State*. London: Humanities Press.

Armillas, Pedro (1987) *La aventura intelectual de Pedro Armillas*. (José Luis de Rojas, ed.) Zamora: El Colegio de Michoacán.

Azarya, Victor, and Naomi Chazan (1987) "Disengagement from the State in Africa: Reflections on the Experience of Ghana and Guinea." *Comparative Studies in Society and History* 29:106-131.

Baker, Christopher J. (1984) "Frogs and Farmers: The Green Revolution in India, and Its Murky Past." Pp. 37-52 in T. P. Bayliss-Smith & S. Wanmali (eds.) *Understanding Green Revolutions: Agrarian Change and Development Planning in South Asia*. Cambridge, ENG: Cambridge University Press.

Bartra, Roger (1975) *Marxismo y sociedades antiguas: El modo de producción asiático y el México prehispánico*. Mexico, DF: Editorial Grijalbo.

_____ (1986) *El modo de producción asiático: Problemas de la historia de los países coloniales* (8th ed.). Mexico, DF: Ediciones Era.

Bernier, Francis (1826) *Travels in the Mogul Empire, Vol. I* (trans. Irving Brock). London: William Pickering.

Boehm de Lameiras, Brigitte (1985) "El origen del estado en el Valle de México." Pp. 235-247 in Jesús Monjarás-Ruiz, Rosa Brambila & Emma Pérez-Rocha (eds.) *Mesoamérica en el centro de México*. Mexico, DF: Instituto Nacional de Antropología e Historia.

_____ (1986a) "El origen del estado en el Valle de México: Marxismo, modo de producción asiático y materialismo ecológico en la investigación del México prehispánico." Pp. 151-160 in Andrés Medina et al., eds., *infra*.

_____ (1986b) *Formación del estado en el México prehispánico*. Zamora: Colegio de Michoacán.

_____ (1987) "La actualidad de los aztecas." Pp. 226-248 in Susana Glantz, ed., *infra*.

_____ (1988) "El origen de las sociedades clasistas y el Estado." Pp. 533-573 in Carlos García Mora (ed.) *La antropología en México, Tomo 3*. Mexico, DF: Instituto Nacional de Antropología e Historia.

Brook, Timothy (1989a) "Introduction." Pp. 3-34 in Timothy Brook, ed., *infra*.

_____, ed. (1989b) *The Asiatic Mode of Production in China*. Armonk, NY: M. E. Sharpe, Inc.

Carneiro, Robert L. (1970) "A Theory of the Origin of the State." *Science* 169:733-738.

Carrasco, Pedro (1978) "La economía en el México prehispánico." Pp. 15-76 in Pedro Carrasco & Johanna Broda (eds.) *Economía política e ideología en el México prehispánico*. Mexico, DF: Editorial Nueva Imagen.

———— (1988) "La organización social prehispánica en el centro de México." Pp. 465-531 in Carlos García Mora (ed.) *La antropología en México, Tomo 3*. Mexico, DF: Instituto Nacional de Antropología e Historia.

Claessen, Henri J. M. (1978) "The Early State: A Structural Approach." Pp. 533-596 in H. J. M. Claessen & P. Skalník, eds., 1978, *infra*.

Claessen, Henri J. M., and Peter Skalník, eds. (1978) *The Early State*. The Hague: Mouton.

————, eds. (1981) *The Study of the State*. The Hague: Mouton.

Claessen, Henri J. M., and Pieter van de Velde, eds. (1987) *Early State Dynamics*. Leiden: E. J. Brill.

————, eds. (1991) *Early State Economics*. New Brunswick, NJ: Transaction Publishers.

Cohen, Ronald (1991) "Paradise Regained: Myth and Reality in the Political Economy of the Early State." Pp. 109-129 in H. J. M. Claessen & Pieter van de Velde, eds., *supra*.

Colburn, Forrest D., ed. (1989) *Everyday Forms of Peasant Resistance*. Armonk, NY: M. E. Sharpe, Inc.

Coupland, Gary (1988) "Prehistoric Economic and Social Change in the Tsimshian Area." Pp. 211-243 in B. L. Isaac (ed.) *Prehistoric Economies of the Pacific Northwest Coast, Suppl. 3, Research in Economic Anthropology*. Greenwich, CT: JAI Press.

Davidson, Basil (1959) *The Lost Cities of Africa*. Boston: Little, Brown.

Dowling, John H. (1968) "Individual Ownership and the Sharing of Game in Hunting Societies." *American Anthropologist* 70:502-507.

Dunn, Stephen P. (1982) *The Fall and Rise of the Asiatic Mode of Production*. London: Routledge & Kegan Paul.

Escobar, Arturo (1991) "Anthropology and the Development Encounter: The Making and Marketing of Development Anthropology." *American Ethnology* 18:658-682.

Evans, Susan (1980) "Spatial Analysis of Basin of Mexico Settlement: Problems with the Use of the Central Place Model." *American Antiquity* 45:866-875.

Fábregas P., Andrés (1987) "El modo asiático de producción en la obra de Angel Palerm." Pp. 147-164 in Susana Glantz, ed., *infra*.

Feuer, Lewis S., ed. (1959) *Karl Marx and Friedrich Engels: Basic Writings on Politics and Philosophy*. Garden City, NY: Doubleday/Anchor.

Gándara V., Manuel (1986) "El modo de producción asiático: ¿Explicación marxista del origen del estado?" Pp. 41-59 in Andrés Medina et al., eds., *infra*.

Gellner, Ernest (1988) *State and Society in Soviet Thought*. London: Basil Blackwell.

Gernet, Jacques (1970) *Daily Life in China on the Eve of the Mongol Invasion, 1250-1276*. Stanford, CA: Stanford University Press.

Gilman, Antonio (1981) "The Development of Social Stratification in Bronze Age Europe." *Current Anthropology* 22:1-8, 17-23.

Glantz, Susana, ed. (1987) *La heterodoxia recuperada: En torno a Angel Palerm*. Mexico, DF: Fondo de Cultura Económica.

Gluckman, Max (1941) *Economy of the Central Barotse Plain*. Livingstone, ZB: Rhodes-Livingstone Institute, Paper No. 7.

———— (1959) "The Lozi of Barotseland in North-Western Rhodesia." Pp. 1-91 in Elizabeth Colson & Max Gluckman (eds.) *Seven Tribes of British Central Africa*. Manchester, ENG: Manchester University Press.

Halperin, Rhoda H. (1989) "Ecological versus Economic Anthropology: Changing 'Place' versus Changing 'Hands'." Pp. 15-41 in B. L. Isaac (ed.) *Research in Economic Anthropology, Vol. 11*. Greenwich, CT: JAI Press.

Hobsbawm, Eric (1964) "Introduction." Pp. 9-65 in Karl Marx (1964), *infra*.

Hunt, Eva, and Robert C. Hunt (1974) "Irrigation, Conflict, and Politics: A Mexican Case." Pp. 129-157 in T. E. Downing & McG. Gibson (eds.) *Irrigation's Impact on Society*. Tucson: University of Arizona Press, Anthropological Papers, No. 25.

Isaac, Barry L. (1990) "Economy, Ecology, and Analogy: The !Kung San and the Generalized Foraging Model." Pp. 323-335 in K. B. Tankersley & B. L. Isaac (eds.) *Early Paleoindian Economies of Eastern North America, Suppl. 5, Research in Economic Anthropology.* Greenwich, CT: JAI Press Inc.

_____ (1991) "Introduction." Pp. 1-15 in *Research in Economic Anthropology, Vol. 13.* Greenwich, CT: JAI Press Inc.

_____ (1992) "Discussion." Pp. 441-452 in D. R. Croes, R. A. Hawkins & B. L. Isaac (eds.) *Long-Term Subsistence Change in Prehistoric North America, Suppl. 6, Research in Economic Anthropology.* Greenwich, CT: JAI Press Inc.

Jungerberg, Rex (1990) "Women's Contribution to Taxation Effort in Chiefdoms and States." Pp. 347-391 in B. L. Isaac (ed.) *Research in Economic Anthropology, Vol. 12.* Greenwich, CT: JAI Press Inc.

Kaplan, Abraham (1964) *The Conduct of Inquiry.* San Francisco, CA: Chandler.

Ke Changji (1989) "Ancient Chinese Society and the Asiatic Mode of Production." Pp. 47-64 in Timothy Brook, ed., *supra.*

Krader, Lawrence (1975) *The Asiatic Mode of Production.* Assen, Netherlands: Van Gorcum.

_____ (1987) "Reflexiones sobre el modo asiático de producción." Pp. 119-125 in Susana Glantz, ed., 1989b, *supra.*

Kurtz, Donald V. (1987) "The Economics of Urbanization and State Formation at Teotihuacan." *Current Anthropology* 28:329-353.

Larken, P. M. (1930) "Further Impressions of the Azande." *Sudan Notes and Records* 13:1 (Human Relations Area Files).

Leach, Edmund R. (1959) "Hydraulic Society in Ceylon." *Past and Present* 15:2-26.

Lee, Richard B. (1976) "!Kung Spatial Organization: An Ecological and Historical Perspective." Pp. 73-97 in R. B. Lee & I. DeVore (eds.) *Kalahari Hunter-Gatherers.* Cambridge, MA: Harvard University Press.

Little, Kenneth (1967) *The Mende of Sierra Leone.* London: Routledge & Kegan Paul.

Marx, Karl (1951) *Articles on India* ("Introduction" by R. P. Dutt). Bombay: People's Publishing House Ltd.

_____ (1964) *Pre-capitalist Economic Formations* (trans. Jack Cohen, ed. E. J. Hobsbawm). London: Lawrence & Wishart.

_____ (1967) *Capital, Vol. I: A Critical Analysis of Capitalist Production* (ed. F. Engels). New York: International Publishers.

_____ (1969) *The 18th Brumaire of Louis Bonaparte.* New York: International Publishers.

_____ (1977) *A Contribution to the Critique of Political Economy* (trans. S. W. Ryazanskaya, ed. Maurice Dobb). Moscow: Progress Publishers.

Marx, Karl, and Frederick Engels (1975) *Selected Correspondence, 1846-1895* (trans. Dora Torr). Westport, CT: Greenwood Press.

Medina, Andrés (1986) "Presentación." Pp. 7-31 in Andrés Medina et al., eds., *infra.*

Medina, Andrés, and Carlos García Mora (1983/1986) *La quiebra política de la antropología social en México, T. I & II.* Mexico, DF: Universidad Nacional Autónoma de México.

Medina, Andrés, Alfredo López Austin, and Mari Carmen Serra, eds. (1986) *Origen y formación del estado en Mesoamérica.* Mexico, DF: Universidad Nacional Autónoma de México.

Mitchell, William P. (1973) "The Hydraulic Hypothesis: A Reappraisal." *Current Anthropology* 14:532-534.

Murdock, George Peter (1967) *Ethnographic Atlas.* Pittsburgh, PA: University of Pittsburgh Press.

Murdock, George Peter, and Douglas R. White (1969) "Standard Cross-Cultural Sample." *Ethnology* 8:329-369.

Neale, Walter C. (1957) "Reciprocity and Redistribution in the Indian Village: Sequel to Some Notable Discussions." Pp. 218-236 in Karl Polanyi, Conrad Arensberg & Harry Pearson (eds.) *Trade and Market in the Early Empires.* Glencoe, IL: The Free Press.

_____ (1973) *Economic Change in Rural India: Land Tenure and Reform in Uttar Pradesh, 1800-1955*. Port Washington, NY: Kennikat Press.

O'Leary, Brendan (1989) *The Asiatic Mode of Production*. London: Basil Blackwell.

Palerm, Angel (1972) *Agricultura y sociedad en Mesoamérica*. Mexico, DF: Secretaría de Educación Pública, SEP-SETENTAS.

_____ (1973) *Obras hidráulicas prehispánicas en el sistema lacustre del Valle de México*. Mexico, DF: Secretaría de Educación Pública/Instituto Nacional de Antropología e Historia.

_____ (1976) *Modos de producción y formaciones socioeconómicas* (*Modes of Production and Socioeconomic Formations*). Mexico, DF: Editorial Edicol.

_____ (1980) *Antropología y marxismo*. Mexico, DF: Editorial Nueva Imagen.

_____ (1990) "Obras hidráulicas prehispánicas en el sistema lacustre del Valle de México." Pp. 185-443 in Angel Palerm, *México prehispánico: Evolución ecológica del Valle de México* (ed. Carmen Viqueira L.; repr. of 1973 edition, *supra*). Mexico, DF: Consejo Nacional para la Cultura y las Artes.

Palerm, Angel, and Eric Wolf (1972) *Agricultura y civilización en Mesoamérica*. Mexico, DF: Secretaría de Educación Pública, SEP-SETENTAS.

Parsons, Jeffrey R. (1987) "El área central de Teotihuacan: Patrones regionales de colonización en el Valle de México." Pp. 37-75 in Joseph B. Mountjoy & Donald L. Brockington (eds.) *El auge y la caída del Clásico en el México central*. Mexico, DF: Universidad Nacional Autónoma de México.

Richards, Audrey I. (1939) *Land, Labour and Diet in Northern Rhodesia*. London: Oxford University Press.

Roscoe, John (1965) *The Baganda* (2nd ed.). London: Frank Cass.

Santley, Robert S. (1986) "Prehispanic Roadways, Transport Network Geometry, and Aztec Politico-Economic Organization in the Basin of Mexico." Pp. 223-244 in B. L. Isaac (ed.) *Economic Aspects of Prehispanic Highland Mexico, Suppl. 2, Research in Economic Anthropology*. Greenwich, CT: JAI Press Inc.

Scarborough, Vernon L. (1991) "Water Management Adaptations in Non-Industrial Complex Societies." Pp. 101-154 in M. B. Schiffer (ed.) *Method and Theory in Archaeology, Vol. 3*. Tucson: University of Arizona Press.

Schaedel, Richard P. (1987) "Control del agua y control social." Pp. 126-146 in Susana Glantz, ed., *supra*.

Scott, James C. (1985) *Weapons of the Weak: Everyday Forms of Peasant Resistance*. New Haven, CT: Yale University Press.

_____ (1989) "Everyday Forms of Resistance." Pp. 3-33 in Forrest Colburn, ed., *supra*.

_____ (1990) *Domination and the Arts of Resistance: Hidden Transcripts*. New Haven, CT: Yale University Press.

Sherman, David (n.d.) "Graduate Paper." MS, Department of Anthropology, University of Cincinnati, 1992.

Skinner, G. William (1964/65) "Marketing and Social Structure in Rural China (I and II)." *Journal of Asian Studies* 24:3-43, 195-228.

Smith, Michael (1979) "The Aztec Marketing System and Settlement Pattern in the Valley of Mexico: A Central Place Analysis." *American Antiquity* 44:110-125.

Snow, Philip (1988) *The Star Raft: China's Encounter with Africa*. New York: Weidenfeld & Nicolson.

Steward, Julian H. (1955a) "Introduction: The Irrigation Civilizations, a Symposium on Method and Result in Cross-Cultural Regularities." Pp. 1-5 in J. H. Steward, ed., *infra*.

_____ ed. (1955b) *Irrigation Civilizations: A Comparative Study*. Washington, DC: Pan American Union, Social Science Monographs, 1.

Sugiura Y., Yoko (1986) "Algunos comentarios en torno a la formación de los estados más tempranos de China; Shang y Zhou y la sociedad hidráulica." Pp. 61-76 in Andrés Medina et al., eds., *supra.*

Tankersley, Kenneth B., and Barry L. Isaac (1990) "Concluding Remarks on Paleoecology and Paleoeconomy." Pp. 337-355 in their (eds.) *Early Paleoindian Economies of Eastern North America, Suppl. 5, Research in Economic Anthropology.* Greenwich, CT: JAI Press Inc.

Wallerstein, Immanuel (1974) *The Modern World-System, Vol. I.* New York: Academic Press.

Wittfogel, Karl A. (1955) "Developmental Aspects of Hydraulic Societies." Pp. 43-52 in J. H. Steward, ed., 1955b, *supra.*

————— (1957) *Oriental Despotism: A Comparative Study of Total Power.* New Haven, CT: Yale University Press.

————— (1963) *Oriental Despotism: A Comparative Study of Total Power.* New Haven, CT: Yale University Press.

Wolf, Eric R. (1957) "Closed Corporate Peasant Communities in Mesoamerica and Central Java." *Southwestern Journal of Anthropology* 13:1-18.

————— (1982) *Europe and the People without History.* Berkeley & Los Angeles: University of California Press.

Zhao Lisheng (1989) "The Well-Field System of Relation to the Asiatic Mode of Production." Pp. 65-84 in Timothy Brook, ed., 1989b, *supra.*

JAI PRESS

Research in Economic Anthropology

Edited by **Barry L. Isaac,** *Department of Anthropology, University of Cincinnati*

Volume 10, 1988, 306 pp. $73.25
ISBN 0-89232-946-7

Supplement 4 - Prehistoric Maya Economies of Belize
1989, 372 pp. $73.25
ISBN 1-55938-051-9

L. Fedick. **Secondary Development and Settlement Economics: The Classic Maya of Southern Belize,** *Peter S. Dunham, Thomas R. Jamison, and Richard M. Leventhal.* **PART IV. SETTLEMENT GROWTH AND ECONOMIC DIFFERENTIATION. Changing Subsistence Economy at a Late Preclassic Maya Community,** *Maynard B. Cliff and Cathy J. Crane.* **Maya Cuisine: Hearths and Lowland Economy,** *K. Anne Pyburn.* **PART V. CONCLUSION. Economic Foundations of Prehistoric Maya Society: Paradigms and Concepts,** *Patricia A. McAnany.*

Volume 11, 1989, 303 pp. $73.25
ISBN 1-55938-020-9

CONTENTS: Introduction, *Barry L. Isaac.* **PART I. ECONOMY AND ECOLOGY. Ecological Versus Economic Anthropology: Changing "Place" Versus Changing "Hands",** *Rhoda H. Halperin.* **Time, Efficiency, and Fitness in the Amazonian Protein Quest,** *Raymond Hames.* **PART II. HOUSEHOLD ECONOMY. Risk Reduction and Variation in Agricultural Economies: A Computer Simulation of Hopi Agriculture,** *Michelle Hegmon.* **Interhousehold Exchange and the Public Economy in Three Highland Philippine Communities,** *Jean Treloggen Peterson.* **Labor Sufficiency, Livestock Management, and Time Allocation on Maasai Group Ranches,** *Barbara E. Grandin.* **PART III. Native Californian Economies. Market Forces in the Creation of Pomo Basketry Style and Pomo Ethnicity,** *John Pryor.* **The Economics of Acculturation in the Spanish Missions of Alta California,** *Paul Farnsworth.* **The Fisheries of Mission Nuestra Senora De La Soledad, Monterey County, California,** *Roy A. Salls.* **Exchange, Subsistence, and Sedentism Along the Middle Klamath River,** *Joseph L. Chartkoff.*

Supplement 5 - Early Paleoindian Economies of Eastern North America
1990, 355 pp. $73.25
ISBN 1-55938-207-4

Edited by **Kenneth B. Tankersley,** *Illinois State Museum* and **Barry L. Isaac,** *University of Cincinnati*

CONTETNS: Series Editor's Preface, *Barry L. Isaac, University of Cincinnati.* **Introduction,** *Kenneth B. Tankersley and Barry L. Isaac.* **PART I. GLACIATED LANDSCAPES. Stone Tools and Economic: Great Lakes Paleoindian Examples,** *Michael J. Shott.* **An Early Paleoindian Cache of Informal Tools at the Udora Site, Ontario,** *Peter L. Storck and John Tomenchuk.* **Interior Paleoindian Settlement Strategies: A First Approximation for the Lower Great Lakes,** *Lawrence J. Jackson.* **Early Paleoindian Economies in the Glaciated Regions of Indiana,** *Don ald R. Cochran, Kris D. Richey, and Lisa A. Maust.* **PART II. UNGLACIATED LANDSCAPES. The Paleoindian Colonization of Eastern North America: A View From the Southeast-**

JAI PRESS

ern United States, *David G. Anderson.* **Paleoindian Economy and Settlement Patterns in the Wyandotte Chert Source Area, Unglaciated South-Central Indiana,** *Edward E. Smith, Jr.* **Late Pleistocene Lithic Exploitation in the Midwest and Midsouth: Indiana, Ohio, and Kentucky,** *Kenneth B. Tankersley.* **PART III. CRITICAL PERSPECTIVES. Environment, Analogy, and Early Paleoindian Economies in Northeastern North America,** *Jay F. Custer and R. Michael Stewart.* **Economy, Ecology, and Analogy: The Kung San and the Generaliaed Foraging Model,** *Barry L. Isaac.* **Concluding Remarks on Paleoecology and Paleoeconomy,** *Kenneth B. Tankersley, Illinois State Museum and Barry L. Isaac.*

Volume 12, 1990, 391 pp. $73.25
ISBN 1-55938-118-3

Volume 13, 1991, 386 pp. $73.25
ISBN 1-55938-365-8

Malaysia, *Conner Bailey.* **Diversity in a Bangladesh Village: Landholding, Occupation, and Economic Mobility of Moslems and Hindus,** *Michael S. Harris.* **Small-Scale Irrigation and the Emergence of Inequality Among Farmers in Central Mexico,** *James H. McDonald.* **Some are More Equal than Others: Labor Supply, Reciprocity, and Redistribution in the Andes,** *William P. Mitchell.* **Capitalism, Socioeconomic Differentiation, and Development in Rural French Polynesia,** *Victoria S. Lockwood.* **PART III. CENTER AND PERIPHERY. Maritime Exchange in the Early Formative Period of Coastal Ecuador: Geopolitical Origins of Uneven Development,** *James A. Zeidler.* **Products and Politics of a Milagro Entrepot: Penon Del Rio, Guayas Basin, Ecuador,** *Michael Muse.* **Highland Center and Foothill Periphery in 16th-Century Eastern Colombia,** *Carl Henrik Langebaek.* **Storage, Access Control, and Bureaucratic Proliferation: Understanding the Initial Period (1800-900 B.C.) Economy at Pampa De Las Llamas-Moxeke, Casma Valley, Peru,** *Sheila Pozorski and Thomas Pozorski.* **The Energetics of Trade and Market in the Early Empires of Mesoamerica,** *Robert N. Zeitlin.*

Supplement 6, Long-Term Subsistence Change
in Prehistoric North America
1992, 452 pp. $73.25
ISBN 1-55938-529-4

Edited by **Dale R. Cross,** *Washington State University,*
Rebecca A. Hawkins, *University of Cincinnati,*
and **Barry L. Isaac,** *University of Cincinnati.*

CONTENTS: Series Editor's Preface, *Barry L. Isaac.* **Introduction,** *Rebecca A. Hawkins.* **PART I. THE MIDCONTINENT. Woodland Traditions in the Midcontinent: A Comparison of Three Regional Sequenecs,** *Mark F. Seeman.* **Subsistence Inferencesfrom Woodland and Mississippian Ceramics: The Central Ohio Valley, CIRCA 1000 BC-AD 1200,** *Rebeca A. Hawkins.* **The Possible Role of Salt Production in Fort Ancient Cultural Development from A.D. 1200 to 1550,** *David Pollack and A. Gwynn Henderson.* **PART II. THE PRAIRIES AND THE PLAINS. Bison and Subsistence Change: The Protohistoric Ohio Valley and Illinois Valley Connection,** *Kenneth B. Tankersley.* **Early Village Formation in the Middle Missouri Subarea of the Plains,** *Dennis L. Toom.* **PART III. THE SOUTHWEST. Pinyon Nuts and Other Wild Resources in Western Anasazi Subsistence Economies,** *Alan P. Sullivan, III.* **Subsistence Change and Architecture: Anasazi Storerooms in the Dolores Region, Colorado,** *G. Timothy Gross.* **Reservoirs and Locational Shifts in Sonoran Desert Subsistence,** *James M. Bayman and Suzanne K. Fish.* **Ceramics, Sedentism, and Agricultural Dependency at a Late Pithouse/Early Pueblo Period Village,** *Vernon L. Scarborough.* **PART IV. THE NORTHWEST CAOST. Exploring Prehistoric Subsistence Change on the Northwest Coast,** *Dale R. Cross.* **The Evolution of Northwest Coast Subsistence,** *R. G. Matson.* **PART V. DISCUSSION.** *Barry L. Isaac. Dale R. Cross*

J A I P R E S S

Volume 14, 1993, 298 pp. $73.25
ISBN 1-55938-575-8

CONTENTS: Preface, *Barry L. Isaac.* **PART I. PREHISTORIC CRAFT SPECIALIZATION. Textiles, Women, and Political Economy in Late Prehispanic Peru,** *Cathy Lynne Costin.* **The Organizational Context of Specialized Craft Production in Early Mesopotamian States,** *Gil J. Stein and M. James Blackman.* **Craft Specialization in Nonstrafied Societies,** *John R. Cross.* **PAET II. HUNTING AND GATHERING. How the Ancient Peigans Lived,** *Alice B. Kehoe.* **Human Foraging in Lowland South America: Pattern and Process of Resource Procurement,** *Ted L. Gragson.* **PART III. LONGITUDINAL PERSPECTIVES. The Annual Market Cycle at Antigua Guatemala,** *John Swetnam.* **Household and Community: The Alexanderwohl Mennoites and Two Counterfactuals, the Amish and Hutterites,** *Jeffrey Longhofer.* **PART IV. METHOD AND THEORY. Altruism and Self-Interest: Towards an Anthropoligical Theory of Decision Making,** *Richard Wilk.* **Retrospective opn the Formalist-Substantivist Debate,** *Barry L. Isaac.* **Representation and Experience in Kula and Western Exchange Spheres (Or, Billy),** *Frederick H. Damon.* **The Concept of Equivalencies in Economic Anthropology,** *Rhoda H. Halperin.*

Also Available:

Volumes 1-'9 (l978-1985)
   +Supplements 1-2 (1980-1986) $73.25 each

> **FACULTY/PROFESSIONAL** *discounts are available in the U.S. and Canada at a rate of 40% off the list price when prepaid by personal check or credit card and ordered directly from the publisher.*

JAI PRESS INC.

55 Old Post Road # 2 - P.O. Box 1678
Greenwich, Connecticut 06836-1678
Tel: (203) 661-7602   Fax:(203) 661-0792